DIETRICH BONHOEFFER WORKS, VOLUME 12

Berlin: 1932–1933

This series is a translation of
DIETRICH BONHOEFFER WERKE
Edited by
Eberhard Bethge†, Ernst Feil,
Christian Gremmels, Wolfgang Huber,
Hans Pfeifer, Albrecht Schönherr†,
Heinz Eduard Tödt†, Ilse Tödt

This volume has been made possible through the generous support of the Lilly Endowment, Inc.; Thrivent Financial Foundation for Lutherans; the Bowen H. and Janice Arthur McCoy Charitable Foundation; the Lutheran Theological Seminary at Philadelphia; and the gifts of numerous members and friends of the International Bonhoeffer Society.

DIETRICH BONHOEFFER WORKS, VOLUME 12

DIETRICH BONHOEFFER

Berlin

1932–1933

Translated from the German Edition
Edited by
CARSTEN NICOLAISEN AND ERNST-ALBERT SCHARFFENORTH

English Edition
Edited by
LARRY L. RASMUSSEN

Translated by
ISABEL BEST AND DAVID HIGGINS

Supplementary Material Translated by
DOUGLAS W. STOTT

FORTRESS PRESS MINNEAPOLIS

DIETRICH BONHOEFFER WORKS, Volume 12

Originally published in German as *Dietrich Bonhoeffer Werke,* edited by Eberhard Bethge et al., by Chr. Kaiser Verlag in 1997; Band 12, *Berlin: 1932–1933,* edited by Carsten Nicolaisen and Ernst-Albert Scharffenorth. First English-language edition of *Dietrich Bonhoeffer Works,* Volume 12, published by Fortress Press in 2009.

The publication of this work was subsidized in part by a grant from the Goethe-Institut Inter Nationes, Munich.

Jacket design: Cheryl Watson
Jacket finishing: Ivy Palmer Skrade
Photo acknowledgments: Dietrich Bonhoeffer, 1932, while teaching a weekend course in Prebelow, cover and p. 49; © Chr. Kaiser/Gütersloher Verlagshaus, Gütersloh, Germany
Book design: HK Scriptorium, Inc.
Typesetting: Ann Delgehausen, Trio Bookworks

Library of Congress Cataloging-in-Publication Data

Bonhoeffer, Dietrich, 1906–1945.
[Berlin, 1932–1933. English]
Berlin, 1932–1933 / Dietrich Bonhoeffer ; translated from the German edition edited by Hans Goedeking, Martin Heimbucher, and Hans-Walter Schleicher ; English edition edited by Larry L. Rasmussen ; translated by Isabel Best and David Higgins ; supplementary material translated by Douglas W. Stott.
p. cm. — (Dietrich Bonhoeffer works ; v. 12)
Includes bibliographical references and index.
ISBN 978-0-8006-8312-2 (alk. paper)
1. Bonhoeffer, Dietrich, 1906-1945—Correspondence. 2. Theologians—Germany—Correspondence. 3. Lutheran Church—Sermons. 4. Sermons, German—Translations into English. 5. Theology. I. Rasmussen, Larry L. II. Best, Isabel. III. Higgins, David Warren Simons. IV. Title.
BX4827.B57A4 2009
230'.044—dc22 2009037987

The paper used in this publication meets the minimum requirements for American National Standard for Information Sciences—Permanence of Paper for Printed Library Materials, ANSI Z329.48–1984.

Manufactured in the U.S.A.
12 11 10 09 08 1 2 3 4 5 6 7 8 9 10

Contents

General Editor's Foreword to Dietrich Bonhoeffer Works

The German theologian and pastor Dietrich Bonhoeffer has become one of the most influential Christian thinkers of all time. Barely twenty-seven years of age when the Nazi regime came to power in Germany, Bonhoeffer emerged immediately as a radical Protestant voice against the ideological cooptation of his church. He was one of the earliest critics of the Nazi regime and an outspoken opponent of the pro-Nazi "German Christians." From 1933 to 1935, he served as pastor of two German-speaking congregations in England, leading them to join the Confessing Church—the faction within the German Protestant church that opposed the nazification of the Christian faith. He returned to Germany to become director of a small Confessing Church seminary and, after the Gestapo closed it, continued to work illegally to educate Confessing clergy. Throughout the 1930s, he attended ecumenical meetings, effectively becoming the voice of the Confessing Church throughout the European and American ecumenical world. In 1939, his ecumenical friends urged him to accept a position in New York. Rejecting the security of a life in exile, Bonhoeffer chose instead to join the ranks of the German conspiracy to overthrow the regime, like his brother Klaus and his brothers-in-law Hans von Dohnanyi and Rüdiger Schleicher. He was arrested and imprisoned in April 1943 and executed in the Flossenbürg concentration camp in April 1945.

In a eulogy published shortly after Bonhoeffer's death, his former professor and friend Reinhold Niebuhr wrote that Bonhoeffer's story "is worth recording. It belongs to the modern acts of the apostles. . . . Not only his martyr's death, but also his actions and precepts contain within them the hope of a revitalised Protestant faith in Germany. It will be a faith, religiously more profound than that of many of its critics; but it will have learned to overcome the one fateful error of German Protestantism, the complete dichotomy between faith and political life."[1]

In the ensuing decades, Niebuhr's prescient insight that Bonhoeffer's life and work offered lasting insights for modern Christian experience and witness has been more than fulfilled. Bonhoeffer wrote hundreds of letters, sermons, and biblical reflections in addition to his published theological works. After 1945, Bonhoeffer's former student and close friend Eberhard Bethge worked with publishers to reissue and translate the books Bonhoeffer had published in his lifetime. In translation, these works—*Discipleship, Ethics,* and *Letters and Papers from Prison*—became classics, finding a wide readership among Christians throughout the world.

Yet there was a growing sense that these works should not stand alone—a realization of the significance of the biographical and historical context of his thought. Bonhoeffer's papers included lecture notes that had been made by his students, documents from the German Church Struggle and ecumenical meetings, circular letters that were sent to his seminarians, sermons, extensive correspondence with theologians and religious leaders in Europe and the United States, and prison writings. Bethge published several early compilations of some of these documents (*Gesammelte Schriften* and *Mündige Welt*) and incorporated additional material into his magisterial biography of Bonhoeffer, which first appeared in English in 1970 and then, in a revised and unabridged edition, in 2000.

Bethge and leading Bonhoeffer scholars in Germany decided to publish new annotated editions of Bonhoeffer's complete theological works, together with most of the documents from the literary estate, including historical documents and correspondence to Bonhoeffer. The *Dietrich Bonhoeffer Werke* series was published by Chr. Kaiser Verlag, now part of Gütersloher Verlagshaus. The first German volume, a new edition of Bonhoeffer's dissertation, *Sanctorum Communio,* appeared in 1986; the final volume, Bonhoeffer's complete prison writings, appeared in April 1998. An index volume (vol. 17) for the entire series appeared in 1999; this volume also included documents discovered after their respective volumes had been published. Whenever possible these documents are integrated into the appropriate volumes of the English edition; documents that continue to be discovered are published in the *Dietrich Bonhoeffer Jahrbuch,* a series published by Gütersloher Verlagshaus.

[1.] Reinhold Niebuhr, "The Death of a Martyr," *Christianity and Crisis* 5, no. 11 (1945): 6–7.

Discussion about an English translation of the entire series began as soon as the first German volumes appeared. In 1990, the International Bonhoeffer Society, English Language Section, in agreement with the German Bonhoeffer Society and Fortress Press, undertook the English translation of the German *Dietrich Bonhoeffer Werke*. The project began with an initial grant from the National Endowment for the Humanities with Robin Lovin serving as project director, assisted by Mark Brocker. An editorial board was formed for the *Dietrich Bonhoeffer Works*, English edition, staffed by Wayne Whitson Floyd Jr., as general editor, and Clifford J. Green of Hartford Seminary as executive director. Wayne Whitson Floyd Jr., at that time director of the Dietrich Bonhoeffer Center at the Lutheran Theological Seminary in Philadelphia, served as general editor from 1993 to 2004, overseeing publication of the first seven volumes as well as volume 9. Victoria J. Barnett, director of church relations at the U.S. Holocaust Memorial Museum, joined the project as associate general editor in 2002 and became general editor in 2004, joined by Barbara Wojhoski, a professional editor who prepared the manuscripts of the final volumes for publication.

The *Dietrich Bonhoeffer Works*, English edition (*DBWE*), is the definitive English translation of Bonhoeffer's theological and other writings. It includes a great deal of material that appears for the first time in English, as well as documents discovered only after the publication of the original German volumes. *DBWE* is a significant contribution to twentieth-century theological literature, church history, and the history of the Nazi era. Particularly in their portrayal of the daily implications of the Protestant Church Struggle in Nazi Germany and the response of Christians outside Germany, these volumes offer a detailed and unique glimpse of Bonhoeffer's historical context and its great challenges for the churches and for all people of conscience.

The translators of the *DBWE* volumes have attempted throughout to render an accurate and readable translation of Bonhoeffer's writings for contemporary audiences, while remaining true to Bonhoeffer's thought and style. Particular attention has been paid to the translation of important theological, historical, and philosophical terms. Bonhoeffer's language and style are often reflective of his age, particularly with regard to gendered language, and this is reflected in the historical and church documents. Nonetheless, in the translations of the early volumes of his theological writings (*DBWE* volumes 1–7), the decision was made to use gender-inclusive language, insofar as this was deemed possible without distorting Bonhoeffer's meaning or unjustifiably dissociating him from his own time.

Each volume includes an introduction written by the *DBWE* volume editor(s), footnotes provided by Bonhoeffer, editorial notes added by the

German and English editors, and the original afterword written by the editor(s) of the German edition. Additions or revisions of the German editors' notes are enclosed within square brackets and initialed by the editor of the respective volume. When any previously translated material is quoted within an editorial note in altered form—indicated by the notation [trans. altered]—such changes should be assumed to be the responsibility of the translator(s). Where available, existing English translations of books and articles in German and other languages are cited in the notes.

Bonhoeffer's own footnotes—which are indicated in the body of the text by plain, superscripted numbers—are reproduced in precisely the same numerical sequence as they appear in the German critical edition, complete with his idiosyncrasies of documentation. In these, as in the accompanying editorial notes, the edition of a work that was consulted by Bonhoeffer himself can be determined by consulting the bibliography at the end of each volume.

Each volume also contains a list of abbreviations frequently used in the editorial notes, as well as a bibliography of archival sources, sources used by Bonhoeffer, literature consulted by the editors, and other works relevant to that respective volume. Each volume also includes a chronology of important dates relevant to that volume, an index of scriptural references, an index of persons with relevant biographical information, and an index of subjects. Bibliographies at the end of each volume provide complete information for each written source that Bonhoeffer or the various editors have mentioned in the current volume.

Bonhoeffer's literary estate—the notes, sermons, and other writings, as well as correspondence, and the personal library of materials that belonged to him and survived the war—was cataloged by Dietrich Meyer and Eberhard Bethge; this catalog has been published as the *Nachlaß Dietrich Bonhoeffer.* Most of the documents cited in the *Nachlaß* are collected in the Berlin Staatsbibliothek, although some documents remain in other archives. All documents listed in the *Nachlaß*, however, have been copied on microfiches that are now at the Staatsbibliothek in Berlin and in the Bonhoeffer collection at Burke Library, Union Theological Seminary, New York. References to any of these documents are indicated within the *DBWE* by the abbreviation *NL*, followed by the corresponding catalog number. Books in the bibliography from Bonhoeffer's own library are indicated by the abbreviation *NL-Bibl.*

Volumes 1–7 of the English edition, which contain only Bonhoeffer's own writings, retain his original organization of the material, either as chapters or as sections or unnumbered manuscripts. Volumes 8–16 contain collected writings from a particular period of Bonhoeffer's life, including correspondence from others and historical documents. With the exception of volume 8, these final volumes are divided into three sections, with the documents in each section arranged chronologically: (1) Letters, Journals, Documents; (2) Essays, Seminar Papers, Papers, Lectures, Compositions; (3) Sermons, Meditations, Catechetical Writings, Exegetical Writings. Documents are numbered consecutively within the respective sections. In editorial notes these items are labeled with the *DBWE* volume number, followed by the section number, document number, and finally the page number, for example, *DBWE* 9, 1/109, p. 000, ed. note 1, would refer to the English edition, volume 9, section 1, document 109, page 000, editorial note 1.

The *DBWE* also reproduces Bonhoeffer's original paragraphing (exceptions are noted by a ¶ symbol to indicate any paragraph break added by the editors of the English edition or by conventions explained in the introductions written by the editor[s] of specific volumes). The pagination of the *DBW* German critical edition is indicated in the outer margins of the pages of the translated text. Where it is important to give readers a word or phrase in the original language, a translated passage is followed by the original, set within square brackets. All biblical citations come from the New Revised Standard Version (NRSV) unless otherwise noted. Where versification of the Bible used by Bonhoeffer differs from the NRSV, the verse number in the latter is noted in the text in square brackets.

The publication of the *Dietrich Bonhoeffer Works*, English edition, would not have been possible without the generous support of numerous individuals and institutions. The verso of the half-title page of each volume provides a list of supporters of that particular volume. The series as a whole is indebted to many individual members and friends of the International Bonhoeffer Society, and to family foundations, congregations, synods, seminaries, and universities. Special thanks are due to the following foundations and donors for major grants: the National Endowment for the Humanities; the Lilly Endowment, Inc.; the Thrivent Financial for Lutherans Foundation; the Aid Association for Lutherans; the Stiftung Bonhoeffer Lehrstuhl; the Bowen H. and Janice Arthur McCoy Charitable Foundation; and Dr. John Young and Ms. Cleo Young. The Lutheran Theological Seminary at Philadelphia and its former Auxiliary provided space and ongoing support. Particular thanks go to our publisher, Fortress Press, and its ever-helpful and skilled staff, particularly its editorial director, Michael West, and his predecessor, Marshall Johnson.

The existence of this series in English and other languages is testimony to the international community of those who have found Dietrich Bonhoeffer to be a profoundly important companion in their own journey. That community would not exist without the wisdom, generosity, and dedication of Eberhard Bethge (1909–2000) and his wife, Renate. Bethge was himself a pastor in the Confessing Church. After 1945, he was convinced that the future of a living church in Germany depended on its addressing its failures under Nazism and in a new understanding of Bonhoeffer's lasting question, Who is Christ for us today?

The editors of this English edition are particularly grateful to the original editorial board of the German edition—composed of Eberhard Bethge†, Ernst Feil, Christian Gremmels, Wolfgang Huber, Hans Pfeifer, Albrecht Schönherr†, Heinz Eduard Tödt†, and Ilse Tödt. As liaison between the German and English editorial boards, Hans Pfeifer has given steadfast and congenial support to his colleagues on both sides of the Atlantic. The editors of the individual German volumes have been generous with their time and expertise. As work on *DBWE* has proceeded, a new generation of Bonhoeffer scholars in Germany has assisted us as well: Christine Kasch, Andreas Pangritz, Holger Roggelin, Christiane Tietz, Ralf Wuestenberg.

We remain grateful to those whose original translations of Bonhoeffer's words introduced most of us to his work. It is only fitting, however, that this English edition be dedicated, finally, to the remarkable group of scholars who over the years have devoted their time, their insights, and their generous spirit to the translation, editing, and publication of these volumes. That dedication should begin with a special acknowledgment of the capable editorial leadership of Wayne Whitson Floyd Jr., who brought eight volumes to publication, and to Clifford J. Green, whose steady hand has guided the project throughout its existence and ensured the financial foundation for its completion.

The translators who have brought Bonhoeffer's words to new life in these volumes are Victoria Barnett, Douglas Bax, Claudia and Scott Bergmann-Moore, Isabel Best, Daniel W. Bloesch, James H. Burtness†, Lisa Dahill, Peter Frick, Barbara Green, David Higgins, Nick Humphrey, Reinhard Krauss, Peter Krey, Nancy Lukens, Mary Nebelsick, Marion Pauck, Martin Rumscheidt, Anne Schmidt-Lange, Douglas W. Stott, and Charles West.

Since its inception, the following people have served on the *DBWE* editorial board: H. Gaylon Barker, Victoria Barnett, Mark Brocker, Keith W. Clements, Wayne Whitson Floyd Jr., Peter Frick, Clifford J. Green, John W. de Gruchy, Barry Harvey, Geffrey B. Kelly, Reinhard Krauss, Michael Lukens, Larry Rasmussen, H. Martin Rumscheidt, and Barbara Wojhoski. The following served on the advisory committee: James H. Burtness†, John D. Godsey, Barbara Green, James Patrick Kelley, Robin W. Lovin, Nancy Lukens, Paul Matheny, and Mary Nebelsick.

In September 1943, Dietrich Bonhoeffer wrote his parents from prison: "In ordinary life we hardly realize that we receive a great deal more than we give, and that it is only with gratitude that life becomes rich. It is very easy to overestimate the importance of our own achievements in comparison with what we owe others."[2] Everyone who has worked on this project will, I believe, find meaning in those words and feel gratitude for Bonhoeffer's life and witness. It is a privilege to have been part of this long, deep, and rich conversation with Bonhoeffer's thought, and to extend that conversation to the readers of these volumes.

Victoria J. Barnett

[2.] *LPP,* 109.

Abbreviations

ACLU	American Civil Liberties Union
BA	Bundesarchiv
BBKL	*Biographisch-bibliographisches Kirchenlexicon*
CA	Confessio Augustana
DB-ER	*Dietrich Bonhoeffer: A Biography* (Fortress Press, rev. ed., 2000)
DBW	*Dietrich Bonhoeffer Werke,* German edition
DBWE	*Dietrich Bonhoeffer Works,* English edition
DCSV	Deutsche Christliche Studentenvereinigung
EKD	Evangelische Kirche in Deutschland
EZA	Evangelisches Zentralarchiv, Berlin
GS	*Gesammelte Schriften*
HA Bethel	Hauptarchiv, Bethel
KJV	King James Version
KGVBl	*Kirchliches Gesetz- und Veordnungsblatt*
Lic.	Licentiate
LKA	Landeskirchliches Archiv
LKA EKvW	Landeskirchliches Archiv der Evangelischen Kirche von Westfalen
LPP	*Letters and Papers from Prison*
LW	*Luther's Works,* American edition
NL	*Nachlaß Dietrich Bonhoeffer*
NRSV	New Revised Standard Version
NSDAP	Nationalsozialistische Deutsche Arbeiterpartei
PAM	*Predigten—Auslegungen—Meditationen* (Chr. Kaiser, 1984–85)
RGBl	*Reichsgesetzblatt*
RGG	*Die Religion in Geschichte und Gegenwart*

RSV	Revised Standard Version
SA	Sturmabteilung
SD	Solid Declaration of the Formula of Concord
SF	*Schöpfung und Fall*
SPD	Sozialdemokratische Partei Deutschland
TRE	*Theologische Realenzyklopädie*
WA	Martin Luther, *Werke*, Weimarer Ausgabe (Weimar edition)
WCC	World Council of Churches
YMCA	Young Men's Christian Association
ZEKHN	Zentralarchiv der Evangelischen Kirche in Hessen und Nassau
ZLB	Zentral- und Landesbibliothek, Berlin

Larry L. Rasmussen

Editor's Introduction to the English Edition

Civilization and barbarism are not incompatible. The university and the church can serve them both well. One might draw this sobering conclusion from *Berlin: 1932–1933.*

Dietrich Bonhoeffer's premonitions of such a fateful turning were already present when President Paul von Hindenburg appointed Adolf Hitler Reich chancellor at noon on January 30, 1933. A charged moment for the nation, it coincided with a decisive transition in Bonhoeffer's own life. "The period of learning and roaming" from 1928 until 1932 "had come to an end" as the twenty-six-year-old lecturer began to teach "on a faculty whose theology he did not share" and to preach "in a church whose self-confidence he regarded as unfounded." Bonhoeffer was becoming part of a society "that was moving toward political, social, and economic chaos," and he knew it.[1]

Eberhard Bethge, looking back at the "learning and roaming" and ahead to Bonhoeffer's deepening involvement in Germany's fate, draws a heavy line here, reflected in the titles of parts 2 and 3 of his biography of Bonhoeffer, "The Cost of Being a Christian" and "Sharing Germany's Destiny," respectively.[2]

[1.] *DB-ER,* 173.

[2.] *DB-ER,* 173–78.

This heavy line is short, spanning only eleven months. Across that compressed period, from November 1932 to October 1933, the documents included in the present volume provide insight into Bonhoeffer's dual work at the university and in the church. Yet neither the university's direction nor the church's, to say nothing of the imperial "Aryan" impulses playing out in the unruly streets of Berlin, was tolerable for him or his family. To a person the Bonhoeffers were aware that their responsibility as citizens remained, even as their society moved toward chaos. They were convinced that Hitler meant war, and it was already clear that, as patriots and people of conscience, they could not withdraw from the challenges facing them. Bonhoeffer nonetheless threw himself into his work and even reaped a certain satisfaction that he carried with him through the fray. As was the case throughout the Bonhoeffer family, much of his energy and activity was directed to unaccustomed resistance and the troubled search for alternatives amid unrelenting crises.

Theology's lure had brought him to this point. Although already torn between pulpit and lectern in Barcelona in 1928,[3] he felt fortunate to take up his prospective academic career as a lecturer (*Privatdozent*) on the theological faculty of Friedrich Wilhelm University in the winter semester of 1931–32; in the same month (November), he began his ordained ministry in charge of a confirmation class in Berlin-Wedding. Still, neither his spirit nor his sense of responsibility was sufficiently nurtured by the university, despite his enthusiasm for his students and the academic subject matter. Instead, the church captured his dedication, so completely, in fact, that even at the university his focus was on the Church Struggle.[4] The university was also the locus of Bonhoeffer's dogged efforts to live the Christian life differently. "It became clear to me that the life of a servant of Jesus Christ must belong to the church," he wrote later, "and step by step it became

[3.] In a letter to Helmut Rößler after he resumed his academic work post-Barcelona, he writes of an impending visit to "my congregation in Barcelona, of which I am very fond, and I feel in general that academic work will not hold me for long. But I do acknowledge that it is quite important to acquire beforehand the best academic training possible" (*DBWE* 10, 1/106, p. 205). See also Clifford Green's discussion of Bonhoeffer's divided loyalties in the editor's introduction to *DBWE* 10. Note especially the sections on Barcelona, Berlin, and New York, 4–43.

[4.] The Church Struggle—*Kirchenkampf*—was the protracted conflict within the Protestant churches over their identity in the new National Socialist state; it turned on bitterly contested church-state issues together with equally contested judgments about the moral and political legitimacy of the Nazi state. See the chapter "Nationalism, Nazism, and the Churches: The Early Period," in Barnett, *For the Soul of the People*, for an account that covers the period encompassed in this volume.

ever more evident how far this had to go. Then came the crisis of 1933. It only confirmed the new direction in which I was heading. And I now also found other people who shared the same vision and goal. The renewal of the church and the ministry became my supreme concern."[5]

Clear traces of this supreme concern wend their way through the pages that follow—in letters, lectures, memoranda, essays, radio addresses, debates, book reviews, confessions, and sermons. But absent a narrative, they are fragments. They are tiles but not a mosaic.

"I no longer believe in the university"

"Then came the crisis of 1933." The years 1932–33 in Germany can still leave the observer baffled—as it did some living at the time—by the spectacle of a civilized society disintegrating into barbarism. Single-factor theories for this catastrophe, while tempting, do not suffice. The mesmerizing power of a charismatic individual, Adolf Hitler, does not sufficiently explain what took place, despite his hold on a fawning population. Nor does National Socialism's ascent as the contagious brutality of thuggish leaders abetted by ignorant mobs.[6] Nor does the explanation of blind adherence to what was, for many, a powerful ideology. This was, after all, Germany—a teacher to the world, a leader in the arts, humanities, and sciences. In science Germans represented the majority of the thirty-eight Nobel laureates from 1905 to 1936. Fourteen were won by German Jews, with Berlin's halls of research and learning again in the forefront. This was also Germany, the nation of poets and thinkers, creators of the twinned ideals of *Bildung* and *Wissenschaft*—character formation through first-rate education and ordered knowledge dedicated to the pursuit of truth.[7] And this was Germany, the home of liberal Enlightenment scholarship, the seeming antithesis of the ecstatic irrationality that would soon prevail. (Bonhoeffer's own university exemplified this rigorous scholarship, through critical, open-minded inquiry and cutting-edge science.) Not least, German theology and philosophy were the most widely read and respected of the day. These disciplines were also popular: fully a thousand students were enrolled in theology at Friedrich Wilhelm University in Berlin when Bonhoeffer began teaching there.[8] The young professor's Christology lectures alone attracted as many as two hundred students.

[5.] *DBW* 14, 1/47, pp. 112–13; see also *DB-ER*, 204–5. Bonhoeffer's letter is from 1936, written to Elisabeth Zinn.

[6.] Isaacson, *Einstein*, 409.

[7.] Stern, *Five Germanys I Have Known*, 16.

[8.] *DB-ER*, 207.

Bonhoeffer, his family, friends, and members of his social stratum all breathed this heady air easily. Thus, he expected to settle into his profession as he took up his teaching post in November 1932.

Yet some German intellectuals contributed enthusiastically to the triumph of fascism. Prominent Protestant theologians whom Bonhoeffer knew and read were among them: Paul Althaus, Gerhard Kittel, Emanuel Hirsch, Friedrich Gogarten, Ernst Vogelsang, Wilhelm Stapel. So were secular philosophers whom Bonhoeffer had mastered (Heidegger was vital to his *Act and Being*). Already in 1930, Klaus Bonhoeffer wrote to Dietrich at Union Seminary in New York, "People are flirting with fascism. If this radical wave captures the educated classes, I am afraid that it will be all over for this nation of poets and thinkers."[9]

Bonhoeffer and his inner circle of university students thus confronted the bewildering decision of doing battle not only with fellow students, the majority of whom demanded a "Germanic" education and flocked to Hitler's racial-ethnic (*völkisch*) community of new promise and national rebirth. They also confronted their esteemed teachers in the one institution that, above all others, merited their respect and carried authority. May 10, 1933, presented a bizarre and unsettling sight, as the summer semester opened with a book burning on the Opernplatz beneath the Humboldt monument, with students and professors joining with SA (Sturmabteilung) members who tossed hundreds of volumes into the bonfire in the name of a national "will to live." Einstein and Mann, Freud and Rathenau, Zweig, Remarque, and Heuss were among the authors whose names were read out in celebration as their works went up in flames.[10] Among the authors whose books were consigned to the conflagration was Heinrich Heine, whose chilling prescience a century earlier would soon come to haunt sophisticated Berlin: "Where they burn books, they will ultimately also burn people."[11]

Berlin: 1932–1933 mirrors this pathos.[12] It also records eerie banality and impending tragedy. Routine duties, commonplace exchanges, the humdrum of daily life all are reflected in this volume. Yet now they become part of a very different story, a story reframing the German world so radically that Bonhoeffer would soon find himself a stranger in his own profession. He lectured to great effect on Christology and conducted courses on cre-

[9.] Klaus Bonhoeffer, letter of November 3, 1930, cited in *DB-ER*, 167.

[10.] *DB-ER*, 279–80.

[11.] The line is from Heine's 1821 play, *Almansor.* The original reference is to the burning of the Qur'an during the Spanish Inquisition.

[12.] See the following documents: 1/44, 1/45, 1/58, 1/64, 1/69, 1/77, 1/95, 1/102, 1/105.

ation and sin, the nature of the church, theological anthropology, recent works in systematic theology, and the question "Is There a Christian Ethic?" Yet he also began to question the allegiances he had taken for granted and the career he had assumed. "I no longer believe in the university; in fact I never really have believed in it—to your chagrin!" he wrote to Erwin Sutz the next year.[13]

Some of his students, like Bonhoeffer also at home with classic German *Bildung* and *Wissenschaft*, found themselves strangers in the emerging society as well. Later a number of them would take the work begun at the university elsewhere, to a very different school of formation and instruction—the Finkenwalde seminary. A new model for theological instruction was already on Bonhoeffer's mind. The same letter to Sutz continues, without interruption:

> The next generation of pastors, these days, ought to be trained entirely in church-monastic schools, where the pure doctrine, the Sermon on the Mount, and worship are taken seriously—which for all three of these things is simply not the case at the university and under the present circumstances is impossible. It is also time for a final break with our theologically grounded reserve about whatever is being done by the state—which really only comes down to fear. "Speak out for those who cannot speak"[14]—who in the church today still remembers that this is the very least the Bible asks of us in such times as these?[15]

In short, Bonhoeffer had decided that "credible Christian praxis and community was more important than his academic career"[16] in almost the same moment he embarked on that career. Moreover, even at the university he sought out men and women who would gravitate to a disciplined community that would share a life of theory and practice beyond the classroom. He took his students on retreat in Biesenthal[17] with some regularity, a rare teaching practice at the time. There he led them in a meditative approach to the Bible and argued for oral confession and a life of communal prayer and obedience. He even broached the subject of Christian pacifism, not a serious topic in either the university or the church at this time, except as the

[13.] *DBWE* 13, 1/147, p. 217.

[14.] Prov. 31:8.

[15.] *DBWE* 13, 1/147, p. 217.

[16.] Wind, *Dietrich Bonhoeffer*, 60.

[17.] A cabin that Bonhoeffer had purchased in a village outside Berlin as a retreat for his university students and confirmation class.

object of vilification.[18] (His own ecclesiastical superior later wrote church authorities that "because the reproach can be raised against [Bonhoeffer] that he is *a pacifist and an enemy of the state,* it might be advisable for the Provincial Church Committee to disassociate itself from him and take measures to ensure that German theologians no longer be trained by him.")[19] Yet here, at the university, were also the "other people who shared the same vision and goal" that he spoke of in a letter to Elisabeth Zinn.[20] He would gladly be a German theologian engaged in their training.

All this drama reflected a recent life-changing turn, a turn to the Sermon on the Mount and to life together as demanding discipleship. Still, Bonhoeffer said nothing to the students about his altered interests and new direction.[21] They simply assumed that their young professor's communitarianism, interpretation of Scripture, pedagogy, and practices had been trademarks of his teaching all along. And well they might have, since Bonhoeffer spoke little of his life journey and was always wary of drawing attention to himself. In the essay "What Should a Student of Theology Do Today?" he even warned these same students against making too much of their own journeys, including their experiences of call and vocation.[22] The advice was a stark contrast to the romantic indulgence of the many

[18.] With the help of his father, Bonhoeffer tried to interest professors at the university in the case of Günther Dehn, a professor of practical theology who was prevented from taking up his duties in Heidelberg and Halle after right-wing students and faculty demonstrated against him. Dehn had given a pacifist lecture and was dismissed in 1933 because he was "a pacifist and a socialist." Bonhoeffer's draft of a petition in the Dehn case, to be sent to the theological faculty in Halle, March 1932, is published in *DBW* 11, 1/40, and will be included in the forthcoming *DBWE* 11. In a letter to Paul Lehmann six months earlier, Bonhoeffer commented on the state of affairs in the universities: "A prelude to what can be expected from the National Socialists at the university is taking place right now in Halle, where the students (and not only the theology students) refuse to continue studying if a recently called pacifist professor of theology, who is an extraordinarily capable man, is not fired immediately [a reference to Dehn]. The intellectual level now entering the universities is simply dreadful" (letter of November 5, 1931, to Paul Lehmann, *DBWE* 11, 1/16a). See also Ernst-Albert Scharffenorth's comment on the Dehn affair in the afterword, p. 493.

[19.] Letter of March 7, 1936, from Theodor Heckel to the regional church council. *DBW* 14, 1/58.

[20.] *DBW* 14, 1/47, p. 113. Strikingly similar ideas about the Christian life, theological education, and the ministry can be found in the letter of September 14, 1933, from Wilhelm Stählin to Bonhoeffer. See 1/100.

[21.] Little noticed in the accounts of these years is that about a third of the "Bonhoeffer group"—i.e., the small group of students who attached themselves to Bonhoeffer and met with him regularly—were female. Wind, *Dietrich Bonhoeffer,* 61.

[22.] See 2/17.

fellow students (and faculty) caught up in the epic adventure of a new Germany set upon a new path.[23]

Yet because this Christian communitarianism, its style and theology, was unconventional, Bonhoeffer was suspect. Colleagues "have the feeling that they have been nurturing a snake in their bosom,"[24] he wrote Sutz. Even a senior colleague who was fond of him lamented Bonhoeffer's preoccupation: "It is a great pity that our best hope in the faculty is being wasted on the Church Struggle."[25] But a "waste" is not how Bonhoeffer viewed the Church Struggle and his search for viable Christian community at the university itself. The concrete form of the church amid grave uncertainty preoccupied him, as did the church's impoverished spiritual formation.

Friedrich Wilhelm University was not the only site of Bonhoeffer's activity. He moved from his parents' house into a room north of the Alexanderplatz, where his confirmation class of fifty boys could drop in, a few at a time, to talk, learn chess, or practice speaking English.[26] They, too, retreated with him on weekends to the cabin in Biesenthal. He said of one session close to their confirmation day, "I have structured the entire class on the basis of the concept of church-community, and the boys, who hear daily from political party organizations, note very well what this is all about."[27] His comments reflected the competing communities of allegiance, even faith. Confirmation Sunday, it turned out, was the same day as the German presidential election, March 13, 1932. Bonhoeffer preached on Jacob at the river Jabbok, the hard wrestling with the night visitor by whom Jacob, though wounded, is given a new name and a new identity, "Israel," the one who strove with God and was blessed. Bonhoeffer ended the sermon with a

[23.] See Bonhoeffer's insightful analysis "The Führer and the Individual in the Younger Generation" (2/9).

[24.] Letter of December 25, 1931, to Erwin Sutz, *DBW* 11, 1/27. Bonhoeffer is writing not only about the students drawn to his seminar and his (suspect) theology; he comments as well on his colleagues: "I almost never see any of the professors, not to my inconsolable regret. Since I returned from Bonn, things here seem even more desolate. Recently on two days, one after the other, I invited first the lecturers and then my students here to the house, and I must say that the students were considerably more interested in theology than the lecturers."

[25.] *DB-ER*, 221, quoting Arthur Titius, professor of systematic theology.

[26.] Bonhoeffer's letter of February 28, 1932, to Sutz has this account: "Since New Year's, I've been living here in the north [of Berlin], so that I can have the boys here every evening, naturally not all at the same time. We eat dinner together, afterward we play something—I have taught them chess and now they're playing it with great enthusiasm. In general, any of them can also come without an appointment. And they all like to come. . . . At the close of each evening I read something from the Bible and following that we have a little catechetics, which is often very serious" (*DBW* 11, 1/39).

[27.] Letter of February 26, 1932, to Sutz, *DBW* 11, 1/39.

repeat of its refrain, combining words of Jacob and Paul: "I will not let you go, unless you bless me! If God is for us, who is against us?"[28]

Bonhoeffer's ecumenical activity also reflected the concern for the church and the ministry in the face of fascism on the march. The liberal and humanist Anglo-Saxon currents of the World Alliance for Promoting International Friendship through the Churches were hardly congruent with Bonhoeffer's postliberal, revelation-centered Word of God ecclesiology. "The hitherto almost universally accepted Anglo-Saxon foundation simply does not suffice,"[29] he wrote in his report on the Cambridge meeting of September 1931, where he was elected one of three European youth secretaries. But the practical efforts of the World Alliance to take its peace work into parishes coincided with his quest for the concrete expression of the church on the compelling issues of the day. It also accorded with his conviction that the church as the body of Christ is a transnational body transcending ethnic-nationalist identities, a body that could rally forces across borders to oppose nationalism and war. Thus Bonhoeffer set his theological reservations aside for the moment to say that "for all the criticism . . . it remained evident that the work of the World Alliance is progressing slowly but surely. It is performing work that has urgency today. It is a work that must fire the heart and soul of every person but at this point we do not yet know how we could pursue it better and faster."[30]

The work "that must fire the heart and soul of every person" was an international order of peace. For Bonhoeffer, this was the concrete command given the church at this moment. It was discipleship as simple obedience to the Jesus of the Sermon on the Mount. But it was not for individual Christians alone. It was for the church collectively, meeting as an evangelical council and as a moral agent, vis-à-vis the state.[31]

Still, back home the church leadership largely supported, rather than resisted, National Socialism. It viewed the rest of Europe as enemies of Germany and therefore refused to make common cause with the ecumenical

---

[28.] *DBW* 11, 3/6, p. 414. The Pauline line, "If God is for us, who is against us?" is from Rom. 8:31; the Jacob sentence, "I will not let you go, unless you bless me," is Gen. 32:26b.

[29.] From "Report on a Conference of the World Alliance in Cambridge," *DBW* 11, 2/1, p. 129.

[30.] *DBW* 11, 2/1, p. 129.

[31.] "Christ and Peace" (2/6) explicitly draws the imperative of peace for the political order from Bonhoeffer's understanding of discipleship as the church's obedience to Jesus in the Sermon on the Mount. The lectures at Finkenwalde that resulted in *Discipleship* (*DBWE* 4) and Bonhoeffer's urging of the church's collective action for peace in ecumenical circles both have their antecedents in this late 1932/early 1933 essay.

movement. The church rank and file followed the same line. Bonhoeffer's efforts at "new ecclesial forms of community"[32] thus created few ripples and left no noticeable mark, at least at the time. The church, nonetheless, remained his center of gravity, more so than the university. He could, and would, leave the university. (He was, in any event, forbidden to teach there after August 1936 and forbidden to live in Berlin after January 1938.) He could not, and would not, leave the church—even when tense, deepening divisions took its leaders and members in very different directions. Some joined the march to fascism with conviction; some fled into a noncommittal neutrality and sought to distance faith from politics. A few voiced resistance in the name of protecting the proclamation of the gospel and church governance of its own affairs. Bonhoeffer personally identified with this latter group, although he believed that the dissenters were neither sufficiently decisive nor courageous.[33]

The tensions within and between these factions fill the pages of this volume. So do the passionate responses of Bonhoeffer, his students and friends. Yet one cannot gainsay that the most widespread and effective allegiances within the church and the university supported the Nazi visions for the resurrection of the humiliated nation.

Such ardent support of fascism by university and church—or, conversely, such lack of resistance to it—nonetheless remains enigmatic, at least for the reader who knows how the story begun in 1932–33 ends. Neither the bourgeois culture that Bonhoeffer cherished nor the socialist revolution making noise in the streets prevented the emergence of evil and the onset of barbarity. Nor were the temples of learning and the citadels of faith mighty fortresses or forces of good. Responses to the rise of National Socialist power varied widely, ranging from active, enthusiastic support for Nazism and its ideology to a dull apathy whereby people focused only on their immediate circle and daily routine, choosing to ignore the unpleasant truths surrounding them. Even today, with hundreds of studies on what happened in Europe between 1933 and 1945, this history leaves us with haunting questions about the path that began in 1933 and culminated in a genocide in which tens of thousands of "ordinary people" who loved their country committed the most unprecedented of crimes.[34] More must be

[32.] Bonhoeffer's phrase in his preface to *Life Together*. See *DBWE* 5:25.

[33.] Throughout 1933, a confessing movement was in the process of formation. With the Barmen Declaration in 1934, it became the Confessing Church.

[34.] The discussion of these factors in what Susan Neiman calls "the technological production of corpses" draws from her chapter "Homeless," especially the section "Mass Murders: Why Auschwitz?" in her book *Evil in Modern Thought*, 250–57.

said, then, especially about the church's entanglement in national renewal and the triumph in both university and church of "the masquerade of evil."[35]

100 Days

"Then came the crisis of 1933." Hitler deftly used his sense of Germany's providential election—and his own—to stir Christian support for what he and others dubbed "the national revolution." In a speech to the Associated Press on February 3, 1933, he described Christianity as "'the foundation of our entire moral health' and the family as 'the germ cell of our ethnic and political body.'"[36] "Positive Christianity" was the slogan in the 1920 Nazi party platform.[37] This slogan and "Kinder, Küche, Kirche" ("children, kitchen, church," describing the appropriate domain for women) became something of a mantra. Largely conservative and nationalistic Protestant clergy and laity, baring their dislike of the liberal-secular Weimar state and the loose morals of the 1920s, responded with displaced yearning for the authority and pride for which Bismarck and the Kaiser were symbols. That yearning was underwritten by acculturated Christianity long accustomed to privilege and standing, standing that had been largely lost among the masses during the Weimar years.[38] In the very early months of National

[35.] Bonhoeffer's phrase in *Ethics* (*DBWE* 6), considered in some detail later in this discussion.

[36.] Cited from Koonz, *Nazi Conscience*, 33. Hitler said much the same in a radio address on July 22, 1933, but was more explicit about what poison must be "burnt out": "The national government will maintain and defend the foundations on which the power of our nation rests. It will offer strong protection to Christianity as the very basis of our collective morality. Today Christians stand at the very heart of our country. We want to fill our culture again with the Christian spirit. We want to burn out all the recent immoral developments in literature, in the theater, and in the press—in short, we want to burn out the point of immorality which has entered our whole life and culture as a result of liberal excess during the past years" (Baynes, *Speeches of Adolf Hitler*, 1:871–72). I am grateful to Jeffrey Pugh for this citation, part of his narrative of Bonhoeffer's life in his *Religionless Christianity*, 27.

[37.] The article on religion in the 1920 Nazi party platform includes the following: "The party as such upholds the point of view of a positive Christianity without tying itself confessionally to any one confession. It combats the Jewish-materialistic spirit at home and abroad and is convinced that a permanent recovery of our people can only be achieved from within on the basis of common good before individual good" (cited from Barnett, *For the Soul of the People*, 32).

[38.] The details of the churches and Nazism can be found in Barnett, *For the Soul of the People*. See especially chap. 1, "Omens," 9–44. Barnett cites these figures for church revival: in 1932, 215,908 members left the Evangelical Church and only 49,700 joined. In 1933, 323,618 joined and 56,849 left (32).

Socialism, the party even encouraged Germans to rejoin the church (they did), and Hitler seemed to offer a pseudo-religious and populist, even mystical, transformation of politics itself. Clergy and laity in turn reciprocated with enthusiasm for what they regarded as the opportunity to re-evangelize the nation and rejuvenate the church. Then, with the burning of the strongest symbol of the German state, the Reichstag, on February 27, 1933, Hitler had the terrorist act he needed to move swiftly from a faltering democracy toward party control and dictatorship (some historians believe that the Nazi party itself was behind the fire). Hindenburg complied by suspending constitutional protection of individual freedoms and imposing restrictions on freedom of speech and association while allowing detention of suspects without trial.[39] The Reichstag Fire Edict (officially the Emergency Decree of February 28) was the first of a series of decrees that consolidated all power under Hitler. (This decree was cited when the Gestapo shut down the Finkenwalde seminary four and a half years later.)

The most critical of these consolidating laws were the Malicious Practices Act of March 21, the Enabling Act of March 23, and the Law for the Reconstitution of the Civil Service of April 7, paragraph 3 of which was the so-called Aryan paragraph. The Malicious Practices Act supplied the judicial measures to prosecute anyone who, "with malice aforethought," put forward reports that might impair the welfare of the Reich; effectively this meant anyone whose criticism of the state might be interpreted as disloyalty. The Enabling Act (officially the Law to Remove the Crisis of the People and the State) suspended the Weimar constitution, giving Hitler dictatorial powers. The evening before its passage, Hitler spoke to the churches, offering the following assurance: "The National Government sees the two Christian confessions [Protestant and Catholic] as the most important factors safeguarding our national heritage . . . in Christianity [we have] the unshakable foundations of our people's ethical and moral life."[40] Finally, with the Law for the Reconstitution of the Civil Service of April 7, "non-Aryans" and anyone whose political loyalty could be questioned, such as socialists and Communists, were banned from the civil service. The first dismissals of suspect professors followed this legislation as well. Taken together with other Aryan legislation, this "reconstitution" wrote racial/ethnic discrimination and ideological conformity into the law of the land.

[39.] For a concise account of these developments, see Field, "Dietrich Bonhoeffer," 390. Pugh's *Religionless Christianity* also has a succinct, accurate account in chap. 2, "A Life among the Fragments."

[40.] *DB-ER*, 268. Bethge cites Hitler's words from Norden, *Kirche in der Krise*, 45.

In less than three months, then, almost everything legally required for the organization of barbarism and brutality was in place. It would be a while before the various sectors of the military, education, religion, the judiciary, and bureaucracy could all be brought into full conformity with the state (the process known as *Gleichschaltung*), and this present volume reflects over and again this fluidity and chaos in society, together with the turmoil in the churches. It also reflects Bonhoeffer's hope that this very restlessness, uncertainty, and transience could mean malleability and opportunity. Nonetheless, the social and political realities were already pieced together for the portentous drama Bonhoeffer later described in *Ethics*. "Today we have villains and saints again, in full public view. The gray on gray of a sultry, rainy day has turned into the black cloud and bright lightning flash of a thunderstorm. The contours are sharply drawn. Reality is laid bare. Shakespeare's characters are among us."[41]

The sharp contours belong to what Bonhoeffer called "the masquerade of evil." Evil gathers to itself its opposite and takes "the form of light, of beneficence, of faithfulness, of renewal, . . . of historical necessity, of social justice."[42] Lucifer appears as an angel of light. Such cunning renders traditional moral options inadequate, which Bonhoeffer then inventoried[43] as impotent in the face of the National Socialist juggernaut. In their stead, the morally perverse triumphs. "At such a time," Bonhoeffer wrote in his passage on Hitler, "the tyrannical despiser of humanity easily makes use of the meanness of the human heart by nourishing it and giving it other names. Anxiety is called responsibility; greed is called industriousness; lack of independence becomes solidarity; brutality becomes masterfulness. By this ingratiating treatment of human weaknesses, what is base and mean is generated and increased ever anew. The basest contempt for humanity carries on its sinister business under the most holy assertions of love for humanity."[44] Such was the victory of the politics of resentment in a proud and offended nation fighting those who would disgrace a beloved *Volk* and *Vaterland*.

Thus, in practice, from 1933 until the collapse of the "Thousand Year Reich" twelve years later, almost every moral act would be illegal and almost every legal act a crime. Those who accused the state of terror would soon

[41.] *DBWE* 6:76.

[42.] *DBWE* 6:77.

[43.] See the section in *Ethics* on the common ethical options and their failure, *DBWE* 6:77–80.

[44.] *DBWE* 6:85–86.

themselves be accused (of treason). And like those they sought to save, Jews and others, they too would become state victims.[45]

But this is to leap ahead. For most Germans, the early months of 1933 did not lay bare what was to come. Yet Bonhoeffer *did* sense that during the winter and spring of 1933 the die was cast. His address "The Younger Generation's Altered View of the Concept of Führer," included in this volume, was broadcast February 1, two days after Hitler's accession to power. Several sermons, also included in this volume, share a similar sense of foreboding and coincide with church elections or other meetings heavy with national import. At least from Bonhoeffer's perspective, the goose-step to catastrophe had begun. Deliberate fear had been stoked in the general population, aroused by the menacing presence of external and internal enemies. Authoritarian leadership and ecstatic patriotism were publicly displayed in great spectacles that used mass media to great effect—all in the name of a primitive unity parading as a grand community, using "the stolen words of true community."[46]

"The stolen words of true community" is Bonhoeffer's phrase in *Ethics*, drafted a decade later. Yet his portrayal there of Nazi ideology and institutionalization is retrospective; it reflects 1933 as well as 1943. The same description of Hitler continues without a break as Bonhoeffer described evil's diabolical ways.

> For the tyrannical despiser of humanity, popularity is a sign of the greatest love for humanity. He hides his secret profound distrust of all people behind the stolen words of true community. While he declares himself before the masses to be one of them, he praises himself with repulsive vanity and despises the rights of every individual. He considers the people stupid, and they become stupid; he considers them weak, and they become weak; he considers them criminal, and they become criminal. His most holy seriousness is frivolous play; his conventional protestations of solicitude for people are bare-faced cynicism. In his deep contempt for humanity, the more he seeks the favor of those he despises, the more certainly he arouses the masses to declare him a god. Contempt for humanity and idolization of humanity lie close together.[47]

[45.] A reference to Bonhoeffer's poem from prison "Night Voices in Tegel" to be published in the forthcoming *DBWE* 8, 3/175.

[46.] Bonhoeffer's observation in *Ethics*, in his profile of Hitler and the Nazi regime's effective use of ideology. See *DBWE* 6:86.

[47.] Ibid.

Early 1933 witnessed not only the denial of human rights and the curtailment of the rule of law mentioned earlier but also active hostility to a free press, together with the systematic invasion of privacy and an excessive reliance on secrecy. Not least, the revived dream of a German empire (*Reich*) moved front and center. The reactions of the German population and its leaders to the perceived humiliations of the (imposed) Treaty of Versailles led to a resurgence of militarism that ultimately culminated in aggressive plans to expand German boundaries. The new national pride in a "master race" also fed a virulent anti-Semitism and, more broadly, a racism that targeted not only Jews but those with genetic and other disabilities, considered "unworthy of life" (*lebensunwertes Leben*), as well as the Slavic so-called *Untermenschen* in the east. Other political and societal scapegoats included homosexuals, Communists, and anyone perceived as a potential threat by the Nazi regime. Germany, now both fighting economic chaos and taking to the streets afire with passion for renewed greatness, had marched to fascism in the space of little more than one hundred days.

The German Christian movement, one of the parties in the Church Struggle, embraced this course with emotion and enthusiasm rarely seen in the normally sober circles of central and northern European Protestantism. The culmination of several nationalist Protestant movements that emerged during the 1920s, the German Christians reached their peak in 1933. In April 1933, Hitler appointed Ludwig Müller, a former military chaplain and enthusiastic German Christian, as his advisor on questions concerning the Protestant church; and in July 1933, the German Christians won an overwhelming victory in the national church elections. Müller became Reich bishop in September 1933, at the "Brown Synod," so named because many church delegates appeared in brown SA uniforms. But even beyond the German Christian movement, the standing Protestant tradition of piety and theological support for nationalism and the powers of the state, together with the privileged status of the Volkskirche, provided ecclesial underpinning for National Socialism. As Bonhoeffer commented to Sutz, the time was long overdue "for a final break with our theologically grounded reserve about whatever is being done by the state."[48] Writing Sutz on April 14, 1933, about the "Jewish question," he remarked that even "the most intelligent people have totally lost both their heads and their Bible."[49] His brother's fear

[48.] *DBWE* 13, 1/147, p. 217.
[49.] 1/38, p. 101.

about losing "this nation of poets and thinkers"[50] had been realized, abetted by "a neo-Lutheran religious enhancement of the idea of nation."[51]

All these conditions, whether plainly documented or implicit in the texts, frame every page of *Berlin: 1932–1933* to the end, when, after the German Christian triumph at the Brown Synod, Bonhoeffer decided to leave his dual work in Berlin and pastor two German congregations in London. His life had taken a turn he did not expect at the very moment when his nation had taken a direction he could not accept. He put it this way to his brother Karl-Friedrich:

> We really have hardly seen each other at all in the last few years, so the days together recently were very good ones for me. Perhaps I seem to you rather fanatical and mad about a number of things. I myself am sometimes afraid of that. But I know that the day I became more "reasonable," to be honest, I should have to chuck my entire theology. When I first started in theology, my idea of it was quite different—rather more academic, probably. Now it has turned into something else altogether. . . . I think I am right in saying that I would only achieve true inner clarity and honesty by really starting to take the Sermon on the Mount seriously. Here alone lies the force that can blow all this hocus-pocus sky-high—like fireworks, leaving only a few burnt-out shells behind. The restoration of the church must surely depend on a new kind of monasticism,[52] which has nothing in common with the old but a life of uncompromising discipleship, following Christ according to the Sermon on the Mount. I believe the time has come to gather people together and do this.
>
> Forgive me for these rather personal ramblings, but they just came to me as I thought about our time together recently. And, after all, we *do* have an interest in each other. I still have a hard time thinking that you really find all these ideas completely mad. Things do exist that are worth standing up for without compromise. To me it seems that peace and social justice are such things, as is Christ himself.
>
> I recently came across the fairy tale of "The Emperor's New Clothes," which really is relevant for our time. All we are lacking today is the child who speaks up at the end.[53]

[50.] From Klaus Bonhoeffer's letter of November 3, 1930, cited in *DB-ER*, 167.

[51.] Heinz Eduard Tödt's phrase in *Authentic Faith*, 118.

[52.] Bonhoeffer initiated this in the cloistered seminary at Finkenwalde; the world knows it in another form, his little book *Life Together*, available in a revised and critical edition in *DBWE* 5.

[53.] Letter to Karl-Friedrich Bonhoeffer, January 14, 1935, *DBWE* 13, 1/193, pp. 284–85.

Bonhoeffer's earlier disinterest in politics had now disappeared, a victim of the ending and the beginning that 1932–33 signaled for him. A Christmas Day letter to Helmut Rößler in 1932 testifies to this, as does another to Reinhold Niebuhr some weeks later, just days after Hitler had been handed the reins of government. In a quite different way, the 1932 address "Thy Kingdom Come!" marks similar terrain.

The letter to Rößler recalls a time when Bonhoeffer voiced his lack of investment in things political. Now that "strikes me as frivolous," he wrote.[54] The letter to Niebuhr laments "a terrible barbarization of our culture, so that here, too, we will need to create a Civil Liberties Union."[55] Niebuhr might well imagine for himself, Bonhoeffer continued, that the current "nationalist magical incantations and exorcisms (military posturing, etc.) will not drive out the ghost of Communism."[56]

"Thy Kingdom Come!" expresses Bonhoeffer's stance differently, in the form of his theological rejection of the standard church/world dualism regnant in many circles, together with a spirited rejection of otherworldliness, pure inwardness, and eschatological postponement. Both church and state belong to the kingdom and to the *ius civitatis* (the civil order). "Thy kingdom come *on earth*," all of it, is the theme (as it is in Bonhoeffer's report on the social gospel):[57]

> Whoever evades the Earth finds not God but only another world, his own better, lovelier, more peaceful world. He finds a world beyond, to be sure, but never God's world, which is dawning in this world. Whoever evades Earth in order to find God finds only himself. Whoever evades God in order to find the Earth does not find the Earth as God's Earth; he finds the jolly scene of a war between good and evil, pious and impious, which he kindles himself—in short, he find himself. He who loves God, loves God as the Lord of the Earth as it is; he who loves the Earth, loves it as God's Earth. He who loves God's kingdom loves it entirely as *God's* kingdom, and he loves it wholly as *God's kingdom on Earth.* And this because the king of the kingdom is the creator and preserver of the Earth, who has blessed the Earth and taken us from earth.[58]

[54.] 1/22, p. 85.

[55.] A reference to the American Civil Liberties Union, about which Bonhoeffer had learned at Union Theological Seminary in conjunction with a terrible miscarriage of racial justice that the ACLU sought to rectify, the 1931 Scottsboro case.

[56.] 1/31, p. 94.

[57.] See 2/4.

[58.] 2/11, p. 288.

Although Bonhoeffer was always a sharp observer of political, social, and cultural developments, he was not always so directly engaged or so insistent upon the church's straightforward, concrete, and collective involvement. Yet it is precisely the church that now must be empirically well informed, concretely political, and decisive, "for others."[59] ("Things do exist that are worth standing up for without compromise. To me it seems that peace and social justice are such things, as is Christ himself.")[60] If the church is not concretely for others, on God's Earth—*as* God's Earth, it is no longer the church. The "Jewish question," above all, had forced the issue, as we shall see.

"The crisis of 1933" had pushed Bonhoeffer's life onto a different course and into a different story, one that Bethge aptly described as "The Cost of Being a Christian" and "Sharing Germany's Destiny."

"Germanism or Christianity"

If this is the historical-biographical context, what is the theological pulse?

By 1932–33, Bonhoeffer had already written his doctoral dissertation, *Sanctorum Communio,* and his postdoctoral work, *Act and Being.* While both were exercises in dogmatics, they shared a theme present throughout this volume, namely, Bonhoeffer's insistence on the concreteness of God's revelation in Jesus Christ in the church. "Christ is the word of God's freedom," he had written in *Act and Being*; "God *is* present; that is, not in eternal nonobjectivity but—to put it quite provisionally for now—'haveable,' graspable in the Word within the church."[61] But now, in 1932–33, the language steadily shifted from the sociological (*Sanctorum Communio*) and epistemological (*Act and Being*) to the ethical and to personal discipleship. This paralleled the attention in his systematic theology to the practices of an intentional communal Christian life. It also paralleled his growing interest in Gandhi's ashram and the disciplines of nonviolence. The boundary between theology, ethics, and Christian practice became porous for Bonhoeffer as he sought the timely concreteness of God's revelation in that circumscribed space in the world where Jesus Christ exists as day-to-day community, namely, the church.[62] Later, in *Ethics,* and under the influence of his involvement

[59.] A reference to Bonhoeffer's formulation in his "Outline for a Book" in *LPP,* 382: "The church is the church only when it exists for others." This document will be published as 4/187 in the forthcoming *DBWE* 8.

[60.] The letter to Karl-Friedrich, cited earlier, *DBWE* 13, 1/193, p. 285.

[61.] *DBWE* 2:91. The emphasis is Bonhoeffer's.

[62.] A reference to the thesis of *Sanctorum Communio* (*DBWE* 1).

in the military-political resistance, the boundaries of discipleship, faith, and obedience systematically expanded from the church to encompass the whole of earthly life as it is lived in various sectors and structures. But intimations of this were already present in 1932–33, as we have seen (in the lines from "Thy Kingdom Come!" for example).[63]

The reader should keep in mind this convergence of theology with ethics and discipleship for several of the essays in this volume—"Christ and Peace," "What Is Church?" "Thy Kingdom Come! The Prayer of the Church-Community for God's Kingdom on Earth," and "The Church and the Jewish Question." Even "Dogmatic Exercises on 'Theological Anthropology,'" reconstructed from student notes, finishes with a discussion of the practices needed to form Christian character.

That said, the best guide to these pages is Bethge. In summarizing Bonhoeffer's work in these years, he captured the movement across this volume precisely, even brilliantly. "Together with the reformers and Karl Barth, [Bonhoeffer] wanted to learn to spell out and teach what 'justification,' 'revelation,' and the 'word of God' were. In the process, however, his interpretation of all three concepts immediately became something tangible as 'peace,' 'commandment,' and 'connection to church' [*Kirchlichkeit*]. Several years later they would be given a different name, remaining for him what they had been: 'justice,' 'discipleship,' and 'life together.'"[64]

"They would be given a different name," but they would remain "for him what they had been." With this in mind, we turn to the documents.

In the afterword to this volume, Ernst-Albert Scharffenorth addresses Bonhoeffer's activity in three arenas: his university teaching, his work in the German Protestant and ecumenical church, and his confrontation with the political questions of the day. A summary of Scharffenorth's work permits us to forgo further comment here, at least regarding some of the documents. The reader can then use this introduction to the English edition and Scharffenorth's afterword in complementary fashion. Also, given the separate treatment of the Bethel confession by Carsten Nicolaisen, together with Scharffenorth's commentary, only a few additional remarks about that important work are needed.[65]

[63.] See, for example, the sections in *Ethics*, "Christ, Reality, and Good: Christ, Church, and World" and "History and Good [1]," *DBWE* 6:47–75 and 219–44, respectively. Readers who wish to trace the influence of Bonhoeffer's military-political resistance on his theology and ethics can consult Rasmussen, *Dietrich Bonhoeffer*.

[64.] *DB-ER*, 219.

[65.] Scharffenorth and Nicolaisen are coeditors of the German edition of volume 12. I am grateful for their part in answering questions that arose in preparing the English edition.

Entering Bonhoeffer's classroom, Scharffenorth guides the reader through Bonhoeffer's critique of the theologians he was teaching—Karl Barth, Emil Brunner, Friedrich Gogarten, and Karl Heim, among others. Since Bonhoeffer's chief theological work was his Christology lectures, his differences vis-à-vis the liberal theology he himself had learned in Berlin from Harnack and Seeberg, on the one hand, and the dialectical Word of God theology of Barth and Brunner, on the other, received special attention. Although liberal theology had been largely discredited, Bonhoeffer wanted to incorporate some elements of it into dialectical theology, a subject still on his mind, and refined, in the later prison letters.[66]

Scharffenorth rightly goes beyond Bonhoeffer's classroom duties at the university and chaplaincy duties at the Technical College to emphasize his part in the debates with the German Christian movement. Although extracurricular, the debates were well attended and took place on university grounds with university students and faculty participating. The newly formed Young Reformation movement chose Bonhoeffer as one of their main speakers for a high-profile confrontation with the German Christians on June 22, 1933, in the large, new assembly hall. Bonhoeffer, for whom opposition to the Aryan paragraph had become the touchstone for truth and the test for a valid confession of faith, asked for a binding conciliar decision. This call for a convened church council to render a decisive verdict of faith on the "Jewish question" was an unexpected request and an unpopular one.[67] Bonhoeffer himself was clear: both the "Jewish question" and the ecumenical imperative of peace demanded a doctrinal decision by the collective church in response to Christ's binding command. Few others were convinced, however.

Scharffenorth goes on to treat Bonhoeffer's engagement abroad. The memorandum on the social gospel, the theses on "Christ and Peace," and Bonhoeffer's considerable correspondence with ecumenical leaders are the relevant documents here. The treatment of the American social gospel reflects Bonhoeffer's turn to ethical questions and his defense of the church's social engagement on its own basis and its own terms (rather than as the state's chaplain and partner). The theses on "Christ and Peace" engage what became the chief ethical theme of Bonhoeffer's ecumenical

[66.] See, e.g., the long letter to Bethge of June 8, 1944, *LPP*, 324–29. A new translation of this letter will appear in the forthcoming *DBWE* 8, 3/161.

[67.] See 1/58, 2/13, and 2/14. In asking for a binding conciliar decision, Bonhoeffer was calling for a council comparable to the early church councils that established doctrine and creeds or, later, that established the official confessions of the Reformation churches. In the 1933 case cited here, the condition of *status confessionis* demanded that the Protestant churches agree upon a valid confession of faith.

involvement, namely, international peace. More will be said about "Christ and Peace" below. Suffice it to note here that the stimulus for this work can be traced back to Bonhoeffer's friendship with the Frenchman Jean Lasserre at Union Seminary, New York. "After meeting Lasserre," Bethge notes, "the question of the concrete reply to the biblical injunction of peace and of the concrete steps to be taken against warlike impulses never left [Bonhoeffer] again."[68]

The ecumenical correspondence traces how the domestic turbulence in 1932–33 affected Bonhoeffer's limited but concentrated participation in conferences abroad. In contrast to the many Protestant leaders in Germany who voiced deep suspicion of the ecumenical movement because it included "internationalists"[69] hostile to Germany, Bonhoeffer was convinced that the German churches must not distance themselves from Christians in the body of Christ elsewhere. He did what he could to inform leaders abroad about church developments at home and seek their support. A vital part of this effort was representing the dissenting Protestant ranks that soon formed the Confessing Church.

Scharffenorth treats Bonhoeffer's confrontation with political questions in various ways. While separate attention will be given Bonhoeffer's sermons in this introduction, the reader will benefit from Scharffenorth's statement of Bonhoeffer's goal: "to confront his listeners directly with what God has to say here and now" and to strengthen "his listeners' faith in overcoming fear."[70] Striking is Bonhoeffer's capacity to respond with con-

[68.] *DB-ER*, 153. Heinz Eduard Tödt has shown that, in addition to Lasserre's influence, Bonhoeffer's peace ethic expresses tenets of the ecclesiology already in place when he went to Union in 1930–31. See the chapter "Dietrich Bonhoeffer's Ecumenical Ethic of Peace," in Tödt, *Authentic Faith*, 112–41. My gratitude to Ernst-Albert Scharffenorth for this reference.

[69.] A 1931 letter by two theologians well known to Bonhoeffer, Paul Althaus and Emanuel Hirsch, was published during the preparatory meeting, in Hamburg, for the meeting of the World Alliance later that year in Cambridge (Bonhoeffer was present at both meetings). The letter was published on the front pages of right-wing papers across Germany. It read: "In this situation, in our judgment, there can be no understanding between us Germans and the victorious nations in the world war; we can only show them that as long as they continue the war against us, understanding is impossible. . . . This lends weight to the demand [that we] break through all artificial semblance of cooperation and ruthlessly acknowledge that a Christian and church understanding and cooperation on the questions of rapprochement among the peoples is impossible as long as the others are waging a murderous policy against our people. . . . Whoever believes that understanding can be better served otherwise, disowns the German destiny and confuses consciences at home and abroad, because this does not honor the truth" (cited from *DB-ER*, 195).

[70.] Afterword, p. 494.

siderable rhetorical skill to the political upheaval of the day while avoiding direct political statements. Bonhoeffer assumed his hearers, guided by the biblical text and its interpretation in the act of proclamation, could draw their own conclusions.

Among the political confrontations Bonhoeffer did address directly, the "Jewish question" merits special treatment. Scharffenorth provides considerable detail, and the reader is urged to give these pages special attention.[71] Not only is the singular significance of the "Jewish question" noted, together with the ways Bonhoeffer confronted it, but a Jewish response *to* Bonhoeffer, published in the *Jüdische Rundschau*, is cited as well. The reporter called attention to Bonhoeffer's enumeration of three ways the church might react to state-sponsored injustice, the ultimate one being to disable the state by force. Since Bonhoeffer's enumeration went well beyond any discussions of the day, we also comment on it below. The remainder of Scharffenorth's treatment of Bonhoeffer and the Jews is noteworthy, including the manner in which the church's position regarding the Jews was, and was not, treated in the versions of the Bethel confession. (See also Nicolaisen's "Concerning the History of the Bethel Confession" in this volume.)

The afterword's lengthiest treatment of civic and ecclesial confrontation concerns, as we would rightly expect, the Nazi rise to power and the events that followed in its wake. Scharffenorth draws from Bonhoeffer's February 1933 letter to Reinhold Niebuhr[72] and then turns to his radio broadcast in the same month, "The Younger Generation's Altered View of the Concept of Führer."[73] Information is provided not only on the radio address and the circumstances surrounding it but also on two follow-up efforts by Bonhoeffer. Like the radio address, these subsequent efforts warned of the dangers that accompanied too much authority in the hands of the Führer. At the same time, Bonhoeffer's remarks provided the basis for a more conservative, that is, more limited, view of the state and "worldly authority." Scharffenorth closes with his own assessment of Bonhoeffer's political engagement, viewed in the context of those tumultuous years as well as later.

The preceding remarks serve as an introduction and supplement to the following discussion.

It may seem odd to begin at the end of the volume, with the sermons. Yet some were delivered early in the period this volume encompasses, in 1932,

[71.] See pp. 495–99.
[72.] 1/31.
[73.] 2/8.

while others were preached as late as July 1933, a few months before Bonhoeffer left for London. All of them, as Bonhoeffer would say about the one on the golden calf and the church of Aaron and Moses, were "becoming incredibly relevant for today."[74] In this same July 17 letter to Sutz, he went on to note that on the Sunday of the church elections he would preach on Matthew 16:18: "You are Peter, and on this rock I will build my church, and the gates of Hades will not prevail against it." Those elections, held July 23, were marked by Hitler's open support for the pro-Nazi German Christians: Hitler took to the radio waves on election eve and urged voters to cast their ballots for German Christian candidates.

Yet the relevance of these sermons, no doubt enhanced by the liberty Bonhoeffer took in choosing the biblical texts, did not begin in mid-1933. A sermon preached on Reformation Sunday the previous year, November 6, 1932, was anything but the usual celebration of the churches' pride in Martin Luther's epochal achievement. Bonhoeffer chose Revelation 2:4–5, 7 as his text. A portion reads: "But I have this against you, that you have abandoned the love you had at first. Remember then from what you have fallen; repent, and do the works you did at first. If not, I will come to you and remove your lampstand from its place, unless you repent."[75] Bonhoeffer's sermon is lined with foreboding and judgment, even national apocalypse. It ends with these words:

> The last hour has almost come for our church. God has been very patient and long-suffering. No one knows that day and hour. It could break out at any moment and sweep everything away. We can already see things happening all around. God has been known to employ the strangest of instruments in working destruction. The story of Jerusalem's destruction by unbelievers is beginning to take on a terrible relevance for us. However it may come—we had better not make up any fine words, today, about the heroic things we would do when such a breakdown comes—let God be the Lord. . . .
>
> And now, when you leave the church, don't think about whether that was a fine or a poor Reformation service, but let us go soberly and do the works that came first. God be our help. Amen.[76]

The "terrible relevance" of "Jerusalem's destruction by unbelievers" came sooner rather than later. On January 15, shortly before Hitler's accession to power, Bonhoeffer preached to the people's mood.

[74.] See 1/67, p. 140.
[75.] Rev. 2:4–5.
[76.] 3/1, pp. 445–46.

> The overcoming of fear—that is what we are proclaiming here. The Bible, the gospel, Christ, the church, the faith, are all one great battle cry against fear in the lives of human beings. Fear is, somehow or other, the archenemy itself. It crouches in people's hearts. It hollows out their insides, until their resistance and strength are spent and they suddenly break down. Fear secretly gnaws and eats away all the ties that bind a person to God and others, and when in a time of need that person reaches for those ties and clings to them, they break and the individual sinks back into himself or herself, helpless and despairing, while hell rejoices.[77]

A February 26 sermon, Bonhoeffer's first after Hitler grasped the reins of government, was emphatic about the singular altar for Christians and the temptation of idolatry. The preacher contrasted the reluctant Gideon with Siegfried, the unconquered Germanic hero figure of the Nibelung saga, who was already being idealized in Nazi propaganda. Bonhoeffer told the congregation that human beings are to be not heroes but humble creatures of God who know the object of their faith, the one and only God.

> In the church we have only *one* altar—the altar of the Most High, the One and only, the Almighty, the Lord, to whom alone be honor and praise, the Creator before whom all creation bows down, before whom even the most powerful are but dust. We don't have any side altars at which to worship human beings. . . .
>
> In the church we also have only *one* pulpit, from which faith in God is preached and not any other faith, not even with the best intentions.[78]

Bethge contrasts Bonhoeffer's Berlin sermon with the scene in the Magdeburg Cathedral, where the dean mounted the pulpit amid a forest of Nazi flags surrounding the altar and announced that the swastika flag "has simply become the symbol of German hope. Whoever reviles this symbol is reviling our Germany. . . . The swastika flags round the altar radiate hope—hope that the day is at last about to dawn."[79]

Bonhoeffer's counter to this "other faith" and its triumphalist hope in

[77.] 3/4, p. 455. Bonhoeffer's text is from Matt. 8:23–27, when "a great storm" arose on the Sea of Galilee and the disciples called to Jesus, "Save us, Lord; we are sinking!"

[78.] 3/5, pp. 462–63. Bonhoeffer's text is Judg. 6:15–16; 7:2; 8:23, in which Gideon says he cannot answer God's call to deliver Israel from the Midianites because he is too weak and fearful.

[79.] *DB-ER*, 257. Bethge is quoting the cathedral dean, Ernst Martin, as cited in *Die Christliche Welt* (1933): 45.

the national revolution could hardly have been clearer. Again the figure is Gideon and his humble army.[80]

> The people approach the victorious Gideon with the final trial, the final temptation: "Be our lord, rule over us." But Gideon has not forgotten his own history, nor the history of his people . . . The Lord will rule over you, and you shall have no other lord. At this word, all the altars of gods and idols fall down, all worship of human beings and human self-idolization. They are all judged, condemned, cancelled out, crucified, and toppled into the dust before the One who alone is Lord. Beside us kneels Gideon, who was brought through fear and doubt to faith, before the altar of the one and only God, and with us Gideon prays, Lord on the cross, be our only Lord. Amen.[81]

The May 28 sermon in the Kaiser Wilhelm Memorial Church on the church of Moses and the church of Aaron was yet another instance of ecclesial-political import. The Young Reformation movement had been founded at the university in early May in response to German Christian agitation. Many church bodies were still ambivalent about their allegiance, or their resistance, to the Nazi platform. They were often confused as well, sometimes bundling contradictions in their proposals as they sought to display their patriotism as well as their unease. The Young Reformation movement, for example, rejected the proposed exclusion of "non-Aryans" from the church yet affirmed the new German state.[82] They also went along with a special office that Hitler himself had commended, the office of a Reich bishop (*Reichsbischof*), and set about to elect Friedrich Bodelschwingh over the German Christian favorite, Ludwig Müller. Against this backdrop, Bonhoeffer preached on the two churches (of Moses and Aaron) to encourage those who would support Bodelschwingh and to draw sharper lines between the German Christians and those, decided or undecided, who were uneasy with them. For Bonhoeffer these lines demarcated idolatry from faithfulness and obedience. The church of Aaron, while priestly and popular, was idolatrous. The church of Moses was the church of the prophet and the demanding, judging Word of God. Yet these brothers belonged to the same contentious, confused people, even the same tribe and clan.

[80.] Coincidentally, this sermon of the first Sunday of Lent was preached the day before the Reichstag fire.

[81.] 3/2, p. 467.

[82.] See 1/44.

> Moses and Aaron, two brothers from the same tribe, with the same blood and the same history, went part of the way side by side and then were torn apart—Moses, the first prophet, and Aaron, the first priest; Moses, the one called out by God, the one chosen without regard for his person, the man who was slow of tongue, the servant of God who lived only by listening to the word of his Lord; Aaron, the man with the purple robe and the sacred crown, the priest who had been consecrated and sanctified, who was supposed to keep the people worshipping God. And now in our story, we have Moses alone, way up on the terrifying mountain with the living God, between life and death with the thunder and lightning, called to receive the law of God's covenant with God's people—and down in the valley the Israelites with their priest in his purple robe, making sacrifices but estranged from God.
>
> Why did Moses and Aaron have to go against each other? Why couldn't they stand side by side and serve God together? Why are the church of Moses and the church of Aaron, the church of the Word and the church of the world, always breaking apart? The answer to this question is found in our text.[83]

The answer found in the text—idolatry—is already signaled at the outset of the sermon.

> When the people saw that Moses delayed to come down from the mountain, the people gathered around Aaron and said to him, "Come, make gods for us, who shall go before us; as for this Moses, the man who brought us up out of the land of Egypt, we do not know what has become of him." Aaron said to them, "Take off the gold rings . . . of your wives, your sons and your daughters, and bring them to me." So all the people took off the gold rings . . . and brought them to Aaron. He took the gold from them, formed it in a mold, and cast an image of a calf; and they said, "These are your gods, O Israel, who brought you up out of the land of Egypt!" When Aaron saw this, he built an altar before it; and Aaron made proclamation and said, "Tomorrow shall be a festival to the LORD." They rose early the next day, and offered burnt-offerings and brought sacrifices of well-being; and the people sat down to eat and drink, and rose up to revel. . . .
>
> The priest against the prophet, the church of the world against the church of faith, the church of Aaron against the church of Moses—this eternal conflict in the church of Christ, and its resolution, is what we are going to hear about today.[84]

[83.] 3/7, p. 473.
[84.] 3/7, pp. 472–73.

The chaos of May 1933 and the decision for Moses or Aaron were hardly the end, however. Indeed, the event in the Church Struggle that would lead to the Barmen confession and the founding of the Confessing Church came soon, when August Jäger, a magistrate, was appointed state commissioner of the Prussian churches to "put an end to the strife within the churches." Jäger was not subtle; any resistance to his appointment of state officials to church offices would be regarded as "treason against the people and the state."[85] Although Reich Bishop Bodelschwingh resigned immediately in protest, Jäger went ahead with his reorganization of the Prussian churches, and on July 2 a proclamation was read in the churches giving thanks to the state for its benevolent intervention. Protests followed and then escalated when a Berlin pastor, Grossmann, was arrested by the SA. Bonhoeffer and his students quickly collected over a hundred signatures for the July 6 "Declaration of the Berlin Pastors."[86] Its almost confessional character is striking. But that aspect matched Bonhoeffer's mood and stance.[87]

The same call to decide, confess, and resist was present in Bonhoeffer's sermon a few weeks later, on July 23. The text, Matthew 16:13–18, is Peter's confession of Jesus as Messiah and Jesus's word that upon this rock he will build his church. "If we had our way," Bonhoeffer began,

> we would prefer to keep detouring around the decisions confronting us. If we had our way, we would prefer not to be dragged into this fight over the church. If we had our way, we would rather not have to keep insisting on our cause and would gladly avoid the terrible danger of self-righteousness over against other people. If we had our way,[88] we would remove ourselves tomorrow, or better, today, join the quiet folk in the countryside, and leave the quarrel and self-righteousness to other people. But—God be thanked—it is not up to us. With God, we get just what we don't want. We are challenged to come out and make the decision; we cannot get out of it. Wherever we take our stand, we must also allow ourselves to be suspected of being self-opinionated, of speaking and acting against the others out of arrogance. We will not be spared any

[85.] *DB-ER*, 290.

[86.] The text is available as 1/65.

[87.] This synopsis of events, with these citations, is taken from *DB-ER*, 290–91.

[88.] I am grateful to Pastor Talitha Arnold, Santa Fe, New Mexico, for suggesting that the cadence found in many of these sermons may reflect the influence of the preaching that moved Bonhoeffer at Abyssinian Baptist Church in Harlem. "If we had our way," used here many times to introduce succeeding thoughts, is an example of a pattern found in other sermons as well.

> of this—making a decision means that we differ with others. Therefore, if we are honest, we will not hide from the significance of this day, today.[89]

Bonhoeffer keenly sensed the turmoil in the churches and its costs. In the face of it, he sought to offer encouragement, hope, and a sure foundation.

> In the midst of the creaking and groaning of the church structures, which have been profoundly shaken and are collapsing and crumbling away here and there, we can still hear the promise of the eternal church, against which the gates of hell shall not prevail, the church on the rock, which Christ has built and continues to build through all the ages. Where is this church? Where can we find it? Where can we hear its voice? Come, all of you who are asking this seriously, you who are left alone and lonely, who have lost your church. Let us go back to the Holy Scriptures, let us look together for the eternal church. Let anyone with ears to hear listen! . . .[90]
>
> Yet it is not we who are to build, but God. No human being builds the church, but Christ alone. Anyone who proposes to build the church is certainly already on the way to destroying it, because it will turn out to be a temple of idolatry, though the builder does not intend that or know it. We are to confess, while God builds. We are to preach, while God builds. We are to pray to God, while God builds. We do not know God's plan. We cannot see whether God is building up or taking down. It could be that the times that human beings judge to be times for knocking down structures would be, for God, times to do a lot of building, or that the great moments of the church from a human viewpoint are, for God, times for pulling it down. It is a great comfort that Christ gives to the church: You confess, preach, bear witness to me, but I alone will do the building, wherever I am pleased to do so. Don't interfere with my orders. Church, if you do your own part right, then that is enough. But make sure you do it right. Don't look for anyone's opinion; don't ask them what they think. Don't keep calculating; don't look around for support from others. Not only must church remain church,[91] but you, my church, confess, confess, confess . . . Christ alone is your Lord, by his grace alone you live, just as you are. Christ is building.[92]

[89.] 3/8, p. 477.

[90.] Mark 4:9.

[91.] "Church must remain church" was the election campaign slogan of the "Gospel and Church" group, which opposed the German Christians in the July 1933 church elections (see Scholder, *Churches and the Third Reich*, vol. 1, illustration no. 59).

[92.] 3/8, pp. 477–81.

This was the last of the sermons that Bonhoeffer preached in Berlin. The day after the church elections (German Christians received 66 percent of the vote), the Young Reformation movement took stock, decided to withdraw from direct engagement in church politics, and moved toward formulating a confessional statement. This was the origin of the Bethel confession, and Bonhoeffer took an immediate leave of absence from the university to work on it with Hermann Sasse.[93] In a sense, all that was left was the vital question of truth, since the question of power had been settled, painfully, by the elections. The decision was to declare the truth by way of a binding confession, in the hope that this would also push the German Christians to state their faith and intentions with doctrinal clarity, for everyone to see. The contrast would be stark and revealing. Bonhoeffer's birthday letter to his grandmother from Bethel posed the issue as he saw it: either "Germanism or Christianity."

> Our work here is very enjoyable and also very demanding. We want to try to make the German Christians declare their intentions. I rather doubt we shall succeed. Even if, at this point, they make concessions in their official formulations, they are under such strong pressure from behind that sooner or later any promises made are bound to break down. It is becoming increasingly clear to me that what we are going to get is a big, *völkisch* national church that in its essence can no longer be reconciled with Christianity, and that we must make up our minds to take entirely new paths and follow where they lead. The issue is really Germanism or Christianity, and the sooner the conflict comes out in the open, the better. The greatest danger of all would be in trying to conceal this.
>
> This has now turned into a long letter, and it's time for me to go to dinner. I wish you a good new year of life, dear Grandmama, and look forward to seeing you soon.[94]

Additional commentary on the sermons is in order. Collectively the sermons share the pastoral vein of confronting fears and encouraging resistance as the faithful act of urgent obedience. They are Bonhoeffer's effort to hear and proclaim what the gospel of Christ commands amid the real living conditions of his parishioners. Like so many documents in this volume, they are also a modern-day version of the perennial Christian conflicts with Caesar. To say "Jesus is our Caesar" (Acts 17:7) was to

---

[93.] For details, see "Concerning the History of the Bethel Confession," pp. 509–13.
[94.] 1/86, p. 159.

make the *faith* community, rather than the *civic* community, the animating center and ground, a choice that Bonhoeffer himself made early in these years and urged others to make. The outcome of the original clash of the Roman imperial *Kyrios* (Lord, or Caesar) with the Nazarene as *Kyrios* was the chronic church/state conflict that has erupted periodically throughout history as national leaders vied for unqualified loyalty, demanded personal sacrifice, and used religion to create and strengthen social cohesion. In Germany's case in 1932–33, however, the battles were within the church as well. They were never between church and state in any simple way, since the church had aligned itself with state and empire both before the Reformation and afterward. Churches occupied a stratum of privilege and found themselves chaplains to the court, keepers of the culture, and agents of national unity. Lutherans especially taught extreme deference to the state. General Superintendent Otto Dibelius, later a member of the Confessing Church, preached the following sermon at a March 21 service celebrating the reconvening of the German parliament (Reichstag): "When it's a matter of life or death for the nation, then the power of the state must be applied thoroughly and energetically, whether abroad or at home. We have learned from Dr. Martin Luther that the church may not get in the way of state power when [the state] does that which it is called to do. Not even when this [power] becomes hard and ruthless."[95] Little further theological legitimation for yielding to the new heroes in the land—and to barbarism—was needed. Indeed, such legitimation came from many quarters, both inside and outside the churches (and the universities). If evil needed a respected vehicle—the state—to mesh malice and brutal insensitivity with detached routine and the ordinary duties of daily life, it was provided here as common fare.

Thus Bonhoeffer's sermons were necessarily two things at once: a call to churchly repentance and to the sharp contours of a strong, independent Christian faith, together with a call to resist Hitler's exploitation of Christian faith for German renewal.[96] Jesus must confront both Caesar and the churches. In different words, and in the language Bonhoeffer now began to use, "cheap grace" must give way to "costly grace" in both church and society.

The call is sharp and clear in yet another sermon, this one from June 19, 1932.

[95.] Cited in Barnett, *For the Soul of the People*, 28.

[96.] The symbols were chosen carefully. The formal celebration of Hitler's ascent to power in 1933 took place in the Garrison Church (Garnisonkirche) in Potsdam, built by Kaiser Friedrich Wilhelm I. "Kaiser" is, of course, German for "Caesar," i.e., emperor.

> Must Christianity, which formerly, in its beginnings, was revolutionary, now be conservative for all time? Must it be that every movement must blaze its own trail without the church; that the church will realize only twenty years later what happened? If this must really be so, then we may not wonder when times in which martyrs' blood will be demanded will come again also for our church.[97]

With this said both about the sermons and from them, we turn to Bonhoeffer and the Jews. Concrete Christian obedience and collective church action in this fateful moment turned, for Bonhoeffer, on the "Jewish question." His response was always deeply theological and sometimes deeply personal as well. When his brother-in-law's father died on April 11, 1933, Bonhoeffer was asked by Gerhard Leibholz to conduct the funeral service. He consulted his general superintendent, who urged him not to hold a service for a nonbaptized Jew in this volatile moment, and Bonhoeffer complied. He confessed his deep regret to his twin sister and her husband.

> I am tormented even now by the thought that I didn't do as you asked me as a matter of course. To be frank, I can't think what made me behave as I did. How could I have been so horribly afraid at the time? It must have seemed equally incomprehensible to you both, and yet you said nothing. But it preys on my mind, because it's the kind of thing one can never make up for. So all I can do is ask you to forgive my weakness then. I know now for certain that I ought to have behaved differently.[98]

In an important sense, he *did* know differently at the time, for theologically he had already staked almost everything on the "Jewish question." The boycott of Jewish businesses, which his grandmother famously ignored as she defied the SA cordon,[99] took place on April 1. Acts of terror, discrimination, and intimidation both preceded the boycott and followed it. The Aryan legislation reconstituting the civil service took place on April 7. Bonhoeffer's essay "The Church and the Jewish Question" was itself written in the course of these weeks, although it was not published until June. Best known for delineating three options of church action vis-à-vis injustice on the part of the state, this essay also views the "Jewish question" as the circumstance that brings the church to *status confessionis*—a state of confession

[97.] *DBW* 11, 3/12, p. 446.
[98.] *DBWE* 13, 1/42, p. 42.
[99.] *DB-ER*, 267.

in which central truths of faith are at stake.[100] Here is the litmus test of the church's very nature *as* church. Conceptually, Bonhoeffer's ecclesiology had turned on the treatment of "the other" since *Sanctorum Communio*'s theology of sociality. But now, in the case of the Jews, the test was existential and the response urgent. "The Church and the Jewish Question" ends with this statement:

> The question here is not at all about whether our church members of German descent can support fellowship with Jews. In reality, it is the duty of Christian proclamation to say: here, where Jew and German together stand under God's Word, is church; here it will be proven whether or not the church is still church. If someone feels unable to continue in church fellowship with Christians of Jewish origin, nothing can prevent him from leaving this church fellowship. But it must be made clear to him, with ultimate seriousness, that he is turning his back on the place where the church of Christ stands.[101]

Bonhoeffer was also clear that idolatry was the issue in the confrontation with the German Christians and the nation's adoration of *Führer* and *Volk.* Again it turned on the "Jewish question," this time in the meaning of Israel's faith for the German nation. Bonhoeffer made the point sharply in his critique of Stapel's book *Der christliche Staatsman: Eine Theologie des Nationalismus* (The Christian Statesman: A Theology of Nationalism) in the "Review and Discussion of New Publications in Systematic Theology."[102] The first commandment is decisive and shows the uniqueness and superiority of "the Israelite nomos" (law) over "the German one." That is, the biblical law and its God stand in stern judgment over against the law of any people. The German people and law are no exception. In Bonhoeffer's words:

> Is there a difference between the biblical Ur-nomos [foundational law] and the German one? Critique: It is the particularity and uniqueness of the Israelite nomos [law] to be constantly opposed to the people's [Volk] nomos. Nor do the prophets belong to the people's nomos. Herein lies its uniqueness. The *prophets* always said: *It is a question of recognizing the critical nomos.* It is thus not a

[100.] See also 2/14, "Memorandum: 'The Jewish-Christian Question as Status Confessionis.'" It should be noted that even if Bonhoeffer acknowledged in this essay that the church was to help all victims, *status confessionis* for him concerned only whether the church would institute an Aryan paragraph and exclude "non-Aryan" members. Nowhere did he say that *status confessionis* arose in the state's treatment of non-Christian Jews.

[101.] 2/13, pp. 206–9.

[102.] See 2/1, p. 370.

> question of effecting the given nomos. *This critical nomos gains its binding form in the first commandment.* Herein lies the Prae of the Israelite [nomos]. It truly depends on God. It is impossible to say that we should worship the national gods first (Yahweh, Jupiter, Thor) and then Christ. We do this again and again, but we should only worship the one God. The idea of the Reich must be directed toward the divine nomos. We cannot serve two gods, the cross and the German Reich. *No acceptance of the given nomos, rather taking direction from God's nomos. The Israelite nomos is superior to the German one because it truly sees the meaning of the critical nomos.*[103]

Bonhoeffer repeated this same point again in the Bethel confession.[104] The first commandment is the anti-idolatry command par excellence. It is a gift of God and Israel, and for those of Christian and Jewish faiths, the law of the German people must be subordinate to it and judged by it.[105]

With Bonhoeffer's stand on the critical role of Israel's law acknowledged, we return to "The Church and the Jewish Question." Its third contemplated response to state injustice—to seize the wheel of the state and bring the state and its injustice to a grinding halt—merits special comment in that it goes beyond any discussions at the time, including those about the church's nature and the issue of idolatry.

Bonhoeffer's political perspective at this time was more conservative and Lutheran than at any later point. "The church has neither to praise nor to censure the laws of the state,"[106] he wrote, even though he also stated that a strong state, as state, needs argument and opposition. He cited the "Jewish question" in particular as a case in which the church had to ask whether the state's actions were legitimate. (The Confessing Church itself did not do so until three years later, in its 1936 memorandum to Hitler. One of the memorandum's seven sections addressed anti-Semitism and a cultivated hatred of the Jews.)[107]

[103.] 2/1, p. 209.

[104.] 2/15, pp. 378–79.

[105.] See ed. note 22 in Bonhoeffer's "Review and Discussion of New Publications in Systematic Theology" (2/1). One of the students, Klara Hunsche, recorded the following as Bonhoeffer's point: "Redemptive God = Creative God. Gnostics on the other hand: Jews' God and God of the NT. We must not split. Nor tear apart Christ's uniqueness. God is one." Contrary to the temper of the times, Bonhoeffer unambiguously rejected any devaluation of the Hebrew Bible and the sovereign, transcendent God of the Jews as the God of all nations.

[106.] 2/13, p. 362.

[107.] See *DB-ER*, 531–37, for a description of the memorandum and an account of the consequences that followed its publication.

Beyond this critical task of using a criterion of justice to hold the state to its legitimate role as state, Bonhoeffer pronounced a second task for the church: to help the victims of any illegitimate, that is, unjust, state action. Although again the treatment of the Jews was the precipitating and pressing case, Bonhoeffer's argument pertained to any persons deprived of their rights in a state bearing either "too much" or "too little" law and order. The argument about rights—specifically their deprivation—found no resonance, however. (Bonhoeffer's decision to go to London was one consequence of the church's silence on this matter.)[108] Despite this silence, or perhaps because of it, Bonhoeffer carried his attention to rights into his later work in *Ethics*, when the subject was still largely ignored by German theologians. After a long complaint about the eclipse of nature in Protestant theology, he wrote of natural life and of bodily integrity as "the foundation of all natural rights without exception." And why? His answer was: "The living human body is always the human person himself or herself."[109] "The most primordial right of natural life," he says, "is the protection of the body from intentional injury, violation, and killing."[110] "Rape, exploitation, torture, and the arbitrary deprivation of physical freedom are all serious invasions of the right conferred on human beings at creation."[111] The rights of natural life are, he continues, "the reflection of the glory of God the Creator in the midst of the fallen world."[112]

The third church responsibility—to seize the wheel itself—followed from the state unscrupulously wielding "too little" or "too much" law and order. Here Bonhoeffer again made his plea for an ecclesiastical council. Regime change was not a step that an individual Christian, such as he, could or should take on his or her own. When eventually he did conclude that he must be part of the military-political conspiracy to overthrow the regime, he did so aware that he was surrendering his reputation in the church.[113]

Readers of the essay "The Church and the Jewish Question" can easily overlook some critical features.

First, although the essay began with conservative Lutheran deference to state authority, and all the standard conservative disclaimers about the church granting the state its due had their echoes here, the essay went further. Bonhoeffer called upon the church to make a collective judgment,

[108.] *DB-ER*, 275.
[109.] *DBWE* 6:214.
[110.] *DBWE* 6:185–86.
[111.] *DBWE* 6:214.
[112.] *DBWE* 6:180.
[113.] *DB-ER*, 275.

via an evangelical council, about the justice and injustice of state actions and then urged not only its officeholders to take corrective action but the church itself as a body to do so (and not only individual Christians).[114] Both the conciliar judgment and the proposed collective ecclesial action went well beyond any conservative response.

Next, recall our earlier observation that these first months of the Nazi juggernaut were a time when the party sought to synchronize state and society with the party platform and ideology (*Gleichschaltung*). That undertaking, however, was not successful everywhere and immediately, by any means, even if a path for dictatorship had been legally cleared in a remarkably short time. A protracted struggle of the party with sectors of the state ensued, some of it violent. Hitler himself laid down the ultimatum: "What can be resolved by the state will be resolved by the state. What, because of its essence, the state is incapable of resolving will be resolved through the movement"[115] (i.e., through the party).

Bonhoeffer's essay was, notably, *not* about the church's response to the *party*. He showed little or no interest in directly engaging the Nazis in argument about their ideology and program. Nor did he think much of church efforts to do so, including the efforts of his friends. ("Naive, starry-eyed idealists like Niemöller still think they are the real Nat. Socialists," he wrote to Sutz.)[116] His appeal, rather, was to the *state* and its responsibilities, specifically in the matter of the Aryan legislation. It was clear what the party wanted. But was it also clear that a legitimate German state had ceased to exist already in early 1933, with nothing left but a shell? In this contested space, and in the shared hope that a legitimate constitutional state could still be rescued, Bonhoeffer made his appeal to the church and its responsibilities: let the state be a proper state; if it is not, restore it to its rightful roles of order and justice.

Bonhoeffer's was indeed a conservative argument.[117] Maltreatment of the Jews and further threat of that in the Aryan legislation had pushed him

---

[114.] See Bonhoeffer's critique of Brunner in 2/1. Brunner was reluctant to argue, as Bonhoeffer did, that the concrete command and concrete action by the church belonged to the very essence of the church. Brunner saw such action as appropriate for Christian individuals, not ecclesial bodies. Bonhoeffer reacted quite strongly and, in an August 1932 letter to Erwin Sutz, said that this ecclesiology and ethic was "a real threat to the substance of the church" (*DBW* 11, 1/79, p. 100).

[115.] Cited in Tödt, *Authentic Faith*, 102. This quotation is from one of Hitler's speeches in September 1935.

[116.] *DBWE* 13, 1/93, p. 135.

[117.] See Bonhoeffer's January 1933 discussion of church and state in 2/7 ("What Is Church?"), where he discusses how the church is both political and apolitical.

to address the state's very foundation and legitimacy. His response was a law-and-order answer involving the legitimate duties of a limited state, limited in its reach by rights it could not abrogate. As a limited constitutional state, it was responsible for a just order. Bonhoeffer's stand on the "Jewish question," then, not only went beyond the point any German churches were willing to venture, namely, to direct intervention. Bonhoeffer was arguing that the Nazi state, precisely because of its measures against the Jewish citizens of Germany, had ceased to function as a legitimate form of authority.

Readers might easily overlook that this line of argument is not distant from Bonhoeffer's later, less hurried reflections on the state in *Ethics*. Nor is it far from the reasons for his participation in a conspiracy to seize the wheel ten years later. Bonhoeffer in fact carried out all three of the courses of action he outlined in 1933, and paid with his life.[118]

Readers might also overlook that while Bonhoeffer outlined church actions, his argument about treatment of the Jews was based on grounds that theologians and the church ignored, namely, that the state's anti-Jewish legislation was based on race identification, not religion. This was a Nazi innovation, and it meant that all the church discussion about Jewish and Jewish Christian religious identity was largely beside the point. Bonhoeffer made this critical race point at the very outset of "The Church and the Jewish Question": "The fact, unique in history, that the Jew is subjected to special laws by the state, *solely on the basis of his race and regardless of the religion to which he adheres*, presents theologians with two new problems, which must be dealt with separately. How does the church judge this action by the state, and what is the church called upon to do about it? What are the consequences for the church's position toward the baptized Jews in its congregations? Both these questions can only be answered on the basis of a right concept of the church."[119] Although Bonhoeffer's ethic at this time was strictly a church ethic, racist laws, which discriminated against Jews on racial rather than religious grounds, demanded a decisive response from the church. (The version of the Bethel confession that Bonhoeffer favored made this point as well.)

There are other critical documents on the "Jewish question" in this volume,[120] but they are more self-explanatory or, when not, ably discussed in

[118.] The discussion of Bonhoeffer's essay is informed by Tödt's *Authentic Faith*, 73–111.

[119.] 2/13, p. 362, emphasis mine.

[120.] See especially 2/14 ("The Jewish-Christian Question as Status Confessionis") and 2/16 ("The Aryan Paragraph in the Church").

the afterword. Suffice it to add some needed detail about events in the late summer of 1933.

The Brown Synod took place in Berlin (more "paramilitary demonstration than synod," Bethge wrote),[121] and the German Christians pushed through a provision that all future clergy were to be of "Aryan" descent and declare their "unconditional support for the National Socialist State and the German Protestant Church."[122] In response, Bonhoeffer and Franz Hildebrandt jointly called for the widespread resignation of clergy. Their view was not supported; as a result, Hildebrandt personally vowed not to preach in any German church, while Bonhoeffer stated that he would work in both university and church circles for an official schism.[123] The choice, to recall the letter to Julie Bonhoeffer, was "Germanism or Christianity," and in any event, the German Christians had not only generated the need for *status confessionis* but had already effected a schism, according to Bonhoeffer. Barth, in response,[124] agreed about *status confessionis.* But he counseled delay: "I am indeed in favor of waiting to see what comes. If there is to be schism, it must come from the other side" (the German Christians). He thought the opposition should await something more doctrinally decisive than the Aryan paragraph before they took action appropriate to *status confessionis.* "It could well happen that the clash will come over an even more central point," wrote Barth.[125] Bonhoeffer and Hildebrandt were disappointed: What could be "more central" to Christian faith and authentic church than rejection of the Aryan paragraph?

What did emerge from the September meetings of the opposition to the Brown Synod was the Pastors' Emergency League. Its commitments were drafted by Bonhoeffer and Martin Niemöller and sent on to Bodelschwingh on September 7.[126] Then, after a related appeal was brought to the national synod,[127] clergy signatures were solicited throughout Germany. By the end of the year they numbered six thousand. In short, what had begun with the Young Reformation movement in May had now become widespread support for a confessing church. And although there was solidarity among clergy and laity regarding opposition to the Aryan paragraph, still, when the Confessing Church was officially established at Barmen in 1934, its confession

---

[121.] *DB-ER*, 306.

[122.] *DB-ER*, 307.

[123.] See the telegram to Henriod, 1/94, and the "Draft for a 'Statement from Opposition Pastors,'" 1/95.

[124.] See the letter to Barth, 1/96.

[125.] See Barth's letter, 1/97, p. 167.

[126.] See 1/95 and 1/102.

[127.] See 1/105.

did not, in contrast to Bethel's, even mention the Jews.[128] Apparently that was not a "central point."

Other Work, Another Style

Not all of Bonhoeffer's work in 1932–33 was so directly tied to political and ecclesiastical turmoil. Nor was it so hurried and immediate, an urgent reply to a critical event. His duties as a lecturer in systematic theology at a German university carried their own demands and style. In the Christology lectures, for example, the dogmatician is at work, revisiting the basic questions of Christology. On display is the powerful clarity of Bonhoeffer's mind in setting forth the fundamental categories of Christian faith (and his own theology) as these developed in the early church and in the Reformation. Although these lectures demanded the most extensive preparation time among his courses, they may well have contributed most to providing the foundation for his own professional life as he moved Christology to the still center of all his thought. All his work from this point forward was affected by these lectures. The communitarianism of *Discipleship* and *Life Together* is a theme of the Christology lectures in that the living presence of Jesus Christ is not only in Word and sacrament but in the church-community and its practices. More immediately, in 1932–33, the focus on the revealed Word of God in Jesus Christ, the center of humanity, nature, and history, positioned Bonhoeffer to resist the orders-of-creation theology that fit so easily with the German Christian appeals of these years. His alternative, the "orders of preservation," relocated all revelation in God in Jesus Christ, de-absolutized the orders of creation as autonomous spheres, and held their reality open to its eschatological fulfillment in Jesus Christ. And in another way that paralleled his lectures on "Creation and Sin,"[129] Jesus Christ as the cosmic Word of God now spoke as and from the center of all creation—humanity, nature, history. Bonhoeffer built upon the thesis of

[128.] Even here, the attention of the Bethel confession concerned only so-called Jewish Christians.

[129.] Published, at the urging of his students, already in late 1933 as *Creation and Fall* (*DBWE* 3). The lectures' title, "Creation and Sin," was changed to *Creation and Fall* for the book to distinguish Bonhoeffer's volume from Emanuel Hirsch's *Schöpfung und Sünde* (Creation and Sin). Hirsch's work used the Lutheran doctrine of the orders of creation to establish a realm of revelation and the presence of God in creation apart from the Word of God in Jesus Christ. Hirsch used the doctrine of the orders of creation as a theological apologetic for Nazi notions of *das Volk* (people and nation) and *Blut und Boden* (blood and soil). Bonhoeffer rejected this on christological grounds and abandoned the term "orders of creation." For a time, as in *Creation and Fall*, he used the term "orders of preservation"—God preserving creation from chaos until its eschatological fulfillment in Jesus Christ. Then, in *Ethics*, he dropped "orders" altogether in favor of "mandates."

Sanctorum Communio that the Christ who exists as church-community is the same Christ who embodies and personifies the new humanity as a whole. This christological breadth, as well as its concentration, lay the groundwork for baseline themes in *Ethics*: "conformation to Christ" and "the realization of reality" across "the whole of earthly life."[130] "In Christ we are invited to participate in the reality of God and the reality of the world at the same time"[131] and never the one without the other. Even the reconsiderations that arose in the new theology of his *Letters and Papers from Prison* can be traced back to the Christology lectures, which ultimately provided the groundwork from which that new theology then tried to answer the question of "who Christ really is, for us, today"[132] when the issue turns on "Christ and the world that has come of age."[133] However open-ended that question may be, Bonhoeffer never moved off the center he established in the Christology seminar. A late prison letter echoes the 1933 lectures: "The key to everything is the 'in him.' All that we may rightly expect from God and ask him for, is to be found in Jesus Christ. The God of Jesus Christ has nothing to do with what God, as we imagine him, could do and ought to do. If we are to learn what God promises, and what he fulfils, we must persevere in quiet meditation on the life, sayings, deeds, sufferings, and death of Jesus."[134] These lectures were as "incredibly relevant" as the sermons,[135] albeit in a markedly different and more enduring way. They worked their effect both within and beyond their own time, setting, and audience. Thus it is not too much to say that Bonhoeffer's Christology was not only the theological ground for his critique of National Socialism; it was the basis for his efforts to find a way beyond the present crisis and beyond the church as well as within it. When, in the face of Nazi ideology and community, the church collapsed as the place where "*Christ may take form among us today and here*,"[136] Bonhoeffer's Christology led him to the conspiracy as the other viable community open for the exercise of vicarious representative action and genuine responsibility.[137] And while his full Christology goes beyond these 1933 lectures, it was in precisely these lectures that his Christology began assuming a more polished form.

[130.] See, as a sample, "Ethics as Formation," in *Ethics* (*DBWE* 6:76–102).

[131.] *DBWE* 6:55.

[132.] *LPP*, 279.

[133.] *LPP*, 327. This letter will be published as 3/161 in the forthcoming *DBWE* 8.

[134.] *LPP*, 391. This letter will be published as 4/192 in the forthcoming *DBWE* 8.

[135.] Cited from the letter to Sutz, 1/67, p. 140.

[136.] *Ethics* (*DBWE* 6:99), Bonhoeffer's emphasis.

[137.] See especially the section of *Ethics* titled "History and Good [2]" (*DBWE* 6: 246–98).

"Thy Kingdom Come! The Prayer of the Church-Community for God's Kingdom on Earth" is a significant work deserving more attention than it has been given to date. In this address, delivered at a November 1932 retreat, Bonhoeffer emphasized the earthly implications of Jesus Christ's message more strongly than ever before. A theme often deemed a breakthrough of the prison letters, namely, the "this-worldliness of Christianity," is present in this work in sensuous fashion, as are the prison letters' praise of earthly loves and the passion of Song of Songs and the Old Testament as a whole.[138] The "earthiness" of the Hebrew Bible that Bonhoeffer found so attractive and wrote of from prison is proclaimed here without qualification. Not least, his own confession in the famous letter after the failure of the coup on July 20, 1944, that "it is only by living completely in this world that one learns to have faith"[139] might easily have been a line in "Thy Kingdom Come!" Although the tone differs from that of the prison letters and the style is more akin to the first portions of *Discipleship*, the substance is much the same as in these other works. True, Bonhoeffer drew from a major source here that he does not use directly in the prison letters or *Discipleship*; namely, Nietzsche and his affirmation of earth and his critique of religion. Yet Bonhoeffer embraced that affirmation and critique as congruent with Christian faith and with it launched an assault on the otherworldliness of religion and Christianity that he continued to the end of his life. With him to the end was also Christian faith as an earth-honoring faith at the center of his own life and loves. A letter to Maria von Wedemeyer includes the following lines: "Our marriage must be a 'yes' to God's earth. It must strengthen our resolve to do and accomplish something on earth. I fear that Christians who venture to stand on earth on only one leg will stand in heaven on only one leg too."[140]

The following excerpt from "Thy Kingdom Come!" expresses, at length, this belief:

> We have been otherworldly ever since we discovered the devious trick of being religious, indeed "Christian," at the expense of the Earth. Otherworldliness affords a splendid environment in which to live. When life begins to be difficult and oppressive, one leaps boldly into the air and soars, relieved and

[138.] See the letter of May 20, 1944, *LPP*, 302–3. This letter will be published as 3/147 in the forthcoming *DBWE* 8.

[139.] See the letter of July 21, 1944, *LPP*, 369–70. This letter will be published as 4/178 in the forthcoming *DBWE* 8.

[140.] In Bismarck and Kabitz, *Love Letters from Cell 92*, 64.

> worry free, in the so-called eternal realm. One leapfrogs over the present, scorns the Earth; one is better than it; indeed, next to the temporal defeats, one has eternal victories that are so easily achieved. Otherworldliness also makes it easy to preach and speak words of comfort. An otherworldly church can be sure that it will in no time at all attract all the weaklings, all those who are only too glad to be deceived and deluded, all the dreamers, all disloyal children of the Earth.[141]

The exegetical lectures on creation and sin that Bonhoeffer gave during the same time period, published already in 1933 as *Creation and Fall*, strike many of the same notes as "Thy Kingdom Come," but as a statement on human nature in the image of God. "Even Darwin and Feuerbach could not use stronger language" than Genesis in asserting that we are "a piece of earth,"[142] Bonhoeffer noted. The human's "bond with the earth belongs to its essential being. The 'earth is its mother';[143] it comes out of her womb."[144] It is God's earth from which we are taken and from which we have and are "body." The body belongs to "a person's essence. The body is not the prison, the shell, the exterior, of a human being; instead a human being is a human body. A human being does not 'have' a body—or 'have' a soul; instead a human being 'is' body and soul."[145] (That is, we are our bodies, ourselves.) "People who reject their bodies reject their existence before God the Creator. What is to be taken seriously about human existence is its bond with mother earth, its being as body."[146] "Flight from the body is as much flight from being human as is flight from the spirit. The body is the form in which the spirit exists, as the spirit is the form in which the body exists."[147] Bonhoeffer ended this section of *Creation and Fall* with the statement that humanity "is the image of God not in spite of but precisely in its bodily nature. For in their bodily nature human beings are related to the earth and to other bodies; they are there for others and are dependent upon others. In their bodily existence human beings find their brothers and sisters and find the earth. As such creatures human beings of earth and spirit are 'like' God, their Creator."[148]

[141.] 2/11, p. 286.
[142.] *DBWE* 3:76.
[143.] A reference to Sir. 40:1b.
[144.] *DBWE* 3:76.
[145.] *DBWE* 3:76–77.
[146.] *DBWE* 3:77.
[147.] *DBWE* 3:78.
[148.] *DBWE* 3:79.

Too little has been made of these 1932 writings, *Creation and Fall*[149] and "Thy Kingdom Come!" in conjunction with each other. Of special note, at least for our time, is that they display Bonhoeffer's significance for ecological theology on grounds that avoid the pitfalls of natural theology and at the same time wholly engage all of creation and ourselves as creatures of earth. What is more, the foundational theme of the Christology lectures—Jesus Christ as the cosmic Christ, Jesus Christ as the center of nature, humanity, and history—also belongs to Bonhoeffer's contributions to ecological theology.

A prison letter sums all this up nicely: "What is above this world is, in the gospel, intended to exist *for* this world; I mean that, not in the anthropocentric sense of liberal, mystic pietistic, ethical theology, but in the biblical sense of the creation and of the incarnation, crucifixion, and resurrection of Jesus Christ."[150]

"Christ and Peace" was a lecture to the Berlin Student Christian Movement near the end of 1932. Although we have only student notes from the lecture, the distinctive Bonhoeffer themes are clear. The Geneva Disarmament Conference of 1932 had broken down just as Bonhoeffer was becoming concerned about jingoistic nationalism at home and was engaged abroad with the peace question. Bonhoeffer began his lecture with the statement: "Once again, the human authorities who sought to build peace upon a political foundation find themselves shipwrecked";[151] he quickly turned from these secular efforts to another approach, this one explicitly a matter of committed faith. What follows is a core statement later seen in *Discipleship* and its uncompromising adherence to the authority of Jesus in the Sermon on the Mount. It is also a presentation of peace as "the opposite of security" and as "the great venture" that "must be dared," to recall Bonhoeffer's address on peace at Fanø the next year.[152]

> To look for guarantees is to want to protect oneself. Peace means to give oneself altogether to the law of God, wanting no security, but in faith and obedience laying the destiny of the nations in the hand of Almighty God, not trying to direct it for selfish purposes. Battles are won, not with weapons, but with God. They are won where the way leads to the cross.[153]

[149.] A full treatment of the salient themes of *Creation and Fall* can be found in the editor's introduction to the English edition and the afterword of *DBWE* 3, pp. 1–17 and 147–73, respectively.

[150.] Letter of May 5, 1944, *LPP*, 286, Bonhoeffer's emphasis. This letter will be published as 3/138 in the forthcoming *DBWE* 8.

[151.] 2/6, p. 258.

[152.] *DBWE* 13:309.

[153.] Ibid.

These sentences from the Fanø address echo "Christ and Peace." Not least, Bonhoeffer's pacifism, self-evident to him at the time, is manifested here: "For Christians, any military service except in the ambulance corps, and any preparation for war, is forbidden."[154] Note also that he states this with the confidence and form he sought from the whole church in this moment, namely, the concrete, binding command rooted in the gospel of the Sermon on the Mount.

From another angle "Christ and Peace" is stark documentation of the place where we began, with Bonhoeffer's letter, in which he remarks, "It became clear to me that the life of a servant of Jesus Christ must belong to the church, and step by step it became ever more evident how far this had to go,"[155] and with Bethge's conclusion that Bonhoeffer's period of "learning and roaming" had come to an end and the trek of costly grace had begun.[156]

There are, of course, other important documents from this crowded, compressed year in this volume. "The Younger Generation's Altered View of the Concept of Führer" and "The Führer and the Individual in the Younger Generation," both from early 1933, are astute analyses of the cultural and political-psychological ethos compelling for so many young Germans in the period just before the Third Reich. The Bethel confession is, as noted, the turn to the question of truth and how to confess it in the most basic, evangelical way after the electoral triumph of the German Christians had demonstrated beyond a doubt the deep disagreement over core elements of Protestant faith itself. It is striking too, as noted earlier, that Bonhoeffer addressed "race" in the Bethel confession since race is *not* addressed in the foundation documents for Bethel, the Bible, and the Lutheran confessions. To include race is a measure of Bonhoeffer's felt need to address this Nazi tenet and reject it explicitly as a matter of faith, whether or not the Bible and church confessions do so.

The final lecture in "Review and Discussion of New Publications in Systematic Theology" concluded with what Bethge reports was Bonhoeffer's most cited biblical verse in 1932: "Judge them, O God our God, for we have no strength to face this great horde which is invading our land."[157] What on the face of it seemed an academic's tour of recent theology evidently

[154.] 2/6, p. 260.

[155.] *DBW* 14, 1/46, p. 112.

[156.] *DB-ER*, 173. The reader will profit from Clifford Green's discussion of "Christ and Peace" in the editor's introduction to the English edition of *DBWE* 10:34–42.

[157.] 2 Chron. 20:12. This is the translation cited in the Bethge biography. The NRSV reads: "O our God, will you not execute judgment upon them? For we are powerless against this great multitude that is coming against us."

served also as a theological map for students facing political upheaval and church confusion.[158]

"Review and Discussion of New Publications in Systematic Theology" also carried intimations of themes to come. The rejection of an ethics of principles in favor of an ethics of command that we find in *Ethics,* and the difference between them, belongs to Bonhoeffer's discussion of Brunner's ethics.[159] "Christian ethics is not an ethics of principles," he states categorically, drawing on Brunner.[160] The discussion in *Ethics* of the ultimate and penultimate is anticipated both in the section on Christian practice[161] and in the discussion of Heim's *Glaube und Denken.*[162] Important terms in *Letters and Papers from Prison—actus reflexus* and *actus directus*—are discussed in the review of Barth,[163] of Tillich,[164] and in Bonhoeffer's own theses on Obedience and Action.[165] In addition to the *actus* terms, the existence of a human religious a priori is part of the Brunner discussion.[166] "Christ and Peace," with formulations akin to those of *Discipleship,* uses the phrase "cheap grace."[167]

In closing, we can do no better than Bonhoeffer himself in a sermon and two letters. The sermon is from London, probably in 1934. It aptly summarizes the point to which Bonhoeffer had come by the time he left Germany in 1933:

> Christianity stands or falls with its revolutionary protest against violence, arbitrariness and pride of power and with its apologia for the weak.—I feel that Christianity is rather doing too little in showing these points than doing too much. Christianity has adjusted itself much too easily to the worship of power. It should give more offence, more shock to the world, than it is doing. Christianity should [. . .][168] take a much more definite stand for the weak than to consider the potential moral right of the strong.[169]

[158.] *DB-ER*, 218.
[159.] 2/1, pp. 209–12.
[160.] 2/1, p. 210.
[161.] 2/2, pp. 231–32.
[162.] 2/5, pp. 243–58.
[163.] 2/2, p. 221.
[164.] 2/2, p. 226. As noted in 2/2, ed. note 79, it is unclear whether Ernst Tillich or Paul Tillich was meant.
[165.] 2/2, p. 227.
[166.] 2/2, p. 218.
[167.] 2/6, p. 260.
[168.] Illegible insert.
[169.] "Sermon for Evening Worship Service on 2 Corinthians 12:9," *DBWE* 13, 3/19, pp. 402–3.

The first letter, to Erwin Sutz and cited earlier, mirrors the sermon content but expresses it differently.

> It is . . . time for a final break with our theologically grounded reserve about whatever is being done by the state—which really only comes down to fear. "Speak out for those who cannot speak"[170]—who in the church today still remembers that this is the very least the Bible asks of us in such times as these?[171]

The second is the letter to Karl-Friedrich, also cited earlier. The first portion quoted here states succinctly where Bonhoeffer's theology and life had arrived after "the period of learning and roaming"[172] had come to an end and "the crisis of 1933"[173] had set in. The remainder, about the emperor, captures 1932–33 in the heart of Berlin and on the edge of untold grief as civilization, in both bland ways and enthusiastic ones, surrendered its considerable powers to barbarism.

> Things do exist that are worth standing up for without compromise. To me it seems that peace and social justice are such things, as is Christ himself.
>
> I recently came across the fairy tale of "The Emperor's New Clothes," which really is relevant for our time. All we are lacking today is the child who speaks up at the end.[174]

Translation Issues

Two major documents in this volume, the Christology lectures (2/12) and "The Church and the Jewish Question" (2/13), reflect translation decisions that have changed them significantly from their earlier English-language versions. To begin with the latter document: a key term in "The Church and the Jewish Question" is *Recht*, which can be rendered "law," "justice," or "rights." Bonhoeffer's specific discussion is about *Recht* and "too little" or "too much" law and order. "Either *too little* law and order or *too much* law and order compels the church to speak," he wrote. "There is too little law and order wherever a group of people is deprived of its rights," [175] he con-

[170.] Prov. 31:8.
[171.] *DBWE* 13, 1/147, p. 217.
[172.] *DB-ER*, 205.
[173.] *DBW* 14, 1/46, p. 113.
[174.] Letter of January 14, 1935, *DBWE* 13, 1/193, p. 285.
[175.] 2/13, p. 364.

tinued, using *Rechtlosigkeit* for what is translated in this volume as "deprived of its rights." In previous English editions, *Rechtlosigkeit* has usually been translated as "lawlessness," lawlessness being the mark of an unjust state. But the issue in 1933 is the deprivation of the rights of a people, namely, the Jews, and the consequences that follow from that. Those rights were in place in the Weimar Republic, and Bonhoeffer was arguing that the state, as a proper constitutional state, was obliged to uphold them. If the state failed to do so, it had ceased to be a constitutional or legitimate state (of course, by the time Bonhoeffer wrote this, the constitution had been abrogated) and the church had the duty to announce this. If severed from the meaning of *Rechtlosigkeit* as the "deprivation of rights," the words "lawless" and "lawlessness" fail to convey the existential specificity of how Jews were treated and Bonhoeffer's argument about the church's concrete actions in light of that. The implications of this translation choice are significant for the continuing controversies about Bonhoeffer and the Jews. That we can have this nuanced discussion about the translation of *Rechtlosigkeit* is thanks to the insights of general editor Victoria Barnett and her close reading of the German text and context. As cited in a footnote to the essay, the German editor of volume 12 confirms this as the correct translation.

The Christology lectures reveal a deliberate choice of words by Bonhoeffer that has not been taken into account in earlier English translations. Translators have always noted Bonhoeffer's emphasis on the "who" question as the right christological one, the "how" question as the wrong one. Bonhoeffer's answer to the "who" question was that Jesus Christ is "the God who became human," for which the German term is *Menschgewordene.* When he spoke of God *becoming human,* he used the word form *Menschwerdung,* though he warned that this was not to be understood as an answer to the "how" question. That is, it is not an explanation of the process of how God became human. (In fact, he regretted that stories of the virgin birth take this turn.) Even more pointedly, Bonhoeffer chose the word *Menschgewordene* over the word *Inkarnation,* a term as standard in German theology as "incarnation" is in English. Not that he questioned the real, bodily existence of Jesus of Nazareth, but *Menschgewordene* includes that concept and more: God took on not only our "flesh," as "incarnation" emphasizes, but our whole humanity. God became fully human.

There is one point in the Christology lectures, however, where Bonhoeffer wanted to emphasize bodiliness. That is in his discussion of the sacrament. Here he used the phrase "*das fleischgewordene Wort Gottes,*" the Word of God become flesh. He wished to make clear that in the sacrament it is not a case of a bodiless Word of God taking on bodily form. Rather, the God who has become human is precisely the Word of God who has become flesh and is now present in the sacrament in the form of a stumbling block, in "humiliation."

"Humiliation" in the Christology lectures translates *Erniedrigung*, a word that in other contexts could also be translated "humbling." But here Bonhoeffer used it consistently in a special theological sense, above all to refer to the cross as the "humiliation" of the God who became fully human. This humiliation is also involved in the church in preaching and sacrament, veiling but not negating the real presence of the resurrected and exalted Christ. It is imperative to note that Bonhoeffer never spoke of God's becoming human per se as "humiliation." On the contrary *Menschwerdung*, "becoming human," is revelation. But in the cross, and derivatively, in the sermon and sacrament, the God-human is humiliated and veiled and a scandal or stumbling block. English readers familiar with Philippians 2 will recall the translation that "Christ Jesus . . . humbled himself" to the point of death on a cross. The *DBWE* editors have chosen, however, to translate Bonhoeffer's christological term in such contexts as "humiliated" rather than "humbled."[176] It was Bonhoeffer's way of emphasizing a potent theological point, namely, that in the very act of becoming *fully* human God in Jesus Christ has taken on *the full reality of human sinfulness*. "Humiliation" captures this better than "humbling."

Hans Pfeifer, Christiane Tietz, Andreas Pangritz, and Clifford Green all noticed Bonhoeffer's deliberate, subtle, and consistent word choices, brought them to our attention, discussed them extensively as emphases important to Bonhoeffer's Christology, and suggested some of the wording used in the discussion here.

Other important translation matters, such as capitalization versus lowercase spelling of "Earth"/"earth" and "Logos"/"logos," are discussed at the appropriate places in the footnotes and need not be given fuller treatment here. Likewise, the nuances of *Heiden* (sometimes translated "heathens," sometimes "pagans," sometimes "Gentiles") and the relationship and overlap of race-based anti-Semitism and religious anti-Semitism (or theological anti-Judaism) are addressed in the footnotes to the documents in which they appear.

The decision whether to capitalize "Word"/"word" merits special treatment. The now-standard guidelines are followed in this volume: the capital-

[176.] In the sentence on p. 348 discussing kenosis, *erniedrigende* is translated "humbling" to distinguish it from Bonhoeffer's normal usage. The "renunciation" by the Logos of divine attributes proposed by the nineteenth-century advocates of kenosis appears from the notes to have been presented by Bonhoeffer as a "humbling" rather than a "humiliation."

ized form, "Word of God," is used when the reference is to Jesus Christ; the lowercase form, "word of God," is used when the reference is to Scripture, its interpretation and proclamation. The capitalized form, "Word of God," however, is also used with reference to the Barthian postliberal, revelation-centered theology that Bonhoeffer wholly embraced at this time. "Word of God" here identifies a theology and theological school, whose presence, meaning, and significance are not clearly conveyed by the lowercase form.

This orthographic decision was influenced by the significance of Barthian theology, which, as the storm gathered in the churches, was defended by Bonhoeffer and many of his students. The dialectical Word of God theology of Barth contrasted with both the liberal theology of Berlin (Harnack and Seeberg) and the orders-of-creation theology of many Lutheran theologians, including some enthusiastic supporters of the German Christian movement. As the theological contestations of these camps played out, the focus of the arguments made and the positions taken was the character and locus of revelation. Agreement and disagreement over core elements of Protestant faith had their litmus test here. For Bonhoeffer personally the concrete revelation of God in Jesus Christ, expressed in the church as the lived practices of discipleship, was the very core of both theology and piety. It is fitting, then, to use "Word of God" whenever the allusion is to the Barthian school.

Finally, the translation of salutations and closings of letters has been an ongoing challenge in the *DBWE* series. In particular, the German form of address used for one's superiors at that time could be quite florid, and Bonhoeffer was attuned to such nuances when he addressed church and university authorities. In such cases, however, a literal translation of the German (e.g., "Honorable, highly esteemed Professor") would not have been used in a comparable English salutation, and we have tried to indicate such formalities in a manner more consistent with English-language customs. Readers, however, should be aware of such nuances.

Acknowledgments

I am deeply grateful to the translators of this volume, Isabel Best and David Higgins; to Douglas Stott, who translated the supplementary material; and to Peter Frick, who translated the Greek terms. I also thank Peter Krey for his early contributions to this volume. The unfailing work throughout of Victoria Barnett, general editor of the English edition of the *Dietrich Bonhoeffer Works*, merits special mention (and applause), as does that of Barbara Wojhoski, whose usual exacting attention has been given to all the details of style and format needed for publication. Expert advice on the text has also come from the coeditors of the German edition of *Berlin: 1932–1933*, Ernst-

Albert Scharffenorth and Carsten Nicolaisen, as well as Hans Pfeifer, Christiane Tietz, Andreas Pangritz, and Clifford Green. Important assistance has been given by staff in the libraries of Union Theological Seminary and Columbia University, New York City; Wesley Theological Seminary, Washington, D.C.; the Lutheran Theological Seminary at Philadelphia; and the Kierkegaard Library at St. Olaf College, Northfield, Minnesota. I am keenly aware of the debt this volume owes all these persons and institutions as well as those who contributed to the parent German edition.

Photograph

The photograph that follows this introduction is a fitting close. Were there an official dedication of this volume, it would be to Bonhoeffer's university students of theology. Here he found those who "shared the same vision and goal"[177] as he turned to disciplined Christian community in response to the impact on him of the Sermon on the Mount and the crisis of 1933. Here were those he first gathered for a life of discipleship and Christian practices that went well beyond the classroom—prayer, confession, meditation, retreats together. Here were those who organized the Young Reformation movement that led to the Pastors' Emergency League and the Confessing Church. Some of them would join Bonhoeffer later as seminarians in Finkenwalde.

There were others who were part of Bonhoeffer's focus on the church and its ministry in 1932–33—his confirmation class, the ecumenical movement, Gandhi and his ashram. But none quite equaled the constituency of his theological students.

We also have these students to thank for arguably the most important pages of this volume, for the Christology lectures are reconstructed from student notes. The students are both a reminder and an embodiment of Bonhoeffer's theology. The *DBW* volumes necessarily focus on their subject, Dietrich Bonhoeffer. Yet that was not his focus. His theology and practice were other oriented and community centered. His enthusiasm for his university students and their subject matter belongs to that theology and practice.

Larry Rasmussen
Santa Fe, New Mexico

[177.] Letter to Elisabeth Zinn, *DBW* 14, 1/47, p. 113.

Bonhoeffer with his Berlin students on vacation in Prebelow, 1932.

Front row, from left: G. Bölte, Albrecht Schönherr, Christoph Harhausen, Reinhard Rütenik, Hilde Pfeiffer

Middle row: K. Vogt, Adele Hoffmann, Bonhoeffer, Helga Zimmermann

Back row: Ursula Weymann, Winfried Maechler, Inge Karding (The young man behind DB with the pen in his mouth is unidentified.)

PART 1
Letters and Documents

1. From Henry Louis Henriod[1] 15

Geneva, November 2, 1932

My dear Bonhoeffer,

How are you getting along? In these difficult times for Germany, my thoughts often turn to you and to those who bear such a difficult responsibility for the objectives of the Alliance, and especially for the attitudes of Christians and the churches in view of the serious current political and economic situation.

Toureille has no doubt let you know of the invitation we received to send a representative to the quadrennial conference of the Student Christian Movement of Great Britain,[2] a very important event that could provide an occasion for us, if you attend, to meet at the bishop of Ripon's office[3] and have an Alliance Youth Committee.

There are two other questions currently occupying my thoughts on which I would like to have your opinion or response: first, that of the commission on publications in which you have agreed to take part[4] and which still needs to define its task. I believe it will be difficult for us, given the current budget, and without actually having discussed it face to face, to formulate a "policy." On the other hand, I believe that we could take some practical steps, which is why I'm sending you a first draft[5] of what I intend to put in the *News Letter* that I will be publishing in the course of this month, on my own responsibility. But it's important for me to know whether the line I'm proposing is what is needed, since beginning in January it will be published conjointly with the Life & Work[6] newsletter. If you could let me have your personal reaction to my "foreword," it would be very helpful.

[1.] Archives of Jørgen Glenthøj, Åbyhøj, Denmark; typewritten copy of a carbon copy missing from the WCC Archives. See also *NL*, A 28,3 (6); typewritten copy. Previously published in *Mündige Welt*, 5:57–59.

[2.] Invitation not extant.

[3.] Arthur Burroughs.

[4.] Bonhoeffer's acceptance not documented. The Management Committee of the World Alliance had named Bonhoeffer to this commission in August 1932 (WCC Archives, box no. 212-003: Minutes of the Management Committee of August 19–20, 1932, no. 34). In September 1933, the Executive Committee was already referring to Bonhoeffer only as a member of the Youth Commission (Minutes Sofia § 30: Reelection of Commissions). [According to Bethge's biography, Bonhoeffer resigned from the publications job in January 1933. See *DB-ER*, 254.—LR]

[5.] Not extant.

[6.] The decision to publish these newsletters was made by the World Alliance Management Committee at the meeting mentioned in ed. note 4 (see WCC Archives, box no. 212-003, Minutes of the Management Committee, no. 33).

¶I also think we should continue our efforts to have occasional publications
16 on this or that important question. It would seem to me, for example, that the question of disarmament would make an excellent subject for a well-conceived brochure that might appear, for example, toward the end of the second part of the Disarmament Conference[7] at a relevant point, so that public opinion might be well enlightened as to the decisions that governments should take. I also think our Commission on Minorities[8] could do a good job, if the ground is well prepared and if we have a bibliography that we can draw on or a brochure or series of brochures dealing with the question.

¶Finally, I would like to see us be able to formulate, in a concentrated but well thought-out way, the goals of the Alliance—a comprehensive and lively concept suitable for the public-relations work we have to do. What sort of written material do you think we actually could and should produce for our youth? The conference at Gland[9] obviously did not reach a very high level and perhaps did not meet the expectations of many of its participants. It was nonetheless an interesting and valuable experience. Smaller and more intimate conferences, where we can go deeper into things, are essential; regional conferences like the one we are planning in the Balkans[10] can also have an important effect. However, apart from such meetings, should we give the youth of the church a chance either to express themselves or to read and discuss certain topics of import today, in the light of present trends in theology, and especially to benefit from the remarkable renewal of interest in the church in certain countries? I have been very encouraged by certain signs that give me hope for a really close cooperation between the Alliance and the Life and Work movement, and beyond that in obtaining
17 active cooperation with particular events, perhaps from Faith & Order, certainly

[7.] The League of Nations Disarmament Conference had begun its work on February 2, 1932, but suspended it in July of that year. The results were greeted with "bitter disappointment" in a resolution of the World Alliance Management Committee. The World Alliance hoped that the resumption of the conference in 1933 would bring "a lasting solution to the disarmament problem" and to that end appealed to regional groups and churches to bring influence to bear on governments, members of parliaments, and public opinion (*Die Eiche* 20 (1932): 323–24).

[8.] The World Alliance appointed a Commission on Minorities only in August 1932 [according to Bethge, however, it was a preexisting "member organization"; see *DB-ER*, 250.—LR]; its purpose was defined at the Executive Committee meeting in Sofia, Bulgaria, in September 1933 (*Handbook of the World Alliance 1935*, 12).

[9.] Refers to the World Alliance Youth Conference, August 24–31, 1932, in Gland, on the shores of Lake Geneva, Switzerland (see also *DBWE* 11, 2/18 and 2/19).

[10.] The World Alliance Management Committee, at the meeting mentioned in ed. note 4, had decided to hold this conference in October 1932 or the spring of 1933 (see WCC Archives, box no. 212-003: Minutes of the Management Committee, no. 37).

from the organized Christian youth movements. My aim would not at all be any sort of confused syncretism, which would be deplorable, but rather to avoid certain duplications of effort, and to enrich our publications or our conferences with valuable presentations on this or that particular point, which would be different from those that come to us officially from the church hierarchy.

My third point is doubtless the one that is of most immediate interest to you, namely, the question of your possible trip to Austria[11] and the grant you will be needing. I was rather reticent when you asked me about it, but since we have some money left in our youth-work budget, I would ask you to let me know between now and the end of November whether you will be able to carry out your plan to go to Austria and how much money you might need. It would not be a large sum, obviously, perhaps 100 to 150 Swiss francs.

I recently had an interesting experience; I was asked to speak at a worship service for youth of the Anglican and Scottish churches in Lausanne, and they gave me a donation of 100 francs for the youth work of the Alliance and of Stockholm.[12] Perhaps I could pass on some extra-budgetary contributions to the pool from time to time and others could do the same, and in this way our youth work could be expanded.

Last, I would like to have your personal opinion about my visit to Berlin.[13] You are doubtless aware that some months ago Siegmund-Schultze asked me to stay for a week afterward at the end of January, during which I believe he would like me to give one or two public lectures. In view of the current political situation and the tension in the air, I wonder whether public lectures given by a French-speaking person from Geneva don't run the risk of encountering great difficulties and leading to rather negative results, especially since my German isn't all that good. I raise the question because Pastor Menn, who was in Geneva for a few days for a committee of the International Christian Social Institute,[14]

[11.] No documentation found on the purpose and dates of this trip (but see 1/34, especially ed. note 4).

[12.] [This is a reference to the ecumenical Life and Work office, founded in Stockholm in 1925.—LR]

[13.] See the postscript of the current letter. [The translation of this part of the letter in *DB-ER*, 254, seems a misunderstanding: it was not the meeting that was to be held in French, but rather Henriod was to give a lecture or two in French following or preceding it. The French, *conferences publiques*, can mean both "conference" and "lecture," and it was the latter that was meant here. Thanks to Isabel Best for this clarification and correction.—LR]

[14.] This was the research office for Life and Work, where Menn worked. See Boyens, *Kirchenkampf und Ökumene*, 1:16.

mentioned some things about the attitude he notes among his colleagues, pastors from different churches. Wouldn't it be better if I devoted all my time, or most of it, to private conversations and meetings of small groups, rather than to public events? I am writing in this vein to Mr. Jordan and would be grateful to have your personal opinion on the subject without too much delay.

18 You surely remember von Oppen? He came to say goodbye this morning; he's returning to Germany and hopes to get in touch with you. Let me remind you of his address: Dietrich von Oppen, Danckelmannstr. 1, Eberswalde bei Berlin. He does not yet have a permanent job, and I was wondering whether you could use him in the work of the Alliance in Germany.[15] What do you think?

Hoping that these lines find you in good health, my dear Bonhoeffer, I send you my best regards.

[Henry Louis Henriod]

P.S. The dates planned for my visit to Berlin, which may well change again, are January 22–29, following the meeting of the Executive[16] and the secretariats. It is possible that we shall reverse the order and start with my visit to Berlin around the seventeenth, and the Executive Committee meeting will be held at the end of January.

2. To Wilhelm Stählin[1]

Dear Professor Stählin:

Both Dr. Schreiber and Superintendent Diestel are very much in agreement that one of the gentlemen from the Potsdam meeting should be invited. As
19 to how the talks went in Potsdam, we have nothing precise to report from

[15.] Bethge (*DB-ER*, 240) assumed that Bonhoeffer got Dietrich von Oppen to participate in ecumenical conferences. However, von Oppen wrote in a letter of January 25, 1989, to Christian Gremmels that Bonhoeffer had neither involved him in the work nor sent him to ecumenical conferences.

[16.] [Refers to the Executive Committee.—LR]

[1.] LKA Nuremberg, Personen XVIII, no. 63; typewritten. From Berlin-Grunewald; not previously published. From Stählin's reply of November 4, 1932 (see 1/3), the date is no later than the beginning of November 1932. This is in reply to Stählin's letter of October 27, 1932 (cf. *DBWE* 11, 1/88.1 and 88.2). This letter concerns an invitation to a theological conference of the Provisional Bureau for Ecumenical Youth Work (see 1/4). The Provisional Bureau had been established in 1931 to help clarify ecumenical issues and promote ecumenical ideas among German Protestant

here.[2] None of our people were invited. We would, however, request that you please send the letters of invitation yourself to those gentlemen whom you consider best suited. As a matter of fact there is probably not much chance that any of them will come. The session is now scheduled to begin at three o'clock on December 8. The rooms will be at our disposal on Saturday [December 10] as well; however, Dr. Schreiber thinks that the participants will not have that much time. Actually I would not know why it should be different from the last time;[3] I would be for continuing the discussions on Saturday. We are still not sure whether Dr. Zoellner will come.

¶Also, Dr. Schreiber asks if you would be so kind as to send the invitation forms to the Church Federation Office[4] as soon as possible, because other invitations with which they are to be sent in one mailing need to go out quickly. Please decide on the exact times yourself. It would seem desirable that Friday evening be kept free.

---

youth. Stählin was the director of this office, the activities of which were "carried out by the administrative office of the German World Alliance in consultation with the Church Federation Office" (Petrick, "Deutsche Mittelstelle," 376–77). Since September 1931, Bonhoeffer had been secretary of the Provisional Bureau, supporting Max Diestel, whose office had "taken over the secretarial tasks" (*DBW* 11:60).

[2.] A detailed report on this confidential discussion between representatives of the German Christian movement and university theologians on the topic "Our Gospel Message in the Era of the German Struggle for Freedom" (*Unsere Botschaft des Evangeliums in der Zeit des deutschen Freiheitskampfes*), held September 21–22, 1932, may be found in the *Reichsbote* newspaper of September 25, 1932 (see also Weiling, *"Christlich-deutsche Bewegung,"* 257–58). In his letter of October 27, 1932, to Bonhoeffer, Stählin said of this "Potsdam religious discussion" that it was "in many ways that which really lies ahead for us," and regretted that it had not been possible "to get Althaus and Rendtorff to negotiate with us beforehand. It would be all the more important now if we could manage to have at least a few of these men who have attacked the ecumenical movement take part in our conversation" (*DBW* 11:114–15). However, neither Althaus nor Rendtorff was invited to the Provisional Bureau's second theological conference (see 2/10) in Dassel. (See Schreiber's handwritten comment on Stählin's letter of November 24, 1932, dated December 13, 1932; EZA, 5/112).

[3.] Bonhoeffer is referring to the first theological conference of the Provisional Bureau for Ecumenical Youth Work, which had been held April 29–30, 1932 (see *DBWE* 11, 2/12).

[4.] The Church Federation Office was the head administrative office of the German Evangelical Church Federation, which the regional Protestant churches of Germany had formed in 1922.

For the rest, it seems as if the Church Federation Office regards our work [as] something akin to a viper in its bosom.[5] But perhaps that's best left until we see each other.

With best regards, I remain respectfully yours,
Dietrich Bonhoeffer

20 **3. From Wilhelm Stählin**[1]

November 4, 1932

My dear colleague Bonhoeffer:

With the enclosed correspondence, the viper reposes once again in the bosom of the Church Federation Office. I am sending the draft of the invitation to you[2] first, asking you to insert the time as well as the address to which registrations are to be sent.

¶I am not clear about the publication of the theses in *Die Eiche*.[3] They are supposed to be in the fourth issue, and since this issue is still not out as of today, it should be simple and cost only pennies to make thirty to forty copies of the theses from the galley proofs, so that each participant has them in hand. If this is possible, would you please add a note about it in the invitation.

¶Three o'clock in the afternoon is really a bit early. It was also not clear to me from your letter whether it is the ecumenical working group[4] that starts its meeting at that hour, or if this meeting will already have taken place. Please also let me know once again whether I should participate in the working group meeting.

I am writing to Dr. Zoellner, Bishop Rendtorff, and Prof. Althaus by this same post. Would you please take care of the invitations to the gentlemen in Berlin?[5] About the lodgings I will write to you later.

With best wishes,
yours,
[W. Stählin]

[5.] On the position of the Church Federation Office, see also Stählin's letter of October 27, 1932, *DBWE* 11, 1/88.1.

[1.] LKA Nuremberg, Personen XVIII, no. 63; carbon copy; from Münster, not previously published.

[2.] Draft invitation not preserved. See final version, 1/4.

[3.] Refers to the articles by Stählin and Zoellner mentioned in 1/4.

[4.] Refers to the German Ecumenical Working Committee, which in addition to members of the Provisional Bureau included the German Committee on Faith and Order and the German Evangelical Mission Committee.

[5.] For the list of names, see 1/5.

4. Invitation from the Provisional Bureau for Ecumenical Youth Work[1] 21

Münster–Berlin, November 1932

The theological conference held on April 29 and 30 this year, which discussed two lectures by former general superintendent Zoellner and Professor Stählin on "The Unity of the Church and the Churches" and "The Unity of the Church and the Nations,"[2] felt that it was urgent to continue, at some later time, the conversation that it had begun there. The German Evangelical Church Federation Office is making it possible for us to have this theological conference discussion in connection with a meeting of the German ecumenical working group,[3] and has again very kindly placed the Church Federation Office meeting room at our disposal. We hope that this conjunction of time and place will make it possible for all the representatives of those associations[4] that are related to us to participate in this conference, and to bring along other members of their associations who are interested in theology.

Accordingly, the Provisional Bureau for Ecumenical Youth Work invites you to its second theological conference on Friday, December 9, 1932, at four o'clock in the afternoon, in the meeting room of the German Evangelical Church Federation Office, 2 Marchstr., Berlin-Charlottenburg 2.

We have the possibility of continuing the discussion on Saturday morning, and we hope that participants will be able to take time to do so. However, in response to several requests from participants with other obligations, Friday evening will be left free. A section from the periodical *Die Eiche* is enclosed for each association, with the request that you familiarize yourself with both the theses and the report on the meeting in April,[5] and also that you bring them with you in December.

It was agreed at the April conference that this time no new lectures would 22
be presented, but rather that these theses, which have now been published in *Die Eiche* (no. 4), should serve as the basis for our continuing discussion.

Following up our previous discussion, we will speak to the two questions that it had begun to address, namely, the place of the nation [das Volk] in

[1.] *NL*, A 28,2 (10); hectograph copy; not previously published.

[2.] Cf. the articles published in *Die Eiche* (20 [1932]) under different titles: Wilhelm Zoellner, "Die *una sancta*" (The one, holy Church; 328–32), and Wilhelm Stählin, "Die Einheit" (Unity; 332–33).

[3.] See 1/5.

[4.] See 1/3, ed. note 4.

[5.] Refers to the articles mentioned in ed. note 2 and Bonhoeffer's report on the first theological conference (*DBWE* 11, 2/12 and 2/13).

theology, and the meaning of the confessions in the context of the ecumenical movement.

We ask that names of participants be registered in advance if possible with the undersigned, Dr. Bonhoeffer, 14 Wangenheimstr., Berlin-Grunewald, who is also ready to provide information.

Signed: Lecturer Dr. Bonhoeffer
Signed: Professor Stählin, ThD

5. To Wilhelm Stählin[1]

Dear Professor Stählin:

I am enclosing a letter from Dr. Schreiber.[2] I don't think you will have any objection to these suggestions.

The German ecumenical working group's[3] meeting is on Friday[4] morning; ours[5] will follow in the afternoon at 3:30. Of course we especially ask you to participate in the morning session as well, and I believe the Church Federation Office would particularly welcome that.

We thought we would send personal invitations to Messrs. Titius, Deißmann, (Richter and Siegmund-Schultze are not in Germany), [O.] Dibelius, Karow, Vits, Schreiber, Heckel, Wahl, Funke, Hinderer, Böhme, Braun (Mis-
23 sion), Philipps, Wilm, Rudolph. If you have any other particular requests, please let me know.[6]

With best wishes, I remain respectfully yours,
Dietrich Bonhoeffer

[1.] LKA Nuremberg, Personen XVIII, no. 63; typewritten. From Berlin-Grunewald; not previously published. Since 1/6 is dated November 11, 1932, Bonhoeffer's letter must have been written before that date.

[2.] Not extant. The content is probably identical to that of the letter mentioned in 1/6, ed. note 2.

[3.] Cf. 1/3, ed. note 4.

[4.] December 9, 1932.

[5.] Refers to the Provisional Bureau for Ecumenical Youth Work.

[6.] Following Bonhoeffer's letter of November 24, 1932, to the Church Federation Office, the list of names was changed once again. Instead of Böhme, Hinderer, Philipps, Rudolph, and Wahl, invitations were now sent to Görnandt, Hosemann, [H.] Sasse, and Weichert (EZA, 5/112; see also Glenthøj, *Zu Dietrich Bonhoeffers Eintritt*, 30).

6. From Wilhelm Stählin[1]

Münster, November 11, 1932

Dear Mr. Bonhoeffer:

Dr. Schreiber had already written to me in the meantime,[2] and I acted according to his wish. I am naturally in agreement with the list of personal invitations. I am not well enough acquainted in Berlin to be able to judge who might still be considered. Recently at a meeting of the YMCA students' working group,[3] I had an excellent conversation with Missions Inspector Weichert and was deeply impressed by his seriousness and broad perspective. But I could understand the reservations against inviting him, because he is a member of the Reich leadership of the Nazi party.[4] But he really is a very different type from someone like Peter.[5]

I am now arranging my time so as to be on hand Friday[6] morning for the 24
meeting of the ecumenical working group.[7]

Yours sincerely,
W. Stählin

[1.] *NL,* A 28,2 (8); typewritten; not previously published.

[2.] Cf. Schreiber's letter of November 9, 1932 (LKA Nuremberg, Personen XVIII, no. 63), in which he proposed changes to Bonhoeffer's draft of the Provisional Bureau's invitation for December 9–10, 1932, and "for procedural reasons" asked for the letter "to be addressed in the heading to the German Evangelical Church Federation Office, but on the envelope to me personally."

[3.] Young Men's Christian Association organizations had existed in Germany on the North American model since 1883. In 1919 they joined together to form the YMCA working group.

[4.] This probably refers to the Reich leadership of the German Christian movement, in which Weichert was in charge of the missions desk. Although it was in principle neutral on church politics, the Nazi party in Prussia had a close relationship to the German Christians at that time (Scholder, *Churches and the Third Reich,* 1:201–16).

[5.] Friedrich Peter, a member of the NSDAP and the German Christians since 1929, had participated in the Provisional Bureau's first theological conference on April 29–30, 1932 (see *DBWE* 11, 2/13).

[6.] December 9, 1932.

[7.] Cf. 1/3, ed. note 4.

6a. To August Wilhelm Schreiber[1]

Dear Councillor Schreiber:

I enclose the most recent letter I have had from Stählin.[2] Might I ask you to kindly let me know what you think of his suggestion to invite Dr. Weichert? Otherwise we now have everything in hand here.

As ever,
Yours sincerely and respectfully,
Bonhoeffer

6b. From Adolf Deißmann to the Junior Teaching Faculty of Systematic Theology[1]

Ev. Theological Faculty
of the
Friedr[ich] Wilh[elm] University
Journal no. 64

Berlin, November 14, 1932

Dear Colleagues:

On the basis of § 42 of our University Charter of March 5, 1930, I am honored to invite you to submit your own personal recommendations for the reappointment of the professorship held by Dr. Titius.

[1.] *NL*, A 2,2 (4); typewritten, signed by hand, on engraved letterhead: "Dietrich Bonhoeffer, MA, Lecturer, University of Berlin, Berlin Grunewald, date (undated), Wangenheimstraße 14, H 1 Pfalzburg 2616"; unpublished. On the letter, a handwritten note by the recipient, dated January 21 (probably actually November 21), saying the letter and its enclosure should be returned to the sender. Schreiber replied to Bonhoeffer's inquiry: "Very much in agreement that Dr. Weichert should be invited." This letter was written between November 11 and 21, 1933. A small slip of paper was found with it, with a penciled note by Schreiber, dated January 21 (probably actually November 20; cf. 1/3–5): "Dear Mr. Bonhoeffer, may I expect to receive the copies of *Die Eiche* soon? The invitations need to be sent!" This indicates that the invitation (1/4) must have been sent later than November 21, 1932. Edited by Carsten Nicolaisen and Ernst-Albert Scharffenorth.

[2.] Of November 11, 1932 (1/6).

[1.] Humboldt-Universität Berlin, Universitätsarchiv, Bestand Theologische Fakultät 178, Bl. 6; typewritten carbon copy. The name of Arnold Stolzenburg has been added to the list of recipients by hand. Edited by Hartmut Ludwig.

Will you please send your recommendations to me in the dean's office by Friday, November 25, at the latest.

With my collegial regards
Yours sincerely,
Signed Dr. Deißmann
Dean

Sent to:
Professor D. Runze[2]
" D. Fabricius
" D. Gruehn[3]
" D. Stolzenburg
Priv. Doz. Lic. Bonhoeffer
Priv. Doz. Lic. Dr. Künneth

7. From Henry Louis Henriod[1]

Geneva, November 18, 1932

My dear Bonhoeffer,

Thanks for your excellent letter of November 11. I am in total agreement with you concerning the essential points that we have to emphasize in our publications. The test issue of the *News Letter*[2] has been printed and is going out tonight. Taken as a whole it is not very coherent, but by nature it is not supposed to look like a review or a periodical. Its chief aim should be the sharing of information, which for me does not exclude the usefulness of including in each issue a short article on questions of principle.

May I ask you to give me your reactions after having read this first International Bulletin? And would you please make contact with the other members of the publications commission, that is, Messrs. Marthinussen, Bach, Craske, Fischer, and Miss Niven, regarding the *News Letter* and all other publications we may find necessary, so that you can pass on to me some proposals and requests to submit to the Executive[3] during our January meeting in Berlin? As to finding

[2.] Georg Runze. See *RGG*, 2nd ed., vol. 4, col. 2143.

[3.] Werner Gruehn. See *BBKL* 20:658–68.

[1.] *NL*, A 28,3 (7); typewritten; reprinted in *GS* 6:279–80. Bonhoeffer's letter of November 11, 1932, which Henriod mentions, has been lost.

[2.] Cf. 1/1.

[3.] Refers to the Executive Committee.

people to write a short article on principles for each newsletter, I think we need to speak first to our president, Lord Dickinson. However, I am tempted to ask Bishop Ammundsen as well for a brief message to put in this same issue. Whom would you suggest from Germany for the next issue? Should I speak to Siegmund-Schultze, or do you have someone else you would like to suggest? I would also like to have younger voices, but we shouldn't forget that the letter will probably appear no more than four times during the year 1933.[4]

As to the grant for Vienna,[5] please send me a precise request before the end of December. If not, the balance we have in the youth-work account will be automatically reabsorbed in the settlement of accounts for the year. If I send you the amount before December 31, that does not mean you cannot use it at the beginning of the following year.

Thanks for your reassuring response concerning the speeches I have been asked to give in Berlin. I have just received a letter from Mr. Jordan. The probable dates for my stay in Berlin, apart from the Executive meeting, are January 17–26. The Executive will doubtless take place immediately afterward.[6] Siegmund-Schultze and Jordan are insisting that I speak in German. In that case I shall have to read my speeches, although in French or in English I could speak from notes.

Like you, I have some reservations about the articles by the bishop of Ripon. Nonetheless, they have certainly helped the cause of the Alliance in British circles.

Thanks again and best wishes,
[Henry Louis Henriod]

[4.] In fact, in 1933 and each subsequent year (until the end of 1938, when its publication ceased), three issues of *Die Kirchen am Werk: Mitteilungen* appeared in German, English, and French. [The English publication was titled *The Churches at Work: News Letter.*—LR] In 1934 between 1,700 and 1,800 copies were printed in German, about 1,600 in English, and about 450 in French (World Alliance, *Annual Report*, 1933–34, 34).

[5.] Cf. 1/1.

[6.] The Executive Committee met January 30–February 2, 1933, in Berlin. Henriod arrived in Berlin beforehand and spoke to students at the university on January 27, 1933, on "National and Transnational Church Work: The Church and the General Crisis" ("Nationale und übernationale kirchliche Arbeit: Die Kirche und die allgemeine Not") (see *Die Eiche*, no. 21).

7a. From Caius Fabricius to Adolf Deißmann[1]

Professor Dr. Fabricius Berlin, November 19, 1932
Berlin NW 87, Jagowstr.

May Your Eminence permit me to offer the following reply to the request I received regarding the successor to Dr. Titius:

Since Dr. Titius continues to be active with uninterrupted energy and without doubt is difficult to replace, I would like to recommend that the reappointment of this position be postponed for at least two years. This would also be a desirable saving of state resources. However, should an earlier appointment appear to be desirable, one should first and foremost look toward Dr. Barth in Bonn, who has very openly won a leading position in theology. The only question here would be whether the intellectual position represented by Barth, with its emphasis on the nothingness [Nichtigkeit] of the human being, which corresponded to the atmosphere of breakdown of the decade that has just ended, will continue to be dominant in the near future or whether it will soon be replaced by other tendencies.

Particularly at this present moment, one must warn against the appointment of a religious socialist.[2] Such a person—as the recent events in Halle[3] illustrate—

[1.] Geheimes Staatsarchiv Berlin-Dahlem, PK, I. HA Rep. 76 Kultusministerium, Va Sekt. 2 [Berlin], Tit. IV, Nr. 44, Bd. IX, Bl. 385; typewritten original with no salutation, handwritten signature. Handwritten notation of the faculty: Tgb. Nr. 83 (upper left), D. Fabricius (upper right). Edited by Hartmut Ludwig.

[2.] Fabricius is referring here to inviting Paul Tillich. [Erich Seeberg had mentioned the possibility of Titius's successor to Paul Tillich and asked his advice. Tillich replied on November 24, 1932: "As far as the chances for me, I naturally would judge this as negatively as you do" (BA Koblenz, Nachlaß Erich Seeberg N 1248/37; Seeberg's letter not extant). It is not known whether Tillich announced his own interest in an invitation to Berlin or whether he was recommended. In 1928, the invitation to Tillich failed due to the opposition of the Evangelical Consistory (BA Koblenz, Nachlaß Erich Seeberg, N 1248: letters of Tillich to Seeberg dated June 21, November 1, and December 1, 1928). On December 11, 1932, Tillich suggested to Seeberg how his appointment in Berlin might possibly be arranged: (1) He would receive a professorship for the philosophy of religion at the Theological Faculty; (2) he would make a promise to the consistory only to examine theologians in philosophy and not to offer any lectures in dogmatics; and (3) the lectures, exercises, and examinations in dogmatics would be assigned to either Caius Fabricius or Arnold Stolzenburg (BA Koblenz, Nachlaß Erich Seeberg, N 1248/37). The editors thank Hartmut Ludwig for this information.—LR]

[3.] The reference here is to the 1931 "Dehn Case" in Halle. See Dehn, *Die alte Zeit, die vorigen Jahre*, 247–85. [Cf. also *DBWE* 11, 1/40, as well as *DB-ER*, 177 and 235–36.—LR]

could have very unpleasant consequences that would lead not to the promotion of scholarship but instead to the disturbance of academic peace.

Your humble servant,
Fabricius

To the Dean
of the Theological Faculty
in Berlin

26 **8. To the Berlin Office of the World Alliance for Promoting International Friendship through the Churches**[1]

Berlin-Grunewald, November 22, 1932

I hereby ask that Rev. Jordan be informed that on Friday, November 25, I shall not be able to attend the meeting because of responsibilities in my work. Would you please also inform Superintendent Diestel that the piece I am writing on the "Social gospel" will be finished in the next few days.[2] The work was substantially delayed by my efforts to obtain references.

Very respectfully yours,
Dietrich Bonhoeffer

[1.] *NL*, Anh. A 7 (4); handwritten; not previously published. This probably refers to the meeting of the Management Committee of the German World Alliance section, announced for "four in the afternoon at the quarters on Albrecht St." (EZA, 51 D V c: Report on the Meeting of the Management Committee of October 29, 1933).

[2.] Cf. 1/13 and 2/4.

9. To Anneliese Schnurmann[1]

Berlin-Grunewald, November 23, 1932

Dear Anneliese,

I have received all your postal checks and am feeling that my self-confidence has been greatly enhanced. You better watch out—I may suddenly run off to India with all this![2]

We've been having some trouble at the youth club. From the first day I
did not think Zimmermann[3] would be up to any good. It seems that he 27
and Albert[4] both have made themselves pretty unpopular with the boys. He recently introduced himself as director of the youth club; he claims he was drunk at the time. I think we'll have to show him the door as soon as possible; otherwise there's going to be a real fight. Apart from that it's still quite pleasant. But we are thinking of moving. This place is getting too small for us. What would you think of that? Two theology students are working with us. There's also a technical student, who would like to earn twenty-five marks a month and would be there three evenings [a week]. Do you think we should do that? He's a friendly fellow and might take Zimmermann's place. Please write soon, because he'd like to know. Hope you enjoy the rest of the semester. For my part, I've already had all I can take.

Yours with all good wishes,
Dietrich Bonhoeffer

[1.] *NL*, A 28,6 (2); typewritten copy of the original from the literary estate of Anneliese Schnurmann, London, which has been lost. Previously published in *GS* 6:226–27. Anneliese Schnurmann's letters to Bonhoeffer have not been preserved among his papers. Schnurmann was a school friend of Susanne Bonhoeffer's and was of Jewish descent; she financially supported Bonhoeffer's social work at the youth club that was founded in fall 1932 on Schloßstrasse in Charlottenburg. See also 1/1 and *DBWE* 11, 1/86.

[2.] Since 1928, Bonhoeffer had been planning a trip to India; he had a particular interest in Gandhi (*DB-ER*, 105). [See also *DBWE* 13, esp. letters 1/154 and 1/158 (from Gandhi to Bonhoeffer).—LR]

[3.] Not identified.

[4.] Not identified.

9a. From Arnold Stolzenburg[1]

With regard to the appointment of the professorship for systematic theology at the University of Berlin, my recommendation begins with the assumption that (1) in light of the entire intellectual situation today, the theological direction that has been determined by the individualistic line of intellectual history is no longer under consideration, and that (2) dialectical theology, despite all the significance given to it in the present, will be determined by the church authorities more narrowly in the future. Thus, the kind of person to wish for would be sought from the direction that is prepared to assimilate the justifiable elements of the dialecticians while at the same time remaining open, to a sufficient degree, to the great tasks of influencing the general culture.

With this in mind (1) Althaus und (2) particularly Frick[2] seem promising to me.

Berlin, November 24, 1932 Dr. Stolzenburg

9b. From Walter Künneth to the Theological Faculty[1]

Berlin-Dahlem, November 24, 1932

To the
Honorable Theological Faculty
of Friedrich Wilhelm University
Berlin NW 7

On the basis of the request by the dean dated November 14, I permit myself, in accordance with § 42 of the University Charter to recommend first

Professor Dr. Karl Barth = Bonn

[1.] Geheimes Staatsarchiv Berlin-Dahlem, PK, I. HA Rep. 76 Kultusministerium, Va Sekt. 2 [Berlin], Tit. IV, Nr. 44, Bd. IX, Bl. 386; handwritten original without address and salutation. Handwritten notation of the faculty: Tb Nr. 85 (upper left), Dr. Stolzenburg (upper right). Edited by Hartmut Ludwig.

[2.] Heinrich Frick. See *BBKL* 2:123.

[1.] Geheimes Staatsarchiv Berlin-Dahlem, PK, I. HA Rep. 76 Kultusministerium, Va Sekt. 2 [Berlin], Tit. IV, Nr. 44, Bd. IX, Bl. 389; original single page with handwritten signature and official stamp. Handwritten notation of the faculty: Tb. 90 (left), Lic. Dr. Künneth (upper right). Edited by Hartmut Ludwig.

for the reappointment of the professorship of Privy Councillor Professor Dr. Titius. Also permit me to recommend further Professor Dr. Friedrich Brunstäd = Rostock[2] as well as Professor Dr. Paul Althaus = Erlangen.

With my greatest respects,
Yours sincerely,
Dr. Künneth,
Lecturer

10. Notice Posted at the Technical College[1]

Berlin-Grunewald, November 25, 1932

To the fellow student who has now felt compelled to remove this notice for the third time![2]

Dear Friend:

Why so secretive and why always the same joke, or why so terribly angry? I'm convinced that you and I are depriving ourselves of a significant experience if our relationship remains so impersonal. Why not come round to see me sometime? We might not do so badly talking with each other. I at least would be happier with that than this sort of acquaintance, which can give neither you nor me any pleasure.

With best regards,
Bonhoeffer

[2.] Friedrich Brunstädt. See *TRE* 7:249–53.

[1.] *NL*, A 29,1 (1); handwritten on letterhead with Bonhoeffer's private address. Previously published in *GS* 6:218.

[2.] Probably the semester program for the student chaplain's office at the Technical College. See also Bonhoeffer's report to the consistory (1/54).

10a. To Adolf Deißmann[1]

Dr. Dietrich Bonhoeffer — Berlin-Grunewald, November 26,1932
Lecturer at the University of Berlin — Wangenheimstraße 14
H 1 Pfalzburg 2616

His Eminence
Privy Councillor Professor Dr. Deißmann
Theological Faculty of the University of Berlin

Your Eminence

Allow me to respond to the request for recommendations for the successor to Privy Councillor Professor Dr. Titius with the following names:
Professor Karl Barth
Professor Werner Elert
Professor Paul Althaus.

Your Eminence
Your most devoted servant
Bonhoeffer

17:115

10b. To Paul Lehmann[1]

Berlin, November 29, [19]32

Dear Paul,

It is certainly no indication of my gratitude to you for your prompt and willing help, and of how valuable it was to me,[2] that I am only writing today to thank you for it. Please forgive me that even today I must be very brief. As soon as I can, I shall write to you properly, you may depend on it. At least

[1.] Geheimes Staatsarchiv Berlin-Dahlem, PK, I. HA Rep. 76 Kultusministerium, Va Sekt. 2 [Berlin], Tit. IV, Nr. 44, Bd. IX, Bl. 388; original single page with handwritten signature. Handwritten notation of the faculty: Tb. 88 (left), Lic. Bonhoeffer (right, under the address). Cf. also 1/30, ed. note 8. Edited by Hartmut Ludwig.

[1.] Center of Theological Inquiry, Princeton, Paul Lehmann Papers; typewritten, signed by hand, with heading: "Dietrich Bonhoeffer, MA, Grunewald, Wangenheimstr. 14"; unpublished. Edited by Ernst-Albert Scharffenorth. [Originally published in *DBW* 17 as number 10a; following the discovery of the preceding letter to Adolf Deißmann, it has been renumbered accordingly.—LR]

[2.] See Bonhoeffer's letter of October 30, 1932, to Lehmann, *DBWE* 11, 1/93a, according to which Lehmann fulfilled a request for material (not found) on the social gospel. For Bonhoeffer's text, see 2/4.

the ten dollars arrived all right at the time.[3] For your tobacco problem I have not yet found a satisfactory solution.[4] Please give my best regards to your wife and to Sutz, and to Brunner if you have the opportunity. For me as well, spring would be the best time for us to get together.[5]

With best regards and sincere thanks,
Yours as ever,
Dietrich Bonhoeffer

11. To Anneliese Schnurmann[1] 28

Berlin-Charlottenburg, December 1, 1932

Dear Anneliese,

I don't know what to think anymore. I gave you my signature before you left.[2] Since then I haven't been asked for it again. I received both of your postal checks, but they included nothing of that nature. I wonder if I'm losing my mind—shouldn't I have received something by now and have sent it along? Things don't usually get lost in the mail. (Although I can prove that I did have such an experience three weeks ago.) So please send it to me again and just say what I am supposed to sign. I should be very sorry to have been the cause of confusion. But I really cannot remember anything like that. At least this card will console you that I haven't gone to India;[3] I'm right here, busy enough to forget all sorts of things. Otherwise everything is fine. We moved yesterday![4] More soon.

Yours, with best regards,
Dietrich Bonhoeffer

P.S. In the meantime I'm covering expenses out of my own pocket.

[3.] According to his letter of February 19, 1932, (*DBWE* 11, 1/37a) to Paul Lehmann, Bonhoeffer sent this amount to pay for the literature requested.

[4.] Specific reference not known, but cf. letter of November 5, 1931, to Lehmann (*DBWE* 11, 1/16a), which mentions the cigarettes that Paul Lehmann usually smoked.

[5.] Paul and Marion Lehmann visited Bonhoeffer in early April 1933 (*DB-ER*, 268–69).

[1.] *NL*, A 28,6(3); typewritten copy of the original from the Anneliese Schnurmann papers, London (which have been lost). Previously published in *GS* 6:227.

[2.] This probably concerns a signature for the financing of the youth club through a post office money account. [Europeans often keep money in a post office account rather than a bank account, since they also pay most bills with postal money orders. Thanks to Isabel Best for this information.—LR]

[3.] See 1/9, ed. note 2.

[4.] Refers to the youth club's move to larger premises (cf. 1/9).

29 **12. To Hans Schönfeld**[1]

Berlin, December 1, 1932

Dear Dr. Schönfeld:

For a paper that I have been asked to write[2] by the German Management Committee of the World Alliance for Promoting International Friendship through the Churches, I need Visser 't Hooft's book, *Background of the Social Gospel*,[3] which I have not been able to get from either the library or the bookstore, or from Haarlem, where it is out of print. Would it be possible for you to help me in any way to get hold of this book, whether a copy that I can buy or one that you could make available to me from a library? I should be very grateful to hear from you soon.[4]

With best wishes, I am yours very sincerely,
Bonhoeffer

12a. To Herbert Jehle[1]

December 1 [1932]

Dear Mr. Jehle,

It is with extraordinary regret that that I must now cancel our appointment. A sudden expert opinion that must be ready by [. . .][2] will not allow me to be free tomorrow. Please forgive me. I hope very much that there will be another occasion soon. Most sincerely I am

yours truly,
Dietrich Bonhoeffer

[1.] WCC Archives, Bonhoeffer box; photocopy of a specially preserved letter. See also *NL*, A 28,3 (14); typewritten copy. Previously published in *GS* 6:248.

[2.] This was the "Memorandum: The 'Social Gospel'" (2/4).

[3.] Refers to Visser 't Hooft, *The Background of the Social Gospel in America*, first published in Haarlem, the Netherlands, 1928.

[4.] Bonhoeffer received the book on December 5, 1932, but sent it back immediately because in the meantime he had obtained it in Berlin (*GS* 6:249; letter of December 5, 1932, to Schönfeld). The return of the borrowed book is confirmed in a handwritten note (dated January 9, 1933) on a typewritten reminder of January 6, 1933 (WCC Archives, World Alliance, Bonhoeffer box; carbon copy).

[1.] Literary estate of Herbert Jehle. Addressed by hand to "Mr. Herbert Jehle, Student of Physics, Friedenau, Benningsenstr. 17, c/o Dr. Dibbers." Edited by Hans Pfeifer.

[2.] Illegible in the original manuscript.

13. To Max Diestel[1]

Berlin, December 3, 1932

Dear Superintendent Diestel:

I had a good deal of trouble finding the reference works I needed. That is why this "paper"[2] is reaching you a week late. I hope that is not too bad.

I remain respectfully yours,
Dietrich Bonhoeffer

13a. To Paul Althaus[1] 11:44

Berlin-Grunewald, December 5

Dear Professor Althaus:

Thank you very much for the *Dogmatik* II![2] It was a very great pleasure for me to receive the book today from you personally. It is strange, but it is the case that one has even more enjoyment in reading something when there is a personal experience connected to it. Let me thank you sincerely for your kindness.

For a long time I have been looking forward eagerly to this second part. Because today this is simply what everything depends upon. And yet so often the courage is lacking to say something about it. And now to have a finished work in such a compact form—it hardly lets one do anything other than jump into it immediately. In spite of the preparation I really should be doing for my lecture tomorrow, I believe I will not be able to resist sitting down with your book for a good part of tonight. But I just wanted to write you right away and thank you for your great kindness.

In grateful admiration, most esteemed Professor, I am very respectfully 11:45
yours,
Dietrich Bonhoeffer

[1.] *NL*, Anh. A 7(5); typewritten; not previously published. Cf. 1/8.

[2.] Refers to the "Memorandum: The 'Social Gospel'" (2/4).

[1.] *NL*, Anh. A 10; photocopy of the handwritten original; the right edge is partially missing. According to a handwritten notation by Eberhard Bethge on the original, the letter was written in 1931. [Because of Bethge's notation, this letter was originally included in *DBW* 11 as 1/23. It is now certain, however, that the letter was written in 1932, and thus it has been moved to this volume. Translation by Anne Schmidt-Lange.—LR]

[2.] Althaus, *Grundriß der Dogmatik*, vol. 2. Since the book was not published until 1932, Althaus must have sent either the proofs or one of his advance copies.

30 **14. To Wilhelm Stählin**[1]

Berlin, December 6, 1932

Dear Professor Stählin:

Dr. Schreiber thinks that twenty minutes would be enough for what we need to discuss. He has another meeting at ten [o'clock] and asks if we could come to his office about twenty to eleven [o'clock]. Is it all right with you if I wait for you between quarter past and 10:30 at the corner of Marchstr. and Am Knie?[2] Otherwise, could I ask you to call me by telephone (Pfalzburg H1. 2616) on Thursday[3] evening? I can certainly make my report very brief, because the theses and the discussion will be available[4] in printed form and a restatement of the theses in even shorter form is not really possible.

With best regards, I remain respectfully yours,
Dietrich Bonhoeffer

14a. From the Provisional Bureau for Ecumenical Youth Work to Adolf Deißmann[1]

Provisional Bureau
for
Ecumenical Youth Work

Münster–Berlin, December 6, 1932
(unfortunately delayed)

The Provisional Bureau[2] for Ecumenical Youth Work is holding its second theological conference at 4:00 p.m. on the afternoon of March 9 in the meeting room of the Church Federation office in Berlin-Charlottenburg,

[1.] LKA Nuremberg, Personen XVIII, no. 63; typewritten; not previously published. This probably concerns a meeting on December 9, 1932, that was to take place before the discussion between representatives of the Provisional Bureau and the Church Federation Office about the ecumenical working meeting in Dassel (cf. 1/4 and 2/10).

[2.] Now Ernst-Reuter-Platz. They were thus to meet very near the Church Federation Office at 2 Marchstr.

[3.] December 8, 1932.

[4.] See 1/4, ed. notes 2 and 5.

[1.] ZLB Berlin, Nachlaß Adolf Deißmann, Nr. 307. Edited by Hans Pfeifer.

[2.] [This office for ecumenical youth work in Germany at that time had no executive power, only the power to organize in ad hoc fashion. On the one hand, this lack of executive power was a clear disadvantage. On the other, Bonhoeffer was thereby given considerable latitude to organize ecumenical youth work as he deemed proper.—LR]

Marchstr. 2. In the first conference it was agreed that this time no new lectures would be held, but instead the published Guiding Principles concerning "Church and Churches," "Church and the People [Volk]," written by Drs. Zöllner and Stählin, which in the interim have been published in issue 4 of *Die Eiche*, are to be the basis of the discussion. The signators of this letter would like most sincerely to invite you to this conference.

A reply to Dr. Bonhoeffer, Berlin-Grunewald, Wangenheimstr. 14, is requested.

signed Professor Dr. Stählin
signed Lecturer Dr. Bonhoeffer

P.S. The theses of the lectures by General Superintendent Emer. Dr. Zoellner und Professor Dr. Stählin are enclosed in the text from April 29 and 30.[3]

15. From Tamotsu Utsugi[1]

Nakamura machi, Fukushima-Ken, Japan, December 6, 1932

Hellow, Mr. Bonhoeffer!

How have you been getting along? In this season of Christmas my happy thoughts carry me back again to our delightful days at Union Seminary in New York, and now I think of you and send my heartly Christmas wishes. I'm studying as ever hard as I have been at Union. We must rebuild up the world by our coopera- 31
tion that the world could never require. Drop me a card often, in English or in Deutsch. New theology of your country is much interesting in our country.[2]

Ever yours
T. Utsugi

[3.] The theses have not been preserved.

[1.] *NL*, C 23; handwritten postcard from Japan; not previously published. Original in English, including errors.

[2.] Presumably Utsugi meant dialectical theology. Bonhoeffer had given an introduction to it ["The Theology of Crisis"—LR] when they were both students at Union Theological Seminary in New York (*DBWE* 10:462–76; cf. *DB-ER*, 157–59).

15a. From Adolf Deißmann[1]

December 7, 1932

To Lecturer Dietrich Bonhoeffer
Berlin-Grunewald, Wangenheimstr. 14

My dear Colleague:

To my regret, only yesterday did I receive the invitation to the second theological conference of the Provisional Bureau for Ecumenical Youth Work, and I can no longer free my calendar for Friday and Saturday of this week.[2] Hence I request that my absence will be excused. I have entrusted Pastor Dr. Hermann Sasse to represent me.

On this occasion I would like to express personally my warmest thanks to you for engaging yourself so actively in ecumenical matters. I hope there will soon be the chance for me to discuss the general situation with you. With the request that you give my best wishes as well to Professor Dr. Stählin and the other friends, I remain

Your very devoted
Adolf Deißmann[3]

16. To Anneliese Schnurmann[1]

Berlin W.8, December 8, 1932

Dear Anneliese,

Now everything should be all right.[2] I am now certain, however, that I never received such a paper[3] in a letter from you.

I paid the first rent of sixty reichsmarks out of my own pocket.[4] The party for the official reopening is today, moreover. It's a pity I have a touch of the flu and can't go. They're having sausages, cake, and cigarettes, too. The

---

[1.] ZLB, Nachlaß Adolf Deißmann, Nr. 307. Edited by Hans Pfeifer.

[2.] Deißmann erroneously read the conference date as December 9, 1932; cf. 1/14a.

[3.] Handwritten signature.

[1.] *NL*, A 28,6 (4); typewritten copy of the original in the literary estate of Anneliese Schnurmann (which has been lost), London. Previously published in *GS* 6:228. Later, after Hitler took power, the police searched the youth club for the card index with the names of its members; the youth work then had to be stopped to prevent persecution of Communist members (*DB-ER*, 231).

[2.] See 1/11.

[3.] Not extant.

[4.] For the new youth club premises.

boys have worked really hard in the past few days, so we surely had to give them a good time. The party cost twenty reichsmarks, which I advanced.

Luckily Zimmerman is gone.[5] He would have upset the whole thing. Evidently he thought he was being watched and hemmed in too much. As for the student from the Technical College,[6] my idea was that he could come three evenings a week, offer stenography lessons, and be helpful in other ways. For this he could be paid fifteen reichsmarks from the funds of the Technical College chaplain's office, and fifteen reichsmarks from you. Let's just try it during January. I think he is very decent.

Unfortunately I get over there far too seldom. So many other things are 32
going on.—So, I'll write myself a check on the post office account for eighty marks. How are the funds holding up? Perhaps I'll just cover the twenty reichsmarks myself.

Yours, with best regards,
D[ietrich] B[onhoeffer]

17. To Irma and Harold Boericke[1]

Berlin-Grunewald, December 12, 1932

Dear Aunt Irma and Uncle Harold,

It's nice when Christmas comes round again and gives one the chance to write letters that one has been wanting to write for a long time. I often hear about you from Grandmama,[2] including the real worries you have had over the past year. At those times I thought about you a great deal, and so often I really intended to write. But the rat race here in Berlin is terrible; one's best intentions often come to naught. So today I would at least like to say to you how heartily I wish that, along with the old year, all your old troubles will become things of the past. I wish with all my heart and for all of you that you, dear Uncle Harold, will soon be completely well and as fit as you were before. I can hardly believe it's now two years since I was there and was able to spend that lovely first week of Advent with you.[3] I'm really

[5.] See 1/9.

[6.] See 1/9.

[1.] *NL*, A 28.1(8); typewritten with a handwritten paragraph added at the end, not previously published.

[2.] Julie Bonhoeffer.

[3.] Bonhoeffer had visited these relatives, who lived in Wynnewood, Pennsylvania, the week of November 27 to December 3, 1930 (see *DBWE* 10, 1/142, ed. note 2).

not exaggerating when I say, even now, that I never felt myself so at home in America as at your house. I shall never forget the restful evenings and the
33 pleasant afternoon at your sisters' house.[4] These are wonderful memories associated with your home, for which I am so grateful.

¶How I'd like to see you all again. But it would probably be more possible here in Germany this time, than over there with you. Wouldn't you like to take another trip to Germany this summer, after you have completely recovered, and include a visit to us? That would be splendid. Be sure to bring Binkie[5] along. What is he up to, and especially what is happening with his love of music? It's getting to be time now when he should really begin to practice if he wants to accomplish something. It was so precious, when I was there, the way the little fellow would listen to the most difficult things and recognize them again. I'd enjoy teaching him to play the piano. And what are Betty and Ray[6] doing? How do they like college life? Wouldn't they like to come over here sometime to learn German?

For us at home everything is going along as usual. Grandmama is still astonishingly active and lively, even though she often considers herself quite disabled. She just expects a great deal of herself. There is such an unusual vitality in her, and we are all glad for every day that we have her with us.

¶With my two jobs I am very busy. The university, that is, the young theological students, make real demands on my time, and so does the practical work in the church. But having a lot to do is something to be thankful for these days. I also greatly enjoy my profession, even though it is becoming clearer to me from day to day how difficult it is to be a good pastor. What especially weighs on my heart right now is the work with unemployed working-class youth.[7] It is here that everything one does is really only a drop in the
34 bucket. It can often be very discouraging to experience here, in one little place, the great hardships that are being felt worldwide. That's what makes it so good when Christmas comes again, even though it seems against all common sense. It calls us anew not to hang onto the darkness and hopelessness, but to take seriously, once again, the message of the light shining in

[4.] According to a letter of May 3, 1991, from Betty Boericke-Imhoff, this refers to the three unmarried sisters [of Harold Boericke]: Clara Auguste (1861–1941), Helene (1865–1962), and Johanna Magdalena Boericke (1868–1949).

[5.] Nickname of Bonhoeffer's cousin, Harold Boericke Jr.

[6.] Sisters of the above-mentioned cousin: Betty Anne and Irma Theresa, who was called Ray.

[7.] Proof of this interest was the youth club project (see 1/9, 1/11, and 1/16).

the darkness and to live in a new way from now on. And I'm always glad for the privilege of knowing that you and I share this way of thinking.

Please forgive me for typing this letter; I did it out of consideration for you.—Please remember me warmly to your two cousins, as well as your sisters, and especially to Binkie. Wishing you a Merry Christmas and a good New Year,

Yours very thankfully,
Dietrich B[onhoeffer]

18. To Renate Lepsius[1]

Berlin, December 14, 1932

Dear Miss Lepsius,

On looking through the translation,[2] I decided, to my regret, that there are so many errors in translation, inaccuracies, and Anglicisms that it would be impossible for me to rework the whole of it in detail. I did go through a sample of it, that is, pages 1–21 and the beginning of the concluding chapter. Some of the errors in the first pages of this excerpt are noted on the enclosed slips of paper.[3] I myself could not recommend publication of such a translation. In my opinion it is not worthwhile comparing the page proofs with the galley proofs. I am sorry that I can only help in such a nega- 35
tive way. I'll return the translation to you by the next post.

With best regards, and thanks for sending the ten copies of *Die Eiche*,[4] I remain yours very respectfully,

Dietrich Bonhoeffer

[1.] EZA 51/P III 1c; typewritten. Previously published in *Mündige Welt*, 5:74, and *GS* 6:249–50.

[2.] Refers to the translation of Bell's book *A Brief Sketch of the Church of England*, which Bonhoeffer had received from Renate Lepsius on October 15, 1932, along with a draft translation (see *DBWE* 11, 1/182).

[3.] Not found with the letter.

[4.] Possibly Bonhoeffer's author's copies of the essay "On the Theological Basis of the Work of the World Alliance," which was published in *Die Eiche* (published in *DBWE* 11, 2/14).

19. To Joachim Kanitz[1]

Dear Mr. Kanitz,

Please send a copy of this[2] to Mr. Rütenik right away. I don't have his address. The way the liturgy has now taken shape for me, I believe it is no longer really possible to have two liturgists and that the same person should both lead the service and give the homily. In fact, the congregation is drawn into the action to such an extent by the responsive readings that I now no longer have any reservations about this.

Thanking you for your offer to help, I remain sincerely yours,
D[ietrich] B[onhoeffer]

36
20. To Wilhelm Stählin[1]

Berlin-Grunewald, December 22, 1932

Dear Professor Stählin:

After our recent conversation,[2] I cannot let Christmas go by without writing to you. Since that time I feel such a new bond with you, even if for the moment all I can say is that the things we talked about then preoccupy me daily, and that I still have a great deal of thinking and living to do in this regard. (I cannot get away entirely from the fear that in my case, the craving to penetrate the mysteries that are closed to us, the craving to "see" prematurely, could keep interfering.)—But now it is Christmas that moves me to tell you this, and to thank you for that midday hour. That conversation, in its unexpectedness and the way it ended so abruptly, was a real gift.

The day before yesterday I held a Christmas service[3] in the church with my seminar students. It was such a joyful time for all of us. I very much wish for you that in this year you might find the same joy. We all need it. The needs of the theology students are so considerable; if only it could be

[1.] *NL,* A 29,1 (4); handwritten draft on the same page as the liturgy mentioned in the letter; from Berlin. Previously published in *GS* 6:210. Written before December 20, 1932 (cf. 1/20).

[2.] Refers to the liturgy for the Christmas service for seminar participants (3/3).

[1.] LKA Nuremberg, Personen XVIII, no. 49; handwritten; not previously published.

[2.] Probably during the conference of the Provisional Bureau (see 1/14).

[3.] See 3/3.

granted us to be of real service to them in the New Year. That is probably a New Year's wish that we both share.

Please give my regards to your son![4]

In sincere gratitude and respect I send you my most cordial greetings.
Yours, Dietrich Bonhoeffer

21. To Karl Barth[1] 37

Berlin-Grunewald, December 24, 1932

Dear Professor Barth:

Before this year closes, I would like to thank you once again for all that I have received from you in the course of the year. The evening here in Berlin[2] and then the incomparably splendid hours spent with you on the Bergli[3] belong to the moments of this year that will remain with me. Please forgive me if I was a burden to you in August[4] with my perhaps too obstinate, and—as you once said—"godless" questions.[5] But at the same time I should like you to know that I know no one else who can free me from these persistent questions as you can, and therefore you are the one with whom I feel I must talk like this. It's hard to say why, but with you I just have this very distinct feeling that the way you see things is somehow the right way. It's just that when I am talking with you, I am brought right to the heart of the matter, whereas before I only kept circling around it at a distance. That for me is the very unmistakable sign that here is where I am right on target. And since nowhere else is this awareness with anything like this intensity, I shall have to keep asking you now and then for the gift of some of your time;

[4.] Refers to Rudolf Stählin, who was studying theology during the winter semester 1932–33 in Berlin and had become acquainted with Bonhoeffer there (see *DBWE* 11, 1/84 and 1/85).

[1.] Karl Barth-Archiv, Basel; handwritten. See also *NL*, A 28,5 (1); typewritten copy. Previously published in *Mündige Welt*, 1:106–7, and *GS* 2:39–40.

[2.] On April 11, 1932, following Barth's lecture in Berlin on "Die Theologie und die Mission in der Gegenwart" ("Theology and Mission in the Present Era"). See also Bonhoeffer's report on the reactions to the lecture from theologians in Berlin, in his letter of May 17, 1932, to Erwin Sutz (*DBWE* 11, 1/59).

[3.] Barth's vacation home by Lake Zürich in Switzerland.

[4.] According to *DB-ER*, 177, and *DBWE* 11 (1/79 and 1/89), this visit did not take place until early September.

[5.] This is evidently how Barth characterized Bonhoeffer's insistence on the church's authority to give concrete ethical directives (see 1/22 and *DB-ER*, 181–85).

at such times, please forgive me. The brief hours that we had together this year have succeeded in steering my thoughts, which are always wanting to sink back into "godless" questions, and keeping them to the point. For this I should like to thank you.

38 We had a fine semester here. We have plenty of students, including even some who really get involved in things.

For the New Year I wish you that the continuation of your work on the Dogmatics,[6] which is a gift to us from our church through you, and on the success of which so much depends, *Deo iuvante et nostris orationibus*,[7] may go well.

In deep gratitude and respect, I remain yours sincerely,
Dietrich Bonhoeffer

22. To Helmut Rößler[1]

Berlin-Grunewald, December 25, 1932

My dear Rößler,

It was really a joy for me to read your good letter.[2] All the years we have been apart seemed to vanish in an instant, and it was as if we stood face to face or side by side, as we did in our student years and even occasionally on the tennis court.[3] It's quite remarkable how a few words have the power to make the years disappear.

¶Yes, you may be right that we were bound to go separate ways, since we are so differently constituted spiritually. It's always good for one's own modesty to see the attitude one has gained, through plenty of hard struggle, regarded as a matter of one's constitution, and certainly it's true as well. But now you yourself are entering into an argument based on objective
39 considerations—and I'm so grateful that you are. Since in my opinion you have in fact picked up the decisive point, I'd like to add a few more thoughts

[6.] Barth's *Church Dogmatics* 1.1 (with a foreword written in August 1932) had just been published.

[7.] "With God's help and our prayers."

[1.] *NL*, A 20,4 (8); as printed in *Dietrich Bonhoeffer: Einführung in seine Botschaft*, 61–63; previously published in *GS* 1:62–65 from the original handwritten letter, which has been lost.

[2.] Not extant. It probably expressed Rößler's reaction to Bonhoeffer's lecture "On the Theological Basis of the Work of the World Alliance," published in *Die Eiche* in 1932 (see *DBWE* 11, 2/14).

[3.] They had known each other since they were students together in Berlin (*DBWE* 9:169 and 439).

to what you said. It is indeed this problem that is giving me no rest these days, and I would like so much to talk through the whole complex of questions with you and get to the bottom of it. In our discussions, I have always felt that we lost no time in arriving at something that was a burning issue for one of us. This has made our conversations especially worthwhile.

In the first place, I think we are agreed on one thing, namely, that our church today cannot utter a concrete commandment. But the question is whether this lies in its nature—that is, within the inherent limitations of the *eschata*[4]—or represents apostasy [Abfall] and loss of substance. I grant you as well that the question is ultimately that of its teaching office and authority. But isn't that precisely what characterizes the authority of the church (as distinct from all other authority)—that it does not begin by having authority, acting on that basis, but rather that its authority derives solely from the "arbitrary" pronouncing of the commandment, provided this is heard as God's commandment, and that with every word it speaks it is putting its entire authority at stake. The authority of the state is not based on its concrete decisions, but the authority of the church rests on these alone. Its decision, however, should certainly not be withheld for fear of gambling away its authority, for fear of chaos (cf. Luther against Erasmus on the demoralizing consequences of teaching predestination!).[5] And this quite apart from the fact that any time the authority of the church has been gambled away by a frightful, catastrophic error of judgment (the decision on which will have to wait till Judgment Day)—I mean really gambled away, in terms of faith in the forgiveness of sins—another authority altogether can become visible, namely, that of God's mercy.

Third, I know I agree with you in not relegating the church to the level of prophecy. (I have just published an article about it in *Christentum und Wissenschaft*,[6] in distinct opposition to Heim's book.[7] What Heim says on this is totally absurd, patently impossible.) The church is more than prophecy (not less!), for it is *Christus praesens*,[8] in the flesh, to be sure, in the form of a human organization, but still, *Christus praesens*. And this Christ has the power to command us, even from within the veil of the church, and being Christ, he gives very concrete commands. You say the law is already there;

[4.] "The last things."

[5.] Cf. Martin Luther, "The Bondage of the Will" (*De servo arbitrio*, 1525), *LW* 33:41, 190, and 293.

[6.] ["Christianity and Scholarship."—LR]

[7.] Cf. the essay "On Karl Heim's *Glaube und Denken*," 2/5.

[8.] "Christ who is present."

the church cannot create a *novos decalogos*[9]—I share your view completely; but what does it mean to proclaim the law in the church? What does "Love your neighbor" mean in the church (and not in the synagogue!)? Is it creating new decaloga to announce the law concretely? Aren't you doing it too, in your own way, every Sunday? The law in the church means concrete commandments; it means communion with God based on the concrete word addressed to me. What it does not mean is that God is distant from me as a matter of principle (as it does in the synagogue!). So what I should have made sure to say in my essay[10] is that, just as the individual is supposed to hear the concrete commandment (just as the pastor should state it, dare to speak it to him during pastoral counseling), so should a congregation or a nation [Volk] also be the subject, the hearer of God's commandment. In 1914 the nation asked the church: What do you say about the war? and the nation hears the commandment. This is precisely where we should not think in individualistic terms.

Two more questions: Do you really think that it's not the church's business to talk about the means used in the fight? Isn't it precisely the "better" righteousness (comparatively!),[11] in essence, to mask the "good"? And as for the question of whether the commandments can be accounted for: we cannot account for the commandment.[12] What can be accounted for, or better, demonstrated, is its content, which can never of itself lead to the hearing of the commandment. I do not want to account for even the commandment to make peace in any other way.

So, I've been trying to express my gratitude for your letter by firing all
41 these questions back at you. I'd be very pleased, very pleased indeed, if you would find the time to reply, because if the problem comes to a head anywhere, it's here. And it's only from here, it seems to me, that one can begin to understand Barth. I have discussed these things with him several times this year,[13] and it was very fruitful.

[9.] "New decalogue (commandments)"; this was Luther's expression to describe what he saw as the capacity of Christians to supersede the Ten Commandments of the Old Testament (see *LW* 34:112–13). Cf. also *DBWE* 9:346 and 359–60.

[10.] See ed. note 2.

[11.] Matt. 5:20 [the Luther Bible says literally, "Unless your righteousness is better than that of the scribes and Pharisees." Thanks to Isabel Best for this note.—LR]

[12.] ["Account for" and "accounted for" in this paragraph is the English rendering of *Begründbarkeit* and *begründen* in the original German. This is accounting for and accountability in the sense of ethical justification. Bonhoeffer does not think there is independent and autonomous ethical and philosophical justification of the commandments; rather, the "justification" of their content, if that word is to be used at all, is in their demonstration in concrete practice.—LR]

[13.] See 1/21.

One more thing: I hope you will not misunderstand the term "disinterestedness" that I let drop a long time ago (I can't even remember that anymore); it now actually strikes me as frivolous. It was only meant to indicate the parameter within which I see these problems through the objective reality of the church.

Forgive my handwriting; I'm struggling with two fountain pens, both of which have been used by someone who is left-handed!

I wish you joy and strength for these busy weeks of the year. Please give my best regards to your wife. Wishing you all a good New Year,

As ever your old friend,
Dietrich Bonhoeffer

23. From Friedrich Siegmund-Schultze[1]

December 27, 1932

Dear colleague Bonhoeffer:

Thank you very much for your work on Bell's book.[2] If I have correctly understood your response, which was forwarded to me by Miss Lepsius, it looks as though the review of the translation will still entail quite a lot of work. But I was not completely clear as to whether you might still be prepared to do it yourself, or if I should look for another qualified person to whom to entrust it. As I see it, the person who undertakes this work will indeed be doing a very great service to our cause. Since making some corrections to the first pages myself in order
to get an idea of it, I have been persuaded that this is so. May I now ask you again 42
to let me know whether you might be able to take two weeks for this task, or should I entrust it to Pastor Guthke, who has an interest in writing? I hope he is up to it; I'd rather see it in your hands.

I have a further request to make of you: would you please send me, as quickly as possible, a short notice about the meeting of the ecumenical Provisional Bureau that took place on December 8–9,[3] so that it can still be inserted in the January issue of *Die Eiche*.[4]

Finally, I should like to ask you now, ahead of time, if you would be willing to work with us on the preparatory committee for the conference on political

---

[1.] Archives of Jørgen Glenthøj, Åbyhøj, Denmark; photocopy of the carbon copy (which has been lost) from the Siegmund-Schultze literary estate, which had a note: "Dict(ated) December 27, 1932," signed by Siegmund-Schultze; from Berlin. Previously published in *Mündige Welt*, 5:75, and *GS* 6:250–51.

[2.] See also 1/18.

[3.] The date is incorrect. The meeting was held December 9–10, 1932 (see 1/4).

[4.] See 1/24.

ethics.[5] I was very interested to hear that you were dealing with Brunner's ethics of the state[6] in your seminar. I'd appreciate a conversation with you sometime about this. I'd be very pleased if it were possible for you to visit me in east Berlin[7] on a Tuesday or Friday morning, or even for you to come to Wilhelmshagen[8] on a Sunday evening. Could we even consider doing this on New Year's Eve? On Friday I'll be in my Berlin office all day; perhaps you'd give me a ring there. I tried to reach you by telephone several times before Christmas, but without success. I'd also be happy to tell you about my trip to America.[9]

With best wishes for Christmas and the New Year, I remain

Yours sincerely,
S[iegmund]-S[chultze]

43 **24. To Friedrich Siegmund-Schultze**[1]

Berlin-Grunewald, January 5, 1932[2]

Dear Professor Siegmund-Schultze:

Many thanks for your kind letter. Unfortunately I have only now received it, on returning from a trip. Concerning the translation, I should like to make the following proposal. At the present time it is almost impossible for

---

[5.] Siegmund-Schultze was planning a large conference for 150–200 participants, to be held at Easter 1933; following the Social Work Association's (Sozialen Arbeitsgemeinschaft) principle of pluralism, representatives of various parties and religions were to speak. However, he decided in the end not to hold this event, because socialist speakers could not be guaranteed freedom to express their opinions (Grotefeld, *Friedrich Siegmund-Schultze,* 117; see also *Die Eiche,* no. 21 [1933]: 301).

[6.] See the October 29, 1932, report of the Executive Committee meeting of the German section of the World Alliance, agenda point 2: "For the winter semester work with students, Dr. Bonhoeffer is again planning to hold discussions at the university on Brunner's ethics of the state" (EZA, 51 D V c; for Bonhoeffer's discussion of Brunner, see 2/1).

[7.] Probably at Fruchtstr. 64, where the offices of the Social Work Association and *Die Eiche* were located.

[8.] At the Ulmenhof, a settlement run by the Social Work Association that had an adult education center, children's homes, a trade school, and apartments for workers.

[9.] Siegmund-Schultze had been on a lecture tour in the United States from the end of October to early December 1932 (see his report in *Die Eiche,* no. 21 [1933]: 8–17).

[1.] Archives of Jørgen Glenthøj, Åbyhøj, Denmark; photocopy of the typewritten letter, which has not been found in the Siegmund-Schultze literary estate. Previously published in *Mündige Welt,* 5:75–76, and *GS* 6:251–52. Reply to 1/23.

[2.] The date should be 1933.

me to do the work myself. But I have someone[3] nearby, a friend of mine who does this kind of work extremely well and reliably, and who would help me out of friendship. I would of course check every questionable passage myself and could consider myself as responsible for the corrections, since I would review every corrected passage. I just don't have time to do every bit of it myself. If you agree with this proposal, then please have the manuscript sent back to me. In that case I should be pleased to help.

May I call on you on one of the coming Tuesdays? I'd be very glad of your advice on some questions I have, and most grateful to you.

The meeting of the Provisional Bureau[4] decided not to make a report, since they spent a large part of the time planning an ecumenical conference that the Church Federation Office is going to hold,[5] and the discussion continued from last time did not bring anything to light substantially new. The above-mentioned planning is to be kept strictly confidential for the time being.

I remain yours very respectfully,
Dietrich Bonhoeffer

25. From Renate Lepsius[1] 44

January 6, 1933

Dear Dr. Bonhoeffer:

Prof. Siegmund-Schultze thanks you very much for your letter and is very pleased that you are prepared in this way to make a review of the Bell book[2] possible. I am sending you herewith the manuscript and a complete copy that we have just received.

[3.] Bonhoeffer refers here to Bertha Schulze, whom Siegmund-Schultze thanked in a letter of April 10, 1933, after completion of the task, "for your substantial work, which has been a great help to me" (EZA, 51 P III 1c).

[4.] [The office responsible, in this instance, for ecumenical affairs.—LR]

[5.] Bonhoeffer is referring to the theological conference of the Provisional Bureau on December 9–10, 1932, which decided to hold the ecumenical working meeting in Dassel (*Mündige Welt,* 5:60–62; see also 2/10).

[1.] EZA, 51 P III 1c; carbon copy; from Berlin; not previously published. Reply to 1/24.

[2.] See 1/18.

Prof. Siegmund-Schultze is also looking forward to seeing you on Tuesday [January 10] during his office hours. Perhaps I might mention that he has to leave promptly at 1 p.m. that day, so it would be good not to arrive too late.

Yours sincerely and respectfully,
Signed R[enate] L[epsius]

26. To Richard Jordan[1]

Berlin-Grunewald, January 11, 1933

Dear Pastor Jordan:

The meeting of the ecumenical Provisional Bureau[2] decided at the time not to make any kind of a report because a large part of the time was taken up—as you doubtless remember—by a confidential discussion of plans for an ecumenical conference,[3] and the actual theological discussion did not lead to new *conclusions* but instead was essentially of a clarifying nature.[4] So I am asking that point 5 be stricken from the agenda of the meeting.[5]

With best regards, I remain respectfully yours,
Bonhoeffer

[1.] Literary estate of Jürgen Winterhager, Berlin; typewritten on letterhead stationery of the student chaplain at the Technical College in Charlottenburg. See also *NL*, Anh. A 7 (6); photocopy; not previously published. The source mentioned in ed. note 5 identifies the addressee.

[2.] On December 9–10, 1932 (see 1/4).

[3.] This conference was held March 6–10, 1933, in Dassel (see also 2/10).

[4.] See 1/24.

[5.] Bonhoeffer refers here to the executive meeting of the German section of the World Alliance on January 20, 1933, to which Max Diestel and Richard Jordan sent out invitations on January 10, 1933 (EZA Berlin, 51 D V c). Agenda point 5 was to have been Bonhoeffer's report on the second theological conference of the Provisional Bureau for Ecumenical Youth Work.

27. To Karl-Friedrich Bonhoeffer[1] 45

Berlin-Grunewald, January 12, 1933

Dear Karl-Friedrich,

I wish you and your family a happy birthday celebration[2] and a good and peaceful New Year. Today I want to use this rare chance to write a letter and tell you a little about what I am doing. The semester has begun again, and preparations for lectures[3] and the seminar[4] are again taking up most of my time. I often have the feeling that housewives must have when they have put a lot of effort into cooking something special and then see it just gobbled up along with the rest. But I simply couldn't see myself giving a poorly prepared lecture; I'd get hopelessly bogged down. The seminar continues to be very pleasant. Every week or two I also have a working group[5] with a few "selected" students, which is one of the best things going on this winter. They are really up to something, and it's very enjoyable.

At the moment I am faced with a rather momentous decision, whether to undertake a parish ministry, which will probably be offered to me in Friedrichshain,[6] in east Berlin, at Easter. Strange how difficult it is to make a choice. Every effort to decide what my own abilities are, whether they lie in this direction or that, simply breaks down. We are really pretty bad at knowing ourselves. The question is whether pastorate and lectureship could be

---

[1.] *NL*, Anh. A 14 (11); handwritten. Partially reproduced in *GS* 3:23–24 from the typewritten copy in *NL*, A 28,1 (7).

[2.] On January 13, 1933, Karl-Friedrich Bonhoeffer celebrated his thirty-fourth birthday.

[3.] Refers to the lectures "Creation and Sin: A Theological Interpretation of Genesis 1–3" and "Review and Discussion of New Publications in Systematic Theology" (2/1). [The "Creation and Sin" lectures were published as *Creation and Fall* (*DBWE* 3) in 1933. The title was changed to avoid confusion with Emanuel Hirsch's 1931 work titled *Schöpfung und Sünde* (Creation and Sin). Hirsch, who joined the Nazi party in 1937, gave strong theological support to its views of *das Volk* and aggressive German nationalism. Bonhoeffer consciously distanced himself from Hirsch and Hirsch's doctrine of creation as revelation.—LR]

[4.] The seminar "Dogmatic Exercises on 'Theological Anthropology'" (2/2).

[5.] See *DB-ER*, 218–19, and Zimmermann, *I Knew Dietrich Bonhoeffer*, 60–62.

[6.] Bonhoeffer had applied for a pastorate at St. Bartholomew's Church in northeast Berlin, District 43. However, on February 28, 1933, the other, older candidate, Dr. Ernst Pätzold, was elected instead (see excerpts from the minutes of the St. Bartholomew Church council, February 2 and 28, 1933, in *GS* 6:256). On Bonhoeffer's plan to take a pastorate in east Berlin, see also 1/48 and *DB-ER*, 231–32.

46 combined—because I don't think I should give up the latter. Klaus[7] says no, Rüdiger,[8] yes. The others aren't saying a word, and neither am I. Being with students is very pleasant, of course, but not completely fulfilling. It's such a small slice of life that one gets to see in them. And that won't do for the long term.[9] So perhaps the next time you all come to Berlin, you will be able to come and see me in the parsonage at Friedrichshain, but perhaps not. It's dreadful not to know what to do.

By the way, do you know that Papa will be speaking on the radio[10] at 7:00 p.m. on the seventeenth and twenty-fourth [of January]? On February 1, I am also supposed to speak.[11] Perhaps I'll be able to welcome you as listeners. You must have heard from the others, so here I have only told you about myself.

Much love to you all,
Yours, Dietrich

28. To Wilhelm Zoellner[1]

Berlin, January 29, 1933

Dear General Superintendent Zoellner:

Thank you very much for your kind invitation to the ecumenical conference on March 7.[2] I shall of course be most happy to attend.

I remain, sir, yours very respectfully,
Bonhoeffer

[7.] Klaus Bonhoeffer.

[8.] Rüdiger Schleicher.

[9.] See also Gertrud Staewen's handwritten letter of January 29, 1933, to Barth and [his secretary] Charlotte von Kirschbaum: "Yesterday evening Bonhoeffer, Fricke, and Theo Jänicke (a student of Bultmann's) were here for good discussions about their work as pastors. It was a very enjoyable evening. I am also attending Bonhoeffer's lectures again. . . . What he actually wants now is to go into full-time ministry, because (like all of us), he very much hopes that you, dear Karl, will be called to Berlin, so that he would then be free to leave the university" (Karl Barth-Archiv, Basel).

[10.] According to the program printed in *Der Rundfunk Hörer* (The Radio Listener) for January 17 and 24, 1933, Karl Bonhoeffer was to speak in a nationwide broadcast at 7:00 p.m. on "Psychological Illnesses."

[11.] See 2/8–9 [and 1/29.—LR].

[1.] EZA, Bestand 5/4040; typewritten. Previously published in *Mündige Welt*, 5:63.

[2.] Refers to the ecumenical working meeting, March 6–10, in Dassel (see also 2/10).

29. Circular Letter to Colleagues and Friends[1] 47

Berlin, February 2, 1933

To prevent a possible misunderstanding on the part of anyone who may have been listening on February 1 at 5:45 [p.m.] to my radio lecture, "The Younger Generation's Altered View of the Concept of Führer,"[2] please allow me to inform you that, because it had gone slightly over time, the broadcast of the lecture was abruptly cut off at a completely inappropriate place,[3] one that could give rise to misinterpretation. The last few sentences, which were of crucial importance to me because they made clear the theological parameters of the discussion, were thus entirely omitted, which must have distorted the whole picture. The lecture is now to be published in a daily newspaper.[4]

Signed,
Bonhoeffer

[1.] *NL,* A 36,3: (a) handwritten draft by Bonhoeffer with list of names in two columns, some with addresses in another's handwriting; (b) carbon copy of typed text. Previously published with list of names in *GS* 6:258–59. According to (a), the message was sent to the following: "Rev. [H.] Sasse, Rev. Jakobi [*sic*], Fendt, Dr. Künneth, Prof. Stolzenburg, Rev. Bronisch-Holtze, Reinold [*sic*] Seeberg, Dr. Pinsk ThD, Technical College, General Superintendent Dr. [Otto] Dibelius, General Superintendent Karow, Superintendent Diestel, Senior Consistory Councillor Heckel, Senior Consistory Councillor Schreiber, President Burghart, Lütgert, Dr. Stange, Rev. Dr. Lilie [*sic*], Rev. Zippel, Superintendent [Richard] Zimmermann, Superintendent [Friedrich] Richter, Pastor Kluge, Pastor Rößler, Rev. Riethmüller, Rev. Peter, Miss Zarnack, Mrs. Staewen, Rev. de Haas, Prof. Stählin, Prof. Siegmund-Schultze, Rev. Jordan, Dr. Damaschke, Chaplain Leise, His Eminence Prof. Tübben [rector of the university—LR], all lecturers, Horst Michael."

[2.] Cf. 2/8 and 2/9.

[3.] Since the Nazis did not undertake the *Gleichschaltung* [the Nazi legal process of "synchronization" or nazification that placed all aspects of German life under Nazi control and direction—LR] of radio broadcasting until March 25, 1933, shortly after the Enabling Act had been proclaimed (see Rexin, *Machtergreifung*), the reason given here must be the real one (despite Bethge's speculation, *DB-ER,* 260). [This counters the very widespread assumption in the literature on Bonhoeffer that Nazi authorities silenced Bonhoeffer's broadcast at the point when it became politically problematic, which is often cited as an early example of Bonhoeffer's opposition to Nazism and of the Nazi regime's response. The German editor of *DBW* 12, Ernst-Albert Scharffenorth, believes that Bonhoeffer, who had never spoken on the radio before, simply went over time and was cut off because the next program had to begin on time.—LR]

[4.] Bonhoeffer's speech was published, slightly abridged, in the *Kreuz-Zeitung* of February 25, 1933. An abridged version also appeared in the February 26, 1933, *Tägliche Rundschau* (in an insert devoted to "Bünde, Hochschulen und Jugend" [Associations,

48 **30. From Karl Barth**[1]

Bonn/Rhine, February 4, 1933

My dear Colleague,

Your kind Christmas letter should not go any longer without an answer. For my part, I am happy just to know that you exist and glad whenever I hear, in a roundabout way through Mrs. Staewen or through the students, about the way you are carrying out the difficult job you have. My sincere thanks also for sending me your article about Heim,[2] and not least of all for the courage and skill with which you defended me in it.

¶For months now I have been increasingly under the impression that a great deal of what seemed in recent years to be a sense of theological unity in Germany was deceptive, and I have expressed myself along these lines to Althaus, Brunner, and Gogarten.[3] I cannot find myself in agreement, in either form or substance, with what I see these "neighbors" of mine pursuing, particularly on these crucial points. Instead, it feels pretty much as though I have been pushed back to that same lonely position from which, and in which, I came riding into this remarkable arena twelve years ago.[4] And it now seems to me even less possible than at that time that this could ever change. It was with grim amusement that I just heard, in a letter from Mrs. Staewen, some indication of what is going on in the Berlin faculty.[5] I'll assume these are "faculty secrets" and therefore say nothing to anyone, least of all to my New Testament neighbor[6] with his burning interest in such matters, but keep my amusement to myself. This is just how things have to go, and it would be almost a miracle if they went otherwise. I am just now

---

Colleges, and Youth]); it was from this source that *Die Furche* (no. 19 [1933]: 158–59) quoted his observations regarding the "authority of the leader or the authority of the office" and regarding the "leader's place in the structure of authorities."

[1.] *NL*, A 28,5 (4); typewritten. Previously published in *Mündige Welt*, 1:107–8, and *GS* 2:40–1. Reply to 1/21.

[2.] Refers to the essay "On Karl Heim's *Glaube und Denken*" (2/5).

[3.] For this finding, see, for example, Barth, *Church Dogmatics* 1.1 (on Althaus, 23, 271; on Brunner, 27–30, 273–74; on Gogarten, 141–46 and 194–97). [Barth was complaining that Althaus, Brunner, and Gogarten were effectively becoming theological apologists for Nazism. See also the discussion of the *völkisch* position of Althaus and Gogarten in Ericksen, *Theologians under Hitler*, esp. their attack on ecumenism, 142–44.—LR]

[4.] Barth was speaking of having left his Swiss pastorate in 1921 to become a professor at Göttingen.

[5.] Refers to the choice of a successor to Arthur Titius, professor of systematic theology. See ed. note 8.

[6.] Refers to Professor Karl L. Schmidt, a close colleague at the University of Bonn.

reading Lietzmann's church history,[7] so I know from the freshest of sources what is still regarded as theology there in Berlin. In the era of Reich Chancellor
Hitler, Wobbermin will be more suitable for Schleiermacher's chair than I would 49
have been. I hear that you took my part on that occasion.[8] Again, I would like to offer you my hand in thanks for that, because I know what you intended and meant by it. Without doubt I would have accepted the position, but how could I not gladly allow such a great and deserving scholar such as Wobbermin to take precedence, and why not be quite content to stay here in Bonn?

¶By the way, for the past week and a half I have been out of action due to the flu and the bad aftereffects of some quinine I took for it. In early March, I shall be going to Copenhagen to give a lecture.[9] Perhaps on the way back, I'll stop off briefly in Berlin, fortunately not for a lecture this time,[10] so no need to worry about being insulted afterward in the Protestant paper.[11] But what if it did happen? The world is in a wretched state, but we shan't let ourselves be counted out yet, shall we?

My best regards to Mrs. Staewen, Mr. Fricke, and any of the good folk whom you might run across there in Berlin. (Would that Edelhoff chap[12] still be around? He's had some books of mine for three years. If he's still there, and you know him and have the opportunity, perhaps you could gently remind him of this.)

With kindest regards, yours sincerely,
Karl Barth

[7.] In 1932, Hans Lietzmann had just published volume 1 of his four-volume history of the early church.

[8.] In her letter of January 29, 1933, to Barth and [his secretary] Charlotte von Kirschbaum, Gertrud Staewen wrote the following on Bonhoeffer's role in the Berlin faculty's discussion about a successor to Titius (see also 1/27, ed. note 9): "Apparently he fought for you like a lion, he and Lütgert. But the Seeberg and Lietzmann families could find nothing better to do, in their autocratic delusion, than to nominate Wobbermin and Wehrung as first and second choices" (Karl Barth-Archiv, Basel). Dean Deißmann had asked Bonhoeffer, "in accordance with §42 of our University's statutes of March 5, 1930," to propose names for a successor to Titius (Humboldt-Universität Berlin, Universitätsarchiv, Bestand Theologische Fakultät, 178). On November 26, 1932, Bonhoeffer proposed Barth, Elert, and Althaus, in that order (Geheimes Staatsarchiv Berlin-Dahlem, Rep. 76, vol. 4).

[9.] On March 10, 1933, Barth gave a lecture in Copenhagen, "Das erste Gebot als theologisches Axiom" (The First Commandment as Theological Axiom), which was published the same year in *Zwischen den Zeiten*.

[10.] See 1/21, ed. note 2.

[11.] Cf. Schubring and Köhler, "Karl Barth über Theologie und Mission."

[12.] According to a letter of November 21, 1988, from Hinrich Stoevesandt, both a Hans and a Willi Edelhoff were among Barth's students.

50 31. To Reinhold Niebuhr[1]

Berlin, February 6, 1933

Dear Professor Niebuhr,

After such a long while during which we have heard nothing from each other and so many decisive things have happened, which I'd often have gladly discussed with you, I wanted to write to you again today. But unfortunately I shan't get as far as a proper letter even this time, since it essentially concerns the following request. My cousin Pastor Dr. Hans Christoph von Hase has applied for a scholarship at Union Seminary for next fall. I should like to tell you some positive things about this man, even though he is my cousin. First, just in general, and in light of my acquaintance with both parties concerned, I believe the seminary would be well advised to bring this man over. He is unusually well oriented with regard to the present state of theology and the churches in Germany and also has an almost passionate interest in politics. He is fit, open, sociable, approachable, has an independent mind, and would certainly gain a great deal from a year at Union. He is also the kind of young person who would later be in a position in Germany to correctly represent what he learned there. That's all I can say with a good conscience, but I think it's enough. If you would speak on his behalf, I should be grateful to you.

It would be precipitous to say even one word about the state of affairs here in Germany. It can scarcely be expected that nothing will substantially change here, whether economically, politically, or socially. But an even greater threat is a terrible barbarization of our culture, so that here, too, we will need to create a Civil Liberties Union in the coming period.[2] You
51 yourself can imagine that nationalist magical incantations and exorcisms (military posturing, etc.)[3] will not drive out the ghost of Communism. People are incredibly naive here in our country. The path ahead for the

---

[1.] Library of Congress Annex, Washington, D.C., Dept. of Manuscripts, Reinhold Niebuhr Papers, box 2, General Correspondence; typewritten; in German. See also *NL*, A 29,1 (5): photocopy. Previously published in *GS* 6:259–61.

[2.] The American Civil Liberties Union (ACLU) emerged in 1920 from an older organization led by Roger Nash Baldwin that defended conscientious objectors; the purpose of the ACLU was to work on behalf of politically and ethnically marginalized citizens. In the 1931 Scottsboro Case, the ACLU obtained lighter sentences for the African American defendants convicted of raping whites. Cf. *DBWE* 6:295, esp. ed. note 181. See also D. O. Johnson, *Challenge to American Freedoms*.

[3.] In its proclamation of February 1, 1933, the new "government to uplift the nation" under Hitler had announced that it would save the country from Marxism and Bolshevism (cf. Nicolaisen, *Dokument*, 1:1–2).

church has seldom looked so gloomy. But a great deal has also changed where you are since I left there. Furthermore, there is no denying that we—especially we here in Europe—are living in an incredibly interesting time, and one might almost not want to exchange it for a different era.

I should be extremely pleased to hear from you again sometime. But you must have an awful lot to do, and that's how it is for me too. It's too bad that friendships have to suffer in this way.

Would you please give my best regards to my friends from my time at Union, especially Jim Dombrowski (whom I would ask please to return my essay on Negro literature,[4] which he must still have).

Please remember me also to your mother and to your wife; and for yourself, please accept my best wishes.

Respectfully, your friend,
Dietrich Bonhoeffer

32. To Ludwig Tübben[1] 52

Your Eminence:

Please permit me to make the following request: As student chaplain at the T.H.,[2] I should like to give a lecture on the topic "The Führer and the Individual in the Younger Generation"[3] on February 23 at 6:00 p.m. at the Technical College. May I ask Your Eminence please to make a small lecture hall available to me for that evening? A reply envelope is enclosed; I respectfully request a reply[4] as soon as possible.

With my most respectful greetings to Your Eminence,
Yours truly,
D[ietrich] B[onhoeffer]

[4.] This probably refers to a short report that Bonhoeffer wrote for Niebuhr's seminar on "Ethical Viewpoints in Modern Literature" (cf. *DBWE* 10, 2/11.2, and *DB-ER*, 162). [James Dombrowski was contacted in 1967, when the letter from Bonhoeffer to Niebuhr was discovered in the Niebuhr papers at the Library of Congress, but he no longer had any knowledge of where the student papers might have been.—LR]

[1.] *NL*, A 29,1 (8): (a) handwritten draft by Bertha Schulze; (b) typewritten copy; from Berlin-Grunewald. Previously published in *GS* 6:219. Bonhoeffer also invited several student contacts; on the invitations he referred to posters giving the location of the lecture hall (see *NL*, A 29,1 [8]). This letter to the rector of the university was probably sent in the first half of February.

[2.] [Technische Hochschule, "Technical College."—LR]

[3.] Cf. 2/9, "The Führer and the Individual in the Younger Generation."

[4.] Not extant.

33. To Friedrich Siegmund-Schultze[1]

Berlin-Grunewald, March 3, 1933

Dear Professor Siegmund-Schultze:

I am sending you enclosed the chapters that have been completed. I shall only be able to send the final portion on Saturday of next week,[2] because I have to leave today and shall be away for a week.[3] In the meantime I have
53 spoken with the lady,[4] and she said she would be willing to rewrite the illegible pages herself if you would send them to her. The pages with fewer corrections are hopefully legible, as you have them in your office. If you are coming to the meeting in Dassel, I should be glad to discuss a few more translation problems with you.

I remain yours sincerely and respectfully,
Bonhoeffer

34. From Henry Louis Henriod[1]

Geneva, March 7, 1933

My dear Bonhoeffer,

I wasn't able to meet Toureille as I had hoped; he is now in Czechoslovakia. He will probably pass through Geneva again when he returns to France. By the way, he wrote me to say that the Franco-English conference will be held as planned at Luneray near Dieppe from April 18 to 20 and will doubtless finish at midday, and that the youth commission would take place the afternoon of Friday, April 21, and all day on Saturday the twenty-second, at Luneray. It is essential that you be present at the commission meeting, so please reserve these dates, and I hope that nothing prevents you from coming.

In view of the terrible restrictions on the budget, for travel expenses we are reimbursing a third-class ticket for both the English and the French. Do you

---

[1.] *NL*, A 28,4 (7); typewritten copy of the original, which has been lost. Previously published in *Mündige Welt*, 5:78, and *GS* 6:252 (cf. also *Mündige Welt*, 5:72–79). On its publication [in German] in 1934, this book by the bishop of Chichester (cf. 1/18), supplemented with articles by other writers, became the first volume in the Ekklesia series edited by Siegmund-Schultze.

[2.] No letter has been found confirming this (but see 1/24, ed. note 3).

[3.] To attend the ecumenical working meeting in Dassel (cf. also 2/10).

[4.] Bertha Schulze, who was helping with the translation (cf. 1/24).

[1.] *NL*, A 28,3 (8); typewritten copy of carbon copy missing from WCC Archives. Previously published in *GS* 6:280–81.

think that you too would be able to travel from Berlin to Luneray in third class, with a sleeper for the night you spend on the train? How much would that cost? It would be paid, needless to say, out of the budget of the youth commission.

I was sorry not to see you again before leaving Berlin.[2] I didn't write to you in Austria because, the evening after we had seen each other,[3] I was informed by Mr. Siegmund-Schultze that another speaker had been chosen for the week in Austria.[4]

These are particularly serious and difficult times, and it is not without a certain foreboding that I am awaiting the Executive Committee meeting in Septem- 54
ber in the Balkans.[5] It is all the more important that the youth are active and can meet, and in order for our Balkan conference[6] to produce all the results we can expect, we need to be able to prepare it together. That's why I must again insist on your being at Luneray on April 21–22.[7]

With best regards, yours as ever,
Henry Louis Henriod

35. From Henry Louis Henriod[1]

Geneva, April 12, 1933

My dear Bonhoeffer,

Thank you for your letter of April 6.[2] I understand the difficulties you are having. I hope that in spite of everything you will be able to come to Luneray.[3] It is the current international difficulties themselves that make it all the more necessary that we meet. In any case, it would be impossible to change the date for the youth commission. Too many people are involved, and all the arrangements

[2.] After the meetings of the World Alliance and the Ecumenical Council [on Life and Work] at the beginning of February 1933.

[3.] Perhaps on January 27, 1933, before Henriod's lecture at Berlin University (see 1/7, ed. note 6).

[4.] The trip "had to be canceled due to the political changes" (*DB-ER*, 253).

[5.] Because of financial problems, an expanded meeting of the Executive Committee was held there September 14–21, 1933, in place of the Management Committee meeting planned for Sofia (World Alliance, *Annual Report*, 1933–34, 1).

[6.] The last of three regional youth conferences, the planning of which Henriod had announced to the youth secretaries on October 28, 1931 (see *DBWE* 11, 1/16).

[7.] Meeting of the youth commissions of the World Alliance and the Ecumenical Council on Life and Work, which voted to merge the two commissions.

[1.] WCC Archives, Bonhoeffer box; carbon copy; not previously published.

[2.] Letter not extant.

[3.] Cf. 1/34.

have been made. I can now tell you, by the way, that before going to Dieppe[4] I'm planning to stop over in Berlin, arriving on Tuesday morning the eighteenth and leaving again on Wednesday evening.[5] I shall have a great many people to see, and not much time, but perhaps it would be possible for you to meet me for lunch, say on Wednesday? I am also asking Mr. Lilje. Please be so kind as to reply to Nils Ehrenström, my colleague from the Stockholm movement (address: Pastor N. Ehrenström, c/o Beuster, 4/II, Monbijou St., Berlin N. 24), who is taking care of the details of my program. I'll be staying at the Christliches Hospiz, by the Friedrichstrasse railway station.

Yours as ever,
[Henry Louis Henriod]

36. To Nils Ehrenström[1]

Dear Colleague:

Mr. Henriod has written to me that you are in charge of the arrangements for his stay in Berlin. He suggests that I have lunch with him on Wednesday [April 19]. However, it would be of the utmost importance to me to speak with him immediately after his arrival here. Perhaps it would be possible for me to meet his train. Would you be so kind as to let me know what time he arrives, or allow me a short time immediately afterward for an important conversation (it would not take longer than half an hour)?[2] I believe that the matter is also rather important to Mr. Henriod.

[4.] More precisely, to Luneray, near Dieppe, France, where the youth commissions of the World Alliance and the Ecumenical Council on Life and Work were to meet.

[5.] Henriod was accompanied by Schönfeld. The purpose of the trip was to gather information about the situation in Germany, through discussions with German representatives of the World Alliance and the Ecumenical Council and other persons. See Henriod's confidential April 1933 report, "Impressions d'Allemagne" (Impressions of Germany), in Boyens, *Kirchenkampf und Ökumene*, 1:291–95. Among other things, he speaks there of the lack of liberty and security, as well as the measures taken by the Nazis that affected the youth and the attitude of the Protestant church toward these measures.

[1.] *NL*, A 28,3 (16); typewritten copy of original letter missing from the WCC Archives; reprinted in *GS* 6:281 (where it is incorrectly identified as a letter to Schönfeld). The addressee can be identified on the basis of 1/35. The present letter was sent from Berlin-Grunewald to Ehrenström's Berlin address, not before April 13.

[2.] According to *DB-ER*, 277–78, this probably concerned the fears that Barth would be dismissed (see also 1/37) and the measures against the Jews throughout the German Reich. Henriod's confidential report (see 1/35, ed. note 5) does not specifically mention a talk with Bonhoeffer, but it does speak of the anti-Semitic measures and the

Might I ask you for an immediate reply?

With all good wishes for a peaceful Easter in these turbulent days, I remain

Yours very respectfully,

Dietrich Bonhoeffer

37. To Karl Barth[1] 56

Berlin-Grunewald, April 14, 1933

Dear Professor Barth:

The word is going around here that perhaps you will not be able to return to Bonn next semester.[2] This rumor is cause for considerable dismay among many people here. Georg Merz, who was here a few days ago, personally told me more about it. Some theologian friends and I are now planning, in such a case, to introduce a petition immediately to avert such a disastrous mistake.[3] Such an undertaking only makes sense, however, if we know something definite about the outcome in your case, so permit me to ask you, on

---

dismissal of professors who were out of favor. In view of contradictory assessments of the seriousness of the situation, Henriod warned against protests from abroad and recommended help from the ecumenical community for the victims of the Nazi regime.

[1.] Karl Barth-Archiv, Basel; typewritten. See also *NL*, A 28,5 (2); typewritten copy. Previously published in *Mündige Welt*, 1:108, and *GS* 2:41–42.

[2.] According to the Law on the Reconstitution of the Civil Service of April 7, 1933 (*RGBl*, pt. 1, 175), not only "non-Aryans" but all civil servants who were not considered politically dependable by Hitler's government could expect "early retirement." As a member of the Social Democratic Party, Barth was among those facing this threat (see also 1/41).

[3.] In her letter of March 24, 1933, to Charlotte von Kirschbaum, Gertrud Staewen wrote that "our circle here"—Bonhoeffer, Fricke, and herself—was "deeply concerned," and further that not only had Bonhoeffer sent an express letter to Barth in Bonn (1/37), but the group had also drawn up "a petition," the "approximate wording" of which she gave as follows: "The undersigned professors and teachers of the Prot[estant] church consider it urgent, in the best interest of the German Prot[estant] church and [of the] G[erman] people, that the prof[essor] holding the chair in theol[ogy] at the Univ[ersity] of B[onn], K[arl] B[arth], be retained as teacher for the church and the next generation of theol[ogy] students. The u[ndersigned] declare that they have themselves received from B[arth] vital inspiration for their church and theol[ogical] work, inspiration that, in its ecclesiastical purity and open-hearted caring for the world, but most crucially in its unsparing biblical seriousness, has helped the undersigned greatly, strengthening their preaching of the gospel and their work. They are convinced that retaining [blacked out, presumably: Barth] as a teacher in the German church will also be a blessing for the German state and people" (Karl Barth-Archiv, Basel).

behalf of all those who are greatly disturbed by this news, to let me know briefly how things stand.[4] Should the occasion arise not a moment should
57 be lost. By the way, the German Christian position toward you doesn't seem to have been clarified yet.

If only this continuing unease doesn't completely disrupt your peace and quiet and your work during these vacation weeks! We think about you a great deal. I should like to thank you once again, very much, for our evening in Berlin.[5] If something like that happened just once a year, then in spite of everything Berlin would still be endurable for a while. I am so eager for the semester to begin.

In sincere gratitude, I remain as ever yours respectfully,
Dietrich Bonhoeffer

38. To Erwin Sutz[1]

Berlin, April 14, 1933

Dear Mr. Sutz:

It's so good of you to keep sending me a greeting now and again in spite of my disgraceful silence.[2] Since I last wrote,[3] there have been a lot of changes here, and we are most likely still in the midst of them. Where it will all come out is still hard to tell. We in the church and the university are the most directly affected. You probably already know that K[arl] B[arth] can no longer be sure of keeping his position. For my part, I shall do anything from here to prevent such a disastrous and irreparable mistake, in fact, I am already working on it.[4] We are about to witness a great reorganization of the churches, which, to all appearances, will not be a bad thing.[5]

[4.] Cf. 1/39.

[5.] According to Gertrud Staewen's letter of February 25, 1933, to Charlotte von Kirschbaum (Karl Barth-Archiv, Basel), Bonhoeffer planned to meet with Barth on March 14, 1933, on the latter's way back from Denmark, "either here at my place or somewhere else" (cf. also 1/30).

[1.] Literary estate of Erwin Sutz, Herrliberg, Switzerland; handwritten. See also *NL*, A 29,4 (11); typewritten copy; *NL*, Anh. A 29 (4); photocopy of the original. Partially reproduced in *GS* 1:37 from *NL*, 29,4 (11).

[2.] These letters to Bonhoeffer have been lost.

[3.] On October 27, 1932 (*DBWE* 11, 1/89).

[4.] Cf. 1/37.

[5.] [April 1933 saw a great deal of activity around the organizational shape and confessional stance of the Evangelical Church. The German Christians wanted to confirm the Führer principle and introduce the Aryan paragraph in the church and called for

It is to be hoped that it will bring about the automatic withdrawal of the German Christians from both of the confessional churches[6]—however 58
regrettable that may be in other respects—and so, *hominum confusione et dei providentia,*[7] we shall once again rescue the church. The Jewish question is also giving the church a great deal of trouble, and here the most intelligent people have totally lost both their heads and their Bible.[8] So it is that demands come pressing upon one from every side, and one hardly gets to

---

new church elections. Hitler took advantage of the church struggles to appoint a military chaplain, Ludwig Müller, as his "confidential adviser and plenipotentiary in questions concerning the Protestant church" (*DB-ER,* 270). Confusion reigned in many provincial church bodies as church/state lines were crossed both by church factions and by the state. Leaders in the existing church administration countered with a proposal to draft a new constitution and organize a single Evangelical Church in place of the twenty-eight independent regional churches. Bonhoeffer's reference to this possible reorganization as not "a bad thing" expresses his hope that it will sharpen issues with the German Christians and the state and lead to a clearer stand and more coherent action on the part of a more unified church. See ed. note 6 on the proposal of one of the church leaders, Wilhelm Zoellner.—LR]

[6.] Bonhoeffer is here referring to hopes and plans to reform the church (cf. Scholder, *Churches and the Third Reich,* 1:280–332). Probably freshly inspired by Zoellner's appeal "to all Lutherans," which had just been published (April 13, 1933), he was counting on the dissolution of the Evangelical Church of the Old Prussian Union and its replacement by a Lutheran and Reformed church. Cf. also Zoellner's assessment of the ecumenical working meeting at Dassel (March 6–10, 1933), in which Bonhoeffer had also taken part (see 2/10). Having noted "that the main difficulties between Lutherans and Reformed concerned not doctrine but rather questions of order," Zoellner observed: "If we had not gotten to the point of artificial union but instead had grown spiritually, we should be ahead today. . . . The only way I see forward is to go back to being educated as Lutherans and Reformed in purely confessional terms. . . . If only we already had a Lutheran and a Reformed synod in Prussia, we'd be much further along" (EZA, 5/100).

[7.] This is an allusion to the Swiss proverb "Dei providentia et hominum confusione Helvetia regitur" (Switzerland is governed by human confusion and God's providence), of unknown origin (Curti, *Schweizer Geflügelte Worte,* 6). Barth had quoted it in the foreword to his *Church Dogmatics* 1.1 (p. vi) and also liked to use it on other occasions (cf. Barth, *Vorträge 1909–1914,* 143, ed. note 6).

[8.] Cf. Bonhoeffer's essay "The Church and the Jewish Question" (2/13). See also Paula Bonhoeffer's letter of April 3–4, 1933, to Hans and Christine von Dohnanyi, which says in part: "I am so often reminded of the 'Tower of Babel' [Gen. 11:1–9]. It was supposed to reach to heaven, and the upshot was that people could no longer understand each other, each one speaking a different language. And what about the 'Tree of Knowledge' [Genesis 3]? Was its fruit really not good for us, and are we supposed to regress from intellectualism back to the primitive? But we need to think about holding onto humanism, as Christ's most urgent command, in response to the question 'Who is my neighbor?' [Luke 10:29]. I do worry a lot about Dietrich. It's time for the church to show that it is still a force in our lives, and fills a need in our lives! It's really making it hard for him" (literary estate of Barbara Bayer-von Dohnanyi).

do any quiet work during the vacation. How I envy you sometimes, or rather
59 how glad I am for you, that you can pursue your work in peace and quiet, which is the one thing on which church work depends. I often long terribly for a quiet pastorate. I always knew you would be a good preacher, without even having heard you and before the Lehmanns[9] also said so. It's a huge responsibility to know that about oneself.

¶Do you plan to stay in Fluntern, or will you go into the wilderness[10] for a few years? Of course you won't be any safer there from me dropping in. At the beginning of June, I have to go to Basel.[11] Couldn't we see each other for a few hours somewhere? That would be *very*[12] nice and a great comfort. Here it's dreadfully lonely even sitting in a whole crowd of people. All good wishes until then! Please be warmly assured that our friendship will always be important to me. That I can't write any more today about the situation here is because, as you know, the privacy of the post is no longer in force.[13]

Farewell for now! With my best regards, yours as ever
Dietrich Bonhoeffer

[9.] Paul Lehmann and his wife had apparently visited Sutz on their way to Berlin (see *DB-ER*, 268–69).

[10.] [Bonhoeffer uses this same phrase about his own decision to seek a parish in London after the Aryan paragraph was introduced into the Prussian church. See his letter to Barth about this in *DBWE* 13, 1/2.—LR]

[11.] To attend the meeting of the German and French sections of the World Alliance, June 8–9, 1933. According to the newsletter of the German section (no. 13, May 1933, p. 13), Bonhoeffer was to participate along with four other Germans. However, at its meeting on May 23, 1933, the working committee of the German World Alliance section named Burghart, Jordan, Siegmund-Schultze, and Bauer as the German delegates (EZA, 51/D V c). Their names appear as German representatives on the participants' list at the Basel meeting (WCC Archives, box 212 009, "Liste des participants à la conférence du 7 au 9 juin"). Therefore, Bonhoeffer did not go to Basel (despite the uncertainty mentioned in *DB-ER*, 283–84).

[12.] Underlined twice in the original.

[13.] Following the Reich president's edict "for the Protection of People and State" of February 28, 1933, basic rights including the privacy of mail and telephone were no longer in force (*RGBl*, pt. 1, 83).

39. From Karl Barth[1] 60

152 Bellevue Street, Bern-Wabern,[2]April 18, 1933

My dear colleague Bonhöffer:

My warm thanks for your letter of the fourteenth [of April 1933] and for all your sympathy. As far as can be known at this point, it actually seems more likely that my work in Bonn can and will go on as usual. I wrote a letter to Minister Rust (indicating that I would not resign from the SPD)[3] and asked him for information about my future.[4] I have yet to receive an answer, but I have heard indirectly that this step did not even make a bad impression at Unter den Linden.[5] Then there is the fact that my name did not appear in the first proscription list,[6] which has just been published; even though it has certainly not been forgotten that less than a year ago I declared myself to be "personally and materially in solidarity" with Günther Dehn.[7] It also appears that all possible authorities have long been working in favor of my staying. So, for the moment, all is as "good" as it could be under the circumstances.

Whether and how I shall be able to adapt spiritually to a Germany that has changed so much will be a different question altogether. And this applies particularly to Zoellner's "Evangelical Church of the German Nation."[8] The name of this promised infant speaks for itself . . . ! But here, too, I can only wait and see,
as calmly as I can manage. I am really glad to see so many signs that the church has 61
changed somewhat and is more on its guard this time than in 1914.[9]

With most cordial greetings to you and all our friends, I remain
Yours,
Karl Barth

[1.] *NL*, A 28,5 (5); typewritten; not previously published. Reply to 1/37.

[2.] This was the home of Barth's mother.

[3.] [Social Democratic Party.—LR]

[4.] See Barth's letter of April 4, 1933, to Rust (in Prolingheuer, *Der Fall Barth*, 233–34).

[5.] Unter den Linden 4 was the address of the office of the Prussian Ministry for Education and Cultural Affairs.

[6.] Barth probably was referring here to information that appeared in daily newspapers following publication of the Law for the Reconstitution of the Civil Service. The *Kreuz-Zeitung* for April 14, 1933, carried on page 1 the report "The Cleansing of Higher Education Begins," which stated that "sixteen lecturers had been suspended." These were almost all lecturers in faculties of law and governmental studies, but included the "theologians Tillich and Dehn."

[7.] When Dehn was strongly criticized for his comments about honoring those who had died in battle, Barth publicly stood by him (Busch, *Karl Barth*, 218).

[8.] An allusion to Zoellner's appeal of April 13, 1933 (see also 1/38, ed. note 6).

[9.] Refers to the enthusiasm for World War I, which, to Barth's indignation, even his German teachers of theology shared (see Busch, *Karl Barth*, 81ff.).

40. To Erich Seeberg[1]

Berlin-Grunewald, April 21, 1933

Honored Professor Seeberg:

Surely I must assume that you are already well acquainted with what I shall tell you here. But I would still like to do so, at the request of several students. Since the suspension of Tillich,[2] efforts are being made in many quarters to keep him on. Today some students who have been NSDAP members for years came to me and told me about their own efforts in this vein. They have had several conversations with officials at the Ministry of Education and Cultural Affairs, which ended in their being asked to collect as many signatures of Nat[ional] Soc[ialist] students as they could and to come back on Wednesday of next week. Meanwhile, some of them have succeeded in getting Knak so interested in the cause that he is already speaking up energetically about it in the ministry.[3] In Tübingen, Heim is supposed to be launching a related action.[4]

¶Now these students have asked me urgently, in connection with their discussions with the ministry, if it would be possible to have a statement from the lecturers on the Berlin faculty about Tillich's scholarly significance, since this is something that would obviously get a lot of attention from the ministry. Even just my own personal gratitude for what I have learned from Tillich on many occasions gives me the courage to turn to
62 you, and ask if you might initiate such a process among the faculty.[5] I myself am cognizant that it is not really my prerogative to make such a request, but for the moment I can see no other way. So please forgive me for doing so. Even at the risk that you have already long ago done something along these lines, I didn't want to fail to have asked you, since the ministry will be deciding this matter by the end of this week.

Again, please forgive me, Professor Seeberg, for disturbing you during your holiday.

I remain yours most respectfully,
Dietrich Bonhoeffer

[1.] BA Koblenz, Nachlaß Erich Seeberg /5; typewritten; not previously published.

[2.] See 1/39, ed. note 6.

[3.] Not documented.

[4.] Not documented.

[5.] There is no documentation in the Humboldt University archives as to whether Seeberg took up this suggestion.

41. To Karl Barth[1]

Dear, esteemed Professor Barth:

You have probably already known for some time, but I wanted in any case to write you immediately that a most reliable source has just told me that in Bonn everything (in N[ew] T[estament] as well)[2] remains unchanged. I am very happy and am sure many are breathing a sigh of relief along with me. That the church here also seems to have played its part[3] must do you good. It's true, as you wrote to me yesterday, that the church is really more on its guard than in 1914, which makes me remember again, with renewed gratitude, your work of the past decade.

I very much wish you a restful conclusion of your holiday and remain, in respect and gratitude, yours as ever,
Dietrich Bonhoeffer

[1.] Karl Barth-Archiv, Basel; typewritten; undated, from Berlin-Grunewald, with handwritten note by Barth: "Postmarked April 22, 1933"; not previously published. Bonhoeffer's reference to Barth's letter of April 18, 1933 (1/39) indicates that this reply was written April 19, 1933.

[2.] Refers to K. L. Schmidt's retaining the chair in New Testament; however, at the end of April 1933, he was forced into retirement, as a member of the Social Democratic Party, and he was finally dismissed in September 1933 from the civil service. Cf. Mühling, "Es hat diese Aussprache nun doch ihren Sinn," 356.

[3.] Not documented.

63 **42. From Théodore de Félice**[1]

Geneva, May 3, 1933

Dear Mr. Bonhoeffer:

The youth commissions of the World Alliance for Promoting Friendship through the Churches and of the Ecumenical Council [on Life and Work] decided to merge their youth committees at their recent session held in Luneray.[2] Please find enclosed the minutes of the joint meeting of the two committees.[3]

As you will see from the minutes, you have been named a member of this new commission,[4] and I hope you will kindly confirm your acceptance.

In fellowship, sincerely,
[Théodore de Félice]

43. To Théodore de Félice[1]

May 5, 1933

Dear Mr. de Félice:

I thank you for your letter, and accept my appointment to the new commission—thank you very much. I look forward to good work together.

I remain respectfully yours,
Bonhoeffer

[1.] WCC Archives, Bonhoeffer box; carbon copy, not previously published. Félice had been elected secretary at the joint session of the World Alliance and Life and Work youth commissions on April 22, 1933 (see literary estate of Eberhard Bethge: Minutes of the "Séance commune de la commission de jeunesse de l'alliance . . . et du conseil oecuménique" [Joint session of the youth commissions of the Alliance . . . and the Ecumenical Council], April 22, 1933, 2).

[2.] Cf. 1/34 and 1/35.

[3.] Cf. ed. note 1.

[4.] According to the minutes (see ed. note 1), it was decided in Luneray that the joint youth commission would be composed of five representatives from each of the two organizations, plus Henriod as general secretary. For the World Alliance, the four members of its youth commission, plus a woman ("plus une représantante du sex féminin") were named as its representatives.

[1.] WCC Archives, Bonhoeffer box; photocopy of a specially preserved typewritten manuscript; from Berlin-Grunewald; see also *NL*, A 28,4 (1); photocopy. Previously published in *GS* 6:282.

44. Appeal from the Young Reformation Movement[1] 64

Call to Convene

The new day of the German nation, given to us by God, calls our Evangelical Church to restructure itself.[2] As members of the Young Reformation movement, we stand behind the appeal of the authorized church leaders, Dr. Kapler, Dr. Marahrens, Dr. Hesse, and the spokesman for the Reich chancellor, Pastor Müller.[3] With reference to the situation at the moment, the following are our current demands:

1. We demand that the decisions to come be based solely on the essence of the church.

2. We demand that the restructuring of the Evangelical Church of the German nation be carried out as soon as possible. The administration and governing bodies of the church are to be set up exclusively according to the new constitution. We reject preliminary elections as an outmoded democratic error.

3. A Reich bishop must be named immediately; this must be done by the existing directorate.[4]

[1.] LKA EKvW, Bielefeld, 5,1, Bestand 53; printed flyer, dated May 9, 1933, according to Scholder (*Churches and the Third Reich*, 1:321). This appeal is a response particularly to the German Christians' Principles of May 4, 1933, which called for a German Reich Church in accordance with the "Führer principle" and the "Aryan paragraph" (Gauger, *Chronik*, 1:77). Bonhoeffer had intended to sign this appeal; see Gertrud Staewen's letter of May 17, 1933, to Barth and Kirschbaum: "It was interesting what Bonhoeffer told me on the phone yesterday evening: he is being treated as an enemy, supposed to be a 'Social Democrat' (which he has *never* been) who stood up for Dehn. And because of this rumor, Jakobi [*sic*] etc. did *not* include him in the appeal from the Young Reformation movement. Stolzenburg is also using this excuse to undermine his (Bonhoeffer's) work as lecturer and wants to get rid of him, because Bonh. has two hundred students even though he lectures at eight in the morning. Such goings on! Bonh. told me I should write to Karl about this with his best regards" (Karl Barth-Archiv, Basel).

[2.] In their positive assessment of the political transition of January 30, 1933, and its consequences for a reform of the church, the Young Reformers were in agreement here with the majority of German Protestants, including the German Christians.

[3.] See the joint press release by the Church Federation authorities and Müller on the evening of May 4, 1933. It noted "a most gratifying agreement" and viewed a reconstruction of the church as possible "if what the various historical confessions have in common is brought to the fore and made central" (Scholder, *Churches and the Third Reich*, 1:311–12).

[4.] After the rejection of preliminary elections, which the German Christians had called for in their Principles of May 4, 1933 (see Gauger, *Chronik*, 1:77), the Young Reformers apparently felt that the Church Federation authorities (see ed. note 3) should name the Reich bishop.

65 4. We want a church directorate composed of clergy, with full authority to take action. This does not exclude but rather includes the collaboration of the congregations. Lively participation in the worship and work of a congregation is the basis for selecting members of church bodies.

5. We want better training for those who are called to preach the Word. Preaching whatever one likes must be replaced by solid doctrinal authority.

6. We wish to reverse the aging trend among officeholders and in the membership of governing bodies, through more efforts to bring in younger persons, especially from those who served in the Great War.[5]

7. We confess our faith in the Holy Spirit, and therefore reject, as a matter of principle, the exclusion of non-Aryans[6] from the church, because it is based on confusion between state and church. The state is supposed to judge; the church is supposed to save.

8. On the basis of the existing church confessions, the church is to give people today the gospel's answer to questions concerning races, peoples, and state. Out of this foundation a new confession will develop, which is needed by the Evangelical Church of the German nation if it is to be more than an interest group.

9. We resist the attempts of a dead liberal theology to reinstate itself again in the church.

10. We demand that the state give the church the influence in the press and radio appropriate to its task for the spiritual uplifting of the people.

11. We call for the Evangelical Church, joyfully affirming the new German state, to fulfill its God-given mission in total freedom from all political influence and also to dedicate itself unshakably to serving the German people.

12. As important as the reform of the church constitution is, we confess nonetheless that, in God's eyes, the life of the people is centered in prayer and in the work of the congregation.

We call upon all those who are of the same mind and the same faith to join us. All pastors and lay Christians who agree with these basic principles are asked to communicate their assent to university lecturer Dr. Künneth, 24 Zietenstr., Berlin-Dahlem.[7]

[5.] [The implication of this reference to veterans of World War I (e.g., Niemöller) was that these would be pastors whose patriotism could not be doubted.—LR]

[6.] The Principles of the German Christian movement called for the Reich Church to be reconstituted as the "Church of German Christians, that is, Christians of the Aryan race" (Gauger, *Chronik*, 1:77).

[7.] According to a letter of December 19, 1988, from Walter Künneth, this address was a temporary office of the Center for Apologetics (of which he was director), which was responsible for drawing up and distributing this appeal throughout the Reich.

The following are among those who have declared their support thus far: 66
Pastor Dannenbaum, Berlin; Dr. Doerne, director of the Preachers' Seminary, Lückendorf/Saxony; Superintendent Görnandt, Potsdam; Senior Consistory Councillor Heckel, Berlin; Professor Heim, Tübingen; Pastor Gerhard Jacobi, Berlin; Gustav Kochheim, Hamburg; Professor Krukenberg, Stettin; Dr. Künneth, lecturer, Berlin; Pastor Lachmund, Blankenburg/Harz; Pastor Le Soeur, Eisenach; Pastor Dr. Hanns Lilje, Berlin; Dr. Müller, Secretary of the DCSV,[8] Berlin; Pastor Müller-Schwefe, Münster/Westfalen; Mrs. Nietzsche, school official, Berlin; Church Councillor Palmer, Blankenburg/Harz; Dr. Anna Paulsen, Berlin; Pastor Riethmüller, Berlin; Professor Karl Ritter, Marburg/Lahn; Professor Schreiner, Rostock; Pastor Georg Schulz, Barmen; Professor Stählin, Münster/Westfalen; Dr. H.-D. Wendland, lecturer, Heidelberg.

45. Appeal from the Berlin Pastors[1]

With a keen sense of our responsibility at the present hour, we are forwarding the appeal on the other side[2] to rally our fellow clergy, congregational leaders, and members, with the heartfelt request that you honor these statements of principle, which we consider to be appropriate for the restructuring of our church, with serious reflection and study.

We are convinced that the expectations that our people bring to the church today can only be fulfilled if its renewal is based solely on the gospel of the German Reformation.[3] For "anyone who thinks he can arrive at a religious reformation by the detour of a political organization only shows that he has no glimmer of knowledge of the development of religious ideas or dogmas and their ecclesiastical consequences" (Adolf Hitler).[4] So 67
it is precisely our living engagement in the building of our nation [Volk] that compels us to rouse our Protestant fellow believers in all earnestness,

---

[8.] [The Deutsche Christliche Studentenvereinigung, or German Christian Student Association. This was a national body of university students, founded in 1897; it was not related to the German Christian movement.—LR]

[1.] LKA EKvW Bielefeld, 5,1 Bestand 53; printed flyer, on the back of the "Call to Convene" (1/44). Misspelled names have been corrected in the text. Previously published from another source, with more signatures, in *Mündige Welt*, 5:92–93. The text of 1/44 ("Call to Convene") is printed on the back of this appeal.

[2.] [I.e., the other side of the paper.—LR]

[3.] [Meaning the gospel as understood by and proclaimed by Luther's Reformation.—LR]

[4.] This quotation is taken from Hitler's *Mein Kampf*, 114 (1999 English ed., trans. Ralph Mannheim).

to make them aware that the church, in order to serve our nation [Volk] today, must justify itself in the light of the confession given to it. This truth takes precedent over the state's political wishes and above all conflicts over church politics. Our church in Berlin is a clear example of how church-community can emerge only where we build on this foundation. Any special efforts that lead German Christendom to bypass this crucially important task will lead us astray and do us harm.

We therefore summon you, in preaching, pastoral ministry, and rallying people together, to present this task to the church-community and win over all vital energies for this cause.

In the confusion of voices being heard today, every clear Yes means a strengthening of this purpose for the church. We therefore ask that pastors and members of congregations declare their agreement to Dr. Künneth, 24 Zietenstr., Berlin-Dahlem.[5]

Babick (Paul Gerhardt),[6] Backhaus (Matthäus), v. Bargen (Ostern), Dr. Bonhoeffer, Dr. Brandenburg (City Mission), Dannenbaum (City Mission), Drüsedau (Tabor), Ehrich (Lankwitz), Dr. Fricke (Golgotha), Geß (Zehlendorf), Goosmann (Adlershof), Herzog (Gustav-Adolf), W. Hildebrand, youth pastor (Lichterfelde), Dr. F. Hildebrandt (Machnow), Jacobi (Kaiser Wilhelm Gedächtnis), Köhler (Pfingstkirche), Krätschell (Mahlsdorf), Kroppenstedt (Siemensstadt), Künkel (Schmargendorf), Kurtz (Zwölf Apostel), Link (Heiland), Lunde (Wilmersdorf), Consistory Councillor Dr. Lütkemann, Magerstädt (Kaiser Wilhelm Gedächtnis), Marczynski (Heiland), Müller-Schlomka (Tempelhof), [Martin] Niemöller (Dahlem), Dr. Pfeiffer (Nathanael), Praetorius (Lichterfelde), Dr. Puttkammer (Teltow), Quittschau (Steglitz), Röhricht (Dahlem), Sasse (Lazarus), Turne (Johannes, Moabit), Werbeck (Johannes, Moabit), Wesenberg (Christus), Zippel (Steglitz)

[5.] See 1/44, ed. note 7.

[6.] Names of local churches and parish districts, and in some cases the occupations of the signers, are given in parentheses. [The parish names have not been translated. —LR]

46. From Théodore de Félice[1] 68

Geneva, May 16, 1933

Dear Mr. Bonhoeffer:

The merger was confirmed after the meeting in London on May 5–6 of the Executive Committee of the Ecumenical Council on Life and Work and the meeting on May 8–9, also in London, of the officers of the International Federation for Practical Work of the Churches[2] had accepted the suggestions made by the youth commissions at their session in Luneray.[3]

I am confirming receipt of your letter of May 5 with many thanks.[4] I am happy to hear that you are willing to serve as a member of our committee.

So the youth week in the Balkans will probably be held in September, and the international youth week in Gland, Switzerland, from August 29 to September 4.

After checking the budget again, Mr. Henriod and I suggest that the travel grants be amended as follows:

Meeting in the Balkans[5]	$125.00 instead of Fr. 600.00
(Toureille's travel not included)	
German-French meeting	$150.00 instead of Fr. 600.00
German-Polish meeting[6]	$150.00 instead of Fr. 600.00
International Youth Week in Gland	$400.00

Should you have any objections to these new figures, would you kindly let me know.

Sincerely yours,
[Théodore de Félice]

[1.] WCC Archives, Bonhoeffer box; carbon copy, not previously published.

[2.] This is incorrect; it probably refers to the special meeting, mentioned in 1/51, of the officers of the World Alliance for Promoting International Friendship through the Churches.

[3.] Cf. 1/42. Henriod commented on the merger in his "Draft Annual Report": "It is to be hoped that this process of *Gleichschaltung* [coordination], which is of moral and material benefit to both organizations, will facilitate increased financial support from those interested in both movements within the Christian constituency of all countries" (World Alliance, *Annual Report*, 1933–34, 33). [Henriod's comment is in English, but he uses the German *Gleichschaltung*, which of course was the name of the Nazi policy to coordinate all aspects of German life.—LR]

[4.] 1/43.

[5.] See 1/34, ed. note 6.

[6.] According to the *Handbook of the World Alliance* 1935, p. 62, this meeting, as well as the German-French one (see 1/59 and 1/74), had to be canceled due to the political situation in Germany.

69 47. To Friedrich Siegmund-Schultze[1]

[Berlin-]Grunewald, May 17, 1933

Dear Professor Siegmund-Schultze:

May I please ask for your advice and help on a personal matter? A young Jewish sociologist, Dr. Landshut, a friend of ours who was Heymann's[2] assistant at the University of Hamburg, has found himself in great difficulty since Heymann's suspension. He had planned to qualify as a university lecturer in May but found out a few days ago that he will not be allowed to do so. His pronounced Jewish appearance would also make working at the university much more difficult. In all likelihood, he will also lose his position as assistant in the next few days. Thus he will be completely without income, with a wife who has severe heart trouble and three children. His last book, *Kritik der Soziologie,*[3] was very well received when it was published. He is a man of the purest scholarship and integrity. With regard to his character, it is worth noting that in 1914, at the age of seventeen, he volunteered for the war, and served on the front from 1914 to 1918. He is a man who feels completely German and is not yet able to contemplate looking for a job outside Germany. He would rather stay here and do any kind of work by which he could possibly support his family, even something completely outside his profession. My question now to you is whether you might be so kind as to make it possible for Dr. Landshut to get in touch with the chairman of the Jewish Welfare Association, Dr. Oldendorf,[4] or possibly with someone in the association's Hamburg office, to discuss his situation there. For myself and those in my family[5] who are close friends of Landshut, it matters very
70 much what happens to him, and I should not like to have failed to ask you earnestly for any help you might be able to provide him.

In sincere gratitude I remain, as always, yours respectfully,
Bonhoeffer

[1.] EZA, 51/H II b 1.2; typewritten, not previously published.

[2.] Correct spelling: Heimann.

[3.] ["Sociological Critique"] published in Munich in 1929.

[4.] Correct spelling: Ollendorf.

[5.] Christine and Hans von Dohnanyi, who knew Landshut from their time in Hamburg.

48. To Johannes von Schneidemesser[1]

Dear Pastor Schneidemesser:

Permit me to turn to you with the following request. I have heard that even before my sermon of May 14,[2] the thinking on the choice of a new pastor[3] appeared to be reaching a consensus. When I agreed to preach on May 14, I asked at the time that it be considered a supply sermon rather than that of a candidate, in order not to make the decision on the calling of a pastor more difficult in any way. It means very much to me not to be the cause of differences of opinion in the congregation, so I would ask, when the vote for a new pastor[4] is taken on Tuesday, that I not be considered as a candidate. Should it happen in the near future that another ministry position
becomes available, one connected with youth work,[5] as things now stand 71
I would gladly be at your disposal for an interview, based on the sermon I preached on May 14.

May I request that you bring this letter to the attention of the congregation.

Yours most sincerely and respectfully,
D[ietrich] B[onhoeffer]

[1.] *NL*, A 29,3; handwritten draft, undated, from Berlin-Grunewald. Previously published in *GS* 6:256–57. There is no final copy in the files of Lazarus-Kirchengemeinde, Berlin; possibly Bonhoeffer never sent this letter, which was written shortly before May 23, 1933. On this second candidacy for a pastorate in east Berlin, see *DB-ER*, 232, and ed. note 3.

[2.] The text of this sermon has not been preserved.

[3.] According to written information of May 2, 1986, from Pastor Steiner at Lazarus-Kirche, this was one of five positions that had become available after November 14, 1932. As of April 11, 1933, the candidates for these positions were Pastor Schwarz, Pastor Wünscher, and Dr. von Baer. Bonhoeffer must have later replaced Baer as a candidate—although this cannot be documented precisely from the files—since he preached on May 14, 1933, the date originally assigned to Baer.

[4.] The vote was taken on May 23, 1933, and Schwarz received the call. He received forty of the seventy-three votes, while thirty-three voted for Bonhoeffer (Minutes Book of Lazarus-Kirchengemeinde, Berlin, p. 154).

[5.] On Bonhoeffer's interest in youth work, see his letters to Anneliese Schnurmann (1/9, 1/11, and 1/16).

49. From Théodore de Félice[1]

Geneva, May 24, 1933

Dear Mr. Bonhoeffer,

Mr. Taul[2] has written us: "As can be seen from the enclosed minutes,[3] the youth commission is planning a week of work together in Geneva,[4] at which there will be two places for delegates from the Baltic states. Would you please send me more information about this, especially about the provisions for travel? In case these are within the limits of my possibilities, I should very much like to participate in this conference."

I am informing Mr. Taul that it was decided in Luneray to ask you to be in charge of representation from the Baltic states, and I am passing his inquiry on to you.

With regard to the financial means at our disposal, the working week is being organized by the London office of the World Alliance for Promoting International Friendship through the Churches, so requests for travel grants should also be made to that office.

Yours very respectfully,
[Théodore de Félice]

72 **50. To Théodore de Félice[1]**

Berlin-Grunewald, May 31, 1933

Dear Mr. de Félice,

Might I please inquire whether the amount that has been set aside for the German-French youth conference is the final amount. In our case, in fact, the sum of three hundred Swiss francs[2] will not make it possible to send

---

[1.] WCC Archives, Bonhoeffer box; carbon copy; not previously published.

[2.] According to the minutes of the April 22, 1933, joint meeting of the World Alliance and Life and Work youth commissions in Luneray (cf. 1/42, ed. note 1), Jaak Taul, a young Lutheran from Estonia, became the youth commission member representing the Baltic states.

[3.] Taul is evidently referring to the minutes of the aforementioned youth commission meeting in Luneray.

[4.] Refers to the International Youth Conference, which met from August 29 to September 4, 1933, in Gland by Lake Geneva.

[1.] WCC Archives, Bonhoeffer box; photocopy of a specially preserved letter; see also *NL*, A 28,4 (2); photocopy. Previously published in *GS* 6:282.

[2.] Bonhoeffer was still proceeding on the basis of the budget made in Luneray and had not taken into account the subsequent (cf. 1/46) increase in the travel grants.

more than four people to this conference, at best. Toureille, to my knowledge, is planning on eight. What do you think about this? May I request an answer soon?

With best regards, yours respectfully,
Bonhoeffer

51. From Henry Louis Henriod[1]

Geneva, June 1, 1933

Dear Colleague:

At a special meeting of managing directors that took place in London on May 8 and 9, the financial situation of the World Alliance was thoroughly discussed in view of the devaluation of the dollar. Among other things, it was decided to hold a meeting of the Executive Committee in Sofia, instead of a conference of the entire working committee, which will save a considerable amount of money. The conference is to take place September 15–19 in Sofia and be followed immediately by a meeting of the secretariat.[2]

It was also decided that the president, the chair of the working committee, and the secretaries[3] are to meet with Dr. Mer[r]ill on September 4–5 in 73
Geneva, to use Dr. W. Adams Brown's visit there, perhaps meeting as well with the bishop of Chichester[4] from Life and Work, to discuss the issues of concern to the two movements.

The members of the Executive Committee, as you know, are Lord Dickinson, Bishop Ammundsen, Dr. Henry A. Atkinson, Dr. Bursche, Dr. Drummond, Mr. Jézéquel, Dr. Mihalescu, Rev. Sandegren, Professor Siegmund-Schultze, Dr. Wissing, and myself.

It was further decided that, besides the eleven members of the Executive,[5] you also should be invited to participate in this conference,[6] as well as one representative from each of the Balkan countries, since they would not otherwise be represented there, and other persons who could provide valuable

[1.] *NL*, A 28,3 (9); typewritten. Previously published in *GS* 6:282–84.

[2.] See agenda points 5 and 6 of the Minutes of the Officers' meeting, London, May 8–9, 1933 (WCC Archives, box 212.003).

[3.] This would mean Lord Dickinson, Bishop Ammundsen, and probably the five international secretaries: Atkinson, Jézéquel, Drummond, Siegmund-Schultze, and Zankow.

[4.] George Bell.

[5.] [Refers to the Executive Committee.—LR]

[6.] Of the Executive Committee in Sofia (cf. also 1/101 and 1/103).

help with preparations for the International Council meeting in 1934.[7] Each country's association will, of course, receive the full minutes of the meeting.[8] This expanded Executive Committee will not consider any resolutions concerning the constitution, but will only make decisions necessary for the ongoing work of the World Alliance and in preparation for its work in the next few years.

The agenda[9] established for the meeting of the working committee will be adopted for this expanded Executive Committee, with a few changes that seemed necessary.

Of the commissions, only the one concerned with minorities will be able to meet.

According to the reports that have been received on military power for the League of Nations, revision of treaties, and disarmament, it will not yet be possible to pass resolutions on these topics; they will be further prepared for the International Council meeting in 1934. The agenda [for Sofia] will, however, be expanded to include the following points:

(a) the question of racial minorities raised by the Dutch and French associations;

(b) a proposal that has been received from representatives of the League of Nations and of the International Labor Organization.

Would you please be so kind as to let me know as soon as possible whether you can participate in this conference?

74 Each participant will be reimbursed for a round-trip second-class fare, as well as meals during travel, that is, up to ten or fifteen francs per day, depending on the financial situation of the World Alliance. All further details will be provided to participants in a timely manner through circular letters.

Yours truly,
Henry Louis Henriod
General Secretary

[7.] This conference was to be held in Budapest. For financial reasons it was finally held on a smaller scale in August 1934 on the island of Fanø in Denmark (see *DB-ER*, 372–92, and *DBWE* 13:304–10).

[8.] [Refers to the minutes of the executive meeting.—LR]

[9.] Not extant. For the agenda of the expanded Executive Committee in Sofia, see 1/101, ed. note 1.

52. From Théodore de Félice[1]

Geneva, June 2, 1933

Dear Mr. Bonhoeffer,

After consultation with Mr. Henrici, I can inform you that the $150[2] placed at our disposal for the German-French gathering will be paid at an exchange rate of 4.40, therefore a total of 660.00 S[wiss] fr[ancs]. You will have to work out with Mr. Toureille how this amount should be divided. It seems right to us, however, that in distributing allowances for travel and meals to German and French delegates, the distance should be taken into account; for example, if the meeting is held in Chaintréauville, one could say two-thirds for the German and one-third for the French. On the other hand, if the meeting is held in Luxembourg, then the French [would] have to receive a correspondingly greater share. I am sending [a] copy of the letter to Mr. Toureille and hope you will succeed in finding more than four delegates for this gathering.

In case you are going to Basel,[3] why not meet with Mr. Toureille, since he also was planning to go there; then you could talk this over face-to-face.

You don't mention the week in Gland.[4] I presume you have been in contact
with Mr. Taul, about whom I wrote you in this regard in my letter of May 24.[5] In 75
our budget for the speakers from Germany, we have included a reimbursement of travel expenses only for you. We assume that the report on National Socialism can be made by one of the German delegates. Should this person require a travel grant, this should be requested—as for all the other delegates—from Mr. Burlingham, World Alliance, Effingham House, Arundel I, London WC2. We hope you will soon be able to notify us of the name of this speaker.[6]

We are working on the invitation for Gland and hope to be able to send you one in the next few days.

What is the status of the German-Polish meeting?[7]

Yours sincerely,
[Théodore de Félice]

[1.] WCC Archives, Bonhoeffer box; carbon copy; not previously published. Reply to 1/50.

[2.] Cf. 1/46.

[3.] See 1/38, ed. note 11.

[4.] Refers to the International Youth Conference in Gland by Lake Geneva, August 29–September 4, 1933; see 1/59, 1/66, and 1/80 for the continued correspondence on this.

[5.] Cf. 1/49.

[6.] Cf. 1/80, ed. note 5.

[7.] Cf. 1/46, ed. note 6.

53. From Théodore de Félice[1]

Geneva, June 9, 1933

Dear Mr. Bonhoeffer,

Mr. Burlingham in London is asking whether you have been informed of the countries and the number of participants for which you are responsible with regard to the study week in Geneva.[2] Mr. Toureille is in charge of this, and since you have never written to me about it, I am informing you that you have been assigned to find four delegates from Germany and two from the Baltic countries.

How many copies of the invitation letter do you want us to send you in German?

Yours truly,
[Théodore de Félice]

76 ### 54. Report to the Berlin Consistory[1]

Report on My Work as a Student Chaplain at the Technical College in Charlottenburg, Winter Semester 1932–33

After what from the outside would appear to be an almost completely unsuccessful summer semester 1932,[2] I decided to take a new approach to gaining entry at the Technical College. Leaving the fraternities to one side for the time being, my attempts to reach the unaffiliated students through lectures, prayer services, and study groups that were announced and held at the Technical College had to be regarded as failures. Participation was almost nil and obviously could not be increased via this approach. So, for the new semester, the only new point of departure left to me was through the student associations [Verbindungen]. A long letter was sent to all the fraternities. It began by pointing out the purpose of a student chaplaincy and then asked that the student ministry be discussed at their meetings

[1.] WCC Archives, Bonhoeffer box; carbon copy, not previously published.

[2.] Refers to the International Youth Conference in Gland, August 29–September 4, 1933.

[1.] EZA, 14/2780; typewritten; from Berlin-Grunewald; a stamp indicates receipt by the Berlin Consistory on June 13, 1933. Previously unpublished. Initialed by Karow and others, with a handwritten note: "This report is not encouraging. But no tree is felled by the first blow. Let's wait and see how it goes."

[2.] Cf. *DBWE* 11, 1/91 and 1/92.

and that they report to me briefly on these discussions. The majority of the replies were completely colorless acknowledgments of my letter, saying that they would call the attention of the fraternity members to the events organized by the student chaplain. Only a few struck a warmer tone and showed any sympathy for the concern expressed; in particular the German Student Association should be mentioned here.[3] By and large the response was not very encouraging. Many groups did not answer at all.

¶No one came to the announced discussions and study groups on "The Crisis of the State and the Gospel" and "Jesus Christ." Devotions had to be 77
abandoned since only one or two students from the Christian Student Association attended. Office hours remained almost entirely without visitors. I actually counseled four students, and I had just as many come to me with financial problems. My request to be informed in case of student illnesses remained unheard.

¶On the other hand, more invitations now came from the fraternity houses, but mostly to their bars[4] and other social events, at which I did not find it appropriate to speak. The danger that a pastor will play a purely decorative role at such events is very great. However, at my explicit request, I was also called upon for lecture evenings. In this way I began a relationship with about eight fraternities, although some of the lectures, due to whatever circumstances in the fraternities, had to be postponed to the next semester. These evenings were actually the most fruitful of the semester, since a lively discussion often followed. Topics requested were Technology and Religion; What Is the Church For?; Church and Popular Culture [Volkstum].[5] The four worship services[6] I conducted in Trinity Church [Dreifaltigkeitskirche] were conspicuously well attended by students.

¶From all this I have concluded that a significant number of students simply have no time to participate in the activities of the student chaplain. This represents one of the great difficulties for a student chaplain in finding a starting point at the Technical College. Two professors who are very influential among the students and with whom I talked about my work confirmed that they thought it almost impossible from the outside to gain any influence on the students, in view of the intense demands made on them by the college. I am becoming increasingly convinced that an attempt should be made to establish a professor's chair in Christian Thought at the Technical

[3.] No such correspondence found among Bonhoeffer's papers.

[4.] Term used for social evenings in student fraternity houses.

[5.] Manuscripts of these lectures have not been preserved.

[6.] Cf. sermons 3/1, 3 /4–5, and 3/8.

78 College,[7] so as to gain influence from the inside in shaping student life. Only when the ground has first been prepared in this way does it seem to me that the work of a student chaplain, who really has to concentrate on the gospel and not get sidetracked from it, can be spared from appearing to fail.

55. To Richard Wienstein[1]

Berlin-Grunewald, June 19, 1933

Dear Ministry Councillor Wienstein:

Permit me, following the conversation that you so kindly had with us today,[2] to report to you briefly about how the assembly went today at the university, according to the information I have received. After the speech by Lecturer Müller from Jena,[3] a resolution was proposed that the student body support Military Chaplain Müller.[4] At this point, in the opinion of some, perhaps 75 percent of the students present, and according to oth-
79 ers, 90 percent, got up and left the hall.[5] Immediately afterward a brief

[7.] This idea was taken up by Karow; see his letter of January 2, 1934, to the Consistory (*DBWE* 13, 1/43).

[1.] BA Koblenz, R 43 II/161; typewritten. See also *NL*, A 38,2 (4,3); copy. Previously published in *Mündige Welt*, 5:94, and *GS* 6:263–64.

[2.] See the Reich Chancellery Memorandum of June 20, 1933 (1/56). Bronisch-Holtze and Bonhoeffer had arranged their reception at the Reich Chancellery through state secretary Hans-Heinrich Lammers, who asked Ministry Councillor Richard Wienstein "to receive the gentlemen and report to me on the outcome of the meeting" (see Lammers's directive of June 17, 1933, to Wienstein in *Mündige Welt*, 5:93, and *GS* 6:262; see also *DB-ER*, 286).

[3.] [Hans Michael Müller, who taught at the University of Jena.—LR]

[4.] [I.e., support Ludwig Müller's election as Reich bishop.—LR]

[5.] This sentence is underlined, probably by Wienstein. Cf. the report in the *Tägliche Rundschau* of June 20, 1933 (reprinted in *Junge Kirche* 1 [1933]: 22, and *GS* 2:54): "Defeat for the German Christians at the University of Berlin: On Monday [June 19, 1933] midday at one o'clock in the Auditorium Maximum of the University of Berlin, the assembly was held, which had been called by the German Student Association to vote on joining the German Christian movement. The assembly went peacefully. When a resolution was read in favor of supporting Military Chaplain Müller for [Reich] bishop, nine-tenths of the audience left the auditorium and, at a rally that followed, submitted themselves to Adolf Hitler's political leadership." [Again, this reveals the ambiguity of the church opposition at that time: although they opposed the German Christians and Müller's candidacy for Reich bishop, they nonetheless supported National Socialism and often made a point of declaring their patriotic loyalty. Cf. 1/44 and 1/45, as well as 1/38, ed. note 5.—LR]

demonstration was held at the Hegel Memorial[6] by the students who had walked out, at which one student gave a *Heil* for the Reich chancellor, the rest following suit. I myself was not present at either the assembly or the demonstration; thus I can only rely on numerous reports from trustworthy students.

With great esteem and gratitude once more for receiving us this morning, honored Councillor Wienstein, I remain most respectfully yours,
Bonhoeffer

56. Reich Chancellery Memorandum[1]

Berlin, June 20, 1933

Concerns: Question of the Reich bishop

Yesterday morning (June 19), I received Lecturer Bonhoeffer and Student Chaplain Bronisch-Holtze. These gentlemen informed me that later that day, at one o'clock in the afternoon, an assembly of the student body was to take place at the University of Berlin, which was to vote on the position of the student body regarding the question of the Reich bishop.[2] On this matter, they said, one section of the student body was severely terrorizing the rest, so that this vote would surely not give a correct picture of the students' views. In reality, the gentlemen said, only a very few students support Military Chaplain Müller. Most support Pastor von Bodelschwingh as Reich bishop. They even said that most National Socialist students support Pastor von Bodelschwingh.[3]

I responded that I would inform the secretary of state about the matter, but that there could hardly be any question of an intervention from this office, because it concerned a student assembly, which was primarily the business of the Prussian Ministry of Cultural Affairs.

[6.] Statue in front of Friedrich Wilhelm University (today Humboldt University) in Berlin.

[1.] BA Koblenz, R 43 II/161; typewritten with handwritten corrections by Wienstein, initialed by Lammers on June 22, 1933. See also *NL*, A 38,2 (4,2); copy. Previously published in *Mündige Welt*, 5:93–94, and *GS* 6:262–63.

[2.] Cf. 1/55, ed. note 5.

[3.] There are two question marks (perhaps inserted by Lammers) in the margin next to the last three sentences.

80 The gentlemen replied that they were also planning to make contact afterward with the Prussian Ministry for Education and Cultural Affairs.[4]

Meanwhile a report (enclosed) has been received from Lecturer Bonhoeffer.[5]

W[ienstein]

57. From Friedrich Siegmund-Schultze[1]

Dear Mr. Bonhoeffer:

I have written to Dr. Landshut, mentioning the Central Welfare Office for German Jews[2] in Berlin.[3] It would be best if he himself contacted this office directly.

Recently Pastor Henriod asked me whom we could suggest for Gland[4] as lecturer on national economic and social political questions. It isn't so easy nowadays to find the right man for this job. I would suggest Dr. Hans Mühle but wanted to know beforehand whether you concur. As you know, Dr. Mühle was the director of our adult education center here, which we had to close this
81 spring.[5] He comes from the Student Christian Movement,[6] was Le Seur's

[4.] According to Bonhoeffer's report at the pastors' conference in Bradford, Yorkshire, on November 28, 1933, a delegation consisting of Bonhoeffer, two storm troopers, and a pastor went to the Ministry for Education and Cultural Affairs, where they met with ministry director Georg Gerullis (*GS* 6:304 and *DBWE* 13:44). Nothing has been found in the state files concerning this visit to the Prussian Ministry for Education and Cultural Affairs.

[5.] Cf. 1/55.

[1.] EZA, 51/D III n 2; carbon copy; from Berlin; with the sender's handwritten signature and a typewritten note: "Dict[ated] on June 21, 1933. Typing of the letter delayed several days" (presumably because of the storm troopers' attack on the Ulmenhof center and the arrest of Siegmund-Schultze; on this see Grotefeld, *Siegmund-Schultze*, 120–28); not previously published. Reply to 1/47.

[2.] The Central Welfare Organization for German Jews (Wohlfahrtsorganisation der deutschen Juden), founded in 1917. In 1932 it had 212 facilities. Its main areas of activity were social support and security, especially for immigrant Jews from Poland and Russia. After 1933, the Central Office was chiefly concerned with emigration possibilities.

[3.] The letter to Landshut was dated June 19, 1933, but was not sent until June 24, 1933 (EZA, 51/H II b 1,1).

[4.] Refers to the International Youth Conference, August 29–September 4, 1933, in Gland, Switzerland.

[5.] Siegmund-Schultze had founded the Ulmenhof Adult Education Center in 1927 to provide continuing education for young workers. It had to be closed in the spring of 1933 after the Berlin city government withdrew support for its work (see Grotefeld, *Siegmund-Schultze*, 114–15). [See also ed. note 1.—LR]

[6.] This movement was started at the end of the nineteenth century, leading to the founding of the German Christian Student Association (DCSV) in 1897. [Again, this organization was unrelated to the German Christians.—LR]

assistant at Hainstein House[7] for several years, then was director of an adult education center in a border region. He was with us for several years and proved himself most capable, even as he did in his earlier positions. I think he would tactfully represent the German situation abroad, which of course is not easy these days. If you agree, please write to me and perhaps at the same time to Henriod, since he was anxious to have a reply soon.

With best regards, I am as ever
[Friedrich Siegmund-Schultze]

58. Minutes of Meeting "The Struggle for the Church"[1]

The Struggle for the Church

Main Speakers: Student Chaplain Bronisch-Holtze
Prof. Fabricius—Berlin (German Christians)
Dr. Bonhoeffer—Berlin
Discussion Leader: Church Councillor Foertsch—Stettin
Discussion Speakers: Prof. Deissmann—Berlin
Prof. Schumann—Halle
Prof. Hirsch—Göttingen
Prof. Sellin—Berlin
Prof. Hermann—Greifswald
Gruschke, grad. in theology
Reppin, grad. in theology 82
Goetz, grad. in theology
Eckardt, grad. in philosophy

[7.] Hainstein House in Eisenach had served since 1925 as a Protestant youth education center and a center for ecumenical encounters. [The reference is to Paul Le Soeur, director of Hainstein House.—LR]

[1.] EZA 50/264a; handwritten, by an unnamed note taker. Previously published in *Mündige Welt*, 5:95–98. According to a report in *Junge Kirche*, about two thousand students attended this gathering, organized by the Protestant Students Working Committee and held at the university in Berlin on June 22, 1933. This report, titled "Der Kampf um die Kirche" ("The Struggle for the Church," published in *Junge Kirche* 1 [1933]: 22–23; partially reproduced in *GS* 2:54–55), stressed that it was surprising "that at such a time as this, both 'Young Reformers' and 'German Christians' had the same opportunities to speak, and debated with one another objectively. . . . This was made possible by the unusually disciplined behavior of the audience, three-fourths of whom sympathized with the Young Reformers." According to Bonhoeffer's report at the pastors' conference at Bradford, Yorkshire, on November 28, 1933, this meeting was held in opposition to the German Christian assembly mentioned in 1/55, ed. note 5. Cf. *DBW* 13:37.

	Lorenz, student of political science
	Dr. Vogelsang—Königsberg
Closing Speaker:	Prof. Lütgert—Berlin

As speaker for the Young Reformers,[2] student chaplain Bronisch-Holtze began with a description of the church situation today. It had changed because of the altered position of the church toward the state. Whereas under the old state,[3] an icy neutrality had been maintained on both sides, under the new state there is no longer neutrality. The state is demanding that the church take part in building the nation.[4] However, instead of the church entering fully into this task, a struggle had begun. The reason for this is that there are two directions here that are now colliding. One of them had its origin in the nation [Volk], or rather in the ethno-nationalist [völkisch] principle; the other originated in the church.[5] The latter the speaker described as quieter and more reserved; it reflects the deadly seriousness of the Christian message. The church is not the nursemaid of the German soul but rather the bearer of God's gospel, revealed in Christ, which is given to all people.

An irrational vitality was hiding in the German Christian movement, vital values that are to be affirmed since they were a critique of liberalism.[6] However, the national dynamic must not be allowed to become an absolute. An omnipotent state would destroy the church and finish by devouring itself as well.

What is the church's task now? It is calling for a nationwide effort, but it would need to be clear about where earth leaves off and heaven begins. Its obligation would be to say soberly and objectively that salvation is not from

[2.] [Members of the Young Reformation movement commonly referred to themselves as Young Reformers. The Young Reformation movement was the precursor to the Pastor's Emergency League, founded in 1933 under the leadership of Pastor Martin Niemöller to oppose the German Christian drive to make the Aryan paragraph part of church law. The Pastor's Emergency League was in turn the precursor to the Confessing Church, which emerged from the Barmen synod in May 1934.—LR]

[3.] That is, before Hitler became Reich chancellor.

[4.] See, for example, Hitler's declaration of March 23, 1933, which said that the rights of the two Christian confessions should "not be infringed"; however, they would be expected to show "for their part, the same respect for the task which this government has set itself, namely, the moral and national uplifting of our people" (Nicolaisen, *Dokumente*, 1:24).

[5.] Refers to the German Christian faith movement and the Young Reformation movement.

[6.] [This and the following three paragraphs record the remarks of Bronisch-Holtze. —LR]

the nation [Volk], but from the merciful redemption we have received through Jesus Christ. The church has made a great mistake in not taking its stand under the cross. There is too much talk of the *ecclesia triumphans*[7] and too little solidarity with the godless brother. The criterion should be "under the cross."

In contrast, the ill-defined demands of the German Christians (the same content in a new form; "undegenerate Christianity,"[8] a religion in accordance with ethno-national traditions) represented an attack on the substance. Rather than a crass departure like that of the Tannenberg movement,[9] however, they had attempted a compromise by trying to make Christ into an idealized human hero. The death of Christ, however, was no human hero's death, but represented the Last Judgment, God's wrath revealed. One must be careful not to muddle these concepts. 83

Through the Aryan paragraph,[10] the church's baptismal vow had been broken. The speaker[11] concluded his remarks with the statement, "Only the Word from the cross unites us internally; all else demonizes the church."

The speaker for the German Christians, Prof. Fabricius, characterized the German Christians as those Christians who saw and humbly recognized the great things that God has done for our nation—this is faith, and their movement is a faith movement—and the Young Reformers as those who, though they did agree, always did so with a "But."[12]

The chief task of the German Christians was to fuse at the deepest level the life of the people with the gospel.[13] This was a two-sided task: first, the German people must be christianized through the *pure* gospel. What Hitler's movement had accomplished outwardly—the destruction of Bolshevism in

[7.] The "church triumphant."

[8.] The call for "undegenerate [*artgemäß*] Christianity" was already found in the German Christian Guidelines of June 6, 1932 (Gauger, *Chronik*, 1:67).

[9.] This is a reference to the Tannenberg Association, a radical *völkisch*-antichurch [neo-pagan—LR] group founded in 1926 by Erich Ludendorff and his wife, Mathilde, which was banned by the Nazis in September 1933.

[10.] With their demand that the Reich Church be the church of "Christians of the Aryan race" (cf. 1/44, ed. note 6), the German Christians had already drawn radical conclusions from the Law for the Reconstitution of the Civil Service of April 7, 1933 (*RGBl*, pt. 1, 245), which contained the so-called Aryan paragraph, although on May 6, 1933, it had been made clear that this Reich law was not to be applied to "officials, employees, and workers of religious societies established under public law" (*RGBl*, pt. 1, 245).

[11.] [I.e., Bronisch-Holtze.—LR]

[12.] Cf. 1/44.

[13.] [This and the following six paragraphs record Fabricius's remarks.—LR]

Germany—the German Christians must do inwardly: the overcoming of atheism. This meant also combating nationalist [völkisch] religions.[14] The danger that these sects would spread had been markedly reduced by the German Christians.

84 ¶The other side of the task consisted in preserving the purity of the German gospel. This meant proclaiming the Good News that we are God's children. We, along with all Indo-Germans, should shout for joy at this news and not be frightened by the cross. Preserving the gospel's purity, however, also meant defending it against judaization; the OT was subordinate to the NT and only worthy of consideration as disciplinarian until Christ came.[15] The speaker mentioned the danger in dialectical theology of being led toward the Old Testament, if such theology became the text itself instead of a commentary on the text as it claimed to be.

The only other task of the German Christians mentioned by the speaker was that of social education.

The final task would be the unification of the church. This was an external matter. The two movements had different ideas about it.

With regard to the Jewish question, it should be noted that the Young Reformers also had an Aryan paragraph.[16] However, the Jewish question is less important in the church than in the state, because the church is not nearly

[14.] The various ethno-nationalist (*völkisch*) religious groups intended to retain elements of Christianity; nonetheless, for them the confession of faith in ethnically defined national identity (*Volkstum*) and race was constitutive (cf. here, for example, Weinel, *Völkische Bewegung*).

[15.] Cf. Gal. 3:24.

[16.] The Young Reformation movement had indeed made a clear decision on the issue of church membership, and in the seventh thesis of their Appeal of May 9, 1933, had fundamentally condemned "the exclusion of non-Aryans from the church" (1/44); however, on the question of whether "non-Aryans" could and should hold offices or pastorates in the church, the Young Reformers were more ambiguous. For example, in the summer of 1933 Walter Künneth publicly expressed the opinion that, in principle, "what determines membership in a Christian church has nothing to do with one's racial origin, but rather with one's faith in Christ as the Lord"; however, he hinted at the possibility that "too prominent a Jewish Christian element in the church . . . might threaten its fulfillment of its duty to the German nation," and offered for consideration "whether, in the coming German Evangelical Church, certain leadership positions ought to be reserved for persons of the German race. In principle, Jewish Christians have the same rights in the church, but in order to avoid trouble, for the sake of love and our mission to our people, it appears that this sacrifice should be asked of them" (Künneth, "Das Judenproblem und die Kirche," 95 and 97–98).

as tainted by the Jews [verjudet] as the state. "We'll be able to deal with the handful of Jews we have."[17]

There was also a difference of thinking with regard to the question of a Reich bishop. The Young Reformers considered an election to be a democratic mistake.[18] In objection[19] it must be said that Hitler himself had let his posi- 85
tion be thus legitimized. Such an election offered the assurance of allegiance.[20] The Catholic Church, too, where the apostolic faith was still as strong as in the monasteries, still held elections. The manner of electing bishops was the most objectionable Vaticanism.[21]

The speaker closed by returning to the difference between German Christians and Young Reformers stated at the beginning of his presentation.

Dr. Bonhoeffer[22] spoke about the meaning of the struggle. If God had involved the church in struggle, it was to encourage humility. There was therefore no place in this dispute for self-justification. Anyone who simply made accusations without any self-accusation had simply failed to understand the meaning of the struggle.

Once again the difference that is described in Romans 14 has become apparent, between the strong and the weak in faith. The strong in faith are those who do not push others out, while the weak are those who try to mark off the church-community. Today it is those of weak faith who have introduced a racial

[17.] According to the *Deutsches Pfarrblatt* (no. 44, 1933) since the Reformation there had been only ninety-eight Protestant pastors known to be of Jewish origin; in 1933, twenty-nine of them were still in the ministry (representing 0.2 percent of ca. eighteen thousand pastors). However, more-recent research had shown that there were really far more than one hundred (Nowak, *Stigma*, 76). [The quotation marks in the text would seem to indicate this was a direct statement by Fabricius. On the number of "non-Aryan" clergy, see also Gerlach, *And the Witnesses Were Silent*, 269n63; and Barnett, *For the Soul of the People*, 133–34.—LR]

[18.] In the second point of their Appeal of May 9, 1933 (1/44), the Young Reformers had rejected elections by an electoral system as "an outdated democratic mistake." The German Christians, however, had called on May 4, 1933, for the election of the Reich bishop, "nominated by German Christians from their own ranks" and by a vote of electors chosen by the votes of church members (Gauger, *Chronik*, 1:77).

[19.] [Fabricius continues to speak here.—LR]

[20.] Fabricius obviously intended this interpretation also to apply to the results of the Reichstag elections of March 5, 1933, in which 51.9 percent voted for the ruling coalition led by the NSDAP [Nazi party], which itself had 43.9 percent of the vote.

[21.] Here the election of Bodelschwingh as Reich bishop by the leaders of the regional churches on May 26–27, 1933 (cf. Scholder, *Churches and the Third Reich*, 1:329–32) was apparently being compared to the election of the pope by the College of Cardinals.

[22.] [This and the following five paragraphs record Bonhoeffer's reply to the previous two speakers.—LR]

law. The strength of the others would now consist in being open to the petition of the weak ones. But the former must watch out, for it is precisely the weak who are the aggressive ones, the reformers.[23]

A faith movement should not trivialize the confession (countering Fabricius's statements about the Jewish question).[24] When this happened in early Christian times, the first council was convened.[25]

And we today should demand that a council be convened. Its decisions should be binding. The last possibility open to Protestantism would then be schism.[26]

It is now the confession that is at stake.[27] There are two points of doctrine to be decided: the doctrine of the church and the doctrine of creation.

The struggle in the church is a great gift, but the greatest gift is peace.[28]

86 The discussion leader, Consistory Councillor Foertsch from Stettin, pointed out that the discussion should take actual practices into account.

As the first of the discussion speakers, Prof. Deissmann remarked that two things made him glad this evening: the debate among the Protestant spiritual leaders and the presence of outside guests. This dialogue was necessary, but it should be an exchange of opinions in a fraternal spirit.

Prof. Schumann from Halle felt that, most of all, both sides needed to venture out of their tensely guarded positions and get back to theological thinking. In his opinion, theology belongs to the local congregation [Gemeinde]. Theological and practical issues are inseparable. What is important today is not to keep talking at cross purposes, not to keep shifting fronts or putting up false fronts, but to come face-to-face over the issue at hand.

At present a great deal is being said about the church, what the church actually is. A Protestant church is a place where God's Word, through the mouths of human beings, meets with faith. Churches do need to have their rules, their order. Here too, the distinction must be made between heaven and earth. We must take care not to idolize the church.

The speaker was opposed to the idea of schism.

[23.] Cf. 2/16.

[24.] [Bonhoeffer is countering Fabricius here.—LR]

[25.] The "council of the apostles" (Acts 15).

[26.] Cf. 2/13 and 2/14.

[27.] Cf. 2/13 and 2/14.

[28.] *Junge Kirche* 1 (1933): 23, reported on Bonhoeffer's remarks in similar words (reprinted in *DB-ER*, 288) and further remarked: "The greatest impact on the meeting were the words of Lecturer Bonhoeffer when he pointed to the possibilities and limitations of a struggle within the church." [This concludes the record of Bonhoeffer's remarks.—LR]

Prof. Hirsch from Göttingen emphasized that the state had torn the people away from contemporary culture.[29] The state[30] cannot take a neutral position toward the church. Either people will have to find a way to cooperate, or the church will become a foreign body. The state and the Führer also have a claim on a person's soul.

Prof. Sellin had three questions for the German Christians, in order to prevent any clouding of the issues:

1. Did the German Christians condone the sentence that spoke of belief in the "sovereignty of the National Socialist state"?[31]

2. Did they condone the Karlshorst decisions of June 17, 1933, especially those in which the men on the church committee were designated as "alien to our people [volksfremd] and church" and demanded the help of the Reich president and Reich chancellor?[32]

3. Did they condone the involvement of political organizations in the elec- 87
tion of a bishop?[33]

After posing these questions, Prof. Sellin called for unity and peace and proposed a one-year truce.

Prof. Hermann from Greifswald characterized the new state as one based on conviction, not merely an authoritarian state that now summoned the church. The church could therefore bring its message all the more joyfully. It could not become the state's high priest and hallow the state's ideas. It is the messenger

[29.] Cf. especially Hirsch, *Die gegenwärtige geistige Lage.*

[30.] [The German here is "Er," which could refer either to Hirsch or to the state (*der Staat*).—LR]

[31.] In their Principles of May 4, 1933, the German Christian movement had demanded among other things that the Reich Church should recognize the "sovereignty of the National Socialist state as a matter of faith" (Gauger, *Chronik,* 1:6). [See also Bergen, *Twisted Cross,* 54–57.—LR]

[32.] A more detailed account on the German Christian meeting held in Berlin-Karlshorst to protest Bodelschwingh's election as Reich bishop, attended by several thousand people, was reported, for example, in the *Schwäbische Merkur* [a southwest German newspaper], (no. 141, June 20, 1933): "In the end a statement was adopted emphatically rejecting the church leaders' decision in the matter of the Reich bishop, because these leaders were no friends of our church and nation, had no spiritual relationship to the German people, and because Bodelschwingh had neither the confidence [of the people] nor the church behind him. The Reich president and Reich chancellor were sent the resolution by telegraph and asked to take measures ensuring that the decisions of the Protestant people on this question concerning their leadership were in accord with those of the nation's chancellor, Adolf Hitler."

[33.] In their agitation against Bodelschwingh's election as Reich bishop, the German Christians had accepted the support of Nazi organizations (cf. Nicolaisen, *Dokumente,* 1:56). [See also Scholder, *Churches and the Third Reich,* 1:336–37.—LR]

of God's gospel. It is visible, but with a trace of the invisible, of the Holy Spirit at work within it. Therefore it is independent. The church also has a mission to the state. It is to preach about sin, a terrifying message. But without this message, there would be no Good News (contrary to Fabricius!).

Gruschke, a graduate student in theology, was of the opinion that Christians had to live within the tension between obeying the state and obeying the church. State and church could not be brought into line [gleichgeschaltet] with each other.

Voting for a bishop should be done only on the basis of one's faith.

Reppin, a graduate student in theology, asked whether being National Socialists obligated us to be German Christians. He thought not, citing a passage in Hitler's *Mein Kampf* that spoke of the church as apolitical and not aligned with any political party.[34]

Goetz, a graduate student in theology, emphasized that the German Christian faith movement had arisen from godlessness, the people's rejection of everything to do with Christianity, from the desperate situation in which the belief is totally lacking that "I can do all things through him who strengthens me, Jesus Christ."[35]

Eckardt, a graduate student in theology, objected to a blurring of the affairs of state with affairs of the church.

88 Lorenz, a student of political science, expressed the belief that the tension between this world and the world beyond could only be bridged by true faith.

The lecturer Dr. Vogelsang from Königsberg said he thought that the old conception of state and of church had been liquidated. On the relationship of the two, bringing them together, he cited Luther's Pentecost sermon of 1529.[36] Here Luther showed that God governed the whole world, through both. Church and state were yoked together, bound to each other as in a marriage. The tragedy of May 23 was that the church had been separated from National Socialism through the insult to the German Christians.[37]

[34.] Cf., for example, Hitler's statement in *Mein Kampf*: "Political parties have nothing to do with religious problems, as long as these are not alien to the nation, undermining the morals and ethics of the race; just as religion cannot be amalgamated with the scheming of political parties" (1999 English ed., trans. Ralph Mannheim), 116.

[35.] Phil. 4:13. [The NRSV does not include the name "Jesus Christ" in this verse. The KJV has "I can do all things through Christ which strengtheneth me."—LR]

[36.] Cf. Luther's works, *WA* 29:344–51.

[37.] This evidently refers to May 26–27, 1933, when the church leaders chose Bodelschwingh as Reich bishop, although the German Christians had named Ludwig Müller as their candidate the week before (cf. Scholder, *Churches and the Third Reich,* 1:329–31).

In his closing remarks, Prof. Lütgert of Berlin pointed out the danger represented by a state church. Church and state had each received a different commission from God. Cooperation was only possible on the foundation of the distinction between them.

59. To Théodore de Félice[1]

June 23, 1933

Dear Mr. de Félice,

I have just heard from Toureille[2] that he has requested more funding for our German-French meeting;[3] otherwise he does not think the conference can be held. With the three hundred francs that have been made available to me, I certainly cannot bring more than four delegates with me to the conference.[4] These days it is not possible to expect people to pay their own travel, board, and lodging costs. I want to convey the same message to you now with regard to the Geneva conference in August.[5] I do not see any 89
possibility of sending youth delegates there without assuring them that we will reimburse their full expenses. Since I cannot under any circumstances urge my friends, who are all very busy with their work, to attend the French conference and then cancel it on them again at the last minute, as Toureille proposes, I would ask you please to be so kind as to give me your view of these matters, as soon as possible. I would certainly think it a pity to cancel the German-French conference, but don't think it would necessarily do any harm to postpone it again for a few months.

With best wishes,
Yours sincerely and respectfully,
Bonhoeffer

[1.] WCC Archives, Bonhoeffer box; photocopy of a specially preserved letter; from Berlin-Grunewald. See also *NL*, A 28, 4 (3); copy. Previously published in *Mündige Welt*, 5:64–65, and *GS* 6:284–85. Reply to 1/53.

[2.] Letter not included in the Bonhoeffer *Nachlaß*.

[3.] This was planned for late July 1933 in France or Luxembourg (cf. 1/52).

[4.] Cf. 1/61.

[5.] The international youth conference at Gland by Lake Geneva, August 29–September 4, 1933.

60. From Kurt Zielinski[1]

Dear Pastor Bonhoeffer,

Begging Pastor's pardon for the delay in replying. I am unemployed but am very much occupied with service to the Hittler [*sic*] Youth, have asked for tomorrow evening [Saturday] off, the twenty-fourth of June, and will be there.[2]

With best regards from your confirmand
Kurt Zielinski

Heil Hittler [*sic*]

90 **61. From Théodore de Félice**[1]

Geneva, June 26, 1933

Dear Sir,

Franco-German Meeting. Your letter of the twenty-third received my full attention: In the meantime I had already had a long discussion on the question with Mr. Henriod after having received the letter from Toureille that you refer to. Whatever the circumstances, I don't think that Mr. Toureille will need more than SF 360 for the French delegation, leaving SF 360 for the German delegation and not just SF 300; the best thing for me to do is to give you my reply to Mr. Toureille:

"I spoke again with Henriod about the problem of subsidies for the French delegation. Obviously, your personal costs should be covered completely. Unfortunately, we don't have a penny to spare. Even after having guaranteed SF 660 for that week, we aren't sure we will be able to access the full amount, but whatever the circumstances you can count on the SF 660. As this indicates, we are unable

[1.] *NL*, Anh. D 1,2 (2); handwritten postcard; from north Berlin; postmarked June 23, 1933; unpublished. There is no information as to Zielinski's identity [except that he was a member of Bonhoeffer's confirmation class—LR].

[2.] Probably in Biesenthal near Berlin, where Bonhoeffer used to meet with confirmands on weekends (cf. *DB-ER*, 229, and Zimmermann and Smith, *I Knew Dietrich Bonhoeffer*, 58). According to a February 4, 1989, letter from Bethge, after the end of the 1933 summer semester the property had to be turned over to the Hitler Youth for its use (cf. also *NL*, Anh. D 1,2 (3); undated typewritten confirmation of the handover of the Biesenthal property, by "Comradeship Leader [Kameradschaftsführer] Albert Gaedicke").

[1.] WCC Archives, Bonhoeffer box; carbon copy; unpublished. Reply to 1/59.

to divert any money whatsoever from another meeting, especially the one in Gland.[2] Perhaps it would be better, as you suggested, to reduce to five the number of participants from each side at Chaintréauville.[3]

"Perhaps you could also mention to the participants that they should nevertheless be careful about what they eat and where they stay, and only pay them a part of their living expenses, increasing by the same amount their travel expenses. . . .

"You can also point out that there are a number of bus connections, which are often less expensive than the train for the same route. . . ."

The proposition to put off the conference would unfortunately not have the effect of placing more money at your disposal, as Mr. Henriod, with whom I spoke concerning your letter, said that we never transfer funds from one account to another in our movement.

I believe that in the meantime you will receive a letter from Toureille[4] that will let you know exactly how much is at your disposal.

Study Week at Gland. As to this meeting, I am anxious to know whether you have found, among the delegates you are sending, the "German speaker"
mentioned in the attachment.[5] You haven't yet let me know whether you want 91
copies of the circular for recruiting your delegates.

In our budget we have provided for a complete reimbursement of your travel expenses, round trip, second class from Berlin to here (we budgeted SF 194; is that enough?) and your living expenses in Gland. On top of that, we proposed a general subvention plan for the delegations to Mr. Burlingham (Effingham House, 1 Arundel Street, London WC2, England) who will make the final distribution, and in that plan Germany is granted SF 200 and the Baltic countries SF 120.

Mr. Taul (Tähe t. 64, Tartu, Estonia) wrote to me on the fourteenth, and not knowing your address, he had written to you using Mr. Stange as an intermediary; I replied to his letter on the nineteenth and advised him to write to you directly.

Yours faithfully,
[Théodore de Félice]

[2.] For the international youth conference in Gland by Lake Geneva from August 29–September 4, 1933.

[3.] The Geneva office had thus decided against Luxembourg as a venue (see 1/52).

[4.] Not in the Bonhoeffer *Nachlaß*.

[5.] Not in the Bonhoeffer *Nachlaß*.

62. From Gertrud Staewen[1]

June 26, 1933

Dear Mr. Bonhoeffer,

Here at my vacation spot, I have just heard that you proposed in a speech that a council be convened.[2] An idea that appears to be really necessary in view of the Babylonian confusion of Christian discourse. What a terrible disgrace, once again, this finale for a Reich bishop.[3] (But perhaps my point of view is too "Reformed"!) But why have we got ourselves onto this political "Führer" level?[4]

Best regards,
Gertrud Staewen

92 ### 63. To Friedrich Siegmund-Schultze[1]

July 1, 1933

Dear Professor Siegmund-Schultze,

Thank you very much for your letter, for your help with the Landshut case, and for your suggestion for Gland. Of course I agree with you. It does indeed seem impossible to me, as I have already written the office, to bring

[1.] *NL*, C 24; handwritten picture postcard; from Niendorf, a resort on the Baltic Sea. Previously published in *GS* 2:55.

[2.] Staewen is referring here to Bonhoeffer's contribution to the discussion on June 22, 1933 (cf. 1/58) [where he called for a church council to determine correct doctrine —LR] .

[3.] Refers to Bodelschwingh's resignation on June 24, 1933, in response to the appointment of the state commissioner for the Prussian regional churches and the lack of support from church leaders (cf. Scholder, *Churches and the Third Reich,* 1:352–55).

[4.] Here Staewen affirms Barth's viewpoint (cf. *Theologische Existenz heute!* 41–45). Bonhoeffer apparently took a somewhat different view of the church opposition's choice of Bodelschwingh as Reich bishop; see also Staewen's letter of June 14, 1933, to Charlotte von Kirschbaum, which said in part: "Even Bonhoeffer was not disturbed at this point by the Young Reformers' tactic in making the choice of a leader for the church part of a political platform, and said that Lutherans could certainly support this bishop. . . . Bonhoeffer thus shares the view of people like Paul Fricke and Frede Fritz, who once discussed these matters here at my place, that all efforts must be devoted to forestalling the [German Christian candidate] Military Müller" (Karl Barth-Archiv, Basel). [Staewen referred disdainfully to Ludwig Müller as "Military Müller" because he had been a military chaplain in World War I.—LR]

[1.] EZA, 51/H II c 4; typewritten, from Berlin-Grunewald; unpublished. Reply to 1/57. The letter was addressed to Siegmund-Schultze in Geneva, since he had been forced to leave Germany on June 21, 1933, for political reasons (see Grotefeld, *Siegmund-Schultze,* 120–30). [See also John Conway, "Between Pacifism and Patriotism."—LR]

people there without reimbursing them for their full expenses.[2] I have been thinking of you a great deal since I heard that you had been suddenly taken ill,[3] and hope you will now be able to have a good rest.

With gratitude and my very best regards,
Yours sincerely and respectfully,
Bonhoeffer

64. Theses by the Student Members of the Young Reformation Movement at the University of Berlin[1]

The present situation in the church calls us to reflect upon our true faith, because the visible church may receive its structure only through faith in the forgiveness of sins.

I. Thesis: We see the Reformation understanding of the gospel as the only basis for any restructuring of the church. 93

The church of the pure gospel lives by faith in the forgiveness of sins alone and knows that it can be renewed by Christ alone through the Holy Spirit. The sign of church renewal is conversion to the pure proclamation and the awakening of the church-community to faith and prayer. The more resolutely it confesses Christ as its Lord, the more audible the voice of the church becomes. This confession includes the belief:

—that any person may be a member of the church, regardless of race or social standing;

—that any reduction of the gospel to a bourgeois confidence in God or a liberal moralism is to be rejected;

—that church offices are to be filled, not on the basis of political considerations, but entirely on the basis of spiritual ones.

[2.] Cf. 1/59.

[3.] Here Bonhoeffer uses the official excuse. Siegmund-Schultze himself gave the state of his health as the reason for going to Switzerland (World Alliance, *Annual Report*, 1932–33, 53).

[1.] EZA, 50/814; hectograph copy, with two comments in different handwritings at the end of the document: "July 4, 1933" and "Berlin." See also *NL*, A 38,2 (6,1); carbon copy. Previously published in *GS* 2:56–57. Without any directive from the Young Reformation movement leadership, "Fighting Leagues of the Young Reformation Movement" had developed spontaneously among the students in opposition to appearances by the German Christians at institutions of higher education (see *Junge Kirche* 1 [1933]: 41). According to information from Wolf-Dieter Zimmermann in a letter of March 26, 1995, this text was first formulated by a group of about twenty members of the "Bonhoeffer circle" on their own; they then edited it, with Bonhoeffer present (see also Zimmermann, *Wir nannten ihn Bruder Bonhoeffer*, 54).

II. Thesis: We wish to answer not to any church political party but rather to the whole church.[2]

Every true church member has a responsibility to the whole church. To be responsible means to bear the guilt of the whole church before God. Only those who are prepared, not to bring accusations, but to take the guilt of others upon themselves, are free of party bias.

III. Thesis: We believe that peace can return to the church only through our reflection together on the cross of Christ.

The loss of peace in our church is the expression of unforgiven guilt. It was on the cross that Christ brought about the forgiveness of sins and effected the peace of the church. Only the church-community that returns to the cross, in recognition of the guilt in which all its members share, will find peace.

Based on this theological consideration, the following is our position in the current situation:

We reject

—any intervention by the state in the church[3] that moves the church away from its true nature;

—the authoritative influence on the restructuring of the church by persons who stand outside the church;

94 —the spiritual leadership of Hossenfelder, of Hoff,[4] and of all those who do not proclaim the gospel in all its purity.

We demand

—the withdrawal of the state commissioners and the restoration of the general superintendents to their pastoral offices;

[2.] [This is a reference to factions within the church that represented different positions regarding church politics. The editors thank Ernst-Albert Scharffenorth for this clarification.—LR]

[3.] By order of Bernhard Rust [Prussian minister for education and cultural affairs—LR] on June 24, 1933, August Jäger, who directed the church department in the Prussian Ministry for Education and Cultural Affairs, was made state commissioner for the regional Old Prussian Union Church. In late June and early July, he then appointed subcommissioners for all the regional churches in Prussia, suspending almost all the general superintendents of the Old Prussian Union Church.

[4.] On June 25–26, 1933, Jäger had named Joachim Hossenfelder as vice president of the Evangelical Consistory in Berlin. There is no documentation that Hoff, leader of the German Christian Student Fighting League, had been named to any position in the church at this point.

—the participation of our chosen Reich bishop, Dr. von Bodelschwingh, in the work of uniting the church;[5]

—a new proclamation of the gospel and celebration of Holy Communion in our worship, at the center of which is the forgiveness of sins.

We pray that God may grant the true communion of saints.

The Young Reformation Students

65. Declaration of the Berlin Pastors[1]

Berlin, July 6, 1933

Declaration of the Pastors of Greater Berlin

On the occasion of the appointment of a state commissioner for the Evange-
lical Church of Prussia,[2] and impelled by our responsibility as preachers of 95
the word of God, we wish to make the following declaration:

1. For us it is self-evident that the Evangelical Church is to serve our nation with complete devotion. But it can serve rightly only when the preaching of the gospel and the life of our congregations is not subjected to political pressure.

2. We demand freedom for the Evangelical Church not on the basis of equality with the Roman Catholic Church,[3] but as a matter of principle,

[5.] In taking office as Reich bishop, Bodelschwingh had also become moderator of the committee to craft a new church constitution; however, he resigned on June 24, 1933. On the entire situation, see Scholder, *Churches and the Third Reich*, 1:329–32.

[1.] BA Koblenz, R 43 II/161; carbon copy with cover letter of July 12, 1933: "To the Reich Chancellor, 106 pastors in Berlin have the honor to present a declaration on the occasion of the naming of a state commissioner for the Evangelical Church of Prussia. The original with the signatures has been presented to the Reich Minister of the Interior. A list of the names of the signatories is enclosed." Initialed and dated by Lammers on July 13, 1933. See also *NL*, A 38,4; photocopy. Previously published in *Mündige Welt*, 5:100–101, and *GS* 6:270–72. On July 5, 1933, Jacobi circulated this statement (which was to be addressed to the Reich president, the Reich chancellor, the Reich minister of the interior, and the Prussian minister for education and cultural affairs) to pastors in Berlin; he enclosed a note that stated: "It has been found that the above-named offices attach a remarkable amount of importance to such statements" (*Mündige Welt*, 5:99). The statement uses the wording of the declaration by Westphalian pastors from the Bielefeld synod of June 29, 1933 (K. D. Schmidt, *Bekenntnisse*, 164–65).

[2.] See 1/64, ed. note 3.

[3.] The Concordat between the Reich and the Roman Catholic Church was agreed on July 8, 1933, and officially signed on July 20, 1933. According to Article 1, the German

because a church is truly Evangelical only if the Holy Scriptures are the unique source of its doctrine and its ethos. Only such a church is in a position to render true service to the state. Thus we demand full freedom for the church's message in the public sphere, including the press and broadcasting, and complete freedom to decide on the form [Gestaltung] for rebuilding the church.

3. We consider the naming of a state commissioner to be an unacceptable violation of the Evangelical Church's freedom.

4. The appeal of June 26, 1933, by the commissioner's appointed president of the Evangelical High Church Council,[4] is for us an infringement of our mission as preachers of the word of God, because it restricts us from showing God's word to be fully relevant to present events. God's word is also the measure of the actions that a church government may take.

5. We protest against the hindering of our general superintendents from speaking to their church congregations as their conscience dictates. We are resolved to persist in our loyalty to our suspended church leaders, and we
96 demand that they be restored immediately to their offices. In principle we are in favor of a renewal of the church leadership, but this must come from the church itself.

6. We object to the appointment of church bodies by the state commissioner, because such oppressive acts will necessarily do great damage to the life of our congregations.

7. In making these demands, we feel that we are in agreement with our Reich chancellor, being acquainted with his position on church questions from his program both in published form and in his speech to the Reichstag,[5] which we have gratefully welcomed.

Antoni, Babick, von Bargen, Bergemann, Bonhoeffer, Borning, Boy, Braun, Brandenburg, Breithaupt, Buchholz, Buhre, E. Bunke, H. Bunke, Draeger, Ebel, Ehrich, Freybe, Figur, Fischer, Fritsch, Gerlach, Goosmann, Graue, Habicht, Häfele, Harnisch, Hartmann, Heinecke, Heintze,

---

Reich guaranteed the church "freedom of confession and the public practice of the Catholic religion" (Nicolaisen, *Dokumente*, 1:190; see also Volk, *Reichskonkordat*, 144–46, and Scholder, *Churches and the Third Reich*, 1:399–401).

[4.] In this appeal, Friedrich Werner, whom state commissioner Jäger had just appointed president of the Evangelical Consistory in Berlin, had warned the pastors of the Old Prussian Union Church that they would be severely disciplined for any activity involving church politics (Gauger, *Chronik*, 1:8).

[5.] Cf. Hitler's *Mein Kampf*, for example, the quotation in 1/58, ed. note 34. In the government declaration made by Hitler on March 23, 1933, he assured the churches that there would be no encroachment on their rights and no change in their relationship to the state (cf. Nicolaisen, *Dokumente*, 1:25).

Herbst, Hildebrand, Hildebrandt, Hitzigrath, Hoffmann, Hollmann, Hollweg, Hülle, Huhn, Jacobi, Jeep, Kirchmann, Kittlaus, Klamroth, Kracht, Kröpelin, Kroppenstedt, Künneth, Kunzendorf, Kurtz, Lilje, E. Lindenmeyer, F. Lindenmeyer, Link, Magerstädt, Maresch, Mähl, Messow, Meumann, Moldaenke, Müller, Nebel, Nehmiz, Niemöller, Pankow, Pätzold, Petersen, Plath sen., Plath jun.,[6] Praetorius, Puttkammer, Quittschau, von Rabenau, Rocha, Röhricht, Rosenau, Schalke, Scharf, Schroeder, Schultz, Schulz, Schwebel, Schubring, Schwencke, Seeberger, Seedorf, Stephan, Stratenwerth, Tromm, Theile, Urbain, Vehse, Violet, Vogel, Werbeck, Werder, Wendland, Dr. Wendland, Wesenberg, Wieck, Wiese, Wilde, Ziemer, Zimmermann, Zippel, Backhaus, Schulze

66. To Théodore de Félice[1] 97

July 17, 1933

Dear Mr. de Félice,

I have just received word from Pastor Taul[2] that he would indeed like to come to the conference in Gland,[3] but that he cannot under any circumstances manage with the financial support proposed to him. Thus he would not be able to come at all. I would therefore like to suggest that, instead of two delegates from the Baltic, for neither of whom the subsidy would in any circumstance be sufficient, we settle for only one. In this way we can offer the entire subsidy allotted to the Baltic countries, 114 francs in all, to Mr. Taul. I would ask you urgently to inform both Mr. Taul and me simultaneously,[4] as soon as possible.

With best regards,
Sincerely and respectfully yours,
Dietrich Bonhoeffer

[6.] Crossed out by hand in this copy.

[1.] WCC Archives, Bonhoeffer box; photocopy of a specially preserved typewritten letter; from Berlin-Grunewald. See also *NL*, A 28,4 (4); photocopy. Previously published in *GS* 6:285.

[2.] Not in the Bonhoeffer *Nachlaß*, but see 1/49.

[3.] See 1/61.

[4.] See 1/76.

67. To Erwin Sutz[1]

July 17, 1933

Dear Mr. Sutz,

Now the semester is almost over, and you have not yet received any reply to your kind letters.[2] Please forgive me, but I think you know yourself why it had to be so. I have been completely absorbed with what is going on in the church. We are now about to come to a decision, which I think will be of
98 the utmost church-political significance. There is no doubt in my mind that the victory will go to the German Christians,[3] and this will very quickly bring into view the contours of the new church, and the question will be whether we can even support it as the church. I am afraid, though, that we are crumbling gradually but steadily, that we no longer have the strength to act together. Then we will be back to small, unauthorized gatherings.

By the way, in May I, too, was preaching on the golden calf, on the church of Aaron and the church of Moses;[4] this is becoming incredibly relevant for today. On the Sunday of the election, I am going to preach on Matthew 16:18.[5]

A few days ago Barth was briefly here in Berlin.[6] He told me how much he enjoyed your visit in Bonn. My personal future may be about to reach a decisive turning point before long. It has been proposed that I go to London, as a German pastor with a special responsibility for ecumenical work.[7] I'm considering it seriously, since I think that precisely in view of the possibilities that have to be envisaged for the church here, it could turn out to be immensely important to establish a close contact with the English

---

[1.] Literary estate of Erwin Sutz, Herrliberg, Switzerland; typewritten, signed with the typed initials "D.B." (perhaps a typewritten copy of the original that has been lost); from Berlin-Grünewald. See also *NL*, A 29,4 (12); copy, and the appendix to *NL*, 29,4; photocopy of a typewritten text from the literary estate of Erwin Sutz; reprinted in *GS* 1:38–39.

[2.] These letters not extant.

[3.] In the July 23, 1933, church elections set by the state. [The Reich law that set the date for these elections was newly enacted and controversial (the state had not previously been involved in church elections); this was the basis for the subsequent argument by the church opposition that the elections were not legitimate. Cf. Helmreich, *German Churches under Hitler*, 140–41.—LR]

[4.] Cf. the sermon of May 28, 1933, on Exodus 32 (3/7).

[5.] Cf. 3/8.

[6.] Barth was called to Berlin on July 2, 1933, to advise Hermann Hesse, the Reformed representative, on the negotiations on a constitution for the German Evangelical Church (Busch, *Karl Barth*, 227–28).

[7.] Heckel had made this proposal to Bonhoeffer (cf. 1/70).

churches. What would you think? Or do you have a nice professorship to be filled there in Switzerland that would be open to me? I may be coming to Geneva at the end of August[8] but don't know yet for sure.

I am in a great hurry, so I'm obliged to be brief.

With greetings and all best wishes,
Yours as ever,
D.B.

68. From Willy Fries[1] 99

July 17, 1933

Dear Mr. Bonhoeffer,

I would like to thank you again most sincerely for the evening on which I had the honor of becoming acquainted with you, in the midst of a central issue of concern to us.[2] Please allow me to take the liberty of sending you a work of mine that appeared this spring.[3] It is an attempt to urge calm.

Very respectfully yours,
Willy Fries

69. Circular Letter "To Members and Friends of the Young Reformation Movement"[1]

It is of utmost importance that we receive precise information on the degree to which the independence of election preparations and the election itself have been compromised. We therefore ask all our members and friends to let us know *immediately* when interference of any kind occurs in their congregations or in others known to them. This includes especially threats from Nazi party groups and directives given by them in which they or their

[8.] To the international youth conference, August 29–September 4, 1933, in Gland by Lake Geneva.

[1.] *NL*, C 24; handwritten postcard, from Berlin-Wilmersdorf; unpublished.

[2.] The specific context here is unknown. In a brief autobiographical statement written later, Fries emphasized that Bonhoeffer "was his teacher for a short time" in Berlin. Fries, *Bilder im Sturm*, 37.

[3.] Fries sent Bonhoeffer his book *Gottlose*, which according to the copyright page had already been published in 1932 (see also *NL-Bibl.* 9, no. 10).

[1.] *NL*, A 38,3 (1); hectographed. Previously published in *GS* 2:58–59. The date is presumed to be July 18, 1933.

agents identify themselves with the "German Christian" list.[2] It is urgent and essential that full and precise details be given. It is possible to contest the election on the basis of the church laws for local church elections, which
100 also apply here.[3] We ask you to provide, besides a precise description of what took place and any newspaper clippings, a specific explanation of the violation of the election law that occurred. These protest statements must be received in multiple carbon copies by July 26, 1933, at the latest, at the office of the Young Reformation movement, Berlin-Dahlem, Ladenbergstraße 20.

We further ask you please to take note of the following agreement and in every case to comply with its content:

To all pastors who support the
"Gospel and Church" candidates' list:

This afternoon a discussion took place between the undersigned and officials of the Gestapo.[4] In consequence of this discussion, we urgently request all colleagues to destroy all privately produced leaflets and to distribute only those received from our Reich office, in order to avoid trouble both for yourselves and for our office, and to ensure that the election takes place in accordance with regulations. There must not under any circumstances be leaflets in circulation that still bear the title "List of the Evangelical Church."

Signed
Jacobi
Dr. Bonhoeffer

[2.] On the influences exerted on the election preparations in favor of the German Christians, see *Mündige Welt*, 5:102–3; *DB-ER*, 293–97; and especially Scholder, *Churches and the Third Reich*, 1:441–47.

[3.] According to Article 143 of the Church Congregational Election Ordinances of May 22, 1928. *Kirchliches Gesetz- und Verordnungsblatt* 1 (1928): 182.

[4.] Cf. *DB-ER*, 295–96 (dated there as the morning of July 18, 1933). Rudolf Diels, head of the Prussian Gestapo, accepted Jacobi's suggestion that the candidates' list of the Young Reformation movement be renamed "Gospel and Church," following an injunction that had just been obtained by the German Christians against a listing under the title "Evangelical Church" (*Junge Kirche* 1 [1933]: 60). Bonhoeffer must have been referring to this conversation when he wrote Siegmund-Schultze on November 6, 1933, that "on the occasion of the church election" he and a colleague had been threatened "by the highest police authority" with being sent to a concentration camp (*DBWE* 13:30).

70. To Friedrich Singer[1] 101

Berlin, July 19, 1933

Dear Colleague:

I am taking the liberty of writing to you with an inquiry and a request. In response to the inquiry from High Consistory Councillor Heckel, I should very much like to come to Sydenham, if you will have me. By this same mail you will receive a letter from Councillor Heckel, giving you information about me.[2] He has asked me to make a brief trip over to see you, if at all possible very soon. Since I shall be in Luxembourg at the end of next week,[3] if convenient for you I should like to come over briefly from there to you in London. Would you please be so kind as to let me know by air mail whether it would suit you for me to visit on Monday and Tuesday, the thirty-first [July] and first [August], and whether we could then discuss all questions with regard to the Sydenham pastorate? I would be staying with an English friend in London.[4]

I would be especially grateful for a reply by return mail, since I am leaving Sunday noon[5] and will be difficult to reach after that. Perhaps you would also be so kind as to send the air mail letter by express; then I think I would get it by Saturday evening.

In the hope of making your acquaintance soon, I remain

Sincerely and respectfully yours,
Dietrich Bonhoeffer

71. From Theodor Heckel to Friedrich Singer[1] 102

Berlin-Charlottenburg 2, July 19, 1933

Dear Colleague:

The various letters received from you in the last few days will be attended to by our office as soon as possible. I hope it will fully reassure you to know one

---

[1.] *NL* A 39,1 (1); typewritten. Previously published in *GS* 2:120.

[1.] 1/71.

[3.] For the Franco-German youth meeting, which was to be held at the end of July 1933 in Chaintréauville, France (cf. 1/61, ed. note 3).

[4.] Identity unknown.

[5.] This was July 23, 1933, the Sunday of the church elections.

[1.] Archives of Jørgen Glenthøj, Åbyhøj, Denmark; photocopy of lost typewritten letter. See also *NL*, A 39,3 (1); typewritten copy. Previously published in *GS* 2:121. [The correspondence mentioned in the first paragraph was recently found and is now part of the

thing—that a decision on your request was sent from here over a week ago but obviously did not reach you. In that letter we informed you that we fully agree with your suggestion that a temporary clergyman be sent, etc. You will receive a reformulation of all this, together with a reply to your most recent letters, in the next few days.

I would like to take this opportunity to communicate the following to you personally. A most outstanding younger clergyman is available as your successor. He is a student chaplain, has already been in America as an exchange student, then as an assistant pastor in Spain, and speaks various languages. Besides, he fulfils, at least halfway if not completely, one desire of yours, in that he is 50 percent Württemberger; his father comes from Württemberg.[2] This colleague is coming over there sometime in the next few weeks—he will write to you personally—and would very much like to have contact with you.[3] I would be very glad if you could also make it possible for him to meet the gentlemen on the congregational council, so they could get an impression of this clergyman, whom I personally like very much and who has proved himself here in various situations. That he is unmarried could be an additional, particularly Pauline advantage.[4]

I am sharing this with you personally in the hope that it will help the situation,
103 and to personally help you, as far as I can, in finding a successor. Please also tell the gentlemen on the congregational council that we will completely follow their wishes, and please explain to them why things have happened in this way; it was not our fault here in the office.

I assure you that I am always at your disposal for a satisfactory solution to the question at hand, and remain,

Yours respectfully,
Heckel

Bonhoeffer collection at the Staatsbibliothek, Berlin (*Nachlaß* 299). It includes Singer's letter of May 23, 1933, to Hermann Kapler, president of the German Evangelical Church Committee, as well as Singer's letters to the committee dated June 19, 1933; July 14, 1933; and July 17, 1933. Singer also wrote a reply to Heckel on July 31, 1933.—LR]

[2.] [A region in southwest Germany.—LR]

[3.] Cf. 1/70.

[4.] Cf. 1 Cor. 7:1 and 7. In his letter of June 19, 1933, Singer had recommended that an unmarried man be sought as his successor, apparently because of the primitive state of the plumbing in the London parsonage (*Mündige Welt*, 5:113).

72. From Arthur Burroughs [Bishop of Ripon][1]

The Palace, Ripon, 21st July, 1933

My dear Bonhoeffer,

You give no address and I hope the one we have filed from last year still serves.[2] Your enclosure[3] I am sending on at once to a Committee just formed in connection with Leeds University,[4] which is making an appeal, a copy of which I enclose.[5] As you will see, the Archbishop of York[6] is President and I am on the Committee. No doubt there will be many cases before us, but I hope your friend[7] may at least be favourably considered.

Yes, I am hoping to be at Gland,[8] though it is not quite certain, and I most particularly hope that you will be there, with a Delegation from Germany. If this falls through, the Conference will be robbed of a great part of its value at the present time.

As to the move suggested to you, it is only you who know how far you would be accepting a narrower sphere of influence by leaving the Student World of Berlin, or on the contrary giving yourself freer scope for development and wider experience. What you say about the disinclination in Germany at present for the 104
goods the World Alliance seeks to supply[9] is perhaps a sufficient reason for coming to England, where you might be available as an interpreter of Germany at a time when such interpreters are badly needed. Anyhow, I personally should be delighted to think we might meet more often, and I shall be anxious to hear your final decision.

[1.] *NL*, A 39,2 (4); typewritten. Previously published in *GS* 2:121–22. Reply to a letter from Bonhoeffer; Bonhoeffer's original letter not extant. Document in original English.

[2.] This letter was sent to the World Alliance address, 44 Georgenstraße, Berlin NW7.

[3.] Undetermined.

[4.] Refers to the Leeds Academic Assistance Committee, which collected funds to support academics who had fled Germany (according to information from Keith Clements in a letter of March 13, 1995).

[5.] Not included in the Bonhoeffer *Nachlaß*.

[6.] William Temple.

[7.] This probably refers to Lothar Richter, who, as the files of the Leeds Assistance Committee show, applied to Burroughs, mentioning Bonhoeffer's name and asking about the possibility of a position at Leeds University (according to information from Keith Clements in a letter of March 13, 1995).

[8.] At the international youth conference, which was to be held August 29 to September 4, 1933.

[9.] [The World Alliance (for Promoting International Friendship through the Churches) was, together with Life and Work and Faith and Order, a branch of the ecumenical movement. Ripon's reference to the "goods the World Alliance seeks to supply"

I have exchanged letters occasionally with Ludwig Simon, and wish we might have him at Gland again.

With best wishes, I am Yours very sincerely,
Arthur Ripon[10]

73. From Friedrich Singer[1]

Forest Hill, London S.E. 23, July 21, 1933

Dear Colleague:

You are welcome to visit me on July 31 and August 1. Couldn't you also take the service on [July] 29?[2] The congregational councils did decide not to have "candidate sermons" and in accordance with this decision will not reimburse you for your journey, but perhaps it would be agreeable to you personally to take the services on Sunday, July 30, in both churches[3] (one sermon will suffice for both). If possible I will convene the call committee of both councils on the Monday,[4] so that you can have a conversation with these gentlemen. However, I urgently need to have a reply from you right away.[5]

Sincerely and respectfully yours,
F. Singer

---

but viewed unfavorably by Germany, was a reference to the liberal, humanist, interfaith, internationalist peace orientation that was then out of favor with German nationalists both within the churches and beyond them. Bonhoeffer himself found the theology of the World Alliance weak and had, a year earlier (July 1932), given a vigorous address at the youth peace conference at Ciernohorské-Kúpele, Czechoslovakia, "On the Theological Basis of the Work of the World Alliance" (*DBWE* 11, 2/14). He argued for a stronger self-understanding of the alliance as "church," on biblical and Reformation grounds, together with the courage to issue concrete, timely commands on the basis of the revelation of God in Jesus Christ. See also 1/101.—LR]

[10.] As is customary in the Anglican Church, the bishop signs with the name of his see rather than his family name.

[1.] *NL*, A 39,2 (1); typewritten. Previously unpublished. Reply to 1/70.

[2.] Probably a typographical error; July 30 is correct.

[3.] In Sydenham and St. Paul's. See also the flyer of July 25, 1933, with the invitation to hear Bonhoeffer's sermon on July 30, 1933, in the German Evangelical Church in Sydenham (*NL*, A 39,3 [6]). Bonhoeffer's sermon has not been preserved.

[4.] July 31, 1933.

[5.] Bonhoeffer sent a telegram on July 23, 1933: "Happy to take sermon arrive Friday [July 28, 1933]" (*NL*, A 39,1 [2]).

74. To Théodore de Félice[1] 105

July 24, 1933

Dear Mr. de Félice,

Whether I will be able to come to Gland from August 29 to September 4 is unfortunately not entirely certain.[2] At the moment I am just asking [for] a reply as to whether, in case of need, I might be able to send someone else to Gland to represent me as youth secretary, or whether that is not possible. It concerns mainly questions of finance.

As to the meeting with Toureille and friends, I was obliged to cancel at the last moment due to urgent circumstances, which I will explain to you at some point.[3]

Might I please ask for a reply very soon to my inquiry regarding Taul?[4]

With kind regards and best wishes,
Yours sincerely and respectfully,
Bonhoeffer

75. From Emil Karow[1]

[Berlin-]Charlottenburg, July 26, 1933

Dear Brother Bonhoeffer,

For the trip that you are planning,[2] I wish you all the best. I'm glad for you to have some time off for a rest. During the past weeks we have all suffered even 106
more from psychological tension than from the physical strain. If you should

[1.] WCC Archives, Bonhoeffer box; photocopy of a specially preserved letter. See also *NL*, A 28,4 (5); photocopy. Previously published in *Mündige Welt*, 5:65, and *GS* 6:285–86.

[2.] To the international youth conference (see also 1/80).

[3.] During the week before the church elections (of July 23, 1933), Bonhoeffer canceled his attendance at the German-French youth meeting, which was planned for the end of July (*DB-ER*, 298); see also 1/70, ed. note 3.

[4.] See 1/66 and 1/76.

[1.] *NL*, A 30,1 (12); typewritten. Previously published in *GS* 2:122–23. Reply to a request for leave (not found) from Bonhoeffer.

[2.] From what follows, it is not clear whether Bonhoeffer had fully informed Karow about his travel plans (to London and from there to Bethel). On August 5, 1933, after his interview at the Sydenham and St. Paul's Churches in London (*DB-ER*, 298), Bonhoeffer went to Bethel [an institution for epileptics in Bielefeld, Westphalia, that had been founded by Bodelschwingh's father—LR] for a preliminary conversation with Bodelschwingh and Merz about the Bethel confession (Carter, *Confession at Bethel*, 71; and C.-R. Müller, *Bekenntnis und Bekennen*, 18; see also 1/77, 1/79, 1/86).

receive this letter before you go to Bethel, please give my best regards to Dr. von Bodelschwingh. Whenever I pass by the house in which he was living a short time ago,[3] I cannot help having painful thoughts. That he was never installed as Reich bishop, and as things are now, never will be,[4] is one of those worrying experiences about which one can only ask why. These times weigh heavy on our shoulders. God alone knows the way that will lead us to the light.

With best regards,
Yours sincerely,
Karow

76. From Théodore de Félice[1]

Le Chambon sur Lignon (H[au]te-Loire), July 27, 1933

Dear Sir,

Already on the twentieth I passed on to Mr. Burlingham your request concerning Taul, because in fact only Mr. Burlingham has the final say in granting subsidies.

If there are financial reasons that prevent you from going to Gland,[2] you can naturally send someone else in your place.

With the same delivery I also received a letter from someone who signed himself Gerhardt Schmidt, Artilleriestrasse 15, Berlin 24, and who asked me for some information on Gland; I replied to his letter and told him to contact you to determine if he could receive a subsidy; he didn't ask me that by the way.

107 I have already learned from Toureille, to my regret, that the planned meeting[3] is impossible. As I had to write anyway to our president, the bishop of Ripon, I let him know.

If you have need of writing me, please note the address at the top of this letter, which, for various reasons, will be my provisional address until around the twenty-fifth of Sept[ember].

I extend my best regards to you, dear sir,
[Théodore de Félice]

[3.] During his brief tenure as Reich bishop, Bodelschwingh lived in Karow's immediate neighborhood, at Marchstraße 2 in Berlin-Charlottenburg (near the present-day Ernst-Reuter-Platz).

[4.] Because the German Christians had won the church elections of July 23, 1933, there was now no doubt that they would have a majority in the National Synod and would be able to get their candidate, Ludwig Müller, confirmed as Reich bishop.

[1.] WCC Archives, Bonhoeffer box; carbon copy; unpublished. Reply to 1/74.

[2.] Félice apparently misunderstood Bonhoeffer's question (see 1/74).

[3.] Refers to the Franco-German youth meeting in Chaintréauville.

77. From Berlin Seminarians to Friedrich von Bodelschwingh[1]

Berlin, July 31, 1933

Dear Pastor von Bodelschwingh:

As a group of young theology students who have seen you as our leader[2] in the church struggle of the last few weeks, we would like to turn to you with a request. We are aware that many people in the ministry and congregations throughout the Reich are concerned about the recent developments in our church, and feel ourselves responsible for making sure that its Christian and ecclesial substance—in the proclamation of the Word and in its life—are not compromised.

We would be grateful if you would convene all these circles so that the struggle is not made harder to bear through isolation than it already is. It is not an established organization that is needed but rather a connection through which each can know what others are doing and above all have a firm sense that we are all working toward the same end.

We would regard it as very desirable if our fundamental wish for our proclamation and, to the extent necessary, our opposition to the men who have now taken over the church's leadership, could be emphasized in the form of a *confession*. This confession would need to be a suitable tool for use in congregations, and at the same time serve as a firm guideline for our entire community.

We thought perhaps the confession should begin by expressing in present-day 108
language, in succinct form, and with easily graspable explanations and examples, the church's response to all the issues currently being disputed (Loci);[3] we also think that all the "loci" should be provided with annotations individually set off from the text, each annotation to include supporting evidence from the Holy Scriptures, from the sixteenth-century confessions that are still in force, and from selected writings of Martin Luther.

It was our thought that you, Pastor von Bodelschwingh, might consult on this with such men of our church who are close to you; for example, Professor Sasse of Erlangen, Lecturer Bonhoeffer of Berlin, and Pastor Jacobi, also of Berlin.

With sincere respect and deep gratitude,
Ulrich Seeger, p[astor], superintendent of studies; Dr. Otto Perels, pastor; Wulf Thiel, grad. theology; Alexander von der Marwitz; Dr. Jürgen Winterhager; Johannes Müller, grad. theology (currently vicar); Gerhard Schneider.

[1.] HA Bethel, 2/39–96, folios 3 and 3a; typewritten. Previously published in C.-R. Müller, *Bekenntnis und Bekennen*, 196.

[2.] Even after he had resigned as Reich bishop, Bodelschwingh was still considered the representative of the church opposition movement against the German Christians.

[3.] Points of doctrine (*Lehrstücke*); a technical term derived from Philipp Melanchthon's first Protestant "dogmatics," *Loci Communes*, of 1521.

78. From the Election Committee of the German Evangelical Churches of Sydenham and St. Paul to the Church Chancellery of the German Evangelical Church[1]

Forest Hill, London SE 23, July 31, 1933

Pastor Dr. Dietrich Bonhoeffer, currently a student chaplain in Berlin and lecturer at the university there, conducted services yesterday, July 30, in both of our churches and today was interviewed by our joint election committee. On behalf of both our congregations, Sydenham and St. Paul's, we request that the German Evangelical Church Committee wish to assign Pastor Bonhoeffer to us as of October 1 of this year, for the time being as acting pastor, for our two
109 churches.[2] We are unanimous in hoping that the provisional assent we have received will very soon become the confirmation of this clergyman as our pastor.

The Pastor: F. Singer

The Election Committee of Sydenham:
P. Voigt A. F. Haydorn

The Election Committee of St. Paul's:
G. Henne J. Streitberger W. Neubert

79. From Berlin Theology Students to Friedrich von Bodelschwingh[1]

Berlin, August 1, 1933

Dear Pastor von Bodelschwingh:

In the past few weeks, a group of young theology students in Berlin has participated inwardly and outwardly in the church struggle.[2] Under the present circumstances, it is more urgent than ever that we not become divided. We are therefore taking the liberty of asking you to assume the leadership in that which needs to be done now.

[1.] EZA Berlin, 5/1316; typewritten. See also *NL*, A 39,3 (3); copy. Previously published in *Mündige Welt*, 5:122.

[2.] Following a provisional notification dated August 15, 1933, the election committee received a copy of the church chancellery's August 31, 1933, letter to Bonhoeffer, as a positive reply (1/91; see also *Mündige Welt*, 5:123–26).

[1.] HA Bethel, 2/36-96, folios 2 and 2a; typewritten. Previously published in C.-R. Müller, *Bekenntnis und Bekennen*, 195.

[2.] See 1/55, 1/58, and 1/64.

As a guideline for our future work, the only possibility is a new confession that lays a foundation and also takes a position on the burning issues of today in the church.

There are two reasons why this confession needs to appear soon. First, it must push the whole church to the formation of a confession, and in this should decisively influence its content. But above all, the recognition or the rejection of our confession, when it is presented to the official church, will clarify our further position with regard to that church.

In our studies and in our lives, we have been more or less decisively influenced by the theology and the personal attitude of Dr. Bonhoeffer at the University of Berlin. We therefore ask you to call upon him, but also Professor Sasse of Erlangen, to do this work.

Furthermore, we consider it urgently necessary that our greatest theologian,
Karl Barth, take a parallel step with the Reformed church. We fervently urge you 110
to do everything you can to promote this as a joint endeavor.

There are a great many students here at the University of Berlin, but also at other universities, who take this same position, and would not fail to offer their cooperation and allegiance.

We pray for our church and keep faith in the promises of our Lord.

Winfried Maechler, student of theology, Berlin-Tegel, as is Christoph Harhausen, Herbert Jehle of Berlin-Schlachtensee, Ernst Tillich of Berlin-Steglitz, Albrecht Schönherr of Berlin-Friedenau, Hilde Enterlein of Falkenhain, Finkenkrug district; also on behalf of Ernst Block of Berlin-Lichterfelde, Lydia Giessler of Berlin-Eichkamp, and Inge Harding of Berlin-Dahlem

80. To Théodore de Félice[1]

[Berlin-]Grunewald, August 7, 1933

Dear Mr. de Félice,

To my immense regret, the state of affairs in the church here prevents me from attending the youth conference.[2] I am needed for the preparation of a confession at Bodelschwingh's,[3] and I cannot decline, as important as the Geneva conference would be to me. But I comfort myself with the thought

[1.] WCC Archives, Bonhoeffer box; photocopy of a specially preserved letter. See also *NL*, A 28,4 (6); photocopy. Previously published in *Mündige Welt*, 5:65, and *GS* 6:286.

[2.] It was to be held in Gland by Lake Geneva, from August 29 to September 4, 1933.

[3.] Refers to the Bethel confession (see 2/15 and "Concerning the History of the Bethel Confession").

that perhaps I will soon have the opportunity to work on ecumenical issues with renewed intensity and with much more time available, from a pastorate to German congregations in London.[4] So for the moment I must give up doing what I want. A friend of mine with experience at ecumenical conferences, Mr. Fritz Söhlmann, will come in my stead and participate as my rep-
111 resentative.[5] If you could be here and experience the situation within our church, you would understand that it is really not possible for me to come.

With warm greetings to all our friends, and all good wishes for a successful conference, I am

Yours as ever,
Dietrich Bonhoeffer

81. From Wolfgang Schlunk[1]

Tübingen, August 12, 1933

Dear Mr. Bonhoeffer:

If I had the possibility, I should be very glad to come to Berlin for the seminar outing[2] and to see you. From here, of course, this is unthinkable. But since I have to send my regrets, I should also like to try and express to you how often, and how very much, I have been thinking back over the semester. Not that I have very much to say in a positive vein, for in the end, the little that one has been able to learn and experience does not represent progress, something gained, but rather only shows what one does not know, or what one always forgets. The only positive thing is that you helped me to "see," even to see that aspect of human beings that is invisible and will forever remain so. The same thing is happening again to me now, as I am reading Prof. Barth's *Letter to the Romans*.[3] But one thing appears inexplicable to me: why do human beings only come forth out of themselves on such rare occasions, only to fall back right away into a

[4.] See 1/70.

[5.] According to *Mündige Welt*, 5:46, Söhlmann then astonished the Gland conference "with an impassioned speech in which he defended National Socialism all the way." [This was a surprise at the time because Söhlmann was the editor of *Der Vormarsch* (which became the journal *Junge Kirche* in the course of 1933), the publication of the Young Reformation movement and a theological journal that was often critical of the German Christians and Nazi encroachment in the churches. More recent research has revealed how nationalistic Söhlmann was; this bias was often reflected in *Junge Kirche* under his editorial direction.—LR]

[1.] *NL*, C 24; typewritten copy of letter not found. Partially reproduced in *GS* 6:266.

[2.] Cf. *DB-ER*, 322, where the seminar outing is dated at the beginning of August.

[3.] Barth's *Römerbrief* (published in English as *The Epistle to the Romans*), first published in German in 1919.

"couldn't-care-less" attitude (I don't know a better term), into boring inertia? Probably there is a theoretical explanation, but what help is that? It seems to me that in practice what we have to do with this question is to live into it; then, without realizing, we will get the answer from life and find ourselves living the answer instead of the question.[4] I'm not trying to propose a theology here. I only wanted to point out the danger of one's reaction after the semester is over, and how good it is to remind oneself of what was helpful during the semester. One ought not to talk out loud about it either, only "keep thinking about it, not talking about it." But I just wanted to say thank you, even if it can only be a 112
reminder of what was probably a much more genuine thank-you, last Sunday in Berlin.[5] The future will show me whether I had the right to write this letter.

Perhaps I should also send greetings to those whom I'd have been glad to see again at the retreat; you will know who they are.

Yours very sincerely,
Wolfgang Schlunk

82. From the Church Chancellery of the German Evangelical Church[1]

Berlin-Charlottenburg, August 15, 1933

I have the honor to inform Your Eminence that the joint Election Committee of Sydenham and St. Paul's Churches in London has written to us with the request that you be assigned to these two congregations as of October 1, 1933, for the time being as acting pastor for both churches.[2]

Their letter also expressed unanimity in hoping that the provisional assent already received would very soon become the confirmation of this clergyman as their pastor. On this basis, and on the basis of your contact with the two congregations,[3] I am authorized to proceed on the assumption that you are prepared to take up the position, for the time being as acting pastor to these two congregations, as of October 1 of this year. For this purpose, I would need a more explicit statement from you as to whether and in what way you think of quitting your present position, or what arrangement you have made in this

[4.] [Paraphrase of Rilke's famous statement from *Letters to a Young Poet*, 21.—LR]

[5.] August 6, 1933. The occasion is not given here.

[1.] *NL*, A 39,2 (7); typewritten. Previously published in *Mündige Welt*, 5:123. According to Article 7, §5 of the German Evangelical Church constitution of July 11, 1933, the chancellery was the highest office of church authority, replacing the previous Church Confederation Council (*RGBl*, pt. 1, 473).

[2.] See 1/78.

[3.] Ibid.

regard.[4] I would be very grateful for a reply to this question as soon as possible, since it is most important to avoid upsetting the two congregations in London in any way.

[Signed on behalf of] Gisevius

113 **83. From Wilhelm Lütgert to Georg Gerullis[1]**

Berchtesgaden, August 15, 1933

To the Minister of Education and Cultural Affairs
Your Honor:

I have just heard from my assistant, Lecturer Dr. Dietrich Bonhoeffer, that he has received a letter from the Church Confederation Council, inquiring whether he would be prepared to accept the pastorate to German congregations in London, which will be vacant as of October 1.[2] This position also includes a special assignment to ecumenical work.

The loss of Dr. Bonhoeffer from his teaching activities would be keenly felt by our faculty as well as by me personally. For a lecturer, he has been unusually successful in his teaching[3] and has had a profound influence on the students. Among younger systematic theologians, he is one of the most gifted, and this is not only my judgment but also that of my other colleagues in the department. He did not study with me but was already here as a lecturer when I took up my position at the University of Berlin.[4] He was Seeberg's student but then developed his own independent thinking under Heidegger's influence.[5] Dr. Bonhoeffer would like to be able to return to academic employment in Germany, and this wish is justified by his definite gift for scholarly work. He previously spent a year as a vicar in Barcelona, then another year at a college[6] in America. I consider it desirable, in the interest of the broadest possible theological education that is based upon more than simply reading, that particularly as a future academic theologian, he gets to know the churches and theology of England as well, since

---

[4.] See 1/83, 1/85, and 1/111.

[1.] BA Potsdam, REM 1262, Bl. 315–17; typewritten, stamped by the Prussian Ministry for Education and Cultural Affairs as received September 5, 1933. See also *NL,* D 5 (1); photocopy; unpublished.

[2.] Bonhoeffer's letter to Lütgert not extant.

[3.] See also the report Gertrud Staewen prepared for Barth (1/44, ed. note 1).

[4.] See *DB-ER,* 121 and 129 (1928–29).

[5.] At the beginning of the 1930s, Lütgert still considered Bonhoeffer a "Heidegger man" (*DB-ER,* 129).

[6.] [This is a reference to Union Theological Seminary, New York City, which is not a college but a graduate professional school.—LR]

he has this opportunity. I have therefore advised him to take a year or so of leave for this purpose, to which the Church Confederation Council will probably give its consent.[7] But he is afraid that if he leaves Germany now, this could hurt his prospects for future academic employment.

I therefore request that when he applies for leave,[8] he be given some form of affidavit, stating that the government also values the work he has done here 114
and does not intend to lose him as a future member of academia.[9] I fear that, without this, he might commit himself to the German congregations in England in such a way as to make his return to academic employment quite difficult. Given the dearth of a new generation of systematic theologians, this would be most regrettable.

With respectful greetings, Your Honor, I remain
Yours truly,
Dr. Lütgert

84. To Friedrich Singer[1]

Bethel/Bielefeld, August 15, 1933

Dear Pastor Singer,

Today I finally received the inquiry from the Church Confederation Council.[2] Now I am only waiting for the notice of my leave from the ministry.[3] But this will surely come, and today I must turn to you with a significant request. I have been invited to an important ecumenical conference in Sofia at the end of September,[4] and I should not like to turn it down. It lasts a fortnight.[5] Would it be possible for me to come on October 15 instead of October 1? Perhaps I am making it quite awkward for you with this request; in that case I would certainly come on October 1. But if this were possible, I should be very grateful.

[7.] See the letter of August 15, 1933, from the church chancellery (1/82).

[8.] Bonhoeffer's application for leave not found.

[9.] [University professors were civil servants.—LR]

[1.] *NL*, A 39,1; handwritten; unpublished.

[2.] 1/82.

[3.] See 1/85 and 1/91.

[4.] Meeting of the Central Committee of the World Alliance [for Promoting International Friendship through the Churches—LR], which was held in Sofia, Bulgaria, September 15–20, 1933 (cf. 1/101 and 1/103; *DB-ER*, 311–18); C.-R. Müller, *Bonhoeffers Kampf*, 57–60).

[5.] [As noted, the conference itself was not a fortnight but September 15–20.—LR]

Then there is another matter. I accepted, of course, with pleasure. But in view of the fact that I have some relatives in Germany in very depressed financial circumstances whom I have been helping regularly,[6] might I inquire once again whether there is some probability that the fifty pounds that was temporarily deducted could be repaid in the foreseeable future?[7]
115 It would be painful for me if, by going away, I left a few families here with significant worries. You will understand. May I please ask you to make sure this matter is settled before you leave? It is so difficult for me to do it myself.

My warmest thanks to you for all your kindness and your hospitality to me.[8] I wish you all the best for these last weeks and greet you as a brother, in gratitude.

Yours sincerely,
D. Bonhoeffer

85. To the Church Chancellery of the German Evangelical Church[1]

Berlin-Grunewald, August 17, 1933

Dear Sir:

For the invitation to me to assume duties at the two London congregations of Sydenham and St. Paul's, allow me to express my thanks to you. I am most willing to take up the position of acting pastor. With regard to my departure from my present employment at the university, I have already written to Privy Councillor Lütgert.[2] He expressed his strong wish to grant me only a temporary leave from my position as lecturer, and he has written

[6.] No documentation for this assertion has been found.

[7.] Bonhoeffer was paid directly by the London congregations.

[8.] During his visit at the end of July–beginning of August (see 1/73).

[1.] EZA Berlin, 5/1316; handwritten. Previously published in *Mündige Welt*, 5:124, and *GS* 6:287. Reply to 1/82. This letter was presumably written from Bethel, where Bonhoeffer was staying during the drafting of the Bethel confession (see 2/15 and "Concerning the History of the Bethel Confession").

[2.] Letter not extant, but see Lütgert's letter to Gerullis (1/83). [Privy councillor was an honorary title at the university.—LR]

to the ministry stating this wish. General Superintendent Karow has also been informed,[3] and I will write to him again.[4] He has already given his consent.

Yours sincerely and respectfully,
Dietrich Bonhoeffer

86. To Julie Bonhoeffer[1] 116

August 20, 1933

Dear Grandmama,

Here I am writing again to wish you a happy birthday, and I had been so sure that this time I would be able to come over at least for the day. But we have not yet finished our work,[2] and it probably won't even be finished by Wednesday[3] evening. However, I hope I will still be able to come up on Thursday[4] for two days.[5] I have to be back in Berlin by Sunday.[6]

¶I hope you will have nice weather for your birthday party this Monday.[7] With the great-grandchildren there as well, you will surely have a delightful time. I also hope you have had such a good rest these last few weeks that you have been able to put the recent disturbances behind you to some extent and can look forward to going back to Berlin. Then we will have at least part of September together in Berlin, in any case, before I go to London. I am trying to postpone my departure to October 15.[8] I accepted the position without committing myself to a specific time.

The time here in Bethel has made a deep impression on me. Here we have a part of the church that still knows what the church can be about and what it cannot be about. I have just come back from the worship service. It is an extraordinary sight, the whole church filled with crowds of epileptics

[3.] Cf. 1/75 and 1/88.

[4.] Letter not extant.

[1.] *NL* A 28,1 (6); handwritten, from Bethel. Previously published in *GS* 2:77–79.

[2.] On the Bethel confession (2/15; see also "Concerning the History of the Bethel Confession").

[3.] August 23.

[4.] August 24.

[5.] To Friedrichsbrunn in the Harz Mountains, where the family was celebrating the grandmother's birthday at their holiday cottage.

[6.] August 27.

[7.] August 21, Julie Bonhoeffer's birthday.

[8.] See 1/84.

and other ill persons, interspersed with the deaconesses and deacons who are there to help in case one of them falls; then there are elderly tramps who come in off the country roads, the theological students, the children from the lab school, doctors and pastors with their families.[9] But the sick people dominate the picture, and they are keen listeners and participants.
117 Their experience of life must be most extraordinary, not having control over their bodies, having to be resigned to the possibility of an attack at any moment. Today in church was the first time this really struck me, as I became aware of these moments. Their situation of being truly defenseless perhaps gives these people a much clearer insight into certain realities of human existence, the fact that we are indeed basically defenseless, than can be possible for healthy persons. And it is just this abrupt alternation, between standing there healthy and falling down sick, which must be more conducive to this insight than being healthy all the time. Today in church I was constantly reminded of Rembrandt's "Hundred Guilder" etching[10] and the gospel stories it illustrates. There is nothing sentimental about any of this; it is tremendously real and natural. It knocks down some of the barriers with which we usually shut ourselves off from this world. Here it simply is a part of one's own life, as it is in reality. It is said of Buddha that he was converted by an encounter with a seriously ill person.[11] What utter madness when some people today think that the sick can or ought to be legally eliminated.[12] It is almost like building a Tower of Babel[13] and must bring vengeance on us. Anyhow, our concept of sickness and health is pretty ambiguous. What we see as "sick" is actually healthier, in essential

[9.] [Although founded to house and treat epileptics, Bethel was established (and remains, even today) as an inclusive community where both staff and patients live; there is a lab school and workshops where teachers and staff are trained in special education and occupational therapy. There is also an accredited seminary for theology students on the Bethel grounds.—LR]

[10.] The Hundred Guilder etching, dated around 1647–49, portrays several incidents in Christ's life (healing the sick, welcoming the children, etc.) as told in Matt. 19:1–2, 13–24. See Rembrandt, *Das Leben Jesu*, 89. [It hangs in the Rijksmuseum, Amsterdam, and is often found in books of biblical paintings. Bonhoeffer also refers to the symbolic power of this etching in a London sermon (*DBWE* 13:272) and the drama he wrote in prison (*DBWE* 7:41).—LR]

[11.] See, for example, Glasenapp, *Non-Christian Religions A to Z*, 44 and 104.

[12.] On July 14, 1933, the Reich government had issued the Law for the Prevention of Children with Hereditary Diseases (Gesetz zur Verhütung erbkranken Nachwuchses), according to which certain persons with inherited diseases were subject to compulsory sterilization (*RGBl*, pt. 1, 529).

[13.] Gen. 11:1–9.

aspects of life and of insight, than health is. And that the two conditions depend on each other is surely an essential part of the plan and the laws of life, which can't simply be changed to suit people's impertinence and lack of understanding.

Our work here is very enjoyable and also very demanding. We want to try to make the German Christians declare their intentions.[14] I rather doubt we shall succeed. Even if, at this point, they make concessions in their official formulations, they are under such strong pressure that sooner or later any promises made are bound to break down. It is becoming increasingly clear to me that what we are going to get is a big, *völkisch* national church that in its essence can no longer be reconciled with Christianity, and that we must make up our minds to take entirely new paths and follow where they lead. The issue is really Germanism or Christianity, and the sooner the conflict comes out in the open, the better. The greatest danger of all would be in trying to conceal this. 118

This has now turned into a long letter, and it's time for me to go to dinner. I wish you a good new year of life, dear Grandmama, and look forward to seeing you soon. My love to Karl Friedrich and Grete,[15] and love and gratitude to you from

Dietrich

87. From Erich Seeberg[1]

Berlin C 2, August 20, 1933

Dear Colleague:

I hereby grant your request for leave,[2] and I would like to express to you my sincere good wishes for your work in London,[3] along with my regret that we are losing you here in Berlin. I hope this will be a temporary situation. How much you are valued by this faculty may be clear to you from the fact that, at

[14.] See Hildebrandt's "Flyer on the Church Elections" (*GS* 2:59–61) and the rebuttals of the German Christian heresies in the Bethel confession (2/15).

[15.] Bonhoeffer's eldest brother and his wife (née Dohnanyi).

[1.] *NL*, A 39,2 (5); handwritten on letterhead stationery from the Protestant Theological Faculty of the University of Berlin. Previously published in *GS* 2:124.

[2.] Bonhoeffer's letter not extant, but see 1/111.

[3.] Cf. 1/82.

our last consultation on proposals for the chair in systematics,[4] you were mentioned by several members with great appreciation. I feel the need to take this opportunity to say this to you.

Sincerely and respectfully yours,
E. Seeberg

119 **88. From Emil Karow**[1]

[Berlin-]Charlottenburg, August 21, 1933

Dear Brother,

I had already heard here at the office that you had the intent to go to London as pastor in a German congregation.[2] For me it is very sad that theologians such as you feel that there is no room for them in the German church. However, your decision will have been influenced positively by the foreign connections created by your ecumenical work. So there is in your case at least an apparent connection. I can only express my heartfelt wish that this work abroad in service to German Protestants will be richly satisfying for you. Perhaps it will give you the opportunity to perform more valuable services for the Protestant church and for Germans than would be possible here. It would be a particular joy for me to see you back in a pastorate here at home in a few years. God be with you and bless you!

Yours as ever,
Karow

89. From Friedrich von Bodelschwingh[1]

Bethel-Bielefeld, August 26, 1933

Dear Dr. Bonhoeffer:

When I left for Soest,[2] I hoped I would still find you here upon my return. But by then you had already gone. So for the moment I can only express to you in

[4.] Refers to the search for a successor to Titius (*DB-ER*, 280). On January 1, 1934, the chair was accepted by Arnold Stolzenburg (not by Wobbermin as erroneously stated in *DB-ER*, 280).

[1.] *NL*, A 30,1 (13); typewritten. Previously published in *GS* 2:123.
[2.] See also 1/75 and 1/85.

[1.] HA Bethel, 2/39–46; carbon copy. See also *NL*, A 38,8 (7); photocopy; unpublished.
[2.] For the Westphalian church's provincial synod, which was meeting August 22–24 in the town of Soest.

writing my sincere thanks for your work[3] here during the past few weeks. I am confident in the hope that this work has equipped us with a good tool for carrying on, in a most profound way, the struggle that is ordained for us.

Unfortunately, when you left you were not reimbursed for your travel 120
expenses as you should have been. So I am having a postal money order sent to you for this purpose, by the same post, in the amount of fifty marks.

I remain as ever,
Yours sincerely,
[Friedrich von Bodelschwingh]

90. From Friedrich Singer[1]

London E 1, August 27, 1933

My dear Colleague:

I have replied in the affirmative to your letter of the fifteenth from Bethel.[2] The congregations had already decided that I would hold my final worship service on September 24, and that the congregations' farewell party for me would be held on the evening of September 25. Now this is postponed, and the question is, should I plan to hold my final worship service on October 8 or 15? The farewell event would then take place on the following Monday evening. After that evening I would prefer not to meet anyone from the congregations again. If this evening event takes place on the ninth, I would not expect you here before October 10, or if it is on the sixteenth, not before October 17. But it needs to be decided as soon as possible. So please let me know when you plan to arrive.[3]

Have you received my registered letter with your permit from the Ministry of Labour?[4]

Sincerely yours,
F. Singer

[3.] On the Bethel confession (2/15).

[1.] *NL*, A 39,2 (2); typewritten; unpublished.

[2.] See Bonhoeffer's letter (1/84); Singer's letter is not in the Bonhoeffer *Nachlaß*.

[3.] See 1/92 and 1/106.

[4.] The cover letter from Singer, which apparently included the entrance visa from the Ministry of Labour (see 1/92), is not in the *Nachlaß*.

121 **91. From the Church Chancellery of the German Evangelical Church**[1]

Berlin-Charlottenburg 2, August 31, 1933

Thank you for your letter of August 17, 1933. Following your telephone call and the information provided, your leave from your duties as lecturer at the University of Berlin has been granted.[2] I therefore inform you that this office is in agreement with your assuming the pastorate of the German Evangelical churches of Sydenham and St. Paul's in London, at their specific request, as of *October 1, 1933* until further notice. The Election Committee of the two congregations has been informed of the same.[3]

You are requested to inform the Chancellery of the German Evangelical Church as soon as you have actually taken up this post, giving your precise address.

I pray God's blessings for your work in London.

On behalf of Gisevius

92. To Friedrich Singer[1]

Berlin, September 1, 1933

My dear Colleague:

Thanks very much for your letter. I accept your proposal that I come to London on *October 17*, with special thanks, for indeed I have a *great* deal to do until then. I have received the entry visa.

With my best wishes and sincere thanks,
Yours respectfully,
(signed) Bonhoeffer

[1.] *NL*, A 39,2 (8); typewritten. Previously published in *Mündige Welt*, 5:124–25. Reply to 1/85.

[2.] See 1/93.

[3.] See *Mündige Welt*, 5:125.

[1.] *NL*, A 39,1 (4); copy of original lost in the files of the church office in Forest Hill. Reply to 1/90.

93. From the Prussian Ministry for Education and Cultural Affairs to Wilhelm Lütgert[1] 122

Berlin, September 4, 1933

Dear Professor Lütgert:

The granting of leave to Lecturer Dr. Dietrich Bonnhoeffer [*sic*] to go to England can only be considered by us as desirable, in terms of foreign policy at the present time. Of course, the ministry would welcome the return of Mr. Bonhoeffer to the university when he comes back from England, for God knows we do not have that many academic teachers who also have experience abroad.

Most respectfully yours,
Gerullis

94. To Henry Louis Henriod[1]

General Assembly finished, all Generalsuperintendents dismissed, only Teutonic Christians admitted to National Synod, Aryan paragraph now in action,[2] please work out memorandum against this[3] and inform press at once,[4] separation at hand,[5] further information in Sofia.[6]

[1.] *NL*, A 39,3 (5); typewritten. Previously published in *GS* 2:124. Reply to 1/83.

[1.] WCC Archives, box 284 (43); carbon copy with heading added: "Copy of a telegram received on the 5th of September at 10 p.m." Previously published in *GS* 2:70. Document in original English.

[2.] See the resolutions of the Old Prussian General Synod of September 6, 1933, which had already been anticipated by those of the Council of Elders on September 4, 1933. The Church Law on the Creation of the Office of Regional Bishop and of Bishoprics abolished the office of general superintendent; the Council of Elders, which now had a German Christian majority, decided that only three of the nineteen delegates to the National Synod could be non-"German Christians." The Church Law on the Legal Status of Clergy and Church Officials adopted the "Aryan paragraph" from the Reich law of July 4, 1933, and made it even stricter (see 1/58, ed. note 10). According to the new church law, even marriage to a "non-Aryan" could be grounds for noneligibility for employment or dismissal of clergy and church officials (cf. *KGVBl* [1933]: 141–44; see also Scholder, *Churches and the Third Reich*, 1:469–73). [*DB-ER*, 307, is in error on this point.—LR]

[3.] This was done in Sofia (see 1/101).

[4.] No documentation has been found on whether this was done.

[5.] For Bonhoeffer and his friend Franz Hildebrandt, with the adoption of the "Aryan paragraph" the General Synod had effectively brought about schism. For them, the next step was "resignations from office, beginning immediately" (*DB-ER*, 307, has "widespread resignations"; see also 1/96; 1/98; 2/14; 2/16; and Zimmermann, *Begegnungen mit Dietrich Bonhoeffer*, 63). [The reference, which is from the essay by Henrietta Bell, is omitted from the English translation of Zimmermann's book (*I Knew Dietrich Bonhoeffer*).—LR]

[6.] See 1/101, ed. note 1.

123 **95. Draft for a "Statement from Opposition Pastors"**[1]

According to the confession of our church, the church's teaching office is bound only to authorized vocations in the church.[2] The Aryan paragraph in the new Church Civil Service Law[3] has given rise to a legal situation that directly contradicts this fundamental confessional principle. It proclaims as church law a condition that is unjust according to the confession and that violates the confession.

There can be no doubt that the ordained clergy affected by the Civil Service Law,[4] insofar as they have not been deprived by formal procedure of the rights of the ministry, should continue to exercise in full the right freely to proclaim the Word and freely to administer the sacraments in the Evangelical Church of the Old Prussian Union, which is based on the confessions of the Reformation.

Anyone who assents to such a breach of the confession thereby excludes himself from the communion of the church. We therefore demand the repeal of this law, which separates the Evangelical Church of the Old Prussian Union from the Christian church.

124 **96. To Karl Barth**[1]

Berlin, September 9, 1933

Dear Professor Barth,

You have written that wherever a church introduces the Aryan paragraph, it ceases to be a Christian church.[2] A great many pastors today agree with

[1.] HA Bethel, 2/39–50; carbon copy, not signed, enclosed with a letter of September 9, 1933, from Niemöller to Bodelschwingh. The archival record also contains Bodelschwingh's notes on a September 7, 1933, telephone conversation with Niemöller with the same wording; this is the basis for dating it September 7, 1933. Bonhoeffer's participation in drafting this is confirmed in a letter of September 8, 1933, from Bodelschwingh to Lücking: "The text was drafted by him [Niemöller] together with Mr. Bonhoeffer and a few others" (Jürgen Schmidt, "Studien zur Vorgeschichte," 65n81). Previously published; reprinted in *GS* 2:70–71 and *DB-ER*, 309–10 (Bonhoeffer's and Niemöller's signatures added).

[2.] Cf. the Augsburg Confession, Article XIV, *Book of Concord*, 44.

[3.] See 1/94, ed. note 2.

[4.] [The reference here is clearly not to the German Civil Service Law of April 1933 (ordained clergy were not affected by that law), but to the parallel church law (*Beamtengesetz*) passed by the German Christian–led national synod, which affected church employees with civil servant status.—LR]

[1.] Karl Barth-Archiv, Basel; typewritten. See also *NL*, A 28,5 (3); typewritten copy. Previously published in *Mündige Welt*, 1:109–10, and *GS* 2:126–27.

[2.] See Barth, *Theologische Existenz heute!* 24–25.

you on this point. Now that which was to be expected has happened,[3] and I therefore ask you in the name of many friends, pastors, and students, please to let us know whether you consider it possible to stay in a church that has ceased to be a Christian church, that is, whether one may continue to exercise within it the office of pastor when that office has become a privilege for Aryans.

¶For the time being we have issued a statement in which we wish to communicate to the church government that by adopting the Aryan paragraph, the Evangelical Church of the Old Prussian Union has separated itself from the church of Christ.[4] We are now awaiting an answer as to whether the pastors who have signed this statement are to be dismissed, or whether one need not worry about saying this sort of thing. Several of us are now very drawn to the idea of a free church. The difference between our situation today and that of Luther, we might say, is that the Catholic Church excommunicated Luther, calling his theses heresy, but our church regime cannot do that because it totally lacks even the concept of heresy. So we cannot simply make our argument from Luther's position.

¶I know there are many who await your opinion, and I also know that most think you will counsel us to wait until we are thrown out. However, some of us have already been thrown out, namely, the Jewish Christians [Juden-Christen],[5] and the same will soon happen to others, on the pretext of reasons that have nothing to do with the church. What will the consequences be for us when the church is truly no longer one community in every place? What about solidarity among the clergy? When will there be a
moment when it is even possible to leave the church? There can be no doubt 125
that a *status confessionis*[6] exists, but what is the most appropriate way today to express what the *confessio* says?—that is not clear to us.

[3.] Resolution of the Old Prussian General Synod of September 6, 1933 (see 1/94, ed. note 2).

[4.] See 1/95.

[5.] [In documents of this era, "Jewish Christians" and "non-Aryan Christians" are the terms most often used to refer to Christians whose family ancestry was Jewish.—LR]

[6.] Approximate translation: "confessional situation," as distinct from the term *casus confessionis* (confessional case) found in the Formula of Concord of 1577. First used in 1930 by Hans Asmussen (cf. Kretschmar, "Barmen 1934," 142). [*Casus confessionis,* or the case of confession, is the more comprehensive term, referring to a struggle for the gospel that covers everything—teaching and confession, articles of faith and doctrine, even a way of life itself. "In *statu confessionis*" refers to a more specific cause of concrete confessional protest, in which such matters as church membership and rules are no longer matters of convenience and doctrinal indifference (*adiaphora*) but are matters in which Christian freedom and the very truth of the gospel is at stake. Both *casus confessionis* and *status confessionis* were debated in the *Kirchenkampf* (Church Struggle) and the Confessing

I am also taking the liberty of sending you a carbon copy of a draft confession that was made in Bethel, and which is to be printed shortly.[7] In Bethel I was expressly requested to ask you sincerely for your evaluation of and corrections to this text.[8] Please forgive us for these two questions, which will take some of your time. But these are the matters that are currently affecting the lives of thousands of our theological students, and which are beyond their capabilities—indeed, beyond those of all of us here. Thank you very much for all the help you can give us.

In deep gratitude and honest admiration, dear Professor Barth, I remain,

Yours as ever,
Dietrich Bonhoeffer

97. From Karl Barth[1]

Bergli, Oberrieden [Switzerland], September 11, 1933

Dear Colleague,

In reply to your kind letter, I would like at least to send you my greetings right away. The draft confession that you mention was not enclosed with your let-
126 ter.[2] But the other questions you ask are serious enough. I have been following from here all that has been happening abroad. Shouldn't we be almost grateful that it all seems to be pushing so energetically toward a crisis? But certainly the question of what happens then can make one's blood run hot and cold. Of course the General Synod's resolution[3] has turned the possibility I was con-

---

Church. In this letter to Barth, Bonhoeffer judges that already in September 1933, there can be "no doubt" about a *status confessionis*.—LR]

[7.] Refers to the "August version" of the Bethel Confession (see 2/15, ed. note 1, and "Concerning the History of the Bethel Confession").

[8.] The German editors were unable to determine why Barth did not receive his copy of the text directly from Bethel on August 31, 1933, like the other experts being consulted, and why Bonhoeffer did not send it to Barth until September 9, 1933.

[1.] Karl Barth-Archiv, Basel; carbon copy. See also *NL*, A 28,5 (6); typewritten copy. Previously published in *Mündige Welt*, 1:110–12, and *GS* 2:127–230. Reply to 1/96. Bonhoeffer answered Barth's letter only on October 24, 1933, from London (*DBWE* 13, 1/2).

[2.] Bonhoeffer had sent the "August version" of the Bethel confession to Barth separately (see 1/96). Barth received the text on September 12, 1933, and wrote Bodelschwingh the next day, thanking him because "you also want to hear from me about this" (Karl Barth-Archiv, Basel). On Barth's evaluation of the Bethel confession, cf. Scholder, *Churches and the Third Reich*, 1:458.

[3.] Of September 6, 1933 (see 1/94, ed. note 2).

sidering into a reality, at least in part. They do not seem willing to go as far as excluding non-Aryans from church membership, or in any case not yet. But this disposition with regard to officials and pastors is already unacceptable, and I, too, am of the opinion that there is a *status confessionis* here.

¶This will indeed mean, first of all, saying to the church government, or to the supposed or actual majority of church members that it represents, by direct communication but also by public proclamation, "In this respect, you are no longer the church of Christ!" And it is clear that this protest cannot be made once for all, but must be made again and again, until the cause has been removed—or until the church responds to the protesters by shutting them out or by silencing them. Thus the step you intend to take seems to me to be the right one. But whatever success it has, it will have to be followed by other appropriate ones. Moreover, I am indeed in favor of waiting to see what comes. If there is to be schism, it must come from the other side. Perhaps it will come immediately, in the form of a response to the protest on behalf of the Jewish Christian pastors. Perhaps this vain doctrine that now rules the church will still have to aggrandize itself through other and even worse errors and distortions. In that connection I have looked at a lot of German Christian literature since I have been here and can only say that I am expecting the worst in every way. It could well happen that the clash will come over an even more central point.

¶In any case one must allow the evil decision that has just been made to have its effect, that is, let the factual situation it has created speak for itself. If people keep on in this way, the day will come when the free church is simply there. Probably it is better not even to play with the idea beforehand. It is too great a responsibility to undertake in terms of wanting to "start" it somehow. I suspect that it is already being secretly mulled over in thousands of places! But we must be among the last actually to leave the sinking ship, if it comes to the point where we can no longer regard it as anything but a sinking ship. Perhaps then one
should not wait, under any and all circumstances, to be excluded or dismissed 127
from office. Perhaps one should then actually "walk out." But that should exist only as an *ultima ratio*[4] for us. In a very, very different sort of troubled situation in the past, in Dibelius's church,[5] we did not allow ourselves to be pushed out immediately, and this was right; instead we registered our protest within the church. Now, in Hossenfelder's church,[6] we are in any case called upon to

[4.] The "very last possibility."

[5.] Refers to the 1931 quarrel between Barth and Otto Dibelius about their differing understandings of the church (cf. Busch, *Karl Barth*, 208); see also Lessing, "'Selbstständigkeit' und 'Freiheit' der Kirche."

[6.] Refers to the German Christian–dominated church, with Hossenfelder as the spiritual vice president of the Evangelical Church of the Old Prussian Union and as bishop of Brandenburg.

make this our first act. Here, too, we shall never have cause to regret having assumed a highly active, polemical position of waiting. Of course I am aware that in doing so, we risk being forestalled by all sorts of characters appearing out of the woodwork with this or that wild new organization. But it will be worthwhile to resolve not to think in terms of tactics at this point, but rather to think, according to our best understanding and ability, in spiritual terms.

I am receiving more and more letters in response to my brochure,[7] almost all agreeing with me, and mostly from people I don't know at all, usually not theologians or theological students, but quite often speaking "in the name of many others." I think we can conclude from this that the supposed unanimity among the "church people" with regard to the present dominant trend does not exist. But heaven knows it's not the time to fight one rumor with another! We cannot be sure but that it would be useless even to start one at this time. This battle will be won by those who save their ammunition at the beginning, but who then know how to employ it ruthlessly and with unerring aim. One day, believe me, one day this whole Hossenfelder mess will disintegrate into so many atoms, leaving an unholy stench behind it . . . I have also read an issue of *Junge Kirche* on this,[8] with gratitude for all the news, but objectively I'm simply horrified at all the tiptoeing around and deceptiveness that is the order of the day here. Can't anyone see that the G[erman] C[hristians] will only laugh at opponents who speak and present themselves this way? God have mercy on the German church if the opposition within it, which is so direly needed at this point, doesn't make itself known with other points and principles, and above all with a very
128 different sort of language than it does in this honest but so timid and muddled way of speaking. I am curious to see what Mr. Lilje has to bring up against me, as he promises here.[9] For the moment I have no regrets about any of the sharp words I have written on this account.[10] I am writing you this to make it clear to you that, in any case, I consider only the most severely principled attitude as good enough to justify any such willingness to wait.

Now I am looking forward eagerly to your draft confession. I won't hide from you that the name "Bethel" makes me a little uneasy. I couldn't stand the middle-of-the-road line that Georg Merz was trying to hold in the most recent issue of

---

[7.] *Theologische Existenz heute!* which appeared in July 1933.

[8.] *Junge Kirche* had been published weekly since June 26, 1933 (nos. 1–14 carried the subtitle "Newsletter of the Young Reformation Movement"). Barth had the most recent issue, no. 11 of September 7, 1933.

[9.] An advance notice of Lilje's position appeared at the end of no. 11 of *Junge Kirche.* It was published in the next issue as "Theological Existence," by Hans Lilje.

[10.] In *Theologische Existenz heute!* Barth had included a critique of the Young Reformation movement (see esp. 30–38).

Zwischen den Zeiten.[11] I certainly could not be part of the "middle-of-the-road free church," which is the best I can expect from that quarter.

Perhaps I will try to write something again, sooner or later. But I am not yet to the point where I'm seeing clearly in my own mind what is actually happening and what needs to happen. I should be most indebted to you if you would keep me informed, from time to time, about what knowledge you have and what you are thinking.

Meanwhile, my very best wishes to you.
Sincerely yours,
Karl Barth

98. From Hermann Sasse[1]

Erlangen, September 12, 1933

Dear Mr. Bonhoeffer,

Your request of September 9 moved me deeply.[2] In my estimation, no step
such as the one that you are considering should be taken before the National 129
Synod is over.[3] If a schism is to come, then there must be a large number of pastors and church members taking this step, and not only in the Old Prussian Union Church, but also in the so-called Lutheran churches. I assume that it is the establishment of the Aryan paragraph that you see as a public violation of the confession, since it means that even the apostles of Jesus Christ, and moreover the Lord himself, who in the flesh was a son of David, would have to leave the ordained ministry of the Prussian church. This new law indeed separates the Prussian church from Christianity. It amounts to blasphemy against the Holy Spirit, which cannot be forgiven in either this world or the next. I am assuming

[11.] Literally, "Between the Times." Cf. Merz, "Mitteilungen und Hinweise." At the time Merz was lecturer in practical theology at the theological school in Bethel.

[1.] *NL*, A 28,7 (1); handwritten. In the empty space, Bonhoeffer noted titles from Luther's writings in indelible pencil: "A sermon on the destruction of Jerusalem, 1526 [actually 1525; *WA* 17/1:380–90]. What the temple of God is. A comforting sermon on the coming of Christ, 1532 [actually 1531; *WA* 34/2:459–82]. On the church, what, who, and where it is and how one can recognize it, 1540 [cf. *WA* 50:507]." This letter was previously published without these notations in *GS* 2:71.

[2.] Not found in Sasse's literary estate. Bonhoeffer had evidently posed the question to Sasse as to whether and when the decision to separate from the church was justified. See also 1/95 and 1/96.

[3.] The National Synod was to meet on September 27, 1933, in Wittenberg. However, it made no decision on the Aryan paragraph, out of concern about protests, especially from abroad (cf. Nicolaisen, *Dokumente* 1:130–32).

that this law will be extended to other regional churches and perhaps to the entire German Evangelical Church. The National Synod will show whether this is the case. This then would be the moment for large-scale collective action.

I would make the following suggestion to you. Send a description of the situation, with a request for counsel and for protection of the Lutheran confession, to Bishop Meiser in Munich, Arcisstrasse 13. Meiser is president of the Association of Lutheran Churches.[4] There must be an urgent final appeal of Prussian Lutherans to the Lutherans in the regional churches. Lay the obligation on Meiser's conscience, as Lutheran bishop, to stand fast until the very end for the Lutheran confession within the entire German Evangelical Church. Perhaps you should also send copies to Marahrens and Schöffel.[5] Here in Bavaria there's still time to fight. Perhaps a copy of this appeal should also go to the Lutheran faculties of theology at Erlangen and Rostock for their discussion and action. I have already arranged that the church Aryan law will be on the agenda of our
130 next faculty meeting.[6] The appeal must carry as many signatures as possible, and declarations of agreement with it must be sent subsequently. You must make the following case: that we no longer have a church government in Prussia that stands up for us, so you Lutheran bishops must do this. The undersigned should refer specifically to the Confessio Augustana,[7] or to the Lutheran confessions, not simply to the confession in general. With this document, the bishops—Meiser in particular—could take a stand at the National Synod, and make it decide whether the church of the Augsburg Confession is still tolerated within the German Evangelical Church.

That is my advice, the great advantage of which is that it challenges the church to take a decision on behalf of all of Germany. Then you would also have the satisfaction of having done everything possible. Its success depends on making a truly serious appeal to the Lutheran bishops' sense of duty to their office.

[4.] The Lutheran regional churches had met in Würzburg on May 27, 1933, and joined together "as a Lutheran branch within the German Evangelical Church which is taking shape"; Meiser was president of its six-person directorate (cf. Braun and Nicolaisen, *Verantwortung* 1:xxvii ff.).

[5.] These two bishops were considered at the time to be among the most prominent Lutherans.

[6.] Possibly Sasse already knew about the Hessian pastors' initiative that had asked the theological faculties in Marburg and Erlangen to give an expert opinion as to whether the introduction of the Aryan paragraph by the Old Prussian General Synod (see 1/94, ed. note 2) was correct according to the Scriptures and the confession. In response, the Erlangen faculty appointed Professors Althaus and Elert to draw up an opinion "on the admission of Christians of Jewish descent to offices in the German Evangelical Church," which was then published on September 25, 1933 (K. D. Schmidt, *Bekenntnisse*, 178–82). [See also Gerlach, *And the Witnesses Were Silent*, 39–41.—LR]

[7.] The Augsburg Confession of 1530, the most important Lutheran confessional text.

Our Bethel confession[8] could also be useful in this regard. But in the section on the Reformation it would have to speak very clearly about the Lutheran confession, which unfortunately is not the case as it stands. I will be discussing this with Merz tomorrow.

Enclosed is my article from the *Th[eologische] Bl[ätter]*.[9] It has been sent to Lutheran bishops both within Germany and abroad, as a call for help.

I am expecting a reply in the next few days from Dr. Nagel in Breslau,[10] with whom I have been corresponding.

I would also like to draw your attention to a publication by Elert, *Ecclesia militans* (Dörffling and Franke, Leipzig), especially the third section, [which] in my opinion has a far too favorable discussion of the new constitution.[11] Elert doesn't know the German Christians, as indeed many people around here who are still in a touching state of naïveté. Also I don't care for the tone of his response to Barth.[12] But you can see for yourself from this piece how optimistically leading Lutherans still view the situation.

Please remember me to our colleagues in Berlin, and put the above *modus procedendi*[13] before them.

As ever yours sincerely,
H. Sasse

99. To Wilhelm Stählin[1] 131

Dear Professor Stählin,

It was really too bad that I wasn't able to have a proper conversation with you the other day.[2] The next day some students came to me, on behalf of a larger group, asking that the question of a Protestant monastic community,

[8.] Cf. 2/15.

[9.] See Sasse, "Die deutsche Union von 1933." [*Theologische Blätter* was a journal. —LR]

[10.] Nagel was president of the Association of Evangelical Lutheran Free Churches in Prussia. [These were the Lutheran churches in Prussia that organized their own church, in protest against the union of Lutheran, Reformed, and United churches in the Old Prussian Union Church.—LR]

[11.] Refers to the German Evangelical Church constitution of July 11, 1933.

[12.] Elert had very didactically rejected Barth's criticism of the Lutheran position on the issue of the Reich bishop (*Ecclesia militans*, 50–51).

[13.] "Way of proceeding."

[1.] Archiv der Evangelischen Michaelsbruderschaft, Kirchberg; typewritten. Sent from Berlin-Grunewald, before September 14, 1933; unpublished.

[2.] This apparently refers to September 6, 1933, following the Old Prussian General Synod, when the Young Reformation movement and the "Gospel and Church" group met

perhaps in the form of a settlement, be raised more seriously. Since I know that this has been an idea of yours for a long time, I should be very grateful if you could let us know whether you have begun yet to move toward anything concrete. I could imagine that this might be the moment, more so than at any time since the days when the monasteries were founded, and I would be truly pleased to join you in thinking further about it.

With all good wishes, I remain,
Yours gratefully and sincerely,
Dietrich Bonhoeffer

100. From Wilhelm Stählin[1]

September 14, 1933

Dear Mr. Bonhoeffer,

I, too, was sorry that we had only such a limited time together, and that it was so disturbed by the fruitless negotiations in the group.[2] To come to a real agreement with you on working personally together on behalf of young people would truly have been more important to me than this church politicking.

There is only one answer I can give to your letter—to urge you as strongly
132 as I can to take a week off and come to our meeting in Marburg.[3] Years ago in Stockholm I had a conversation with Althaus, during which I urged him to come to our meeting in Berneuchen,[4] but he was going to Riga to give a lecture. Years later he said to me: That was a mistake in terms of church history, that I went to Riga instead of Berneuchen. Please, don't you make this mistake. We will be dealing not with statements or even with confessions but with bringing people together. Perhaps you can get the conference in Bethel[5] postponed or just not

---

together for a discussion but were unable to agree on a united course of action against the German Christian movement's resolutions (see 1/100; *Mündige Welt,* 5:87; Stählin, *Via Vitae,* 276–78; Scholder, *Churches and the Third Reich:* 1:480–82).

[1.] Archiv der Evangelischen Michaelsbruderschaft, Kirchberg; carbon copy; from Münster. See also *NL,* A 28,2 (9); typewritten copy. Previously published in *GS* 6:275–76. Reply to 1/99.

[2.] Cf. 1/99, ed. note 2.

[3.] The annual meeting of St. Michael's Brotherhood, which was always held around Michaelmas, September 29 (see also Stählin, *Via Vitae,* 313–32).

[4.] On this conversation between Stählin and Althaus when they attended the Universal Christian Conference on Life and Work in Stockholm in 1925, see Stählin, *Via Vitae,* 317.

[5.] The second conference of those involved in the drafting of the Bethel confession was supposed to take place at the beginning of October (but see "Concerning the History of the Bethel Confession").

attend this time. (I hardly need mention that we cannot postpone a gathering of sixty to seventy people who have been preparing all year for just this day.)

The idea of a monastic settlement is still hanging in the air. We have very definite concepts and plans for it, and last winter were at the point of carrying them out when the political upheaval[6] forced us to put off all such plans. We have need of a place where young theology students (I think also those not studying theology) can be trained to serve the church in a particular way. Three things are essential in this training: a strictly organized community life, which teaches certain particular forms of brotherly living alongside and with one another; physical work, if at all possible in garden or field, under the direction of trained deacons (in any case that is what we had arranged); and finally an equally strictly organized worship life, with quite specific meditative exercises that really offer people spiritual experience. We thought and still think that such a plan could be combined with running a retreat center, where church members could receive the sort of church schooling we try to offer at our retreats.

These are our plans. Finding an appropriate place is not as easy as it might look at first glance; we have accumulated a certain amount of experience as to what is required. It would be relatively easy to find a director. Finally, as to finances, we think the retreat center should be self-supporting with regard to day-to-day expenses, and even make a little extra money. The young men would have to live very simply, in work-camp style.[7] One or another of the regional
churches would probably be willing to employ a theologically trained person as 133
director. Almost the most important consideration would be to be able to start with a really useful first cohort for this monastery, who would set the right style from the beginning.

You see the extent to which we have already thought these things through. It would be a very, very fine thing if you could enter into this plan. So please, at all costs, come to Marburg.

Yours sincerely,
Wilhelm Stählin

[6.] Refers to Hitler's becoming Reich chancellor on January 30, 1933.

[7.] On Stählin's educational youth work for the Federation of German Youth Clubs (later the Federation of Christian German Youth), see also Stählin, *Via Vitae,* 179–87, 310–13. Voluntary work camps with educational goals had developed within the youth movement after 1926 and served as examples for the work camps set up by the Brüning government in 1931 to combat youth unemployment. The Nazis subsequently turned this into obligatory work service for men and women aged eighteen to twenty-five.

101. Statement by the Executive Committee of the World Alliance for Promoting International Friendship through the Churches[1]

Sofia, [15–20] September 1933

The members of the Executive Committee of the World Alliance meeting at Sofia, September 15th to 20th, 1933, taking note of the fact that racial discrimination in any part of the world, whether because of colour or on other grounds, constitutes a great danger to peace and the welfare of humanity, considers necessary an emphatic declaration, in which the super-racial character of the Gospel is avowed.

[1.] The World Alliance, Minutes of meeting held at Sofia, Bulgaria, September 15–20, 1933 (enlarged Executive Committee). Agenda item 27: "Racial Minorities," with the introduction: "The question of racial minorities was considered and after discussion the following resolution was *agreed to*." Document is in the original English. Previously published in *Handbook of the World Alliance 1935*, 36–37. The ecumenical bulletin *Die Kirchen am Werk*: *Mitteilungen* (no. 3 [October 1933]: 8ff.) contains the official German translation (giving different dates for the conference), which, however, is less precise with regard to the Aryan paragraph than the English version. Following a commentary by Siegmund-Schultze, *Die Eiche* printed another free translation into German (no. 21 [1933]: 379ff.). Regarding Bonhoeffer's evaluation of the statement and its possible consequences, see Bishop Ammundsen's communication of January 12, 1934, to Siegmund-Schultze (EZA Berlin, 51/L 6a/3): "In Sofia, as far as I know, the German representatives made no attempt to prevent a resolution being adopted, although it is true that they proposed that it be put in purely ecclesiastical rather than political terms. One of them, Dr. Bonhoeffer, even said to me that he was very grateful for the resolution; now he would really be able to go back to his friends with a result that was a valuable expression of Christian community and could strengthen their biblical stance." In a private report to Bell of October 5, 1933, Ammundsen wrote about Sofia: "The German delegates were Prof. Richter and the young Privatdozent at Berlin, Dr. Bonhoeffer. He is a splendid fellow, sincere, utterly earnest, decided not to compromise with antibiblical measures. He is on the left wing of the opposition. He had himself attended the Prussian General Synod and in a private circle he gave a description of the proceedings of this 'synod of robbers.' Our friend Dr. Brown turned quite round, when he heard how tyrannical had been the behaviour of the majority. Also Richter was after these experiences much more firm than at Zürich; both he and Bonhoeffer were courageous enough to vote for the resolution" (Schjørring, *Ökumenische Perspektiven*, 44). Another accent was set by Lord Dickinson in a letter of October 22, 1933, to Siegmund-Schultze: "To day I met Pastor Hoffman in London and he told me that Bonhoeffer has been appointed to a church in London. When we were at Sofi[a] I was informed that he had a choice between returning to Germany to be interned in a concentration camp or accepting some work abroad. He was doubtful whether he ought not to go home and take his chance; it is evident now that he thinks it best to remain away" (EZA Berlin, 51/D 8e/2). See also 1/110, Bonhoeffer's correspondence with Siegmund-Schultze (previously published in *Mündige Welt*, 5:66–68), and Henriod's notes in his diary (*GS* 2:73). On the World Alliance statement, cf. *DB-ER*, 311–16; Boyens, *Kirchenkampf und Ökumene*, 1:66–69; C.-R. Müller, *Bonhoeffers Kampf*, 57–60.

As members of many churches representing different cultures and com- 134
ing from many lands, but all united in a common allegiance to our Lord 135
Jesus Christ, we confess with shame our many sins of transgression against our brothers of other races and colour. In a feeling of brotherhood and responsibility with all the Churches of the world, while recognising the right of every country to safeguard the integrity of its own national life, we are nevertheless deeply concerned by the treatment inflicted upon persons of Jewish origin and connection in Germany.

We especially deplore the fact that the State measures against the Jews in Germany have had such an effect on public opinion that in some circles the Jewish race is considered a race of inferior status. We protest against the resolution of the Prussian General Synod and other Synods which apply the Aryan paragraph of the State to the Church,[2] putting serious disabilities upon ministers and church officers who by chance of birth are non-Aryan, which we believe to be a denial of the explicit teaching and spirit of the Gospel of Jesus Christ.

102. Draft for a Petition to the National Synod of the German Evangelical Church[1]

In the name of . . . pastors, I have the following statement to make:

The Prussian General Synod and other regional synods, through the introduction of the Aryan paragraph into the Protestant church,[2] have
placed themselves in opposition to the Christian confession. The work of 136
Paul is thereby negated and Jewish Christianity is reinstated. The Third Article[3] is thereby set aside, and a part of the church-community is designated

[2.] Following the example of the Prussian General Synod, during September 1933 other regional churches dominated by German Christian majorities had introduced Aryan paragraphs (see Scholder, *Churches and the Third Reich*, 1:476–79).

[1.] ZEKHN, 62/1020; typewritten, with corrections in various handwritings. A handwritten note in upper right-hand corner, "Bonhoeffer—Hildebrandt 24/9," confirms authorship and date. Previously published in *Mündige Welt*, 5:110, and *GS* 6:276–77. See also 1/105; *DB-ER*, 318–19; and Gertrud Staewen's communication of September 25, 1933, to Charlotte von Kirschbaum: "Bonhoeffer is extremely depressed about the situation in the church. Obviously, as he says, *almost* all those who a short time ago were willing to stand fast on 'G[erman] C[hristian]' matters are now in retreat, so that one can only fear the worst for the National Synod" (Karl Barth-Archiv, Basel).

[2.] See 1/94, ed. note 2.

[3.] [Refers to the Third Article of the Nicene Creed. The Aryan paragraph would effectively set aside the confession "We believe in one holy catholic and apostolic Church," as well as "We acknowledge one Baptism for the forgiveness of sins."—LR]

as second-class Christians. Ordinations are thereby revoked without a scriptural reason for doing so, and the pastoral ministry becomes a privilege.[4] Fraternal relations among Christians are thereby arbitrarily[5] destroyed. There is no room here for the preaching of the apostles, nor for our Lord Jesus Christ himself. We therefore cannot recognize a synod that proposes such a resolution as a Christian synod, nor a church that acts upon such a resolution as a church of Christ.[6]

Under the pressure of the use of force, all those who are determined not to waver in their insistence on the confession of the true church have joined together as a league of pastors whose purpose is to oppose to the last any such break with the gospel and to protest against any violation of conscience.[7]

We demand that the National Synod revoke the introduction of the civil service law in all the regional churches, and we submit the following petition:

That the National Synod, at this its first session, refusing to yield its competency to other authorities, immediately state its position on the resolutions of the regional synods with regard to the Aryan paragraph, and that it do so by roll-call vote.[8]

[4.] "and . . . privilege" crossed out by hand, thus eliminating a characteristic remark of Bonhoeffer's (cf. the reference in 1/96 to the ministry as "a privilege for Aryans").

[5.] "Fraternal relations among Christians are" changed (by Niemöller?) to "The communion of the faithful is"; "arbitrarily" crossed out.

[6.] This last sentence, "We therefore . . . Christ," crossed out.

[7.] On September 11, 1933, the pastors remaining faithful to the confession throughout the Reich had joined together in the Pastors' Emergency League, in which they committed themselves, among other things, to "protest unconditionally" against any violation of the confession as it stood (cf. Scholder, *Churches and the Third Reich,* 1:482). By September 21, 1933, the Pastors' Emergency League already had 1,300 members (Gauger, *Chronik,* 1:101).

[8.] The issue of the Aryan paragraph was, however, not dealt with at the National Synod (see also 1/105, ed. note 1).

103. Report to the Ministry of Foreign Affairs from the German Legation in Sofia[1] 137

Sofia, September 26, 1933

Re: Conference of the World Alliance for Promoting International Friendship through the Churches

From September 15 to 20, a conference of the World Alliance for Promoting International Friendship through the Churches took place in Sofia.

Participants in this conference of the World Alliance, to which all the churches except the Catholics belong,[2] were Lord Dickinson (England), Bishop Ammundsen (Denmark), Pastor Henriod (Switzerland), Dr. Atkinson (USA), Dr. Drummond (England), Pastor Jézéquel (France), Prof. Mihalescu (Romania), Rev. Sandegren (Sweden), Prof. Richter (Germany), Dr. Wissing (the Netherlands), Prof. von Boer (Hungary), Prof. Alivisatos (Greece), Prof. Janitsch (Yugoslavia), Prof. Zankoff (Bulgaria), Dr. Gay (Italy), Pastor Toureille (France), Dr. Bonhoeffer (Germany), Pastor Bouvier (Switzerland), Msgr. Visarion (Albania), Prof. Fischer (Austria), Prof. Adams Brown (USA). Also numerous members of the Bulgarian clergy participated in the various events.

This conference has no particular political significance, even though the participants obviously believed that they should be particularly zealous in discussing political issues, such as protection of minorities, disarmament, and the way the
race problem is being dealt with in Germany.[3] The Bulgarian delegates, how- 138
ever, discussed the issue of minorities particularly in great detail. I am enclosing

[1.] EZA, 5/81; carbon copy of a typed copy, sent by the Ministry of Foreign Affairs on October 12, 1933, to the German Evangelical Church. Previously published in *Mündige Welt*, 5:341–42. On the meeting, in which thirty people participated, see 1/101, ed. note 1; *DB-ER*, 311–16; Boyens, *Kirchenkampf und Ökumene*, 1:66–69.

[2.] The World Alliance did not see itself as either a confessional or a supra-confessional organization of churches. Its members were not the individual churches but rather national councils of churches, whose task it was "to enlist the Churches, in their corporate capacity, in a joint endeavour to achieve the promotion of international friendship and the avoidance of war" (*Handbook of the World Alliance*, 7). Roman Catholics were, in fact, not represented in the World Alliance. But a number of other churches were not represented either, such as the Russian Orthodox Church. In 1933 there were thirty-seven national councils in the World Alliance, representing almost exclusively Protestant churches in North America, Australia, and Europe (see *Handbook of the World Alliance*).

[3.] See 1/101. According to the self-understanding of the World Alliance, it was indeed not to concern itself with purely political issues. For example, with regard to the work of the Commission on Minorities, Prof. Alivisatos had warned against creating the impression "that the Alliance is dealing with politics" and recommended that problems be judged "from a purely moral and religious point of view." This led to a resolution

these speeches to the extent that they were published in the press.[4] Apart from that, little of the confidential deliberations reached the public eye. The two German representatives, Professor Richter and Dr. Bonhoeffer, who both left immediately after the conclusion of the congress, agreed to provide detailed information to the relevant offices in Germany after arriving home. The wording of the unpublished resolutions will be included in the information that Mr. Richter and Mr. Bonhoeffer will make available in Berlin.[5]

In discussions on disarmament and on the race question in Germany, the German representatives countered attacks against Germany from the French, Swiss, and Anglo-Saxon side. In response to the reproach that the present regime in Germany represented a hindrance to disarmament, Prof. Richter emphasized that Germany was not pursuing any goals involving aggression.

139 The debate on the Aryan question was especially animated. Here it was particularly the representatives of the Anglo-Saxon church who took the view that the Aryan laws in Germany are not reconcilable with Christian teaching and beliefs. And here as well the German representatives both tried to take a position that did justice to German interests. However, they told me that it was out of the question to persuade the congress that the use of the Aryan paragraph in the church was above reproach from a Christian standpoint. Nevertheless, the two gentlemen tried to prevent the adoption of a resolution that condemned the Aryan laws in general. Finally, a resolution was formulated that deplored the effects of the Aryan laws in Germany and spoke out against the use of these laws within the church.

---

somewhat later that "in accordance with the basic constitution of the alliance the question of minorities will be dealt with primarily from the religious and moral standpoint" (cf. Minutes of the Sofia meeting, agenda point 26 [published in *Handbook of the World Alliance*], and 1/101, ed. note 1).

[4.] These enclosures not found in the file. The Austrian Franz Fischer (Fischer, "Eindrücke von der Konferenz in Sofia") reported that the "World Alliance leaders in Bulgaria . . . knew how to give our conference a grand and official significance." In addition to a reception by the king of Bulgaria, there were events for mass participation by the local people, as well as "regularly appearing, detailed articles in the newspapers, often prominently reporting on our deliberations." The *Annual Report* of the Alliance said, "The meeting proved to be one of the most appropriate and successful means of propaganda for the ideals of the Alliance ever made in Bulgaria. . . . The whole press of the country reported fully on this meeting and also on the resolutions adopted by the Executive Committee" (World Alliance, *Annual Report*, 1933–34, 11).

[5.] No such written communications have been found. But see Max Diestel's [as German World Alliance Association President—LR] report of October 28, 1933, to the German Evangelical Church (*Mündige Welt*, 5:343–44).

The Bulgarian press was not especially well disposed toward the conference; it was repeatedly emphasized that the church should concern itself with things other than politics.

The venue being considered for the next conference in 1934 is Budapest.[6]

sgd. Clodius

104. From Wolfgang Schlunk[1]

Tübingen, September 26, 1933

Dear Mr. Bonhoeffer,

I cannot leave your letter[2] unanswered, even at the risk of not knowing what to say. Above all I must tell you how surprised I was that you took the time to write to me, and how grateful, if that is the right word, for your speaking openly, the way you have always done with us, letting us share in this one great concern. You gave only a slight indication of it, but that said clearly enough that all was not in the letter as it stood, but rather between the lines. I can well imagine how long the time must seem to you since the semester ended. You have become 140
a different person since then. How right you are to say that we down here are completely outside history in the making.[3] We aren't experiencing it along with you; all we do is read fine reports in the newspapers, the background of which not many people will recognize. If you up there are having a schism, it will be the same as in earlier times, heresy being equivalent to a crime against the state. But what use would it be? Our Christians here don't have the courage to take a stand, that is, only a few would dare to follow; most wouldn't have the slightest notion of what it was actually about. They'd shake their heads, and that would be it. It will be difficult for you to go on working in the church, and outside the church there will hardly be any possible employment left for you in Germany. You could take up a pastorate somewhere, but there you wouldn't be able to say what you need to say, and that would be even more painful. The university will chase you out pretty soon in any case, if I may say so. If you were to go abroad,

[6.] See 1/51, ed. note 7.

[1.] *NL*, C 24; typewritten copy of original, which has been lost. Partially reproduced in *GS* 6:266–68.

[2.] This letter (undoubtedly Bonhoeffer's reply to 1/81) not extant.

[3.] In contrast to other churches, especially the Evangelical Church of the Old Prussian Union, the regional churches of Württemberg and Bavaria had at that point been spared the far-reaching church political dispute, because the German Christians had agreed to respect the authority of the church leadership in those regions.

your possibilities for returning would certainly be in doubt. And you wouldn't give up your profession, either. Perhaps there is one way out—to go into mission work for a few years. You would have the possibility that when you came back, the situation would be calmer and clearer; for the moment, opposition is of no use at all. What I am mainly thinking is that Professor Heim here was in China for many years as a missionary,[4] and it certainly did him no harm. It would be a way out, but not a cowardly one of shirking one's duty. The only other way would be to go abroad, but I shouldn't advise it. The state is now forbidding and preventing any sort of opposition, even if it were God's commandment, and it is. But the state is now going against God, even if it says: God with us. The gospel is simply supposed to orient and adapt itself to the nation [Volk] here in our country; there is no question of anything else.

How is the situation for me? We are always, in any case, both following the same invisible line; for us as well, there is no question of anything else. The circumstances that are driving you out of the church will possibly take me to that point as well, when it comes down to it. If I should ever become a pastor, I know too in which church it would be. As long as everything still remains unclear, especially down here, as long as those studying theology aren't forced into any-
141 thing, whichever way it goes, I shall finish my studies. But if I had to get out, there would unfortunately be a definite difference; you have a personal reputation, but I? Perhaps you would expect more of me, but that is the truth. While grateful for everything I have learned, I would try for a change; not for a different course of study, but for a different life, for some human occupation.

Forgive me for saying it, but I envy you your faith (Professor Schlatter would laugh at anyone who said such a thing!). But I want to do as you have told me. Please don't trouble yourself with a reply!

With sincerest thanks,
Yours,
W. Schlunk

[4.] This is incorrect; Karl Heim had merely traveled in China for several weeks in 1922, in connection with the Peking conference of the World Christian Student Federation (Heim, *Ich gedenke der vorigen Zeiten*, 142–86).

105. Statement of the Berlin Pastors "To the National Synod of the German Evangelical Church"[1]

To the National Synod of the German Evangelical Church

The National Synod in Wittenberg is to introduce a new chapter in the history of our Protestant church. In this hour we raise our voice in the name of two thousand Protestant pastors.[2]

The National Synod must not give the impression, through its solemn 142
character, that it represents a united church, as long as our congregations are torn apart by the deepest conflicts. We see the outbreak of this dissension as God's judgment upon our church. We know that we ourselves stand under the same judgment, and are willing to bear it together with all those who, like us, bow before the judgment that God has spoken, so that the Lord Christ may turn again to us.

The National Synod is meeting in the same place where Luther, in his Invocavit sermons, raised objections, based on the gospel, against the turning of Christ's church into a false church.[3] So we may rightly expect that

---

[1.] *NL*, A 38,6; printed flyer. Previously published in *GS* 2:74–76. Niemöller sent the flyer to the National Synod on September 27, 1933 (EZA Berlin, 1/A4/18, with notes of the same date "To be distributed" and "Done"). In Wittenberg itself "the petition signers" sent a local telegram, during a break in the proceedings at 3:30 p.m., to Bishop Ludwig Müller, which said: "We ask that in your closing speech to the synod, you respond to the petition of two thousand pastors, so that the synod may fulfill its assigned task and these pastors whose conscience is hard-pressed may be accorded an answer from you" (ibid.). Müller did not respond to the flyer. Nevertheless, out of concern especially about the effect on opinion abroad, and after the intervention of state secretary Bernhard von Bülow, Müller did not yet introduce the Aryan paragraph into the Reich Church (Scholder, *Churches and the Third Reich*, 487–88). The final version of the statement was the result of several drafts by Otto Dibelius, Friedrich Müller of Dahlem, and Martin Niemöller, among others (but see also 1/102). Bonhoeffer was among those who edited the final version on September 26, 1933, in Niemöller's parsonage; he handwrote the sentence indicated in ed. note 5 in one of the drafts (ZEKHN, 62/100; cf. also *Mündige Welt*, 5:88, and Bonhoeffer's report of November 28, 1933, to the pastors' conference in Bradford, Yorkshire [*DBWE* 13, 1/20.1]).

[2.] This was approximately the number of members at the time in the Pastors' Emergency League, which had been founded September 11, 1933; the Berlin pastors claimed to be speaking on behalf of the PEL members (J. Schmidt, "Studien zur Vorgeschichte des Pfarrernotbundes," 67; and *Mündige Welt*, 5:86–89).

[3.] In the Wittenberg *Stadtkirche* (City Church; *DB-ER*, 319, is incorrect that it was the castle church). Luther's Invocavit sermons of 1522 (*LW* 51:70–94) were directed against Karlstadt's Radical Reformation measures in Wittenberg, which did not take account of "weak consciences." [Karlstadt urged that the divine law of Scripture be determinative for both secular society and the church and proposed radical reform toward this end.

not all the synod delegates will timidly remain silent about these contested issues today, especially since we know that many of them feel the same weight upon their consciences that we feel. And should none of them have the courage, we call upon the Lutheran bishops, especially the intended Reich bishop,[4] to speak a clear word for the sake of the truth. At its first National Synod the church should confess the gospel not only in words but in deeds, by deciding the questions put before it in accordance with the gospel.

So that the church may not set out on its new path with hidden guilt,[5] we declare, for the sake of truth and of love, the following:

1. The way in which new rules are being introduced into the church and applied there has brought deep spiritual distress to countless numbers of serious Christians. At crucially important synods, the present majority has denied the minority's representatives their right to thorough discussion and
143 freedom of speech,[6] even on questions that affect the church's innermost essence and its mission. For several months the life of the church has been under pressure from the force exerted by one group within the church. The church of Jesus Christ must not be allowed to be turned into a kingdom of this world by the rule of force and the denial of fraternal love.

2. With the silent consent of the new church government, laws are being made and put into force by regional synods that are contrary to the Holy Scriptures and the confession of the church. Here the Aryan paragraph in particular must be mentioned.[7] We have realized that the regional churches that have introduced such laws are preempting the German church's legislation for the entire Reich, and we demand that the National Synod not cede its authority to others, but rather use it to revoke such regional church legislation as is contrary to our confession. The gospel must not be allowed to be restricted or countermanded by human laws.

3. The ministry of the church is being put in the greatest danger by the persecution of pastors and church officials who are unable to follow

---

Luther's convictions about freedom and evolutionary change would not impose such strictures upon all.—LR]

[4.] The National Synod was to elect the Reich bishop; the sole candidate was Ludwig Müller.

[5.] "So that . . . guilt" added by hand to a draft version by Bonhoeffer (see ed. note 1).

[6.] Especially at the Prussian Provincial Synod at the end of August 1933 and its General Synod of September 5–6, 1933, the German Christian majority party had refused to allow any speakers for opposing opinions to take the floor (cf. Scholder, *Churches and the Third Reich,* 1:466–73).

[7.] Cf. 1/94, ed. note 2, and 1/101, ed. note 2.

the group that currently rules the church. This means that the ministry is placed under such pressure from human beings that the servants of the Word are in danger of violating the commandment, "We must obey God rather than any human authority!"[8] and becoming instead the servants of human authorities. We demand that the National Synod adopt clear resolutions to assure the full freedom of the Protestant proclamation and those who carry it out. The church's proclamation must not be compelled to bow to any human demands.

In this grave hour, in which a heavy crisis of conscience impels us to make this protest, we solemnly resolve before God to do everything in our power that the message of salvation may be preached among us pure and unsullied, as the revelation of the living God in Christ.

We resolve to carry out this our mission as servants of the Word, bound 144
by none other than the Holy Scriptures, according to the understanding given in the confessional writings.[9]

We resolve to do everything in our power to make room in our church for the spirit of truth and love, to counter openly all untruth and lack of love, and through our ministry to make real, for ourselves and our congregations, the community of those who belong to Christ.

Therefore we will not stop our struggle against everything that destroys the church in its essence.

We will not stop protesting loudly and clearly, far and wide, against any violation of the church's confession.[10]

We will not stop or falter in our work, in loyal obedience to our ordination vows, for the upbuilding of the German Evangelical Church.

We put our trust in the Lord of the church and pray that he may give our church, of his Spirit and his peace, the gift of new life!

Berlin, September 27, 1933

Bonhoeffer, Burckhardt, Figur, Fricke, Grüneisen, Hildebrand, Hildebrandt, Hitzigrath, Jacobi, Eduard Lindenmeyer, Friedrich Lindenmeyer, Link, Messow, Moldaenke, Müller-Dahlem, Niemöller, Petersen, Praetorius, Puttkammer, Schwebel, Stupperich, Wendland-Steglitz

[8.] Acts 5:29.

[9.] This sentence corresponds to the first point in the Pastors' Emergency League statement of principles (cf. K. D. Schmidt, *Bekenntnisse*, 77).

[10.] Taken from the second point in the Pastors' Emergency League statement of principles.

145 **106. To Friedrich Singer**[1]

Berlin, September 30, 1933

My esteemed, dear Colleague,

The time is drawing nearer when I shall be relieving you of your work. As you suggested, I plan to arrive in London on the seventeenth [of October], and to preach there for the first time on the twenty-second [of October]. Might I take this opportunity to inquire whether you intend to leave any furniture in the apartment, which I could then purchase from you? What about the kitchen furniture, for example? When do you expect to return to Germany? I hope you will not have cause to regret the exchange that we are now making. I am looking forward very much to seeing you again soon and beginning work.

With greetings and good wishes for your last weeks there, and my thanks, I am

Sincerely yours,
(sgd.) Bonhoeffer

107. To Theodor Heckel[1]

Berlin-Grunewald, October 4, 1933

Dear Councillor Heckel:

I have just spoken with the Reich bishop about my assignment to London.[2]
146 He said he would work out the final decision together with you. I therefore respectfully state once again my position, as I presented it to him this morning, as follows:

[1.] *NL,* A 39/1 (5); typewritten copy of letter that has been lost, unpublished. See also 1/92.

[1.] EZA 5/1316; typewritten. See also *NL,* A 39,1 (9); carbon copy. Previously published in *Mündige Welt,* 5:126, and *GS* 2:125. See also Heckel's note for the file of October 6, 1933 (1/108).

[2.] According to a letter of October 6, 1933, from Forell to Eidem, Bonhoeffer "was summoned by the Reich bishop and asked whether he still stood by his signature [to the statement of September 27, 1933; see 1/105], which Bonhoeffer affirmed, quoting Article 7 of the Augsburg Confession, but when he proceeded to recite the entire article in Latin, M[üller] got a bit hot under the collar and suggested postponing the conversation until later" (*Mündige Welt,* 5:127–28; cf. also *DB-ER,* 321–22). See also Bonhoeffer's description of this conversation with the Reich bishop in his letters of October 24, 1933, to Barth (*DBWE* 13:23–24), and of November 6, 1933, to Siegmund-Schultze (*DBWE* 13:30).

I am not a German Christian and cannot honestly represent the German Christian cause abroad. Of course my first duty would be as pastor to the German congregation. But I believe that my connections with leading circles in the English churches resulting from ecumenical work, as well as my personal interest in the ecumenical task of the churches, would make it inevitable that I be called upon to take a position on issues of the German church and the German Christians, because people will come to me with questions in this regard.

It goes without saying that I will speak and act out of full political loyalty to Germany. My family origin as well as my connections, of both family and friendship, with leading National Socialists such as my cousin, State Counselor and Trustee for Labor[3] Count von der Goltz, will no doubt attest to this.

I would rather be obliged to give up going to London than arouse any lack of clarity about my position. I hold this to be a self-evident act of loyalty to our church.

May I please request that you keep this letter on file?

Sincerely and respectfully,
Your faithful servant,
Dietrich Bonhoeffer

108. Memorandum from Theodor Heckel[1] 147

Berlin, October 6 [1933]

Lecturer Dr. Dietrich Bonhoeffer has been in touch with the Reich bishop in order to ensure complete clarity regarding the decision on his assignment.[2] He presented the reasons why it would be impossible for him, in his position abroad, to represent the cause of the German Christians.[3]

[3.] During the Nazi era, "Reich Trustees for Labor" were officials in the Reich Ministry for Labor whose duties included helping to "keep the peace in industrial relations" in the nazified economy—especially with regard to wage rates and the settling of social [or labor—LR] disputes by extralegal means (Brackmann and Birkenhauer, *NS-Deutsch*, 159).

[1.] EZA Berlin, 5/1316; typewritten. Heckel added here that his memorandum should be "sent directly to the personnel files," i.e., not go through the usual office channels. Reprinted in *Mündige Welt*, 5:127.

[2.] [To London.—LR]

[3.] See 1/107.

The Reich bishop then asked the undersigned to come for a specific discussion of the matter. The circumstances were investigated thoroughly. The Reich bishop decided that Lecturer Bonhoeffer's assignment could proceed but expressed his expectation that the confidence that this represents in Lecturer Bonhoeffer would be honored on his part as well.

The undersigned then conducted a further thorough discussion with Lecturer Bonhoeffer for this purpose. There was agreement that Lecturer Bonhoeffer's duty would be, first and foremost, to assemble and tend to his two congregations, that it would not be appropriate for him to bring the internal German church conflicts into his work; moreover that, to the extent that ecumenical relations came into the picture, he would endeavor, as in his previous ecumenical work, to focus in a positive way on the theological seriousness and the difficulty of the questions being raised today.

Lecturer Dr. Bonhoeffer has agreed with this memorandum for the files.

Heckel

148 **109. From Paul Theodor Jensen**[1]

Königsfeld, Black Forest, October 7, 1933

Dear Dr. Bonhoeffer:

Your name was given to me by Privy Councillor Deißmann. Thus I am taking the liberty to send you the enclosed invitation for the formation of a working group.[2] May our work be of service to our church and to the communion of saints.

Yours sincerely,
Dr. P. Th. Jensen

[1.] *NL*, C 24; handwritten, with two enclosures; unpublished.

[2.] It appears from the enclosed circular letter that Jensen, as chair of the German Committee of the Lausanne Faith and Order movement, proposed (in addition to Bonhoeffer) Martin Dibelius, Wobbermin, Zoellner, Sasse, Renkewitz, and Lang to "chair working groups of our German Committee." These working groups were to do theological study on the doctrine of grace, the sacraments, and the nature of the church in preparation for the [Faith and Order] conference being planned for Oxford in 1937 [following the Life and Work Conference there, but later moved to Edinburgh—LR]. See *Ökumenisches Jahrbuch 1934/1935*, 185. [See also Hodgson, *Second World Conference on Faith and Order*, 5 and 7—LR].

110. To Ove Valdemar Ammundsen[1]

Berlin-Grunewald, October 10, 1933

My esteemed Bishop Ammundsen:

Just a brief note to say that I am well.[2] I am leaving for London on Sunday,[3] and from there, when I have more time, I shall have many things to tell you.[4]

With warm greetings—please remember me also to your daughter, Miss 149
Esther Ammundsen[5]—and with gratitude, I remain

Yours sincerely,
Dietrich Bonhoeffer

111. From Emil Karow to the Berlin Church Consistory[1]

[Berlin-]Charlottenburg, October 14, 1933

Lecturer Dr. Bonhoeffer, who is assigned to me as a city vicar, informed me on August 15 that he had received an inquiry from the Church Confederation Office as to whether he was prepared to take up the pastorate of Sydenham and St. Paul's Churches in London as of October 1, 1933. A short time ago I received the news from him that the matter has now been settled and that he is leaving for London on October 12.[2] I do not know whether, in the rush of preparing to leave, Bonhoeffer has given his notice to you, and whether the church chancellery will accordingly notify the consistory. I am therefore hereby notifying you of Bonhoeffer's departure.

Karow

[1.] Royal Library, Copenhagen; literary estate of Bishop Ove Ammundsen; unpublished.

[2.] This is probably a coded message that neither the World Alliance resolution from Sofia (cf. 1/101, esp. ed. note 1: communications from Dickinson and Ammundsen about Bonhoeffer's stance in Sofia) nor the statement by Berlin pastors to the National Synod (1/105) had had negative consequences for Bonhoeffer (as indicated by 1/107 and 1/108).

[3.] October 15, 1933.

[4.] No such letter from Bonhoeffer has been found.

[5.] Bonhoeffer had met her in 1931 at the World Alliance Youth Conference in Cambridge (according to J. H. Schørring, Aarhus).

[1.] EZA Berlin, 14/22503; typewritten. Cf. also *NL*, D 11 (73); photocopy; unpublished. No documentation for Bonhoeffer's communication to Karow referred to here has been found.

[2.] See, however, 1/110.

PART 2
Essays and Lectures

A. Winter Semester 1932–1933

1. Lecture: "Review and Discussion of New Publications in Systematic Theology" (Student Notes)[1] 153

Review and Discussion of New Publications in Systematic Theology[2]

[1. Introduction to the current state of theology
2. Karl Heim, *Glaube und Denken*
3. Paul Schütz, *Säkulare Religion*
4. Karl Barth, *Fides quaerens intellectum*
5. Friedrich Gogarten, *Politische Ethik*
6. Hinrich Knittermeyer, *Grenzen des Staates*
7. Alfred de Quervain, *Das Gesetz des Staates*
8. Wilhelm Stapel, *Der christliche Staatsmann*

[1.] Literary estate of Eberhard Bethge; notes of Hilde Pfeiffer; sixty handwritten pages. There are five additional sets of shorter or incomplete notes or summaries made by students; see *NL*, B 4,1: Notes of Udo Köhler, fifty-one handwritten pages; *NL*, B 4,2: Notes of Hanns Rüppell, thirty-three handwritten pages (only after December 13, 1932); *NL*, B 4,3: Notes of Klara Hunsche, fifty-nine handwritten pages (incomplete); *NL*, B 4,4: Notes of Wolf-Dieter Zimmermann, thirty-one handwritten pages; from (abbreviated) notes made by Ferenc Lehel; there is a typewritten transcript made by Ilse Tödt. *GS* 5:302–40 provides a reconstruction of the lecture using the notes of Hunsche, Köhler, Lehel, Rüppell, and Zimmermann (see *GS* 5:588). Bonhoeffer's preparatory notes and lecture manuscripts have not been preserved. Bonhoeffer presented the lecture (not listed in the course list) in one-hour segments (*DB-ER*, 217). According to Pfeiffer, he began on Tuesday, November 8, 1932, and finished on February 21, 1933, concluding with the critique of Brunner's ethics as well as a brief reference to the recently published Altona confession (see *DB-ER*, 218). The section of Pfeiffer's notes containing the discussion of Heim has not been included here, as these notes—like other students' notes—only roughly reflect Bonhoeffer's presentation (see *GS* 5:301). On Bonhoeffer's description and estimation of Heim, see 2/5.

[2.] [Unless an English translation exists, the German book titles are given in the text and notes. An unofficial translation can be found after each title in the bibliography. —LR]

9. Emil Brunner, *Das Gebot und die Ordnungen*
10. The Altona confession][3]

154 Heim, Brunner, Gogarten, Stapel, Schütz, Quervain, Gutmann,[4] Otto: *Sünde und Urschuld,*[5] Hirsch: *Schöpfung und Sünde.*[6]

1. Introduction to the Current State of Theology
The current lively discussion takes place against the background of a question that Karl Barth raised in his 1922 *Letter to the Romans*:[7]

1. Only God himself can speak his Word, *deus dixit,*[8] i.e., it is a question of the beginning that God himself made. Human words came afterward. The Word of God cuts vertically through human words. He said it in Jesus Christ and God speaks this Word anew, again and again, and it should be seized anew, again and again, in faith. It is not a word of continuity, but one descending vertically from above.

2. God is only in the revelation, God wants and wanted to speak in Christ. God is the way from eternity into time; there is no way from below to above, which is why the way from above to below cannot be proven. It is only faith that proves itself.[9]

3. For this reason, human speech must always be dialectic. Because I, in my thoughts, must go from below to above, I must always relate them to the way from above to below. I must therefore say God—Not God. Revelation—

[3.] [This was the "Wort und Bekenntnis Altonaer Pastors," an early protest (January 11, 1933) against German Christian theology by a group of Protestant pastors in Altona, a suburb of Hamburg. See Helmreich, *German Churches under Hitler,* 128.—LR]

[4.] According to Hunsche: Gutmann, *Freies Menschentum aus ewigen Bindungen* (not discussed).

[5.] Otto, *Sünde und Urschuld* (not discussed).

[6.] Hirsch, *Schöpfung und Sünde* (not discussed). In Hunsche's notes the following additional references are given: Gogarten, *Ich glaube*; Heinrich Vogel, *Allein und auch*; as well as E. Stanley Jones, *The Christ of the Indian Road.* Hunsche concludes the list of references with the words: "General Comments. Journals *Zwischen die Zeiten* and *[Zeitschrift für] Theologie und Kirche.*"

[7.] Bonhoeffer was referring to the second revised edition of Barth's *Commentary on Romans,* published in 1922; first edition was published in 1919.

[8.] "God has spoken." [This discussion is an instance of Bonhoeffer's embrace of Barth's Word of God theology and its doctrine of revelation. Regarding the capitalization of "word," the reader is reminded of the comments in the introduction, in the section on translation issues.—LR]

[9.] Zimmermann correctly notes: "Evidence = Faith. He believes in the self-evidence of God."

Non-Revelation. I—Not-I.[10] I cannot simply say God's word; rather God speaks when God so desires.

4. This verticality of God means judgment of all human beings throughout the world. The pious too live under God's No, as otherwise they would 155
not have to come to us. Their coming to us is an expression of the Yes. Between judgment and forgiveness, God himself speaks.

A church is Evangelical because it hears that God is protesting, not because it is protesting. Human beings no longer have any καύχημα.[11] As God comes to the world, this shows that the world cannot come to him. That they have to keep to the Word that comes from him. This Word is judgment and forgiveness. This Word is brought forth in the proclamation.[12]

5. All theological thought is eschatological because it is always a matter of the coming, and not of the existing, tangible God. The coming is the coming from the ἔσχατα[13] to me at a certain moment. God's transcendence and immanence is the same. God truly came into history; God is entirely immanent as the coming God. However, God is only there where he speaks his Word, not where I look for him. Because God comes here and there during worship, for this reason God is immanent. The rug has been pulled from under the feet of human beings; they are quite simply in the hands of the Word.

All critique [of Barth] consists of saving a last καύχημα for human beings. It is said: in religious inwardness, in pious knowledge of God I have God himself.[14] Now pushed into the background by three [new] streams of thought: 1. Phenomenology/Heidegger, 2. Critical Philosophy/Grisebach, 3. The ethno-nationalist movement [Völkische Bewegung].[15] Both

[10.] Zimmermann adds: "The absolutely opaque middle; it lies between my two statements."

[11.] "Object of fame, something one can be proud of."

[12.] This section is probably a summary of point 4 at the beginning of the lecture of November 15, 1933.

[13.] "The last [things]."

[14.] According to Köhler and Lehel, Bonhoeffer is referring here to Schaeder's critique of Barth (see Schaeder, *Das Geistproblem der Theologie*).

[15.] After the First World War, the *völkisch* (ethno-nationalist) movement, the roots of which lie in the nineteenth century, was represented primarily among the political parties by the NSDAP (which published the *Völkischer Beobachter* after 1920). Aside from that, there were religious groups and individuals such as Mathilde Ludendorff, who turned sharply against Christianity or aimed for an ethno-nationalist reform of the church (German Church movement) and theology (Maurenbrecher, *Der Heiland der Deutschen*). Wilhelm Stapel, whom Bonhoeffer also deals with, belongs in this group. [See also Bergen, *Twisted Cross*, 14.—LR]

156 deal with the problem of the natural human being in his pre-belief.[16] On the one hand, a strong emphasis on Christian matters and, with that, timidity, reservation, without a real clarification. The two currents share this. It is a protest against Barth's interpretation of natural human beings. Their interests lie in trans-subjective ontology.[17] Both are interested in the sober, the objective, that is wholly within the world. When theology speaks of the judgment of all humans, this is seen as a violation of their territory. The natural human being protests and feels dishonored as God's creation. Philosophy: philosophy is anthropology, theology should no longer call into question what philosophy has to say about natural existence. Both groups look back to the natural order of creation.[18] In Barth's interpretation of revelation, one no longer finds the way into life. Where Barth speaks of the godlessness of man in good and evil, the question arises of what we should do then; therefore the ethical problem.[19]

The teachings on creation, redemption, and sanctification are the three starting points for the ethical problem. Arising from the order of creation is the question: What is the people [Volk], the action of the people, the goal of the people? The pressing question is no longer one of soul and God, but rather of people and God. Thus the question of the state [is also raised]. What is the authority of the state and what relation does it have to God's authority? Creation and revelation [in Jesus Christ] must never be played
157 against each other.[20] It is a matter of a *theologia naturalis*.[21] It is a ques-

[16.] The reference here is to the new currents of thought, on the one hand, and Barth's critique of religious inwardness, on the other.

[17.] Hunsche adds: "Barth's." Zimmermann has instead: "They ignore the anti-subjective in Barth's theology." Hunsche adds: "The decisive element in Barth is continually misunderstood; see the case of Dehn in Halle [see Dehn, *Kirche und Völkerversöhnung*; see also the documentation concerning the Dehn case in Huber and Huber, *Staat und Kirche* 4:785–803]. The 'misunderstood Barth': often due to Barth's unclear way of expressing himself."

[18.] Hunsche adds: "This debate extends well beyond the interest of theology: *Die Tat, Tägliche Rundschau*. Where is the point on which these turn?" [Hunsche refers to Nazi daily newspapers.—LR]

[19.] According to Zimmermann and Hunsche, in the following Bonhoeffer was interested in distinguishing an ethics anchored in the Trinity from "demands to base the ethics in the order of creation."

[20.] Köhler at this point: "Also an important problem: How to reconcile the thought that creation and Jesus Christ were the same revelation of God?" Zimmermann: "There is only *one* revelation. For this reason merger of creation and revelation in Christ . . . Trinity of thought on God must become unity."

[21.] "Natural theology." According to Hunsche, this related to philosophy, whereby with ethno-nationalism, the problem of "order of creation and revelation" is raised.

tion of the God of creation and the God of redemption. The uniqueness of God's revelation of creation and redemption.[22]

Barth sets three limits:[23]

1. Recognition of the truth in Christ as that truth of the free path of God to human beings that excludes all human paths.

2. The absolute judgment that the coming and death of God in the flesh is pronounced for all flesh. All flesh is judged through the death on the cross.[24]

3. Only God can speak of himself; all human talk of God is false.

Yet even theology that feels itself bound by these limits must live in the world.[25] For this reason, Heim rejects Barth: He is not able to live with this theology. And who can live with this theology? Aren't we misunderstanding the theology at this point? Is this not a confusion of theology and church? What is the church? Is it not its task to say God's word in a specific situa-
tion?[26] On the one hand: a question of the order of creation, of ethics, 158
of natural man and natural order. On the other hand: a question of the church.

[22.] Instead of the last two sentences, Hunsche has: "Redemptive God = Creative God. Gnostics on the other hand: Jews' God and God of the NT. We must not split. Nor tear apart Christ's uniqueness. God is one."

[23.] According to Hunsche, Köhler, Lehel, and Zimmermann, Bonhoeffer had adopted Barth's view. Thus in Köhler, for example, on 1: "We are sure of one thing, God speaks to us when and where he will." Or on 3: "A further limit, beyond which we cannot go is that God speaks."

[24.] According to Hunsche, Lehel, and Zimmermann, here Bonhoeffer said, "*religio caro est*" (religion is flesh).

[25.] In Lehel this statement is followed by a reference to H. M. Müller in *Zwischen den Zeiten* (1931). Referred to here is his review of Heim in the essay "Priester und Laie." There Müller posed the question to Barth as to how "man . . . as believer" should decide "in the conflicts of the world" when the gospel, as Barth interprets it, is not "of positive import in terms of social ethics" (385).

[26.] Zimmermann adds to this question: "The church must be able to pronounce specific commandments in specific situations." There then follows—only in his notes—remarks concerning the relation of theology and preaching, in which it is essentially said: "Theology does not provide rules for life, instead reflecting in abstraction. The church must speak concretely. Every theologian should also preach! It is unavoidable. When preaching, he must provide rules for life. Theology taken from the Bible and the revelation of the Word of God. I cannot discover sitting at a desk how he will reveal himself to me. The act of working with the Bible is different when preaching."

[2. Karl] Heim, *Glaube und Denken*[27]

[3.] Paul Schütz, *Säkulare Religion*[28]
1. Systematic section[29] 2. Schleiermacher-Blumhardt section.[30] Question of the purity of faith. Critique of overstepping of the limits of faith, where the human being wishes to be *sicut deus*.[31] This is the moment when humans place their acts under the protection of the absolute and claim: this is acting in a Christian manner. Secular religion is a crossing of escha-
159 tological barriers through religious works.[32] We cannot act in a Christian manner; we can only believe. There is no religious work; there is only mercy. When I wish to have a Christian effect on the world, then I am doing that which only God can do.

Different types of secular religion:

1. Imperial religion. Humans are God. It is the mission of the West in the East, a mission of the idea of power.

2. Capitalist religion: Capitalism and a certainty of salvation are foster brothers.[33] Both are (a) appropriation of property, (b) appropriation of God. For this reason, Bolshevik protests against a capitalist Christianity are

[27.] The presentation and critique of Heim—the subject of three lectures starting November 29, 1932—have been skipped over, as explained in ed. note 1. It should be noted, however, that selected notes offer a general characterizing of Heim: Pfeiffer ("No cheap apology. But apology nonetheless. However, Heim fundamentally strives not to sell out the revelation. Nor does he try to sell out the conceptual difficulties. Heim can think with us, can raise questions, can doubt") and Zimmermann ("He who makes an apology places himself on the other's territory, doubting [the church doesn't do that]"). Lehel's recollections are similar; Bonhoeffer recommended that he read Heim's *Glaube und Denken* with the words: Heim is not "indulging in cheap apologetics"; his "alternative, belief or despair," however, was "wrong" (Zimmermann and Smith, *I Knew Dietrich Bonhoeffer*, 69). According to Pfeiffer, Bonhoeffer concluded this section of his lectures with a reference to the literature mentioned in 2/5 as well as the review of Heim by H. M. Müller, *Priester und Laie*, and by Diem, *Glaube und Denken*.

[28.] Rüppell refers to "Georg Merz in *Z[wischen den] Z[eiten]*, the most recent issue." Referred to here is Merz's discussion of Schütz's interpretation of Blumhardt (see Merz, "Christoph Blumhardt").

[29.] Schütz, *Säkulare Religion*, 1–100.

[30.] Ibid., 101–224.

[31.] "Like God."

[32.] According to Hunsche and Rüppell, Bonhoeffer here refers to page 53 of Schütz's book; according to Zimmermann, he refers to pages 53 and 55.

[33.] Schütz, *Säkulare Religion*, 24, refers in turn to Max Weber's *Protestant Ethic and the Spirit of Capitalism*.

justified. The same is true for young blacks in America.[34] Context: in religious action we justify history.[35] Religious works destroy faith. The church has become a machine. The church becomes a synagogue, the law. Mercy, on the other hand, arises when humans sleep.[36] An awakened church is already a sect.

Sect-Works-World as opposed to Church-Revelation-Faith. The church does not create; it preaches the gospel. There is only one kind of action, but that is a simple action.[37] To act under the gospel is essentially hidden action. No chilianism, rather life under the ἔσχατον. The purity of faith excludes religious action.

[Critique:]

1. Ordinary works and religious acts cannot be distinguished by humans. [Even] ordinary actions are planned, conscious acts. Ordinary works are seen by God as religious acts, as obedience.

2. Criticism can only be relative. Criticism of the purity of faith, of religious actions is [only justified as] a dialectical critique.[38] 160

3. The church as Christianity proclaims and fulfills the will of God.[39]

4. This fulfillment is twofold, the obeyed commandment and the commandment not obeyed. In the former case [it] is an act in the name of God, [in the latter an act totally within the realm of the profane].[40] Christian action and profane action are both possibilities that should not be seen as absolutes.[41]

[34.] This statement does not come from Schütz, who instead talks about the "religious ideology of political acts . . . in the pro-British Boer policy in South and East Africa" (24). The reference to the view of African Americans in the United States is placed in parentheses in Rüppell—probably to indicate that this was Bonhoeffer's own observation. [Cf., e.g., *DBWE* 10:421–22.—LR]

[35.] Zimmermann and Köhler add: "and ourselves."

[36.] Schütz, *Säkulare Religion*, 57–58, speaks of "faith as the sleep of creation."

[37.] According to Zimmermann, Bonhoeffer refers here to p. 74 of the book under discussion.

[38.] Zimmermann adds: "Absolute critique from God"; similarly Lehel. Hunsche continues: "Religious acts are not evil; rather humans are evil. Here in Schütz a false absolutism." Similarly Köhler and Zimmermann.

[39.] Hunsche, Köhler, and Zimmermann all record the first half of this sentence exactly the same: "Church proclaims mercy and commandments."

[40.] Added according to Rüppell.

[41.] Zimmermann concludes with: "No position (Heim and Schütz) to be seen as absolute. Two possibilities: never anticipate God's judgment."

[4.] K. Barth, *Fides quaerens intellectum*[42]
Barth declares his support for Anselm. Theology is thought tied to the church. The basis is *fides quae* and *fides qua credo.*[43] Theology is thought within the framework of the church. *Intelligere*[44] arises from thinking about the given credo. Theology begins with the προσλόγιον[45] (credo). Theology is not [thought] a priori but rather knowledge bound by the *credo.* Because I can only speak of God where God wants to speak, within the framework of the church. There is [a][46] false solidarity among the theologians with the unbelievers. [True] solidarity can be justified only [in speaking to the unbeliever] as if the unbeliever were part of the church. I can only speak to others as though they have received God's forgiveness.

161 Barth says there is no knowledge of the end (Heim). Theology is thought bound to the "Credo." Theology has the *fides qua creditur* as its precondition. Theology is God's address, somehow embedded in prayer. *Intelligere* arises from a previously affirmed credo. *Intelligere* because in every *credere*[47] there is *intelligere. Intelligere* belongs to the *credere.* Theology is based on the model of the *credo* [consisting] of [parts] a, b, c, d, e, f. The theological process is that of taking out c and demonstrating, using the other parts, that this part c is part of the *credo* ([that] [has] an inner logic) whereby paradox stands at the beginning. In the assumption that God exists the question arises *quo modo*[48] God exists. That is Anselm's proof of the existence of God.[49]

How does an unbeliever react to this? Heim would ask. In reply [Barth says]: it would be irrelevant to offer the unbeliever other proofs than those we have faith in. That is, speaking to an unbeliever as if he were a believer, with the nonsinner as if he were a sinner, with an atheist as if he were in

[42.] "Faith seeking understanding." In this work, Barth drew extensively on Anselm of Canterbury's work *Proslogion* (see F. S. Schmitt, *Proslogion*).

[43.] A reference to *fides quae creditur* and *fides qua creditor,* i.e, a distinction between the content of the faith ("the faith that is believed") and the act of faith ("the faith through which is believed").

[44.] "Understand."

[45.] *Proslogion,* or "discourse." [Here it means address, specifically prayer to God, the form in which Anselm casts his writing. "Credo" refers to the fact that Anselm's argument aims to understand what he and the church believe about God. Hence Anselm called the work "faith seeking understanding," the title Barth also used for his own exposition. —LR]

[46.] In the notes mistakenly "no."

[47.] "Faith."

[48.] "In what manner."

[49.] This section is probably a review at the beginning of the lecture of January 10, 1933.

the church would be more reasonable. This "as if" is the "as if" of God's mercy. The atheist must be spoken to in the solidarity of standing together in God's mercy. Thus not, as [in] Heim to meet the atheist at his level. God can be proven theologically [only] within the framework of the church. The revealed name of God is a precondition: *aliquid quo nihil maius cogitari potest.*[50] The antithesis: God [does not] exist is taken *ad absurdum* and thus the positive existence is proved. If the revealed name were only seen as *esse in intellectu,*[51] it would thus be even [greater] as *esse in re.*[52] Thus the *esse in re* would be higher than the *esse in intellectu*. Then there would be something higher. We do not enter the church when we are not already in, according to Heim.[53]

[5.] Friedrich Gogarten, *Politische Ethik,* Jena, 1932 162
(To be read: p. 166[–70] Intermezzo) Luther: The human being should serve God in his station [Stand] and not in smug works. Gogarten wishes to regain this insight for our times. This is Gogarten's starting point. Heim's ethical approach begins at the level of natural thinking without God. Gogarten: God is good to evil humans. Two poles: First the doctrine of justification. Second, the political existence in which the human being finds himself.[54] In linking the two poles, the question of being good is answered. The human recognizes since the end of the war [that he is subject to a foreign power].[55] For this reason we raise questions about this foreign power, about Christian faith. The world is a broken power; it is disintegrating. This is due to the autonomous human of the Renaissance. From this the machine [arose]. Now the human is in service to the machine. For this reason the individual is a mass of atoms, a mass that consumes itself, a chaos. The only power that can bring this chaos under control once again

---

[50.] "That than which nothing greater can be conceived" (cf. Schmitt, *Proslogion*).

[51.] "Being in intellect."

[52.] "Being in reality."

[53.] Bonhoeffer's chain of reasoning is more clearly expressed in Hunsche: "Precondition the knowledge of the *revelation of the name of God*: *aliquid quo nihil maius cogitari potest.* Antithesis 'God does not exist' is argued *ad absurdum.* Then the [above-mentioned] prerequisite applies. If the revealed name were only *in intellectu,* then beyond it something greater could be thought of *in re.* From the prerequisite of the revelation it cannot be concluded: God does not exist. The *positive* proof lies in the revelation. The church is the prerequisite, unlike in Heim, who first located himself outside and then sought to move into the church."

[54.] See Rüppell: "Doctrine of justification and that human beings discover themselves as existing politically: These are the two poles in Gogarten."

[55.] Gap has been filled using Köhler. See also Hunsche: "Collapse of the *humanitas* since the war, enslaved to a foreign power"; similarly Rüppell.

is the state. The state limits evil. The state is sovereign with *auctoritas*[56] over humans. The human being, who can only thus exist within the state, is therefore [only] a political existence. Human action is only political action in [the] orders [of society]. Being good means taking responsibility in political existence. Only in life in the state do we live in a manner pleasing to God. Only the state offers a humane existence.

163 [Three Problems] 1. Individualistic and political ethics; 2. The meaning of ethical demands in political ethics; 3. State and society ([see also Gogarten's essays:] "Illusionen," "Wider die Ächtung der Autorität").[57]

Re: 1: For individualistic[58] ethics:

[(a)] The human being is free and has rights and powers over himself.

(b) The human being is human when he is in and for himself.

(c) The human being is imperfect but is good and neutral. He is made good by the possibilities for being good that he carries within himself.

(d) The human being is spirit. Human nature exists in one's stance vis-à-vis nature.[59] The human is the "ego" in contrast to the "id."[60] He has control over both.

(e) The human being is responsible only to himself. The human being, in his being in-and-for-himself [An-und-für-sich-Sein], is the measure of all things. The goal is the full realization and fulfillment of the self. He should do good. Here a link with utilitarian ethics. The human being is what he can be [. . .],[61] [understood in relation to] his possibilities.

[In contrast, a] political [ethic states]:

a. The human being is what he is in relation to other humans, he is dependent on other humans, is not alone. The human is essentially a political being (ζῷον πολιτικόν: Aristotle). Hegel's thought is individualistic. [Having taken up] the idea of I-You is Gogarten's service to theology.[62]

[56.] "Authority."

[57.] ["Illusions" and "Against Respecting Authority."—LR]

[58.] In the notes incorrectly as "individual."

[59.] Added in Hunsche: "Govern nature, Ritschl." Similarly Zimmermann.

[60.] [Elsewhere in this text *das Ich* is translated as "self"; here, however, it is "ego" and "id" that are being contrasted.—LR]

[61.] One word illegible.

[62.] According to Hunsche, Rüppell, Köhler, and Zimmermann, Bonhoeffer sees individualistic thought as having begun earlier and also refers to forerunners of Gogarten's concerns. See also, e.g., Zimmermann: "Since orthodoxy always individualistic thought. At first in Jacobi, speaking about I and You; then Feuerbach (anthropological).

b. The human being is not free but rather always in a political situation.[63]

c. In his dependence on other humans, the human individual recognizes that he is radically evil, unable to do good.[64] Evil is not wanting to be dependent on others and not wanting to be there for others. Evil is the desire to be good on one's own. In his attempt to do good, the human being is bad. 164

d. The ethical phenomenon exists in the relation between humans. Ethical terms need to be translated from individualistic ties to political ones.

Re: 2: There is a dual sense [to the ethical demands in political ethics]: (a) a "Thou shalt" sense, (b) a "One does this and that" sense.[65]

1. The human being is addressed unconditionally in the "Thou shalt" sense and conditionally in the "One does this and that" sense. One cannot avoid the Thou.

2. We need to be told the "Thou shalt" sense; the "One does this and that" sense goes without saying.

3. The "One does this and that" sense addresses the human being as good; the "Thou shalt" sense addresses the human being as evil. Here the human being himself is challenged.

4. The "One does this or that" sense demands something concrete, something to be done. "Thou shalt" never demands anything concrete; [rather it makes demands on me].[66]

5. The "One does this or that" sense make demands of my Self, my person; the "Thou shalt" demands me, myself. "Thou shalt" is a demand of

Gogarten takes up this term. He draws on M. Buber. Then community with Grisebach." [Bonhoeffer employs the language of I-You in *Sanctorum Communio.* And while he refers here to Gogarten's use of Martin Buber's *I and Thou*, published as *Ich und Du* in Germany in 1923, there is no indication that Bonhoeffer drew directly from it. See Clifford Green's discussion of this in the editor's introduction to *DBWE* 1:5–6.—LR]

[63.] Zimmermann and Hunsche add that it was "decreed" for humans.

[64.] Zimmermann adds: "With their good and evil qualities, they become enslaved to the power of evil."

[65.] [The distinction of "Thou shalt" from "One does this and that" is as follows: "Thou shalt" conveys the structure of the divine command itself; "One does this and that" conveys a general ethical insight about individual behavior, with no sense of divine command intrinsic to it.—LR]

[66.] Supplemented from other notes. See, e.g., Rüppell: "'Thou shalt' makes demands on me, demands that I cannot fulfill. They are *speculum peccati* [mirror of sins], p. 152: 'Exposing evil is the true ethical phenomenon.'" See also Zimmermann: "Sermon on the Mount, Old Testament: 'Thou shalt not.' According to Jesus's interpretation, these you *must* break. The irremovable evil existence is exposed. (Jesus's interpretation too is specific, *not* principle)."

authentic [eigentlich] quality; "One does this or that" is of inauthentic quality, and confusing the two is dangerous. "Thou shalt" speaks to my being (page 47 on truth and lies). A lie is not the truth, but it lives from the truth. An exposed lie can no longer be a lie. Similarly with evil. Ethics only exists because there is evil. The reverse fails to recognize that the human being
165 is evil. The human being, shown to be evil, can only live in the πόλις. The πόλις saves the human being from the depths of ruin.

The two demands of "Thou shalt" and "One does this and that" come together in the state. How does my exercising my right to vote, my function as family member, obtain ethical quality? The "One does this and that" has ethical quality [only to the extent] that it can be placed within the "Thou shalt" demand, subordinate to it. I must hold you in check because you are evil; in this respect it has ethical quality. The sense of the "One does this and that" demand is in maintaining humans' [external] obedience. The "Thou shalt" demand on the other hand has true ethical quality.

In Gogarten, the Christian is actually secondary.[67] Christian belief has the function of illuminating and receiving from the other side what is stated about the real and the unreal.

The concept of the good: being good to a human being. Luther's understanding of justification consisted [according to Gogarten] of the point that God is good to human beings. Doing good means recognizing that God is good to me and thereby a direct recognition of one's own evil. Being good means letting God be good to me. The good occurs today in the state. Because of sin, God continually creates a new order, which is the state.[68] Political ethics arises necessarily out of the recognition of the irreversible power of evil. In fulfilling my duties as a citizen, I am also doing work pleasing to God; I am also doing the work of God's creation. This does not, however, justify the human being, who always remains evil.

[Re: 3]: The state is the order that is there for the sake of the human being. Social crisis is [in reality] political crisis.[69] The crisis can be solved only when the human being is forced back into his own orders. The state is not
166 the kingdom of God, but the subduing of evil powers. The state guarantees

[67.] According to Köhler and Rüppell, Bonhoeffer referred here to Gogarten, *Politische Ethik*, 115.

[68.] Clearer in Hunsche: "The good arises in the state. God creates the order in which I can live."

[69.] Köhler adds: "The state contrasts with community, being contrasts with action, political contrasts with social"; similarly Zimmermann.

freedom in obedience. It is not glory but rather honor that befits the state. Honor and morality are linked. Honor finds its guarantee in it.

State and church: The task of the church vis-à-vis the state, that it preserves the knowledge of evil. The "Thou shalt" demand.

Appreciation: Reformed, Lutheran: (a) the human being exists in mercy and vocation. Mercy in the church, vocation in the state. (b) The state's authority comes from God. In our Reich constitution: The authority of the state comes from the people.[70] Gogarten also separates the state from enthusiasm. The rediscovery of the You.[71]

Critical reservations: Gogarten ignores the ambiguity of the state. He proclaims a Christian conservatism. That is Lutheran, but not from the New Testament. The state can be seen as the order of evil. A Christian can say that he can make use of this order.[72] Because a revolutionary is fundamentally wrong, the state is relatively right.[73]

Luther and the Catholic Church reject revolution.[74] Luther quite clearly and radically. In the Enlightenment, revolution was recognized as a right. Resulting from this was the theology [of the Erlangen School]:[75] 167

[70.] See Article 1 of the Weimar constitution: "The authority of the state comes from the people" (Horst Hildebrandt, *Verfassungen*, 69). Hunsche lists the first position from which Gogarten distances himself: "popular sovereignty as a natural right (the first sentence of the constitution is wrong; the state gains its authority not from below, but from above. Rejected by Catholicism and Protestantism)."

[71.] Hunsche more extensively: "Against enthusiasm? (radical opposition to the state, establishment of the state on the Christian commandment to love one another. Sermon on the Mount). In both built from below (1. antiquity, 2. post-Lutheran)."

[72.] Zimmermann notes: "a. It can be seen as *the* order of evil. To do the greatest possible evil without destroying yourself (Hobbes). When that is accepted, however, then this order can be drawn from God in his service. b. Order, existing, receives its justification from God."

[73.] Hunsche (the only one to mark the following as "Digression: revolution and conservatism in Christian ethics") adds: "as a reference to God, who alone can preserve and revolutionize," while "the revolutionary thinks he can escape the circumstances as such."

[74.] Zimmermann adds: "Thomas [Aquinas]: Tyrant = rebel; for this reason, tyrants must be overthrown." Similarly in Rüppell, Hunsche, and Lehel. See also Wünsch, "Christentum und Revolution."

[75.] Supplemented from the other notes (see, e.g., Hunsche: "Erlangen School: Do not participate in revolution, rather *adapt to the existing order*"). On this subject see the essays of the systematician of neo-Lutheranism at the University in Erlangen, Franz Frank, *System der christlichen Sittlichkeit* 2:437–38.

You cannot participate in revolution. However, a Christian submits to every order. The revolution as a relative right vis-à-vis the relative right of the state.[76]

Gogarten no longer recognizes any limitations with regard to the Christian state. The tyrant himself is a revolutionary, according to Thomas. Erlangen position: the Christian does not recognize but submits to the revolution. The error of Christian conservatism: it ignores a better justice. The right of the state is relative; thus there is a relative right of revolution as well. *A better justice* is to be found based on the Bible and from that [follows] relative critique, not radical critique (see the enthusiasts) of the state.[77]

Critique of [Gogarten's determination] of the political existence of the human being: for the time being actually placed within the state. [However] is there no tension for the Christian between the Christian order of love and the state's order of force? Official [acts] have no right per se; rather, on the basis of the Christian commandment to love, the orders must be seen in their relativity.

[On the problem of distinguishing ethical demands:] the demands
168 on "one"[78] are the material of ethical commands. [This could mean:] 1. Totally: then the church would be included as well, then there is no longer a concrete Christian demand. 2. Or it is only the state's "one" that is meant. Then there would be a Christian "one" next to the state "one." Then there would be a Christian parallel to the state ethic. The "Thou shalt": in its political acts, does the "Thou shalt" really[79] aim toward (greater justice)?

[On defining the relationship between] state and church: Not only does the church recognize state order; it also preaches the lasting breach of this

---

[76.] In other notes, reference is made here to Adolf von Harnack, although not always in exactly the same manner (Zimmermann: "A. v. Harnack—relative right of revolution"; Hunsche: "Adolf von Harnack. The relative right of the new as opposed to the existing"; Rüppell: "Neutrality—Adolf von Harnack thus"). On Harnack's programmatic, positivist position to the new political order after 1918, see, e.g., his letter of September 24, 1925, to Wilhelm Stapel: "I made my stand on the foundation of the constitution because I must *act* and try to reintroduce as many good things from the past as possible." Harnack rejected inactive waiting for "a better democracy" and a retreat "into an ideological critique" (A. v. Zahn-Harnack, *Harnack*, 483–84). The following section is probably a review with which Bonhoeffer began his lecture of January 31, 1933.

[77.] According to Hunsche and Zimmermann, Bonhoeffer here mentions Dehn and his stand on war (see also ed. note 21).

[78.] [Refers to Bonhoeffer's earlier distinction between the demands on the individual as a member of society (the "One does this or that" referred to on pp. 201–3) and the demands that God's command places upon our very selves (the "Thou shalt"). —LR]

[79.] Zimmermann adds: "formally and materially."

worldly order through the miracle of resurrection. This order only exists in relativity. Between law-synagogue and enthusiasm[80] stand church and state. The church indicating the state as an order called into question.[81] The two are mutually limiting, recognizing each other, both providing justice. That is the relation of church and state.[82]

[6.] Hinrich Knittermeyer, *Grenzen des Staates*,[83] 1932
He wishes to describe the particularity of the German situation. Germany lies between East and West. This intermediary position should be preserved. In Western thought, church and state each have their own powers. In the East, church and state are merged. Germany must find the proper German critical intermediary solution between these two radical solutions. If the church were to place itself under the external protection of the state, the result would be a state church precisely for the sake of the freedom of the state and the boundaries of the state. Thus the church would be less free than the earlier state church and the state with less authority than before. The church must be a critic of the state and the state a critic of the church.
The outward form of the church must be based entirely in the state, can- 169
not have an independent life. The state, on the other hand, must receive authority from the protection of the church. Church and state are fatefully linked in Germany.[84]

[7.] Alfred de Quervain, *Das Gesetz des Staates: Wesen und Grenze der Staatlichkeit*[85]
According to him, the limits of the state are in created reality.[86] This is [however] never unambiguous reality. It is always in a kind of twilight. It could be precisely that which [needs to be] destroyed. Doesn't trace itself

[80.] Rüppell explains: "Where miracles become absolute = enthusiasm" and "synagogue, where order becomes absolute." Similarly Zimmermann and Hunsche.

[81.] Zimmermann: "State as preserving order; eschatological but an order broken and rescinded by the resurrection."

[82.] Hunsche concludes with the sentence: "Church not simply there to support the state. Friction between church and state natural."

[83.] ["The boundaries of the state."—LR]

[84.] The other sets of notes also confine themselves to a (variously accentuated) presentation of Knittermeyer's position. According to Merz (*Mitteilungen*, 376), Knittermeyer was one of those working for *Zwischen den Zeiten* who joined the German Christian movement in 1933.

[85.] ["The law of the state: Essence and limit of statehood."—LR]

[86.] As the other students' notes also show, Bonhoeffer did not describe Quervain's position in his lecture and limited himself to a critique. See Zimmermann ("Knittermeyer [is] Reformed. Created reality remains in twilight between creation and sin.

back to the creation, rather reflects on everything from the perspective of the cross of Christ.

[8. Wilhelm] Stapel, *Der christliche Staatsmann: Eine Theologie des Nationalismus*[87]
Not a well thought-out book, [but] a major thread. Theological book from a layperson, good use of Luther.[88] It is a dangerous book. It cannot keep its promises. Stapel aims to justify and provide foundations for the ideas of the Reich theologically. However, his scholarship is a radical critique of everything[89] that exists.

170 Orientation: Christian-conservative, imperial populist front. It is a question of the German testament. How can we be Christians without breaking with the Reich? How can a statesman serve the Holy Trinity without denying his natural God? First historical, second critical, third decisive part.

Re: 1. Summary p. 118.[90] Doubts as to whether the description of Luther[91] is correct.

Re: 2. Critical part. The ethical attempt to found a Christian state. There are reasons from ethics and religion for a Christian state. There is no Christian state, only Christians in the state. There is no Christian morality. The Sermon on the Mount was essentially teaching for disciples. It talks about a kingdom from another world. There are historically different so-called Christian moralities. Morality only exists on the basis of natural biological conditions; there are countless differentiated moralities. Religion: A Chris-

---

Requires interpretation. Can perhaps be destroyed. Limited only by the church through miracles") and Rüppell ("Quervain sees the limits of the state in the created reality [family, marriage, Volk, culture!]. But never an unambiguous created reality, there is always conflict between being and the created. Only the church can be the limit of the state, with its preaching of the breakthrough on the cross").

[87.] ["The Christian statesman: A theology of nationalism."—LR]

[88.] Only Zimmermann: "Stapel studied Luther." Rüppell: "Conglomerate of essays! Much good, much pathos. Theological book by a layman. Return to Luther!" Köhler: "No clear terminology. A theological book by a layman! Wilhelm Stapel knows his Luther."

[89.] In the draft: "an" corrected by Rüppell.

[90.] Here Stapel looks back at the first, historical part of his book.

[91.] See Stapel's chapter on Luther, 75–98 of *Der christliche Staatsmann.* According to Stapel, Luther's teaching on the state could be summed up as "metaphysics of patriarchy" (96; in parentheses in original). In a critique of modern discourse about individual rights, Stapel states: "When Luther gives preference to the judgment of natural patriarchal mediation over legal decisions, it is an expression of a biologically healthy sense" (97).

tian state must be a union, a kingdom of love. However, the state is force. In the state, however, there are Christians.

Part 3: decisive part. Metaphysics of the state. Analogy between the terms "king" and "God": 1. In God's kingdom as in the state it is a question of lordship. 2. Structure: structure of delimitation. God's kingdom is faced by that of Lucifer, from this [follows the contrast between] friend and enemy.[92] 171
3. Problem of law. In God's kingdom there are laws just like in the state.

His *doctrine of the nomos* is important. 1. Every people [Volk] has its nomos.[93] There must therefore be a German nomos. 2. The Sinai nomos is only exceptional in that Christ was born among this people. This nomos has no ethical significance, only a religious one. 3. The Israelite nomos was fulfilled by Christ. In the German nomos is there something to be fulfilled,[94] something fulfilled by Christ? Does every people have something to be fulfilled, δικαίωμα? Does Jesus also fulfill the νόμοι of other peoples or only the νόμος of the Jews? The δικαίωμα is fulfilled in the ἀγάπη.[95] The δικαίωμα is the receptiveness of the soul for redemption.[96] How can the δικαίωμα of the German people be compared with that of the Jews? First, God enters into the people as nomos, Yahweh the God of the people, Zeus, Jupiter, Thor (pp. 182–83). Under the Christian cathedral is a heathen crypt. National gods and national *nomoi* have their justification. At the level of the crypt is the νόμος τῶν ἐθνῶν and at the level of the church the νόμος τοῦ θεοῦ, for which the crypt provides the foundation. The constitution of the state is an act of mercy by God toward the world.

The health of ethics depends on biological health.[97] The Germans are an imperial people. The Reich is a precondition for Christ's appearance. With the Reich are bound a number of hypostases. True morality is

[92.] According to Zimmermann, Rüppell, and Lehel, Bonhoeffer mentions Carl Schmitt here. Stapel welcomed Schmitt's idea of "the contrast of friend and enemy as the nature of the political" (170). On Schmitt, cf. his text on the concept of the political, published as a 1927 essay and already reprinted independently twice by 1933. He begins with the sentence: "The specific political distinction to which political actions and motives can be reduced is that between friend and enemy" (Schmitt, *Concept of the Political,* 26).

[93.] "Law."

[94.] Added above the line: δικαίωμα (statute). In Stapel (175–76), beginning with Rom. 2:26 and 8:4, this is understood as "that which, in law, points toward fulfillment through Jesus Christ."

[95.] "Love."

[96.] See Stapel, 180.

[97.] Köhler on the "ethics of the state" in Stapel: "The Decalogue will be biologically resolved." The same in Lehel, similarly Zimmermann.

renown. The Kaiser stands over against Christ. Christ and the Kaiser belong together. In the end, the Kaiser will lay down his crown on Golgotha.[98]

Conclusion: Imperium Teutonicum.[99] Nationalism must be overcome by a new imperialism.

172 Nomos teaching: 1. There are only Volks-νόμοι; they all exist at the same level, even the Israelite nomos. 2. The νόμοι are the consequences of the fall. They are directed toward the redemption; they shall be effected by God. 3. The German nomos is the realization of the Reich. However, it must be effected and redeemed.[100]

Bonhoeffer's critique: the concept of nomos justifies the given reality as such. Stapel defends the radical autonomy of existing reality (because there are rich and poor, they must be preserved, class struggle, war, etc.: "see, it is very good").[101] Existing reality as such is very good.[102] Stapel, on the other hand, would say: It is a matter not of the orders of creation but rather of the orders of sinfulness. But this is spurious reasoning. They gain their continuity and clarity like the orders of creation.

Critique: Stapel does not understand the Christian concept of law. He understands it as something given, existing. *But law is nomos turned against the order of sin.* Critique of every natural nomos. Christian nomos opposes the biological nomos, which only claims to be the true nomos. *Nomos* is a *critical* term. Stapel's thought is Catholic.[103] *Catholic* thought separates the people's nomos from the superior nomos, but each retains its rights.[104] *We* see everything given in a critical light, as everything existing is seen only in relation to God. There is no world in which the people's nomos is valid and

[98.] See Stapel, 245, on the end of "world history": "The Kaiser will remove the crown from his head and lay it on the cross of Golgotha."

[99.] See Stapel, 246–73. Zimmermann adds: "(historically good!)." Köhler adds: "a victory hymn. Who can challenge the Germans?"; see also Stapel's statement on "the special dignity of the German people [Volk]" (226), which, after stating that Germany is the "mother of the peoples" (enclosed in parentheses in original) continues with the rhetorical question: "Who can compare with this people?" (267).

[100.] This paragraph probably contains Bonhoeffer's summary of Stapel's teaching at the beginning of the January 24, 1933, lecture.

[101.] A reference to Gen. 1:31a ["God saw everything that he had made, and indeed, it was very good"—LR].

[102.] Hunsche summarizes everything with the sentence: "Stapel's thesis is the radical autonomy of everything existing. Renewal of the idea of the unbroken *unambiguous order of creation.*"

[103.] According to Rüppell, Hunsche, and Lehel, Bonhoeffer referred here to the positive critique of Stapel by Eschweiler, "Zehn Gebote und Naturgesetz."

[104.] Zimmermann: "No two-stage system, *Volk* nomos–church nomos. That is Catholic. Catholicism distinguishes nature-supranatural. Nature seen in the light of the supranatural (in the light of mercy and promise)."

another where the nomos of love is valid.[105] The νόμος τοῦ θεοῦ is always a critique of the νόμος τῶν ἐθνῶν.[106]

Stapel is correct when he opposes Althaus in saying: It is impossible and arbitrary to place the Israelite Ur-nomos apart from the nomoi of other peoples.[107] Is there a difference between the biblical Ur-nomos and the German one? Critique: It is the particularity and uniqueness of the Israelite nomos to be constantly opposed to the people's nomos. Nor do the prophets belong to the people's nomos. Herein lies its uniqueness. The *prophets* always said: *It is a question of recognizing the critical nomos.* It is thus not a question of effecting the given nomos. *This critical nomos gains its binding form in the first commandment.* Herein lies the Pre of the Israelite [nomos]. It truly depends on God. It is impossible to say that we should worship the national gods first (Yahweh, Jupiter, Thor) and then Christ. We do this again and again, but we should only worship the one God. The idea of the Reich must be directed toward the divine nomos.[108] One cannot serve two gods, the cross and the German Reich. *No acceptance of the given nomos, rather taking direction from God's nomos. The Israelite nomos is superior to the German one because it truly sees the meaning of the critical nomos.*[109] 173

[9.] Emil Brunner: *Das Gebot und die Ordnungen: Versuch einer protestantischen Ethik.*[110]

First comprehensive ethical work of dialectic theology. It includes general and specific ethics. The most valuable part is in the appendix: an examination of the current situation. Unlike Barth: he has a very pressing concern, *a concern for eristic* (which used to be called apologetic). ([See:] *Zwischen den Zeiten*: "Die andere Aufgabe der Theologie.")[111] Discussion with others, with nontheologians. Brunner particularly believes the questions that come from jurists and doctors are essential. 174

[105.] Zimmermann: "Everything existing in relation to the *one* God's judgment. *One* world, in which the nomos of love and the nomos of the *Volk* apply."

[106.] "God's law—law of the *Volk.*"

[107.] According to Hunsche, Bonhoeffer here refers to "*Deutsches Volkstum,* January (1933): Althaus/Stapel." [This was Stapel's reply to Althaus and Eschweiler, titled "Juden, Heiden und Christen" (Jews, Gentiles, and Christians).—LR]

[108.] See Rüppell: "The idea of the Reich is directed toward God's law, which found its end and its fulfillment in the cross."

[109.] Lehel writes at the beginning of this section: "The exceptional nature of the Jewish nomos is not discussed."

[110.] [Published as *The Divine Imperative: A Study in Christian Ethics.*—LR] The correct subtitle is *Entwurf* [draft] *einer protestantisch-theologischen Ethik.*

[111.] See *Zwischen den Zeiten* 7 (1929).

I. Unity of mercy and commandment,[112] faith and obedience, promise and demand, indicative and imperative.

II.[113] Natural ethics can be defined by principles, but not Christian ethics. It is not an ethics in the form of laws since the commandment of love is not a principle; it is God's love itself. Christian ethics is not an ethics of principles.[114]

III. Law and commandment: biblical laws remain laws until God's call transforms them into commandments. Only I myself know God's commandment; no one [else] can tell me. We can never know the commandment in advance. What we say always remains law.[115]

IV. The human being on his own [only] knows God's law; he does not know it as commandment. For this reason, he does not know why he exists: love. We should not do anything, rather receive something. When we do good, we open ourselves to this gift. Commandment is the obedient imitation of the acts of the Creator and Redeemer. Accepting and rejecting, recognizing and not recognizing the given as coming from God is the content of the commandment.

[V.] Law is principle, commandment the concrete word of God.

VI. The commandments of the Bible bear witness to the specific commandments of yesteryear. The biblical commandments have a negative sense; they contain references to the totality of God's demands. Ethics can therefore not be casuistic. Ethics can only prepare the decision.

VII. Law presents itself as legality, as radical law, as Christian law (as instructions for the believers)—(*triplex usus legis*).[116] What does law mean
175 for the Christian? It has the character of advice. Thus also the *tertius usus legis*[117] is only preparation for his actual acts. But it is something necessary.

VIII. The human being is only good in the obedience of faith, because God alone remains the subject of good acts; the human is to let God be God (pp. 156–59, [distinction between] conscience and faith).

[112.] [The German *Gebot* can be translated "command," "commandment," even "directive" or "requirement." The choice here is "commandment," and the meaning is, as the text says in V, "the concrete word of God" (for a specific time and place). Bonhoeffer and Brunner both consider the commandment in this sense to be an authoritative directive that requires obedience. They differ on whether the church, rather than individual Christians, can know and issue the concrete commandment. Readers should note that this use of "commandment" differs from its reference to the Ten Commandments.—LR]

[113.] The remarks for this point were entered later in the draft, after point IV.

[114.] Hunsche adds; "Christian ethics is the science of human acts determined by God's acts." Similarly Köhler, Rüppell, and Lehel.

[115.] Hunsche adds: "through hearing the commandment."

[116.] "Threefold use of the law."

[117.] "Third use of the law."

IX. The commandment of the Creator speaks of self-affirmation; the commandment of the Redeemer speaks of self-denial. Here too we [humans only] speak of the law affirming and negating life; each individual is free to decide.

X. The commandment unfolds in law. The specific commandment cannot be described; the commandment can be spoken of only in law. This law has three forms: 1. *iustitia civilis,*[118] 2. humility, 3. greater justice (guidance). These instructions deal with something relatively better, but it gains an absolute character in the specific commandment. What should I do? Remain in your vocation.[119] That is, vocation is only for the Christian community. Status quo. In vocation you can have a good conscience. Having this good conscience is not the same as being justified.

XI. In the community commandment as threefold law: 1. official duty, 2. absolute law, radical, 3. the law of love.

XII. The Christian in the community: 1. Remain in solidarity with the worldly society. 2. There is prophetic social critique. 3. There are exceptional acts by the community in proclamation and acts of love.

XIII. The church proclaims the gospel and the commandment, commandment as sharpening of the conscience (p. 546). The specific commandment is not given with the church's proclamation (p. 559): "When someone, in the hour of the commandment, understands clearly, he should say it"[120] (individualistically).

XIV. The concrete orders are to be examined for their sense of commu- 176
nity. Threefold law within the community as well.

[Summary characterizing Brunner:] 1. Establishment of ethics from justification. Mercy and commandment are one. Then the church should be able to proclaim the commandment with full authority. This Brunner denies. 2. Overcoming of the law of principle by the concrete commandment. 3. Law = framework, within which the commandment is free. 4. Fundamental ethical categories are left to the individual. Herein lies the basic problem.

[118.] "Civil justice."

[119.] According to Zimmermann and Hunsche, Bonhoeffer referred here to 1 Cor. 4:4.

[120.] Brunner first stated: "The Church ought to give the world some instruction on the subject of the secular 'orders'" (*Divine Imperative,* 559). Later on the same page Brunner writes: "The Church ought to exercise a prophetic office, the office of a 'watchman.'" This leads Brunner to conclude: "[O]n occasion the individual preacher may and indeed must demand concrete decisions. He may and indeed must do this when he clearly perceives the Divine Command for that particular moment. To-day, too, there is the possibility of a prophetic calling through which an individual has to proclaim the Divine Command, for that moment, to the Church. No one can assume this responsibility for himself, but we ought to be prepared for such an eventuality" (559–60).

Critique:

1. Can the church command, with full authority, in the same way as it can forgive?[121] Principle is not commandment, but according to Brunner the church can only speak of principles. There are cases in which a united church-community asks: what should we do? Here the individualistic question would be resolved. Here the pastor must indeed risk a concrete commandment, under the promise that the church is included in the forgiveness of sins.

2. How does the church speak the commandment? The pastor is bound to the church, which in turn is subject to the council, which itself needs forgiveness of sins.

3. What should the church proclaim as commandment? Are there concrete demands as proclamation? Only where this question is asked by an existentially threatened church-community is there a concrete commandment. The principle is hypocritical.[122]

177 [10.] The Word and Confession of the Altona Pastors (Hans Asmussen, in *Der Vormarsch*, 1933; student notes)[123]

This concerns the clarification of the relations between church and civic life from a Reformation standpoint. It aims to be a confession,[124] not a

---

[121.] Lehel adds: "When commandment and gospel are the same, then this must be true. The church must also pronounce specific commandments." Hunsche continues: "If commandment and gospel are the same, then this must be true. Objection: The commandment remains different for everyone. Answer: The church-community comes as one and asks: What should we do?"

[122.] Rüppell at greater length: "Generally the social commandments of the church and others remain principles! Either specifics or stay silent. Only speaking of principles is hypocritical!" Similarly Hunsche.

[123.] Issue 2 (February 1933) of the journal *Vormarsch* contains Asmussen's essay on the so-called Altona confession (34–36) as well as the text of that statement (titled "Das Wort der Kirche zur Not und Verwirrung des öffentlichen Lebens" [The church's statement on the crisis and disarray of public life], 3–43). In Bonhoeffer's library there is an issue of the *Niederdeutschen Kirchenzeitung* of May 1, 1933, which also contains "Das Wort der Kirche zur Not und Verwirrung des öffentlichen Lebens." Inserted in this copy is a reprint of the Altona confession in the *Hannoverischen Sonntagsblatt* [1933], no. 4, with the title "a remarkable statement." Five Altona pastors, including Asmussen, had written this statement after the violent riots that preceded the July 1932 parliamentary elections (the so-called Altona Bloody Sunday, July 17, 1932). Starting with an understanding of the church as "the flock . . . called by God's given word in which Christ is truly present" (Article 1), the tasks of the political parties (Article 2) and the states (Articles 3–5) are defined. The Altona confession was presented to the presiding bishop, Adolf Mordhorst, on December 19, 1932, and signed by twenty-one pastors (Scholder, *Churches and the Third Reich*, 1:179–80 and 184–86). [The text reproduces not the actual essay from *Der Vormarsch*, but rather the Berlin students' notes about Bonhoeffer's remarks about Asmussen's remarks.—LR]

[124.] According to Köhler and Hunsche: "Confession in the sense of Augsburg Confession."

church declaration. It hovers between confession, teaching, and declaration. "Church exists only where there is the church-community of Christ. . . .["][125] No claims to be a political party. Church released from demands for an inauthentic decorative function.[126] Distinction from all chiliastic expectations.[127] 4. The role of the state. 5. Keeping the commandment.

From a Reformation standpoint some things need correcting. Cases of conflict between the church and the state are again[128] seen as cases of conflicts of the individual.

The church should speak to the world, bear witness in the church-community (thus the term [*confession*] not well chosen). What is the relation between church and commandment? Qualified silence is better than 178
speaking in principles. Either give concrete commandments or remain silent. Compare Psalm 11:19:[129] "Do not hide your commandment!" and [2 Chron. 20:12:] "We do not know what to do, but our eyes are on you." That is also a possibility for the church, but a humble church.

[125.] Origin of quote not provided.

[126.] See Article 1 of the Altona confession, "Von der Kirche" (Concerning the church). [The reference here is to a sentence in Article 1 that opposed the "misuse" of the church when the church was used to add a ceremonial tone to "military, state or political rallies."—LR]

[127.] See Article 2 of the Altona confession, "Von der Grenzen des Menschen" (On the limitations of human beings). There, the "dream of the coming worldly kingdom of justice, peace, and general welfare in all its deviations" was theologically criticized. The next two sentences in the text describe the focus of Articles 4 and 5 of the Altona confession.

[128.] See also Rüppell: "Some things need to be corrected. Conflict of the individual with the state. That is individualistic"; and Hunsche: "Correct some things. Conflict of the individual with the state instead of the church-state conflict."

[129.] [The reference is actually to Ps. 119:19: "Do not hide your commandments from me."—LR]

2. Dogmatic Exercises on "Theological Anthropology" (Student Notes)[1]

Theological Anthropology[2]

We examine an element of the human person, the soul, the believing soul in light of the precondition of God's revelation. A problem left open in current theology![3] Brunner: Lecture: "Biblical Psychology," [in:] *Gott und Mensch: Vier Untersuchungen über das personhafte Sein.* 1930.[4]

179 Themes:[5]
I.[6] The human being as creature and as structure:
Substance and soul—resolution of the concept of self—finiteness and substance (delimitation vis-à-vis the philosophical "soul." This is structure; in contrast to that is being-creation, being-in-relation).

[1.] Literary estate of Eberhard Bethge; student notes of Hilde Pfeiffer; handwritten manuscript; fifty pages. See also *NL*, B 6,1; student notes of Wolf-Dieter Zimmermann; handwritten manuscript; twenty pages (with gaps, contains a more detailed outline than Pfeiffer). The "fragment of student notes by Klara Hunsche" (*NL*, B 6,2) relates to the themes of the lecture series but cannot be fitted into the structure as shown by Pfeiffer and Zimmermann and has therefore not been referred to here. From Bonhoeffer's own notes, only handwritten theses on the sections "Obedience and Action" and "Sin and Errors" have been preserved (*NL*, A 31,2; incorrectly listed there as part of the "seminar" of the summer semester 1932), which here replace the relevant student notes by Pfeiffer (see below pp. 226–27 and 228–31). Previously published in *GS* 3:62–165. *GS* 5:341–58 provides, under the title provided by Eberhard Bethge, "Problems of a Theological Anthropology" (see also *DB-ER*, 212), a reconstruction of the lecture series using the only notes available to him, those of Zimmermann (which are brief and just use key words). According to Pfeiffer, Bonhoeffer probably began the series on Wednesday, November 2, 1932, and concluded on February 22, 1933 (see ed. notes 6 and 109).

[2.] [In deference to present standard categories in theology, "anthropology" is used here as the translation for "Psychologie." Bonhoeffer is reviewing works on examining human nature, and that field is now commonly referred to as "theological anthropology." "Psychology" is nonetheless retained when the reference is to discussions appropriate to the field of psychology as a science. It is also retained where it has been rendered "psychology" in English translations of the texts Bonhoeffer cites. Readers may note that Eberhard Bethge used "theological anthropology" in his reconstruction of Bonhoeffer's lectures. See ed. note 1.—LR]

[3.] Zimmermann adds: "In contrast with Bultmann; Heidegger. No philosophical preparatory course in theology."

[4.] [Translated as *God and Man: Four Essays on the Nature of Personality*.—LR]

[5.] Bonhoeffer apparently only dealt with a selection from the following list of themes.

[6.] On the left edge the date: "11. 23." 1932. Since Pfeiffer subsequently refers to a seminar on November 9, 1932 (see ed. note 12), this is probably a mistake (correct: "11/2").

II. Immediacy and Reflection
Reflection on belief, on thought, on action. Is reflection already the fall? Five-part answer:

1. Self-knowledge (a) in classical philosophy, (b) in Reformation and pietistic church hymns, [(c)] Luther's judgment of himself (Holl) 1540–1545 Letters,[7] [(d)] Augustine's confessions, [(e)] Paul—Psalms

2. Faith and devotion: Barth—Hans Michael Müller, Schleiermacher ("Act and Being")[8]

3. Knowledge, thought, and understanding: γνῶσις and νοῦς in the New Testament—interpretation of 1 Cor. 2—*credo ut intelligam*[9] in Anselm, in Barth, in Hegel

4. Obedience and action

5. The sinner and transgressions (*desperatio*[10] in Luther and Kierkegaard)—dichotomy and trichotomy in Paul—the individual and individuality—Schelling—Kierkegaard

III. The heart and Christian character—doctrine of Christian perfection: Paul, John—Augsburg Confession, Schleiermacher, Ritschl—hymns of sanctification, the concept of *cor*[11] in Luther—ethics in the nineteenth and twentieth centuries

[Immediacy and Reflection][12] 180
Brunner: "Biblical Psychology."[13] Scientific psychology cannot be practiced without preconditions of worldview. Naturalist psychology, e.g., James Joyce: *Ulysses.*[14] [William] James: *The Varieties of Religious Experience* ([translated by] Wobbermin).[15] Fichte: The self [Ich] is the creator of the nonself. Kant: The self is always linked forward and backward. The self runs

[7.] The reference here is to Karl Holl, "Martin Luther on Luther" ("Luthers Urteile"); see also Bonhoeffer's "Seminar Paper on Luther's Feelings about His Work" (*DBWE* 9:257–84).

[8.] Bonhoeffer had already dealt with Müller in *Act and Being*, to which he refers elsewhere in these lectures (see *DBWE* 2:86 et passim).

[9.] "I believe in order to understand."

[10.] "Despair."

[11.] "Heart."

[12.] Beginning of the notes from November 9, 1932.

[13.] In Brunner, *God and Man: Four Essays on the Nature of Personality*.

[14.] Published in English: 1922; German translation: 1927.

[15.] See James, *Varieties of Religious Experience*. See also Bonhoeffer's 1931 class report, *DBWE* 10:238, 2/13, esp. ed. note 1.

between the boundaries of transcendental apperception and the thing-in-itself. The self can never think itself.[16]

Romantic psychology means grasping the vital essence of humanness before it becomes a mask.[17] Naturalist psychology: soul is a multiplicity of individual phenomena, which can be observed like a film. Idealistic psychology: The subject cannot be observed; the self flees, is not an objective entity. Fichte: the self is a totality resting in itself, an infinitely large sphere. Kant: The self runs here and there. Destruction of this view: the self must have overcome this boundary (see above) in order to know it (Hegel).[18] The boundaries are those of your own reason; for theology: the boundary of the act of revelation is once again *my* boundary.[19] A boundary is an act of decision, where it is up to me to stop. Idealism denies that there are any boundaries within thought. The boundary becomes an object, and thus once again I am beyond it. Kant resolves into Fichte;[20] it continues *ad absurdum*. In all three views the self can know itself, knows about itself, knows.[21]

181 In reflection the human being removes himself from reality. I retreat from that which I hold off. Reflection: I divide myself into subject and object. The act of existing: the self identifies with itself. The self, which gives itself totally to God. Structure is a self-contained totality, not in-relation-to.

Self-knowledge[22] in pietist and Reformation church hymns[23]

Reformation church hymns[24] always say: I exist as a whole.[25] Pietist church hymns: My soul—thus a possibility to look to ourselves, while the Reformation church hymns truly see what happens within the entire human being. [The Reformation human being] knows himself through that which

[16.] Zimmermann here refers to Hinrich Knittermeyer, *Mensch der Erkenntnis*.

[17.] The notes from November 23, 1932, begin with the following sentence. In Pfeiffer erroneously dated November 22. The lecture of November 16 was apparently canceled for a public holiday, the Day of Repentance and Prayer (Buß- und Bettag).

[18.] Zimmermann: "Hegel: Dialectic. The self [*Ich*] returns to itself. Ring."

[19.] On the term "boundary" (*Grenze*), see *DBWE* 3 [esp. ed. note 15, p. 85. See also below 2/7, ed. note 2.—LR]

[20.] The reference here is to Fichte's critique of Kant's transcendental self.

[21.] The following is crossed out in these notes: "understand oneself from oneself."

[22.] Following this term, Zimmermann writes: "Human condition—act of God.—Wittenberg Hymnal—Hallesches." ["Hallesches" refers to the pietist movement centered in Halle.—LR]

[23.] Beginning of the notes from November 30, 1932.

[24.] Zimmermann refers to the hymns "Mitten wir im Leben sind [mit dem Tod umfangen]" ("In the very midst of life," *Lutheran Hymnal*, no. 265) and "Aus tiefer Not" ("From the depths of woe I cry," *Lutheran Hymnal*, no. 230).

[25.] [That is, existential circumstances affect the entire person.—LR]

happens to him, through the things that confront him. If he wants to know himself, the person of the Reformation looks beyond himself; the pietist looks to his soul. "And though if I may have erred through weakness, sin is not my master"[26] (Gellert, rationalism) error, sensuality.[27]

Luther's self-knowledge.[28] To experience no temptation [Anfechtung][29] is the worst temptation of all for him. He acts under the pressure of necessity. He experienced duty as a burden; awareness of being a tool. In renown he sees that which must repel the Christian. Self-knowledge always has the sense of a confession. As a tool, he also affirms himself. He admits that Christ is working within him. He sees his gift from God. He under- 182
lines the involuntary nature of his experience of [temptation], as if coming from outside. The human being is either in the hands of God or in the hands of the devil. The concept of temptation [Anfechtung] is important for Luther's self-knowledge.

In this he comes to understand that the world of experience is an ambiguity; Satan too can transform himself into an angel (2 Cor. 11).[30] For him, this is fundamental. For this reason, every inner experience can be temptation by God or the devil. The comprehension of the Word[31] that we encounter emerges out of this experience. The Word comes and says that beyond the ambiguity of experience is the explicitness of the Word of God of mercy and judgment. Luther's self-knowledge comes not from ambiguous temptation but rather from the Word of God. Temptation *alone* would cause the human being to despair, because he could never be sure. Next

[26.] From the hymn "Wie gross ist des Allmächt'gen Güte" ("How great is the Almighty's goodness"). In the Protestant hymnal for Brandenburg and Pomerania, the second half of verse 5 is as follows: "If my body lives in my soul, it pushes me to do my duty, and although I err through weakness, sin does not govern me" (*Evangelisches Gesangbuch*, no. 609).

[27.] Zimmermann also includes key words on Paul Gerhardt and Friedrich Schleiermacher.

[28.] In the following Bonhoeffer apparently refers to Holl's interpretation of Luther (see ed. note 7), which is mentioned in Zimmermann.

[29.] [*Anfechtung* is a key category for Bonhoeffer as well as Luther. It is properly rendered as "temptation" provided its force is underscored as an "assault by temptation" or "spiritual assault." The connotation is an assault from without that causes one's heart to doubt God and to engage in a battle with the demonic. It is not "temptation" as the passing lure of some attractive vice.—LR]

[30.] See verse 14, "Even Satan disguises himself as an angel of light."

[31.] ["Word" is not always capitalized. It is when it is a christological title, i.e., when it refers to the revelation of God in Jesus Christ as the Word who brings the gospel "word" of "mercy and judgment" (to cite Bonhoeffer's interpretation of Luther). It is not capitalized when it is a reference to the Bible as the word of God or when it is a reference to the interpretation of Scripture, such as the preacher's proclamation.—LR]

to the Word stands the church. When the church is behind him, then he must do it. Where his work is considered, his person is suspended [ausgeschaltet].[32] Luther can say that he is the *peccator maximus*[33] and immediately thereafter that he is the tool of God, that I must do this work, God acts through me. (For us, this does not come into consideration, this separation of person and work. We can no longer simply say that we act as those called by God, that we do this work as compelled by God.)

Luther is in fact confronted by a dual God. [Therefore Luther as human being can also be viewed quite differently:] as someone through whom God acts, who recognizes the errors of the church fathers, for example, and as *peccator maximus*. He [is] incomprehensible to himself—no human being can comprehend himself.

Systematic Summary[34]

1. (Brunner): The human being knows himself only in his existence
183 in relation to something. Existence always only in relation to something. Existence as created existence is being-in-relation-to (see Kant?),[35] is not structure (see romantic psychology).

2. It is possible that this being-in-relation-to is the structure of the human being. This implies: the human being is predisposed religiously. The first is understood in fulfillment, the second in the encounter with the first. This structure then turns existence into something being, existing, demonstrable. Thus I am speaking of human beings with the religious a priori. The first: *actus directus*, the second: *actus reflexus*.[36]

The Reformation.[37] Luther draws his self-knowledge from the future, pietism from the past. Self-knowledge in Augustine: Evil in humans is evil will, not substance. The human being who is autonomous [versus] the human being with knowledge of revelation. The human being is a sinner

[32.] [*Ausgeschaltet* literally means "turned off," the way a light would be turned off. —LR]

[33.] "Greatest sinner." In the Luther letters mentioned by Bonhoeffer (see ed. note 7), there is the phrase *peccator pessimus* ("worst sinner"; see *Luthers Briefwechsel* 14:3013, 53).

[34.] Zimmermann also includes the following seven points; there is no heading. Thus it can be assumed that this, like the following summary (see especially the theses in Bonhoeffer's handwriting on "Obedience and Action" and "Sin and Error") were part of Bonhoeffer's lecture.

[35.] Zimmermann: "(Kant; transcendental)."

[36.] Distinction between direct consciousness and the consciousness of reflection (see *DBWE* 2:158–61).

[37.] Beginning of the notes from December 7, 1932. The following paragraph is in brackets in the manuscript.

through and through; the human being can do nothing. The human race is in a position to practice asceticism before the multiplicity.[38] His original question: What is the human being? In the pre-Christian period, to be a human was to have a split existence. This split disappears in the Christian Augustine; he knows himself as one creature. He has a different image of that which he finds before him.

3. Creation is not being but rather a condition of being. The creaturely is not what already exists but rather the structure. The created is beyond the sphere of objects. Self-knowledge is not reproducible knowledge of objects.[39]

4. What is the relation of this created entirety to existing conditions (soul, flesh, desire, struggle, serenity, et al.)?

5. Answers:

a. From existing reality I draw conclusions about the person. The existing becomes criterion for the nonexisting.

b. There is no relation between the two.

c. The human being is whole in himself [einer als ganzer], as spirit, soul, body. The human being as a whole being is the created.

d. From this [it follows] the person should be directly interpreted from 184
the state of already existing, the ontological being [Struktur-Sein], and vice versa.

6. Where does this split, between that which we find before us and that which we don't find before us, come from? That comes from reflection that turns away from God.[40] For this reason, proof is in philosophy; it can imagine a unified point, no split.[41]

7. That is the problem of the human's own being. One's own being, which encompasses the creatureliness and ontological structure, is a being from God. There is no possibility of a formal ontology. Being is always in relation to Being, thus *analogia relationis,* not *entis.*[42] Because he has his being from God, the human being understands himself not through himself but through God.[43]

[38.] The notes here are unclear, as are those of Zimmermann. [Here we have simply translated the German text as it stands, which is very unclear as to its meaning.—LR]

[39.] Instead of this sentence, Zimmermann has: "Self-knowledge is not objective, but only in knowledge of God."

[40.] Zimmermann instead of the subordinate phrase: *cor curvum in se* (the heart turned in on itself); see also ed. note 98.

[41.] Zimmermann instead of the last two words: "interpret the one from the other."

[42.] "Analogy of relationship, not analogy of being."

[43.] Zimmermann concludes this point with: "Being thus only in relation to God as forgiven or damned. The human being has his own being from God and from others."

[Self-Knowledge in the Bible]
Self-knowledge in the Psalms: Faced with God's creation, the human being trembles with fear in his nothingness. The psalmist sees himself as having succumbed to sin even before he has become responsible. He is simply dependent on God. It is not the self [Ich] that the human being wishes to describe.

Discussion [of individual psalms].[44] 1. The psalmist sees himself in his history. 2. The psalmist see himself as a sinner. God's wrath is inferred from the human situation.[45] 3. The psalmist understands himself through that which he finds before him, works, from his just nature. Convictions, the inner life, fall away. It is a matter of the work that has been done.[46]

185 Self-knowledge in Paul: 1 Cor. 4:3–4: "I do not even judge myself. I am not aware of anything against myself, but I am not thereby acquitted."[47] In the first sentence, which says: I keep your commandment, he is like the psalmists.[48] Paul [here] looks at his work, at where he finds himself. However, apart from where he finds himself, he sees himself as a sinner, as unjust in his relation to God.

Faith and Devotion in Barth[49]
Faith is a gift of God over which we have no disposal. Devotion is a state. The free God stands opposite the God bound to some institution. Barth's free God is the Pauline justification.[50]

Conduct: What is the process by which I know the free God in faith? Now the [self] splits itself for the Pauline, Reformation, Barthian ways of thinking. God himself creates faith in us; it is an act of God in which God remains entirely the subject, while at the same time we ourselves are affected. It is a matter of God's freedom and our freedom.

[44.] According to Zimmermann this was a critique of Ps. 8:5; Ps. 51; and Ps. 119.

[45.] Zimmermann adds: "Is the Israelite thinking that Job protested against."

[46.] Zimmermann concludes the section on the Psalms with: "Different from pietistic existence: Revelation for *the* people [and not] individualistic revelation. Ps[almist] never speaks of progress that he makes. Pietism = process of sanctification. [In the] Psalm ethos plays little role (inwardness disappears)."

[47.] Preceding this Zimmermann mentions Rom. 7.

[48.] Zimmermann: "Is absolutely Jewish, like the Psalmist. Paul revokes it with the following sentence. That can be said before God; he finds nothing; even when we point to error, that stills lies on the same plane. Being depraved, totally, is the opposite. Continuation not in view of his work, but out of the relationship itself to God."

[49.] Beginning of the notes from December 14, 1932.

[50.] Zimmermann: "Barth: Old-new human; gift of God's freedom; God is always free. That is Paul's justification." [The abbreviated phrasing here and in Bonhoeffer's text means the following: Barth's God is the God of Paul's doctrine of justification by grace through faith.—LR]

[Theses on Faith and Devotion]

1. The problem of devotion is the problem of awareness in faith, of consciousness in reflection. It is *actus reflexus* = the form of consciousness in which I [make] my faith explicit; the *actus directus* is the form of consciousness in which the intentionality placed by Christ is placed on Christ. The faith of the child in baptism is not an *actus reflexus*; it is an *actus directus*. One should not think naturalistically here (Hofmann).[51] A baptized child must 186
believe in the form of a consciousness, which is not an *actus reflexus*.

[2.] Faith means *actus directus*. Devotion means *actus reflexus*. Devotion is possession; faith is acceptance of the freedom that presents itself.[52]

3. In Barth, the self breaks apart: old self—new self. In Bultmann too: however [here it is a matter occasionally of] whole self now, whole self now, whole self now.[53] In Barth, the continuity of the old self and the new [is] conceived at the expense of the whole self. In Bultmann, the continuity of the whole self [is] conceived at the expense of the new self.[54] Continuity is the totality of existence.

4. The problem of devotion is the problem of existential continuity.[55]

5. Existence should not be conceived as either being or nonbeing. For the being-in-the-world [Dasein] of human existence, a new term needs to be found that overarches being and nonbeing. If no such term is found, then continuity disappears.

6. Existence should not be conceived of as either objective or nonobjective. For existence is personal-being [Personsein], i.e., it is a being-from and a being-related-to-God.

7. The given reality in its ambiguity—because it is subject to reflection—must be understood from the totality of existence. It cannot be the bearer of existence and continuity. The given reality cannot serve as guarantee of continuity. The bearer of existence is personal-being in its totality.

[51.] Johann Christian Konrad von Hofmann, *Encyklopädie der Theologie*, 95 (entry on baptism with water), offers no proof for Bonhoeffer's thesis. Probably Bonhoeffer here is following Kattenbusch, who suggested that the Erlangen School had an understanding of baptism as "natural effect" (Kattenbusch, "Taufe," 422).

[52.] Zimmermann writes under (2): "Critique of devoutness comes from knowledge of God's free mercy. Devotion = property. Faith = assumption of freely given. Existence = existential and nonexistential = personal being."

[53.] See also Bultmann's understanding of faith as "an ever new act" as response to the event of God's word (Bultmann, "What Does It Mean to Speak of God?" 65).

[54.] Zimmermann characterizing Bultmann and Barth: "Continuity of old and new self at the expense of the continuity of total self (eschatological existence in Barth = the same)."

[55.] Zimmermann under (4): "Problem of devotion = existential continuity. Continuity of the total self; continuity of the old and new self each for itself."

187 8. Faith is the historical act of devotion, qualified by a Christ-directed intentionality established by Christ himself. Faith is in devotion, because existence is in the given reality before us. The existential statement can only be understood on the basis of the ecclesial statement. Existence is possible not as isolated existence but only as existence in the church.

9.[56] The continuity of the historical person is not in the devotion that already exists but instead in the personlike church. "I believe in the forgiveness of sins" has its continuity in that in the church it is said, "Your sins are forgiven."

Human existence has continuity only through the other person. We are imaginable only as bound to our neighbor.[57]

10. Criticism of devotion remains relative criticism insofar as it is said that devotion, of itself, is not faith. There can be absolute criticism of devotion only in the presence of Christ himself, where he accepts devotion as faith. As faith is and remains veiled in devotion—as Christ and the church-community—this necessarily calls for human devotion as a commandment.[58] I only come to faith in that I previously avoided it.[59]

11.[60] The obscuring of faith with the veil of devotion obscures faith for us, who stand in its reflection. Faith remains, however, the *prius* of devotion; thus faith is not a corollary of devotion.[61]

12. What is being faithful in continuity? Continuity = connection, unity. Which manner of devotion, what does it mean to be faithful? As continu-
188 ity of Christian existence lies in the church, therefore the specific form of devotion that corresponds to it is faithfulness to the church [Kirchlichkeit] (Hebrews).[62] The primary expression of faithful existence is the faithfulness to the church, the holding fast to the gathered community. This holding together as community is the being faithful of Christian existence. This contrasts to pietistic and orthodox existence.

[56.] Beginning of notes from December 21, 1932.

[57.] Zimmermann concludes this point with the sentence: "One can never ask individualistically. We *are* only in the church."

[58.] Zimmermann adds: "Walk before me, and be blameless" (Gen. 17:1).

[59.] Zimmermann at this point: "Faith = act, in which the believer participates in the church; says, however, that he was previously part of it and did not hear the word (i.e., broke away)." In the following only Zimmermann provides notes, which conclude with a reference to Schleiermacher (central statement: "For Schleiermacher only a problem of devotion").

[60.] Beginning of notes from January 11, 1933.

[61.] Zimmermann on faith: "not dependent on or conditioned by devotion."

[62.] See Heb. 10:21–25.

Pietism: abiding by the inner nature of salvation. Orthodoxy: abiding by pure doctrine. The concrete form of Christian existence: faithfulness to the church has something in common with these: 1. The notion of graphic concrete discontinuities. Continuities of faith always breached by its discontinuities.[63] 2. The ambiguity of all positions of faith.[64] This continuity is distinguished from other continuities because it takes seriously the historical form of revelation, the church, and because it takes the neighbor seriously, through the visible ties to the place where I live as a believer. Reflection in every act of devotion is here quite exclusively taken into the service of the immediate; it is attending the gathering, holding oneself out to God's Word alone. *The faithful manner of Christian existence is attending church.* Attending church is commanded, but only so that the human being, as believer, knows he is justified by God. (Christ is the church.) Even faithfulness to the church is not free of ambiguity.

The problem of thinking. The act of thinking is the second level of reflection. The first level is devotion.

νοῦς[65] and γνῶσις[66] [in the New Testament]
In Paul, the νοῦς, unlike the σάρξ[67] and ψυχή,[68] is something related to God. However, it is corrupted by sin, and only turns toward God under 189
the effects of πνεῦμα.[69] The νοῦς is the point of contact for the πνεῦμα, unlike γνῶσις, νοῦς is purely reflective thinking. The difference between γιγώσκειν[70] and faith. If one thinks one has gnosis, then one has absolutely no gnosis. The same for faith.[71]

[63.] Zimmermann adds: "Inner salvation of pietists broken by acts of sin. Inwardness is not yet continuity. Nor is keeping to the pure teaching."

[64.] Zimmermann adds: "All veiled belief (can also be from Satan. Going to church is totally subject to ambiguity)" and indicates the following as contrast in the understanding of pietism and orthodoxy.

[65.] "Understanding."

[66.] "Knowledge."

[67.] "Flesh."

[68.] "Soul."

[69.] "Spirit."

[70.] "Knowing."

[71.] In the manuscript follows: "[ידע = to know = create]"; in the gap above the line: "Ps. 12." [In the manuscript, the Hebrew verb ידע means in this and other biblical contexts "to know sexually." Bonhoeffer makes a distinction between *nous* and *pneuma*, on the one hand, and *gnosis, sarx*, and *psyche*, on the other. His allusion to the Hebrew verb here appears to suggest the ambiguity of the faith-knowledge relationship, by connecting "knowing" to "flesh." The editor thanks Clifford Green for this insight.—LR]

In gnosis lies "vision." It is the perception of the sense of an image, somehow an intuition, which is implicit in faith, i.e., the believer sees what he sees, the Lord on high; the nonbeliever sees nothing.[72]

νοῦς is πνεῦμα turned toward other humans. νοῦς is the quality of humans. It [is] captured through Christ. The Christian, who has πνεῦμα, has νοῦς as the organ of the spoken message. First Corinthians 14:[73] νοῦς is available; γνῶσις is not available; it is not property, not structure. Reflection of the capacity of revelation. It is a direct event. This directness only occurs along the path of the indirectness of νοῦς (similarly the directness of the proclamation occurs only along the path of pure doctrine). The νοῦς is conditioned by the community. νοῦς word, congregation. νοῦς = πνεῦμα turned toward the congregation.

Gnosis is a particular form of faith through knowledge and vision. Faith, because he believes, he sees. The foolishness of wisdom, this Paul knows as believer, that is gnosis.

What does "dialectic" mean?

Because God is free (Barth: because God is subject), for this reason the human being can never capture God in his thoughts. Given this premise, Barth says: This fact can only be expressed in thought in that the positive expression within the circle of thought is contradictorily negated. This
190 shows that God's freedom cannot be captured. Thinking is a circle: the human being as subject can only think in terms of objects; objects, however, are things placed at the disposal of the human being. Everything with which the human is confronted becomes an object. For this reason, one can only hint at the free nature of God. For this reason, one speaks [without dialectic] of God always [as] a false God, because he is captured in the circle of thought: How can God's freedom be expressed? Through positive-negative statements. However, God cannot be captured with dialectic either; dialectic is not a method.

Solution: This thinking, essentially false, does [not] occur in the proximity of the reality of God, in the framework of the preaching church. Thus, for good theology it is important that this humble character of thinking is better maintained in hearing the reality of the Christ preached in the

[72.] In the following paragraph the notes from January 18, 1933, begin.
[73.] See verses 14–17.

church than it is by means of some particular method.[74] The theologian should let himself be humbled in the church in order to subsequently practice true theology. He doesn't go to church with just any theology; rather, his existence is determined by being a humble listener of the preaching. As method, every method is immodest. *Fides quaerit intellectum:*[75] insofar as the Christian has this, he is a theologian.

Hans Michael Müller's critique of Barth[76]

Barth is a catholic theologian (line: Anselm, Barth, Schleiermacher) because of faith as given in Barth. Faith cannot be assumed, because it is the particular gift of God. [It is in] relation to Grisebach's "present,"[77] which is the epitome of contingency; it is the reality unviolated by thought.
Where God speaks, creates, there the contingent occurs. In making reality 191
a precondition of my thinking, I allow it a place in my thoughts; applied to faith: in making faith a precondition, I transform a historical place into a sacred one. That is Catholic. In Protestantism, every place is profane for the sake of the δικαιοσύνη θεοῦ.[78] Müller expects γνῶσις of theology, i.e., it should tell the truth of God. Barth says that theology is not able to express the truth. In theology, according to Barth, objective materials are processed by the νοῦς, since theology is an aid. However, in Barth there is also an existential aspect. Initially presentation of correct doctrine in the service of the church's proclamation, but then an existential question. Theology is the church's knowledge; it stands between both preachings. Theology and preaching are mutually corrective.

Hegel: He demands objective concept of substance, oriented to revelation. Subjective, objective, absolute spirit. Faith is the religious idea as such. 1. *Reflection is gnosis in Hegel.* 2. Grisebach: Exclusion of reflection and pure theology of gnosis. 3. Other possibility: Exclusion of gnosis, pure theology of reflection. 4. Theology of reflection, but located within the church. Gnosis and faith belong closely together.

[74.] The notes here are unclear. What is meant is that the truth of theology cannot be ensured methodologically but is totally dependent on the presence of Christ in the sermon.

[75.] "Faith seeks understanding."

[76.] Beginning of the notes from January 25, 1933. Bonhoeffer drew on H. M. Müller, "Credo, et intelligam."

[77.] H. M. Müller, "Credo, et intelligam," 173, with reference to Grisebach, *Gegenwart*, rejected Barth's dialectic as determined "by pathos of existentiality."

[78.] ["Righteousness of God."—LR]

Obedience and Action[79]

Meant as contrast: Obedience and doing works. Paper by Tillich.[80]

1. Person. 2. Self-determination. 3. Belonging together. Obedience only among people. Is freedom grounded in belonging or vice versa? Belonging and freedom are bound, at the same time, in a personal relationship. Only
192 through the Word are my belonging and my freedom possible. Love and recognition reversible. Faith and obedience assumes a You.

The problem as such. Parallel problem of faith and devotion. What is the relation between the obedient nature of the human being as *actus directus* and concrete acts, [to] doing the act as *actus reflexus*? What is the relation between obedience as seen by God and *bona opera*?[81]

[Bonhoeffer's original theses on "Obedience and Action"]

1. Obedience means to belong to a person in that you listen to his or her words. Obedience means belonging in the form of hearing.

2. Biblically: Obedience means belonging to God in the form of hearing God's word. Because God's word is creative, because it is *verbum visibile,*[82] for this reason the word itself creates in the hearing what it presents. There is no division between hearing and acting. Hearing is acting, both as a creation of the word of God.

3. Dynamic instrumentalism must be rejected—it is an image inappropriate to the facts (even though it runs through all theology since Paul); because in it the fundamental opposition of God and the human being is dissolved and thus mysticism (mysticism of the will, of sanctification) is unavoidable. Acting is then always something that comes out of hearing (faith), something second to hearing, while it is exactly that hearing, the reception of the word itself. Hearing *is* acting.

4. If hearing is originally acting, then the word is something that addresses the human being in his entire existence, body and soul; then the human being is still undivided in πνεῦμα, νοῦς, σῶμα,[83] in hearing and doing, in passivity and activity, in act and being.

5. The human being in *status corruptionis*[84] is determined by Adam's hav-
193 ing wanted to "do" something for God, that his action inexplicably broke

[79.] Beginning of the notes from February 1, 1933.

[80.] It could not be determined whether this was a report by the student Ernst Tillich or a report on a paper by Paul Tillich.

[81.] "Good works."

[82.] "Visible word."

[83.] "Body."

[84.] "State of corruption/sin."

away from his hearing. Thus humans are divided in hearing and acting. The problem is: how does God's word now approach these divided humans?

6. God's word has remained the same, but for the sake of the human being it is now issued in the isolated form of the preached word. The totality of God's word is preserved in the sacrament, to be sure, but the sacrament, for its part, requires interpretation in spoken preaching, which is only captured by the ears of the people who hear. How does the word heard by the ear move to action, to completion? That is the theological-anthropological question. Through the third level of reflection (the first: I know myself before God in devout acts; the second: theological reflection on the heard word and the act; the third: practical reflection on the consequences of that which has been heard).

7. Obedience remains *actus directus*. Acting is the third level of reflection. Obedience is in hearing the word, in fulfillment of the word, in faith. In hearing the word, the human being, as one who is aware of his original unity in faith, knows that he is simultaneously called to the impossibility of achieving this unity and to do something. This act (which remains purely reflection, there is no "simple action," vegetating, sleeping, eating . . .) is obedience, is *actus directus*, to the extent that its necessity and impossibility are known in the same manner, i.e., to the extent that it occurs in faith. (That is not identical with the question of *acceptatio*.[85] God can reject the obedient; that is, it is up to God to accept the obedient.)

8. Obedience is hearing the word of God, faith, and nothing else. The word is fulfilled in *status corruptionis*, in faith, i.e., in the hearing of fallen humans. The word, as *verbum visibile* in the sacrament, is visible only to believers. Obedience hears the word, acting follows the word; thus church practice is justified as the first commandment of action. The faithfulness to the church is genuine when it is aware of its necessity and its impossibility.[86]

Sin and Transgression[87] 194

When the topic is sin, discernment extends to something that already exists, that is, to an existing transgression. (The thinking is as follows: it lies before devotion, acting, transgression. Thinking begins with this fact, goes back and seeks to define the sin; thus, the transgression, seen from the nature of

[85.] "Acceptance."

[86.] End of Bonhoeffer's original theses, which replace the student notes to "Obedience and Action." The underlining of some passages in the original has generally not been indicated here.

[87.] Beginning of the notes from February 8, 1933.

sin, loses its importance. Then the thinking goes further back, to the act, to the transgression.) Thinking on sin begins with despair as the point of experience.

Despair in Luther: For Luther, despair means the end of human existence. The human being stands alone when faced with a moral decision, before the wrath of God. Despair drives him into the abyss, thus robs him of his possibility of existence. The powers of temptation [Anfechtungsmächte] seem hypostasized. Faced with despair, he has a feeling of the constricting world, of being afraid. There is a complete silence from a wrathful God. The human being is all alone. The devil's hands and feet are the abominable facts of God's wrath.[88]

Experience of *esse peccator*[89] and falling ever again into sin. The human being must constantly enter into infernal doubt, as long as he himself endeavors to do something. The human being must resign himself to despair. But God takes the despairing human in his hands.

Günter Jacob: Der Gewissensbegriff Luthers[90]

Theodosius Harnack: Luther[91]

[Despair in] Kierkegaard:[92] That which is Christian is incommensurable. The self before God characterized by its existentialism. Despair is the sick-
195 ness unto death.[93] This sickness of the spirit is different from that to which a psychiatrist refers. Despair is the primary characteristic of the existence of persons of spirit. The Christian must enter into conscious awareness to the highest possible degree of despair in order to overcome reflection.[94] Revelation is a paradox, a stumbling block for humans. The human being does not wish to understand it, because sin revolts against the destruction

---

[88.] According to the information from the Luther Archives, Tübingen, provided on February 26, 1994, no evidence for this sentence can be found in Luther's writing.

[89.] "Being a sinner."

[90.] See Jacob, *Der Gewissensbegriff in der Theologie Luthers.*

[91.] See T. Harnack, *Luthers Theologie.*

[92.] The *DBW* 12 note reads: "On the concept of doubt, cf. the evidence in Kierkegaard, *Registerband,* pp. 132–33." [This is an index volume to the main German edition of Kierkegaard's works. The English reader can find the discussion of doubt in the works cited in the *Registerband,* namely, Kierkegaard's *Concept of Anxiety* and *The Sickness unto Death.*—LR]

[93.] See Kierkegaard, *Sickness unto Death,* 24 (title of chapter C in the first section is "Despair Is the Sickness unto Death").

[94.] [Bonhoeffer is referring to Kierkegaard's juxtaposition of "immanence" (or immediacy) and "reflection." Kierkegaard warned against succumbing to reflection in a

of understanding. Knowing oneself to be a sinner is a necessary prerequisite for the highest form of existence in faith. Sin is a position, not a negation;[95] it is the eternal thorn in human flesh. Christianity demands the strictest consciousness of sin. Remaining in sin as a permanent state. In the transition from despair to faith lies the dialectical moment. Original sin is an existential problem, not a cosmic problem. Sinning is a free act here (for us) as it was there (Adam). "An eternal individual guilt weighs on humans."[96] Original sin is guilt in spite of coercion. Consciousness of sin shows the eternal break, the unbridgeable gap between human and God, but it is, on the other hand, the way into Christianity.

Luther's *desperatio*: He knows why it overcomes him. In Luther the concept of despair is seen psychologically and theologically; in Kierkegaard it is the existential reality of human beings, i.e., he applies the concept of despair as well to those who know nothing of it. This *desperatio* is structurally seen. How are the two views related? Luther uses "God's wrath." What is the relation between the *desperatio*, which is bound to transgression (Luther), to that which was original, there before the transgression? They are not mutually exclusive.

[Theses on] Sin and Transgression[97]

(1) The dogmatic problem: Sin as being and as act. Sin as being cannot be seen as being, as already existing, from which an act follows. Both in 196
personal-being, as humanity and as self.

(2) The knowledge of sin is objective-nonobjective knowledge. Like all knowledge, it arises from an object, from the transgression. This is only then recognized as sin when the individual transgression is immediately understood as the fall of my entire existence from a relation with God, i.e., when I understand myself as *cor curvum in se*.[98]

---

kind of self-preoccupation that represented a retreat from the immediacy of existential reality.—LR]

[95.] See Kierkegaard, *Sickness unto Death* (pt. 1, 156–57), chapter 3: "Sin Is Not a Negation, but a Position."

[96.] According to information from the Søren Kierkegaard Research Center, Copenhagen, received by the German editor, June 27, 1995, no evidence of this sentence can be found in his writings.

[97.] Bonhoeffer's original theses on sin and error. Bonhoeffer here drew on arguments from *Act and Being* (see *DBWE* 2, esp. pp. 136–50).

[98.] See Martin Luther, "Lectures on Romans" (1515–16, *LW* 25:291ff.).

(3) There are two forms of the knowledge of sin: (1) sinful knowledge of sin, (2) Christian knowledge of sin.

[To] (1) Reproach of the conscience, regret, *contritio activa,*[99] not wishing to die, but instead to live in sin. This reflection is the death of the "spiritual human," the new self. With respect to conscience every sin = transgression! For it is the ability of the human being to improve himself that is being addressed.

[To] (2) "To consider one's sin in Christ" . . . "Seek yourself only in Christ and not in yourself and you will find yourself in him" (*LW* 42:106). "Out of your conscience in Christ." Here knowledge of sin is infinitely sharpened and simultaneously done away with, death and life, because life, therefore death. Sin not = transgression, rather *cor curvum in se,* I believe that I am a sinner. *Contritio passiva*[100]—reflection in Christ. Faith remains repentance. But this reflection is now the eternal death of the old human (as reflection in sin was the death of the new human). Faith is dying, dying daily. The final reflection is [the text stops here].

(4) The Christian will obediently enter daily into this dying and will, here too, assume the existing transgressions. For him, they obtain the dual sense of sin and the reference to sin. The Christian will not remain stuck on the transgression; he will not overestimate himself, i.e., he will not let it distract his view from his fallen existence; he will not let the magnitude of the sins disappear into it; he will not underestimate it, i.e., he will recognize
197 it as his act. He will be attentive to the transgressions but will be even more attentive to the word of the church, which marks him as a sinner, condemns him, and exonerates him.[101]

Christian Character[102]
Faith—devotion; obedience—act; sin—transgression: Somewhere in between lies Christian character.

Reinhold Seeberg, *System der Ethik:*[103] The Christian being-good of humans is to be ascertained. It becomes a preferred habit to turn disposition into acts. In Christian character, faith and love mature. "Christian character consists . . . of the habitual ability to internalize God's rule."[104] Here faith and mercy become directly visible. The "act" exists here. Faith is a

[99.] "Active regret."
[100.] "Passive regret."
[101.] End of Bonhoeffer's original theses. Emphases not marked.
[102.] Beginning of the notes from February 15, 1933.
[103.] See for the following esp. § 40–42.
[104.] Seeberg, *System der Ethik,* 99.

part of character. Character is a *habitus*[105] gained through practice. Christian character would then be a *habitus* gained through Christian practice.

Christian practice (earlier, virtue).

1. Christian *habitus*: *Habitus* is something that the human being has. The human being is determined furthermore by the *esse* and *fieri* (*pati*).[106] The human has neither his *esse* nor his *pati*. His *esse* is his *pati*. However, *habere*[107] is part of the *esse*, but not in the sense that the *habere* is a *habere* of the *esse*. It is a *habere* of conditionality, desires. The human being has that which can be possessed. Having is the behavior of the *esse*. Christian *habitus* is the behavior, the Christian *esse*.

2. The Christian *esse* is being a sinner and forgiven in faith. Christian *habitus* is the behavior of faith.

3. Christian *habitus* falls under the category of that which we find before us [vorfindlich], but is not identical with it, rather subordinate. That which we find before us and that which we do not is not the contrast between the old and the new human being. The old human being is just as much already 198
there and not already there [vorfindlich und nicht vorfindlich] as the new human being. The division into that which is already there and that which is not is the act of the old human being. Nonetheless, the whole human being stands in *habere* and *esse*, but in such a way that the *habere* is a manner of being of the non-preexisting *esse* (the *habere* is already present).

4. The *habitus* must be explained from the *esse*. As, however, the *esse* cannot be had, the *habitus* cannot simply be formed from the *esse*. The *habitus* is formed in its awareness of the character of being had by the *esse*. Part of the nature of Christian *habitus* is that it continually annuls itself, i.e., it is part of its nature to be aware of being penultimate, compared to the finality of the *esse* of faith, and that it does not take itself so seriously.

5. The *habitus* of Christian character distinguishes itself from that of individuality in that it is gained through practice. The practice that forms the Christian *habitus* must begin with [letting it find itself] in the penultimate.[108] It is a practice of formed humans to look beyond themselves.

6. Christian character therefore carries within it a basic element of neglecting itself. The knowledge of myself as sinner, this knowledge of my

[105.] "Permanent state/position." [In Catholic doctrine *habitus* is a metaphysical quality that exists in opposition to *Dispositio*. *Habitus* is permanent and *dispositio* is transitory; there are multiple subdivisions of both.—LR]

[106.] "Being and becoming (suffering)."

[107.] "To have."

[108.] Gap filled using Zimmermann's notes.

justification makes character formation into something secondary, penultimate, yet significant as practice.

7. Which practices form Christian character?[109] Not ethic, description. Practices (virtues) of Christian character:[110]

1. Exercising faithfulness to the church, participating in Word and sacrament. Receiving it, allowing oneself to be addressed. To be silent in the domain of the church. Letting go of oneself (externally),[111] bearing ([one's own and the][112] burdens of others), admitting one is wrong. Internally: humility, patience.

199 2. Practice of piety, of devotion itself: practiced by reading the Bible, by meditation, by prayer. That is, turning outward. However, it must not remain *opus*,[113] but rather it must refer to myself, i.e., stance of being turned outward and remaining responsible. Prayer [only][114] upon receiving the heard word of God.

3. Practice of recognizing sin: 1. in the recognition of exploring conscience, of having to judge oneself in order to give expression to God's judgment; 2. however, always being able to silence the conscience. Specifically saying: In the face of the continuing reproach of the conscience: be quiet now. Not being ordered around by the conscience.

4. Practice of service: 1. [In the] practice of asceticism (i.e., moderation); 2. practice in the freedom (of not being bound) (problem of sexual ethic is problem of asceticism). Practice in freedom as expression of breaking through against the ties of pietistic strictness and narrowness. The Christian lives in the tension described in 3. and 4. A similar tension must occasionally arise in 1. and 2. but nowadays the absence of church and of faith and prayer is carelessness.

George Bernanos: *Sous le soleil de Satan*[115] (for spiritual exercises). When asceticism wants to enslave me, I must practice freedom.

[109.] Pfeiffer incorrectly dated the following as April 22, 1933.

[110.] Zimmermann on the relation between practice and character: "Practices (virtues); found character and come from it. In which is it preserved?"

[111.] Supplemented using Zimmermann.

[112.] Supplemented using Zimmermann.

[113.] "Work."

[114.] Supplemented using Zimmermann.

[115.] *Under Satan's Sun*; published in Germany in 1927.

The reflection of character is, on the one hand, an expression of the *cor curvum in se* and, on the other hand, a sentence from Jesus Sirach is true: "Respect your soul, but in humility."[116]

3. Review of Robert Jelke, *Vernunft und Offenbarung*[1] 200

"The relation between reason and revelation is materially an exclusive one" (103). This is the thesis of this work. The author draws on Luther for this and, in a historical section, shows how the material use of reason for knowledge of revelation was, before Luther, certainly permissible; how Luther then rediscovered the original understanding of revelation in its exclusive material relationship to reason; and how, beginning with Melanchthon, a turning away from Luther arose; and how, in turn, the material use of reason spoils the term "revelation." This continues into contemporary theology, and the entire so-called dialectical theology[2] is accused of working "with material thinking" (95). "Here the knowledge of God and revelation is nothing more than the pure knowledge of reason. Here it is not God who is in the center, but rather the human being" (45). Here theology is based on a philosophy of existence, which is why the attempt is made to "demonstrate with reason the transcendence of reason in revelation" (65), and in doing so both revelation and reason are offended. The paradox that God's "revelation [is][3] entirely God's work and at the same time human knowledge" (99) is thus either left unresolved or is not understood by the dialecticians. Here reason holds sway over revelation, and this is because a distinction has not been made between formal and material reason. This distinction, however, is absolutely necessary "if an indisputable solution to the problem of revelation and reason is to be found" (96).

[116.] Sir. 10:28a. Zimmermann includes this chain of thought, more extensively, before the four points on preserving character. In doing so he refers to "1 Cor. 4:4 = penultimate of conscience." Later there is a citation: "But when you fast, put oil on your head and wash your face" (Matt. 6:17).

[1.] ["Reason and Revelation."—LR] From *Theologische Literaturzeitung* 57 (1932): 563–65. Previously published in *GS* 3:134–37. [The page numbers given in parentheses in the text refer to pages in Jelke's book.—LR]

[2.] Jelke differentiates between two "main groups" of dialectical theology. Barth and Brunner are taken as representative of the first, Bultmann and Gogarten of the second (Jelke, *Vernunft und Offenbarung*, 49).

[3.] Omission in the manuscript not marked.

It is quite a different question as to whether one understands the problem of reason and revelation as a problem of philosophy and theology, or as a problem of theology and faith, or as one of knowledge and faith, and a clear distinction should be made between such questions; however, as the
201 work under discussion does not make these or similar distinctions, it must be assumed that the proposed solution relates to all three questions. This is to be kept in mind.

The second, systematic, section of the work is dedicated to the development of the thesis. In an explanation of the nature of reason, objectifying individual contents of consciousness is called the a priori of the spirit, its "most valuable ability" (76). It is only in this act that self-consciousness arises. This function of reason's understanding, in the sense of *ratio*,[4] is part of all knowledge (78 [–79]), thus of religious knowledge as well. A religious a priori must draw on a theoretical one, but it of course leads independently beyond this in that its material is no longer the unformed given, but that which has already been formed by the theoretical a priori. The "religious employment of reason" (87) thus forms, for the spatial-temporal determinants of the self, the respective contrasting determinants—thus: limitation—limitlessness, finiteness—infinity, restriction—separation (87). It would be wrong to say that the religious a priori is the active and the material the passive (90). Rather, the religious a priori functions only through stimulation by the material. It is only to be understood as "the formal possibility of religious formation of ideas" (93). To this extent it is totally passive and totally formal. "Revelation occurs not through reason but within the realm of reason" (94), but this is formal reason, which does not aim to be systematic but rather consists of absorbing and forming the material available. That which can be gained here from the concept of reason is then correspondingly drawn from the concept of revelation (103 to 140), with the result that the concept of revelation demands "the ability of the human soul to imagine and comprehend the infinite with the aid of the finite" (134). Jelke thinks it is especially necessary to raise the question of the certainty of the reality of that given in religious knowledge and answers it with a reference to the immediate experience of faith. Here, as before, one can see the realistic starting point of Jelke's theory of religious knowledge.

202 Without wishing here to enter into the question of the possibility of speaking of an "unformed material" and so on, the central question must be raised as to whether the distinction between formal and material reason, on which the entire argument is based, is philosophically possible and

[4.] "Reason."

theologically useful. Assuming it is correct to say that the first a priori is the ability to objectify, that basically it is always somehow a question of a subject-object relation, this then entails that the "material" is already included in a system arising from reason and that it will not be released from it, so that it is no longer even possible to speak of "material." This means reason, with its first act, has taken total control. There where humans reasonably speak of "I" or "it" is already the world where the "material" is subject to reason. That is the result of Kantian and idealistic philosophy. Reason as a circle closed on itself cannot be "used"; it draws everything irresistibly into the circle it governs. It must, however, be made completely clear that theology is already decisively prejudiced if we can only think of God, know God, in objectification. It may be true that we cannot think in any other way, but precisely that will be our undoing, because God thus appears no longer as the free Lord but as the summit of our system of objects of reason. The distinction between formal and material reason is philosophically and theologically a failure because formal reason extends the system beyond its proper field and prejudices. And now the accusation that Jelke seemingly turned against the dialecticians can be turned against him; and the question must be raised: Is it not at the very point where one is aware of the error of *all* (also formal) reason and then—because one cannot think, also theologically, without reason—one takes up this ragged, malformed tool as it is, in full awareness, *in order* not to be able to do something well? Is it not precisely here that Christian modesty about reason, the penance that reason must do, is truer than where this radical insight fails and continuous attempts are made to discover something good in this defective means—and then
rely upon this good and feel secure within it? It is because Barth knows 203
that *all* reason is nothing and that he can nonetheless not do without it; it is because of this that he can speak "in accordance with reason" more courageously and more freely than those who wish to preserve reason as a last resort. Everyone must be aware that behind all impartiality stands a radical critique of reason, which can come never from reason but rather only from revelation. Reason that criticizes itself remains a partial critique that leaves a modest remainder—and be it "formal reason"—for itself. Reason that lets itself be oriented by revelation is totally oriented, and just because of that, toward something new applied in its temporary office. It is from this starting point that other possibilities of interpreting Luther in relation to this problem will arise.

4. Memorandum: "The 'Social Gospel' (Soziale Evangelium)"[1]

The Social Gospel[2]

1. *The "social gospel" in America*
Because adherents of the "social gospel" are most interested in and participate most in international Christian work, the view is commonly held in
204 Europe that it is *the* American Christianity. This is mistaken. Numerically, those who reject the social gospel in America are greater. However, the living church forces generally profess it, at least in its moderate form. Its church opponents are usually fundamentalists (strong financial support from capitalist circles—which reject the social gospel, but also important theological reasons [see below]) and adherents of individualistic revival Christianity. The spiritual influence of the social gospel on American intellectual circles is greater than that of any other church influence. In the North more than in the South. The Fed[eral] Council [of Churches of Christ in America], an association of thirty-three denominations, is strongly influenced in its work by the social gospel.

2. *The intellectual context of the social gospel*
State and church fundamentally separated. No financial support (but tax breaks etc. so that radical supporters of the social gospel see the de facto dependence of the church on the state as one of the main problems), no religion classes in public schools; however, congressional sessions open with

[1.] EZA, 621/41; mimeographed copy. See also *NL*, A 34,1; carbon copy. Previously published in *GS* 1:104–12. Texts such as Bonhoeffer's memorandum were intended to encourage "fruitful detailed work and intensive recruitment" among members and groups of the German branch of the World Alliance (*Die Kirchen am Werk*, no. 1, 13). In addition to Bonhoeffer's memorandum, the following papers were included among the "short, brief collections of materials by experts with citations of all relevant literature on the topics dealt with": "Our Position on Non-Christian Religions, Draft by Prof. Dr. Witte, Berlin" and "The Position of Christians on Questions of Nationality and Race, Draft by Mission Inspector Walter Braun" (*Mitteilungen der deutschen Weltbundvereinigung*, no. 13 [May 1933]: 13). The paper on the social gospel was originally to have been done by Hermann Sasse. As he was prevented from doing so, Bonhoeffer took on the task of preparing this text "by December" (Report on the meeting of the working committee of the German branch of the World Alliance for Promoting International Friendship through the Churches, October 29, 1932, EZA, 51/D V c). See also 1/8 and 1/13, as well as Bonhoeffer's report on his year of study at Union Theological Seminary, especially the section on pragmatism and social work (*DBWE* 10, 1/181, esp. pp. 310–12 and 317–19).

[2.] [A draft of this essay was written by Paul Lehmann, at Bonhoeffer's request. Bonhoeffer's request of October 30, 1932, to Lehmann can be found in Green, *Bonhoeffer*, appendix, 332, and was also published in *DBW* 17:112–14. The letter will be included in *DBWE* 11 as 1/93a.—LR]

a prayer, in the schools often regular prayers. Because the church depends completely on the activity of the congregation, there is strong general interest in the church and a close fusion of public with church interests, with all the consequences for the dominance of the pew over the pulpit.[3] Parallel
to a separation of church and state, there is a close link between church and 205
society. For this reason throughout American history there has always been significant participation by the church in the formation of public opinion. (Revolution, Civil War, end of slavery, Prohibition laws enacted mainly due to Methodists' influence!) The contact of the church with the world of labor has therefore not broken off to the extent that it has in Germany. American workers are not antichurch (only recently, especially among young blacks, because the church is one of the most difficult hurdles to the solution of the racial question). Nonetheless, at the beginning of the nineteenth century, radical social and economic change was so profound that the church was in danger of losing contact. The rise of mechanization demanded a rethinking of Christian social teachings. For individualistic American thinking, which is based on individual performance, mechanization, the "impersonal" economic system, created a special problem. The capitalistic conservatism of the pioneer years required an adjustment.

3. *The history of the social gospel*

In its general tendency not originally American (Kingsley,[4] Stöcker,[5] 1891 encyclical).[6] Combination of a number of sources: Methodism (human efforts to bring about God's kingdom on earth), Unitarianism; Darwin and Spencer (theory of evolution, eudemonistic social ethic, the two easily united, development of humanity to its greatest potential, to God's kingdom on earth); pragmatism (the truth lies in the effect, in success [truth works]; every human being has the potential for improve-
ment, theory of environment); Calvinist influence questionable. At most 206
a Calvin secularized by the Enlightenment and the theory of evolution. (Tracing both capitalism [Max Weber][7] as well as social gospel back to

[3.] Visser 't Hooft, *Background of the Social Gospel*, 20n1, quotes from the July 15, 1926, issue of *The Christian Century*: "There is a tyranny of the pew over the pulpit in America which is not paralleled in other Protestant nations and which only the stoutest heart can defy."

[4.] Refers to Charles Kingsley, one of the leaders of Christian socialism in Great Britain who opposed the effects of Manchester liberalism in the mid-nineteenth century.

[5.] Refers to Adolf Stöcker, a leader of the Christian social mission movement in Germany, who was concerned with the "social question" in the 1870s.

[6.] Refers is to the social encyclical *Rerum Novarum* of Leo XIII of May 15, 1891.

[7.] See Weber, *Protestant Ethic*.

Calvinism[8] doubtful.) First great teacher of the social gospel is Walter Rauschenbusch (German-American, longtime pastor on the east side of New York,[9] then professor of church history in Rochester). 1907 *Christianity and the Social Crisis* his first, pioneering work of the social gospel, makes overwhelming impression (further literature see below). Especially influential among Methodists. 1908 Federal Council publishes [*The*] *Social Creed of the Churches.*[10] Rauschenbusch promotes a moderate social gospel, recognizes, on the one hand, those places in the New Testament referring to the individual, but underlines the religious, not the social aspect (Sherwood Eddy).[11] On the other hand, later writers see all of Christianity in Jesus's social proclamations (Ellwood,[12] Harry F. Ward), indeed eliminate the specifically religious elements and arrive at a pure evolutionary humanism (Ames and the Chicago School).[13] In spite of realistic and open descriptions of conditions, because of the fundamental optimism of Rauschenbusch and his friends—among the younger an ever more skeptical pessimism (Reinhold Niebuhr, Kirby Page). The influence of Continental Christian socialism (Ragaz, Tillich) is slowly undermining evolutionary thinking and the belief in the fundamental goodness of the human being. However, here too the American spirit is putting up strong resistance. The social gospel, in its original form, is currently past its prime in America. However, its basic motives and directions still have broad influence in church life.

207 4. *The concept of the social gospel*

The concept is enigmatic. For Rauschenbusch it is a return to the original gospel, to the religion of Jesus, his message of the kingdom of God and brotherhood among human beings, and its application to the current social crisis. For Ames a radical combination of religious and social humanitarian

[8.] According to Visser 't Hooft, *Social Gospel,* 7, this derivation was widespread and typical for the views of European Lutherans.

[9.] ["The east side of New York" is incorrect. Rauschenbusch's parish was in Hell's Kitchen, on the west side.—LR]

[10.] This edition was expanded in 1912 (*Social Creed of the Churches;* see 5–7).

[11.] Bonhoeffer's bibliographical references for Eddy, Ward, Niebuhr, and Page are at the end of this memorandum.

[12.] See Ellwood's *Reconstruction of Religion* and *Christianity and Social Science.*

[13.] The reference here is to Edward Scribner Ames. In addition to Ames, Shailer Mathews and Henry Nelson Wieman were members of the Chicago School. They all taught at the University of Chicago Divinity School and supported a "naturalistic theism" (Shaw, "Naturalistic Theism").

thought.[14] The foundations of the social gospel arise in great part from a constructive sociology (Ward developed from sociology the teaching of mutual aid as ethical principle of society, seeing it at the same time as the central idea of Jesus and the prophets), in part in close relation with theology, e.g., insight into the ethical and religious tensions in the New Testament (Reinhold Niebuhr). The social gospel is "application of Christian principles to society and application of social principles to Christianity" (Visser 't Hooft).[15] It is in this general form that the social gospel is most widespread, in its radical sense only very limited.

5. *Teachings of the social gospel*

1. The social gospel is social *gospel*. The gospel entirely relates to the human being in his current situation, i.e., in the social crisis ("Christ must be the Lord of all or he is not Lord at all," Sherwood Eddy).[16] There is no 208
ethical neutrality in social life. Mammon or Christ. The exclusiveness of the *social* gospel is accented differently.

2. Today's social structure is materialistic, atomistic, individualistic, capitalistic. Its greatest crime is its undermining of the value of human personality among the oppressed. Here the church must get involved.

3. The church must get behind the dogmatic theology that conceals the real Christ; to the religion of Jesus, that was essentially determined ethically and socially. Not teaching about Christ, but Christ's teaching. It is the high point of biblical proclamation, which previously had its high point in the prophetic [Prophetentum] ethic.

4. Christianity is an ethical religion (or even only an ethic); the Decalogue and its interpretation in the Sermon on the Mount form its center.

5. Jesus is God's revelation, to the extent that he embodied his teaching in his life. His cross is the symbol for his complete devotion to the ideal of brotherly love, his resurrection the symbol for the eternal truth of this value.

6. The central term of Jesus's proclamation is the kingdom of God, willed *on earth*. The emphasis is on the latter. The kingdom of God means the

[14.] Shaw writes: "Ames' early position seems to have identified the divine with the spirit of the social group, following Durkheim. In his book *Religion* (1929), this concept provides the starting point of his discussion, but it is broadened to include nature as generated and supporting group values" ("Naturalistic Theism," 300).

[15.] See Visser 't Hooft, *Background of the Social Gospel*, 16: "The social gospel, therefore, . . . is more than an application of Christian principles to society; it is also an application of social principles to Christianity."

[16.] See Eddy, *Facing the Crisis*, 201.

fatherhood of God and brotherhood among human beings. Its realization occurs through the step-by-step work of Christianity in history. (Sometimes it is taught that in the development of God's kingdom, God too grows and develops.)[17] God is immanent in the world, not transcendent.[18]

7. The history of the kingdom of God on earth provides a develop-
209 ment from imperialism to internationalism, from monarchy to democracy (Rauschenbusch: "The worst thing that could happen would be that God remained an autocrat, while the world advanced towards democracy"),[19] from individualism to collectivism. That is the eschatology. The dualism of two worlds is changed into a monism of an evolutionary theory of history. The teaching of eternal life and immortality are not dealt with here.

8. Despite the radical critique of the current situation, the fundamental optimism that the world can be won for Christ, the social order rebuilt, and the kingdom of God created leads to a high level of activism that rejects every doubt and declares all neutrality to be unchristian. The human being is, if not originally good, then at least neutral (fundamentally sound, Rauschenbusch),[20] i.e., capable of improvement; his sin is his resistance to the social gospel and can be overcome through ethical living. This corresponds to the understanding of history.

9. The social gospel is a gospel of action, realistic, practical. "Not dogma, but life; not theology, but religion."[21] Theology is here generally understood as fundamentalist-orthodox. It is rejected for the following reasons: God's transcendence, Christ's teaching, the teaching on sin, dualist eschatology, neutrality toward the orders of the world.

10. Rebuilding the social order is conceived concretely in the imitation of the form of the family. In the family there is no profit motive, competi-

---

[17.] Probably Bonhoeffer was referring here to the Chicago School, which understood the divine as "not ontologically transcendent of the natural world" (Shaw, "Naturalistic Theism," 299).

[18.] See Visser 't Hooft, *Background of the Social Gospel*, 179: "The moralization and humanization of the doctrine of God thus leads naturally to the idea of pure immanence."

[19.] Visser 't Hooft, *Background of the Social Gospel*, 178, quotes this sentence from Rauschenbusch as typical of an understanding widespread in the social gospel literature.

[20.] See Visser 't Hooft's characterization of the social gospel movement: "[S]in is not conceived as inherent in human nature. On the contrary human nature is 'fundamentally sound' (Rauschenbusch)" (*Background of the Social Gospel*, 62).

[21.] The source of this sentence could not be found. A similar position was also current among European Christians in the World Alliance and in Life and Work. Thus, for example, Hermann Kapler coined the phrase: "Doctrine divides, service unites" (Weiße, *Praktisches Christentum und Reich Gottes*, 197).

tion, and in its place is the principle of mutual aid.[22] It is on this basis that 210
the new society of the brotherhood of mankind[23] should be built.

6. *Appreciation and critique*

1. The unrelenting seriousness with which the practical social problems are shown here, and with which Christians are called on to serve, is the decisive contribution of American Christians to the understanding of the Christian message in the entire world. The personal and sober passion of those involved in the social gospel demand a decision of everyone who comes into contact with it.

2. The social gospel consciously aims at the world of laypeople, rejecting all ecclesiastical considerations.

3. Taking seriously the kingdom of God as a kingdom on earth is biblically sound and is justified compared to an understanding of the kingdom as one beyond.

4. Nonetheless, the biblical message is not clearly imparted.

(a) The eschatological understanding of the kingdom, as one that God can create and brings in contrast to the world, has disappeared.

(b) From this follows a fundamentally different understanding of history. There is no concept of evolution in the New Testament. The end of history is not the coming into being of the kingdom of God on earth but the deepest gap between Christianity and the world.[24]

(c) Sin is not an unpleasant side effect of human existence; rather it corrupts the innermost core of human beings.

(d) Christ is the mediator who reconciles the human being with God and forgives his sins. Cross and resurrection as acts of God are therefore the center of history.

(e) God is not the immanent progressive ethical principle of history; God is the Lord who judges the human being and his work, he is the absolute sovereign (God's kingdom is not a democracy!).

5. The optimism, the ideology of progress does not take God's com- 211
mandment seriously (Luke 17:10). It is modern enthusiasm [Schwärmerei]. It fails to recognize human limits; it ignores the fundamental difference between a kingdom of the world and God's kingdom.

6. The ideal of international, democratic, collectivist life together on the basis of the value of individuals (notice the inner contradiction!) is

[22.] English "mutual aid" in the original.

[23.] English "brotherhood of mankind" in the original.

[24.] See also *DBWE* 9:264 and 320.

not identical with the kingdom of God; it is the ideology of the Enlightenment, which admittedly is quite justified compared to other ideologies. The attempt to model the social order on that of the family is based on a lack of insight into the difference between community, society, state.

7. The contempt for theology is outrageous. Rauschenbusch's own "theology for the social gospel" clearly shows, like its successors, that a lack of obedience to Scripture is characteristic for the teaching of the social gospel.

7. *Bibliography*[25]

Walter Rauschenbusch. *Christianity and the Social Crisis*. [New York, London,] 1907.

[Idem. *For God and the People:*] *Prayers of the Social Awakening*. [Boston, New York, etc.,] 1910. (German: *Für Gott und das Volk:* [*Gebete der sozialen Erweckung*. Translated by Minna Griebel und Heinrich Frick, with an appendix by Conrad Henry Moehlmann and a picture of Rauschenbusch. Göttingen, 1928]).

[Idem.] *Christianizing the Social Order*. [Boston, New York,] 1912.

[Idem. *A*] *Theology for the Social Gospel*. [New York,] 1917 (German: *Die religiösen Grundlagen der sozialen Botschaft*. [Translated by] Clara Ragaz. [Zürich,] 1922).

R[ichard] H[enry] Tawney. *The Acquisitive Society*. [New York, 1920].

H[arry] F[rederick] Ward. *The New Social Order* [*: Principles and Programs*. New York,] 1923.

[Idem.] *Our Economic Morality* [*and the Ethic of Jesus*. New York,] 1929.

[Idem.] *Which Way Religion?* [New York,] 1931.

[George] Sherwood Eddy: *Facing the Crisis* [*: A Study in Present Day Social and Religious Problems*. New York, 1922].

212 Kirby Page. *The World Tomorrow*. (Journal of the social gospel movement; published with R. Niebuhr.)

Reinhold Niebuhr. *Does Civilization Need Religion?* [*A Study in the Social Resources and Limitations of Religion in Modern Life*. New York,] 1928.

[Idem.] *Leaves from the Notebook of a Tamed Cynic*. [Chicago, New York, 1929].

Shailer Mathews. *The Church and the Changing Order*. [New York, London, 1907].

[25.] Bonhoeffer's bibliography has been standardized and completed. [Because Lehmann drafted this essay at Bonhoeffer's request, he may also have compiled this bibliography. The books listed here are included in the bibliographical section "Literature Used by Bonhoeffer" at the end of this volume, but it cannot be assumed that he had read them all.—LR]

H[enry] E[merson] Fosdick. *Christianity and Progress.* [New York, Chicago, etc., 1922].

The Social Creed of the Churches. Published by H. F. Ward. [New York, 1912].

W. A. Visser 't Hooft. *The Background of the Social Gospel in America.* [Haarlem, Netherlands,] 1928.

Arthur Titius. "Der angelsächsische Aktivismus und Luther." [*Die*] *Christliche Welt*, July 1926.

Karl Müller. *Der biblische Reich-Gottes-Gedanke im Lichte des Weltkrieges.* [Neukirchen, 1920].

Erich Stange. "Das Ergebnis der Aussprache über das Reich Gottes in Stockholm." [*Pastoralblätter für Predigt, Seelsorge und kirchliche Unterweisung*], 1926.

Heinrich Frick. *Das Reich Gottes in amerikanischer und deutscher Theologie der Gegenwart.* [Gießen, 1926].

[Chester Carlton] McCown. *The Genesis of the Social Gospel* [*: The Meaning of the Ideals of Jesus in the Light of Their Antecedents.* New York, London,] 1929.

[Joyce Oramel] Hertzler. [*The*] *History of Utopian Thought.* [London,] 1923.

[Ernst] Troeltsch. [*Die*] *Soziallehren der christlichen Kirchen* [*und Gruppen.* Tübingen, 1912].

5. Essay: "On Karl Heim's *Glaube und Denken*"[1] [[1]] 213

On Karl Heim's *Glaube und Denken*

Karl Heim writes his new book out of solidarity with the modern human being, his questions, his sicknesses, and his despair. Only out of genuine solidarity with those asking the questions is it possible to think concretely, and if one makes a scientific principle out of this, there is always the danger that questions and answers will be dictated by that solidarity. This, however, would mean that the book would essentially reflect the viewpoint of the generational conflict. It is curious that Heim himself does not avoid

1. I refer to the table of contents in Robert Winkler, *Christentum und Wissenschaft*, 273–74. [This note and the following unbracketed footnotes in this document are Bonhoeffer's own notes.—LR]

[1.] From *Christentum und Wissenschaft* 8 (1932): 441–54. Previously published in *GS* 3:138–59. Bonhoeffer refers to vol. 1 (*Glaube und Denken: Philosophische Grundlegung einer christlichen Lebensanschauung*) of Karl Heim, *Der Evangelische Glaube und das Denken der Gegenwart.* He also takes into consideration Heim's reactions to his critics (see *Die Furche*, 1932; and *Zeitschrift für Theologie und Kirche*, 1932) as well as—see Bonhoeffer's footnote 7—Theophil Steinmann's argument that Heim wanted "the self to be somehow constant and thus a quantity existing for itself quite removed" (*Zeitschrift für Theologie und Kirche* [1932]: 42–43). [The meaning of "Glaube und Denken" is "Faith and Reason."—LR]

this, but instead, quite the contrary, in his Furche essay[2] consciously situates himself here. He sees himself united with the "people of the postwar period who have not forgotten the shaking of the foundations that we once experienced" (*Furche*, p. 145); he sees himself misunderstood by those "who themselves have never in their life experienced an earthquake in which the foundations of their own lives were shaken" (*Furche*, p. 145) and who see God as the gable of a solid house (*Furche*, p. 152). The latter seem to misunderstand him because here it is a matter of a "contradiction of experiencing God and self-judgment" (*Furche*, p. 152). Heim thus consciously burdens his work not only with the heavy load of the generational conflict but also with the truly serious contrast of a quite different "experience of God." This point needs to be kept in mind in order to confront Heim at the level at
214 which he wishes to be understood, and the question must then be raised as to whether the alternative through which he defines his position is correct and how, seen from a possible third position, his book arrives at its end. The answer to this question can only be given at the conclusion.

Heim takes up the modern human being's question, which is oriented to the meaning of being in general, his "ultimate question." Heim speaks as he does because today "everyone senses that it is a matter of the ultimate"(v). He is not concerned at all about the independence of the disciplines—thus the philosophy-theology problem seems secondary to him in view of the seriousness of the situation and the question. "The struggle for the ultimate" creates a "community of fate" (22) out of which a response can be formulated. This sovereign overstepping of the boundaries of the sciences will have to demonstrate its worth in the course of the book, as every new science owes its existence to a similar overstepping of boundaries. One would completely miss Heim's point if one sought, in a doctrinaire manner, to reproach him for such so-called overstepping of boundaries, thereby employing premises that Heim does not share; instead, here too one has to approach Heim at his level and follow the entire development of his thought impartially, in order to then ask at the end if a new "science of the ultimate," which succeeds in making traditional distinctions meaningless, is justified or whether it is only a new name for the same old thing.

The "question of the ultimate" is the question about the conditions of life on which being is based; it is plainly the "radical question" and as such the question about God (31–32). However, the radical question is at the same time the question of meaning, which is aimed at being, or to be more exact: in which being is located. Thus for Heim the question of God is the

2. "Gott oder Verzweiflung," *Die Furche*, no. 2 (1932): 143ff.

question of meaning (320). In that ontological and noological interpreta-
tions of the ultimate question meet, the ontological-noological question
of "why" emerges as its concrete form. The question of "why" is here the
transcendence question, the "ultimate question." Of itself, the question of
the "ultimate" could be quite differently interpreted than in Heim. The
transcendental reduction to the thinking subject is one possibility, where the
question of meaning is directly contained in the question of being, as the
origin and the thinking and asking self are identical. The *ontological* reduc- 215
tion to the being [Sein] of the existing [Seiende] may understand the ques-
tion of meaning as a way of being of the existing, and thus to take it into
being, although it becomes clear here—as is the case in Heidegger—that
the question of meaning absorbs the question of being, and being is violated
by an existence that asks for meaning, whereby these reciprocal movements
of including meaning-questioning subjects in being and excluding being
in meaning-questioning subjects can be seen as endlessly self-reproducing.
These two embedded systematic possibilities of interpreting the "question
of the ultimate" are joined by a third, the critical-transcendental possibil-
ity. The questioning and thinking self cannot be absorbed into being and
cannot absorb being; rather it sees itself in action as limited both forward
and backward. It "is" only in moving forward and backward and bumping
up against a boundary, without eternalizing the encounter. It is "between,"
"in-relation-to," but it finds the "ultimate" neither in turning in on itself nor
in extending itself infinitely, to the given, to reality. Rather, it "is" respec-
tively only "in relation to" itself and to the "ultimate," whereby it basically
does not even know how it should ask about the ultimate. It "is" "between"
the ultimate. It "is" therefore in the very critique of the "ultimate question."
However, because through this statement this critique once more becomes
a systematic one, precisely this "ultimate question" is in turn posed and
replied to negatively. These three possibilities of the question about the
ultimate, which cannot be reduced to each other, show equally that there
is no "ultimate question." Rather, the first philosophical question as such is
always the ultimate question, and this movement of questions thus cancels
itself out. Therefore, Heim's terminology of transcendence ("the existence
by its very structure is open to receive things from a direction over which it
itself has no control," 356) is not necessarily given with the ultimate ques-
tion as such (even as a true noological or ontological question of mean-
ing). Ultimately the question of meaning as the "why" question, which is
the question of transcendence for Heim, cannot be a true philosophical
interpretation of the ultimate question. This all is admittedly no more than
that which Heim himself knows, namely, that he has not bound himself to a 216
certain discipline, for example, philosophy, with his question.

Heim's discovery, which empowers him to enter into full solidarity with human questions about the ultimate and at the same time to be indifferent in the disputes about the boundaries between theology and philosophy, is the concept of *dimension*. In it, the concerns of philosophy and theology are "canceled out" [aufgehoben].[2] The dimensions are the ultimate spheres of distinction within the *ens indistinctum*[3] (54, 48), which are only disjunctively expressible in the sentence of the excluded third through an either-or logic; they include the ultimate relationships I–It, I–You, I–God. Using this dimensional scheme, a proper understanding and a proper order of the ultimate question is made possible. Being is located in all dimensions respectively, is located therefore before the ultimate question as well. As, however, the "totality of being"[3] cannot immediately be made visible, Heim employs the method of a hypothetical destruction. However, already at this point the question arises: What is the reason for the *ens indistinctum*, for "unfashioned being" as divided among the dimensions, or for the "totality of being"? The ultimate ontological backdrop of Heim's thinking, onto which the dimension scheme is entered, is formed. It is the brackets surrounding the dimension scheme. There is no doubt that the idea of God must therefore also appear against this backdrop. This sheds light on the possibilities and limits of the dimension scheme. The dimensions have been brought to a common denominator that, left uncritically in the background, alone makes possible the design of the dimensions and holds the concept of dimension together.

Heim's method of a hypothetical destruction must at first examine the "totality of being." It is in this that God is contained. Only thus is it possible to abstract from the "ground of being," from God, and thus to observe the other dimensions unbound. It is characteristic that Heim here employs the
217 image of a tower, the foundation of which is God.[4] This foreknowledge of the "totality" includes in it the individual dimensions that must always be seen in relation to the totality, that is, truly as dimensions that are part of a basic ontological structure, "unfashioned" or not. And it is here that the basically neutral concept of dimension becomes dangerous in that, as the uncritically accepted basic ontological structure, it does violence to the *ens* of reality. That which is immediately attractive in the concept of dimension,

3. *Theologie und Kirche* (1932): 183.

4. *Theologie und Kirche*, 176–77.

[2.] [*Aufgehoben* can mean both canceled out in the present form and at the same time gathered up, even fulfilled, on a different level. This Hegelian use is common in German philosophy.—LR]

[3.] "Undifferentiated being."

namely, that things that cannot be coordinated nonetheless form a coordination system, is exactly its danger. Thus it can be seen that the originally mathematical concept of dimension can only be introduced with considerable violence. For the mathematical concept of dimension it is essential that between two dimensions an identical x can be identified as the place where the two dimensions meet. "*One* dimension is no dimension" (p. 70).[4] The point of the line on which the vertical lies remains the identical point of two dimensions. This is what Heim means when he speaks of dimensional splitting.[5] But it is at this point that the metaphor fails, that is, the transfer of the mathematical term implies an uncritical interpretation of reality. That in the I–It dimension the point now lies in the present (I) dimension as well as the past (It) dimension as identical x, is a metaphysical construction that coordinates that which cannot be coordinated. That this x "*ens indistinctum,*" identical with itself, should form the identical point now in the I dimension as well as in the It dimension, is uncritical ontology, a flight from the specific radical exclusivity of present and past. A dimensional relationship between present and past, I and It, arises only from the It, from the past, i.e., it "is" not "there."[5] Here is the point at which Heim's "critical" understanding of the present must either be abandoned or completely altered. It is simply not possible "to take one step backward from Grisebach's criti- 218
cal stance" without fundamentally transforming the critical stance into a dogmatic one. There where—behind Grisebach's "reminiscent" talk of the present—two dimensions can be constituted, present and past, I and It—there is where precisely what Grisebach meant by "present"[6] is cancelled out. Heim himself fights the conclusion, drawn from the reality of the permanent transition from present to past, that there is a passing "I essence" (163ff.), since this would lose sight of the fulfillment itself. Yet he does the same thing with Grisebach. And indeed Heim, unlike Grisebach, has no right to this defense because he thereby explodes the concept of dimension.

5. I can focus on only one page here. Equally questionable is the concept of paradox and polar relations. The disjunctive question as logical expression for a dimension is also a necessary but not sufficient determinant.

[4.] Bonhoeffer's emphasis.

[5.] [This is phrased similarly to Bonhoeffer's well-known sentence in *Act and Being*: "There is no God who 'is there' [Einen Gott, den 'es gibt,' gibt es nicht]; God 'is' in the relation of persons, and being is God's being person [das Sein ist sein Personsein]." *DBWE* 2:115.—LR]

[6.] See Grisebach, *Gegenwart* (especially chap. 12, 513–95).

If Heim therefore feels that something is not right here, then he must drop the concept of dimension in order to be free for a truly critical question. And when Heim objects that this in turn shows that we are only capable of thinking in the objective, in the I–It dimension, it is exactly his concept of dimension that is responsible for this. The "I as constant nonobjective reality"[6] and the coordination system of things that cannot be coordinated is one and the same thing, which means an entry into a metaphysical system and thus remaining stuck in the It dimension.[7]

Whether Heim succeeds in advancing beyond I–It thinking must be shown in his interpretation of the I–You dimension. This dimension begins where "resistance experiences" arise in the crossing over from present to past—(is not a quite vivid "present" experience being made from this quite "obscure" process?)—that is, where the event divides into action and passion, and where I and You come face to face. This I–You dimension stands "vertically" on the converged I–It dimension and on the individual I and
219 the It dimension. Initially two relationships arise: I–You (through the I dimension) as *direct* meeting in the fulfillment of becoming, of the present; I–You (through the It dimension) as meeting in the It world, in the past, in the "word." In this complete disintegration of the statements, the ontologically determined concept of dimension must provide the brackets. "They are the two sides of one and the same meeting" (260). This sentence requires interpretation or it is a senseless claim. An interpretation, however, can be made possible only through an uncritical ontology: becoming cannot be separated from having become, "the present passes continually into the image of the past" (260). This statement, however, means an extension beyond the present, which can come only from a systematic ontology (located behind the dimension scheme) of an *ens indistinctum*—whether this is the I, the fulfillment, the other I—an anticipation that leaves neither I, nor present, nor You, nor It there where it exists. Thus, however—and this was the essential point—the You is not left in its essential freedom; rather it is torn out of the inevitable present–past (I–It) dialectic. The You in the It world and in the I–You relationship is reduced to an identical nonobjective basic structure that is no longer accessible to critique. Where, however, do these statements on this identical x (in this case "You") come to us from? Heim made his task easy for himself and, on the other hand, irresolvable, in that he understands the "You" "in all cases" as the "other I" (206). It is precisely this which should not be said here. If the You is an I, not only is

6. *Theologie und Kirche*, no. [correctly: p.] 179.

7. I would thus reverse Steinmann's objection and say that the dissolution of the I myth has not been carried far enough.

it fundamentally unexplorable for me, but this very question negates the I–You relationship. It implies an attempt that is the same as an evasion. The equation You = other I is just as inadmissible as the other: other I = You. "You" is the boundary that is absolutely impenetrable for my I. Neither the other sees "me" as other than as You, nor "I" see the other than as You. I never see myself as You (this contra p. 276ff.); I remain only I, and the other remains only "You." I can certainly reflect on the I form of the other, but in doing so have lost sight of the other as You.[7] If the You were truly primarily an "other I," then that would quite justifiably exist which cannot justifiably 220
exist: "basically we are both of equal birth because we are both similar as humans and as creations" (Löwith[8] quoted in Heim, p. 429; see p. 345). Such a "basically" does not, however, exist; for in the "basically" we already abandon the I–You relationship and enter into an I–"other I" relationship in which the factual You situation is not even realized, because we have led the You back to an uncritical ontological structure that "I" no longer wish to call into question. The "other I" lies totally in the It world: the paradox of the "two centers" in one world arises only through a false identification of "You" and "other I." Neither for the "You" nor for the "other I" does a paradox arise *here*. The "other I," which includes the You, is metaphysical construction, coordination of that which cannot be coordinated.

A few further questions may be allowed: When I only become I with regard to You, how can I then assume that the You of the other is "I" in this sense? Or should the fact that someone becomes "You" to me also mean that I, too, become You to him, that is, that he becomes an I? What does the definition of the You as the other I mean for the concept of God? It is thus once more the same point at which the dimensional split takes place for Heim, making the fundamentally uncritical ontology visible, and catching and absorbing the present as well as the You into his coordination system, because the abrupt fall of the one as well as the other into the infinite is intolerable.

In the following we would like to put aside for the moment all the objections raised up to now and reexamine Heim's presentation on this point, for it is here with the question of God that a decision must be made. Heim takes the previously presented coordination system, which "stood under a common denominator" (320), puts it all in brackets and asks whether "before the bracket . . . a plus or minus should stand," if the numbers have

[7.] [The reader may wish to consult Bonhoeffer's explication of the I–You relationship and the Christian concept of person in *Sanctorum Communio*. See *DBWE* 1:51–54. —LR]

[8.] See Löwith, *Das Individuum*, 135.

a negative or positive value, if "it is an expression of despair or one of God's creations." At this decisive point in the first volume, then, Heim's concern—
221 which oddly is hardly mentioned thereafter—is the rationale for the doctrine of creation. Heim also calls this latter relation a dimension, as it is only disjunctively expressible in the question: "Does God or despair have the ultimate word? Can the question of meaning be answered positively or negatively?" (320). Here Heim in deepest solidarity joins the human beings of today—really of today?—who are tossed to and fro between two answers; and now he utilizes his utterly amazing power of synthesis, by truly taking up the human being's question, on the one hand, and not withholding any part of the answer from him, on the other. First the question must be quite clearly analyzed. The ultimate question is that of meaning, which extends to cover the entire structure of existence. "What is it all about?" (303). Before this ultimate question lies the path of the infinite process of relativization, in which the human being views everything that has become as only one possibility, in the place of which something else could exist—and so on, to which he must direct the question of "why." This relativistic question should arise directly from the process of thinking. With respect to this it must be said: The question why is *this* not different? not only no longer has any logical sense—because it would no longer be "this" (general example: Why "is" being not nonbeing? Because it is then not "being")—but is the cancellation of thinking itself; it is the impossible thought; it is not a legitimate question in the philosophical process; the thinking is directed toward that which is identical with itself and bound to it. It can therefore arise only as the philosophical question of transcendence. However, Heim too places great worth in not yet defining the relativistic question as the question of the pure (sense) dimension, because in it no value judgment is expressed (295, 305). Only when we define this situation as accidental, arbitrary, desperate, where I suffer from this existence, have we entered into the ultimate question and dimension. However, it is precisely here that Heim seems to have trouble with a clear delineation of the dimensions. While at the beginning the question of the relativistic "why" is defined as the radical question, as the new dimension (282–83), directly thereafter this question is neces-
222 sarily inferred from the process of objectification of thought (286), with the conclusion that above and beyond this question there is an ultimate question that arises (295), one that in itself is not given with the knowledge of the contingent character of existence (305), the question that arises from the practical situation of life, which understands suffering as chance and action as arbitrary and which asks about the value judgment of these events. However, the extent to which the relativistic question can be posed without this question of meaning is truly unclear; that is, the extent to which the

question of suffering—why is my fate as it is and not different?—can be distinguished from the relativistic question. The question itself remains the same, the one I ask myself about the "why." It would therefore be the "why" question that my ultimate question would have to express, and it is precisely here that the connection to the true philosophical question is torn away. Philosophical reflection always absorbs the question of "why" into the question of the meaning of being, which I dispose of in my question. A radical-relativistic "why" is not legitimate philosophically. Whether it is theologically possible remains to be considered.

Heim does not want to accept the connection between the relativistic and the ultimate question because he wants to establish a dimensional contrast between those who have fallen into secularism and the others, who "suffer from existence." "Between those who suffer from relativism but who see no way out and those who also suffer from it but believe they have found a way out there exists, initially, complete agreement on the question that is concerned. Both are located in the same dimension" (307). The dimensional contrast arises between those for whom relativism is a natural state and those for whom it causes suffering or provides relief. Those for whom it causes suffering or provides relief are in the same dimension. Their common question is the question about God, about the relief from suffering from the question of "why," from chance and the arbitrary nature of existence. In order to develop a dimensional difference in the relation to God, Heim needs to claim that this suffering is "certainly not a priori of our being. . . . From our existence itself there is no direct path to this suffering.
The suffering from existence is thus, in religious terms, a gift of mercy" 223
(309). However, it seems to me that Heim has already robbed himself of the right to this—in my view quite correct—claim through his interpretation of the "ultimate question." Herein lies the decisive point for an evaluation of Heim's work.

We need to go back a bit. Heim wants to lay the foundations of a *Christian* view of life, that is, here he wishes to be taken at his word, putting aside all arguments across disciplines. Where Heim speaks of the ultimate dimension, of the I–God relation, we therefore must simply pose the question: is Heim here speaking "in a Christian manner" of God and God's relation to human beings or not?

Heim sought, on the one hand, and avoided, on the other, the disturbing proximity of the "ultimate question" to the relativistic one. It is a matter of questioning the contingent existence in its entirety. Existence poses questions about its "why" in action and in suffering. And because it is unable to offer an answer that can provide grounds for the contingent (it would otherwise have to be the Creator himself), it has doubts about the sense of

its specific being and calls for healing. Heim asks: what must occur so that a healing is possible? The answer, which is easily constructed, must be that existence is credited with eternal meaning in this ultimate dimension, so that it sees its suffering not as chance but as guidance, and its actions not as arbitrary but as a task. In order for existence, always threatened as it is by the fall into infinity, to find an ultimate foundation, two statements must be made: God, this ultimate foundation, must be the absolutely "unconditional" (in contrast to the contingency of thc It-world), and, second, "the eternal and all-present You" (in contrast to the You-world located in It). Thus all existence has "gained the calm of eternal necessity" (357). The ultimate question is answered. Existence has gained a positive sign. The alternative of the ultimate dimension is thus despair or God, the meaninglessness of existence or the meaning of life. And with this, the dimension scheme has achieved its completion. It has provided proof that the weight
224 of the entirety of being would collapse if God did not support it. That is all that is possible in a metaphysic of the ultimate things.

We can summarize our concerns in two conceptual groups: *First,* what is the meaning of the concept of dimension in the question about the ultimate dimension? *Second,* what is Heim talking about when he speaks of despair and of God?

In view of what has been said, a dimension can be expressed logically only in the form of a disjunctive question. Because in this world there is no way to decide, however, attention is drawn to the fact that an answer can only be given from another dimension, that is, the possibility of opening onto a further dimension remains possible in each case. This, however, creates difficulties for the notion of an "ultimate" dimension. The either-or of the ultimate relationship is, according to Heim, the question of meaning: God or despair (320). Given the existential impossibility of deciding, the answer must be able to allow the opening up of another dimension, which explodes the either-or. A dimension beyond the "ultimate" dimension, however, is a thought impossible to consummate, that is, the term "ultimate" dimension is itself by definition impossible to consummate. Heim seems to sense this when he says that the ultimate dimension is not one among many but rather the dimension of the dimensions (321). This concept, however, if taken seriously, is empty both mathematically and philosophically. It negates the concept of dimension. The destruction of this concept becomes even clearer where Heim says that where the decision is made for God, the "dimensions have filled [themselves] with positive content" (335). This no longer has any meaning, however, and we realize that the dimension scheme has come to the end of its usefulness. The same conclusion is evident in the understanding of the dimensional split (339). The relationship to God is certainly not

a certain view of the self (*Theologie und Kirche*, 179), nor one that includes all other views, whereby the self remains a "constant, nonobjective reality"; rather this continuity certainly cannot be expressed philosophically and is rather only believable through the Word of God, who is the Creator, destroying the old self and creating the new one. Thus the very point of identity at which the dimensional split must be demonstrated (the acting self) is not 225
an ontologically provable reality, being instead an act of revelation by God the Creator alone, which is not accessible ontologically and cannot be captured in any system of coordinates. The concept of dimension in its uncritical ontology defies the understanding of revelation. Here Karl Heim's two concerns clash, the question of serving equally the natural human being in solidarity and the answer of the Christian revelation.

What are the consequences of this for Heim's *Christian* statements? First, that he recognizes the "why" question of those suffering from existence as the question for God, that is, as the question to which God provides the answer. The answer fits somewhere into the framework of *this* question (358). Question and answer lie, of course, in the same dimension. If we object that this would mean forgetting that humans can only ask about God when they are found by God, Heim would reply that is why he has already defined *this* question as God's gift of mercy. This raises the question of whether this last sentence is true. Despair about the contingency of existence is the despair not of the human being who asks about God, but of the one who asks about the "meaning of life" in the form of an answered "why." In this question of "why" and meaning, however, it is not human existence that is at stake, since the question circumvents the reality of evil. That is why it cannot ask about God. Concerning the meaning or meaninglessness of life, the human being may promote himself as one who is able to interrogate life itself about its meaning and meaninglessness and who, even in meaninglessness, is still able to maintain an unchallenged existence with a heroic attitude. Despair about meaninglessness is the ultimate successful escape from the necessity of having to exist and certainly not an entering into one's own existence. It is only in the despair about evil, about my evil, in which I confront the world and the You, that my existence is at stake. Only from my evil can I no longer save myself. The question is no longer one of meaning or meaninglessness, but one of life or death, one of mercy or judgment. The answer to this question may also not deliver that through which my existence gains "eternal meaning." The answer through which my existence gains "eternal meaning" may also not deliver me from this question. What do I care about the eternal sense of an existence that certainly cannot be mine if I do not know whether my evil has been forgiven, whether before God I must live 226
or die? Rather the great danger arises that I once again avoid my evil with

the excuse that it has "eternal meaning." The question of whether a stroke of fate is meaningful or meaningless does not touch "me" when "I" am not aware of forgiveness. It becomes a matter of purely metaphysical interest, a stoic attitude toward life by which I deny my existence. The first word of God, the first answer, from which alone the question about God can arise, is the smashing of the human question about "worth," about the "sense" of human existence, as a question of "why." The question is stuffed back into the human's mouth, and he is told that in this question he asks about himself, that he is looking for himself and not God, and indeed that he denies God as the Lord and that is why he is evil. The ultimate dimension in which the human being thinks he is open "for reception from a direction over which he[9] has no control" (356), the question about the sense of existence and its answer, is the grasp of the human being, in which he wishes to pull himself back from the fall. And judgment is made upon this *entire* human being, with all his life's meaning and meaninglessness. In his existence he is evil and must die. And it is only here that one can truly speak of despair; but not so that despair and belief were to stand "in the same dimension," opposite to "secularism," because both are concerned with the question of meaning; rather, despair now appears as hostility toward God, as evil, that is, as an attack by the devil even there where, as "consoled despair," it seizes God's mercy in God's anger. It is here that the possibility of speaking of despair and belief as the same dimension collapses completely. God and the devil are not a dimension in which the human being stands; rather they are opponents, victor and vanquished, mutually negating each other; and the human being is obsessed with one or the other. Despair is the archenemy of belief. Every dialectical consolidation is just as impossible here as it is with God and the devil. It is not a matter of the "meaning of existence," but rather that of God's victory and the destruction of the devil. Despair is the devil's victory, when God does not vanquish the devil and create belief.
227 The healing of despair, that is, faith, is God's victory over the devil, over my evil, not, however, the knowledge that my fate is direction and my action a commission. From here, the concepts of despair and faith, as Heim uses them, are exposed in their true meaning. They are interpreted out of the solidarity with the unaffected existence of the human being who is posing the question of meaning, and must for this reason have quite dangerous consequences in an attempt at a Christian interpretation. If the question of despair is why am I suffering this? why do I do that? the answer that brings healing must be: because that is how God is leading me, this is God's commission. But thereby something very terrible has happened. First, it is

[9.] In Heim: "it" (i.e., existence).

forgotten—and this too out of solidarity—that the devil is also working on my fate. Second, it is forgotten that it is precisely here that the devil can transform himself into the angel of light.[10] More must in fact be said to this point, for it is simply not true as Karl Heim presents it. Rather, this immediate commission of God is not so clearly given that I myself, as I heed it, must not constantly move from calling upon the commanding God to the merciful one. Heim's insistence on concreteness is therefore misguided, because it seeks to "heal" the human being who asks about meaning and not the human being who is desperate. He should know what he has to do in order to overcome the fear of his lack of knowledge, and precisely here he is kept away from the knowledge of evil within himself, itself responsible for this lack of knowledge. The "commission" is not "redemption from (genuine)[11] despair" (365)—it only redeems from the question of meaning. Rather, it is the gospel that is spoken to evil, not distinct from the commandment, but in such a manner that the hearing of the commandment always points back to the hearing of the gospel about the evil.

This sheds light on Heim's debate with Karl Barth, which is somehow central for him, and it becomes clear that here a real injustice has occurred. In this debate, Barth is not only not encountered; he is not even taken seriously. Heim thinks that it is Barth's ultimate, perhaps not conscious, inten- 228
tion to speak of God in the sphere of abstraction to protect himself from God *in concreto.* (We will intentionally skip over all the individual accusations against Barth because they are, to a great extent, not true and indeed have Barth saying quite the opposite of what he has long said.) Why—Heim says—does Barth otherwise not provide a specific answer to the question of what I should do? It is with this question, one which for Barth is completely incorrect as a theological question, that the concerns of the two men become evident. Barth admits, without hesitation, that he, too, is not "safe from the . . . sin" of making "God into an object of reason" (311), that inherent in his first principles is the risk of being "an ultimate safeguard against God and God's involvement in our life" (423).[12] His saying that he is not safe from this danger and that he always thinks with this danger in mind is characteristic of his theology. He knows that the *concretissimum* can only be spoken by the Holy Spirit and that every *concretum* of human words remains an *abstractum* when the Holy Spirit has not said them, and this sets the limits for his theological efforts. By way of contrast, where Heim says that he is nonetheless able to speak of God in the dimension scheme—even if it is

[10.] See 2 Cor. 11:14.

[11.] Bonhoeffer has added "genuine."

[12.] In the latter two quotes, Bonhoeffer does not use Heim's emphasis.

only formal-ontological (what advantage do statements on the "absolute" and the "You" actually have over any other metaphysical speculation?)—he must also somehow think he is able to say the *concretissimum*—as the content of the given form. Heim's accusation against Barth turns immediately back on him. Yet Heim believes that he can sustain this through the power of his concept of dimension, and that does not work.

The problem of the boundary between philosophy and theology, which for Heim is not a main concern here, is resolved for Heim so that the "science of the ultimate" provides the forms, "the general category of revelation" (th[eology] a[nd] c[hurch], 189), the ultimate question, while in theology one must only speak of content, of specific revelation, of the
229 answer. Heim could perhaps also say that this reflects the fact that creation could be spoken of without Christ (to the extent that this volume contains teachings on creation). In any case, however, Heim speaks of God already within the framework of the dimension ontology, and it is precisely this that is impossible. One cannot speak of the category of revelation different from the revelation in Christ himself; all talk of absolute and relative is seriously only possible from the cross. Otherwise something else completely different is meant, such that it would no longer be able to provide a framework for the specific revelation. The ontological dimension as framework for revelation makes talk of revelation, of God, and of humans within this scheme impossible. Because Heim's entire outline is based on an uncritical ontology, on the basis of which one speaks of the human being and his relation to God, that which is said about the human being in revelation is missed. Only from the perspective of revelation can it be seen that there is no general determinant of being for the human that does not come solely through the determination of being sinner or forgiven and that God "is" the Creator, the Holy, and the Merciful, and that here a genuine ontology would have to be introduced.

We have tried to encounter Heim where he would like to stand and not to categorize him here or there in a doctrinaire manner. However, if we ask ourselves where Heim stands, then we must say that he stands at a place where no human being can stand. The "science of the ultimate" is solely God's knowledge; viewed by the theologian it is philosophy and viewed by the philosopher it is theology, and it is in fact neither of the two. *The "why" question is the impossible middle ground between philosophy and theology.* Heim, even with his dimension scheme, has not managed to convince us that there is a way to this "ultimate" position by way of philosophy and theology.

The depth of his solidarity with the contemporary human being is demonstrated by Heim, the thinker who wishes to base everything on revelation, in that he takes his "ultimate question" to be the question of God; it would nonetheless be true solidarity if he would totally swallow it in view of the Word, God's answer.

It is not a matter of playing out the debate with Heim as a generational 230
problem. In what has been said here neither of Heim's types is meant to be justified. And yet of course it depends somehow on Heim's view of the human being, not in terms of generation, but ultimately in the objective consideration based on the revelation in the Scriptures. Heim's human being who asks the question of God is one who, through the chance and arbitrariness of his existence, has been shaken to the core, tortured, torn, full of despair, and who now, because he knows God's answer, will be freed from his suffering in the world, but only to be pushed into an immeasurable suffering, suffering as God's commission. The human being who knows of God is a prophet (337), with all the circumstances bordering on madness of such a person. He is a martyr in obedience against the absolute, abandoned without defense to the attack of the entire world (362), prepared to die as a poor fool abandoned by all in a hopeless situation (338), "the whole world can cover you with filth when only you have God's smile" (329); and at the same time this human being is the person who always hears in obedience the accent of eternity in his actions, who always receives the certainty: "this path must be traveled in the name of God" (336). Something inside us protests against this image of the human being. The Bible did not speak of humans like this. Certainly, who could say that all the things that Heim talks about here could not or should not be true? But are we not captured here by the tremendous horror of religious *titanentum*?[13] Can we really speak of these things like *that,* of martyrdom, of the suffering of God's prophets, of hearing the commandments at every hour? What does Heim wish to say to the person who confesses that it is not like that at all for him, but that he nonetheless believes, who in his day-to-day life is not frightened by the fates of the prophets and martyrdom, who indeed shyly and soberly is afraid of saying and thinking too much about such important things? Who knows hours, weeks, years, in which he does not hear the 231
accent of eternity in his actions, who goes his way with fear and trembling in the lack of knowledge of the commandment that asks him to go in the name of God, but in prayer for forgiveness? Who faces the nothingness of his existence, who despairs of his guilt, and who nonetheless in faith—for once not shaken—"is happy in his work"[14] because this is his portion?

[13.] See Barth's statement in his interpretation of Rom. 7 that "the sinfulness of the creature [becomes] acute in the titanic human potential of religion" (*Epistle to the Romans,* 236).

[14.] Eccl. 5:18.

Should *this* really be the issue when speaking of the questions of the human being and the Word of God, should for us the knowledge of the possibility of the different position here serve for anything other than as evidence of the unity of God's Word? Because, however, Heim's entire book has become the expression of a quite specific position—and who among us can criticize that—it is perhaps necessary to pinpoint this question in particular, certainly not because of some generational problem or other reasons of differences in religious positions, but because of the biblical proclamation of the gospel, aimed at *evil.*

This seems to me to be the most honest way to express real gratitude for a great work, by entering into the working and reworking of the questions that have been posed to the best of one's ability. If in doing so different judgments arise, the admiration for the work achieved remains unaltered.[15]

17:116 **6. Lecture: "Christ and Peace" (Student Notes)**[1]

Christ and Peace[2]

"You shall love the Lord your God with all your heart, and with all your soul, and with all your mind." This is the greatest and first commandment. And the second is like it: "You shall love your neighbor as yourself."[3]

Once again, the human authorities who sought to build peace upon a political foundation find themselves shipwrecked.[4] It would be good to reflect

---

[15.] See also the positive estimation of Heim in the student notes of the lecture "Review and Discussion of New Publications in Systematic Theology" (2/1, ed. note 27).

[1.] *NL,* A 32,9 (1); typewritten manuscript, which is based on the lost student notes of Jürgen Winterhager for the lecture Bonhoeffer is said to have given in December 1932 for the ecumenical working group of the German Christian Student Association [the German branch of the World Student Christian Federation; it was not connected to the German Christian movement—LR] (*NL,* A 32,9 [2]; Jürgen Winterhager to Eberhard Bethge, June 24, 1957.) Previously published in *Mündige Welt* 5:69–71 and *GS* 5:359–62. [The text as published here is based on the final completed text from *DBW* 17, which is identical to the original text in *DBW* 12 but has three additional paragraphs at the conclusion. Also, the text published here includes additional notes by Ernst-Albert Scharffenorth, who edited the version in *DBW* 17.—LR]

[2.] In the left-hand margin, "1932" is written in Bethge's handwriting.

[3.] Matt. 22:37–39 (this reference is in Bethge's handwriting).

[4.] If Bonhoeffer is referring here to the failure of the Geneva disarmament conference in the summer of 1932, the date given by Winterhager for the lecture (December) might have to be corrected. Cf. also Heimbucher, *Christusfriede—Weltfrieden,* 94.

on this, and not to be too amazed, for *worldly authorities* are set up by human beings and thus do not constitute absolute authority.

There is only one *authority* who has spoken definitively on this question, and that is *Jesus Christ.*

It is true that Christ has not given us specific rules for our conduct in every possible complex political, economic, or other situation that may arise in human life. However, this does not mean that the gospel of Jesus Christ does not give a clear answer to the problems that confront us. To the simple reader of the Sermon on the Mount, what it says is unmistakable.

Let us begin at the very center of the New Testament, so that we can subject these questions to the first and greatest commandment and to
the preaching of our Lord. Let us not pull one single word about worldly 17:117
authority out of the whole context of the New Testament,[5] thereby failing to recognize that Christ proclaimed the reign of God, which the entire world, including its governance [Obrigkeit],[6] meets with hostility.

Let me first discuss a few points that can easily be occasions for misunderstanding.

(1) It was not Christ's concern to change the conditions he found in this world in order to bring about security, peace, and quiet. Much less should we think that *we* can do away with outward sins and the horrors of war through political treaties. As long as the world is free of God, there will be wars.

Christ was much more concerned that we should love God, that we become disciples of Jesus, as we are called to do through the promise of the Beatitudes,[7] and that we thus become witnesses for peace.

This *discipleship of Christ* arises [from] and is based entirely on simple *faith,* and inversely, faith is only true in discipleship.[8] So these words are addressed to the faithful, but the world is judged by Christ's witness to peace. Faith, however, must be simple; otherwise it will bring about reflection rather than obedience; the left hand will know what the right hand is doing, and this is not discipleship, which knows nothing of good or evil. Moreover, only such discipleship [encompasses] the right attitude toward those who have given their lives in war.

[5.] Refers to Rom. 13:1.

[6.] [In this essay we have translated *Obrigkeit* with "authority" in most instances; as mentioned previously, however, it can also mean "governance" or "government." That appears to be Bonhoeffer's meaning here. For a discussion of the translation of this term elsewhere, see *DBWE* 16:503, ed. note 5, and 636, ed. note 10.—LR]

[7.] Matt. 5:3–12.

[8.] These ideas hint at those developed later in *Discipleship*; cf. *DBWE* 4:63–64.

So there are no possibilities at the human level to organize or to build peace. Indeed, human attempts to do so by political means can become domination of self-glorifying human beings and thus be sinful. There is no *guaranteed* peace. A Christian can only dare to make peace through faith. So there is no direct way to make all people brothers and sisters; the way to one's enemy is only through prayer to the Lord of all peoples.

(2) Conversely, the relationship between *law and gospel* is often misunderstood. Here the gospel is understood as the message of forgiveness of
17:118 sin that doesn't address the citizen or indeed deal with any aspect of the earthly life of human beings. The human being is told that he is a sinner but is not called to lay aside his sin and sinful connections. If we do not walk the path of obedience, if we sin in confidence that grace exists, how shall we take seriously the grace of the forgiveness of sins, or even take prayer itself seriously, and believe in God with pure hearts? At that point we are asking for cheap grace. We are forgetting, in the justification of the sinner through the cross of Christ, the cry of the Lord, who never justifies sin.

The commandment "You shall not kill,"[9] the word that says, "Love your enemies,"[10] is given to us simply to be obeyed. For Christians, any military service, except in the ambulance corps, and any preparation for war, is forbidden. The belief that sees freedom from the law as meaning you can do anything you like outside the law is a human belief and defies God. Simple obedience knows nothing of good and evil but lives in discipleship to Christ and does its good works as a matter of course.

(3) The commandment to love is addressed to us Christians first of all in the sense that we *ourselves* have peace with every other person, as Christ did when he preached peace to his congregation, using the example of making peace with one's brother or with one's neighbor, or the example of the Good Samaritan. If we do not have this personal peace, we cannot preach peace to the nations [Völker]. And most people who are annoyed by hearing about peace among nations already question the love for one's personal enemies.

So when we speak of matters of peace, we must always keep in mind that relations between two nations are deeply analogous with relations between two individual persons.

The things that stand in the way of peace are in both cases thirst for power, pride, the drive to seek fame and honor, as well as arrogance and feelings of inferiority, fear of other people, and the struggle for living space

[9.] Exod. 20:13.

[10.] Matt. 5:44.

[Lebensraum][11] and for bread. What is sinful for an individual person, however, can never be a virtue for a *nation* [Volk].

That which is proclaimed as gospel to the church, to the church-community, and to individual Christians is spoken as judgment on the world. But if a nation [Volk] will not listen to this commandment, Christians from within that nation are called to be witnesses to it. 17:119

But let us take care that we, who are miserable sinners, preach peace out of love, and not out of zeal to bring about security, to pursue a political end.

(4) Peace with whom? True peace can only be in God and come from God. This peace is a gift given to us with Christ, that is, peace is inseparably bound up with the gospel. So peace can never consist in reconciling the gospel with religious worldviews. Jesus said: "I have not come to bring peace, but a sword."[12] Forgiveness of sins is granted to sinners who repent, who have lost their way, and we should love them, not judge them. The commandment serves as judgment for the defiant sinner. But there is no reconciliation with sin, any more than with a false doctrine. In the struggle between the gospel and these earthly powers, the Christian becomes separated from father and mother.

The Christian's struggle is therefore a struggle for the cause. In the conflict with the enemy of the gospel, the Christian's *weapons*, however, are[13] faith and love, which are purified in suffering. How much more so than in quarrels that are only about earthly possessions.[14]

What[15] does this greatest and highest commandment tell us? It calls upon us to love and makes the love of our neighbor a *parable* for our love of God. We do not *truly* love God unless we love our neighbor as ourselves. Our love for our neighbor is not *pure* if we do not love God in and with him. Love is self-seeking if it does not seek God and God's commandments. In the pure love with which God first loved us is the peace that Christ gives (John 14:27), which is promised in the Beatitudes. Pure love, however, would rather see a defenseless brother be killed than to see his soul, or our own,

[11.] *Lebensraum* was a concept used in Nazi propaganda [and became policy—LR] to legitimize the eastward expansion of the Reich (Brackmann and Birkenhauer, *NS-Deutsch*, 121).

[12.] [Matt. 10:34.—LR]

[13.] The German here is singular; it was corrected by hand (by Bethge?) to "are."

[14.] It is unclear in the manuscript as to whether this last word is "possessions" or "virtue."

[15.] The text from this point on was omitted in the versions published in *GS* 5:362 and *DBW* 12.

17:120 stained with blood. Pure love, in obedience to the fifth commandment,[16] gives up its life for a brother, whether he is on this side or on the other side.[17] Pure love quite simply cannot lift up a sword against a Christian, because that would mean to lift it against Christ.

When we confront these individual questions, the thought that always comes is that following Christ means very simply, Go and do likewise—do as the Lord himself did. The question of whether God actually commanded *us* to do these things is the serpent's question.[18] What we learn from the commandment is what Christ would have done in this or that concrete situation.

And let us be glad: "Little children, you are from God, and have conquered them; for the one who is in you is greater than the one who is in the world" (1 John 4:4).

235 7. Essay: "What Is Church?"[1]

What Is Church?

What church "is" can only be said if we say both what it is from the viewpoint of human beings and what it is from the standpoint of God. Both belong inseparably together. It is in this dual nature that it exists. Thus we are talking about not what the church should be and that means, in other words, what we should make of the church today, but rather what it [is] when it "is." This is the essential point.

Church is a part of the world, a lost, godless, cursed, vain, evil world;
236 and evil world in its most potent form, because in it the name of God is

[16.] According to the numbering in the Lutheran Catechism: "You shall not kill!"

[17.] Here Bonhoeffer is protesting against the trend within German Protestantism at the time to confine the commandment to love one's neighbor to one's own people and fatherland, so that church memorial plaques honoring soldiers who had died in war could be adorned with the words of John 15:13 ["No one has greater love than this, to lay down one's life for one's friends"]. In a 1928 speech to his congregation, Günther Dehn had objected to this equating of the death of soldiers with Christ's sacrificial death (see Dehn, *Kirche und Völkerversöhnung*, 21–22). Because of the massive criticism of this position, in 1930 Dehn was turned down for a professorship at the University of Heidelberg. He was able to continue teaching only with protection against the protests of National Socialist students (cf. Bonhoeffer's draft of an article on the Dehn case in *DBWE* 11, 1/40, as well as the comments on the controversy in the afterword to *DBW* 11), and he lost his position at the end of summer 1932 (Bizer, "Der 'Fall Dehn'").

[18.] Cf. Gen. 3:1.

[1.] From *Der Vormarsch* 3, no. 1 (January 1933): 8–10. Previously published in *GS* 3:286–91. See also *NL*, 32, 4(a); carbon copy with typewritten comment: "(for the *Vormarsch* January 1933)."

misused, because in it God has been made into a plaything, the false idol of human beings, indeed eternally lost, the epitome of the antichristian world, praised when the church forsakes the final solidarity with the evil world and strikes up against the world. However, the church is to some extent qualified world, qualified by God's own entry into it and for it, through God's revelatory, merciful word that God has taken under his wings and will not let go of those who have fallen prey to the world and who are at its mercy. Church is the presence of God in the world; truly in the world, truly a present God. Church is not consecrated shrine; it is from God for the world called to God, which is why there is only *one* church in the world.

Church is an institution for preserving Christian piety and morals. It "must" be kept for the people—otherwise it gets carried away. It "serves" public life, order, the state. It is an institution that is not a good model of organization, not very influential, not very impressive, in need of improvement in the extreme. However, church is a ministry [Amt] from God, a ministry of proclamation, the message of the living God. From it come commission and commandment; in it arise eternal ties; in it heaven and hell clash; in it the judgment on earth takes place. Because church is the living Christ and his judgment. The preached and preaching Christ, proclaimer and proclamation, ministry and word. Church is the awakening of the world through a miracle, through the presence of the life-creating God calling from death into life.

Church is a union of religiously inclined, interested people who curiously enjoy expressing their religiosity in this form of church. Today they generally belong to a social class that is neither particularly spiritually lively nor a particularly future-oriented creative force, but rather offers a certain contentment with their own achievements as its most pronounced characteristic. Here the atmosphere is relatively thin and the horizons restricted. Not a lot seems to take place. More "happens" in the cinema; it is more interesting. A small group rises up; they no longer feel so contented; they push open the window; they are the "activists," the "reformers"—something that every association needs and produces now and again. However, the 237
church is fellowship, the church-community of the saints, freed by God from isolated existence, each one belonging to the other, giving themselves, accepting responsibility because it was placed on them by God; a community through sacrifice, prayer, and forgiveness, shattering the chains of isolation, the reality of being together and for one another, love, fraternity. All that from God. God, the living Christ, founded the community; it is his people called from the world by his Word, bound to him as the sole Lord in faith, bound to their brothers in love.

Church "is" always both things simultaneously; those who see only one of the two do not see the "church." Church would be a term much easier to employ, both by its enemies as well as its friends, if we only needed to name one of its two aspects. In its particular duality, however, it escapes the grasp of its enemies as well as its friends. It would already be a great advance if the two statements on the nature of the church could be interpreted so that the first said what the church is and the second what it should be. Then we would have something tangible for our church activities. But this is completely denied us. That church "is" from God in all its apparent plerophory[1] of the aforementioned, all this makes the church a church. This, however, is then a stab in the back of our all-too-complacent desire for reform. God, not we, makes the church into that which it is. In the end we want to get around this difficulty by saying that there are somehow two churches under discussion here. Yet this would miss the decisive point. It is one and the same church, its visible form and its hidden divinity. As it is one and the same Lord, the carpenter's son from Nazareth and the Son of God.

As God's church in the world, the church proves its worth through nothing other than properly spreading the message of the gospel, through properly proclaiming grace and commandment. And just as an aside: We suffer not from too much preaching but from too much false preaching.
238 Equally, we suffer from having forgotten that those who bring nothing into the church get nothing out of it, that is, that we falsely hear the preaching. Thus, in the church it is a question of spreading the Word of God in the world, of witnessing to the breaching of the world and its laws through the revelation of God's resolve and goodness in Jesus Christ. The church speaks of miracles because it speaks of God. From eternity into time, from life into death, from love into hate, from forgiveness into sin, from healing into suffering, from hope into doubt. This it does in full knowledge that its message disconcerts, but also that its own task is irreversible.

With the proclamation of the commandments and the grace of God, the church finds itself at the boundary [Grenze], at the boundary of human possibilities that has now been broken through from above.[2] However, in speaking of breaching this boundary, this worldly order, the church—which

1. Full of hope (correctly: "plenty").

[2.] [The German word *Grenze* can mean "limit" (or "limitation") and "boundary," i.e., it can describe the line of demarcation between two entities or the limits on those entities as they encounter this boundary. In the following passages the word is used in both ways; Bonhoeffer also describes how God transcends the limit of human possibilities. These distinctions arise frequently in Bonhoeffer's thought. For more on the nuances of translation of this term, see the discussion in *DBWE* 3:85, ed. note 15.—LR]

as a human institution stands entirely within these boundaries—knowingly points to these laws, these worldly orders, the destruction, and obliteration of which it is empowered to witness by God. For this reason, the church's preaching is of necessity "political," that is, it is directed at the political order in which humans are bound. Yet precisely in this "political" sense it is first of all the critical limit [Grenze] of all political actions. The church is the limit of politics,[3] which is why it is eminently simultaneously political and apolitical. Because it witnesses this breached boundary, the church points to the limited, to the law, to order, to the state. Church is only in relation to the state. Church limits the state; state limits the church.

The first political word of the church is the call to recognize one's own limits, to sobriety. The church names this limit sin; the state names it reality; both tend to call it, with different accents, finiteness. Politics in its finiteness—that is the first eminent political word of the church, and this word releases the church from party politics, places it in the essentially[4] "political" sphere in political independence from parties. It must be observed: the first word of the church is not Christianization of politics!—that would 239
be in turn a misunderstanding of the boundary—but instead the recognition of finiteness![5] Is there a second word of the church on politics? Here opinions divide. A concrete commandment can be taken from the church, and enforcement of this commandment—perhaps even through creating a political party—is a fundamental possibility. However, here too it can only be a question of a *concrete* commandment within the boundaries set by finiteness and by what is proper to the state, not on a program that misunderstands the boundaries of Christian political ideology.[2] Self-examination down to the smallest detail is always necessary as to whether this commandment was correctly heard or not. It would always be necessary to ask whether this commandment really requires a political party or whether clearheadedness does not demand that existing parties be used, that is, whether it is really worthwhile risking the highly political substance of a church, which in its first word is beyond party politics, by entering in the second word into party politics. A mistake here severely damages the political substance

2. That is, it can only initially concern the desire to serve the people and state, not the desire to rule. The desire to rule may at most arise from tactical necessity (t[he] edit[orial staff]).

[3.] Carbon copy: "polis."

[4.] Carbon copy: "actually."

[5.] [Bonhoeffer is quite explicit on this point throughout his writings on the church-state relationship; see, for example, his essay "State and Church," probably written in 1941, in *DBWE* 16:509–10.—LR]

of the church and thus its substance in general. Nonetheless, the second word with all its consequences cannot be excluded as an ultimate possibility for the church. No one should see the limits here more clearly than the church, which stands at the boundary that has been broken through from above. It thus follows of necessity that nothing would be more destructive and detrimental for the Protestant church in the current situation than if, as the last politically unspent force in Germany, it unthinkingly let itself be used in party politics. That would certainly mean its end. That this danger confronts the other possibility, that the church today truly has a second political word, a commission, and that it will be tortured and torn apart in the agony of party politics—this dilemma summons the church in its political responsibility and decision.

240 **8. Essay: "The Younger Generation's Altered View of the Concept of Führer"[1]**

The Younger Generation's Altered View of the Concept of Führer

Why all these constant questions about the younger generation, about their thoughts, their hopes, and their strengths?[2] Why these questions at a time when, as never before, it is practical ability, acquired skills, and well-qualified knowledge that are important: that is, experienced adults and certainly not youth? Is it the anxious curiosity of insecure parents who want to know how things will continue after they are gone that finds its expression here? Is it the sensationalism of our times, which is as impatient for the "new" associated with the younger generation as it is for the latest in summer fashion? Is it an unnatural basking in their own reflection on the part of youth themselves, made vain by old fools because of their uniqueness and beauty? Often, indeed normally, it is all of these together, which is

[1.] From *Der Rundfunk Hörer* 10, no. 5 (Friday, January 27, 1933): 4; with the introduction: "Dr. Dietrich Bonhoeffer, Student Chaplain at the Technical College Charlottenburg, who will be speaking on the 'Altered View of the Concept of Leader' among the younger generation next Wednesday (February 1, 1933) in the Berliner Funkstunde at 5:30 p.m., has sent us the following remarks on this topic." See also *NL*, A 36, 1(a): handwritten; *NL*, A 36, 1(b): carbon copy; *NL*, 36, 1(c): photocopy from the *Rundfunk Hörer* (erroneously listed as reproduction from the *Funkstunde*). Previously published in *GS* 2:19–21. See also 2/9.

[2.] In his radio presentation "The Younger Generation in Literature" (see 2/9, ed. note 1), Giselher Wirsing spoke of an "exaggerated ideology of youth" (from the partial reprint of the *Täglichen Rundschau* of March 5, 1933, in *Beiblatt Bünde, Hochschule und Jugend*). For an assessment of youth in the Weimar Republic, see also Thomas Koebner, *Mit uns zieht die neue Zeit.*

why, when there is a hint of such things, these questions should be avoided altogether. They don't ask; they provoke. The younger generation finds it degrading to be simply an object of curiosity. Only where they can assume there is a serious willingness to help them understand their own particular situation, tasks, strengths, and limits will they speak of their concerns, not to satisfy curiosity, but for the sake of their responsibility.

It is certainly a healthy sign that the edginess with which these ques- 241
tions were pursued a few years ago has been replaced by a greater sense of calm. There is a very sound reason for this: the problem of the younger generation, at least in its very provocative form as a "father and son" problem, has been overcome, on the one hand, because this battle has been fought out. On the other hand, however, there has also been a major shift in the entire way of looking at things. Today—in contrast to the period ten years ago—the younger generation is no longer interested in being young and in its right to youthfulness. Instead, they see themselves as included together with their parents in serving a common future, although each in his own way. Then as today, however, the guarantor for justice, sense, and success is the "Führer." The image of the "leader," as it arose in the youth movement, has undergone considerable transformation in the recent past, but it has ultimately become the only common denominator for the youth in all their desires, the symbol of the younger generation. The political, ideological, and religious ideas of the younger generation are symbolized in the image of the "Führer," and its transformation mirrors their emotional and political history. Where does this particular fire, this brilliance, and this pathos contained in the concept of leader as used by the youth of today come from? Those in their forties can assure us that in their youth such talk of a leader was completely unknown. Does the call for a leader arise from knowledge that the power of things over people has become so great and so destructive and so chaotic that only a great figure would be able to restore order and unity? Or does talk always necessarily turn to a leader when, given the awareness of the political necessity of surrendering the ideal of the individual and the engagement of human beings as a mass, as collective, everything one was forced to surrender is transferred onto the ideal of the leader and is rediscovered in him, magnified immeasurably? What other explanation is there for the peculiar tension between a cult of
personality and collectivism? Or is the call for a leader a logical reflection 242
both of our current political situation as well as of a certain youthful way of looking at life in general? That is, is it historically and psychologically necessary? And if this is the case, what are its limits? To what extent is leading and being led healthy and genuine, and when does it become pathological and excessive? Only those who give careful consideration to these questions

can understand something of the nature of "the ideology of the 'Führer'" [Führertum] and something of the behavior of the younger generation. Among today's youth leaders, almost everything depends on having a good sense of direction, going beyond the vague and fantastic in order to have a clear vision. The health and rectitude of young people are at risk. To this extent, ideal and illusion are close neighbors.

9. Lecture: "The Führer and the Individual in the Younger Generation"[1]

The Führer and the Individual in the Younger Generation

If today we take up a question from among the problems of the younger generation, we can only do so if we ourselves [are] sure of having overcome
243 the unpleasant self-reflection with which this sort of subject has been dealt with countless times, if we do not take a sensationalist approach . . . and do not take ourselves too seriously—but rather take this on as an attempt at

[1.] *NL*, A 36,4 (1); typescript with handwritten remarks and additions by Bonhoeffer. Previously published in *GS* 2:22–38. See also the shorter version *NL*, A 36,2: radio address "The Younger Generation's Altered View of the Concept of Führer" (i.e., the radio version); *NL*, A 36, 2(a): handwritten; *NL*, A 36, 2(b): typescript with handwritten remarks above right "Lic. Dr. Bonhoeffer (Dietrich) Rund[funk-] Vortrag Funk-St[un]de am 1.2. [1933 um] 17.45 Uhr" [Dr. Bonhoeffer (Dietrich) Radio Lecture *Funkstunde* on February 1, 1933, at 5:45 p.m.]. See also literary estate of Eberhard Bethge, "The Younger Generation's Altered View of the Concept of Führer" (eight-page typescript that is closer to *NL*, A 36, 2[a] than *NL*, A 36, 2[b]). The radio version was presented on February 1, 1933, over the Berliner Rundfunk (see *Der Rundfunk Hörer* 10, no. 5 (1933): 5: "17.45 [o'clock] The Younger Generation. The Younger Generation's Altered View of the Concept of Führer. Speaker: Dietrich Bonhoeffer"). In the column "Kritische Wochenrückschau" of the above-mentioned radio magazine, Bonhoeffer's lecture was later assessed: "Dietrich Bonnhöffer [*sic*], the student chaplain at the Technical College and lecturer of theology, shows the transformation of the concept of leader among German youth. They were well-formed sentences that one hopes to be able to read at leisure in print" (*Der Rundfunk Hörer* 10, no. 7 [1933]). According to written information of May 20, 1994, from the Deutsche Rundfunkarchiv in Frankfurt am Main, no recording of Bonhoeffer's talk exists. Bonhoeffer's contribution was the second in a six-part series *The Younger Generation,* which, according to the program printed by *Der Rundfunk Hörer,* also included the following contributions: January 11, 1933: "The Younger Generation: Rural Youth in New Ties," speaker: Ludwig Rese; January 18, 1933: "The Younger Generation: A High School Student Does Not Study," speaker Werner Lucke; February 8, 1933: "The Younger Generation: The Chances for Apprentices," speaker: Arnold Rocholl; February 15, 1933: "The Younger Generation in Literature," speaker: Giselher Wirsing; February 22, 1933: "The Younger Generation: The Importance of the Berlin Student House," speaker: Herbert Gutjahr (see also 1/29). The second, considerably longer, version [of Bonhoeffer's talk]

critical self-reflection in the service of a greater good.[2] Three brothers, of whom the eldest was born in 1900, the second in 1905, and the third in 1910, who are therefore thirty-three, twenty-eight, and twenty-three years old, embody the difference today between three generations. They all, however, belong to that which we like to call the "young generation"—the eldest, who reached maturity during the war, the second under the impression of the years after the collapse, and the third in a still-untitled epoch, let us say since 1926. The rush of historical events has accelerated the speed of the change in generations by nearly a factor of 10. A period of three to five years separates the generations today. We must speak of a generational change when the ranks of young people of the same age invoke one rea- 244
son for their general intellectual position, thereby setting themselves apart from the older generation as an independent group shaped by a particular experience—and where, on the other hand, those who are older are already engaged in the strange process of clarifying their own range of experience and intellectual position. The greatest difficulties in the current debate with and within the younger generation have their roots in this same inner disunity.[3] The *first*: people who have experienced death, who have, so to speak, stepped daily out of death into life, who have come to know life as action and profit, and who thus have a very special range in their thinking and desires. They are characterized, on the one hand, by an almost injurious hardness toward their own lives and acts and those of others and, on the other, by a strong affirmation of life and responsibility toward others' lives. This generation of youth who experienced war exists as a closed group vis-à-vis their younger brothers. Whether conscious or not, their entire stance is the expression of an unachievable superiority over the others; there is almost an expression of mockery on the faces of these youth marked by life and death, a mockery of those who are completely inexperienced, who live without really knowing what it means. There is an invisible

with an altered title (*NL*, A 36,4 [1] = lecture version) was presented at two Berlin universities: on February 23, 1933, at the Technical College (see 1/32) and at the beginning of March 1933 at the request of Theodor Heuss at the College of Political Science (*DB-ER*, 206). Alterations in the text mentioned in the following are based on a comparison of the radio address with the longer versions. To illustrate Bonhoeffer's statements, appropriate statements are included in the footnotes from Gründel, *Die Sendung der jungen Generation*, and Lesser, *Von deutscher Jugend*. See also Hartmann, *Die Junge Generation* (10–16), who, however, had not yet dealt with the problem of political leadership, and Lilje, "Die evangelische Jugendführung," which in 1932 had already referred to "the oft-dealt with example of the *politicization* of today's youth" (290).

[2.] Entire paragraph: handwritten addition in the lecture version.

[3.] With the following sentence the first major insertion begins.

but impenetrable barrier between those who fought in the war and those who are only a little younger, who reached maturity during the period of collapse. This is felt even more greatly among the younger ones than among the older. For the first postwar generation there is nothing more impressive than the fact that among them live these men who have escaped from the world of death. There is something frightening, worrying, terrifying in this knowledge. And the strange silence that lay over this world in the first postwar years, replaced only some years later by a no longer very original talkativeness, strengthens the awareness of the unapproachability of this world for all the others.

It was under pressure from this generation of war veterans that the
245 younger generation grew up. They have two main characteristics: On the one hand, they have been given the knowledge that their older brothers acquired firsthand, and thus they have been made aware of life in its entirety, with all its uncertainty and dubiousness. On the other, this problem differs from the question facing the older ones in that the latter experienced it themselves in the middle of a situation of responsibility, that is, one they continually had to overcome in their lives. The problem for the younger ones was not bound to responsibility and was therefore radical, and at the same time they had to push to create a situation of responsibility in which this problem could be experienced. Thus the younger ones, due to this contrast with the older ones, were led to be actively constructive, and less to responsibly accept and tolerate the given, to freely create their own way of life out of their radical critique.

With the end of the era of the youth movement [Jugendbewegung]—in the largest sense of the term—that is, at the moment that this second group of youth accepted the responsibility of professional life, today's youngest generation arose. Without being aware of it, they know that life cannot be constructed out of the radical problematic. It does not therefore become unproblematic, as is often said, because the inheritance from their older brothers is too much a part of them, but the focus of their problems has shifted; indeed one could say that the problem has split. The ultimate questions of life are answered with silence—in deliberate opposition to the talkativeness of the preceding generation—a silent alliance with the reality in sport, travel, does not permit curiosity and sensation for the problem to arise for itself, without our being able to say that this silence is a deathly silence. On the other hand, the problem of life turns from a general question to a concrete one with respect to the time for political action. And to this point it must be said that the youngest generation's sense of reality has and is becoming a metaphysic of reality. Reality is not taken as that which it is; there is
246 no reflection on what it can and cannot be; rather, reality is taken as what it

should be; it is naively held to be open to any development and construction; in it the elements of God's kingdom on earth are seen in the process of coming into being. Where this metaphysic of reality is bound to an awareness of the concrete political difficulties, there arises a political-chiliastic way of thinking like that which generally characterizes the youngest generation.

It is now understandable that, on the intellectual battlefield where these three young generations find themselves together with the older generation, that is, where these four generations struggle against one another, the situation is as unclear as it appears today. However, for an understanding of the decisive contemporary cultural-political and other questions, it is necessary to keep in mind these divisions brought about by the historical developments, for which no one is to blame.[4]

Nonetheless a few generalizations may be made about the younger generation as a whole. They reached maturity during a period of history during which the previously well-established Western world came apart at the seams—war, postwar period, crisis. Thus the inner task facing them could only consist of the attempt to avoid being pulled into a complete collapse and instead to find the foothold that would allow them a continued existence. Three impressions shaped their move toward this foothold: first, in the collapse they experienced the triumph of objects over humans, of machines over their creators. Technology, which was intended to master nature, had been turned against defenseless humans and thus robbed of its essential meaning![5] Second, the impotence of the entire existing political, intellectual, and religious ideology seemed to have been proven, and third, the millions who fell in the Great War, the revolutionizing[6] masses of the postwar period, and the million-strong army of unemployed during the crisis must have given the younger generation a convincing impression of the meaninglessness and complete isolation of the individual and of the blunt power of the masses. The masses and lifeless objects appeared to have 247
emerged from this collapse as victors. In neither, however, was the younger generation able to find the foothold that could help sustain their lives in this chaos. A sense of the individual and the sense of true community seemed to have been completely destroyed.[7] An individualistically formed autonomous[8] personality and an idea separated from the reality of the [. . .][9]

[4.] End of the first insertion.

[5.] This sentence is not in the radio version.

[6.] In the radio version and in the handwritten manuscript: "revolutionary."

[7.] This sentence not in the radio version.

[8.] In the radio version instead of the last three words only: "individualistic."

[9.] One word illegible.

life went bankrupt. It was out of this crisis that an impassioned call arose for new authority, new ties, for community.[10] The common concern of the younger generation as a whole vis-à-vis the older generation can be seen in the opposition to an unreal individualism and the attempt at a new, meaningful common life.[11] The extent to which an unreal individualism is being contrasted here with an equally unreal collectivism will be examined later. A quite simple fact of experience led initially to this opposition, namely, that at the turn of the century and later the educated classes were unable to deal with the important problems of life, both public and private. The lost war made this latent crisis obvious. Germany came apart at the seams. And the younger generation found itself more or less abandoned and having to fend for itself. The problem of the meaning of the defeat in intellectual
248 historical terms was taken up and discussed, with the conclusion that the answer was to be found by overcoming the lack of community among Germans, and that the defeat had to lead to a new sense of community, to new bonds, new authority.[12] Fairly and unfairly, this was suggested to the older generation. These concepts naturally underwent a superficial schematization: individualism, liberalism, personality became terms of denigration for something generally misunderstood that people did under other names. These, however, are natural processes and not to be taken too seriously. Hidden behind these words was a serious desire, intended to lead people from the individual to the collective, from lack of attachment to interdependence, from a lack of authority to new authority.[13] This new authority, however, could only be imagined in terms of a new human being, one not

---

[10.] With the following sentence, the second major insertion begins.

[11.] Lesser understood the push for "the peoples' community" (*Volksgemeinschaft*) as a concern that brings youth together, "whether they" think "nationalist or socialist." They therefore apply it to "the affectations of the older generation, as if the peoples' community existed already, or still." The "better, intellectual youth" know that "a new human being is needed, a complete change is needed and a turning away from all liberal and progressive solutions and misstatements, from all relativism, rationalism, which were so characteristic of the recent unfortunate epoch. And the human being must again give himself to the eternal forces, the forces of the eternal and divine, live from them and order his state, his economy, his community accordingly" (*Von deutscher Jugend*, 133–34).

[12.] Lesser quotes from his sources on the attitude of nationalist youth toward the state: "The youth are entering into politics at a moment in which a miserable twelve-year system of muddling and cover-ups is collapsing. The great threat that parliamentarianism, pseudodemocracy, economy of special interests, corruption, inefficiency, and bad management pose to people and state become painfully obvious. The older generation, with their prewar thinking, failed when faced by the monstrous European crisis." He added, "[A]nd the socialist-communist youth speak no differently, even when they are not saying the same thing in many cases" (*Der deutsche Jugend*, 181).

[13.] End of the second addition.

disconnected from the reality of life, based on a new idea of life overcoming the isolation of individuals. The ideal of the leader was thus outlined. Authority in the form of the leader—it was in this demand that the younger generation liberated itself from the burden forced upon it.[14]

With the postwar youth movement, the idea of the leader in its new form 249
spread throughout Germany for the first time.[15] This was the movement's
first creative act, one through which these youth also prompted their elder 250
brothers to act; the younger ones became the creative force for the elder

[14.] Lesser writes, "[C]oncerning the Führer question, which preoccupies and stirs up so many young people, a question that also causes no little" confusion, which [he says has the following consequence]: "With extreme impatience, many young people today confuse the great nation-forming leader with this or that party leader—only few truly intellectual youth avoid this confusion. These intellectual youths understand with the certainty of God's mercy that only the superior human being is the salvation of the world, that he whose myth is the continuing source of fecundity and fruitfulness for the race, is a true leader of the people. . . . Only a superior human being is leader and ruler: he of utterly radiant, world-encompassing, all-comprehending spirit, a fundamentally sage heart, utterly masculine, all infusing action, utterly suprapersonal, visionary will of Earth, he is creator of the people, the nation; in him the divine spirit and earthly kingdom are one" (*Der deutsche Jugend*, 189). Lesser saw Stefan George as this leader of German youth (190). In another sense he named him as "the only true leader, the creator of the new world and the new values," together with Friedrich Nietzsche and his contemporary Rudolf Pannwitz (89); see also his warning against false leaders and saviors, "who preach against the false spirit of the age in order to then do business with this false spirit" (342). Lesser thus did not see Adolf Hitler as the expected great leader. Gründel, too, protested mightily against Hitler's claim to be the long-awaited leader of the German revolution. Although he gave his approval to the National Socialist German Workers' Party as the "party of youth" (Gründel, *Die Sendung der jungen Generation*, 302), he doubted whether the hoped-for leader existed among the National Socialist leadership. Gründel described "the outline of the coming *great leader*" (435) and commented: "We thus now know that our century has a major 'hero's role' to grant, perhaps the most significant for the last thousand years and that this role, in the deeper sense and with the will of history, falls to Germany. However, none of us should yet feel himself chosen for this role. Not one of us has the stature demanded by this role. Neither exaggerated self-praise nor an 'impressive vote count' coming out of parliamentary ballot boxes can change this fact. The coming great leadership is not a matter for parliament. The rise to power will occur—and this lies in the exceptional nature of the matter and the historical situation—neither through elections nor through any 'legitimate' or manipulated 'inheritance,' but instead through a very rare synthesis of the people's desires and inherent power. Here there is 'no searched for, no elected leadership, but only an evolving one' (Erwin Guido Kolbenheyer)" (434).

[15.] Lesser writes on "Leader and Followers" among the members of youth associations [a reference to the young people who had joined one of the many youth associations and clubs in that era—LR]: "The fundamental experience of an association is the polarity of leader and followers. . . . It is in this that the youthful members of associations oppose contemporary opinion, held by the vast majority of the peoples who see in the leader only an elected civil servant, only recognize these and denigrate any other form

ones.[16] Naturally, there have always been leaders. Where there is community there is leadership. However, here we are interested only in the particular form that the idea of the leader took in the young generation, and here is a first characteristic: previously, leadership had found its expression in teachers, statesmen, fathers, that is, in the given social structure and offices, but now the leader has become a completely autonomous form. The leader has become totally divorced from an office; he is essentially and only leader.[17] What does this mean? While leadership was previously based on bonds, it is now based on choice. This is understandable, as the bonds from which any previous leader could arise have become obsolete. Thus the problem of leadership, one of the oldest problems of community altogether, became concentrated in the problem of the *leader*. For both parties[18] leadership [Führung] remains something neutral, neutered—or to be more specific, objective; the ideology of the leader [Führertum] relates to the person of both parties. Leadership arises through superiority in something objective, through office, knowledge, ability; with the leader, it is essentially a dominance of the person.[19] For both it is a question of power relations, for leadership superiority in something objective, for a leader in the dominance of his person. Thus it is quite clear that there can be a more rational basis for leadership than for the ideology of the leader. It is inherent to
251 the ideology of the leader that it cannot be rationally based. That is both

---

of leadership as 'undemocratic' and 'romantic.' The youth in these associations, however, view themselves as being at one with the great creators of the German people when they rescue the concept of leader from the quotidian-societal to carry it into the metaphysical, beyond all politics and social necessities, as they certainly do not close themselves to experiencing something holy in the erotic experience of the leader, without which life would remain irreverent" (*Von deutscher Jugend*, 20–21). Gründel wrote on the "coming *leadership*": "It is not leadership as vainglory, but rather leadership as holy office. Never would this new leadership be, for example, an absolutism in the sense of aristocratic divine mercy or oriental despotism. Both would be radically un-German. That which Ernst Moritz Arndt unsuccessfully demanded a century ago is all the more true today: 'Away with the base fatalism that calls to us: the strong should rule and the weak serve; a higher voice calls: the just should lead and the free will obey!' It is the leadership [*Führertum*] of the best as holy office and the free following of the entire people, who serve the greater goals of society" (*Die Sendung der jungen Generation*, 409–10).

[16.] This sentence not in the radio version.

[17.] With this sentence, the third major addition begins.

[18.] [The leader and the follower.—LR]

[19.] Lesser on the leader among members of youth associations: "A leader is not an arbitrary, self-serving commander; leading also means serving and listening. . . . They follow, they imitate, they listen with all their soul only to those who demand the utmost and the hardest of themselves and live as models, as it is only in such a leader that the sense and nature of the association is contained" (*Die deutsche Jugend*, 21).

its strength and its limitation. For leadership it is essentially a question of "what," and for the ideology of the leader a question of "who"; the object of leadership is those who are being led, the view is from above to below; the object of the ideology of the leader is the leader himself, the view is from below to above. Thus a sociologically interesting new phenomenon has been introduced into the structure of authority. The leader as autonomous form has its own particular sociological place. We will conclude our thoughts here by systematically defining the sociological place of the leader—in the modern understanding of the term. First, in the historical developments of the last decades, the concept of leader has undergone an essential transformation, and this we need to examine.[20]

The leader in the sense used in the youth movement arose from a small group; he was not one of those in charge, but a person elected by the group. It was the good, the inwardly noble, who were to be raised up by the group and entrusted by them. The group is the cradle of the leader. It gives the leader everything, including authority. It is the person of the leader onto which all authority, honor, and glory of the group are transferred. Leadership [Führerschaft] is not an office independent of the person. The group expects that a leader who emerges from the group will embody the group's ideals. This task, in itself impossible, is made easier for the leader in that the group that produced the leader regards that person in the light of their ideals. They are looking not at his reality but at his purpose. It is essential for the image of the leader that the group does not see the face of the past but only regards him from behind; as the figure of the one who strides forward, the leader's humanity is veiled in his form of leader [Führergestalt]. In the youth movement, however, this leader was meant to be essentially human; it was on the leader's ideal humanity that these youth sought their foothold and a fulfillment for their collapsing personal lives. The leader
was meant to be the friend whom one worshipped, loved, for whom one was 252
willing to sacrifice everything. The leader was meant to be that which they had failed to find in their fathers or teachers.[21] These are the two major factors that must be considered in any discussion of the concept of leader: the individual and the father, that is, the given, existing office here. The symptomatic problem of the youth movement was the father-and-son problem. It was here that an explosion was repeatedly sparked off. The father was replaced by the leader, the authority of the father denied in favor of the authority of the leader; the leader was placed above the father; the father

[20.] End of the third addition.

[21.] With the following sentence, the fourth major addition begins.

would only be an authority when he himself became a leader of youth. Thus the individual is freed from his ties to the existing order and becomes free to choose, completely free; the leader then becomes—in a very particular way in the youth movement—the leader of his own heretofore undiscovered, better self. In the election of the leader, the individual is liberated to himself. In the leader, the one who is led sees his own ideal human self. In the youth movement the group and the leader are essentially a mere extension of one's own self; for all the searching for community and authority, it is essentially a matter of the individual's own soul, which then plunges into the supposed You, only to find itself in every mirror. The sociological category of the individual, with its unbridgeable eternal individuality, as well as the sociological category of the father, that is, the given order, was swallowed up in the first form of the idea of leader in a broad, extended new individualism. Thus the terms "responsibility" and "order" were subsumed in a free, self-legislating individual.[22] In the youth movement—one can say today—it was always only a matter of a new, *individual* soul; the leader of the youth movement was the leader for a spiritual-human fulfillment of the
253 individual. It was because of this definition that the fate of the leader was repeatedly a tragic one. One wanted to see the entire ideal humanity of the leader; one didn't want merely to be permitted to see him as the progressive one. Here, however, where the leader was to be leader in the totally human sense and where he himself understood his task as only personal and not objective, it was unavoidable that both the led and the leader saw through the illusion of such an unlimited ideology of leader. The secret of the leader's authority was unveiled and destroyed, and it was in naked humanity that leader and led separated. Authority collapsed, and with it loyalty and obedience. All that was left was a romantic memory.

The youth movement of the war and the postwar generation was replaced by that of the third—today's youngest generation—at the same time that their supporters had to enter professional life. These young people, originally instilled with a greater sense of reality than their elder siblings and more certain of their direction, saw the hopelessness and meaninglessness of their own futures and those of their fellows most particularly in the political crisis. Thus the aim of these new youth was initially much more concrete and clearly defined than that of their elders; and to a much greater extent the lack of authority in political thought and action was seen as the ultimate cause of all that was bad. The call for political authority, however, in view of the apparently complete failure of previously existing

[22.] End of the fourth addition.

order and conditions,[23] had to become the call for a great person,[24] for a political leader, and in this call—this is the most significant and specific factor—the differences in generation among the youth suddenly disappeared; indeed, the "father-and-son problem," which was the central focus of the youth movement, was completely overshadowed; emphasis was placed no longer on the differences but on common obligation. The form of political leader lost its familiarity; friendship was replaced by comrade- 254
ship, dedication replaced by obedience. The individualistic remnants of the youth movement have been overcome.[25] That is to say, a strange transfer has occurred. The individual sees his duty in unconditional obedience to the leader. The individual is totally dissolved; he becomes a tool in the hands of the leader; the individual is not responsible; it is the leader who is responsible. In his faith in the leader, the individual surrenders ultimate responsibility to the leader, just as for Catholics their faith in their church includes belief in the justness of its commandments and its guarantee for my obedience. In this submission, this disconnection [Ausschaltung][26] of the individual, individualism is truly overcome, but it reappears in the form of the transfer to the new. That which the individual must surrender is transferred from all individuals onto the form of one person who is the leader. The individual is renounced in favor of the leader. The leader is that which no one else may be, an individual, personality. The relation of the led to their leader is that of the transfer of their own rights onto the leader. As such, it is a form of collectivism that turns into an individualism of the nth degree. For this reason the true sense of community, which is based on the responsibility of individuals to hold one another responsible, does not find its fulfillment here. However, let us continue with the description of this concept of leader.[27] The leader is placed at an enormous distance from the led but—and this is the decisive point—the leader is only such as the one elected by those he leads. Having come from them, the leader receives authority only from his retinue, from below, from the people. The spirit of the people [Volksgeist]—it is imagined—brings the leader out from its

[23.] Instead of "In view of . . . conditions" in the radio version: "in view of the general collapse of forms and order."

[24.] The last four words were not in the radio version.

[25.] With the following sentence, the fifth major addition begins.

[26.] [Bonhoeffer's audience would have heard the linguistic contrast of *Ausschaltung* (disconnection) to *Gleichschaltung*. *Gleichschaltung*—switching everything into the same gear, bringing everything into alignment—was a central policy of the National Socialist regime.—LR]

[27.] End of the fifth addition.

metaphysical depths and raises him to great heights.[28] This leader, aris-
255 ing from the collective power of the people, now appears in the light as the one awaited by the people, the longed-for fulfillment of the meaning and power of the life of the Volk. Thus the originally prosaic idea of political authority is transformed into the political-messianic idea of leader that we see today. All the religious thinking of its supporters flows into it as well. Where the spirit of the people is a divine-metaphysical factor, the leader who embodies this spirit has a religious function in the true sense of the term, becoming the messiah, and thus his appearance heralds the dawn of the fulfillment of ultimate hope, and with the kingdom that he brings in his wake, the eternal kingdom comes closer. While the religious attitude of the group toward their leader in the youth movement could be related to the pietistic ideal of community, the political-messianic idea of leader is closer to the ideal of a universal kingdom of God on earth, which was the goal of enthusiasm and the French Revolution and has been repeatedly taken up ever since.

But it is exactly this idea that is decisively rejected in the young generation. For all the unanimity in their call for political authority, there are the deepest of divisions as to the exact nature of this authority. This is the fundamental question: Authority of the leader or authority of the office? And this brings us to the most burning question of the day. The leader has authority from below, from the led; the office has authority from above; the authority of the leader depends on the leader's person; the authority of the office is beyond personality; authority from below is self-justification of the people; authority of the office is recognition of given limits; authority from below is authority lent; authority of office is original authority. The key word of the authority of the leader is the Reich; [29] the key word of the author-

---

[28.] See the citation [of Lesser] in ed. note 15. Lesser also reports on the complaint of the nationalistic youths, "that the spirit of the people today has been completely overwhelmed," and of the lack of unity in these circles about "who embodies the spirit of the people today; while most of them see it embodied in one or another fanatical political leader, a small minority among them . . . say that German and people [Volk] in the highest and purest sense is not embodied by this or another overly idolized politician, but by [Stefan] George, whom many refer to but few follow" (*Von deutscher Jugend*, 117) .

[29.] Lesser on the meaning of the concept of *Reich* among youth: "Some youth who, unlike many others, are attracted neither by Russia nor by Italy, would like Germany to grant itself a form of state arising from German nature, a form that corresponds neither to the democracy of which they are suspicious nor to the dictatorship of which they are equally suspicious, but rather something radically new, which combines the oldest fruitfulness with creative orientation toward the future. It is the idea of a holy Reich of all Germans that moves them" (*Von deutsche Jugend*, 187). The concept of Reich was used by

ity of office is the state.[30] For the problem of the individual this means the following: In the authority of the office, the individual experiences his self will over against the existing ties, his ordered place in the world, his inability to determine his destiny, and at the same time his responsibility in the very place where he finds himself. Authority of office means limitations on the individual in his individual freedom, restrictions, calling attention to the other, to reality. Authority of the leader means for the individual: the free choice of obedience, radical surrender of his right as individual, and nonetheless measureless, limitless freedom of the individual according to the law of transfer. Admittedly, however, neither the limited nor the unlimited individual is as such the individual in his indestructible unity and responsibility, and neither obedience toward the father nor submission to the leader can establish the community in which You and I are truly related to each other. Neither the office nor the leader is, as such, the ultimate given condition.[31] 256

Nonetheless, the following must initially be said concerning this conflict: the concept of "authority" contains, from its origin, the idea of authorship. Authority is more original than those for whom it is authority. I can therefore only recognize authority as the authority set over me. The authority that I allow others to have over me is basically only my own authority. It is for this reason that the one is true and limited authority, and the other is lent and in danger of becoming excessive. It is for this reason that I am under the control of the one authority, and from the other I can free myself
only by myself, and I gain worth from myself. There is a decisive difference 257
between the authority of the father, the teacher, the judge, the statesman, on the one hand, and the authority of the leader, on the other. The former have authority from their office and only through it; the leader has authority only by virtue of his person. The authority of the former can be infringed, violated, but it continues to exist; the authority of the leader is constantly at risk; it is in the hand of his followers. I can choose the leader, but I cannot choose a father and a teacher; I submit to the authority of the leader; I am subordinate to the authority of the father and the teacher. Father, teacher, statesman are essentially not leaders but rather administrators of

Friedrich Hielscher in 1931 as a program and also plays an important role in Wilhelm Stapel (see 2/1). Already in 1923 Arthur Moeller van der Bruck, in his book *Das dritte Reich* (originally titled *Die dritte Partei*), coined the term that gained wide acceptance and, through the offices of Otto Straßer, became the term for National Socialist claims to power.

[30.] With the following sentence, the sixth major addition begins.

[31.] End of the sixth addition.

their office. Those who expect something else do not see the reality, are dreamers. With their idea of leadership, they are certainly dependent on a historical necessity as well as on a necessity arising from a certain youthful sense of life, and there remains only the final fundamental question of the place that the "leader"—in the most portentous sense of the term—takes in the construction of authority and the place from where the individual comes to that authority. People and especially youth will feel the need to give a leader authority over them as long as they do not feel themselves to be mature, strong, responsible enough to themselves fulfill the demands placed in this authority. The leader will have to be responsibly aware of this clear restriction of authority. If the leader understands his function differently from that thus established, if the leader does not repeatedly provide the led with clear details on the *limited nature* of the task and on their own responsibility, if the leader tries to become the idol the led are looking for—something the led always hope from their leader—then the image of the leader shifts to one of a misleader,[32] then the leader is acting improp-
258 erly[33] both toward the led as well as toward himself. The true leader must always be able to disappoint. This, especially, is part of the leader's responsibility and objectivity. The leader must lead the led from the authority of the leader's person to a recognition of the true authority of order and office. The leader must lead the led into responsibility toward the social structures of life, toward father, teacher, judge, state. The leader must radically reject the temptation to become an idol, that is, the ultimate authority of the led. In all soberness, the leader must confine himself to the task at hand. The leader serves the order of the state, the community, and the service of the leader can be of incomparable value; indeed it can be essential.[34] This, however, only as long as the leader keeps strictly to the task. The leader temporarily takes decision-making powers from the individual but must always remember that this state is a *temporary* necessity and must always remind the led of this. The leader should accept this self-deprivation of rights, self-incapacitation in order to lead the individuals back to their responsibility. To the responsibility of human beings belongs, however, the responsibility vis-à-vis the others, vis-à-vis existing orders, of adapting, ordering oneself, accepting limits. It is thus the case that the leader accepts in their stead

[32.] After the comma, the sentence in the radio version breaks off.

[33.] In the handwritten version as well as in the first typewritten version found in Bethge's literary estate (see ed. note 1), instead of "improperly" there is the stronger formulation "criminally." Bethge's assumption that this change was made by the radio editor in charge (*GS* 2:35) cannot be proven.

[34.] With the following sentence, the seventh major addition begins.

that responsibility toward the order and offices of life that the followers are
not capable of, and fulfills it for them. While the led believe and hope that
their leader is the epitome of an autonomous human being, the masterful
human being who is totally free, the leader must be aware that because of
the followers, the leader is the most bound, the one most burdened with
the responsibility for the orders of life, the epitome of a servant. It is quite
obvious that here neither the idea of the individual nor the idea of the
community is given due justice, that instead both here are in a historically
and psychologically necessary but penultimate stage of development. The
leader serves the office. However, this service in office is itself only a pen- 259
ultimate matter. In the authority of office, the individual experiences his
bonds, his limits, but also his responsibility. However, here too, the human
being is not seen for what he is. It *can*[35] be the case that the individual is
in the right vis-à-vis the office, since it is not the ultimate authority. From
where can the individual take this right vis-à-vis the office? Nowhere else
than there where he sees that the office is the penultimate authority with
respect to an ultimate unutterable authority, with respect to the authority
of God. And from this authority the individual truly knows himself to be an
individual. It is to God that the individual is responsible. And this individu-
ality of standing before God, this submission to the ultimate authority, is
destroyed when the authority of a leader or an office is seen as the ultimate
authority. The irrefutable indication of this inevitability of individuality for
the human being is this: that he must die alone, that he must bear his own
body, his suffering and guilt as an individual. Only before God does the
human being become what he is, an individual, free, and at the same time
bound in responsibility. And each individual knows that he is placed among
other individuals, that he is bound to them, that he exists in community.
Community of individuals, not a melting together of I and You, the strict-
est distinction and therefore the strictest responsibility for each other and
only for this reason, where the human being becomes an individual before
God, community, the community of suffering, of guilt, of death, and of life.
There is currently a terrible danger that, in the crying out for authority, for
a leader or office, we forget that the human being is an individual before
the ultimate authority, and that everyone who misappropriates this breaks
an eternal law and takes on superhuman responsibility, which in the end
will crush him. The eternal law of individuality before God is terribly venge-
ful when offended and perverted.[36] Thus the leader points to the office;

[35.] Twice underlined in the draft.

[36.] End of the seventh addition.

leader and office, however, to the ultimate authority itself, before which
260 Reich and state are penultimate authorities.[37] Leader and office that turn
themselves into gods mock God and the solitary individual before him who
is becoming the individual, and must collapse. Only the leader who is in the
service of the penultimate and ultimate authority merits loyalty.

10. Discussion Paper for the Ecumenical Conference in Dassel[1]

The Concept of Confession from the Standpoint of the Concept of Truth

Between the concept of truth and that of confession lies the concept of the
Word in Protestant thinking. Truth is to be understood as the truth of the
261 Word, and here it is a matter of the clear, unambiguous, comprehensible
spoken word. In the church this Word is with us in two forms, as the Word
of God itself, which appears *ubi et quando visum est deo*,[2] and as the word

---

[37.] The following sentence is not in the radio version.

[1.] EZA, 5/100 (text is identical to EZA, 635/13), Bl. 61 and 122–23; typescript. See also *NL*, A 34,9; carbon copy (excerpt from a draft sent to a participant for correction) with extensive handwritten corrections by Bonhoeffer. Previously published in *GS* 1:179–91. According to Zoellner's words at the beginning of the ecumenical conference in Dassel (March 6–10, 1933), it was a question of creating a committee to advise the German Evangelical Church Committee and thus to prevent it from coming under the influence of anti-ecumenical currents aligned with a particular church faction. Under the general heading of "common viewpoints for German ecumenical work," on which Stange gave an introduction on the evening of March 6, 1933, the following topics were then discussed March 7–10, 1933. 1. "The Question of Truth in Ecumenical Work" (paper by Otto Zänker and Wilhelm Stählin; Bonhoeffer's paper "The Concept of Confession from the Standpoint of the Concept of Truth" was part of that debate); 2. "The Unity of the Church and Its Proclamation: The Current State of Ecumenical Discussion and Starting Points for Its Continuation" (paper by Hanns Lilje and Hermann Sasse); 3. "Measures to Deepen and Spread the Ecumenical Front within the German Church" (paper by August Marahrens and Max Diestel, during which Bonhoeffer made his comments on the theological divisions in the ecumenical movement); 4. "The Ecumenical Movement in Its Relation to Contemporary National and International Currents" (paper by Johannes Eger and Wilhelm Stählin). As Zoellner reported to the Church Federation Office on March 13, 1933, among the nineteen participants there was "considerable unanimity on the main question." With regard to the conference agenda, Zoellner, Stählin, and Kurt Dietrich Schmidt planned to formulate a series of topics with the "main lines of unanimity," which would then be followed by "individual publications . . . in the sense of this conference and its topics" (*Mündige Welt* 5:63). This plan never came to fruition, probably because of the political and church changes in Germany.

[2.] "When and where God pleases" (see the Augsburg Confession, Article V, *Book of Concord*, 41).

of the confessing and speaking community in which the gospel is properly taught—*pure docetur.*[3] The two are merged inseparably and united. Where truth appears in the Word, it is the Word of God and the word of human beings at the same time. The word of human beings in the church, however, is always somehow intrinsically related to doctrine, and this with the accent on "pure" doctrine. It is from this starting point that the notion of doctrine becomes constitutive for the concept of confession; "proper" doctrine has a theological precedence over all questions of the proper constitution. This leads to a decisive defense against all confessional relativism, on the one hand, and against an absolutism, as is true for the Catholic Church, on the other. In Protestant understanding, confession has, paradoxically, a relative = absolute character in one. This leads me to characterize ecumenical dialogue thus: that those involved seek to open themselves to the others with the Word of God expressed in human words, in doctrinal teaching, that they, with their human words and human understanding, humbly let themselves be called into question, that they take the criticism of the others, and that in this criticism they allow themselves to be directed toward their mutual dependence on God's living grace. The confessional word of every individual remains absolute and relative at the same time. It is in confessional profession and in human modesty, in order to be fully open to others, that ecumenical dialogue takes place. The proof that confessional seriousness is entirely preserved can be seen in the fact that even in ecumenical work the *concept of heresy* is regaining currency. The loss of this term means serious cost to confessional substance.[4]

[3.] "Taught purely" (see the Augsburg Confession, Article VII, *Book of Concord*, 43).

[4.] In his closing statement, Stählin, beginning with the idea that "Paul [was] mostly acoustically talented, while John was generally visually so" and that therefore "with the emphasis on the 'Word' of God in Protestant theology, arising from Romans, the acoustic image [is] so central, indeed more absolute . . . than anywhere else," underlined his "decisive objection to Bonhoeffer" and said: "Yes, I confess that for me the terrible danger of the expression 'Word of God' has never been more frighteningly evident than today. Two things, which are radically different, are being confused here. First, the 'Word of God' should be the God that comes to us, and then comes our human attempt to witness this light, word, this creative force of the Father in human speech. If and to what extent our human speech, as we are taught theologically, is the absolute primary and central means for our bearing witness to God's coming into the world, is an extremely difficult theological question, which cannot be answered by referring to certain impressions and experiences. The question arises very seriously as to whether there are not other forms of bearing witness that are indispensable, so that the Word's form of bearing witness (which no human could ever imagine replacing) is not misinterpreted as a merely conceptual communication, but remains credible as witness" (EZA, 5/100, Bl. 68–69).

262 [On theological conflict in the ecumenical movement]
I hold that which Schmidt-Kiel said[5] not only to be theologically correct but also to correspond to concrete experience. The theological difference truly extends to the very depths. At the ecumenical youth meetings in recent years, this recognition has repeatedly been the final honest result that could be achieved. How should we view and overcome this difference? Only with the original Reformation idea that the church of the gospel is a church that is always penitent. The particularity of the Lutheran message is the recognition of the penitent church. On the one hand, this recognition
263 is absolutely important; but, on the other, the church in particular, as the object of this message, must always repent, that is, it must humbly listen to the other. An absolute claim and at the same time humility are included in the concept of penitence in the Lutheran understanding of the church. The term *Una sancta*[6] is only imaginable in this paradoxical form. It is wrong, by contrast—and arises historically from Romanticism and not from the Reformation—to think of the concept of church organically, that is, to understand the confessions as parts of the whole, as different branches on a tree. This is wrong because this talk of the relation of the part to the whole assumes that it is possible to make a statement about this whole. However, this is exactly what we cannot do; we know nothing of the church other than its founding through the Word of God that calls to repentance and the gospel; we know about the church only in the form of our confession; we do not see a universal church. All this remains free speculation and devalues the truth claims of the confession. The concept of partial truth completely destroys the concept of truth. Any organic notion of church dissolves the true claim of the confession. It is not only non-Reformation but also unbiblical. The *tertium comparationis*[7] in Paul's image of the body is the idea of service of the one for the other, not the relation of the part to the whole. It

[5.] In the discussion of the question of whether the unity of the church was more profound in the confession of the early church (*altkirchlichen Bekenntnis*) than in the community in word, Kurt Dietrich Schmidt argued that "the substance of words" is "different." In saying this, he did not intend to "demand a unity of theology." However, he was more concerned with the idea that the "Catholic concept of God" was fundamentally different from the Lutheran one: "For the Catholics, God is the just. It was on this concept of God that Luther was ruined. When the Augustinians say: we are agreed about God, in fact the agreement is only about words. Among the Reformed, one can see a similar situation" (EZA 5/100, Bl. 117–18). [Schmidt was a professor at the university in Kiel.—LR]

[6.] "The one, holy [church]."

[7.] [The third aspect of the comparison.—LR]

is a Lutheran concern to criticize the romantic notion of the church that is widespread in the ecumenical movement and thus to clear the way for a true understanding of the confession and the *Una sancta*.[8]

11. Essay: "Thy Kingdom Come! The Prayer of the Church-Community for God's Kingdom on Earth"[1] 264

Thy Kingdom Come!
The Prayer of the Church-Community for God's Kingdom on Earth

We are otherworldly[2] or we are secularists, but in either case this means that we no longer believe in God's kingdom. We are hostile to the Earth, because we want to be better than it,[3] or we are hostile to God, because

[8.] Stählin, who spoke right after Bonhoeffer, was convinced of "a complete inadequacy of all spoken forms of expression" as "the form of the curse that lies over all humanity." He referred to the problem that the theological school language was "utterly incomprehensible for the vast majority of our contemporaries"—which is why the unconventional attempt of the Altona confession (see 2/1) was met with "relief and attentiveness." He found the "contemporary confusion of language . . . that we mean different things with the same words . . . bearable only because (in contrast to Bonhoeffer's statement!) language, in fact, the expressible doctrine of the Church, is always a form of the church's witness only in relation to the other forms of witness that are essential to the church." Although, according to Stählin, the "primary significance of the word" could not be disputed, he did not wish to understand this significance "merely ritualistically, by appealing to a purported command (Karl Barth: We have not been commanded to play the organ, but indeed to preach), but rather from the nature of language and its special connection to a spiritual content of meaning." This led him to a further statement in relation to Bonhoeffer: "The biblical allegory of the body must be understood much more tangibly and comprehensively (in contrast to Bonhoeffer, in agreement with Zoellner). When speaking of different parts of a body, this certainly also means the mutual relations of office and service; but this image of body is not exhausted when it is used only in reference to mutual service. 'Division of labor' (Acts 6) and mutual service are only then possible and meaningful because parts that should serve one another *are parts of the body of Christ*" (EZA, 5/100, Bl. 124–25).

[1.] From *Das kommende Reich*, 27–43; reprinted in *GS* 3:270–85. The essay is based on a lecture of November 19, 1932, that was part of the eighth "devotional retreat" of the Protestant Continuing Education Institute for Women (Evangelische Mädchen- und Frauenbildungsanstalt) in Potsdam-Hermannswerder (*Das kommende Reich*, 43, and *Protestantenblatt* 66 [1933]: 446). See also *NL*, A 32,3; handwritten draft with multiple corrections, mentioned in selected cases in the footnotes.

[2.] Bonhoeffer here takes up Nietzsche's expression and ideas (see Nietzsche, *Thus Spake Zarathustra*, esp. 56–60).

[3.] "Better . . . it" replaced "because it is too strong for us."

God robs us of the Earth, our mother.[4] We flee the power of the Earth, or we hold hard and fast to it. Either way we are not the wanderers who love the Earth that bears them, and who only truly love it because it is on it that they travel toward that foreign land that they love above all;[5] otherwise
265 they would not be wandering at all. Only wanderers of this kind, who love the Earth and God as one, can believe in God's kingdom.

We have been otherworldly ever since we discovered the devious trick of being religious, indeed "Christian," at the expense of the Earth. Otherworldliness affords a splendid environment in which to live. When life begins to be difficult and oppressive, one leaps boldly into the air and soars, relieved and worry free, in the so-called eternal realm. One leapfrogs over the present, scorns the Earth; one is better than it; indeed, next to the temporal defeats, one has eternal victories that are so easily achieved. Otherworldliness also makes it easy to preach and speak words of comfort. An otherworldly church can be sure that it will in no time at all attract all the weaklings, all those who are only too glad to be deceived and deluded, all the dreamers, all disloyal children of the Earth. When the explosions start, who among us is not so human that he won't quickly mount the chariot that descends from the sky with the promise of taking us to a better world on the other side?[6] What church would be so merciless, so inhuman that it wouldn't deal compassionately with this weakness of suffering human beings—thereby saving their souls for the kingdom of heaven? The human being is weak and cannot bear having the Earth so near, the Earth that supports him. He cannot stand it because the Earth is stronger than him, and because he wishes to be better than the evil Earth. So he wrests himself from it and refuses to take it seriously. And who can blame him—unless it be the have-nots, in their envy? The human being is weak and this weakling is susceptible to the religion of otherworldliness—should we deny him, should the weak individual remain without aid? Is that the spirit of Jesus Christ? No, the weak human being should receive help and receives it from Christ. But Christ does not want these weaknesses; rather Christ makes the human being strong. Christ does not lead him into the otherworldliness of religious escapism. Rather, Christ returns him to the Earth as its true son.

[4.] "Because . . . mother" replaced "because it is our homeland."

[5.] "Bears . . . love" replaced "and who nonetheless love the land they are going to much more."

[6.] A reference to Elijah's ascension (cf. 2 Kgs. 2:11).

"Do not be otherworldly, be strong!"[7] 266

Or we are children of the world. Those who feel that what has been said up to now does not apply to them at all should give heed to whether what now follows does not strike painfully home. We have succumbed to secularism, and here I mean the pious, Christian secularism. Not godlessness or cultural Bolshevism[8] at all, but the *Christian* renunciation of God as the Lord of the Earth. Here we can see that we are bound to the Earth. We have to deal with it. There is no escape. Power confronts power. World confronts church; worldliness confronts religion.[9] How could it be otherwise than that religion and church are forced into this struggle, this controversy? Moreover, faith is compelled to harden into religious convention [Sitte][10] and morality, and the church into an organization of action for religious-moral reconstruction. Thus faith arms itself because the powers of the Earth compel it to do so. After all, we are to represent God's cause. We need to build ourselves a strong fortress within which we can dwell safe and secure with God. We build the kingdom. We can also live quite well with such cheerful secularism. The human being—including the religious person—enjoys a good fight and putting his strength to the test. Who would begrudge him this good gift of nature—unless it be the have-nots in their envy? This pious secularism also makes it possible to preach and say nice things. The church may be certain, if only it makes a somewhat more spirited effort, that it will soon have all the brave, determined, well-meaning, all the all-true sons of the Earth on its side in this happy war.[11] Which
upright human being would not gladly represent God's cause in this wicked 267
world and do so as the ancient Egyptians are said to have done? They carried the images of their gods against their enemies[12]—in order to hide behind them. But in this case the human being wants to hide not just from

[7.] Here there is an exclamation mark in the handwritten draft.

[8.] Originally a term for the new proletarian, revolutionary art in the Soviet Union; here generally derogatory with respect to modern art and literature in the period after the First World War. [German nationalists, especially the Nazis, used "godless or cultural Bolshevism" to fan the flames of anti-Communism; it was also a code word in the propaganda of that era for the "worldwide Jewish conspiracy." In his arguments throughout this period, Bonhoeffer often took the slogans of his opponents and critiqued them.—LR]

[9.] In the first correction replaced by "faith," then reinserted.

[10.] "Faith . . . convention" replaced "Religion may solidify into convention."

[11.] This is a wordplay on the dictum of the "fresh, happy war," which Heinrich Leo wished for in the 1850s, in order to be rid "of the European mess of peoples" (see, e.g., *Volksblatt für Stadt und Land* 10, no. 61 (1853); see Büchmann, *Geflügelte Worte*, 369).

[12.] A reference for Bonhoeffer's statement here could not be found.

the enemy, from the world, but from God, from that God who destroys the mask created for him on earth, who does not wish for human beings to assume his role on earth in loud, boastful strength—just as the strong acquire the weak. On the contrary, God manages his own cause and, by free grace, accepts humans or not. God intends to be Lord on Earth and regards all exuberant human zeal on his behalf to be a real disservice. Our Christian secularism lies precisely in our readiness to earn God his right in the world, only to escape from him, and in our love of the Earth for its own sake and for the sake of this struggle. But we do not thereby elude God. We are brought back under God's dominion.

Become weak in the world and let God be the Lord!

Now, however, otherworldliness and secularism are simply two sides of the same coin—*namely, the lack of belief in God's kingdom.* He who would flee from the world, seeking in the kingdom a place removed from his troubles, does not believe. Nor does the one who presumes that he must establish a worldly kingdom. Whoever evades the Earth finds not God but only another world, his own better, lovelier, more peaceful world. He finds a world beyond, to be sure, but never God's world, which is dawning in this world.[13] Whoever evades Earth in order to find God finds only himself. Whoever evades God in order to find the Earth does not find the Earth as God's Earth; he finds the jolly scene of a war between good and evil, pious and impious, which he kindles himself—in short, he finds himself. He who loves God, loves God as the Lord of the Earth as it is; he who loves the Earth, loves it as God's
268 Earth.[14] He who loves God's kingdom loves it entirely as *God's* kingdom, and he loves it wholly as *God's kingdom on Earth.* And this because the king of the kingdom is the creator and preserver of the Earth, who has blessed the Earth and taken us from earth.

But—this blessed Earth has been cursed by God. We live on cursed ground that yields thorns and thistles;[15] but—Christ has entered into this cursed Earth; the flesh Christ bore was taken from this ground. On this ground the tree of the curse stood,[16] and this second "but" establishes the kingdom of Christ as God's kingdom on this cursed ground. This is why

[13.] "Which is dawning" replaced "but never God's world, which is dawning in this world."

[14.] The following is crossed out: "If you ask yourself: is God's kingdom infinitely far away? then the reply is: Yes but only because it is already here among us. If you ask your-self: Is God's kingdom here, the answer is then: yes but only because it is always there."

[15.] See Gen. 3:17–18.

[16.] See Gal. 3:13.

the kingdom of Christ is a kingdom that has been lowered into the cursed ground from above.[17] It is there, but like a hidden treasure in the cursed field. We pass over it unaware, and this not-seeing becomes a judgment on us. You saw only the field, saw its thistles and thorns, maybe even its seeds and grain, but you did not find the hidden treasure in the cursed ground. Indeed, this is the true curse that is a burden upon the ground of the Earth; not that it yields thistles and thorns, but rather that it hides God's countenance, so that even the deepest furrows in the Earth do not unveil for us the hidden God.

If we are to pray for the coming of the kingdom, we can pray for it only as those wholly on the Earth. Praying for the kingdom cannot be done by the one who tears himself away from his own misery and that of others, who lives unattached and solely in the pious hours of his "own salvation." The church may have hours in which it can sustain even that, but we cannot. The hour in which the church prays for the kingdom today forces the church, for better or worse, to identify completely with the fellowship of the children of the Earth and world. It binds the church by oaths of fealty to the Earth, to misery, to hunger, to death. It renders the church completely in solidarity with that which is evil and with the guilt of their brothers. The hour in which we pray today for God's kingdom is the hour of the most profound solidarity with the world, an hour of clenched teeth and trembling fists. It 269
is not a time for solitary whispering, "Oh, that I might be saved." Rather, it is a time for mutual silence and screaming, that this world which has forced us into distress together might pass away and Your kingdom come to us. It is the eternal right of Prometheus to love the Earth, the "Earth, which is the mother of us all" (Sir. 40:1); this allows him to draw near the kingdom of God in a way that the coward fleeing to other worlds cannot.

No one can pray for the kingdom who imagines himself in bold utopias, in dreams and hopes of the kingdom, who lives his ideologies, who knows thousands of programs and prescriptions with which to heal the world. We should look at ourselves very carefully when we catch ourselves thinking such thoughts, and in doing so we will be in for a surprise. None of us knows what we basically want, so let us pose a very simple question: How do you really imagine your kingdom of God on Earth? How do you really want the people to be? Should they be more moral, more pious; should they be more homogeneous? Should they be less passionate; should they no longer be ill and hungry, no longer subject to death? Should there no longer be the

[17.] The following is crossed out: "Since then it is there, but only as God alone is there, namely, in that God always goes to humans and allows humans to find God."

smart and the stupid, the strong and the weak, the poor and the rich? It is truly amazing that as soon as we honestly pose this question and attempt to answer it, we are no longer able to provide even one. We want the one all right, and then again, for good reasons, we do not want it either. With a little honesty and some serious thought, it is simply not possible to come up with any kind of utopia for a kingdom of God on Earth. The possibility of thinking in universal terms, of seeing the big picture, fails us. All our longing to transform the cursed field into a blessed one, to regain it, fails because it is God who cursed the ground, and it is God alone who can retract this word and bless the Earth again. We must awaken from the state of intoxication with which the poison of the cursed ground has drugged us and become sober. The Earth wants us to take it seriously. It will not let us escape, not into the salvation of otherworldly piety nor into the utopia of this-worldly secularism. Instead, it comes right out and shows us how it is
270 enslaved in finiteness. Its enslavement is our enslavement; with it we, too, are subjected.

Death, loneliness, and desire—these are the three powers that enslave the Earth. Better, they are the one force, the adversary, the evil one, who will not surrender the rights he has gained over the fallen creature. Yet it is the force of the curse that came from the mouth of the Creator. And for this reason we cannot get beyond our death, our loneliness, and our desire with our utopias—they all belong inextricably to the cursed Earth. But in fact we are not supposed to get beyond them at all. Rather, the kingdom comes *to us* in our death, in our loneliness, in our desire. It comes where the church perseveres in solidarity with the world and expects the kingdom from God alone.

"Thy kingdom come"—this is not the prayer of the pious soul of the individual who wants to flee the world, nor is it the prayer of the utopian and fanatic, the stubborn world reformer. Rather, this is the prayer only of the church-community of children of the Earth, who do not set themselves apart, who have no special proposals for reforming the world to offer, who are no better than the world, but who persevere together in the midst of the world, in its depths, in the daily life and subjugation of the world. They persevere because they are, in their own curious way, true to this existence,[18] and they steadfastly fix their gaze on that most unique place in the world where they witness, in amazement, the overcoming of the curse, the most

[18.] "Persevere . . . are" replaced "persevere—not from vitality, but rather because they are simply there—and cannot forget that God has also blessed the cursed and will bless them again, because God created them and because in the resurrection of Jesus Christ God defeated the power of the Earth, performed the absolute miracle."

profound yes of God to the world. Here, in the midst of the dying, torn, and thirsting world, something becomes evident to those who can believe, believe in the resurrection of Jesus Christ. Here the absolute miracle has occurred. Here the law of death is shattered; here the kingdom of God itself comes to us, in our world; here is God's declaration to the world, God's blessing, which annuls the curse. This is the event that alone kindles the 271
prayer for the kingdom. It is in this very event that the old Earth is affirmed and God is hailed as lord of the Earth; and it is again this event that overcomes, breaks through, and destroys the cursed Earth and promises the new Earth. God's kingdom is the *kingdom of resurrection* on Earth.

We resist this kingdom with our hypocritical lack of faith. We place limits on God by declaring with false humility that God cannot come to us because God is too great and God's kingdom is not meant for this Earth, that God and God's kingdom are in the eternal hereafter. But what humility could presume to define the limits of God's action—the limits of the one who died and rose again? This humility is nothing other than the poorly concealed pride of those who think they know what God's kingdom is and who then, in equally poorly concealed zeal, wish to perform the miracle themselves. They themselves wish to create the kingdom of God, and they see the coming of the kingdom in the strengthening of the church, in the Christianizing of culture and politics and upbringing, and in a renewal of Christian moral convention. In this way they thus fall once again under the curse of the Earth in which the treasure of the kingdom of God is *hidden*. Who wish to deceive themselves so completely that they do not see that it is God alone who effects this breakthrough, this miracle, this kingdom of resurrection.

It is not what *God* could do and what *we* could do that forms the basis of our prayer for the coming of the kingdom, but what God *does* for us and what God will do for us again and again. It is God's kingdom for the Earth, on the Earth under the curse; it is overcoming the law of death, loneliness, and desire in the world; and it is wholly God's kingdom, God's actions, God's word, God's resurrection. It is truly the miracle, God's miracle, of breaking through death to life, and it is the miracle that supports our faith and our prayer for the kingdom. Why should we be ashamed that we have a God who performs miracles, who creates life and conquers death? We ourselves are a god who cannot perform miracles. If God is truly God—then God is God, then God's kingdom is miraculous, the epitome of miracles. Why are we so anxious, so cautious, so cowardly? God will shame us all when one 272
day he lets us see things that are a thousand times more miraculous than anything seen until now. We will feel shame before the miraculous God. Thus we look upon God's miraculous acts and say: Your kingdom come to

us. The petition for the kingdom is not the begging of the anxious soul for its salvation. It is not Christian trimming to be used by the world's reformers. It is the plea of suffering and struggling communities in the world, on behalf of the human race, asking that God's glory be manifest in it. Not I and God, but we and God, we ask today. Not that God dwell in my soul, but that God should create the kingdom in our midst; that is our prayer today. How does God's kingdom come to us? No differently than God comes, in overcoming the law of death, in the resurrection, in miracles, and at the same time in the affirmation of the Earth, in entering into its order, its communities, its history. The two belong completely together. For only where the Earth is fully affirmed can its curse be seriously broken through and destroyed; and only the fact that the Earth's curse is broken through allows the Earth to be taken truly seriously. In other words God directs the Earth in such a manner that God breaks through the law of death. Thus God is always the one who binds [bekennen][19] himself to the Earth and the one who overcomes its curse. The Earth to which God is bound is the Earth that God preserves, the fallen, lost, cursed Earth. God binds himself to Earth as God's own work.[20] But where God is, there is God's kingdom. God always comes with the kingdom. God's kingdom must follow the same path as God. The kingdom comes with God to the Earth, and it is among us in no other way than a dual form: as the kingdom on Earth for all, the ultimate kingdom of resurrection, of miracles, breaking through, negating, overcoming,
273 destroying all human works, which are subjected to the curse of death; and at the same time the kingdom of order, which affirms and preserves the Earth with its laws, communities, and its history. *Miracle* and *order* are the two forms in which God's kingdom on Earth presents itself and in which it is scattered. The miracle as the breaking through of all order, and the order as the preservation in preparation for the miracle. But also the miracle completely veiled in the world of orders, and order maintained by virtue of its limitation by the miracle. The form in which the *kingdom of God* is

[19.] [Bonhoeffer uses *bekennen* here. The common meaning would be "to declare, proclaim, confess." Here, however, the context mandates the less-common usage of "binding" and "freely allying." God declares for Earth in the strong sense of freely binding to Earth.—LR]

[20.] The following is crossed out: "There remains however he who proclaimed Earth, the historical Jesus of Nazareth, his divinity hidden, completely veiled; one would not say: look, look there he is, and who is it then [but he—LR] who overcomes the curse of the Earth, visible to all believers. People can become [word illegible] in many ways. No explanation is sound. The God who comes to us still remains the hidden One, even in his miracle, in his resurrection."

attested as miracle we call—the *church*; the form in which the kingdom of God is attested as order we call—the *state.*

The kingdom of God exists in our world exclusively in the duality of church and state. Both are necessarily linked to each other. Every attempt to control the other ignores this relationship of God's kingdom on Earth. Every prayer for the coming of the kingdom to us that does not have in mind both church and state is either otherworldliness or secularism. It is, in any case, a lack of faith in the kingdom of God.

The kingdom of God takes form *in the church,* insofar as the church gives witness to the miracle of God. The ministry of the church is to witness to Christ's resurrection from the dead, to the end of the law of death of this world under the curse, and to the power of God in the new creation.

The kingdom of God takes form *in the state* insofar as the state recognizes and maintains the order of preservation of life and insofar as it accepts responsibility for preserving this world from collapse and for exercising its authority here against the destruction of life. Not the creation of new life, but preservation of existing life is its ministry.

Thus the power of *death,* of which we spoke, is destroyed in the church through the authoritative witness to the miracle of the resurrection; it is restrained in the state through the order of the preservation of life. With its entire authority, with which it alone is responsible for the order of life, the
state points to the church's witness to the breaking up of the law of death in 274
the world of resurrection. And the church, with its witness to the resurrection, points to the preserving, ordering action of the state in the preserved world of the curse. Thus they both bear witness to the kingdom of God, which is entirely God's kingdom and wholly a kingdom for us.

The kingdom of God takes form in the *church,* insofar as here the loneliness of human beings is overcome through the miracle of confession and forgiveness. This is because in the church, in the communion of saints created by the resurrection, one person can and should bear the guilt of the other, and for this reason the last shackle of loneliness—hatred—is shattered and the community is established and created anew. It is through confession, a miracle that defies explanation, that all previously existing community is shown to have been illusory, is annulled, destroyed, and broken through, and that here and now the new community of the resurrection world is created.

The kingdom of God takes form in the *state,* insofar as here the orders of existing communities are maintained with authority and responsibility. So that humanity does not collapse through the will of the individual who wants to go his own way, the state pledges to preserve the order of the community, marriage, family, and nation [Volk] in the world of the curse. The state does not create new communities, but it maintains the existing ones; that is its office.

In the church the power of *loneliness* is destroyed in the act of confession; in the state it is restrained through preservation of communal order. And in turn the state, in its limited range of action, points to the final miracle of God in the resurrection, just as the church, in its authoritative witness to God's breaking through to the world, points to the preservation of order in the world under the curse.

The kingdom of God takes form in the *church* insofar as the power of *desire* is transfigured through the witnessing of God's miracle. Human desire, which is turned in on itself, is judged, destroyed, nullified in the proclamation of the cross and the resurrection of Jesus Christ. On the body of Christ on the cross our desire is judged. Yet, at the same time, transfig-
275 ured and created anew in the resurrection world, where it becomes the desire of one person for another, for God and the brother, for love, peace, happiness, blessedness.

The kingdom of God takes form in the *state* insofar as here human desire is restrained with authority and responsibility, is kept within the order, to the extent that each is protected and preserved from the desire of the other. However, desire is not destroyed, only restrained, so that it may prove its value and bear fruit in the service of the community of the fallen world. Here, too, is love—although always immersed in the possibility of hate; here, too, is joy—but never without the bitter awareness of its transitory nature;—[and] salvation—but always at the edge of despair.

The power of desire is *overcome* and *transfigured* in the church, *restrained* and ordered in the state. Here, too, the limited range of state action points to the authoritative testimony of the church, just as the church points to the order of the state, which fulfills its office in this cursed world.

The church limits the state, just as the state limits the church. And both must remain aware of this mutual limitation and support this tense juxtaposition, which should never be a coalescence. Only thus do both *together*, and never one alone, point to the kingdom of God, which is here attested in such a splendid twofold form.

This consideration does not remain theoretical, however, but becomes truly serious at the point where between church and state we speak of a *people* [Volk]. Because the people are called to the kingdom of God, they have a place in both state and church. As a result, the people, indeed we ourselves, now become the setting in which their encounter[21] takes place.

[21.] [That is, the encounter of church and state.—LR]

We ourselves become those who are called, on the one hand, to take seriously the limits and, on the other, where the limits truly collide and produce sparks, to perceive the living heart of God's kingdom itself. When we pray: Thy kingdom come! we are then praying for the church, that it might bear witness to the miracle of the resurrection, and for the state, with its authority, that it may defend the orders of the preserved world of the curse. That the church has its office solely in relation to miracle and that the state has its office solely in relation to order, and that between church and state the people of God, Christendom, live in obedience—that is the prayer for God's kingdom on Earth, for the kingdom of Christ.

Christ's kingdom is God's kingdom, but God's kingdom in the form 276
ordained for us; not as a visible, powerful empire, as the "new" kingdom of the world,[22] but as the kingdom of the other world that has entered completely into the discord and contradiction of this world. At the same time it appears as the powerless, defenseless gospel of the resurrection, of miracle, and as the state that possesses authority and power that preserves order. Only in the true relation and delimitation of the two is Christ's kingdom reality.

This may sound somber, but then it should, and only thus does it call us to obedience. Obedience toward God in the church and in the state. The kingdom of God is found not in some other world beyond but in our midst.[23] It seeks our obedience despite contradictory appearances, and then it constantly seeks, through our obedience, the miracle, like lightning allowed to flash from the perfect, blessed new world of the final promise. On Earth, God seeks to be honored by us in the other, and nowhere else. God plants his kingdom in the cursed ground. We must open our eyes, become sober, obey God here. Come, you that are blessed by my father, inherit the kingdom![24] This the Lord says to none other than those to whom he said: I was hungry and you gave me food, I was thirsty and you gave me drink. Just as you did it to one of the least of these who are members of my family, you did it to me.[25]

Because God's kingdom is to exist eternally, God will create a new Heaven and a new Earth.[26] But truly a new *Earth.* It will then be God's kingdom on Earth, on the new Earth of the promise, on the old Earth of the creation. This is the promise: that one day we shall behold the world of

[22.] See also the debate with Wilhelm Stapel (2/1).

[23.] See Luke 17:21.

[24.] See Matt. 25:34.

[25.] See Matt. 25:25 and 40.

[26.] See 2 Pet. 3:13; Rev. 21:1.

the resurrection, which we here comprehend in the words of the church and to which the state points. We shall not remain divided, but God will be all in all. Christ will lay his kingdom at God's feet,[27] and the kingdom of the consummation will be at hand. The kingdom where there will be no
277 more tears, no more sorrow, no more crying, no more death.[28] It is the kingdom of life, of community, of transfiguration. And there will no longer be church or state; rather, they will return their offices to the One from whom they originally received them, and God alone will be the Lord as the Creator, the crucified and resurrected One, and the Spirit that reigns in his holy community.

Thy kingdom come. Thus we pray also for that ultimate kingdom in the certainty that his kingdom has already dawned among us. It comes even without our prayer—says Luther,[29] but in this prayer we ask that it may also come among us, that we not be left outside.

The Old Testament tells the strange story of Jacob,[30] who has fled his homeland, from the land God promised, and has lived abroad for many years in a state of enmity with his brother. Then, one day, he can no longer stand it; he wants to return home to the promised land, the land of God's promise; he wants to return to his brother. He is on his way; it is the last night before he is to enter once again into the promised land. Only a narrow river still separates him from it. As he prepares to cross it, he is stopped. Someone wrestles with him in the dark, someone he does not recognize. It seems Jacob is not to reenter his homeland; he is to be pinned down and to die at the gate to the promised land. But incredible powers come upon Jacob, and he fights back against his attacker and takes hold of him and does not let him go until he hears his attacker say: "Let me go, dawn is breaking." With his last ounce of strength, Jacob refuses to let his attacker go: "I will not let you go unless you bless me." It seems to him then as if the end had come, so hard his attacker struggles against him. Yet at that moment, he is blessed, and the attacker disappears. Then the sun rises upon Jacob, and limping from one hip, he enters into the promised land. The way is clear; the dark door to the promised land had been blown open. The curse had been transformed into a blessing. And now the sun rises upon him. That for all of us the way into the promised land passes through the night, that we too only enter it as those strangely marked with scars from the struggle

[27.] See 1 Cor. 15:24–28.

[28.] See Rev. 21:4.

[29.] See the interpretation of the second petition of the Lord's Prayer in Luther's Large Catechism (*Book of Concord*, 446–48).

[30.] See Gen. 32:22–29.

with God, the struggle for God's kingdom and grace; that we enter into the 278
land of God and of our brother as limping warriors—this we Christians share with Jacob. And we know, too, that the sun is destined for us as well. This allows us to bear with patience the time of wandering and waiting and believing that has been imposed on us. But this we know more than Jacob, that it is not we who must go, but rather that God comes to us. Our consolation today, on the eve of All Souls' Day,[31] is that Advent and Christmas follow. That is why we pray: Thy kingdom come to us as well.

[31.] November 20, 1932.

B. Summer Semester 1933

12. Lectures on Christology (Student Notes)[1] 279

Christology

[Introduction

I. The Development of the Christological Question

II. The Person and Work of Christ

[1.] *NL*, B 7,3; transcribed by Gerhard Riemer in 1960 for *GS* from his shorthand notes of 1933; the original notes were destroyed by Riemer in 1960. The fifty-two-page typescript is arranged in chapters, with a few handwritten corrections by Riemer, and shows a number of gaps. Some of these he filled in by hand, with question marks by several. Other notes or transcriptions of this lecture that have been preserved are by Otto Dudzus (*NL*, Anh. B 1, handwritten, 94 pages); Hartmut Gadow (*NL*, B 7,2, typewritten, 30 pages); Ferenc Lehel (typewritten transcription by Ilse Tödt, 34 pages); Hilde Pfeiffer (handwritten, 87 pages, Sammlung Rannenberg-Pfeiffer, Lüneburg); Marga Sperling (typewritten transcription, 28 pages, literary estate of Eberhard Bethge): Wolf-Dieter Zimmermann (*NL*, B 7,1, handwritten, 25 sheets). The accounts by Hilde Enterlein and Klara Hunsche, which in addition to those of Gadow, Riemer, and Zimmermann that were used for the reconstruction of these lectures in *GS* 3:166–242, were not available to the *DBW* editors. Only two undated pages of notes in Bonhoeffer's hand have survived, on early Protestant Christology (see *NL*, A 54,13). [Readers of the earlier English translation of the Christology lectures (published as *Christ the Center*, 1966) should note the somewhat different approach used to arrive at the text of Bonhoeffer's lectures. *Christ the Center* was a composite reconstruction that utilized the notes of many students. The translation here is, as indicated, based substantially on the transcription of one student, Gerhard Riemer, with materials drawn from the notes of others where they share substantial agreement or offer a supplement. The two approaches explain most of the differences in this text from that of *Christ the Center*.—LR] According to the university catalog, Bonhoeffer lectured on Wednesdays and Saturdays from 8:00 to 9:00 a.m. According to information from Pfeiffer et al., the lectures were held from May 3, 1933, to the Saturday before the church elections, July 22, 1933 (contrary to *DB-ER*, 293). A comparison of the topics and dates in the available lecture notes points to the conclusion that Bonhoeffer canceled the lectures on June 3 and 10 and on July 19. The lectures are reprinted here beginning with an outline by the *DBW* 12 editor that has been reconstructed from the notes by Gadow, Pfeiffer, Sperling, and Zimmermann, among which there is extensive agreement. Riemer's notes, which are structured somewhat differently, then follow. Unlike the source, the text here normally gives Greek words in Greek characters.

Part 1. The Present Christ—The *pro-me*[2]
I. The Form[3] of Christ
1. Christ as Word
2. Christ as Sacrament
3. Christ as Church-Community
280 II. The Place of Christ
1. Christ as the Center of Our Existence
2. Christ as the Center of History
3. Christ as the Center of Nature
Part 2. The Historical Christ
I. Access to the Historical Christ
II. Critical Christology or Negative Christology
1. The Docetic Heresy
2. The Ebionite Heresy
3. The Monophysite and the Nestorian Heresies
4. The Modalist and the Subordinationist Heresies
5. What Has Been Gained from Critical Christology
III. Positive Christology
1. The One Who Became Human
2. The Humiliated[4] and Exalted One]

Introduction
[I.] The Development of the Christological Question
Mystagogical silence is prattle.[5] The silence of the church is silence before the Word. In proclaiming Christ, the church falls on its knees in silence before the inexpressible, the ἄρρητον. To speak of Christ is to be silent, and to be silent about Christ is to speak. That is obedient affirmation of God's revelation, which takes place through the Word. The church's speech

[2.] "For me."

[3.] ["Form" is the translation of *Gestalt* here. It refers to an integrated structure and pattern that comprises a whole and is more that the sum of its parts. Bonhoeffer refers to the *Gestalt* of Christ extensively in *Ethics*. See especially the section "Ethics as Formation," in *DBWE* 6:76–102.—LR]

[4.] [The German term here is *der Erniedrigte*. For a discussion of the nuances of our translation of the German verb *erniedrigen* and its variations, see the editor's introduction to this volume.—LR]

[5.] [Edwin Robertson, in *Christ the Center*, simply calls it "mystical silence" and explains it as "the soul secretly chattering away to itself." If that is the meaning, the words for it are not in the Bonhoeffer text here. However, it does contrast well with Bonhoeffer's topic, the silence of the church before the objective Word.—LR]

through silence is the right way to proclaim Christ. σιωπῇ προσκυνείσθω τὸ ἄρρητον (Cyril).[6]

To pray is to keep silent and at the same time to cry out, before God in both cases, in the light of God's Word. Christology, as the doctrine about Christ, is a rather peculiar area of scholarship, [to the extent that] Christ is the very Word of God. Christology is doctrine, speaking, the word about 281
the Word of God. Christ is the Logos of God. Christology is logology. It is knowledge par excellence. From outside, Christology becomes the center of knowledge. The Logos we are talking about here is a person. This human person is the transcendent.

This means two things: first, that wherever the idea of the Logos is considered to be its ultimate reality, there can be no true understanding of the central character of Christology; second, that Christology, with its claim to be the center of the sphere of knowledge, stands alone. It cannot point to anything other than the transcendence of its object. The fact that the Logos became flesh, a human being,[7] is the prerequisite, not the proof. It has to be so, because the transcendent is always only the prerequisite for our thinking, never the proof. For as an object providing proof it would no longer be the transcendent.

Only scholarship that knows itself to be within the realm of the Christian church could agree here that Christology is the center of the realm of scholarship itself. That means that Christology is the invisible, unrecognized, hidden center of scholarship, of the *universitas litterarum*.[8]

All scholarly questions can be reduced to two fundamental questions: First, what is the cause of X? Second, what is the meaning of X? The first question covers the realm of the natural sciences; the second, that of the arts and humanities. The object X is grasped by natural science by being understood in its causal relationship with other objects. The object X is grasped by the arts and humanities by being understood in its relationship of meaning with other known objects. In both cases it is necessary to understand a classification of relationships; how does this object X fit into the classification that I already have at hand?

[6.] "Let the inexpressible be honored with silence." Probably not quoted from Cyril, but rather a sentence formulated by church history professor Adolf von Harnack (see his *Dogmengeschichte*, 240, and his *Lehrbuch*, 2:349, where this sentence appears, in both cases without reference to any source). [The English sentence that parallels these citations from the German reads: "We must live in the feeling of this secret." See A. von Harnack, *History of Dogma*, 4:175.—LR]

[7.] Cf. John 1:14.

[8.] "Universe of scholarship."

How is it possible to classify an object? This is important for the question of Christology. The object is defined, recognized, and understood by means of its possibilities, by means of its "how," by the immanent logos of
282 human beings. The final prerequisite is determined by the human logos. But what if the final prerequisite is subject to doubt? What happens if it is claimed that the human logos is dead, condemned, superseded? What answer does the human logos give, after having been told that it is the final prerequisite? The logos repeats its old question, that of how this demand can be met within history. Thus the logos stays with the question of "how." The logos sees that its autonomy is being threatened from outside. It meets the demand made upon it by negating itself. That is the last thing it has the power to do. It is what Hegel did in his philosophy. Thus what the logos does under attack from the other Logos represents not philistine self-defense but rather a great insight into its power of self-negation, for self-negation signifies the self-affirmation of the logos. So it appears that the attack on the final prerequisite has failed, for the logos has assimilated the counter Logos [Gegenlogos] into itself.

But what happens if the counter Logos suddenly presents its demand in a wholly new form, so that it is no longer an idea or a word that is turned against the autonomy of the [human] logos, but rather the counter Logos appears, somewhere and at some time in history, as a human being, and as a human being sets itself up as judge over the human logos and says, "I am the truth,"[9] I am the death of the human logos, I am the life of God's Logos, I am the Alpha and the Omega?[10] Human beings are those who must die and must fall, with their logos, into my hands. Here it is no longer possible to fit the Word made flesh into the logos classification system. Here all that remains is the question: Who are you?

This is the question asked by horrified, dethroned human reason, and also the question of faith: Who are you? Are you God's very self? This is the question with which Christology alone is concerned. Every possibility of classification must fall short, because the existence of this Logos means the end of my logos. He[11] *is* the Logos. He *is* the counter Word. We are now talking about "Being"! The question of "who" is the question about tran-
283 scendence. The question of "how" is the question about immanence. But because the One who is questioned is the Son himself, the immanent question of "how" can never comprehend him. Not "how" is it possible for you

[9.] John 14:6.

[10.] See Rev. 1:11 [1:8 in the NRSV and RSV; not repeated in verse 11 as in KJV. —LR]

[11.] [That is, Jesus.—LR]

to exist?—that is the godless question, the serpent's question—but rather, "who" are you? The question of "who" expresses the otherness of the other. At the same time the "who question" interrogates the very existence of the one asking it. With the "who question," the person asking is queried about the limits of his or her own being. If the person asking must hear, in reply, that his or her own logos has reached its limits, then the questioner has encountered the boundaries of his or her own existence. To sum up: the question of one's existence is the question of transcendence.

In our everyday speech, the question, "Who are you?" does exist. But it can always be dissolved into the "how question." Tell me *how* you exist, tell me *how* you think, and I'll tell you who you are.

The "who question" is the quintessential religious question. It is the question that asks about the other person, the other being, the other authority. It is the question about love for one's neighbor. The question of transcendence, of existence, is the question about the neighbor; it is the question about [being] a person. That we are always asking the "how" question shows how we are chained to our own authority. It is the *cor curvum in se* (Luther).[12] When we ask, *Who* are you, we are speaking the language of the obedient Adam, but we are *thinking* the "how" of the fallen Adam.

But can *we* then really ask the question, *who*? Can we, when we ask *who*, really mean anything other than *how*? No, we cannot. The mystery of *who* remains hidden from us. The ultimate question for critical thinking is that it *must* ask *who* but it *can* not. That means that one can legitimately ask *who* only after the self-revelation of the other to whom one puts the question has already taken place, after the immanent logos has already been superseded. That is, the question of *who* can only be asked on condition that the answer has already been given. And this in turn means that the christological question can only be asked, as a scholarly question, within the sphere of the church, and the prerequisite for it is the fact that Christ's claim to be 284
the Word of God is a just claim. There is only one possibility for me to be truly searching for God—that I already know who God is. There is no such thing as blindly setting out to search for God. I can only search for what has already been found. "You would not seek me if you had not already found me" (Pascal).[13]

[12.] "The heart curved in upon itself"; cf., for example, Luther's "Lectures on Romans," 1515–16 (*LW* 25:291 et passim) .

[13.] See Blaise Pascal: "Tu ne me chercherais pas, si tu ne m'avais trouvé" (*Pensées and Other Writings*, 336). Dudzus's notes here also cite Augustine, probably referring to the sentence that Bonhoeffer liked to quote from the beginning of the *Confessions*: "Inquietum est cor nostrum, donec requiescat in te" (Our heart is unquiet until it rests

With that the place where our work must begin is clearly indicated. In the church, where Christ has revealed himself as the Word of God, the human logos asks the question: Who are you, Jesus Christ? Logos of God! The answer is given. The church receives it every day anew. It is up to the human logos to understand the question as it is given, and to reflect upon and analyze it as it exists. But it remains always the question, "Who."

Two questions are prohibited:

(1) Whether the answer that is given is the right answer. This question has no right to be asked, because there can be no authority for our human logos to cast doubt on the truth of this Logos. Jesus's own witness to himself, then and now, stands on its own and substantiates itself. The "that" in "that God was revealed in Christ" cannot be theologically questioned.

(2) The second prohibited question is how the "that" of the revelation can be *conceived.* This question leads in the direction of trying again to get behind Christ's claim, and to ground it on our own. In doing so, our own logos is presuming on the role of the Father of Jesus Christ himself, when all we actually know is the fact of God's revelation.

Having *excluded* these two questions, what we have is the question of *who,* the question of *being,* of the essence and nature of Christ. So the christological question is in its essence an ontological question. Its purpose is to bring
285 out the ontological structure of the *who,* without getting caught in either the Scylla of the "how question" or the Charybdis of the "that question." The early church foundered on the "how question," modern theology since the Enlightenment on the "that question." Luther, Paul, and the New Testament stayed on track through the middle.

To go back to the question with which we began: in what way is the christological question the central question of all knowledge? Insofar as it alone poses the question of existence as an ontological question about the being of Jesus Christ; insofar as the ontological question asked here is the question about the being of the person Jesus Christ; insofar as the ontological question asked here is the question of the being of Christ's person as clearly being the revealed Logos of God. Only on the basis of having been judged by this Logos can the old logos learn anew to comprehend the relative rights to which it is entitled. Only from the question of transcendence does the human logos receive the rights peculiar to it, its necessity and also

---

in you). See also *DBWE* 9:292, ed. note 57, and *DBWE* 4:174, ed. note 226. [The full passage reads: "You arouse us so that praising you may bring us joy, because you have made us and drawn us to yourself, and our heart is unquiet until it rests in you" (Augustine, *Confessions,* 39). See also *DBWE* 3:69–70.—LR]

its limits. In this way, Christology as logology becomes that which makes all knowledge possible.

But this is only the formal side of the matter; the side that deals with content is more important. Let us ask again what happens if the claim of the counter Logos is questioned. The human logos kills the Logos of God, the Word become human, which it has just questioned. Because the human logos does not want to die itself, the Logos of God, which is death to the human logos, must die instead. The Word become human must be hung on the cross by the human logos. Then the person who was causing the worry has been killed, and along with that person, the question.

But what happens when this counter Word, though it has been killed, raises itself from the dead as the living, eternal, ultimate, conquering Word of God, when it rises up to meet its murderers and rushes at them again, appearing as the Resurrected One who has overcome death? Here the question, "Who are you?" becomes most poignant. Here it stands, alive forever, over and around and within humankind. The human being can still fight against the Word become human and kill him, but against the Resurrected One the human being has no power. We ourselves are now the ones who stand convicted. Now our question has been turned around.
The question we have put to the person of Christ, "Who are you?" comes 286
back at us: who are you, that you ask this question? Do you live in the truth, so you can ask it? Who are you, you who can only ask about me because you have been justified and received grace through me? Only when this question has been heard has the christological question been definitively formulated.

For the human being, the question of existence is the question of transcendence. Transcendence is the boundary of the being that has been given to me. The question that asks about my existence, and calls it into question, is also the question of transcendence, because it is with reference to transcendence that my own being is called into question; in theological terms, because it is only with reference to God that human beings know who they are. If the "who question" is the only question I ask that goes beyond my own being, then this is the only question that asks about transcendence and existence. The "who question" cannot be answered by human beings themselves. Even existence cannot provide the answer, because the existence of a human being cannot go beyond its own limits but remains entirely within its own frame of reference and mirrors itself to itself.

Human beings destroy the Who standing over against them. Who are you? people ask Jesus. Silence is his reply. Human beings cannot wait for the answer. They kill him. The logos cannot bear the presence of the counter Logos, because it knows that one of them must die. So the human logos kills the Jesus Christ Logos who has appeared before it and challenged it, and goes on living with the unanswered question of existence and transcendence. But the counter Logos, which has risen from the dead, can no longer be killed by human beings. They either are not aware of him at all, or they are aware of him as one who asks them, Who are you? Since Christ is the Son, the question asked of Christ, Who are you? has been answered.

But what does all this mean in concrete terms? Human beings today still cannot get around the figure of Jesus Christ. They have to deal with him. Take Socrates and Goethe, for example. It may be that our education depends on the confrontation with these two. But on our confrontation with Jesus depend life and death, salvation and damnation. From an outside point of view, this is not understandable. It is from the church that we
287 learn that the sentence on which everything else depends is this: "There is salvation in no one else."[14] The encounter with Jesus has a different cause than does the encounter with Socrates and Goethe. One can get past the person of Goethe, because he is dead. [The encounter with Jesus Christ is different.] The attempts to face up to this encounter and at the same time avoid it are thousandfold.

For example, in the world of the proletariat Christ may appear to be as finished off as the church and bourgeois society as a whole. There seems to be no occasion for giving Jesus a qualified place. The church is the stultifying institution that sanctions the capitalist system. But this is not the case. The proletariat actually disassociates Jesus from his church and its religion. When the proletariat says that Jesus is a good human being, it means more than the bourgeoisie means when it says that Jesus is God. Jesus is present in factory halls as a worker among workers, in politics as the perfect idealist, in the life of the proletariat as a good human being. He stands beside members of the proletariat as a fighter in their ranks against the capitalist enemy.[15]

Dostoyevsky portrays the idiot as a Christ figure.[16] The idiot does not isolate himself, but he is awkward and gives offense. He associates not with the powerful but rather with children, who like him. He is mocked, and he is loved. He is the fool, and he is the wise one. He is the one who bears all things and forgives all things. He is the revolutionary, and also the one

---

[14.] Acts 4:12.

[15.] On the question of proletarian attitudes toward Christ, Dudzus formulates as follows: "Jesus is here regarded as the great human being, the great example, the first socialist or communist." The terms "socialist" and "communist" are also found in the notes of Gadow and Pfeiffer. See "Church and Proletariat" in *Sanctorum Communio, DBWE* 1:271–74.

[16.] See Dostoyevsky, *The Idiot.*

who goes along with everything. He is the one who, through no intent of his own, calls attention to himself by his very existence, so that the question pops up again and again, Who are you? Are you an idiot, or Jesus Christ himself?

One could also read Gerhart Hauptmann's novel about Emanuel Quint.[17] Or think of Grosz and his distortion of Christ.[18] Here in the end we also have the question, Who are you really? So Jesus Christ passes 288
through our time, through different stations and occupations in life, always being asked anew, Who are you? and yet always, when some person is aware of having confronted this question, being killed anew. These are all attempts to be finished with Christ. Even theologians do the same. Everywhere the Son of Man is betrayed with the kiss of Judas.[19] Wanting to be finished with Christ means that now and then we kill him, crucify him, commit shameful acts against him, kneel before him with the scornful and say, "Greetings, Rabbi!"[20]

There are only two possibilities when a human being confronts Jesus: the human being must either die or kill Jesus. Thus the question, Who are you? remains ambiguous. It can also be the question of those who realize, as soon as they ask the question, that they themselves are meant by it, and instead of hearing the answer, hear the question in return: Who then are you? Only then is it the question of those judged by Jesus. The "who question" can only be asked of Jesus by those who know that it is being asked of them. But then it is not the human beings who are finished with Jesus, but rather Jesus who is finished with them. Strictly speaking, the "who question" can be asked only within the context of faith, and there it will receive its answer. As long as the christological question is one asked by our logos, it always remains within the ambiguity of the "how question." But as soon as it stands within the act of faith, it becomes a form of knowledge, which has the possibility of posing the "who question."

There are two contrasting types of authority in the world: the authority deriving from office, and the authority inherent in the person. When these two authorities confront each other, then the question posed to the authority of the person is "What" are you? The "what" means, what office do you hold? The question of the individual person to the person in authority is

[17.] See Hauptmann, *Der Narr in Christo Emanuel Quint*.

[18.] Cf. George Grosz, *Ecce Homo*. Gadow, Sperling, and Zimmermann also mention the sculptor Wilhelm Groß. [The student notes may be confusing the sculptor Groß with the Communist George Grosz and his portrayal of Christ. The latter better fits Bonhoeffer's discussion here. My thanks to Hans Pfeifer for this observation.—LR]

[19.] Cf. Matt. 26:48–49.

[20.] Cf. Matt. [26:49 and] 27:29.

where do you as an individual get your authority? The answer is from myself, since I recognize your authority over me. Both questions about authority are derived from the "how question." All people are holders of some office, of some community, of themselves. Even prophets are only bearers of the word; they are not the word itself.

What happens, then, when someone appears who claims not only to
289 bring the divine office and Word but actually to be that very office and Word? That is, not only to have authority but to be authority itself? Here a new existence breaks into our existence. Here the highest authority in the world, that of the prophet, is superseded. This is no longer the saint, the reformer, the prophet, but rather the Son himself. Here we no longer ask, What are you, where do you come from? Here the question asked is that of the very revelation of God.

[II.] The Person and Work of Christ

Christology is not soteriology. How are the two related? In his *Loci* of 1521, Melanchthon says: "Hoc est Christum cognoscere, beneficia eius cognoscere, non, quod isti (the Scholastics) docent, eius naturas, modos incarnationis contueri."[21] This refers the christological question back to the soteriological question and settles it there. "Who" Christ is, is known solely on the basis of his works. In consequence, Christology as such would be considered superfluous. This has been an epoch-making view and was fully developed by Schleiermacher and Ritschl.[22] For systematics the question is do the works interpret the person or the person the works?

Luther says that everything depends on whether someone is a good person.[23] If the person is good, then the works will be good, even if it appears to be otherwise. If the works are good, this does not allow for any conclusion to be drawn about the person. Works can appear to be good and still be the work of the devil. The devil can appear as an angel of light.

Any other view of the human person leads to justification of the person through works. Luther's thinking is that it is the person through whom the
290 works are to be interpreted. However, it is also true that we do not really recognize the person; only God does so. "The Lord knows those who are

[21.] "For by them [sin, law, grace—LR] is Christ properly known, if indeed this is to know Christ, to wit, to know his benefits and not as they [Scholastic theologians—LR] teach, to perceive his natures and the mode of his incarnation" (Melanchthon, *Loci communes of Philip Melanchthon*, 68).

[22.] Cf. Schleiermacher, *Christian Faith*, 377–424; Ritschl, *Christian Doctrine* (on the rejection of the Chalcedonian doctrine and the two natures: 280–82).

[23.] See, for example, *The Freedom of a Christian* (1520) (*LW* 31:360).

his."[24] There is no access to the works except through the person. [However,] our access to the person is barred by God's mysterious predestination. The attempt to grasp the person through his works cannot succeed, because the character of works remains ambiguous. There is no access to the human person, other than the person's decision to reveal himself. I cannot get to another person unless that person reveals himself to me. This self-revelation of one person to another, however, in reality takes place in the church of Jesus Christ, in the event of the forgiveness of sins, when one presents oneself to another as a sinner, confesses oneself to be a sinner, and receives from the other forgiveness for one's sin.

These thoughts are applicable to Christology. Only when I know who has done any particular work do I understand these works. Everything depends on knowing whether Jesus Christ was the idealistic founder of a religion or the very Son of God. This is no less than a matter of life or death for a human being. If Jesus was only the idealistic founder of a religion, I can be uplifted by his work and feel the urge to follow his example, but my sins are not forgiven me. In that case God is still angry with me, and my life is forfeit to death. In that case the works of Jesus would lead me to utter despair over myself.

But if the works of Christ are God's own works, then I am not called to do exactly as God does, to emulate God; instead, I am affected by these works as one who could in no way perform them myself. At the same time, through this discovery, through these works, through this Jesus Christ, I have found the God of mercy. My sin is forgiven me, and I am no longer in the realm of death, but rather in that of life. Thus it depends on the person of Christ, whether his works perish in the old world of death or last eternally in a new world of life.

But how is the person of Christ to be recognized, other than through his works? This objection contains the deepest error of all. Even the works of Christ are not unambiguous. They are open to the most varied interpretations. Christ's works permit the interpretation that he is a hero, that 291
his cross represents the consummate act of a courageous man who is true to his convictions. There is no point in the works of Jesus to which one can unambiguously refer and say that here Jesus can truly be recognized, unambiguously and without doubt, as the Son of God on the basis of his works. This is the issue, that the Son entered into the flesh, that he wants to do his work within the ambiguity of history, incognito. This incognito is the basis for the two reasons why it is impossible to recognize the person of

[24.] 2 Tim. 2:19.

Jesus through his work; first, because it is never possible, in human terms, to draw conclusions about a person from his works, and second, because Jesus is God, and direct conclusions about God on the basis of history are never possible either.

But if this way to knowledge is closed to me, then there is only one other way by which I can try to approach Jesus. This can happen only in relation to that place where his person reveals himself to me as he really is. Only through Christ's own revelation do I have opened to me his person and his works.

In this way, the christological question is shown to have theological priority over the soteriological question. I must first know who it is who does something before I can know what it is that the person has done. Nevertheless, it would be wrong to conclude that person and works should be considered separately. We are talking here only about the connection between the knowledge of works and the knowledge of the person, not about the real connection between person and works. The separation is only necessary for reasons of theological method. For the theological question, by nature, can only be asked of Christ in his whole being. It is the Christ of history, the whole Christ, whom we ask and who answers. But Christology asks not about what Christ has done but rather who Christ is. To put it in the abstract: The personal ontological structure [personale Seinstruktur] of the whole, historical Christ is the subject matter of Christology.

[Part 1.] The Present Christ—The *pro-me*

As the Crucified and Risen One, Jesus is at the same time the Christ who is present now. This is the first statement: that Christ is the Christ who is pres-
292 ent in history. He is to be understood as present in time and space. *Nunc et hic*,[25] the two flow together in the concept of the church. Christ in his person is indeed present in the church as person. Thus the presence of Christ is there in the church. Only because Christ is the Christ who is present are we still able to inquire of him. Only because proclamation and the sacraments are carried out in the church can we inquire about Christ.

This has been subject to two serious misinterpretations. The presence of Christ was understood, on the one hand, as the influence that emanates from him, extending into the church-community—thus not Christ himself, but the effective influence he has had in history. This is a dynamic understanding of Christ—he is seen as an energy in history that is not lost but goes on communicating itself. The presence of Christ can be seen here as

[25.] "Now and here."

belonging to the category of cause and effect. Or, on the other hand, the attempt is made to reach across history to keep bringing the image of Christ into view; the image is either that of the Enlightenment and rationalism, or that of the inner life of Jesus, as sketched by Wilhelm Herrmann.[26] One sees the image face-to-face. (Often these two observations go hand in hand, as they do for Schleiermacher.)[27] Ritschl subscribes to the former; Herrmann, his student, to the latter.[28]

Here lies an error common to Christology [of this kind]; in both these interpretations, Christ is seen only in terms of his influence in history. Christ is essentially power here, δύναμις, but not person. Christ is understood in terms of his works, not in terms of his person. This power can be conceived in different ways, be it as historical power or as the image of Jesus 293
as the ideal human being shining forth anew, that is, as ideational power. Here the historical power corresponds more to the temporal character of Jesus's presence, while the image corresponds to its spatial character.

If the Christ who is present is seen in this way, Christology misses its point, because it represents Christ as power but not as person. This is also the case when efforts are made to speak of the personality of Jesus. *Personality*, in this context, means the opposite of what is meant by *person*. For personality is the fullness and harmony of the values that are summed up in the phenomenon of Jesus Christ. Personality is by nature an apersonal concept. Personality is realized in the concepts of power and value, that is, it is realized within history. The person, however, is beyond power and value, beyond influence and image. In asking about personality, one asks "how" and "what"; in asking about person, one asks "who." If Jesus, in his essence, is a power, then his being is no more than his works and his person no more than what he has done. Then conclusions about his person can only be drawn from his works. The ultimate ground for [rejecting] this view of Christ's presence is that such an interpretation does not take into account

[26.] Cf. Herrmann, *Communion of the Christian with God*, chap. 2.

[27.] Cf. *Christian Faith*, § 88 (364–65), where Schleiermacher describes, under point 3, the communication of the "sinless perfection" of Jesus as an "experience . . . made up of two elements," "one of which belongs to the personal consciousness and the other to the common consciousness." The first he sees as the effect of the community's image of Christ on the individual, the second as the "impulse" toward perfection coming from the historical life of the community.

[28.] Bonhoeffer evidently drew this conclusion from Ritschl's central concept of Christ's influence as a primal image within and upon the Christian community (see Ritschl, *Christian Doctrine*, 280–82); on Herrmann, see his *Communion of the Christian with God*, pp. 62, 64, and 93–97.

the resurrection of Christ. It would see Jesus Christ only as dead and gone, the way we might think about Goethe or Socrates. Only where the risen Christ is understood as the ground and the prerequisite for Christology is it possible to grasp his presence as person. The person of Jesus Christ is, in fact, its own work.

Luther tried to make the concept of Christ's presence understandable in terms of the concept of his ascension. By virtue of sitting at God's right hand, Christ is able to be present to us. "When he was on earth, he was far away from us here. Now that he is far from earth, he is near to us."[29] Christ's ascension means that, with Christ's distancing, his presence everywhere becomes possible. Because human thought is afraid of the resurrection, theology pushes it aside, as Ritschl[30] and Herrmann do,[31] or thinks
294 of it symbolically, like Schleiermacher.[32] Paul says, "If Christ has not been raised, your faith is futile and you are still in your sins."[33] To be present means to be in the same place at the same time (presence). We are talking about Christ's ability to be simultaneously present to us all. Even as the Risen One, Jesus remains the human Jesus. Only because he is human can he be present to us. But that he is eternally with us here, eternally with us in the now—that is his presence as God. Only because Jesus is God can he be present to us.

The presence of Jesus Christ compels the statement that Jesus is wholly human, as well as the other statement that Jesus is wholly God—otherwise he would not be present. Thus, from the presence of Christ arises the twofold certainty that he is both human being and God. Therefore it is impos-

[29.] Cf. Sermon on Ascension Day (1523) (*WA* 12:562, 25–26).

[30.] Ritschl's understanding of the "awakening and exalting of Christ" as "attestation" that "in his death the purpose of his life was not lost, but fulfilled" (*Unterricht*, §25) was evidently interpreted by Bonhoeffer as an abandonment of the doctrine of *Christus praesens*. [The corresponding section in *Three Essays*, "Instruction in the Christian Religion," is 231–32.—LR]

[31.] In critically rejecting the church's usual talk of "facts that we must take on faith" (*Der Verkehr des Christen mit Gott*, 2–6) [the cited words are apparently Bonhoeffer's paraphrase, rather than a direct quotation; there is no corresponding passage in the English translation of Herrmann's book, *The Communion of the Christian with God*.—LR], Herrmann made a clear distinction between the New Testament stories about Jesus, including the story of his resurrection, and the "gospel" in the sense of the meaning for salvation of the person of Jesus (80). Later he emphasized the connection between them, recognizing the Easter appearances of Jesus as having an "imperishable importance for the Christian community in every age" (Herrmann, *Systematic Theology*, 127).

[32.] See Schleiermacher, *Christian Faith*, § 99 (p. 418), according to which Christ's sitting at the right hand of God does not "depend on a visible resurrection or ascension" but rather expresses the "peculiar and incomparable dignity of Christ."

[33.] 1 Cor. 15:17.

sible to ask how the human Jesus can be simultaneously with each of us—as if this Jesus could exist in isolation! It is just as impossible to ask how God can enter into time—as if such an isolated God could exist! The only question that makes sense is: who is present, who is with us here and now? The answer is: the human-God Jesus. I cannot know who the human Christ is if I do not simultaneously think of the God-Christ and vice versa. God in his timeless eternity is *not* God. Jesus Christ in his humanity, limited in time, is *not* Jesus Christ. Instead, in the human being Jesus Christ, God is God. Only in Jesus Christ is God present.

The starting point for Christology has to be the God-human. Time and space determine not only the humanity of Christ but also his divinity. The God-human who is present in time and space is veiled in the ὁμοίωμα σαρκός[34] (Rom. 8:3). The presence of Christ is a veiled presence. But it is
not God veiled in the human being; instead, the whole God-human is hid- 295
den, and it is the principle of hiddenness that is the ὁμοίωμα σαρκός.

This means the problem has shifted: it is not the relation of God and human in Jesus Christ, but rather the relation of the God-human, as already given, to the ὁμοίωμα σαρκός. The God-human is present in the form of the σάρξ, the form that is a stumbling block.[35] The hidden form in which Christ is *present* is, for us, the church's proclamation. Jesus Christ as the already existing God-human is present to the church alone in the scandalous form of its preaching. The Christ who is proclaimed is the real Christ. It is not the hiddenness of God that is the stumbling block but rather the

[34.] The Greek words mean "likeness of flesh." [The student notes include only the Greek for "likeness of flesh" and not the full phrase from Paul, which is "in the likeness of sinful flesh" (ἐν ὁμοιώματι σαρκὸς ἁμαρτίας). It is impossible at this juncture to know whether the shortened version is Bonhoeffer's intention or student shorthand. See, however, ed. note 171 below for Bonhoeffer's treatment of the Greek phrase *homoioma sarkos* in the context of his discussion of the humiliation of Christ.—LR]

[35.] [The reference is to Paul in 1 Cor. 1:23: "but we proclaim Christ crucified, a stumbling block to Jews and foolishness to Gentiles." Bonhoeffer draws the distinction between God taking human form and the utter humiliation *of* the God-human, Jesus Christ, in his death on a cross. For Paul, dying on the cross as a criminal is the offense and a "stumbling block" since, for the Jews, the Messiah would usher in the kingdom in triumph; he would not suffer the death the Romans had reserved for the worst offenders. Thus the Exalted One is the Humiliated One, as a criminal on the cross. Likewise, the Humiliated One is the Exalted One. For Bonhoeffer, becoming human, God taking on bodily form, is not the offense. God is glorified in the humanity of Jesus Christ. Yet this humanity is present in its veiled nature in the humiliation of Jesus Christ on the cross. That is the offense and the stumbling block. Hence Bonhoeffer's comment below: "A careful distinction must surely be made between the humanity of Christ and the humiliation of Christ." Cf. Bonhoeffer's subsequent discussion of this in the section "Christ as Sacrament," pp. 319–23.—LR]

hiddenness of the God-human. A careful distinction must surely be made between the humanity of Christ and the humiliation of Christ. Jesus Christ is human both as the Humiliated One and as the Exalted One. Jesus Christ is a stumbling block only as the Humiliated One. The doctrine of the stumbling block has its place not in the doctrine of God's taking human form but rather in the doctrine of the God-human's humiliation. Here, in the humiliation of the God-human, is where the ὁμοίωμα σαρκός belongs. For us, this means that the presence of the God-human as the Resurrected One, that is, the Exalted One, is at the same time the presence of the humiliated Christ.

As *presence* in the threefold form of Word, sacrament, and church-community, the basic question of the presence of Christ is not answered. The question is not, how can the human Jesus, or the God Jesus, be simultaneously here? The question must be, by virtue of what personal ontological structure is Christ present to the church? If one answers, by virtue of his God-humanity, that is correct but still needs explication. It is the "*pro-me*" structure. The being of Christ's person is essentially relatedness to me. His being-Christ is his being-for-me. This *pro-me* is not to be understood as an effect that issues from Christ or as a form that he assumes incidentally, but is to be understood as the being of his very person. The very core of his person is *pro-me*. This is not a historical, factual, or ontic statement, but rather an ontological one: that is, I can never think of Jesus Christ in his
296 being-in-himself, but only in his relatedness to me. This in turn means that I can think of Christ only in existential relationship to him and, at the same time, only within the church-community. Christ is not in-himself and also in the church-community, but the Christ who is the only Christ is the one present in the church-community *pro-me*. This *pro-me* should not be forgotten; according to Luther, "Because it is one thing if God is present, and another if he is present in you."[36] It is not only useless to meditate on a Christ-in-himself but godless, precisely because Christ is not there in-himself, but rather is there for you. From this perspective one can comprehend Melanchthon's aversion to Christology.

All theology and all Christology condemn themselves if they do not say right from the beginning that God and Christ can only be Christ *pro-me*. Where this *pro-me* has been assumed, there the specific work begins. But

[36.] See "Word and Sacrament III," *LW* 37:68. [The German text is somewhat different from the English in *Luther's Works*; a more literal translation of the German would be: "There is a difference between when God is there and when he is there for you."—LR]

here theology has deserted its God. It has either carried on with Scholastic substance and condemned being-there-for-you to simply being-there, or else it looks only at Christ's actions, his effects. And yet what is decisive about the *pro-me* structure is that, with it, both the being and the works of Christ are maintained. Being-there-for-*you* comes together with being-*there*-for you. The presence of Christ as the *pro-me* is his real being-for-me.

The *pro-me* structure means three things for the relation of Christ to the new humanity:

(1) Jesus Christ, as the one who is *pro-me*, is the beginning, the head, the firstborn within a large family.[37] So the *pro-me* structure refers first of all to the historical Jesus.

(2) He is there for his brothers and sisters in that he stands in their stead. Christ stands for his new humanity before God, that is, he takes their place and stands in their stead before God. If this is so, then he *is* the new humanity. There where the new humanity should stand, he himself stands, by virtue of his *pro-me* structure. That means he *is* the church-community. He is no longer acting *for* it, on its behalf, but rather *as* it, in his going to the cross, dying, and taking the sins of the church-community upon himself. Thus in him the new humanity is crucified and dies. 297

(3) Because Christ acts as the new humanity, he is in it, because it is in him, because in him God both judges the new humanity and pardons it.

The God-human Jesus Christ is the one who, in his *pro-me* structure, is present in his person to the church as Word, sacrament, and church-community.

I. The Form [Gestalt] of Christ

1. Christ as Word

(1) That Christ is the Word means that he is the truth. Truth is only in the Word and through the Word. Spirit is, to begin with, Word and not power, action, or feeling. "In the beginning was the Word. . . . All things came into being through him."[38] Only as Word is the Spirit power and action. "The word of God is . . . sharper than any two-edged sword, piercing until it divides,"[39] it destroys. The Word of God carries within it the lightning that destroys and the rain that makes alive. As Word of God, it is the truth, which destroys and creates. God, of course, has the freedom to walk in ways unknown to us, and the freedom to choose other ways of self-revelation.

[37.] See Rom. 8:29 and Col. 1:18.

[38.] John 1:1 and 3.

[39.] Heb. 4:12.

But God wanted to reveal himself in the Word. God cannot speak to human beings otherwise than through this Word. God has bound himself. And God's Word never changes—that is not God's way.

(2) That Christ is the Word, and not a stone, means that Christ is there for the sake of humankind. Because the human being has a logos, therefore God encounters the human being in the Logos. Therefore the human being [is] the Homo sapiens. The truth of the human logos therefore originates in the Word, because the Word alone communicates clear and unambiguous meaning. Clarity and lack of ambiguity are of the essence of the Word. The Word interprets itself according to its nature. This clarity and consonance is the reason why it is universally valid. By entering into this human logos, Jesus Christ was humbled. Here it must be said that the Logos of God
298 is not to be identified with, or analyzed by, the human logos.

(3) Christ as the Word of God is distinguished and separated from the human logos in that he is the Word in the form of the living Word to humankind, whereas the human word is word in the form of an idea. These are the structures that the word as such can have: a word spoken to us, or an idea. But the two are mutually exclusive. Our human thinking still knows only the form of the word as idea. The word in this form can include the idea of openness to all. The idea is there. A human being can accept it in full freedom, can make it his own. If it is applied to Christ, it would mean that the "idea of God" that is embodied in Christ is directly accessible by any person at any time. The person needs only take possession of it.

The complete opposite is true, however, of the word that is not an idea, but rather a word spoken to us. The word as idea remains essentially within itself, but the word in the form of address is only possible as word between two persons, as speaking and response, responsibility.[40] It is not timeless but rather takes place within history. Thus it is not generally accessible to anyone at any time but rather happens there where it is spoken to someone by another. This word is wholly subject to the freedom of the one who speaks. By nature it is a one-time event, a new event every time. By its character as word spoken by one to another, it desires community. By its character as truth, it seeks this community only by bringing the other person into the truth. Truth here is something that takes place between two persons,

[40.] [The German term for "responsibility" is *Verantwortung*, from *antworten*, "to answer" or "to reply." As Bonhoeffer indicates, "responsibility" is thus inherently relational, a concrete time-bound and place-bound answering to and answering for; it is accountability to, with, and for others.—LR] not something eternally at rest within itself. Truth happens only in community[41] between two persons.

¶Christ as Word of God in the sense of word spoken to us does not mean Christ as timeless truth, but rather as truth breaking into a concrete moment, as God's speaking to us. Thus Christ is not timelessly and universally accessible as an idea; instead, he is heard as Word only there where he allows himself to be heard. That means it is entirely within his freedom to reveal himself to me or to hide himself from me. Christ is revealed only when and where it pleases the Father in heaven.[42] Christ as the Word expresses both the contingent character of his revelation and his commitment [Bindung] to humankind. Christ is by nature, as God's Word spoken 299
to me, *pro-me.*

(4) This prerequisite determines what the content will be. Christ is not a new concept of God or a new moral teaching. Christ is, instead, God's Word personally addressed to the human being, calling him to responsibility. That is the meaning of the statement that Christ is commandment and forgiveness. The important thing is not whether this is an old or a new commandment, or whether we have ever heard about it before or not; the important thing is where forgiveness really takes place. It is because here forgiveness really takes place that Christ is, in his person, the Word of God.

(5) The relationship of the Word to the person of Christ can be thought of in different ways. Christ can be thought of as the bearer of the idea, and Christ can be thought of as prophet. That would mean that God speaks through Christ. Christ *speaks* the Word instead of *being* the Word. The important thing here is not his personality but his mission. To see Christ in this way contradicts the New Testament, for there Christ says of himself, "I am the way, and the truth, and the life."[43] This is what happened—the quintessential, unique possibility of God's revelation was in him who, in his person, is the Word.

(6) This Christ who is the Word in person is present in the word of the church or as the word of the church. His presence is, by nature, his existence as preaching. His presence is not power or the objective spirit of the church-community out of which it preaches, but rather his presence is preaching. If this were not so, the sermon would not have the exclusive status that

[41.] ["Community" is the translation here of *Gemeinschaft.* This again underscores Bonhoeffer's point about the relational character of revelation and truth. "Communion" would be another possible translation.—LR]

[42.] Cf. the Augsburg Confession, Article V.

[43.] John 14:6.

the Reformation gives it. The sermon is the poverty and the riches of our church. The sermon is the form of the present Christ to whom we are committed, whom we are to follow. If Christ is not wholly present in the sermon, the church breaks down. The human word and God's Word are not simply mutually exclusive; instead, God's Word, Jesus Christ, as the Word of God that has taken human form, is the Word of God that has humbled itself by entering into the human word. That is why Luther says, "This is the human
300 being to whom you should point and say, this is God!"[44] We say, this is the human word to which you should point and say, this is God! The two statements mean the same thing. For I cannot point to the human being unless I am pointing to this Jesus. Christ is in the church as the spoken Word in the form of both sermon and sacrament. Two statements with the same meaning stand side by side. I could not preach if I did not know that I am speaking *God's Word*, and I could not preach if it were *I* who is supposed to be speaking God's Word.

2. Christ as Sacrament

Here there are two things to be said. First: Christ is wholly Word, and the sacrament is wholly Word. Second: The sacrament is different from the Word in that it has its own right to exist in the church as sacrament.

(1) The sacrament is Word of God, for it proclaims the gospel, not as a wordless action, but as action that is made holy and given its meaning by the Word. The promise of "forgiveness of sins" makes the sacrament what it is. Whoever believes in the Word in the sacrament has received the sacrament wholly.

(2) The Word in the sacrament is the Word in bodily form. The sacrament does not represent the "Word," for only that which is not present can be represented. The sacrament is the form of the Word that, because God speaks it, becomes sacrament. The bodily form of the sacrament exists only through the Word, but only as Word, as Word in bodily form. The sacrament, in the form of nature, engages human beings in their nature.

The fallen creation is no longer the creation of the first Word. The "I" is no longer that which God called "I." The *people* is no longer *people*; *history* is no longer *history*; *church* is no longer *church*. With that the continuity
301 between Word and creature has been lost. That is why the natural world is no longer a transparent world. That is why the whole creation is no longer

[44.] Here as elsewhere Bonhoeffer picks up from Hildebrandt a free quote from Luther. Cf. Franz Hildebrandt, *EST*, 82: "I point to this human being and say, this is God." The passage here is cited from "The Babylonian Captivity of the Church" (1520, *LW* 36:35): *"Hic homo est deus, hic deus est homo"* (This man is God, this God is man).

sacrament. Sacrament exists only where God, in the midst of the world of creatures, names an element, speaks to it, and hallows it with the particular word God has for it by giving it its name. Through God's speaking to it, this element becomes what it is. This is what happens in the Lord's Supper; God hallows the elements of bread and wine by speaking the divine word. But the name of God's Word is Jesus Christ. It is through Jesus Christ that the sacrament is hallowed and given its meaning. By his Word, God has bound himself to the sacrament, that is, Jesus Christ is one who is bound by the sacrament. The God-human Jesus Christ is wholly present in the sacrament. As God spoke at the creation, "'Let there be light'; and there was light,"[45] so the Word addressed to the sacrament becomes [reality.][46]

(3) As Jesus Christ, the sacrament is essentially Word. The church's answer to [the understanding] of Christ as *doctrina*,[47] as generalized truth, is to maintain that Christ is sacrament, which means that in his essence, he is not *doctrina*. This refutes the error that Christ is only an idea and does not exist in both history and nature.

But not everything in nature or everything in bodily form is destined to become sacrament. Christ's presence is limited to preaching and sacrament. Why do we have precisely these sacraments? The Protestant church answers, because they are actions instituted by Jesus Christ. This should not be understood in the sense of historicism. Actions instituted by Jesus Christ should not mean anything but that, as Christ exalted and present, he gave them to his church-community. The number of sacraments in which Christ is present, and what is his will, still need no other grounds than their institution by the exalted Lord, thus purely positivist grounds. However, they are not symbols, but Word of God. They do not *mean* something—they *are* something.

(4) The sacrament is not the hiddenness of a bodiless Word of God in a body, so that the sacrament would constitute a second becoming-human
of God. Instead, the Word of God made flesh, the God who has become 302
human, the God-human, is present now in the sacrament in the form of the stumbling block.[48] The sacrament is not the becoming-human of Christ but rather the ultimate humiliation of the God-human. This is analogous to what was said earlier, that Christology is primarily asking, not about the possible union of divinity with humanity, but rather about the hiddenness

[45.] Gen. 1:3.

[46.] Incomplete sentence in the original text.

[47.] "Doctrine" or "teaching."

[48.] [The reference is to Paul. Cf. 1 Cor. 1:23 and the discussion on pp. 313–14 above. —LR]

of the God-human who is present in his humiliated state. God is revealed in the flesh but hidden in the stumbling block. Consequently, the question of Christ's presence in the sacrament can be analyzed not as the question of the humanity and divinity of Christ but rather as the presence of the God-human in humiliated form, as the stumbling block.

(5) A maze of problems has arisen in Protestant theology because the wrong questions were asked. On one hand, the question was about the possibility of the presence of Christ's humanness in the sacrament; on the other, it was about the relation between Christ's being-there [Dasein] and Christ's being-*pro-me.* In the words of institution of the Lord's Supper, Christ himself expressed that he wants to be present to his church as a human being. According to Luther, there is nothing more to say about it.[49] This was the recognition that Christ as human being must be there if his works are to do us any good. Everything depends on the concurrency and presence of the human being Jesus Christ in his church. Thus for Luther the entire gospel depended on Christ's words of institution.

This was contested by saying that Christ was he who had ascended to heaven.[50] The Reformed churches said this. Luther at first unleashed his scorn for it: God must not be imagined as confined by space, like a bird in a cage.[51] The Reformed say that Christ remains only as Logos-person outside the sacrament of the body of Christ. Christ in his bodily form is not the Logos.[52] He remains extra, outside it.

303 Luther answered the Reformed question in the form of his doctrine of ubiquity.[53] He said that it is the body of Christ that, as the body of the God-human and in its communication with the divine nature itself, has taken on divine characteristics. The body of Christ is not bound by its bodily nature but is present everywhere simultaneously as the *genus majestaticum.*[54] The resurrected body of Christ is everywhere. Luther speaks of three different ways of being in a place:[55]

[49.] See, for example, *WA* 17/2:134, 13–36 (interpretation of the "is"' [*ist*] in the *Fastenpostille,* 1522).

[50.] Sperling adds: "*Extra calvinisticum,* is result of the 'how' question."

[51.] See "That These Words of Christ, 'This Is My Body,' Still Stand Firm against the Fanatics" (1527), *LW* 37:73.

[52.] Riemer inserts a handwritten question mark by "Logos."

[53.] Pfeiffer adds here: "which he ought not to have done, it's a 'how' question."

[54.] "The kind related to majesty."

[55.] See Luther's "Confession concerning Christ's Supper" (1528), *LW* 37:214.

(a) Something can be in a place *localiter, circumscriptive.*[56]

(b) Something can be in a place *diffinitive.*[57] This, he said, is the way angels and demons are present.

(c) Something can be in a place *repletive,*[58] that is, there where something is everywhere and yet not measurable in any place.

This is the way in which Christ is present. He is everywhere, and yet we cannot get hold of him. He is not in the bread like straw in a sack;[59] instead, this *in* must be thought of in a theological, spiritual way. He is there, but he is only there where he reveals himself through his Word. Luther says: "It is merely for the sake of revelation. He is everywhere. But you will not catch him unless he offers himself to you and he himself gives the bread meaning for you through his Word. You will not eat of him, unless he wants to reveal himself to you."[60] Christ is even in the rustling leaves, as Luther says,[61] but his presence is not obvious; he is not there for *you*, not *pro-me,* so you cannot grope for him in the rustling leaves.

What do these statements mean for Christology? Here Christology truly becomes eucharistic Christology, that is, Christology derived from the Lord's Supper.

To the "how" question of Christ's presence, Luther has two different answers: (a) the doctrine of ubiquity in the sense of substance; (b) but 304
Christ is only there when he wants to be there for you. This is the doctrine of ubivolipresence.[62] Both doctrines are impossible metaphysical hypostatizations. In each of them, one element of the reality has been isolated and made into a system. Neither the one statement nor the other does justice to the facts of the matter, which must include the being-there-for-*you* and the being-*there*-for-you of Christ. The doctrine of ubiquity teaches an existence of Christ outside revelation. In this way, revelation becomes an incidental state of an existing substance. The ubivolipresence teaches the presence of Christ not as a characterization of his person but rather as a promise,

[56.] "Spatially, circumscribed."

[57.] "Without limitations."

[58.] "All-embracing."

[59.] Luther objected to the view "that Christ's body can have no other way to exist in heaven than the 'local' mode, like straw in a sack" ("Confession concerning Christ's Supper" [1528], *LW* 37:228).

[60.] Freely quoted from "That These Words of Christ, 'This Is My Body,' Still Stand against the Fanatics" (1527). See *LW* 37:68–69.

[61.] See Sermon on Ascension Day (1526) (*WA* 20:382, 24–26, 29–30).

[62.] Concept as used by Reinhold Seeberg, *Dogmengeschichte* 4/2:523–24 (used there as a characteristic of Chemnitz's Christology).

derived from Jesus's words, of his will to be present. Both fail to understand Christ's presence as Christ's way of being. Neither the doctrine of ubiquity nor the doctrine of ubivolipresence can express the presence of the God-human person as the exalted and humiliated Christ. They are theologically inadequate to do so. Both doctrines are necessary consequences of the "how" question in Lutheran territory, that is, of the Reformed question within Lutheran theology. This conceptual *aporia*[63] is nevertheless better, more honest and objective, than the rationalist simplification in Schleiermacher's theology, in which the content is measured and conformed to the form of the "how" question.[64]

(6) Who is the Christ who is present in the sacrament? This is the way the question must be put. The God-human, the Exalted One! Jesus exists in such a way that he is the one who is present in the sacrament *existentialiter.*[65] His being the sacrament is not a particular desire he expresses nor a characteristic, but rather he exists by nature as sacrament in the church, and this because he is the Humiliated One. His being sacrament is his being humiliated in the present. It is not an incidental aspect of his God-human substance, but rather his existence is a humiliated existence.

305 What is the distinction between the Christ who is present *in* and *as* sacrament and the Christ who is present *in* and *as* Word? None. It is the one forgiving and judging Christ who is Word and remains so in both cases. In the sacrament Christ is present to us in the sphere of our body's tangible nature. Here he is by our side as a creature, in our midst as a brother among brothers and sisters. As sacrament he is the restored creation of our spirit-bodily existence; he is the new creature, and in such a way that he is the human being humiliated in bread and wine. Because he is the new creature in the bread and wine, therefore bread and wine are the new creation. Bread and wine are, by nature and *realiter,* the new food for the person who receives them in faith. As newly restored creation, they are no longer anything in and for themselves, but rather for that person. This being-for-the-person is their being newly created. Christ is present in the sacrament simultaneously

[63.] [From the Greek, "without passage." In classical rhetoric *aporia* means placing a claim in doubt by arguing both sides of an issue. In Bonhoeffer's discussion here, the meaning is that of a final conceptual impasse.—LR]

[64.] Bonhoeffer apparently drew this conclusion from Schleiermacher's criticism of traditional christological formulations (cf. §§ 95 and 99; on the Chalcedonian formula, § 96, 1–3; on the *communicatio idiomatum,* § 97, 5). These notes do not indicate to what extent Bonhoeffer took into consideration that the first theorem of Schleiermacher's Christology (§ 96) says: "In Jesus Christ divine nature and human nature were combined into *one* person" (Schleiermacher, *Christian Faith*).

[65.] ["Existentially."—LR]

as creator of all nature and as creature. As Creator, he is present as *our* Creator, who, through this new creation, makes us ourselves into new creatures. The question, "how" can this be? must be turned into the question, "who" is this who does so? And the answer is the historical, crucified, resurrected, heaven-ascended Jesus of Nazareth, the God-human, but here revealed as brother and Lord, creature and creation.

3. Christ as Church-Community

As Word and sacrament, Christ is present as church-community. The presence of Christ as Word and sacrament is related to Christ as church-community, just as reality is related to form. Christ is the church-community by virtue of his being-*pro-me.* He takes action as the new humanity. The church-community, between his ascension and his second coming, is the form he takes. What does it mean that Word and sacrament are the church-community?

Word exists as the word of God's church-community, that is, it exists in time and space. It is not just the poor words of human doctrine, but the mighty Word of the Creator. By speaking, it creates the form of the church-community. Church-community is Word of God, insofar as Word of God is God's revelation. Only because the church-community is itself Word of God can it understand the Word of God alone. Revelation can be understood 306
only because it has been revealed. Word is in the church-community insofar as the church-community is that which receives the Word.

The sacrament, too, is in the church-community and is present as church-community. It does have, beyond the Word, a bodily form. This form in which it becomes bodily present is the body of Christ himself, and as such it is at the same time the form of the church-community.[66] It is not a mere *image*; the church-community *is* the body of Christ. It is so in reality. The concept of the body as applied to the church-community is not a functional concept referring to the members but is instead a concept of the way in which the Christ exists who is present, exalted, and humiliated.

Insofar as the church-community is the church-community, it no longer sins. But it remains in the world of the old Adam, and as such it still lives in the aeon of sin. Christ's being as the church-community is, like his being as Word, a being in the form of the stumbling block.

[66.] According to Pfeiffer, Dudzus, Gadow, Sperling, and Zimmermann, Bonhoeffer referred here to 1 Cor. 12 [12–30] and to Ephesians 5 [23–32]. Zimmermann explains: the separation of members from the "head," or Lord, in Ephesians should be understood as "not originally Paul's," but also "not in contradiction" to Paul's view.

II. The Place of Christ

If we ask about the place of Christ, we are asking about the "where structure" within the "who-structure" of the Christ. Where this structure can be demonstrated, it provides the theological proof that Christ's incidental appearance in space and time is his manner of existing as a person, as the risen Lord. Where does he stand? For me, he stands in my place, where I should be standing. He stands there because I cannot, that is, he stands at the boundary of my existence and nevertheless in my place. This is an expression of the fact that I am separated, by a boundary that I cannot cross, from the self that I ought to be. This boundary lies between my old self and my new self, that is, in the center between myself and me. As the limit, Christ is at the same time the center that I have regained. As boundary, the boundary can only be seen from its other side, outside the limit.
307 Thus it is important that we human beings, in recognizing that our limit is in Christ, at the same time see that in this limit we have found our new center.[67] It is the nature of Christ's person to be in the center. The One who is in the center is the same One who is present in the church as Word and sacrament. If we bring the question of "where" back into the question of "who," the answer is given: Christ, as the one who is being-there *pro-me*, is the mediator. That is Christ's nature and way of existing.

Being in the center means a threefold being-there:

(1) being-there for humankind,

(2) being-there for history,

(3) being-there for nature.

This is the Christ *pro-me* translated into the "where structure." Christ's status as mediator must be proven in that he can [be] seen as the center of human existence, of history, and of nature.

1. Christ as the Center of Our Existence

The center of our existence is [not] the center of our personality. This is not a psychological statement, but rather an ontological[-]theological one, because it refers not to our personality but rather to the persons we are before God. Christ is not the center that we can see is here but rather the center according to our faith. In the fallen world, however, the center is at the same time a boundary. Human beings stand between law and fulfillment. We have the law but not the possibility of fulfilling the law. Christ as the center means that he is the fulfillment of the law. Thus he is both the

---

[67.] [The meaning and uses of "boundary" and "limit" (*Grenze* is Bonhoeffer's word for both here) is discussed in 2/7, ed. note 2, of this volume and in *DBWE* 3:85, ed. note 15.—LR]

limit of human life and the court in which humankind is judged. But Christ is not only the end of our existence—its limit—but also the beginning of the new existence, and that means the center. That Christ is the center of our existence says that he is the judgment and the justification.

2. Christ as the Center of History

Any attempt to substantiate philosophically the idea that Christ is at the center of all religions, or that he is the limit or the end of all religion, must be rejected. Even here, we are not dealing with preexisting historical space. This means that all questions about Jesus as absolute are not the right questions, for these questions are comparing Christ with all other relative phe- 308
nomena. This would mean that the proof would remain always connected to a relative question. The question about absoluteness is the liberal, distorted question.[68]

Christ is at the center of history by being both its boundary and the center, that is, history lives between promise and fulfillment. History carries a promise for us, that of becoming God's people, and also the promise of the Messiah. This has become a living promise everywhere. History lives toward the fulfillment of this promise alone; this means history is essentially messianic history. The meaning of history is nothing other than the coming of the Messiah. But it is subject to this promise as an individual is subject to the law, that is, it cannot fulfill the promise by itself. History wants to glorify itself in the Messiah. History is struggling [toward] the impossible fulfillment of a degenerate promise. History knows about its messianic destiny but is defeated by it. There is only one place where the idea makes any headway, against the current of the messianic promise, that the Messiah cannot be the preexisting center in the midst of history's space but is and must be the hidden center of history put there by God. Thus Israel stands alone among nations with its prophetic hope. Thus Israel becomes the place where God fulfills this promise.

¶ That Christ is the Messiah cannot be proven; he can only be proclaimed. This statement means that in Christ the messianic expectation of history is crushed as well as fulfilled. It is crushed because its fulfillment is hidden. It is fulfilled because the Messiah has truly come. The meaning of history is swallowed up in an event that takes place in the deepest desolation of human life, on the cross. History finds its meaning in the humiliation of Christ. Here, every other claim that history might make is

[68.] Bonhoeffer had already discussed this theological statement critically in his lecture on the "History of Systematic Theology" (*DBWE* 11, 2/3), with special reference to Berlin professor Ernst Troeltsch (*Absoluteness of Christianity*).

finished, condemned, destroyed. History, with all its promises, has reached
309 its boundary here. By its nature it has come to an end. But with that the boundary is simultaneously once again the center. In this way also, Christ is here seen to be the limit and the center of history's being. In the place where history should also stand, Christ stands before God. Thus he is also the mediator of history.

The church should be understood as the center of history. The church is the center of a history that is made by the state. The church must be understood to be the center, the hidden center, of the state. The church, as the Christ who is present, gives proof of its being in the center not by being visibly at the center of the state, not by being a state church. Not through its visible position [within] the realm of the state does the church prove what its place is in the state, [but] only in that the church judges and justifies the state, assuming that it is the nature of the state, through actions that create law and order, to bring the goals of its people nearer to fulfillment. Thus in every state, behind the idea of creating order, the messianic idea lies hidden.

The church, as the center of the state, also constitutes the limit of the state, because the church recognizes and must preach that the entire promise, from a human point of view, was broken on the cross of Christ. The church thereupon becomes the fulfillment of the state's history, because in the cross it is the fulfillment of both the law and the state. The church proclaims, in the cross, both the affirmation of law and order and its ultimate breaking and abolition by God's entering into history and having to die within history.

As a result, there has been a new relation between state and church since the historical event of the cross. The state has existed in its truest sense only since there has been a church. The true origin of the state is only found together with the church, on the cross, insofar as the cross fulfills and affirms law and order and at the same time breaks through it. As a result, the cross of Christ is doubly present to us, in the forms of both the church and the state. Christ himself is present to us, takes shape, only in this twofold form, but is only present to us if we live by his cross. This is why Luther can say that the state is the "kingdom of God on the left hand."[69]
310 As long as Christ was on earth, he alone was the kingdom of God. Since he was crucified, it is as if his form [Gestalt] is broken into the right hand and

[69.] See Luther's interpretation of Psalm 109 (1518) (*WA* 1:692, 8–12) and his sermon of December 15, 1532 (*WA* 36:385, 6–11).

the left hand of God. He can now be recognized only in twofold form, as church and state. Christ as the center of history is the mediator between the state and God in the form of the church. But Christ as the center of history is just as much the mediator between the church and God, for he is also the center of the church, insofar as the church is the center of history.

3. Christ as the Center of Nature

Christ is the new creation. As the new creation, Christ makes all other creatures into the old creation. Nature is subject to the curse of God upon Adam's field, whereas it was nature's original role to be and to proclaim God's Word. But as the fallen creation it is now dumb, in servitude, not free, a creature in subjection, a guilty creature that has lost its freedom, a creature awaiting a new freedom with eager longing. Thus nature is between servitude and liberation, between servitude and redemption. Nature will receive its freedom not through reconciliation but through redemption. What are natural catastrophes if not nature's dim desire to free itself, to make itself into a new creation?

In the sacraments of the church, the old creation is set free from its servitude and obtains its new freedom.[70] Christ cannot be proved to be the redeeming creation within nature; he can only be preached as such. The enslaved creation is, however, only redeemed into hope. In this enslaved creation a sign is set up in which the elements of the old creation become the elements of the new creation. To what extent? To the extent that they are set free from their dumb condition, from their interpretation by humankind. These elements themselves speak and say what they are. Only in the sacrament is Christ the center of nature, as the mediator between nature and God.

In summary we can say that to call Christ the center of human existence,
of history, and of nature—these are never abstract matters and are never 311
to be distinguished from one another. It is a fact that human existence is both history and nature. Christ as the center means that Christ, as the mediator for the creation in its servitude, is the fulfillment of this law, the liberation from this servitude for the whole human being. Christ is all this only because he is the one who stands in my place, in my behalf before God, *pro-me.* Christ as the mediator is precisely the end of the old, fallen world and the beginning of the new world of God.

[70.] Thus correctly noted by Gadow. Riemer noted incorrectly: "In the sacraments of the church the old creation is placed in servitude to its new freedom."

Part 2. The Historical Christ

I. Access to the Historical Christ

The Christ who is present today is the historical Christ. He is the Jesus of history. If this were not so, then we would have to say with Paul that our faith would be in vain,[71] for then the substance of our church would be taken away.

The distinction that liberal theology tries to make between the Jesus of the Synoptic Gospels and the Christ of Paul is dogmatically and historically impossible. Why? The preaching of the church would be an illusion if this distinction between Jesus and Christ were possible. But the distinction is also historically impossible. Liberal theology up to 1900 can be described as an indirect, unintended, and therefore even more emphatic confirmation of precisely this dogmatically necessary statement. Liberal theology is itself undermined by its own conclusions. It has nullified itself; thus it makes way for the statement with which we began, that Jesus and Christ are the same. For liberal theology stands and falls, first of all, by its distinction between Jesus and Christ. It considers Christ to be the Jesus who is enthusiastically idolized by the church-community. Jesus is not Christ in his own being, in his own person, but rather in his effect upon others. The judgment of Jesus's church-community [about Jesus Christ] must be kept strictly separate
312 [from Jesus's actual being], says liberal theology.[72]

¶Scholarly research was supposed to discover and bring forth this historical Jesus. But that was not the result it obtained. It did not prove possible to write a historically credible biography of Jesus. Then the research on Jesus's life came to a conclusion with Albert Schweitzer's dictum that the search for the historical Jesus is an impossibility.[73] And Wrede recognized that a historical Jesus in the sense of a biography of Jesus is unimaginable, since even the Synoptic Gospel writers depended on the faith of their church-communities as their source.[74]

This ending of liberal theology with Wrede has a twofold significance:

a. on the negative side, the actual undermining of its own presupposition, namely, that Jesus is someone other than the Christ;

[71.] See 1 Cor. 15:17. [King James translation, used for reasons of familiarity. The NRSV reads: "If Christ has not been raised, your faith is futile."—LR]

[72.] See Ritschl, *Christian Doctrine of Justification and Reconciliation*, 280 (direct value judgments) and 282 (divinity of Christ as expression of his high esteem by the church-community).

[73.] See Schweitzer, *Quest of the Historical Jesus.*

[74.] See Wrede, *Messianic Secret.*

b. on the positive side, that from now on the New Testament can only be correctly interpreted historically if its own presupposition is taken seriously, namely, that Jesus is the *Kyrios*, the Lord.

So there are the two ways out: remaining on the historical level, to see this *Kyrios*-Christ-cult [Kultus] and the other view of Jesus alongside each other, or to make the transition from the historical level to dogmatic studies. The result of the historical research is that Jesus cannot be separated from Christ. So it does not work to distinguish between the cult of Jesus and the religion of Christ. That result was all the more surprising because faith and research appeared to be opposed to each other. So, after pursuing liberal theology to its final outcome, one finds history and dogmatics allied once again. History has worked out anew the dogmatic assumptions of the New Testament: that the Christ who is present to us, the Christ whom we proclaim, is the historical Christ.

Martin Kähler, in his book *Der sogenannte historische Jesus und der geschichtliche, biblische Christus*,[75] proposes both theses, that the biographical research on Jesus was a wrong track to pursue, and that the Christ whom we preach
is the historical Christ. This means that dogmatics says the same thing that 313
historical theology subsequently recognized. Thus the cardinal assertion that Jesus is the Christ is confirmed by history against its own will.

But to what degree does this dogmatic assertion depend on historical confirmation? What would happen if historical criticism at some later stage made such a dogmatic assertion impossible? What would become of our faith? Two things are to be said here. On the one hand, dogmatics does need the certainty of Jesus Christ's historical existence, that is, that Christ present and the historical Christ are identical. On the other hand, however, the question must be asked, How can dogmatics be certain of this historical truth? Can history ever sustain dogmatic assertion? If it were not so, how should we ever be able to find an access to the historical figure of Jesus Christ? Thus we need either history that is *historia sacra*[76]—but this is not a good option, [either] theologically or empirically—or there must be an access to history from outside history. To put it another way, how can I be

[75.] [Published in English as *The So-Called Historical Jesus and the Historic Biblical Christ*.—LR]

[76.] "Sacred history." [The Latin term refers to a particular stream of historical events understood by those within the community of faith to be the history of salvation. Secular historians interpreting the same events would not deem these events to be qualitatively different in this way, i.e., "sacred," and would not use the term or recognize this distinctive narrative set within a broader history.—LR]

absolutely certain of the historical fact of Jesus Christ? Answer: an essential aspect of historical research is that it no longer considers any individual fact as an absolute. Never does everything depend on one fact alone. Every individual fact preserves an element of chance. Its absolute validity cannot be proven. If Jesus never lived, the church and our faith are damned; we would be far away from God.

Let us ask again: How can I be absolutely certain of the historical fact of Jesus Christ? Evidently this is too much to ask of the historical method. Our answer is

a. Historical research cannot absolutely deny a fact, any more than it can affirm one. Thus the existence of Jesus Christ cannot be absolutely denied, though one can indeed question it and say it is *probably* not so. The historical truth of Jesus Christ can therefore neither be denied nor affirmed with absolute certainty.

b. Absolute certainty about a historical fact is *in itself* not to be had; it
314 remains a paradox. Only for the church is it essential, constitutive. What does that mean? It means that the historical fact is not in the *preterite,* but rather the present tense; that precisely that which happens by chance is the absolute, that precisely the past is that which is present; that the historical is that which is simultaneously here and now. When we can bear this contradiction, then the historical becomes an absolute. But the assertion that the historical is simultaneously present is made historically possible only through faith in the miracle that God accomplished in Jesus's resurrection.

There is no historical [historisch] access to the person of Jesus that can oblige us to believe. Access through the historical [geschichtlich] Jesus is only possible through the Risen One, through the Word by which Christ resurrected bears witness to himself. It is not so, as Wilhelm Herrmann says, that our conscience in its distress encounters Jesus in our inner life, and that through this encounter we become convinced that Jesus existed in history.[77] Instead, it is the Risen One who himself creates faith and makes possible our access to the historicity of Jesus. After that, it is irrelevant whether history says Christ existed or not. Through faith, history is recognized by eternity, not by itself or from within itself.

Here we must keep in mind that the witness to Jesus as the Resurrected One is none other than that which is handed down to us in the Bible. Thus,

[77.] See Herrmann's explanation that one concludes, having experienced the present influence of the image of Jesus, that the "more general features of the common story in the portrait of Jesus" in the Bible can be relied upon (*Communion of the Christian with God,* 59). This assumption was based on the insight that the "absolute truth" of the image of Jesus does not depend on the "relative truth obtained by historical research" (64).

as persons of faith, we remain sober and objective. We have to read this book of books with all our human resources, and even as we do so, we remain in the profane world. This is very difficult ground on which we stand. For it is difficult to preach about words that history cannot prove were actually spoken by Jesus.[78] On the other hand, verbal inspiration means to deny the 315
Christ who alone is present as the Risen One. Inspiration from the literal words [Verbalinspiration] is a poor surrogate for the resurrection. It eternalizes the historical, instead of recognizing the historical as coming from God's eternity and God's resurrection. Only if we are prepared to make our peace with this veiling of the truth within history do we know that the historical-critical method is, for us, a belief in [sentence incomplete].[79] But through the Bible in its fragility, God comes to meet us as the Risen One. Thus as long as we live on earth, we must go ahead and use historical criticism, inadequate though it is. For us, the historicity of Jesus has both aspects, that of history and that of faith. The two are linked together by our saying that this is the way the historical Jesus humbled himself, and that the [historically] incomprehensible Jesus is [as Christ] the object of faith.

The understanding of the risen Lord as a historical figure is the object of the following observation. Ancient history [actually, the early church] assumed Christ to be a historical figure and did not speak of Christ present, the Risen One, because it took this for granted. For us, this assumption has gradually shrunk, almost to the vanishing point. That is why we have to begin with Christ present.

[II.] Critical Christology or Negative Christology

This is the part of Christology that seeks to make the incomprehensibility of the person of Jesus Christ comprehensible. That which is incomprehensible is not to be turned into something comprehensible; rather, that which can be comprehended should serve to let stand that which we cannot comprehend. And in critical Christology, the goal of our effort to comprehend is the incomprehensible. It is critical because it tests every assertion about Christ against this limitation. The conclusions of critical Christology are therefore of a negative nature. This is why we say that we are speaking here

[78.] Here the notes of Sperling and Lehel include a reference to Thurneysen. Pfeiffer has "Historical concern about the Bible is like a man walking on ice floes, jumping from one verse to the next, knowing that one will really reach the promised shore" (for this image, see Thurneysen, "Schrift und Offenbarung," 28).

[79.] But see Pfeiffer's notes: "Faith knows that it will find Christ in this humble condition, and having found [him], faith will then be strengthened by the humble circumstances." The notes here by Dudzus, Gadow, and Lehel are similar.

of "negative Christology." Afterward, in the last section, we will develop a positive Christology.

316 Approaches to a positive Christology have always been launched by individual theologians. The decisions of the councils, however, expressed only the conclusions of critical Christology. The progress made between one council and the next was always due to the appearance of men who worked on positive Christology. The official church makes critical Christology its business—setting limits, issuing negative statements—because in the church, the proclamation of the living Christ is always taking place alongside the decisions of councils.[80]

¶For us the concept of heresy no longer exists, because there is no longer a doctrinal authority vested in councils. Our ecumenical councils of today[81] are anything but councils, because the word heresy has been struck from our vocabulary. And yet the concept of heresy is a necessary, nonnegotiable factor for the confessing church.[82] Doctrine must always be set over against false doctrine; otherwise one does not know what doctrine means. However, care must be taken that the concept of heresy be one that is used by the church out of love, not out of lack of love. For if I do not speak the truth to my brethren, I am considering them as heathens;[83] if I do speak the truth to them, I am doing it out of love.

1. The Docetic Heresy

This is the attempt to make the incarnation of Christ so comprehensible that Jesus Christ is understood as only the appearance of the godhead in history. Christ's humanness is only the garment, the wrapping, the means by which God speaks to humankind, but is not of the essence of God's nature.

[80.] Dudzus's notes are clearer: "Positive Christology is always the work of individual theologians, while the limits on this impetus are set by the councils. Why? Because positive Christology is continually happening through preaching and the sacraments."

[81.] Bonhoeffer meant the councils of the ecumenical movement (cf. his appeal to "the one Great Ecumenical Council of the Holy Church of Christ," *DBWE* 13:309).

[82.] According to the notes by Dudzus, Pfeiffer, and Zimmermann, Bonhoeffer referred here to the Augsburg Confession [CA] of 1530. Pfeiffer: "In the CA, *docent* [they teach] is always, rightly, set over against *damnant* [they condemn]."

[83.] ["Heathens" is the translation of *Heiden*. It occurs with some regularity in the Christology lectures and the Bethel confession in this volume, as well as in other volumes—the prison poem, "Christians and Heathens," e.g., forthcoming in *DBWE* 8. Although it is sometimes translated as "pagans," the preference here is "heathens." "Pagans" often carries the connotation of another (pagan) religion, while "heathens" may mean simply non-Christian. In some contexts, notably related to New Testament texts, it is translated as "Gentile."—LR]

"Jesus the human being as God's stained-glass window"[84] is a shorthand formula for expressing the docetic heresy. This heresy is as old as Christianity and is still alive today. 317

This heresy gets its strength from two motives.

The first is an abstract idea of God, a doctrine of God that prefers to leave the human element to one side. The godhead is already known before its revelation, the truth is already known as an absolute idea; therefore its [meaning][85] is independent of all human nature. The origin of this thinking lies in the antithesis between idea and appearance [Erscheinung]. The docetic heresy is the typical heresy of Greek thinking, which can be generally designated as pagan thinking and which historically is the opposite of Jewish thinking. The latter had no place for docetism, because it lacked the presupposition regarding idea versus appearance.

The second motive is a certain way of thinking about redemption. The early church put it this way: human nature must be redeemed by Christ, meaning the individual human being who, in his or her individuality, has fallen. Or, as Schelling said, individuality is sin.[86] It is the destiny of human beings to return, from captivity to individuality, to their true nature. This human nature is now common to all people. By nature they are all one. Thus redemption can be nothing other than the liberation of human beings to their true nature, in which the unity and naturalness of the entire human race is reestablished. "O human, become your essence!" says Angelus Silesius.[87] Here he is saying the same thing that was said by the early church and later by the idealists.

When the Bible speaks of Christ's becoming human for our redemption, the becoming human is to be understood as nothing other than the
prerequisite for redemption, as God's taking on the nature and essence of 318
humanity, but not as God's becoming a human being in the sense of individuality. Because God takes on only the essence of humankind, human beings are redeemed and restored to their original essence. The question

[84.] [The German word here, *Transparent*, actually refers to a kind of treated paper that allows light to pass through; the meaning here is that through Christ the outline of God is evident—"through a glass darkly" (1 Cor. 13), as it were.—LR]

[85.] Gap in the text, into which Gadow wrote "truth or meaning" by hand.

[86.] Probably confused with the criticism of "self-will" in Schelling (cf. Schelling, *Philosophical Investigations*, 55).

[87.] See Silesius: "O human, become your essence, for when the world passes away, the accidental is gone, but the essence remains" (*Cherubinic Wanderer*, 58). [The translation reads: "Eternal essence be! The world will fall away, the accidental perish, essence alone will stay." Trans. altered by Isabel Best.—LR]

then is how can God become fully human by taking on only the general nature and essence of humankind, and not the individuality that is ours? For the early church, what was decisive was that God could not become an individual human person, because then God could not redeem humanity, and [the human being] would fall back into sin. The crucial thing is that God takes on human nature.

This is the starting point for the teaching of Apollinaris of Laodicea, one of the ablest and most influential dogmaticians of the early church. He taught that the God-Logos had taken on the whole nature of humankind, with flesh and soul, but had not taken on the νοῦς[88] of a human being, that which governed the human being as a personality. Thus God's appearance in human nature is becoming human, but with[89] the elimination of the individuality that is characteristic[90] of human nature.

This refined variety of docetism was immediately detected by the church at that time and was condemned as a heretical doctrine.[91] For then Christ would not be fully human; the becoming human of Christ would be altogether annulled and with it redemption itself. It had to be acknowledged that, in truly becoming human, Christ had taken on not only the σάρξ[92] and ψυχή,[93] but also the νοῦς of a human being. Thus the problem was posed as to how Jesus the human being could be understood as an individual person with νοῦς, yet the unity of Jesus Christ's person could be affirmed.[94]

[88.] "Mind."

[89.] The text has erroneously "without."

[90.] The text has erroneously "individuality that relates" (cf. Zimmermann: "the principle of individuality turned off").

[91.] First in Rome in 377, then in Antioch in 379, and finally in 381 at the Ecumenical Council of Constantinople (Mühlenberg, *Apollinaris*, 364).

[92.] "Flesh."

[93.] "Soul."

[94.] [Attention to Bonhoeffer's choice of words is important here. His words correspond to his vital distinction of "who" from "how" elsewhere in these Christology lectures. In the English language the incarnation of God is understood as God become human in Jesus of Nazareth, but Bonhoeffer chooses *Menschwerdung* and *der Menschgewordene*—God become human, God having become human, in Jesus of Nazareth—to answer the "who" question in all its particularity. By contrast, the German word for incarnation—*der Fleischgewordene* [the Incarnate One]—answers the "how" question: God is incarnate by becoming flesh. "Becoming flesh" is, in German, a general notion focused on "how"; "becoming human" in this person Jesus is a personal notion focused on "who." Given Bonhoeffer's argument that "how" is the wrong question and "who" is the right question, the reader should recognize the importance of Bonhoeffer's deliberate choice—*der Menschgewordene* rather than *der Fleishgewordene*; God become human rather than God incarnate.—LR]

¶So the following progression becomes essential. The νοῦς is recognized as being necessary. But in the church's orthodox thinking, one suffered from the thought that this meant being human in the sense of fallen human individuality. So one shifted the problem. One now taught that it was [im] 319
possible to accept that this Jesus in human form could have only one hypostasis, only one way of being. The [human] hypostasis [of Jesus] would be existing enhypostatically in the divine hypostasis. So Jesus's manner of existing was God's manner of existing. If Jesus [as a human being] had a hypostasis of his own, the result would be that Jesus and Christ could not be held together.

In this doctrine of "en-hypostasia," it is important for us to see that in this final rearguard action by early church dogmatics against docetism, docetism in a refined form had nevertheless crept into the early church dogmatics itself, even into orthodox dogma itself. For what is the doctrine of en-hypostasia if not an ultimately concealed form of docetism?[95]

Where docetism goes astray is in its concept of redemption, in which a distinction is made between human nature and a human being's actual, personal way of being. It can be demonstrated that [in] every abstract doctrine of God and in every concept of redemption, there is at bottom the same presupposition, namely, the opposition between idea and appearance. The appearance of the human being is his individuality, and the idea of the human being is his human nature. The appearance is that which is incidental, and the idea is the substance. Jesus as a human being is incidental, as opposed to the substance that is God. Thus there is a philosophical presupposition in docetism. If one does not rid oneself of this presupposition—about idea and appearance—one will never be free of docetism in some form.

The earliest form of docetism is represented by the gnostics, specifically Basilides and Valentinus. Basilides taught that there is no way to reconcile the idea of Christ with the human being Jesus. The unity between them was only ephemeral and was dissolved at the crucifixion. At the crucifix-
ion, Jesus ascended to heaven and triumphed over the devil. Jesus was a 320
real human being. Only quite incidentally was he the basis for the aeon Christ.[96]

[95.] According to the notes of Gadow, Dudzus, and Sperling, at this point Bonhoeffer criticized Emil Brunner's positive acceptance of the doctrine of enhypostasia (cf. Brunner's *Mediator*, 265–68). For Adolf von Harnack (*Outlines of the History of Dogma*, 298), the said doctrine contained "a more refined Apollinarianism," while Karl Barth, *Christliche Dogmatik*, 264, has a positive assessment of this doctrine.

[96.] ["Aeon" is "spiritual being." The reference to "aeon" in Gnosticism is to the various emanations of God. Two of these are Jesus and Sophia, who constitute the *pleroma*,

Valentinus and his pupil Apelles taught that Jesus's body came from heaven and was not a body born of a human being. Jesus only passed through Mary. Saturninus of Antioch, however, said that Jesus was an imaginary figure. He was never born. What all three have in common is their indifference to Jesus. What is important is the idea and its development. It does not matter who he was or whether he even existed.

The early church stood against this, because it knew what the docetists of every age have forgotten, namely, that Christ was not an idea but rather an event. It is not the idea of a Redeemer that must be proclaimed, but rather Christ who must be understood as having become human. Only he can redeem real human beings. Everything depends on Jesus's existence in history. The intention was then to bring the history of Jesus into harmony with the idea of God. This is where the reductions[97] came in. The ultimate reduction was the doctrine of the "en-hypostasia." This was the insurmountable remnant of orthodox dogmatics, with the docetic presupposition.[98] In the theological formulation, the becoming human remains conceived, in the final analysis, as incidental compared to the substance. Yet docetism was condemned as faulty.

Docetism has openly emerged again in recent Protestant theology, though in a different form. There is a new interest in the historical Jesus. There one must see the speculative concept of history. In this way of thinking, history is the carrier of certain religious ideas—it is the appearance of an idea that is above and beyond history. One of these values is, for example, the idea of the religious personality, the personality with a strong and unclouded "God-consciousness" (cf. Schleiermacher).[99] Christ is the representative of this idea, he who embodied it in history.

321 ¶Why is this docetism? Because, once again, it is not the real human being, but rather an image of the human being obtained from a particular concept of history, which is then applied to Jesus. One starts with a particular religious idea that one already has and applies it to this historical Jesus. Thus it is decisive that Jesus as a historical person is reduced to the embodiment of a religious idea. Here his becoming-human once again becomes the means to an end.

---

or regions of light. In gnostic teaching of the Jesus aeon, Jesus is not truly, fully human. —LR]

[97.] [That is, of the historical Jesus.—LR]

[98.] Sperling's notes here are probably clearer: "The doctrine of enhypostasia . . . is the insurmountable remnant [of docetism within] the attempt to overcome docetism."

[99.] Schleiermacher, *Christian Faith*, § 94 [385].

In Ritschl's Christology this appears very clearly. He says that Christ can only be described as God through a value judgment by his church-community.[100] The church-community addresses him as God, and only through this judgment by the church-community does Christ become God. Ritschl distinguishes between the being-judgment and the value judgment, that is, the church-community has a scale of values with which it comes to the historical figure of Christ and attributes these values to him. Such values, which Christ embodies, are named by Ritschl as mercy, faithfulness, lordship over the world. Jesus as a human being is the appearance of these values.

From this point on, all liberal theology must be understood in the context of a docetic Christology. Liberal theology only wanted to see, in Jesus, the embodiment of a certain doctrine. Thus the humanity of Jesus is basically not taken seriously, even though liberal theology has so much to say about Jesus as a human being. The idea of Jesus's humanity bypasses here the reality of Jesus as a human being, confuses the ideal of his humanity with its reality, in short, makes his humanity into a symbol.

The most brilliant exposition of docetism is found where the concept of idea versus appearance has been brought to perfection, in the work of Hegel. Here, the appearance is *necessarily* the taking shape of the idea. For Hegel, the becoming human is not illusion [Schein] but rather *essential* appearance [Erscheinung], the *necessary* appearance of God in history.[101] God appears by necessity. That is the nature of God. God is only God by appearing in history. It is precisely this *necessity* of the incarnation, God's
becoming human, that is dangerous. It makes a principle out of something 322
that cannot and should not be a necessity.

¶That God becomes a human being is, of course, that which is in principle incomprehensible; otherwise it is not a real human being about which we are speaking but rather the idea of one. God's becoming a human being is not a necessity that follows from God's self. Such a thesis, once again, misses the whole human being as a historical reality. God's becoming a human being is that which is impossible, incomprehensible, God's coming into history in a way that cannot be deduced from God. God and humanity cannot be drawn together [in this relationship] as a necessity.

[100.] See ed. note 72.

[101.] See, for example, Hegel, *Philosophy of History*, 415, on the "incarnation of God in Christ." For Bonhoeffer's critique of Hegel, see also I. Tödt, *Dietrich Bonhoeffers Hegel-seminar*, 11.

The work of Biedermann, a Hegelian, announces the dissolution of christological dogma.[102] Jesus of Nazareth is a replaceable figure. Christ only represents a principle. Although Biedermann denies it, this makes Jesus's humanity, his historical reality, incidental to the divine substance. With this, docetism in a pure cultural form makes its appearance in the Protestant camp.

The church must reject every form of docetism. Along with it, we must refuse every form of Greek idealistic thinking to the extent that it works with the distinction between idea and appearance. For with this distinction such idealism abolishes the first premise of all theology, that God, out of mercy freely given, truly became a human being, rather than becoming, out of necessity, the realization of some human principle. The rupture in every kind of docetism is its closeness to rationalism.[103]

2. The Ebionite Heresy

The Ebionite heresy does not derive from a heathen philosophy, for which the dogma of becoming-human is foolishness. It sees in the cross of Christ the stumbling block, the slander, the dishonoring of God. Its root is in Israelite thinking, [the critique of] the exalting of a man to divine status. Its starting point is a strictly monotheistic belief in God. For the Ebionites,
323 it is blasphemy to place anyone else at the same level as the *one* God. Nor is it acceptable to think of Jesus as a form in which God appeared. Israelite thinking does not countenance any metamorphosis of God as heathen-Greek-docetic thinking does. There is no possibility of giving up the monotheistic God, but rather Jesus is God's creature, thus a real human being. This is the advantage of the Ebionite heresy over docetism; its God is the God of the Bible. God is not a God of metamorphosis. But the relationship of God to this human being cannot be recognized in any way as an identity of being. The Ebionite heresy rejects the supernatural birth, on the one hand, and the preexistence of Christ, on the other, and thus rejects his divinity altogether.

Christ's significance comes through his baptism. It is here that he is accepted as the Son of God who does the will of the Father. Jesus is not one with God in substance but rather receives his status as God's Son. A development takes place in him. He *is* not God but rather becomes God, and becomes more and more so as the Spirit takes possession of him. Christ

---

[102.] See Biedermann, "Kritik der kirchlichen Christologie," *Christliche Dogmatik*, 403–52.

[103.] Perhaps incorrectly noted. Pfeiffer has "What is so captivating is the nearness to rationalism."

becomes God through the Holy Spirit. This becoming-God is made visible for Jewish Christians, for Ebionite heretics, in that Jesus fulfills the law through his obedience unto death. Christ is designated sometimes as God, sometimes as the prophet of truth. Jesus Christ is a human being who has been raised to divine rank. The leitmotif of Israelite thinking is the preservation of the distance between Creator and creature. The leitmotif of heathen thinking is the disregard of the Creator and creature. There, where the human being is considered a servant and a creature, and where metamorphosis is excluded from the beginning, [you have] Ebionite thinking.[104] The Israelite idea of Jesus—Jesus is the human being elevated to Messiah—and the Greek idea of Jesus—Jesus was half divine—are very similar. Yet the heathen thinking is of docetic origin, while the Israelite thinking is Ebionite.[105]

The Monarchists were concerned with preserving the unity of God. This 324
is what interested Paul of Samosata. He gives short shrift to the divinity of the created man Jesus Christ and sees Jesus's divinity in nothing other than his willingness to bind himself to the Father. He thinks of the Spirit as an impersonal power at work in Jesus. Jesus's baptism is his calling to be the Son of God. There is a development here. Paul's teachings were condemned as heretical by the church[106] because they diminish the divinity of Jesus.

Liberal theology likes to refer to Paul of Samosata as a forerunner.[107] There are indeed analogies, but the reference is not justified, for liberal theology is not by nature Ebionitic but rather docetic. It recognizes the human being precisely as being of infinite value. This faith in the value of the human being is the characteristic point. This assertion also tends toward the cult of heroism and of genius.

¶What we have in Ebionitism is the all-obedient servant whose glory is to glorify God. Ebionitism, despite its superficially great similarity to docetic liberalism, is thus substantially superior to it, because it keeps the real human being in concrete terms, Jesus the human being, in view. Our entire salvation begins with Jesus the servant. Ebionitism keeps the real human

[104.] Sperling adds: "the biblical attitude of the Ebionites."

[105.] The transition to the passage that follows is indicated only by Sperling ("Tracing the Ebionite heresy in the history of dogma") and Dudzus ("The Ebionite line often converges with the docetic in the history of dogma").

[106.] At a synod in Antioch in the year 268 (Altaner and Stuiber, *Patrologie*, 214).

[107.] See, for example, Harnack's judgment in 1924: "In the fragments of the Sabinus speeches we have the most valuable pieces from the ancient history of dogma, pieces on which we can reflect and with which we can empathize in their entirety." Harnack added that Ritschl had greeted them "with enthusiastic delight" nearly fifty years previously (A. von Harnack, "Die Reden Pauls," 151).

being and the Creator God in view. The crucial thing is this: that the Ebionites do not find the way from the *real* Creator God to the *real* servant. The church must reject Ebionite thinking as heresy, because it undoes Christ's work of salvation by seeing Christ as a true human being but not *simultaneously* as true God.

In summary, it must be said that the concept of God's becoming human is
325 negatively determined in such a way that its theological interpretation must reject any diminishment of full humanness or full divinity. God as human being, and human being as God, must be held together in our thinking at the risk of sacrificing the rationality of such an assertion. The positive statement on the becoming human must tread a middle path between the docetic and the Ebionite heresies. Between the two "how" questions of docetic and Ebionite theology, we must keep our eyes on the "who" question.

3. The Monophysite and the Nestorian Heresies

How must we conceive of the Person of God, if Christ really became a human being? Here we have arrived at the issue of the divinity of Christ. Within the doctrine of the God-humanness of Christ, the Monophysite and Nestorian heresies developed.

(a) [According to the Monophysites:] the meaning of the person Jesus for salvation history requires that the events of salvation history be fulfilled in human nature. It is crucial that human nature, our nature, be entirely accepted by God. The key word is the ἕνωσις φυσική.[108] Christ is not an individual person; instead, he put on human nature like a garment. He did suffer and thirst and weep as we do, but he did so because he *wanted* to, not because it was his *nature*. For the devout believers of the early church, everything depended on the establishment of this unity between the human and the divine natures. For if God's nature had not been revealed within our human nature, how then could our nature have been made divine, been redeemed and healed!

(b) [For the Nestorians:] the facts of the matter according to the *Bible* are different. Here we read that Jesus was an individual person, with all the weaknesses of a human being as such, a human being who did not claim to be omniscient. Here the issue is apparently Christ's humanness. This humanness is to be understood in the fullest, realistic sense as a τέλειο̃ ἄνθρωπος.[109] It is important here, however, that two distinct natures
326 be present in Christ, and not a unity of substance, for the latter would be

[108.] "According to the oneness of nature."

[109.] "Perfect human being."

an offense against the Creator. We have here a ἕνωσις σχέτικη, that is, a [unity] of attitude, a uniting of the human will with God's, thus the distance between God and human being[110] and there is no transformation. In contrast to the Monophysite view, the element of salvation history is set aside entirely. For how should human nature there become a new creation, if one cannot believe that the two natures were united in Christ!

The struggle over the doctrine of the two natures became a passionate one. For the Nestorians it was a deeply serious matter.[111] The Monophysites taught the mystery of the unity of divine and human nature; the Nestorians made a plain distinction between them, emphasizing the rationality of two entities over against the mystery of their unity. With the former, the mystery of the deification of the human; with the latter, the ethos of the servant's will gradually raising itself toward God, yielding itself to the will of God. In the one, the brighter glow of passion, the greater fervor, the more tenacious insistence; in the other, greater clarity and sobriety of thinking. On one hand, the priestly figure, like an Athanasius (who was not yet one of them); on the other hand, the laity, the ascetics who took an Arian line.

Inevitably it came to conflict and radicalization. On the Monophysite side, the moment of decision arrived when Eutyches of Constantinople confessed: my God is not of the same nature as we; he has no σῶμα ἀνθρώπου, but rather ἀνθρώπινον.[112] Christ is not an individual person; rather, he is human in essence. This radical assertion serves to defend and to settle the question of μία φύσις.[113] The Nestorians took the debate to new heights [of indignation and rejection] with the assertion that Mary should no longer be called the birthgiver[114] of God.

These are the two boundaries between which the real assertion about the mystery of Christ takes place. Monophysitism had to be rejected as heresy because it allowed the human nature of Christ to be swallowed up
in the divine nature. Furthermore, it led to speculation about the nature 327
of God and of the human being, through which the identity of God with the human[115] is ultimately expressed. Nestorianism had to be rejected

[110.] [That is, the distance is maintained.—LR]

[111.] This is misleading. Sperling's notes are clearer, distinguishing between the "greater seriousness about salvation history" of the Monophysites and the "greater biblical seriousness" of the Nestorians.

[112.] Roughly: "he had no human body but something like a human body."

[113.] "One nature."

[114.] [Theotokos.—LR]

[115.] [That is, in Christ.—LR]

because it allowed the humanity and divinity to be so torn apart that the unity of Christ's person could no longer be conceived, so that one could no longer speak of God's becoming human.

In opposition to both these fronts, the classical formulation of the doctrine of Christ as God-human was established in the Chalcedonian formula of 451. It is said: ἕνα καὶ τὸν αὐτὸν Χριστόν . . . ἐν δύο φύσεσιν.[116] [That is to say:]

a. ἀσυγχύτως (without confusion)

b. ἀτρέπτως (without change)

c. ἀδιαιρέτως (without distinction, contradicting the Nestorians)

d. ἀχωρίστως (without separation)

The concern here is the fully divine and the fully human nature. There is only *one* Christ. But he has two natures.

What is being said with the Chalcedonian formula is this: *that all options for thinking of all this together and in juxtaposition are represented as impossible and forbidden options.* Then there is no longer any positive assertion that can be made about what happens in Jesus Christ. In him we are to think of all possibilities [about God and human being] at once. Thus the matter itself is left as a mystery, for we cannot enter into it within the parameters of positive thinking. We can only enter in faith. All forms of thought are outside the realm of possibility. This means that from the Council of Chalcedon onward, it is no longer permissible to talk about the human and
328 divine natures of Jesus Christ as about things or facts.[117] Thus one cannot think of a concept of God and draw a line there. To draw such a line is not permitted.[118]

[116.] "One and the same Christ [, Son, Lord, Only-begotten] in two natures" (Wickham, "Chalcedon," 672) [actually quoted from Ayer, *Source Book for Ancient Church History*, in Walker, *History of the Christian Church*, 139—LR].

[117.] According to Sperling, in characterizing this critique of Chalcedon, Bonhoeffer used the formulations "material concepts and options," "thinking in terms of substance," "speculation on nature." Zimmermann's notes are similar. Harnack criticized the "four bald negative terms" of Chalcedon, in part by saying, "a theology which, in what is for it the most important of all questions, has recourse to mere negatives, is self-condemned." He also found that the "real mystery" was here "shoved aside by a pseudo-mystery which in truth no longer permitted theology to advance to the thought of the actual and perfect union" (A. von Harnack, *History of Dogma*, 4:222–23 [this appears in the German editions in vol. 2.—LR]). For Reinhold Seeberg's somewhat more balanced judgment, see his *Lehrbuch*, 2:246–47.

[118.] Gadow adds: "*Dei providentia et hominum confusione* (through divine providence and human confusion) as the Swiss constitution says [this is incorrect; see 1/38, ed. note 7] the Chalcedon formula was put together." Zimmermann and Sperling have only the Latin quotation.

These negative formulations started a movement [in theological thought]. For theology had to abide within these conceptual tensions. That simply made things hard for the struggling theologians.[119]

In its peculiar form, Chalcedon cancels itself out. The Chalcedonian formula itself reveals the limitations of its own concepts. It works with the concepts regarding the natures[120] and demonstrates that these concepts are inappropriate and heretical forms. It brings the concept of substance that underlies this thinking to its high point and immediately goes beyond it, by saying that from now on assertions about the substance of Jesus Christ will no longer be permitted. If here a continuation of Chalcedon is conceivable, it is no longer a continuation of the thinking about relationships between natures, but rather something else, which we will take up later.[121] The Chalcedonian formula is an objective, living assertion about Christ that goes beyond all conceptual forms. Everything is encompassed in its very clear yet paradoxical agility [Lebendigkeiten].

The Chalcedonian formula was followed by a far-reaching development; people wanted to go beyond it. The orthodox and Protestant formulations said that Christ is one person in two natures (for example, this was already Tertullian's view).[122] This was considered valid from then on. Thus was Chalcedon to be interpreted, with the soteriological leitmotif, on the one hand, and the biblical leitmotif, on the other. The representation of Christ's nature must also include the understanding that this God is completely
human. Then how can it be true that Jesus is omnipotent, present, and yet 329
only a human being? This question must be answered in such a way as neither to question the divinity of Christ nor to eliminate his humanness. Here the conceptual scheme of two natures in one person became crucial.

(c) The doctrine of the *unio hypostatica*.[123] The presupposition for this doctrine is that the integrity of both natures must be preserved: the divine nature in its fundamental and unchangeable essence, and the human nature in its finitude and changeability. These two [assertions] are first made in isolation from each other—precisely that which was forbidden by Chalcedon—and in such a way that the human nature, right from the start, no longer retained its completely human character.

[119.] Incorrectly noted? No parallel statement found in the other sources.

[120.] [That is, the natures of Christ.—LR]

[121.] This means the doctrine of the two states [of Christ: that of humiliation and that of exaltation—LR], which Bonhoeffer accepted as positive; cf. pp. 314 and 355–60.

[122.] See A. von Harnack, *History of Dogma*, 269: "really Tertullian had already used the formulas 'nature' [= substance] and 'person.'"

[123.] "Unity of the person."

The first assertion is thus the one that has both natures joining together in a *unitio.*[124] It is characterized by the divine nature's defining of the human nature. The divine nature is active and suffuses the human nature, which is passive, as fire does to iron. The result of the union is the *unio personalis,* that is, the henceforth indissoluble bond between the two natures. That means that the λόγος no longer exists otherwise than in the σάρξ. God is no longer other than the one who has become human. God is bound up in the human being.[125] The result of this indissoluble bond between Logos and flesh is the *unio naturalis,* the union of divinity and humanity. The *communio naturarum*[126] is expressed in the *propositiones personales.*[127] That is to say, the concrete existence of one nature is expressed by the concrete existence of the other nature. We may say that God is the human being, but not that divinity is humanity. The two natures remain separate. But the concrete existence of God and that of the human being must be expressed by each other.[128]

330 What is crucial, however, is that the union of the two natures develops a *communicatio idiomatum,*[129] that is, a sharing of the individual attributes of the two natures. This is conceived in the following terms:

(1) *The genus idiomaticum.*[130] This says that whatever is true of the one nature or the other can be said to be true of the person as a whole. Thus, Jesus Christ was born or Jesus was born. Jesus suffers or Christ suffers. Jesus Christ suffers.

(2) *The genus apostelesmaticum.*[131] Whatever can be asserted about the person of Jesus [Christ] can be said of each of the two natures of Jesus [Christ]: Jesus Christ cleanses us from sin, or the blood of Jesus Christ [cleanses us]. We now can also speak of the relationship of the two natures to each other, as if divinity and humanity had an immediate relationship with each other. For Luther the crucial term is

[124.] "Union"; the text has, incorrectly, "unio" (unity).

[125.] [That is, Christ.—LR]

[126.] "Communion of natures"; the text has, incorrectly, "communio naturalis."

[127.] "Statements about the person."

[128.] Incorrectly noted? Cf. an undated note by Bonhoeffer: "The concrete existence of each nature can be predicated by the concrete existence of the other: 'the human being (Jesus Christ) is God'; God is the human being (in Jesus Christ), but not 'divinity is humanity'" (*NL,* A 54,13).

[129.] "Impartation of qualities to each other." According to Dudzus, Bonhoeffer described this teaching as "a very astute speculation."

[130.] "Of the sort that refers to properties [of the two natures]."

[131.] "Of the sort that refers to activities [of the person]." Bonhoeffer had noted for himself that "both natures are involved in every action of Christ's ministry. 1 John 1:7" (*NL,* A 54,13; undated).

(3) *The genus majestaticum.*[132] This asserts that the attributes of the divine nature can and must be expressed by the human nature. Jesus is all-powerful; Jesus is ever-present. It is based on the "*est*"[133] in the doctrine of the Eucharist. The *genus majestaticum* is at the core of Lutheran theology. But conflicts arise here with the assertions in the Bible. This is precisely where we come very close to the danger of Monophysitism, that is, the transformation of the human nature into the divine nature.[134]

The Formula of Concord says in its article "Concerning the Person of Christ": "Since both natures are personally united (that is, united in one person) we believe, teach, and confess that this union is not a connection or association of the sort that neither nature shares things with the other personally (that is, because of the personal union), as if two boards were 331
glued together, with neither giving the other anything or receiving anything from the other. Instead, here is the most complete communion, which God truly has with this human being; out of this personal union and out of the most complete and most indescribable communion that results from it flows everything human that can be ascribed to and believed about God and everything divine that can be ascribed to and believed about the human Christ. The ancient teachers of the church have explained this union and communion of the natures using similes of a glowing iron and of the union of body and soul in the human being."[135]

Reformed theologians raise three objections against Lutherans:

(1) That the person of Christ as portrayed here is not the figure of the Redeemer of whom the New Testament speaks.

(2) That Lutheran thinking has envisioned a change in God. This is not possible, because God's essence as such can never be that of human beings. The essence of each remains separate from the other, but the two [natures][136] become one.

(3) That Lutheran Christology is no longer speaking of the real humanity of Jesus.

[132.] "Of the sort that refers to the majesty [of God]." Bonhoeffer had noted for himself: "Matt. 18:20; 17:2. Miracle of forgiveness of sins 8:7" (*NL* A 54,13; undated).

[133.] "Is." Cf. also Franz Hildebrandt's *EST.*

[134.] Zimmermann and Sperling use the term "deification [*Vergottung*]" in this connection.

[135.] See the Formula of Concord, Epitome VIII, 5 (*Book of Concord,* 510).

[136.] The text has, incorrectly, "persons." It concerns the unity of the person in the context of the distinction of nature and essence. See also Sperling: "The two natures are not united in any other way than indirectly through the person" (Lehel and Zimmermann have similar formulations).

Reformed thinkers assert, in opposition, that the λόγος does not enter into the σάρξ in such a way that it no longer exists outside the σάρξ. The λόγος remains in its Trinitarian relationship[137] and thus apart from the flesh. There is, then, no indissoluble bond with the σάρξ. Consequently, there is a development in the human nature. There is no *genus majestaticum*, that is, no deification of human nature [Vergottung], because the sentence begins: *finitum incapax infiniti.*[138] The two natures are not united in any other way than indirectly through the person, that is, what can be said about one of the two natures can be said of the person.

But what does Reformed theology make of the New Testament assertions that Jesus Christ had the authority to say, "This is my body"?[139] This is where the concept of ἀλλοίωσις[140] comes in. This is all to be understood
332 in its symbolic expression.[141] Luther was vehemently opposed to this idea, because it does not allow the Word to stand as Word. The Reformed say that the Logos is everywhere, but in a particular place as God-human. In Reformed Christology, the emphasis is on preserving clearly what belongs to God and what to humanity. The emphasis is on the pure humanity of Christ. Lutherans reply that in Reformed thinking, the two natures relate to each other like two boards glued together.[142] But if true unity is lacking, redemption is called into question. Finitum capax infiniti non per se sed per infinitum.[143] The criterion by which this is decided must be the Bible. The abstract separation of the two natures here is, like their abstract unity, unbiblical.

Luther spoke of the divinity and humanity of Jesus as if they were one nature. He felt it was important to see Christ's humanity as divinity. This is the origin of the doctrine of *genus majestaticum*, which teaches that Christ's human nature is suffused by the divine and receives the attributes of the divine nature. Luther does not keep Jesus separate from Christ; at least, he often does not do so. Because the danger was sensed here that one might

[137.] [That is, to the other two persons of the Trinity.—LR]

[138.] "The finite cannot take on the infinite." [Bonhoeffer's discussion reflects a major difference and point of conflict in the Reformation debate between Lutherans and Calvinists. The former argued that "the finite can take on the infinite," the latter that "the finite cannot take on the infinite."—LR]

[139.] Matt. 26:26.

[140.] "Change" or "to be transformed."

[141.] Text unclear. It refers to Zwingli's understanding of Matt. 26:26 in a symbolic sense, with which one of Luther's writings took issue (see ed. note 36).

[142.] See the above quotation from the Formula of Concord (ed. note 135).

[143.] "The finite cannot take on the infinite by itself, but only through the infinite."

find oneself talking of a deified human being, this doctrine of the *genus majestaticum* was complemented [by] the doctrine of the two states of Christ. This Jesus Christ had submitted to two different states, the *status exinanitionis*[144] and the *status exaltationis*.[145] This doctrine of the two states makes it possible to speak of the historical Jesus and the Redeemer Christ Jesus together as one. According to orthodox Lutheranism, the subject of the *exinanitio*, the one who is humiliated, is the one who has already become human, not the one in the process of becoming human. The one who has become human freely accepts and enters into his humiliation [Ernied- 333
rigung]. Christ's nature, endowed with divine properties, humbles itself [sich erniedrigen]. The humiliation of Christ is an attribute only of the one who has become human, not of the Logos itself. Humiliation means that as long as he lived on earth, Jesus did not exercise his divine attributes in his human nature. Here the question is how this nonexercise of divine attributes is to be understood. Do we really have here a renunciation, an emptying of the divine attributes, in the humiliation,[146] or is it a veiling of the divine powers in Jesus, making them invisible? Thus the doctrine of the two states of Christ led to the argument between the *kenotic* and the *cryptic* thinkers. Those who took the former view were called the kenotics. They say that Jesus really renounced his divine attributes; the cryptics said that these were only veiled.[147]

The cryptics insisted on the identity of the one who became human, who exists in eternity, with the God-human as the one who is humiliated. The Exalted and the Humiliated One must be the same; else all would be lost. The one who must suffer would be, simultaneously, the one who would not have had to suffer. The objection is, if that were so, then Christ did not really suffer, did not really die; it would only have been an illusion that he really died. Cryptic Christology would then be a docetic Christology. It is far more a matter of a real κένωσις, as in Philippians 2.[148] Christ really

[144.] "State of humiliation."

[145.] "State of exaltation."

[146.] [That is, of Christ.—LR]

[147.] On the Lutheran argument over "kenosis" between the theological faculties of Tübingen and Gießen in the seventeenth century that is described here, Bonhoeffer had noted for himself: "Cryptics—Tübingen, Hafenreffer based on Brenz; kenotics—Gießen 1617, Mentzer [based] on Chemnitz; question whether Christ participated in the universal rule of God while on earth. Tübingen: κρύψις χρήσεως [veiling of power]—danger: docetism—concern: unity of the person [of Christ]; Gießen: κένωσις χρήσεως [renunciation of power] = *extra calvinisticum*—danger: division of the person [of Christ]—concern: preservation of [Christ's] human nature" (*NL*, A 54,13; undated).

[148.] Phil. 2:7.

died. One can speak not of a κένωσις κτίσεως,[149] but rather of a [κένωσις] χρήσεως.[150] Christ is said to have been continually suppressing in himself the exercise of his divine attributes. If that is so, one said elsewhere, then
334 the reality of the renunciation is lost. Then this, again, would only be an illusion.

Cryptics and kenotics eventually agreed on an unpretentious formulation: The humiliated Christ made use of his godly attributes when he wanted to and did not use them when he did not want to.[151] The issue of the κτίσις[152] of the divine attributes was put aside. In either case, one sees a glimmer of the divine attributes (but this can cause harm to the concept of faith). Here the entire christological problem is shifted to a different level. It is now concerned with the one God-human, but in two different states (this is important to the kenotics), with the identity of the God-human and yet in two different forms of being God-human, one veiled, one visible.

The doctrine of kenosis [was] taken up again in the nineteenth century, revived by Thomasius and Geß. Kenosis had the same appeal for them (uniting Christ with the Logos image) as for the Lutherans.[153] They shifted it by applying it to the Logos rather than the God-human. The Logos, humbling itself, becomes a human being. What does this turnaround signify? A simplification of the understanding of Christ. For the modern kenotics, the renunciation of the divine attributes takes place in the beyond, in a metaphysical act of the Logos. The historical picture of Jesus Christ is thus freed from the inner violence of needing to repress them.

But this raises the question of what kind of renunciation it was. Thomasius says that God has both relative and immanent attributes. The immanent attributes are those that belong to God's absolute nature. The relative attributes concern God's relationship to the world. These include God's being all-powerful, ever-present, and all-knowing. God's immanent attri-
335 butes are holiness, love, truth. For Christ it is only valid to say that he bore

[149.] "Renunciation of properties."

[150.] The text has, incorrectly, "κτίσις χρήσεως" (renunciation of the exercise [of power]).

[151.] This was the formula imparted in Leipzig in 1624 (Bauke, "Christologie II," 1629).

[152.] "Possession."

[153.] Gap in the text, in which Riemer wrote by hand, with a question mark: "Doctrine of condescension / *Exinanitio* [humiliation]." According to Sperling, the concern was to recognize that both the old Lutheran and the new Lutheran doctrines of kenosis had the same motive ("uniting the constructive understanding of Christ with the Synoptic Gospels").

God's immanent attributes, not the relative ones. Thus Jesus Christ as a human being was not [all-powerful,] ever-present, all-knowing, but he did possess the truth, the love, and holiness of God.[154]

Geß is not happy with this; he goes further. He says that in Christ God renounces his entire divine nature, that in Christ God entirely gives up being God, and only through the gradual self-awareness of Jesus returns to self-understanding as God.[155] Biedermann called this the consummate kenosis of the mind,[156] of which nobody could make any sense.

None of [these] attempts[157] succeeded. First of all, they diminish the divinity of Jesus by having only a part of him become human through God becoming human. But everything depends on the whole of God, the Omnipotent and Glorious One, being the one who becomes human and who comes to meet us in Jesus. This is one of the first statements in theology—that wherever God is, God is wholly there. Second, they do not make the humanity of Jesus understandable. They fill it out with some divine characteristics, making it the form of a demigod living on earth. The kenosis doctrine tries to play down the divine nature. The divine and human [natures] are attuned to each other in such a way as to make them fit [each other]. A concept of the divine and a concept of the human are worked out and put together in such a way that they cannot get away from each other. They must match without the slightest unevenness. If the smallest detail is not right, the whole point is missed.

This whole attempt[158] misses the point, in its very conception, for the following reasons:

(a) If we compare the results it obtains with the Chalcedonian formula, we see that the attempt has again been made to evade the contradictory, [mutually] exclusive opposites, and to try and even them out. These theologians thought they could define *in abstracto* the divine and human 336
natures in such a way that they had to fit into each other. This would simplify the problem. The recognition of the real Jesus Christ was turned into a construction.

[154.] Cf. Thomasius, "Die Menschwerdung als Selbstbeschränkung des Sohnes Gottes," in *Christi Person und Werk*, 1:409–45.

[155.] Cf. Geß, "Die Entherrlichung des Logos" (344–66) and "Die Entwicklung des Sohnes auf Erden" (367–99), in *Das Dogma von Christi Person und Werk*.

[156.] Cf. Biedermann, *Christliche Dogmatik*, 232–33.

[157.] [That is, at clarification.—LR]

[158.] [At explanation.—LR]

(b) The doctrine of kenosis is, for Lutheran dogmatics, a necessary complement to the *genus majestaticum*, with which the kenotic theologians juxtapose a *genus tapeinoticum*.[159] This amounts straightaway to a rejection of the doctrine of the two natures altogether, since it goes beyond the negative definitions at which the Chalcedonian formula had arrived. Here we have a construction of the affirmation of Christ, and not the unvarnished assertion of the "who." Here the question is the "how." The Chalcedonian formula is an answer to the "how" question, but it is an answer in which the "how" question has already been surmounted. In the Chalcedonian formulation, the doctrine of the two natures has itself been surmounted. We must carry on in this Chalcedonian sense. This can only happen when we have overcome our way of thinking about the divinity and humanity of Christ as objects that are before us, when our thinking does not begin with the two natures in isolation, but rather with the fact that Jesus Christ is God. The *is* may not be interpreted any further. It has been established by God and is therefore the premise for all our thinking and not subject to any further constructions.

Since the Chalcedonian formula, we can no longer say, how shall we think about the difference of the two natures and the unity of the person? but rather: who is this human being who is said to be God?

4. The Modalist and the Subordinationist Heresies

Here we are dealing with assertions about the person of Jesus Christ as that of the God who became human in his sonship to God, in his *homoousia*. If we could not speak of the *homoousia*, none of what we have said up to now would make any sense.

The concept of the ὁμοουσία has gone through various transforma-
337 tions. Here ὁμοουσία means not similarity of substance but rather identity of substance.[160] Why is it necessary to assert this? Because this is the only way to maintain the biblical witness to the revelation of God in Jesus Christ, because this is the only way we can speak of revelation. Revelation presupposes that the God revealed to us is identical with God himself; otherwise we would have not a revelation of God but only an appearance or an idea. So, to say that Christ became a human being compels us to say that Christ is identical with God in substance. Any attempt to depart from

[159.] "Of the sort that refers to lowliness."

[160.] The concept of ὁμοουσία was imposed at the Council of Nicaea (325 CE), although at first there was no uniform interpretation of it in the theology of the Eastern Church. [See Wiles, *Archetypal Heresy: Arianism through the Centuries*—LR]; Loofs, "Arianismus," esp. 33; and for more recent research, Ritter, "Arianismus," 704–11.

this toward a ὁμοιούσιος[161] goes straight in the direction of the Arian ἀνόμοιος.[162]

The subordinationists were concerned with preserving the unity and monarchy of God. These would be destroyed if a second God had to be accepted. Therefore Jesus had to be thought of as ἀνόμοιος, dissimilar to God, or at most as ὁμο[ιούσιος], like God. This seems to be the only way to preserve the unity of God, though certainly a unity at the expense of revelation, since we can only speak of revelation when we are talking about a human being of the same substance as God. Then this would not be a revelation in the decision about my life that is being made. It is an either-or question: the unity of God or revelation.

This puts before us the profound error of any subordinationist Christology. For this is precisely not the way to preserve the unity of God; rather, it breaches it. If Christ is understood as a human being who is exalted to the rank of God, who in his substance is not God but human and nevertheless is revered as God, if there is a demigod standing between God and humankind, this demigod totally contests the unity of God. It opens the door wide to polytheism. Modern Arianism has revered Christ as a genius or a hero and thereby breaches the content of the revelation.

A clear attempt to think of the unity of Christ and revelation together is 338
what we have in modalism.

The modalists. For the modalists, Christ is the πρόσωπον of God, that is, the form in which God appears. The question for us is, does this take the concept of revelation seriously? The concepts of revelation and monotheism represent a challenge each to the other. As God's revelation, Christ is either identical in substance [to the Father], or revelation gets thrown out along with monotheism. Both are wrong, Christ as πρόσωπον and as the adoptionist theory. The particularity of Christ's person is that he is God's revelation; it is identity of substance between the Son and the Father. Two natures—one person; two states [Stände]—one God-human; two divine persons—Father and Son, and yet one God.

5. What Has Been Gained from Critical Christology

We should distinguish between the [following] boundaries drawn against the false Jesus Christ. On the one hand, limits against false theological content; on the other, against inappropriate ways of thinking.

[161.] "Similar in substance."

[162.] Refers to Arius's assertion that the Logos was in every way unlike the *ousia* of the Father.

Those characterized as false theological content are those that attempt to assert [something] about Jesus Christ with unambiguous directness. Whoever, for the sake of Jesus's full humanity, sees Christ's divinity only as an ultimate, virtuoso human achievement is condemned as an Ebionite. Whoever speaks of the unity of Jesus Christ's person without speaking of its being God-human is rejected as a Monophysite or a Nestorian. The point of critical theology is to indicate the limits of every assertion as [they are found] in the actual reality of Jesus Christ.

What we have here is a particular way of thinking within which theological thinking takes place. All the thinking of the early church was based on the fundamental concept of nature. Liberal theologians say that it was the introduction of the concept of nature that has corrupted all of dog-
339 matics.[163] But it must be said in opposition that nothing is further from being a product of Greek thinking than the Chalcedonian formula. In the early church οὐσία is not to be thought of as the antithesis of nature and ethos. οὐσία really means here the essence of God, what God is all about, the entirety of God. The error of the *ousia* concept lies not in the twisting of the moral understanding into a physical understanding but rather in that it speaks of the nature [Wesen] of God and human nature in the theoretical manner of an onlooker, as if these were two material things, normally distinguished from each other, which only come together in Jesus Christ. But the relation between God and human being should be understood never as the relation between two things but [only as that] between two persons. Nothing can be known about [either] God or human being, until God has become a human being in Jesus Christ.

The advantage of the *ousia* concept, over against the dynamic understanding [of the Logos] (as in Paul of Samosata), rests in the fact that the nature concept understands salvation straightaway as universal. Consequently, the reality of salvation can be spoken of differently from the way it is conceived if nature itself is seen as deified. The dynamic view also assumes two separate natures. It *constructs* the God-human, rather than letting the fact of the God-human stand as the presupposition. And letting this stand is precisely the result that Christology achieves [in the Chalcedonian formula]! The forms of thinking shaped by materiality are rejected. Critical

[163.] According to Pfeiffer's notes, Bonhoeffer mentioned Albrecht Ritschl here. Emil Brunner also protested against the "modern interpretation of the dogma of the divine nature of Christ" (Brunner, *Mediator*, 249–65). He meant the "modern conception of this dogma introduced by Ritschl and Harnack" (249), which he then criticized almost entirely with reference to Harnack.

theology does not admit them, in that it points to the fact itself. Only at this point do we begin to know who God is.

What has been gained from critical theology can be summed up in three thoughts:

(1) It has gone beyond the one unambiguous positive assertion about Jesus Christ; instead it has opened this assertion into two that stand over against each other (in the Chalcedonian formula).

(2) It has overcome material thinking in Christology; this has been overcome in an immanent sense, in that material thinking has come up against 340
its own limitations. Material thinking reaches its limit at the point where it has to acknowledge that the opposite, contradictory assertion is just as necessary as its own assertion. When this limitation is acknowledged, then there is space for that which is actually, factually true.

(3) It has gone beyond the "how" question. This has been overcome in an immanent sense, since the "how" question subverts itself. The result of critical theology is the recognition that this "how" of relationship is impossible to think through.

How can we now construct a positive Christology on the foundation of this critical Christology?

III. Positive Christology

1. The One Who Became Human [der Menschgewordene]

Who is this God? He is the God who became human as we became human. He is completely human.[164] Nothing human is foreign to him.[165] The human being that I am is what Jesus Christ was also. We say of this human being, Jesus Christ, that he is God. This does not mean that we already knew beforehand who God is. It also does not mean that the assertion that this human being is God adds something onto his being human. God and human are not thought of together through a single concept of nature. The assertion that this human being is God means something else altogether. This person's being God is not something added onto the being human of Jesus Christ. It is not a continuum, into which Jesus Christ just manages to extend himself, but rather this assertion that this person is God *is the vertical Word from above* that neither takes anything away from nor adds anything to

[164.] Gadow adds: "Christ, too, had his own human hypostasis, his existence as a human being." According to Zimmermann and Sperling, Bonhoeffer also expressed here his opposition to the doctrine of enhypostasia (Sperling: "Protest against any teaching of enhypostasia").

[165.] [An allusion to the famous saying from Terence: "Nihil humanum mihi alienum," "nothing human is alien to me."—LR]

Jesus Christ, but rather qualifies this entire human being as God. *It is God's*
341 *judgment about this human being!* It is God's Word, which takes this human being Jesus Christ and qualifies him as God. But the essential difference [between him and all other human beings] is that the Word of God that comes from above is at the same time right here in Jesus Christ himself. Because Jesus is himself God's judgment about him; he points both to himself and to God.

This does away conclusively with the attempt to unite two isolated existing realities. We believe that Jesus the human being is God, and that he is so as *the* human being, not in spite of his humanity or beyond his humanity. It is Jesus Christ the human being who ignites faith. Jesus Christ is God, not in a divine nature, but rather God in our faith alone, thus no longer in a way that we can touch and describe. If we are to describe Jesus as God, we would not speak of his being all-powerful or all-knowing; we would speak of his birth in a manger and of his cross. There is no "divine nature" as all-powerful and ever-present.

We have the reports of Jesus's birth and of his baptism side by side. [In the][166] birth narrative, the focus is on Jesus himself; in the baptism story, the focus is on the Holy Spirit coming from God. The difficulty in thinking of both these stories together, of birth and baptism, is in the doctrine of the two natures. If we leave that out, then we are speaking in the one instance of the Word of God being in Christ, and in the other of the coming down of the Word of God spoken over Christ. The child in the manger is God.[167] The naming of Jesus as God's son at his baptism is the confirmation of the earlier event. If we speak of the human being Jesus Christ as we speak of God, we should not speak of him as representing an idea of God, that is, in his attributes as all-knowing and all-powerful, but rather speak of his weakness and manger.

We should speak not of God becoming human [das Menschwerden] but of the God who became human [der Menschgewordene], for the former is a "how" question, to be found in the old doctrine of the virgin birth. The
342 biblical witness is uncertain with regard to the virgin birth. If the biblical witness really [gave] this as a fact, the dogmatic lack of clarity about it would have nothing to say. The doctrine of the virgin birth is supposed to express how God becomes human [Menschwerdung]. But does it not result

[166.] The text has "The."

[167.] According to Gadow and others, Bonhoeffer referred here to the verse "A manger choosing for a throne / While worlds on worlds are yours alone" in Luther's Christmas hymn "All Praise to You, Eternal Lord" ("Gelobet seist Du, Jesu Christ"), *Lutheran Book of Worship*, no. 48.

in the decisive point being missed, that Jesus became like us?[168] This question remains open, because the Bible leaves it open.

God who became human is the God of glory; God glorifies himself in the human [Gott verherrlicht sich im Menschen]. This is the ultimate mystery of the Trinity. From "now unto eternity,"[169] God regards himself as the God who became human. God's self-glorification in the human is thus the glorification of the human, which shall have eternal life with God the Three in One. Therefore, it is not right to see God's becoming human as judgment upon humankind. God remains human even after the judgment. God's becoming human is God's message about the glorification of God, who honors himself by being in human form.

God's becoming human means first of all simply the revelation of the Creator through the creature. It is wrong to derive the God's becoming human from an idea, such as the idea of the Trinity.[170] When we speak of God's becoming human [Menschwerdung Gottes] as glorifying God, we are not talking about a speculative idea of God. Every idea of God on which the doctrine of God's becoming human [die Lehre von der Menschwerdung] could be speculatively based is impossible, because the relationship of the Creator to the creature is conceived [as] a necessity.

Why does that sound so improbable and strange to us? Because God's becoming human in Jesus Christ does not visibly glorify God; because God who became human is the Crucified One.

2. The Humiliated and Exalted One 343

To speak of Jesus's being humiliated is not to put any limit on his divinity. It is a question put to Jesus as a human being, about his way of existing as a human being. To be humiliated does not mean to be *more* human and *less* God, and to be exalted does not mean to be *more* God and *less* human. Both in being humiliated and in being exalted, Jesus remains wholly human and wholly God. The assertion that he is God must be made in the same way in his being humiliated as in his being exalted. In his death, Jesus does not reveal any of his divine attributes. To the contrary, he is a dying human

[168.] Dudzus noted, in part: "We [should] speak not of God becoming human [Menschwerdung], because that focuses on the 'how,' but rather of the God who became human [Menschgewordene], the 'who' question. The 'how' question is behind the hypothesis of the virgin birth."

[169.] Ps. 41:14 [13] et passim. [Bonhoeffer's text differs from the NRSV translation, which is "from everlasting to everlasting."—LR]

[170.] This takes issue with Hegel (cf. *Philosophy of History*, 412–14, and *Lectures on the Philosophy of Religion*, 1:77).

being, despairing of God. And of this one we say, this is God. God is not concealed in Christ as a human being but rather is revealed as God-human. But this God-human is veiled in his existence as the Humiliated One. In Christ's being humiliated, we are talking about neither divinity nor humanity, but rather the ὁμοίωμα σαρκός.[171] For this is cast off when he is exalted, but his humanity remains.

The question now is who is the God-human who is humiliated? The doctrine of God who became human [Menschwerdung] and the humiliation of Christ must be kept radically separate. Taking on the humiliated way of life is an act of the God-human. It is not to be separated in time from the act of having become human, but rather the God-human of history is always, already, the God-human who is humiliated, from the manger to the cross.

How is Jesus's particular way of existing as the Humiliated One expressed? In that he has taken on sinful flesh. The conditions for his humiliation are set by the curse, the fall of Adam. In being humiliated, Christ, the God-human, enters of his own free will into the world of sin and death. He enters there in such a way as to conceal himself [there], so that he is no longer recognizable visibly as the God-human. He comes among us humans not in μορφὴ θεοῦ[172] but rather incognito, as a beggar among beggars, an outcast among outcasts; he comes among sinners as the one without sin, but also as a sinner among sinners. This is the central problem for all Christology.

344 The doctrine that Jesus was without sin is not just one word [logos], one doctrine [among others], but rather the central point that decides everything. The question is this: Did Jesus, as the God-human who is humiliated, enter wholly into human sin? Was he a human being like us, with our sinfulness? If he was not, then did he really become human at all? Can he help us human beings at all? And if he was as we are, in the same peril in which we are, how can he help us escape that peril?

What we need to understand is what is meant by the ὁμοίωμα σαρκός. This is the true image of the human σάρξ. His σάρξ is our σάρξ. What is essential about our σάρξ is our vulnerability to temptation, our self-will. Christ took on all the mortifying aspects of being human; otherwise he could not help us in our σάρξ. Then how was he different from us? The first answer is, not at all. He is a human like us and is tempted as we are, even

[171.] "Fleshly form", or "likeness of flesh". [These paragraphs develop the theme of the humiliation of Christ, frequently using the Greek phrase *homoioma sarkos,* which Bonhoeffer previously introduced; see p. 313 and ed. note. 34. Here the shorthand version seems clearly to indicate the full phrase from Rom. 8:3, "likeness of sinful flesh." Bonhoeffer underscores that Christ exists as the Humiliated One "in that he has taken on sinful flesh."—LR]

[172.] "Godly form."

more than we are. In his σάρξ too there was a law, which was opposed to the will of God.[173] It was a constant struggle for him. He also did things that appeared to be sins. He gave a hard answer to his mother in the temple; he evaded his opponents' questions; he called for resistance against the ruling castes of the pious and of people. In people's eyes, he must have looked like a sinner. So he entered in, to the extent of being unrecognizable.

But what is all-important is that *he* was the One who entered therein, who did this and that, which the onlookers in his life could only reckon as transgressions. And because this *One* is Christ, these assertions must be seen in another light. It is the true human σάρξ that he bears; that is why the σάρξ is stripped of its rights. He is afraid like us; he is tempted as we are and thus is under the same condemnation as we are. But because *this One* is subject to the same condemnation as we, therefore we are saved. As *the One* who he is, Jesus was afraid like us. On this basis, of *the One* who he is, we must dare to make and to endure all the most scandalous assertions about this God-human who has been humiliated.

For our sake [God] made him to be sin.[174] Christ is the very *peccator pessimus*.[175] Luther even said that Christ was a robber, murderer, and adulterer like ourselves, because he carries our sins. But *he* is at the same time the One who is without sin, the Holy One, the Eternal, the Lord, the Son of the Father.[176]

We cannot speak of balancing these two assertions against each other, as if it were yet possible to tear Jesus, in his humiliated state, from the ὁμοίωμα 345
σαρκός. He lets the law have its way and takes from it and upon himself sin and the power of sin. He is in the ὁμοίωμα σαρκός, yet without sin, tempted as we are in the ὁμοίωμα σαρκός, yet without sin. The statement about his being without sin goes astray if it is focused on the deeds of Jesus that have been reported to us. These actions took place within the ὁμοίωμα σαρκός. We can and should see in them the ambiguity of good and evil. If someone prefers to remain incognito, it is an offense to say, "But I saw you right away." Therefore we should not base his being without sin on his actions. The statement about Jesus being without sin in his actions is not a judgment within a moral system but rather a recognition, through the eyes of faith, of the One who does these things, the One who is without sin for all eternity.

[173.] [An allusion to Rom. 7:23.—LR]
[174.] 2 Cor. 5:21.
[175.] "Worst sinner."
[176.] See, for example, *Operationes in psalmos* (1519–21) (*WA* 5:602, 21–35).

The statement about Jesus being without sin is not a moral pronouncement but rather an insight of faith.

The God-human who is humiliated is the stumbling block to the pious human being and to the human being, period. What is scandalous is the lack of historical clarity of this God-human. The most incomprehensible thing for the pious is this human being's claim to be not only a believer in God but the Son of God. Hence the authority with which Jesus says, "But I say to you,"[177] and, "Your sins are forgiven."[178] If Jesus's human nature had been deified, people would have accepted this claim. If he had done signs and wonders on demand, people would have believed him. But when it comes down to cases, he withdraws. That creates a stumbling block. But everything depends on the fact that he did so. If he had replied to the question, are you the Christ? by doing a miracle, then the statement that he became a human being like us would no longer be true, since at the decisive moment an exception would have been made. That is why Christ's incognito had to become even more impenetrable, the more urgently people asked whether he were the Christ.

This means that the form of the stumbling block is the form that makes possible all our faith in Christ. That is, Christ in the form of stumbling block is in the form of *Christus pro nobis.* Because Jesus wants to be our freedom, he must first become a stumbling block for us before he can be our
346 salvation. Only by being humiliated can Christ become *pro nobis.* If he had documented himself by performing miracles, we would indeed believe, but then Christ would not be our salvation, because that would not be faith in God become human but only recognition [of a supposedly supernatural event]. But that is not faith. Faith exists when I yield myself to God, [to the extent that] I will wager my life on God's Word, even and especially there where it goes against all visible appearances. Only when I give up having visible confirmation do I believe in God. The only guarantee that faith can bear is the Word of God itself.

Christus pro nobis is the Christ who reconciles me with God, and that is only possible through this stumbling block and through faith. The stumbling block, which we accept, is that our faith is continually tested. But this teaches us to pay attention to the Word. Faith comes through temptation.

From this point, how are we to understand that Jesus performed miracles? Didn't that jeopardize his incognito? Liberalism replies that miracles are

[177.] As in Matt. 5:22.
[178.] As in Matt. 9:2.

ghost stories of their time.[179] We reply that the miracles of Jesus do not jeopardize his incognito. The ancient religious world was full of miracles. That is to say, the realm of miracles is not identical with God's realm. The realm of miracles is only superior to that of humankind. The category to which miracles belong is not that of God but rather that of magic. When Jesus performed miracles, he was preserving his incognito in a world of magic. Doing miracles did not serve to authenticate him either; to the contrary, people thought his power was demonic.

The believing community, however, saw in him that the kingdom was near. That still did not lift his incognito for those who did not believe. The unbeliever speaks of magic and means the world in its ambiguity. The believer speaks of the kingdom of God. Our age, which does not believe in magic, is inclined to consider miracles as an unambiguous, visible manifestation of the divine. The miraculous itself is still ambiguous and needs 347
interpretation. It can be interpreted through faith or through lack of faith. The unbeliever does not see God in the miraculous; only the believer does so. Faith that cleaves to the incognito sees, in these miracles, something of the glory of God. "We have seen his glory."[180] Only *in faith* is there seeing.

The Humiliated One is *pro nobis* only as the Exalted One. Only in seeing him as the Risen One, the Exalted One, do we know this incognito God-human. We have the One who was born as a baby as the Ever-Present One, the One laden with sin as the One without sin. So the converse must also be true: we can have the Exalted One only as the Crucified One. The resurrection of Christ does not get us around the stumbling block. Even the Risen One remains the stumbling block for us. If it were not so, he would not be for us. Jesus's resurrection does not jeopardize the incognito. We only believe in the resurrection of Jesus if we do not take away Jesus Christ as the stumbling block. Only the disciples see the Son of God. They see with the eyes of blind faith, because as believers who see nothing they become, as such, those who see, in their belief in God's glory.

Between the humiliation and the exaltation of Christ lies the historical fact of the empty grave. This is one of the most decisive elements in Christology. What does the story of the empty grave mean before the report of the resurrection? If the grave is really empty, then it is the visible authentication of the resurrection. If it is not empty, then Christ was not resurrected. It

[179.] By this assertion, Bonhoeffer could mean the outright criticism of the miracles by rationalism and the Enlightenment, but not liberal theology, which never gave up the concept of miracles (see Seeberg, "Wunder"; and Herrmann, *Offenbarung und Wunder*).

[180.] John 1:14.

seems as though our "resurrection faith" is bound up with the story of the empty grave. If the grave were not empty, we would not have our faith.

This is the final stumbling block, which we have to accept as believers in Christ. Either way, there is a stumbling block. The impossible possibility that the grave was empty is the stumbling block of faith. The affirmation of the empty grave is also a stumbling block. Who is going to prove to us that the disciples did not find Jesus's body? Here once again we cannot get around the stumbling block. To the very end, even through the empty
348 grave, Jesus remains incognito, in the form of a stumbling block. Jesus does not emerge from his incognito, not even as the Risen One. He will not lay it aside until he comes again, for the Last Judgment. Then he will come visibly as the Eternal, the God who became human, in divine power and glory.

With the humiliated Christ, his church must also be humiliated. It cannot seek any visible authentication of its nature, as long as Christ has renounced doing so for himself. Nor may it, as a humiliated church, look upon itself with vain self-satisfaction, as though being humiliated were the visible proof that Christ is with it. There is no law here, and the humiliation of Christ is not a principle for the church to follow but rather a fact. Even the church can be high, and it can be lowly, if only both conditions occur for the sake of Christ. It is not good for the church to hasten to proclaim its lowliness. But it is not good either for the church to hasten to proclaim its greatness and power; it is only good for the church to seek forgiveness for its sins.

Even the church, as the presence of Jesus Christ—God who became human, was humiliated, resurrected, and exalted—must receive the will of God every day anew from Christ. For the church, too, Christ becomes, every day anew, an offense to its own desires and hopes. The church must stumble every day anew over the sentence, "You will all become deserters because of me,"[181] and it must hold on to the promise, "Blessed is anyone who takes no offense at me."[182]

[181.] Matt. 26:31.
[182.] Matt. 11:6.

13. Essay: "The Church and the Jewish Question"[1] 349

The Church and the Jewish Question

Luther, 1546: "We would still show them the Christian doctrine and ask them to convert and accept the Lord whom they should by rights have honored before we did. . . . When they repent, leave their usury, and accept Christ, we would gladly regard them as our brothers."[2]

Luther, 1523: "If the apostles, who also were Jews, had dealt with us Gentiles as we Gentiles deal with the Jews, there would never have been a Christian among the Gentiles. Since they dealt with us Gentiles in such brotherly fashion, we in our turn ought to treat the Jews in a brotherly manner in order that we might convert some of them. For even we ourselves are not yet all very far along, not to speak of having arrived.[3] . . . But when we are trying only to drive them by force . . . how can we expect to work any good among them? Again, when we forbid them to labor and do business and

[1.] From *Der Vormarsch* 3, no. 6 (June 1933): 171–76 (the quotes from Luther at the beginning and end may have been inserted by the editor [they are not in the three drafts written by Bonhoeffer—LR]). Previously published in *GS* 2:44–53. See also the *Niederdeutsche Kirchenzeitung* 3, no. 13 (July 1, 1933) (reprint without the closing quote from Luther). The published manuscript has not been preserved. The carbon copy found in *NL*, A 37,3a (without the quotes from Luther at the beginning and end of the published version), with handwritten additions and corrections (see also *NL*, A 37,3b; carbon copy without these), is apparently an earlier, shorter version, but which does include Bonhoeffer's preliminary versions without significant changes, as follows: for part I and the first paragraph of part II, a handwritten manuscript (*NL*, A 37,2) that is obviously a response to the beginning of discrimination against the Jewish population, especially the April 17, 1933, Law for Reconstitution of the Civil Service, which includes the so-called Aryan paragraph (*RGBl*, pt. 1, 175); for part II, a carbon copy with six theses (*NL*, A 37,1, with handwritten corrections and a longer handwritten addition at the end), which Bonhoeffer had already prepared for discussion in the Berlin pastors' group (see *DB-ER*, 273) in late March/early April 1933. For details on the composition, content, and controversies in interpretation of this essay, see Smid, *Deutscher Protestantismus und Judentum*, 419–85. [The editors call the reader's attention both to the differences between Bonhoeffer's drafts of this essay and the published version, and to some significant corrections made here to previous English translations. At present it is impossible to determine the editorial history of the published essay, particularly whether the changes were suggested by Bonhoeffer or someone else; given the extensive attention this essay receives, however, this would be a worthwhile research project. Regarding the differences, cf. ed. notes 9, 12, 13, 15, 18, 19, 23, 25, 26, 27, and 28. The editors thank Professor Peter Hoffmann for his very helpful suggestions regarding the translation.—LR]

[2.] Martin Luther, *Eine Vermahnung wider die Juden* (1546), *WA* 51:195, 25–27. [This essay was not translated in the English *Luther's Works* edition.—LR]

[3.] Luther, "That Jesus Was Born a Jew," *LW* 45:200–201.

have any human fellowship with us, thereby driving them into usury, how is that supposed to make them better?"[4]

350 The fact, unique in history, that the Jew is subjected to special laws by the state, solely on the basis of his race and regardless of the religion to which he adheres, presents theologians with two new problems, which must be dealt with separately. How does the church judge this action by the state, and what is the church called upon to do about it? What are the consequences for the church's position toward the baptized Jews in its congregations? Both these questions can only be answered on the basis of a right concept of the church.

I.[5]

There is no doubt that the church of the Reformation is not encouraged to get involved directly in specific political actions of the state. The church has neither to praise nor to censure the laws of the state. Instead, it has to affirm the state as God's order of preservation [Erhaltungsordnung][6] in this godless world. It should recognize and understand the state's creation of order—whether good or bad from a humanitarian perspective—as

[4.] Ibid., 229.

[5.] In the carbon copy (*NL*, 37, 3a) there is a handwritten note here: "*Ahasver peregrinus*" (wandering Ahasuerus). According to a legend dated back to the early seventeenth century, the shoemaker Ahasuerus was condemned to wander eternally because he had driven Jesus away from the wall of his house when Jesus, exhausted by carrying the cross, leaned against it. This legend rendered Ahasuerus as a symbolic figure for the fate of the Jewish people, homeless after the crucifixion (cf. Liefmann, "Die Legende vom Antichrist"). [As Liefmann's essay on this legend suggests, the "wandering Jew" story became a central motif in the anti-Jewish teachings that converged with anti-Semitism.—LR]

[6.] [Bonhoeffer here uses "order of preservation" in explicit contrast to "order of creation." As in *Creation and Fall,* given as lectures in the winter semester of 1932–33, he is countering natural theology and its misuse, which was to bolster the Nazi platform of "blood and soil." "Orders of creation" was being used by conservative Lutheran theologians and the German Christians in a natural theology that yielded autonomous orders, such as the state and family, apart from the revelation of God in Jesus Christ. Paul Althaus, for example, published a pamphlet, *Theologie der Ordnungen,* which argued that the German nation, or *Volk,* belonged to God's ordering of creation. "Orders of preservation," in contrast, removes the ordering of the world understood apart from Jesus Christ and locates it in the activity of God to preserve the world from chaos, in anticipation of its end, its redemption in Jesus Christ. God's ordering is thus understood eschatologically, not from its past or present "in nature." For an extensive discussion of the use of "orders of creation" at this time, see Ericksen, *Theologians under Hitler,* 98–104. See also the editor's introduction to *DBWE* 3, 11–12, for Bonhoeffer's explicit choice of "orders of preservation" as the alternative.—LR]

grounded in God's desire for preservation in the midst of the world's chaotic godlessness. This judgment by the church on what the state does stands quite apart from any moralizing and is to be distinguished from every sort of humanitarianism, because of the radical separation between the place of the gospel and the place of the law. The actions of the state[7] remain free from interference by the church. This is not a schoolmaster-like or peevish objection on the part of the church. History is made not by the church but rather by the state. But it is certainly only the church, which bears witness to God's entering into history, that knows what history is and therefore what the state is. And precisely out of this knowledge the church alone bears wit-
ness to God's *breaking into* history through Christ and lets the state go on 351
making history. Without doubt one of the historical problems that must be dealt with by our state is the Jewish question, and without doubt the state is entitled to strike new paths in doing so. It remains for the humanitarian associations and individual Christian men who see themselves called to do so,[8] to make the state aware of the moral aspect of the measures it takes in this regard, that is, should the occasion arise, to accuse the state of offenses against morality. Every strong state needs such associations and such individual personages and will foster them with a certain amount of reserved encouragement. Insight into the finer art of statecraft will tell the state how to make use of this advice in a relative sense. In the same way, however, a church that is regarded essentially as a cultural function of the state will interfere in the work of the state with advice of this kind, and all the more wherever the state incorporates the church more substantially, that is, by relegating essentially moral and educational duties to it.

But the true church of Christ, which lives by the gospel alone and knows the nature of state actions, will never interfere in the functioning of the state in this way, by criticizing its history-making actions from the standpoint of any sort of, say, humanitarian ideal. The church knows about the essential necessity for the use of force in this world, and it knows about the "moral" injustice that is necessarily involved in the use of force in certain concrete state actions. The church cannot primarily take *direct* political action, since it does not presume to know how things should go historically. Even on the Jewish question today, the church cannot contradict the state *directly* and demand that it take any particular different course of action. But that does not mean that the church stands aside, indifferent to what

[7.] In the handwritten version (*NL*, A 37,2), this is followed by "in all circumstances."

[8.] The carbon copy (*NL*, A 37, 3a) has "people," corrected by hand to read "men."

political action is taken. Instead, it can and must, precisely because it does not moralize about individual cases, keep asking the government whether its actions can be justified as *legitimate state* actions, that is, actions that create law and order, not lack of rights and disorder.[9] It will be called
352 upon to put this question as strongly as possible wherever the state seems endangered precisely in its *character as the state* [Staatlichkeit], that is, in its function of creating law and order by force. The church will have to put this question with the utmost clarity today in the matter of the Jewish question. This does not mean interfering in the state's responsibility for its actions; on the contrary, it is thrusting the entire burden of responsibility upon the state itself for the actions proper to it. Thus the church spares the state any moralizing reproach, referring it instead to the function ordained to it by the One who sustains the world. As long as the state acts in such a way as to create law and order—even if it means new laws and a new order—the church of the Creator, Reconciler, and Redeemer cannot oppose it through direct political action. Of course it cannot prevent individual Christians, who know that they are called to do so in certain cases, from accusing the state of "inhumanity"; but as church it will only ask whether or not the state is creating law and order. In doing so the church will, of course, see the state as limited in two ways. Either *too little* law and order or *too much* law and order compels the church to speak. There is too little law and order wherever a group of people is deprived of its rights; although in concrete cases it will always be extraordinarily difficult to distinguish actual deprivation of rights from a formally permitted minimum of rights. Even under serfdom a minimum of law and order was preserved, and yet if serfdom were reintroduced now it would represent deprivation of rights. It is remarkable that Christian churches tolerated serfdom for eighteen hundred years, and

[9.] [Here and in the following passages *DBWE* general editor Victoria Barnett has recommended a significant change to previous translations of this essay. The German word *Recht* can be translated as "justice," "law," or "rights," depending on the context. But the standard translation of *Rechtlos* and *Rechtlosigkeit* is "without rights" or "deprivation of rights." Only with regard to a state (*ein rechtloser Staat*) would *rechtlos* be translated as "lawless" or a "lack of law and order"—the implication being that this is a state without justice. This nuance is crucial to following Bonhoeffer's argument throughout this essay, for he is arguing that a state that deprives citizens of their rights (as was the case in the era of serfdom, which he subsequently gives as an illustration) is "lawless" in its very essence because it is exercising its God-given authority in an illegitimate manner, and hence (as he argues in the paragraphs that follow) the church may be called upon to challenge the legitimacy of that state. The German editor of this volume Ernst-Albert Scharffenorth concurs that this is the correct translation.—LR]

only in an era when the Christian substance of the church could at least be called into question were new rights created, with the help of the churches (but not significantly or even solely due to their help).[10] Nevertheless, for the church today, a step backward in this direction would be the expression 353
of a lawless state. From this we may conclude that the concept of rights is subject to historical transformations, which has the effect of affirming the state's proper right to make history. It is not the church but rather the state that makes and changes laws. At the other extreme from too little law and order, there can be too much law and order. This would mean the state developing its use of force to such a degree as to rob the Christian faith of its right to proclaim its message. (This does not apply to restriction of free conscience—that would be the humanitarian version, which is an illusion, since every state in its life impinges on the so-called free conscience.) This would be a grotesque situation, since it is from the Christian proclamation and faith that the state receives its own rights, so that it would be dethroning itself. The church must repudiate such an encroachment by the state authorities, precisely because it knows better about the state and the limits of its actions. A state that threatens the proclamation of the Christian message negates itself. There are thus three possibilities for action that the church can take vis-à-vis the state: *first* (as we have said), questioning the state as to the legitimate state character of its actions, that is, making the state responsible for what it does. *Second* is service to the victims of the state's actions. The church has an unconditional obligation toward the victims of any societal order, even if they do not belong to the Christian community. "Let us work for the good of all."[11] These are both ways in which the church, in its freedom, conducts itself in the interest of a free state. In times when the laws are changing, the church may under no circumstances neglect either of these duties. The *third* possibility is not just to bind up the wounds of the victims beneath the wheel but to seize the wheel itself.[12]

[10.] As the mention of serfdom shows, Bonhoeffer was referring here in the first place to the liberation of German peasants from their masters toward the end of the eighteenth century. Admittedly, churches did not participate actively in this change in the German states, whereas the abolition of slavery in the United States can be traced [in part] to criticism by Quakers and Methodists, among others. Cf. Bonhoeffer's memorandum on the "social gospel" (2/4).

[11.] Gal. 6:10.

[12.] [This is the famous phrase "dem Rad selbst in die Speichen zu fallen," often translated as "to fall within the spokes of the wheel." As German editor Ernst-Albert Scharffenorth notes, however, Bonhoeffer and his readers would have understood this as

Such an action would be direct[13] political action on the part of the church.
354 This is only possible and called for if the church sees the state to be failing in its function of creating law and order, that is, if the church perceives that the state, without any scruples, has created either too much or too little law and order. It must see in either eventuality a threat to the existence of the state and thus to its own existence as well. There would be too little if any one group of citizens is deprived of its rights. There would be too much in the case of an attack, coming from the state, on the nature of the church and its proclamation, such as the obligatory exclusion of baptized Jews from our Christian congregations or a ban on missions to the Jews. In such a case, the church would find itself in *statu confessionis*,[14] and the state would find itself in the act of self-negation. A state that incorporates a church that it has violated has lost its most loyal servant. But even this third kind of action by a church, which in a given case leads it into conflict with the existing state, is only the paradoxical expression of its ultimate recognition of the state, for the church itself is aware that it is here called upon to protect the state from itself and to preserve it. For the church today, the Jewish question poses the first two possibilities as challenges of the hour, which it has a duty to meet. The necessity for immediate political action by the church must,

---

the act of detaching a cart or wagon from the horse pulling it. In any case, the meaning clearly is to bring the apparatus of the unjust and illegitimate state to a halt. "To seize the wheel itself" is the English phrase; for this reason, we use that translation here.—LR]

[13.] This is the reading in the manuscript (*NL*, A 37, 2, p. 9); the published version has "indirect," taken from the *Niederdeutsche Kirchenzeitung* and *GS* 2:48. This error was pointed out by Ernst Feil in 1971 (*Theologie Bonhoeffers*, 264, ed. note 105. [The English translation of Feil, *Theology of Dietrich Bonhoeffer*, does not include this same footnote, but it does note the correction in endnote 37, pp. 223–24.—LR] The correction first appeared in Huber and Tödt, *Ethik im Ernstfall*, 245–50).

[14.] ["In *statu confessionis*" refers to a state of confessional protest in which such matters as church membership and rules are no longer matters of convenience and doctrinal indifference (*adiaphora*). Rather, they are matters in which the very "truth of the gospel and Christian freedom are at stake." The key passage in the Lutheran confessions that stands behind Bonhoeffer's reference is the following: "We believe, teach, and confess that in a time of persecution, when an unequivocal confession of the faith is demanded of us, we dare not yield to the opponents in such indifferent matters. . . . For in such a situation it is no longer indifferent matters that are at stake. The truth of the gospel and Christian freedom are at stake. The confirmation of open idolatry, as well as the protection of the weak in faith from offense, is at stake. In such matters we can make no concessions but must offer an unequivocal confession and suffer whatever God sends and permits the enemies of His Word to inflict on us" (Formula of Concord, Epitome, Article X/6, *Book of Concord*, 516).—LR]

however, be decided by an "evangelical council" as and when the occasion arises and hence cannot be casuistically construed beforehand.[15]

The measures of the state against Judaism [das Judentum], however, have for the church a very particular context. The church of Christ has never lost sight of the thought that the "chosen people," which hung the Redeemer of the world on the cross, must endure the curse of its action in long-drawn-out suffering. "The Jews are the most miserable people on earth. They are plagued everywhere, and scattered about all countries, having no certain resting place" (Luther, *Table Talk*).[16] But the history of suffering of this people that God loved and punished will end in the final homecoming of
the people Israel to its God. And this homecoming will take place in Israel's 355
conversion to Christ. "When the hour comes when this people, humbled and repentant, lets go of the sins of its fathers, to which it has been clinging with terrible obstinacy to this day, and begs for the blood of the Crucified One to come down to reconcile them, the world will be astonished at the wonders God has wrought! has wrought for this people! And the scoffing Philistines will be just so much filth in the street and dry straw on the rooftops. Then God will gather this people together out of all nations and bring it back to Canaan. O Israel, who is your equal? Blessed is the people whose God is the *Lord*!" (Menken, 1795).[17] The conversion of Israel is to be the end of its people's sufferings. From this perspective, the Christian church trembles at the sight of the people Israel's history, as God's own free, terrible way with God's own people. We know that no state in the world can deal with this enigmatic people, because God has not yet finished with it. Every new attempt to "solve" the "Jewish question" comes to grief because of the meaning of this people for salvation history, and yet such attempts have to be made again and again. The church's knowledge of the curse that weighs upon this people takes it far beyond any sort of cheap moralizing. Instead, it knows itself as the church that is unfaithful to its Lord over and over again, and that it shares in the humiliation that it sees in this outcast people, and full of hope it views those Israelites who have already come home, who have come to faith in the one true God in Christ, and it knows it has a bond with them as brothers and sisters. That brings us to the second question.

[15.] The paragraph that follows appeared only in the published version. [It is not in any of Bonhoeffer's three drafts of the essay.—LR]

[16.] See *WA*, Tischreden, 3:36, 16–19. English translation is from *Table Talk*, "Of the Jews: DCCCVIII," http://biblestudy.churches.net/CCEL/L/LUTHER/TABLE_TA/TABLE_45.HTM.

[17.] Menken, "Über Glück und Unglück der Gottlosen," in his *Schriften*, 7:97.

II.[18]

The church cannot allow the state to prescribe for it the way it treats its members. A baptized Jew is a member of our church. For the church, the Jewish question is therefore different from what it is for the state.[19]

356 From the point of view of Christ's church, Judaism is never a racial concept but rather a religious one. Rather than the biologically dubious entity of the Jewish race, it means the "people Israel." It is God's law that constitutes the "people" Israel; thus one can *become* a Jew by accepting the law. But in the racial sense one cannot become a Jew. At the time of the great Jewish missions to the Gentile world, there were various steps toward becoming a Jew (Schürer III 1909, pages 150ff.).[20] In the same way, being a Jewish Christian is a religious and not a racial concept. The Jewish Christian mission also extended to Gentile regions (see Paul's opponents in the Letter to the Galatians).[21] There were Gentile Jewish Christians and Jewish Gentile Christians.

From the point of view of Christ's church, therefore, Jewish Christians are not people of the Jewish race who have been baptized Christians, but rather *Jewish Christians* in the church's sense are those who see their belonging to the people of God, to the church of Christ, as *determined* by their observance of a divine law. Gentile Christians, on the other hand, see no other prerequisite for their belonging to the people of God, to the church of Christ, than being called to it by God, through God's Word in Christ.

This alone was the difference in understanding with regard to the appearance of Christ, to the gospel, which led to the first division in Christ's church into Gentile Christianity and Jewish Christianity (council of the apostles).[22] This division was understood by some as an unendurable heresy and by others as a schism that could be endured.

An analogous occurrence today would be a case in which a church group within the church of the Reformation made church membership dependent on observance of a divine law, for example, racial uniformity among the members of a congregation. By making this requirement, the people

---

[18.] The carbon copy (*NL*, A 37, 3a) has here a handwritten addition: "Modern Jewish Christianity."

[19.] [This paragraph is not in Bonhoeffer's drafts of this section. Both drafts begin with "From the point of view of Christ's church, Judaism is never a racial concept." The drafts also differ in that each paragraph is numbered.—LR]

[20.] Schürer, *Geschichte des jüdischen Volkes*, 3:150–88, esp. 172ff.

[21.] See Gal. 1–4, esp. 4:8–11 and 21–31.

[22.] See Acts 15:1-29 and Gal. 2:1–10.

concerned would become a type of Jewish Christian, regardless of whether they actually belong to the Jewish race or not. Let us then suppose that these Jewish Christians of the modern type *withdraw* from the Gentile Christian congregation and establish their own church community bound by laws. It 357
would, however, be ecclesiastically impossible for persons in this congregation who are racially Jewish then to be excluded, on the grounds that they spoil the claim to be Jewish Christian through the law. For that would mean claiming that a Gentile Christian congregation is Jewish Christian, a claim that the congregation would rightfully have to refuse.

To exclude persons who are racially Jewish from our ethnically German church would mean to make it into a church of the Jewish Christian type. Such exclusion is therefore not possible in the church.

Only the presence of congregations of foreign origin already in Germany, that is, French, English, and so on, allows us to conclude that there would be no ecclesiastical obstacle to Christians of Jewish origin coming together voluntarily to form their own congregation (as happened with the Jewish Christian Alliance in London in 1925).[23] But in no case may a Gentile Christian congregation whose members are of German descent be compelled to exclude Gentile Christian Jews who are already members in it, quite apart from the difficulty of proving that these Jews are not Germans (cf. Stöcker's thesis that Jews become Germans through baptism).[24] Such compulsory exclusion would always mean a genuine church schism, even if it is done as a purely corporate organizational measure, because it would make racial uniformity a church law to be fulfilled as a requirement for fellowship in the church. The church community *doing the excluding* would thus be constituting itself as a *Jewish Christian* community.[25]

[23.] The phrase in parentheses was added only in the published version. According to Otto von Harling, "Judenmission," 468–69, the "international Jewish Christian Alliance in London, 1925" was founded to "bring Jewish Christians together in Jewish Christian congregations without removing them from the context of the Jewish people."

[24.] This reference expanded in the carbon copy (*NL*, 37, 3a) in Bonhoeffer's handwriting. On Stoecker's thesis, see W. Frank, *Hofprediger Adolf Stoecker*, 102: "Even though he also reproached the Jews with being a nation within a nation, Stoecker as a Christian clergyman could not give up the standpoint that 'being reborn in the Spirit overcomes racial distinctions.'" [Stoecker was among the most prominent Lutheran anti-Semites of the late nineteenth century, and his writings were cited extensively in the Third Reich. —LR]

[25.] [This marks the conclusion of Bonhoeffer's first draft (*NL*, A 37, 1b). The second draft of this section includes the final paragraph that follows in Bonhoeffer's handwriting (*NL*, A 37, 1a) and additional handwritten comments in the margins.—LR]

358 The question here is not at all about whether our church members of German descent can support fellowship in the church with Jews. In reality, it is the duty of Christian proclamation to say: here, where Jew and German together stand under God's Word, is church; here it will be proven whether or not the church is still church. If someone feels unable to continue in church fellowship with Christians of Jewish origin, nothing can prevent him from leaving this church fellowship. But it must be made clear to him, with ultimate seriousness, that he is turning his back on the place where the church of Christ stands, and that with that he himself is bringing about the Jewish Christian idea of a religion of law, that is, he is lapsing into a modern type of Jewish Christianity.[26] It still remains an open question whether or not such a division can be seen as an endurable schism. Furthermore, one must be extraordinarily unobservant not to notice that any behavior other than the just-mentioned one on the part of our church toward baptized Jews would meet with far-reaching[27] lack of understanding among our church people.

(Manuscript completed on April 15, 1933)

"There is no other rule or test for who is a member of the people of God or the church of Christ . . . than this: where there is a little band of those who accept the word of this Lord, teach it purely and confess it against those who persecute it, and for that reason suffer what is their due."

Luther on Psalm 110, v. 3[28]

[26.] "That is . . . Christianity" was added in the published version; it is not in Bonhoeffer's drafts.

[27.] The carbon copy (*NL*, A 37, 3a) has "most far-reaching."

[28.] From Luther's sermon of May 10, 1535, on Psalm 110 (*WA* 41:145, 31–34). This concluding quotation appeared only in the published version [i.e., in *Der Vormarsch*. It is not in Bonhoeffer's drafts in the Nachlaß.—LR]

14. Memorandum: "The Jewish-Christian Question as Status Confessionis"[1] 359

The Jewish-Christian Question as Status Confessionis[2]

In the just published "Outlines" of the new church constitution it is implied that this law guarantees the exclusion of non-German baptized Christians from positions of ecclesiastical leadership.[3] This clause impels us to draw
attention again to the question that is of fundamental significance for the 360
Church in view of the pending decision of all the Synods.

[1.] From Macfarland, *New Church,* 69–71. Previously published in *Mündige Welt* 5:103–4 and *GS* 6:272–74. According to Jørgen Glenthøj, Bonhoeffer dictated this text in English directly to Jürgen Winterhager, who served several times as Bonhoeffer's conduit to Macfarland for material on the Church Struggle; thus there was probably never a German original (*Mündige Welt* 5:86; cf. also C.-R. Müller, *Bonhoeffers Kampf,* 19ff.). The date for this text is presumably mid-July (see ed. note 2) rather than late July (as Müller claims, ibid.).

[2.] In April 1933, Bonhoeffer had already referred to the exclusion of baptized Jews from Christian churches as a *status confessionis* for the church (2/13, p. 366). [On the meaning of *status confessionis,* see 2/13, ed. note 14. The question as to whether the Aryan paragraph constituted a *status confessionis* for the German Evangelical Church was a central issue at the beginning of the Church Struggle and became the bitter dividing line between moderate church leaders and the more radical members of what would become the Confessing Church; see *DB-ER,* 308–9.—LR]

[3.] Here Bonhoeffer is referring to a news item, "Main Outlines of the Constitution," in the Evangelical Press Service, which was published with variations in the text in the daily newspapers after July 13, shortly after the signing of the German Evangelical Church constitution on July 11 but before its publication on July 15–16, 1933. The *Völkische Beobachter* (no. 194, July 14, 1933) wrote: "Since the new German Evangelical Church is not a state church, the church constitution does not include an Aryan paragraph. The Aryan paragraph concerns the necessities of the Volk, while the new church's constitution is determined by the Protestant requirements that come from the gospel ["by . . . Protestant requirements" is missing in the *Reichsbote,* no. 157, July 14, 1933]. This does not prohibit the church from defending itself against non-Germanic [*artfremd*] influences, especially within the church leadership. Thus this defense affects theological students, the church's future leaders, but it does not affect the membership of Christ's church. Sharing in the sacraments, the communion [the *Jüdische Rundschau* of July 28 had "the communion of the sacraments"] and everyone's participation in worship are self-evident in a Christian church. The question of ethnic conformity [*Artgemäßheit*] in church leadership is to be determined not through the constitution but through regulations affecting theological study." The Reich's Ordinance on Implementation of the Law Prohibiting Overcrowding in German Schools and Universities of April 25, 1933, limited the number of new "non-Aryan" school pupils or university students to 1.5 percent, the percentage they represented in the general population; however, in the course of efforts to reduce the number of pupils or students already present, up to 5 percent of "non-Aryans" could still be retained (*RGBl,* pt. 1, 226, erroneously reported in Adam, *Judenpolitik im Dritten Reich,* 70). See also 2/16, ed. note 4.

The Aryan paragraph in the form contained in the first program of the 'German Christians,'[4] is a "*status confessionis*" for the Church. Nothing is more dangerous than for us to allow ourselves to be hoodwinked by statements as to its relative harmlessness. The constantly repeated effort to befog the questions relative to it is intended to keep us from seeing clearly the fact by the very substance of which the Church is endangered, and thus wrest out of our hands the decision for which we are responsible to the Church alone. Do not let us be deceived by all sorts of material considerations about the significance or insignificance of the matter, and lose sight of its spiritual substance, which demands a spiritual decision.

The exclusion of the Jewish Christians from our communion of worship would mean:

The excluding Church is erecting a racial law as a prerequisite of Christian communion.[5] But in doing so, it loses Christ himself, who is the goal of even this human, purely temporal law.[6] The Christian Church cannot deny to any Christian brother the Christian communion which he seeks. A Church which excludes the Jewish Christians puts itself under the Law; it is then a Church of Jewish Christian type.

A Christian Church cannot exclude from its communion a member on whom the sacrament of baptism has been bestowed, without degrading baptism to a purely formal rite to which the Christian communion that administers it is indifferent. It is precisely in baptism that God calls man into this concrete Church and into its communion.

361 The question whether an Aryan paragraph is endurable by the church boards is to be distinguished from the first question. But here, too, a certain laziness and indifference must not be allowed to cloud the issue. Pastors are not state officials. Hence, official regulations cannot be applied to them under any circumstances. Concerning admission to the ministry, as to other church positions, only ecclesiastical viewpoints are decisive, i.e., right doctrine, Christian conduct, and spiritual endowments alone qualify for the ministry. It is therefore an ecclesiastical impossibility to exclude, as a matter

---

[4.] Bonhoeffer is obviously not referring to the German Christian guidelines of May 26, 1932, which did not yet contain any "Aryan paragraph." The call for the Reich Church to be established as a "church of German Christians, that is, Christians of the Aryan race," first appears in the Ten Principles of the German Christian Faith Movement of May 4, 1933 (Gauger, *Chronik der Kirchenwirren*, 1:77). [The "Ten Principles" was simply a revision of the earlier ten-point guidelines. See also Bergen, *Twisted Cross*, 23–24.—LR]

[5.] This statement had already appeared in the essay "The Church and the Jewish Question" (2/13, pp. 368–69, and reappears verbatim in the Bethel confession (2/15, pp. 419–20) and in the theses on "The Aryan Paragraph in the Church" (2/16, pp. 425–26).

[6.] See Rom. 10:4.

of principle, Jewish Christian members from any offices of the Church. It is a different matter if, from case to case, consideration is shown for the weakness of others, so that, for instance, a preponderantly "German Christian" parish will not have a Jewish Christian assigned to it as sole pastor.[7] But even here the possibility remains open of doing just that—for ecclesiastical reasons, on principle. And from this principle, relatively unimportant as it may seem, hangs the very substance of the Church itself. With exclusion of the Jewish Christians from the communion of worship, he who realizes the nature of the Church must feel himself to be excluded also. How can he who holds a church office administer that office if he knows that there are in the communion brethren of fewer rights to whom such office is not open because of their race? Will he not then best safeguard his Christianity and his churchliness by preferring to be where the most despised brethren are, and no longer sit at the head of the table, "among those who are first"?[8]

On a church whose substance, whose essential nature has been violated, the blessing of God can no longer rest—despite the honest and best intentions of individual members. May we here make a clear decision, responsible only to the Church of Christ!

[7.] [Cf. Gerlach, *And the Witnesses Were Silent*, 36–38 and 77–78. A shameful part of the record of many church leaders, even in the Confessing Church, was their support for allowing congregations to decide whether they could "handle" a "Jewish Christian" pastor. Martin Niemöller supported this as well. Cf. 2/16, ed. note 16.—LR]

[8.] See Matt. 20:16.

362 **15. The Bethel Confession**[1]

[Draft

Contents

On the Holy Scriptures

On Creation and Sin

1. Belief in the Creator and Natural Knowledge
2. The Orders
3. The Law
4. Sin

On Christ

On the Holy Spirit

On Justification and Faith

The Church of Christ]

August version

Contents

I. On the Holy Scriptures

II. What Is Reformation?

III. On the Trinitarian Nature of God

IV. On Creation and Sin

1. Belief in the Creator and Natural Knowledge
2. The Orders
3. The Law
4. Sin

V. On Christ

VI. On the Holy Spirit and the Church

1. On the Holy Spirit
2. On Justification and Faith
3. (a) On the Church
   (b) Ministry and Confession
4. Church and People [Volk]
5. Church and State
6. The Church and the Jews
7. On the End of All Things[2]

[1.] Draft: HA Bethel, 2/72–6/21 (carbon copy of typewritten text with handwritten corrections by Bonhoeffer). August version: HA Bethel, 2/39–209 (hectographed copy as sent by Bodelschwingh on August 31, 1933, to some twenty persons for expert opinions). Both versions printed in C.-R. Müller, *Bekenntnis und Bekennen*, 82–117. See also *NL*, A 38,7 for what Bethge called the "first" version (printed in *GS* 2:91–119), actually an almost verbatim copy of the August version that Bonhoeffer had made in Berlin (*GS* 2:80; cf. also C.-R. Müller, *Bekenntnis und Bekennen*, 15 and 118–69, where it is reprinted). Only the first two versions of the confession are reproduced here, since Bonhoeffer did not support the later revisions—the November version (C.-R. Müller, *Bekenntnis und Bekennen*, 118–69) and the one publicized in late 1933/early 1934 (reprinted in K. D. Schmidt, *Bekenntnisse*, 105–31; C. R. Müller, *Bekenntnis und Bekennen*, 171–93). On the drafting and editorial history of the Bethel text, see "Concerning the History of the Bethel Confession." [Margin number with R = right column in *DBW* 12; with L = left column.—LR]

[2.] If one accepts Stratenwerth's handwritten notes on the copy of the November version sent to Zoellner on November 10, 1933, those responsible for the various sections of the August version are as follows: I. Bonhoeffer and Sasse; II. Merz; III. Bonhoeffer; IV/1 through VI/2. Bonhoeffer and Fischer; VI/3a. Stratenwerth; VI/3b. Merz; VI/4–5. Stratenwerth; VI/6. Vischer and Merz; VI/7. Stratenwerth (HA Bethel, 2/39–209, 12; facsimile reprint in Carter, *Confession at Bethel*, 295; see also C.-R. Müller, *Bekenntnis und Bekennen*, 36).

On the Holy Scriptures

The Holy Scriptures of the Old and New Testaments are the sole source and norm for the doctrine of the church. They constitute the fully valid witness, authenticated by the Holy Spirit, that Jesus of Nazareth, who was crucified under Pontius Pilate, is the Christ, Israel's Messiah, the anointed King of the Church, the Son of the living God.

Everything the church teaches must be measured solely by this guiding principle of the Holy Scriptures[3] and be revealed as pure doctrine through it alone. The Holy Scriptures alone witness to the divine revelation, which occurred as a one-time, unrepeatable and self-contained history of salvation. We know about this history only from the prophetic and apostolic words of the Old and New Testaments, and the church can proclaim the revelation only by interpreting this word that bears witness to it.

The facts of salvation history to which the Scriptures bear witness (i.e., the election of Israel and the condemnation of its sin, the revelation of the Law of Moses, the incarnation, the teachings and deeds of Jesus Christ, his death on the cross and his resurrection, the founding of the church) are unique revelatory acts of God, which the church has to

I. On the Holy Scriptures 363

The Holy Scriptures of the Old and New Testaments are the sole source and measure of the doctrine of the church. They constitute the witness, valid in its entirety, that Jesus of Nazareth, who was crucified under Pontius Pilate, is the Christ, that is, Israel's promised Messiah, the King of the Church, the Son of the living God.

All church doctrine must be measured solely by the Holy Scriptures and be revealed as pure doctrine through it alone. The Holy Scriptures alone witness to the divine revelation. They reveal a one-time, unrepeatable, and self-contained history of salvation, beginning with the promise given to the fallen Adam and culminating in the founding of the church. The church proclaims this history as God's revelatory act, meant for us. In bearing witness to these acts of God, the Scriptures are God's word to us. The church can proclaim God's revelation only by interpreting this word, which bears witness to it.

The history to which the Scriptures bear witness is salvation history, that is, the history of salvation, which
God brings to the world. It does not 364R
present the people in the Bible as holy 364L
but only shows that, despite their unworthiness, they were called into the church, for the salvation God had prepared for them. The full understanding of this history begins with

[3.] "The Holy Scriptures" inserted in Bonhoeffer's handwriting.

proclaim as such and as valid for us today as well. It is in bearing witness to these acts of God that the Scriptures are God's word spoken to us; it is not because they contain general religious truths and statements that are merely illustrated by using these facts as examples.[4] The Scriptures are the only witness to the revelation because only in them does Christ testify to himself as the Word of God made flesh.

In accordance with the confessions of the Protestant churches of the Reformation period, we reject the false doctrine, in whatever form it may occur, that Christ may also tes-
365 tify to himself outside the Scriptures and without them, and that the Holy

the New Testament, testifying to the culmination of God's plan for salvation in the incarnation, words, deeds and miracles, death and resurrection of Jesus Christ, and in the founding of the church. The Old Testament is the word of God, because it is the one God who calls Israel to be the church, who is rejected by Israel and who founds the church of the New Covenant.

The Holy Scriptures constitute a whole. They have their unity in Jesus Christ, the Crucified and Risen One, who speaks throughout the Scriptures. We are not the judges of God's word in the Bible; instead, the Bible is given to us so that through it we may submit to Christ's judgment. Only through the Holy Spirit do we hear the word of God from the Bible. But this Spirit itself comes to us only through the word of the Holy Scriptures in their entirety, and therefore can never, except by enthusiasm,[5] be separated from this word.

In accordance with the confessions of the Protestant churches of the Reformation period, we reject the false doctrine, in whatever form it may occur, that Christ may also testify to himself outside the Scriptures and without them, and that the Holy

[4.] These statements come at a point further along in the August version (p. 378).

[5.] ["Enthusiasm" refers to the experience of the Anabaptists and the radical Reformation, whom Luther referred to as *Schwärmer* (enthusiasts). For them the direct experience of the Holy Spirit was authoritative for the Christian life. That claim is rejected here because it separates the word of the Holy Spirit from the binding word of Scripture.—LR]

Spirit may be given without the external words of preaching founded on the Scriptures, and without the sacraments. (A.A.[6]5: "Damnant Anabaptistas et alios, qui sentiunt spiritum sanctum contingere hominibus sine verbo externo per ipsorum praeparationes et opera." Smalcald Articles III/8: "In short, enthusiasm clings to Adam and his children from the beginning to the end of the world—fed and spread among them as poison by the old dragon. It is the source, power, and might of all heresies, even that of the papacy and Mohammed. Therefore we should and must insist that God does not want to deal with us human beings, except by means of his external Word and sacrament. Everything that boasts of being from the Spirit apart from such a Word and sacrament is of the devil."[7] "Et in his, quae vocale et externum verbum concernunt, constanter tenendum est Deum nemini spiritum vel gratiam suam largiri nisi per verbum et cum verbo externo et praecedente, ut ita praemuniamus nos adversum enthusiastas, id est spiritus, qui jactitant se ante verbum et sine verbo spiritum habere et ideo scripturam sive vocale verbum judicant[,] flectunt et reflectunt . . .")[8]

Spirit may be given without the external words of preaching founded on the Scriptures, and without the sacraments. (A.A.[6] 5: "Damnant Anabaptistas et alios, qui sentiunt spiritum sanctum contingere hominibus sine verbo externo per ipsorum praeparationes et opera." Smalcald Articles III/8: "In short, enthusiasm clings to Adam and his children from the beginning to the end of the world—fed and spread among them as poison by the old dragon. It is the source, power, and might of all the heresies, even that of the papacy and Mohammed. Therefore we should and must insist that God does not want to deal with us human beings, except by means of his external Word and sacrament. Everything that boasts of being from the Spirit apart from such a Word and sacrament is of the devil."[7] "Et in his, quae vocale et externum verbum concernunt, constanter tenendum est Deum nemini spiritum vel gratiam suam largiri nisi per verbum et cum verbo externo et praecedente, ut ita praemuniamus nos adversum enthusiastas, id est spiritus, qui jactitant se ante verbum et sine verbo spiritum habere et ideo scripturam sive vocale verbum judicant[,] flectunt et reflectunt . . .")[8]

[6.] Should be "C.A." The quotation following is the last paragraph of Article V of the Augsburg Confession of 1530: "Condemned are the Anabaptists and others who teach that we obtain the Holy Spirit without the external word of the gospel through our own preparation, thoughts, and works" (*Book of Concord*, 40).

[7.] See Smalcald Articles of 1537, "Concerning Confession," *Book of Concord*, 323.

[8.] "In these matters, which concern the spoken, external Word, it must be firmly maintained that God gives no one his Spirit or grace apart from the external Word,

366 We reject the false doctrine that tears apart the unity of the Holy Scriptures, that claims to separate God's words from human words for its own arbitrary reasons.[9] The unity of the entire Holy Scriptures is Jesus Christ, the Crucified and Risen One, who speaks throughout the Scriptures wherever and whenever he wants. We are not the judges of God's Word in the Bible; instead, the Bible is given to us so that through it we may submit ourselves to Christ's judgment. Only the Spirit hears the Word of God from the Bible. But this Spirit itself comes to us only through the word of the Holy Scriptures in its entirety and therefore can never, except by enthusiasm [Schwärmerei], be separated from these words.

We reject the false doctrine that consults the Scriptures only as a historical document that gives examples of certain generally valid truths. It is a denial of the uniqueness and the historicity of God's revelation to draw conclusions about the election of any other people, or perhaps of all peoples, from the election of Israel as God's chosen people, or to conclude from God's giving the Law of Moses to Israel that the laws of all nations

We reject the false doctrine that considers the Scriptures to be a mere historical document expressing only general religious truths and containing the values of religious convention, illustrated by the facts it reports.

We reject the false doctrine that presents the history of salvation as a parable, for example, that the election of Israel as God's chosen people can be applied to any other people, or perhaps to all peoples. This is a denial

---

which goes before. We say this to protect ourselves from the enthusiasts, that is, the "spirits," who boast that they have the Spirit apart from and before contact with the Word. On this basis, they judge, interpret, and twist the Scripture or oral word according to their pleasure" (Smalcald Articles, "Concerning Confession," *Book of Concord,* 322. Cf. Augsburg Confession, Article V, *"De confessione,"* or "Concerning Confession").

[9.] This sentence, in revised form, introduces the last paragraph of section I in the August version (see p. 380).

are given to them by God.[10] The saving acts of God in the Bible are significant not as examples or symbols, but rather as subjects of the church's proclamation of the unique revelation of God.

of the uniqueness and the historicity 367
of God's revelation.

We reject, for the same reason, the false doctrine that concludes from God's giving the Law of Moses to Israel that the laws of all nations are given to them by God (the doctrine of the Nomoi).[10] The saving acts of God in the Bible are not examples or symbols, to be interpreted as such, but rather revelation to be proclaimed.

We reject the false doctrine that tears apart the unity of the Holy Scriptures, rejecting the Old Testament or even replacing it with non-Christian documents from the ancient pagan history of another people.[11] For the unity of the Holy Scriptures in their entirety and *their* unity alone is Christ.

For the same reason we reject the false doctrine that recognizes the Old Testament only as the Bible of Jesus, that is, of the original Christian church, and recognizes its validity only in that context (religious anti-Semitism).[12]

[10.] The doctrine of *Nomoi* (laws) that are specific to each *Volk* was developed especially by Wilhelm Stapel. For Bonhoeffer's critique of Stapel's Nomos doctrine, see 2/1. [See also Bonhoeffer's remarks to the German overseas pastors' conference in Bradford, England, in 1933, *DBWE* 13, 1/20.1, p. 48 and ed. note 32, as well as his later essay on "State and Church," *DBWE* 16, 2/10, esp. p. 507, ed. note 28.—LR]

[11.] This sort of thinking, which was partly adopted by the German Christians, was especially advocated by the German Church League, founded in 1921 (see the overviews of the "*Völkisch* Religious Movement," in *Materialdienst* 5:177–93, 209–32, and Mohler, *Die Konservative Revolution*, 171–98). [See also Bergen, *Twisted Cross*, 28 and 144.—LR]

[12.] [The use of the phrase "religious anti-Semitism" is striking here. In many sectors of the Confessing Church, as well as in some of the later historiography on the

368 We reject every attempt, for one's own arbitrary reasons or based on one's personal devotional experience, to separate God's words from human words in the Holy Scriptures. Luther's saying that the Holy Scriptures are God's Word wherever they bring us Christ[13] does not give us room to arbitrarily choose whatever we want from the Scriptures. The entirety of the Scriptures as they have been collected in the canon brings us Christ. But the Holy Spirit may reveal Christ to us anywhere in the Scriptures and at any time. The Holy Spirit that speaks to us through a word in the Holy Scriptures is always the spirit of the whole of the Holy Scriptures and thus can never be confused with one's own pious experience in selecting whatever one pleases. Instead, Christ as Lord of the Scriptures must be brought to bear on the Scriptures wherever the Scriptures are in danger of being used against Christ. But such freedom to use the Holy Scriptures comes only from submission to the written word in its entirety. (Cf. Luther's Preface to the Letter

Church Struggle, a distinction is made between traditional teachings against Jews and the racialized political anti-Semitism of National Socialism. In reality, of course, these prejudices overlapped, and in German Christian ideology they came fully together; the German Christians explicitly combined theological anti-Judaism with political anti-Semitism. Thus, it is remarkable and significant that the Bethel confession here makes the point that Christianity's appropriation of the Hebrew Scriptures—i.e., recognizing them as God's word only insofar as they are part of the larger narrative of Christian salvation history (predicting Jesus's coming and his life)—means dismissing any integrity of their own as the Holy Scriptures of the Judaic faith. Here (and in the third paragraph back, about Israel's election) is one of the few places where Bonhoeffer seems to draw an explicit connection between traditional Christian theological prejudices against Judaism with Nazi anti-Semitism, since that is the word he uses.—LR]

[13.] See his Preface to the Epistles of James and Jude (1522), *LW* 35:395–96.

of James, 1522.) This humble submission expresses the realization that the Word of God is never in my power but rather receives power over me from God, that God's Word for me is always a foreign one.

II. What Is Reformation?

Our forefathers sacrificed the outward unity of the Christian church to the supremacy of the Holy Scriptures and the preaching of free grace. Therefore, church in the Reformation sense is essentially Protestant church.
It is to be distinguished from any 369
church that renounces, for the sake of any historical development, the constant appeal to the word of God as witnessed in the Scriptures. As the congregation of Jesus Christ, it is and remains just as fundamentally church and is to be distinguished from the sort of Protestantism that equates the church with any national, cultural, or religious movement. The essence of the Reformation is consciousness of the Holy Scriptures, submission to the Holy Scriptures. For the Reformation, Martin Luther is the teacher who is obedient to the Holy Scriptures. To see what he did as the birth of the German spirit[14] or the origin of the modern concept of freedom, or as the foundation of a new religion, goes against his own word.[15]

[14.] The misunderstanding of Luther's work of reformation as the work of the "impetuous, freedom-seeking German spirit" and revelation of the "creative power of the German spirit" in the writings of Wilhelm Dilthey had already been criticized by Georg Merz in 1932 (Merz, *Freiheit und Zucht*, 32).

[15.] [The historical context of this polemical sentence is important. The 450th anniversary of Luther's birth was celebrated with great fanfare in the fall of 1933. Celebrations,

He fought against blind overestimation of human reason and rejected as a temptation of the devil the human delusion that one could come to God through one's own spirit, without the divine Word. However, since he knew he had been sent to help the German nation to be more fully Christian,[16] he also served, and still serves all nations today, as an evangelist.

III. On the Trinitarian Nature of God

The church teaches that Father, Son, and Holy Spirit are distinguished as three persons within one divine Being and nature, the one and only God, who
370 created heaven and earth; that the Father was begotten by no one, the Son by the Father, and the Holy Spirit proceeds from the Father and the Son (Smalcald Art. I, Iff.),[17] which is the greatest mystery in heaven and earth (F.C. II, VIII, 34).[18] This is the Trinitarian God revealed to us human beings in Jesus Christ, so that the entire Holy Trinity points to Christ as to the Book of Life (F.C. II, XI, 66).[19] The Scriptures testify that no one comes to the Father except through Christ (John 14:6); no one comes to the Son unless drawn by the Father (John 6:44); no one can say that Christ is Lord except by the Holy Spirit (I Cor. 12:3); the Holy Spirit is sent out from the Father

including one in Wittenberg, linked Luther to the new *deutsche Geist*. The German Christians as well as the Nazi leadership made much of this.—LR]

[16.] Allusion to Luther's letter of 1520 "To the Christian Nobility of the German Nation" (*LW* 44:123–217).

[17.] *Book of Concord*, 300.

[18.] Formula of Concord, SD VIII, 34, *Book of Concord*, 622.

[19.] Formula of Concord, SD XI, 66, *Book of Concord*, 651.

On Creation and Sin

1. Faith in the Creator and Natural Knowledge

The church teaches that God created the world in the beginning out of nothing and is its Lord. We receive this faith only through the proclamation of the revelation of the Trinitarian God, as witnessed to us by the church on the basis of the Holy Scriptures. Pious natural knowledge is not capable of comprehending God as Creator and the world as creation. It can recognize that there must ultimately be a first cause for the world's existence but cannot understand this to be an act of the Creator's free will. God's relationship to the world is, however, not that of a first cause to its effect, but rather that of Lord to creature. Natural knowledge begins with the world and derives the existence of God from it. Faith begins

and the Son (John 15:16; 14:26). So the Trinitarian God is recognized by faith as Father through the Son, as Son through the Father, as Father and Son through the Holy Spirit, as Holy Spirit through the Father and Son. No power of human reason is able to solve this mystery of God's self-revelation as the Trinity.

We reject any attempt to dismember the revelation of the Trinitarian God, to claim to understand the creation or reconciliation or redemption as a concept on its own. Instead, we have in Christ alone the whole revelation of God as Three in One, Creator, Reconciler, and Redeemer.

IV. On Creation and Sin 371

1. Faith in the Creator and Natural Knowledge

The church teaches that God created the world in the beginning out of nothing and is its Lord. We receive this faith only through the proclamation of the revelation of the Trinitarian God, as witnessed to us by the church on the basis of the Holy Scriptures. In this sense, as given by this witness, pious natural knowledge cannot deceive itself that it comprehends God as Creator and the world as creation. For it deduces the existence of the Creator from the creation, and of the first cause from its effect. God becomes the reason that the world exists. Natural knowledge therefore remains mired in the unresolved contradictions of the world. It continues to see God as awe inspiring, enigmatic, dark, or terrifying. It comes to

with God and the Word of God and clings to it despite the arguments against it from worldly knowledge. In the face of death and the evil in the world, faith in God as Creator can arise not from the world itself but only from God's own revealed words. Natural knowledge remains mired in the unresolved contradictions of the world. It continues to see God as enigmatic, dark, and terrifying. Right away it becomes involved in the problem of the divine Majesty's secrets, which the servant is not supposed
372 to know or try to discover. It comes to grief with the questions it asks of God. Faith knows that the contradictions can be resolved only through redemption, through a new creation by the Creator.

Faith, which begins with God, and natural knowledge, which begins with the world, are no longer one and the same because we are no longer at the beginning—that is, because the world is no longer visibly and unambiguously the Word of God. For Adam, faith and natural knowledge were one and the same. The fall into sin lies between us and the beginning. Through Adam's fall, the whole world came under God's curse. "Cursed is the ground because of you."[20] We live on that cursed ground. Under the curse, God's blessing is now hidden; under God's wrath, the grace of God is concealed. God's blessing and grace have never been more clearly

grief with the questions it asks of God or becomes lost in speculation on the divine Majesty's secrets, which the creature is not supposed to know and cannot discover. Natural knowledge can never, by simply hoping, recognize God as the living Lord who calls upon human beings and challenges them in their thinking, their will, and their deeds. Faith begins with God and the Word of God. In the face of death and the evil in the world, faith can arise not from the world itself but only from God's own revealed words. That faith that is brought about by God knows that the contradictions and enigmas can be resolved only by redemption through a new creation, that is to say, by the Creator.

Faith and natural knowledge are therefore no longer one and the same because we live in a fallen world, that is, because the world is no longer visibly and unambiguously the Word of God. The fall into sin lies between us and the beginning. Under the curse, God's blessing is now hidden; under God's wrath, the grace of God is concealed. In the fallen creation, God and the devil are both at work in everything that happens. God's blessing and grace are no longer clearly visible to our eyes in this fallen world. Therefore, in order to recognize God, we are entirely dependent on God's self-revelation, as witnessed to us by the Scriptures and proclaimed through

[20.] Gen. 3:17.

visible in this fallen world. In the fallen creation, God and the devil are both at work in everything that happens. Therefore, in order to know God, we are entirely dependent on God's self-revelation, as it comes to us through the church's proclamation according to the Scriptures. Not through any interpretation of events in the world, but only in obedience to the word of God in the Scriptures can we know the Creator.

We reject the false doctrine that we can know God as Creator and Father without knowing Christ. For without Christ we can think of God only as an angry despot.

We reject the false doctrine that this world must be fully affirmed, just as it is, as the original creation according to the will of God. If we thought of the world as unscathed by sin, it would contradict the Bible's affirmation that sin is mortally dangerous.

We reject the false doctrine that struggle [Kampf] is the fundamental law of creation, for struggle is a consequence of the fall and is forbidden by the commandment of peace. We reject the false doctrine that certain events in history are to be clearly interpreted as visible expressions of God's grace or of God's wrath and evaluated as such. The high points of history and national progress, and to

the preaching of the church. Only in obedience to the word of God in the Scriptures can we know the Creator, and not through any interpretation of events in the world.

We reject the false doctrine that
we could know God as Creator *and* 373R
Father without knowing Christ. For 373L
without Christ the Creator becomes an angry despot. All our trust in the almighty rule and goodness of God is then only a hope without assurance.

We reject the false doctrine that this world, just as it is, corresponds to the original creation according to the will of God and must therefore be fully affirmed. If we thought of the world as unscathed by sin, it would contradict the Bible's affirmation that sin is mortally dangerous.

We reject the false doctrine that struggle [Kampf] is the fundamental law of the original creation, and that an aggressive attitude is therefore God's commandment arising from the original creation. Struggle presupposes the condition of being friend or foe.[21] This condition arises only from the existence of good and evil. The goal of this struggle, to annihilate one another, is a consequence

[21.] Allusion to Carl Schmitt's definition of the concept of the political (cf. 2/1, ed. note 92).

an equal degree periods of decline, call us to repentance and thanksgiving and represent both judgment and grace. Any equation of historical greatness with the grace of God is broken completely and for all time at the cross of Christ.

374L We reject the false doctrine that in a particular "hour of history" God is speaking to us directly,[22] for it is enthusiasm [Schwärmerei] to think that one understands the will of God without the express words of the Holy Scriptures, to which God is bound.

We reject, as an enthusiastic interpretation of history, the false doctrine that the voice of the people [Volk]

of the fall, according to which good and evil are no longer separate in a human being. Therefore, no struggle with evil, that is, with sin, may ever be aimed at the person who carries the evil, for evil is at work on both sides. The fight must be against evil as such. From the human viewpoint there is no promise of victory in this fight. The victory over evil is the end of all
374R things, for God is all in all. It is not human beings who will bring about the end time; it will be decided by the sovereign will of God. Then the peace of God, in God's kingdom, will begin. It will not be a quiet and motionless peace, but rather the undisturbed reign of God beyond human history, beyond our human understanding of war and peace.

We reject the false doctrine that in a particular "hour of history" God is speaking to us directly[22] and is revealed in direct action in the created world, for it is enthusiasm [Schwärmerei] to think that one understands the will of God without the express words of the Holy Scriptures, to which God is bound. ("God said, 'Let there be the people [Volk]!' and there was the people."—Hossenfelder)[23]

We reject, as an enthusiastic interpretation of history, the false doctrine that the voice of the people [Volk]

[22.] Cf., for example, the German Evangelical Church constitution of July 11, 1933, the preamble of which begins: "At the hour in which God has allowed our German people to experience a great turning point in history" (*KGVBl* 1933, 2; Nicolaisen, *Dokumente,* 1:185). [Bonhoeffer is here critiquing the church for embracing the Nazi theme of a "great turning point" and "hour of history" for Germany under Hitler's leadership.—LR]

[23.] At the Reich conference of the German Christian faith movement, April 3–5, 1933 (cf. Gauger, *Chronik der Kirchenwirren,* 1:73).

could be the voice of God.[24] "They shouted in reply: 'Not this man, but Barabbas!'" "Hosanna!" "Crucify him!"[25]

2. The Orders

The church teaches that God has patience with human beings, allowing them to live in the fallen world and sustaining them there. To preserve human beings from their unbridled selfishness and keep them from destroying themselves, God imposes firm orders on human life. These are not the orders of the original creation but rather orders by which God keeps humankind alive for the sake of its future in Christ and the new creation. These orders of preservation are therefore of no value in themselves, but only in relation to the end to which God will bring humankind, to the new creation in Christ. Their only meaning is that human beings may and must live in accordance with them until we are redeemed. They are the valid orders of God but have no ultimate validity. They have already been broken down and overcome, from the perspective of the end of history.

could be the voice of God.[24] It is the voice of the people that cries both "Hosanna!" *and* "Crucify him!" "They shouted in reply: 'Not this man, but Barabbas!'"[25]

2. The Orders 375

The church teaches that God has patience with human beings, allowing them to live in the fallen world and sustaining them there. To preserve human beings from their unbridled selfishness and keep them from destroying themselves, God imposes firm orders upon human life. These are not the orders of the original creation but rather orders by which God keeps humankind alive for the sake of its future in Christ and the new creation. These orders of preservation are therefore of no value in themselves, but only in relation to the end to which God will bring humankind, to the new creation in Christ. Their only meaning is that human beings may and must live in accordance with them until we are redeemed. They are the valid orders of God but have no ultimate validity. They have already been broken down and overcome, from the perspective of the end of history. The orders remain, but their form changes with the course of history.

[24.] August Jäger and Ludwig Müller made similar statements at a July 12, 1933, rally that followed the completion of work on the German Evangelical Church constitution; the press published various versions of this on July 14 (see the daily *Völkischer Beobachter*, no. 195, and *Der Reichsbote*, no. 157. See also Hildebrandt's flyer for the church election (*GS* 2:59) and Schneider, *Reichsbischof Müller*, 145.

[25.] See John 18:40, and Mark 11:9 ("Hosanna!") as well as Mark 15:14 ("Crucify him!").

The orders that we have been given are those of gender, marriage, the family, the nation, property (work and the economy), and government. Human beings cannot escape from any of these orders, nor can any of them be transferred or transformed into another. Marriage remains marriage; the nation [Volk] remains the nation; government [Obrigkeit]
376L remains government. No aspect of
376R any of them can be changed by any historical upheaval. No order regarding race is found in either the Bible or the Lutheran confessions. In this regard, we are referred to Acts 17:26, to the origin of the human race in one common ancestor.[26]

The orders that we have been given are those of gender, marriage, the family, the nation, property (work and the economy), profession, and government. Human beings cannot escape from any of these orders, nor can any of them be transferred or transformed into another. Marriage remains marriage; the nation [Volk] remains the nation; government [Obrigkeit] remains government. Furthermore, the Bible and confessions understand the human race as one united race in its origin and its final destination (Adam–Christ, Acts 17:26). A human being is a human being, and this unity of the human race calls for our obedience. In the course of history this unity has unfolded as numerous tribes and peoples. But the modern concept of race is not found in either the Bible or the confessional writings. The tribes of Shem, Ham, and Japheth, who were the sons of one father, are not the final boundaries of communities based on bloodlines but rather become thoroughly mixed together. This is the context for the significance given to "thy strangers that are . . . within thy gates" in the Old Testament.[27] Whether they are welcome or not, they are simply there. To speak of the Creator God, who made the entire human race, is to speak of the humanity that exists

[26.] [That the Bethel confession addresses race, when it is not a subject "in either the Bible or the Lutheran confessions," is Bonhoeffer's rejection of Nazi racial ideology. —LR]

[27.] Deut. 24:14. [The KJV is cited here, in part because this phrasing is more familiar and in part because it is closer to the German.—LR]

Because of the demands of the various orders, human beings find themselves in the midst of continuous conflict. This conflict is for us the most highly visible proof that the world is in need of redemption. Worldly authority has the responsibility for resolving the world's conflicts, and it alone defends its legal system by the sword.

Christians receive these orders, which keep human beings alive and preserve them for their future in Christ, in faith from the hand of our Creator. The orders call us to thanksgiving and repentance. Christians know that besides the resolution of conflicts by the state, to which we bow in obedience, the church's proclamation assures us of the ultimate resolution of all conflicts through redemption in Christ.

We reject the false doctrine that in this fallen world there could be any orders of ultimate significance that would not be included under God's curse as a result of the fall and could thus be recognized and affirmed as

over and above the distinct peoples. That means, "the stranger that dwelleth with you shall be unto you as one born among you, and thou shalt love him as thyself . . . I am the Lord your God" (Lev. 19:34).[28]

Because of the demands of the various orders, human beings find themselves in a continuous tension. This tension is for us the most highly 377
visible proof that the world is in need of redemption. Worldly authority has the responsibility for resolving the world's tensions, and it alone defends its legal system by the sword.

Christians receive these orders, which keep human beings alive and preserve them for their future in Christ, in faith from the hand of our Creator. The orders call us to thanksgiving and repentance. We know that besides the resolution of conflicts by the state, to which we bow in obedience, the church's proclamation assures us of the ultimate resolution of all conflicts through redemption in Christ.

We reject the false doctrine that in this fallen world there could be any orders of ultimate significance that would not be included under God's curse as a result of the fall and could thus be recognized and affirmed as

[28.] In his reply to Gerhard Kittel, who had argued in *Die Judenfrage* (The Jewish Question) that a repeal of the Jews' equal rights as citizens was justified (see also ed. note 92), Martin Buber cited not only Lev. 19:33–34 but also 24:22 ("You shall have one law for the alien and for the citizen: for I am the Lord your God") and Num. 15:16 ("You and the alien who resides with you shall have the same law and the same ordinance"). Buber saw in these statements in the Hebrew Bible a "*magna carta* of Biblical faith" that was binding on "all peoples" (Buber, "Offener Brief an Gerhard Kittel," 249).

the original, unbroken orders of creation. For this would make it possible for humankind to return to a world without sin and would make Christ's death on the cross superfluous.

We reject the false doctrine that because the orders of the fallen world mentioned above are not ultimately valid for Christians, they could therefore be a matter of indifference for us or without any validity at all. We therefore reject every attempt[29]
378 to make of the gospel of love a law for the construction of a new, harmonious society. "At the same time, it permits us to make outward use of legitimate political ordinances of whatever nation in which we live. . . . For the gospel does not destroy the state or the household but rather approves them, and it orders us to obey them as divine ordinances. . . . Accordingly, we have repeated these things so that even outsiders may understand that our teaching does not weaken but rather strengthens the authority of magistrates and the value of civil ordinances in general" (A.C. 10, Art. 16).[30]

We reject the false doctrine that could consider any particular corporative order as belonging to God's orders of creation. According to Luther's teaching, human society is

the original, unbroken orders of creation. For this would make it possible for humankind to return to a world without sin and would make Christ's death on the cross superfluous.

We reject the false doctrine that because the orders of the fallen world mentioned above are not ultimately valid for Christians, they could therefore be a matter of indifference for us or without any validity at all. We therefore reject every attempt to make of the gospel of love a law for the construction of a new, harmonious society. "At the same time, it permits us to make outward use of legitimate political ordinances of whatever nation in which we live. . . . For the gospel does not destroy the state or the household but rather approves them, and it orders us to obey them as divine ordinances. . . . Accordingly, we have repeated these things so that even outsiders may understand that our teaching does not weaken but rather strengthens the authority of magistrates and the value of civil ordinances generally" (A.C. 10, Art. 16).[30]

We reject the false doctrine that could consider any particular corporative order as belonging to God's orders of creation. According to Luther's teaching, human society is

---

[29.] Corrected in Bonhoeffer's handwriting: "We therefore reject any solution."

[30.] This is actually not from the Augsburg Confession, but from the Apology of the Augsburg Confession, XVI: "Political Order," *Book of Concord*, 231–33. [In *DBW* 12:378, Bonhoeffer's quotation of the initial sentence paraphrases the passage from the *Bekenntnisschriften*. Our translation here follows the corresponding text in *The Book of Concord*. —LR]

indeed ordered, but in such a way that the same person belongs simultaneously to various orders or groups (*ordo oeconomicus,*[31] *politicus, ecclesiasticus*). To say that a certain historical form of society is based on natural law and is therefore an ultimate order would be to fall back into Catholic social teaching.

We reject the false doctrine that would make obedience to the orders dependent on whether the person who embodies them is a Christian. It is not whether the authorities are Christian or heathen but whether they have a right concept of their worldly office, which obligates us to obey them as God's order. "[The gospel] . . . commands us to obey the present laws, whether they were formulated by pagans or by others" (A.C. 16).[32]

We reject the false doctrine that holds that we ourselves are able to restore the orders of creation, which have been destroyed by sin, to their

indeed ordered, but in such a way that the same person belongs simultaneously to various orders or groups (*ordo oeconomicus, politicus, ecclesiasticus*). To say that a certain historical form of society is based on natural law and is therefore an ultimate order would be to fall back into Catholic 379
social teaching.

We reject the false doctrine that would make obedience to the orders dependent on whether the person who embodies them is a Christian. It is not whether the authorities are Christian or heathen but whether they have a right concept of their worldly office, which obligates us to obey them as God's order. "[The gospel] . . . commands us to obey the present laws, whether they have been formulated by pagans or by others" (A.C. 16).[32] "Christians therefore are obliged to be subject to political authority and to obey its commands and laws in all that may be done without sin. But if a command of the political authority cannot be followed without sin, we must obey God rather than any human beings" (Acts 5:29; C.A. Art. 16).[33]

We reject the false doctrine that holds that we ourselves are able to restore the orders of creation, which have been destroyed by sin, to their

[31.] Inserted in Bonhoeffer's handwriting: "ordo oeconomicus." These orders are listed above, p. 388, as "those of gender, marriage, the family, the nation, property (work and the economy), and authority."

[32.] From the Apology of the Augsburg Confession, *Book of Concord,* 231.

[33.] From the Augsburg Confession, Article XVI: "Concerning Civic Affairs," *Book of Concord,* 50.

original purity. Only in Christ can the world be restored; not until the new creation will it again stand in visible purity before its Creator. "God alone can separate human nature and the corruption of this nature from each other" (F.C. I.I.III).[34]

380 3. The Law

The orders preserve the world until its end according to God's will. The orders are equally well known to both heathens and Christians. They are to be distinguished from the law of God. In the law, God speaks through revelation to each human being personally. It represents God's claim to be Lord among humankind, in which we are called to offer up our complete devotion and love for God and our neighbor. The law is revealed in the Bible in numerous particular demands; these do not have the meaning for us of principles to be applied but rather carry the authority of true witness to the Lord who commands us freely. The Ten Commandments and the Sermon on the Mount are in agreement on this. The church therefore proclaims the law of the Scriptures, not as a principle for us each to apply in different ways, but as the concrete claim made on us by God as our Lord, which binds us again and again to the one Lord revealed in the Bible. A Christian receives God's law only as it is proclaimed in the

original purity. Only in Christ can the world be restored; not until the new creation will it again stand in visible purity before its Creator, for "God alone can separate human nature and the corruption of this nature from each other" (F.C.I.I.III).

3. The Law

The orders preserve the world until its end according to God's will. The orders are equally well known to both heathens and Christians. They are to be distinguished from the law of God. In the law, God speaks through revelation to each human being personally. It represents God's claim to be Lord among humankind, in which we are called to offer up our complete devotion and love for God and our neighbor. The law is revealed in the Bible in numerous particular demands; these do not have the meaning for us of principles to be applied but rather carry the authority of true witness to the Lord who commands us freely. (The Ten Commandments and the Sermon on the Mount are in agreement on this.) The church therefore proclaims the law of the Scriptures, not as a principle for us each to apply in different ways, but as the concrete claim made on us by God as our Lord, which binds us again and again to the one Lord revealed in the Bible. A Christian receives God's law only as it is proclaimed in the church according

[34.] "F.C. I.I.III" in Bonhoeffer's handwriting, replacing the incorrect "Apology." Quotation from the Formula of Concord, Epitome I.3: "Concerning Original Sin," *Book of Concord*, 489.

church according to the Scriptures. Only through the Holy Scriptures does the Christian also understand the orders, within which he lives, as God's law. The Old Testament law differs from the laws for living and the orders of other peoples in that it is given to Israel as people of God, as the people chosen to be the church. Therefore, it is to be made the subject not of comparisons but only of proclamation.

We reject the false doctrine that the orders of nations could be the same as the law of God.[35] This only applies to the Old Testament law of the people Israel. For Israel is both people and church. It alone is chosen. That this is fact is expressed in the difference between the laws of all other peoples and the Ten Commandments. The latter's uniqueness is found in the first commandment, which denies any attempt to call upon any other orders as if they were God's law. The entire law of Israel is valid only by virtue of this first commandment. The first and second tablets of the Ten Commandments form an indissoluble unity and are to be proclaimed only as such. The Christian who wants to live in obedience to the orders as if they were the law of God can do so only on the basis of the proclamation of the biblical law.

to the Scriptures. Only through the Holy Scriptures does the Christian also understand the orders, within which he lives, as God's law. The Old Testament law differs from the laws for living and the orders of other peoples in that it is given to Israel as the people of God, as the people chosen
to be the church. Therefore, it is to 381R
be made the subject not of compari- 381L
sons but only of proclamation.

We reject the false doctrine that the orders of God in the nomos of nations could be the same as the law of God.[35] This only applies to the Old Testament law of the people Israel. For Israel is both people and church. It alone is chosen. That this is fact is expressed in the difference between the laws of all other peoples and the Ten Commandments. The latter's uniqueness is found in the first commandment, which denies any attempt to call upon any other orders as if they were God's law. The entire law of Israel as the people of God is valid only by virtue of this first commandment. The first and second tablets of the Ten Commandments form an indissoluble unity and are to be proclaimed only as such. The Christian who wants to live in obedience to the orders as if they were the law of God can do so only on the basis of the proclamation of the biblical law.

[35.] See ed. note 10.

4. Sin

The church teaches that human beings, by freely transgressing against God's law, have fallen away from God; subsist in the misery of sin, decay, and death in their whole nature and all their doings; and have lost the image
382 of God that was in them. The confessions say "that there is nothing sound or uncorrupted left in the body or soul of the human being, in his internal or external powers. Instead, as the church sings, 'Through Adam's fall human nature and our essence are completely corrupted.'[36] The damage is such that only God alone can separate human nature and the corruption of this nature from each other" (F.C. I.I.III).[37] With the confessions, we are also teaching that human beings are not only sick but dead to all that is good, and that from birth they are without faith, without fear of God, full of evil desires, and subject to the righteous wrath of God.

We reject the false doctrine that sin is merely cutting oneself off from the organic context of life. That would mean that everything we do within the organic context of life is good and without sin. But this would deny the biblical view that the organic world as well has been destroyed by the fall into sin; it would be to idolize the organic

4. Sin

The church teaches that human beings, by freely transgressing against God's law, have fallen away from God; subsist in the misery of sin, decay and death in their whole nature and all their doings; and have lost the image of God that was in them. The confessions say "that there is nothing sound or uncorrupted left in the body or soul of the human being, in his internal or external powers. Instead, as the church sings, 'Through Adam's fall human nature and our essence are completely corrupted.'[36] The damage is such that only God alone can separate human nature and the corruption of this nature from each other" (F.C. I.I.III). With the confessions, we are also teaching that human beings are not only sick but dead to all that is good, and that from birth they are without faith, without fear of God, full of evil desires, and subject to the righteous wrath of God.

We reject the false doctrine that sin is merely cutting oneself off from the organic context of life. That would mean that everything we do within the organic context of life is good and without sin. But this would deny the biblical view that the organic world as well has been corrupted by the fall into sin. There are actions "that do not break apart the organic context

[36.] A hymn (1524) by Lazarus Spengler, which begins, "Durch Adams Fall is ganz verderbt menschlich Natur und Wesen" (*Book of Concord*, 488–89).

[37.] "F.C. I.I.III" in Bonhoeffer's handwriting, replacing the incorrect "Apology." (Quotation from the Formula of Concord, "Concerning Original Sin," *Book of Concord*, 488–89. See ed. note 34.)

world. There are actions that do not break apart the organic context of life but are still sinful because they are unloving. Sin is rebellion against God's absolute claim to be Lord through the law of love.

We reject the false doctrine that speculates that creation and sin both originate from the same principle, so that sin would be simply another side of creation. Creation and sin are total opposites and can never be derived one from the other. They can be seen as God's world and the devil's world, although certainly God is also Lord over the devil. The gnostic attempt to understand sin as necessary is only an excuse for sin, as if black were white; it gives people the possibility of justifying themselves, does away with reconciliation through Christ's death on the cross, takes all seriousness out of the contrast between good and evil, and thus leads to loss of discipline.

of life"[38] but are still sinful because 383R
they are unloving. Sin is rebellion 383L
against God's absolute claim to be Lord through the law of love.

We reject the false doctrine that speculates that creation and sin both originate from the same principle, so that sin would be simply another side of creation. Creation and sin are total opposites and can never be derived one from the other. They can be seen as God's world and the devil's world, although certainly God is the "One who overcomes" even the devil. The gnostic attempt to understand sin as necessary is only an excuse for sin, as if black were white; it gives people the possibility of justifying themselves, does away with reconciliation through Christ's death on the cross, takes all seriousness out of the contrast between good and evil, and thus leads to loss of discipline.

We reject the false doctrine that would see sins only as moral or biological errors or imperfections or ignorance, which human beings could correct by doing better the next time. Our sins brought Christ to the cross, and only through the death of Christ are sins forgiven (F.C. II, I, 487–91).[39]

[38.] Source of quotation not found.
[39.] See Formula of Concord, *Book of Concord*, 487–91.

384L *On Christ*

The church teaches that Jesus Christ is Son of God and Son of David, true God and true human being, the Sinless One in the sinful flesh, and the sole salvation of humankind; that the world without Christ is lost before the wrath of God. We teach that Christ is the end and the fulfillment of the law, the forgiveness of all sins, the victory over death, the solution to every problem, and that he alone is the turning point of the ages. Jesus was crucified for the sake of the guilt of all people and through their lack of faith, and resurrected that we might be made righteous. With the Holy Scriptures and the confessions we call him our Lord, because he "redeemed me, a lost and condemned human being. He has purchased and freed me from all sins, from death, and from the power of the devil, not with silver and gold but with his holy, precious blood and with his innocent sufferings and death. He has done all this in order that I may belong to him, live under him in his kingdom, and serve him in
385L eternal righteousness, innocence, and
385R blessedness, just as he is risen from

We reject the false doctrine that because of sin human beings are no
384R longer God's creatures. For Christ went to the cross for the sake of humankind and there bore witness to God's love for God's fallen creatures (F.C. II, I, 488).[40]

V. On Christ

The church teaches that Jesus Christ is Son of God and Son of David, true God and true human being, the Sinless One in the sinful flesh, and the sole salvation of humankind; that the world without Christ is lost before the wrath of God. We teach that Christ is the end and the fulfillment of the law, the forgiveness of all sins, the victory over death, the solution to every problem, and that he *alone* is the turning point of the ages. Jesus was crucified for the sake of the guilt of all people and through their lack of faith, and resurrected that we might be made righteous. With the Holy Scriptures and the confessions we therefore call him our Lord, because he "redeemed me, a lost and condemned human being. He has purchased and freed me from all sins, from death, and from the power of the devil, not with silver and gold but with his holy, precious blood and with his innocent sufferings and death. He has done all this in order that I may belong to him, live under him in his kingdom, and serve him in eternal righteousness, innocence, and

[40.] See Formula of Concord, *Book of Concord*, 488.

the dead and lives and rules eternally" (Small Catechism, Art. 2).[41]

We reject the false doctrine that Jesus appeared as a "flare of Nordic light" in the midst of a world tormented by signs of decay.[42] Christ is the reflection of God's glory (Hebrews 12)[43] in the midst of the world and the Son of David who was sent to the lost sheep of the house of Israel.[44]

We reject the false doctrine that says we confess Jesus as our Lord because of his heroic devotion.[45] He is our Lord only because he is sent by our Father, the Son and Savior crucified and resurrected for us. With the confessions we hereby reject the error of the new Arians,[46] "that Christ is not true, essential God by nature, of one eternal divine essence with God the Father and the Holy Spirit, but that he is merely adorned with divine majesty under and alongside God the Father" (F.C. I, XII, 28).[47]

We reject the false doctrine that the cross of Jesus Christ may be regarded as a symbol for a generalized religious or human truth, as expressed in the sentence, "The public interest comes before private

blessedness, just as he is risen from the dead and lives and rules eternally" (Small Catechism, Art. 2).[41]

We reject the false doctrine that Jesus appeared as a "flare of Nordic light" in the midst of a world tormented by signs of decay.[42] Christ is the reflection of God's glory (Hebrews 12)[43] in the midst of the world and the Son of David who was sent to the lost sheep of the house of Israel.[44]

We reject the false doctrine that says we confess Jesus as our Lord because of his heroic devotion.[45] He is our Lord only because he is sent by our Father, the Son and Savior crucified and resurrected for us. With the confessions we hereby reject the error of the new Arians, "that Christ is not true, essential God by nature, of one eternal divine essence with God the Father and the Holy Spirit, but that he is merely adorned with divine majesty under and alongside God the Father" (F.C. I, XII, 28).[47]

We reject the false doctrine that
the cross of Jesus Christ may be
regarded as a symbol for a general- 386
ized religious or human truth, as
expressed in the sentence, "The
public interest comes before private

[41.] *Book of Concord,* 355.

[42.] This phrase was used by state church commissioner Jäger in an appeal to vote in the July 18, 1933, church elections (cf. Gauger, *Chronik der Kirchenwirren,* 1:91).

[43.] Should probably be Heb. 1:3.

[44.] See Matt. 15:24.

[45.] See the German Christian guidelines of May 26, 1932, which confessed "a faith in Christ appropriate to our race [*artgemäß*], as we see in him the German Lutheran spirit and heroic devotion" (cf. Gauger, *Chronik der Kirchenwirren,* 1:67).

[46.] "Of the Arians" inserted by hand (by Bonhoeffer?) in this manuscript.

[47.] *Book of Concord,* 522.

interest" (Wieneke).[48] The cross of Jesus Christ is not at all a symbol for anything; it is rather the unique revelatory act of God, in which the fulfillment of the law, the judgment of death on all flesh, and the reconciliation of the world with God are carried out for all people. Therefore, the death of Jesus is not to be compared with any other sacrificial death, and the passion of Jesus Christ should not be compared with the passion of any other person or people. Christ's passion and cross can only be proclaimed as God's judgment and mercy on the entire world.

We reject the false doctrine that would make the crucifixion of Christ the fault of the Jewish people alone, as though other peoples and races had not crucified him. All races and peoples, even the mightiest, share in the guilt for his death and become guilty of it every day anew, when they commit outrage against the Spirit of grace (Heb. 10:29).[49] "Thy grief and bitter passion were all for sinners' gain; mine, mine was the transgression, but
387 thine the deadly pain."[50] "The Lord

interest" (Wieneke).[48] The cross of Jesus Christ is not at all a symbol for anything; it is rather the unique revelatory act of God, in which the fulfillment of the law, the judgment of death on all flesh, and the reconciliation of the world with God are carried out for all people. Therefore, the death of Jesus is not to be compared with any other sacrificial death, and the passion of Jesus Christ should not be compared with the passion of any other person or people. Christ's passion and cross can only be proclaimed as God's judgment on and mercy for the entire world.

We reject the false doctrine that would make the crucifixion of Christ the fault of the Jewish people alone, as though other peoples and races had not crucified him. All races and peoples, even the mightiest, share in the guilt for his death and become guilty of it every day anew, when they commit outrage against the Spirit of grace (Heb. 10:29).[49] "Thy grief and bitter passion were all for sinners' gain; mine, mine was the transgression, but thine the deadly pain."[50] "The Lord

[48.] In 1933, German Christian leader Friedrich Wieneke had drawn the following connection between the cross of Christ and the 1920 Nazi party program: "We are exhorted by the cross, by the law of Christ, to bear one another's burdens (Gal. 6:2). It is this law, after all, which is the source of that true socialism that sums up Hitler's program in the words: 'The public interest comes before private interest'" (Wieneke, *Deutsche Theologie im Umriß*, 109).

[49.] For a different reading of this verse in the paragraph on "The Church and the Jews," see ed. note 89.

[50.] From Paul Gerhardt's chorale "O Sacred Head, Now Wounded," in the traditional translation (*Lutheran Book of Worship* [1978], 116.2).

has laid on him the iniquity of us all" (Isa. 53:6. A.C. XIII, 8; XXIV, 56).[51]

On the Holy Spirit

The church teaches that the Holy Spirit, true God for all eternity, is not created, not made, but proceeds from the Father and the Son; that the Spirit is given to humankind only through the external Word and the sacraments of the church; that through the Spirit those persons are drawn from all nations [Völker] whom God has chosen, who will belong to Christ's church; that the Spirit teaches, judges, punishes, and creates faith, conversion, and renewal in human beings.

We reject the false doctrine that the Holy Spirit can be recognized without Christ in the creation and its orders. For it is always as proceeding from the Son that the Holy Spirit judges this fallen world and establishes the new order, above all nations, of the church as the people of God. Only because the Holy Spirit proceeds from the Father *and* the Son does the church receive its mission to all nations. The rebellion against this teaching about the Holy Spirit is an ethno-nationalist [völkisch] rebellion against the church of Jesus Christ. C.A. I: "Rejected, therefore are all the heresies . . . which hold that . . . the 'Holy Spirit' is a created motion in all creatures."[52] Ap. XXIV: "For

has laid on him the iniquity of us all" (Isa. 53:6. A.C. XIII, 8; XXIV, 56).[51]

VI. On the Holy Spirit and the Church

1. On the Holy Spirit

The church teaches that the Holy Spirit, true God for all eternity, is not created, not made, but proceeds from the Father and the Son; that the Spirit is given to humankind only through the external Word and the sacraments of the church; that through the Spirit those persons are drawn from all nations [Völker] whom God has chosen, who will belong to Christ's church; that the Spirit teaches, judges, punishes, and creates faith, conversion, and renewal in human beings.

We reject the false doctrine that the Holy Spirit can be recognized without Christ in the creation and its orders. For it is always as proceeding from the Son that the Holy Spirit judges this fallen world and establishes the new order, above all nations, of the church as the people of God. Only because the Holy Spirit proceeds from the Father *and* the Son does the church receive its mission to all nations. The rebellion against this teaching about the Holy Spirit is an ethno-nationalist [völkisch] rebellion
against the church of Jesus Christ. 388R
C.A. I: "Rejected, therefore are all
the heresies . . . which hold that . . . 388L
the 'Holy Spirit' is a created motion in all creatures."[52] Ap. XXIV: "For

[51.] Apology of the Augsburg Confession, *Book of Concord*, 220, 268.

[52.] The Augsburg Confession I/6, *Book of Concord*, 36. [In the draft version Bonhoeffer has summarized this section from *The Book of Concord*; the ellipses are his.—LR]

the Holy Spirit works through the Word and the sacrament."[53] Art. Sm. III, VIII.: ". . . it must be firmly maintained that God gives no one his Spirit or grace apart from the external Word which goes before. We say this to protect ourselves from the enthusiasts, that is, the 'spirits,' who boast that they have the Spirit apart from and before contact with the Word."[54]

On Justification and Faith

The church teaches that godless humankind can find its way to a merciful God only through faith in Jesus Christ, who was crucified and resurrected as intermediary for us. This faith is given by the Holy Spirit through Christ's word. Against human reason, against the pride of the flesh, against conscience, faith clings solely to the biblical word of the promise of God's grace. It is through this faith alone that we are justified (C.A. IV).[55]

We reject the confusion of trust in God with faith.[56] There is a heathen
389 way of trusting in God that is limited to ideas of divine providence, an

the Holy Spirit works through the Word and the sacrament."[53] Art. Sm. III, VIII.: ". . . it must be firmly maintained that God gives no one his Spirit or grace apart from the external Word which goes before. We say this to protect ourselves from the enthusiasts, that is, the 'spirits,' who boast that they have the Spirit apart from and before contact with the Word."[54]

2. On Justification and Faith

The church teaches that godless humankind can find its way to a merciful God only through faith in Jesus Christ, who was crucified and resurrected as intermediary for us. This faith is given by the Holy Spirit through Christ's word. Against human reason, against the pride of the flesh, against conscience, faith clings solely to the biblical word of the promise of God's grace. It is through this faith alone that we are justified (C.A. IV).[55]

We reject the confusion of trust in God with faith.[56] There is a heathen way of trusting in God that is limited to ideas of divine providence, an

[53.] Apology of the Augsburg Confession, XXIV/70, *Book of Concord*, 271.

[54.] Smalcald Articles, III, Article VIII/3, *Book of Concord*, 322.

[55.] See the Augsburg Confession, *Book of Concord*, 39–40.

[56.] This statement was directed especially at repeated remarks made by Ludwig Müller; see, for example, his estimation of Hitler's "devoutness" (*Der Reichsbote*, no. 144, June 26, 1933; *Evangelium im Dritten Reich*, no. 23, June 25, 1933) or Müller's sermon in the Berlin Cathedral on July 2, 1933 (*Evangelium im Dritten Reich*, no. 148, July 4, 1933). See also Bonhoeffer's report [to the pastors' conference] in Bradford on November 28, 1933: "From Müller one keeps hearing about trusting in God and assuming one's responsibility" (*DBWE* 13:48), attributed there to Müller's speech to the National Synod, reprinted in Norden, *Der deutsche Protestantismus*, 110–14.

immodest confidence that fearlessly claims God's mercy as something to be taken for granted and asserts to all the world its own justification by God. This confidence is fixated on what is going on in today's world and knows nothing of faith in the future, in the end of all things in Christ. In contrast, Christian faith in Luther's sense is wholly bound to Christ as the Word of God, Christ who goes with us to judgment, allows us to die before God, and in his unseen mercy and power calls us back to life. Christian faith knows of God's wrath and is repentant, fears God and sees God's grace as the miracle of miracles that the world cannot comprehend. Thus Christian faith is always oriented toward the end of the world. Heathen trust in God sees God as a nameless power to which one must submit, as destiny. Christian faith recognizes God, revealed in Christ alone, as the living, holy, just, and merciful Father and Lord. For a Christian, to trust in God means to accept this world obediently from the hand of the God who is revealed in Christ, to take Christ's cross upon oneself and to carry it in the power of the promise that at the end of all things God will create a new heaven and a new earth. Heathen trust in God lives with reference to the world and its fate, while Christian trust in God lives with reference to the end of all things, the last days.

We reject as Israelite thinking the teaching that at the Last Judgment

immodest confidence that fearlessly claims God's mercy as something to be taken for granted and asserts to all the world its own justification by God. This confidence is fixated on what is going on in today's world and knows nothing of faith in the future, in the end of all things in Christ. In contrast, Christian faith is wholly bound to Christ as the Word of God, Christ who goes with us to judgment, allows us to die before God, and in his unseen mercy and power calls us back to life. Christian faith knows of God's wrath and is repentant, fears God and sees God's grace as the miracle of miracles that the world cannot comprehend. Thus Christian faith is always oriented toward the end of the world. Heathen trust in God sees God as a nameless power to which one must submit, as destiny. Christian faith recognizes God, revealed in Christ alone, as the living, holy, just, and merciful Father and Lord. For a Christian, to trust in God means to accept this world obediently from the hand of the God who is revealed in
Christ, to take Christ's cross upon 390
oneself and to carry it in the power of the promise that at the end of all things God will create a new heaven and a new earth. Heathen "trust in God" trusts in the fateful laws of the world, while Christian trust in God lives by the certainty that the Lord who will judge the world on the appointed day is the God who promises mercy.

We reject as Israelite thinking the teaching that at the Last Judgment

God will ask people only whether they have been "decent folk."[57] This is a basic misunderstanding of the gospel's meaning and of the faith in Luther's sense. In judging humankind, God intends only to ask whether we have believed in Christ, and this faith is to justify each of us before God. This faith is the work of God, and it bears fruit in the good works for which God prepared us beforehand, cf. Eph. 2:10. We reject the doctrine that the meaning of the gospel is lighthearted trust in God, knowing one's duty, and the will to conquer. The meaning of the gospel is to repent (to turn back, to change one's mind) and to believe in the good news of the kingdom of God in Christ.

God will ask people only whether they have been "decent folk."[57] This is a basic misunderstanding of the gospel's meaning and of the faith in Luther's sense. In judging humankind, God intends only to ask whether we have believed in Christ, and this faith is to justify each of us before God. This faith is the work of God, and it bears fruit in the good works for which God prepared us beforehand. (Cf. Eph. 2:10.) The fruits of faith include trust in God and the sense of one's duty. But this must in no way be confused with faith itself. One cannot assume that someone has faith on the basis of his or her trust in God and sense of duty. Both can be false images, temptations, thus the work of the devil in a
391 person. Faith that is totally the work of God does not look for the fruits of faith but looks only to its Lord. It lives not with reference to itself but only with reference to Christ. The meaning of the gospel is not lighthearted trust in God, knowing one's duty, and the will to conquer, but rather repentance (turning back) and daring to believe in the kingdom of God in Christ.

[The Church of Christ]
The church of Jesus Christ, as it has understood itself since New Testament times, is not one among many

3(a). On the Church
The church is the body of Jesus Christ. The Crucified and Risen One is the Lord who created and still cre-

[57.] This probably refers to a formulation in Ludwig Müller's speech on the evening of his fiftieth birthday, on June 25, 1933: "On Judgment Day the Lord God won't ask whether we were Catholics or Protestants, but whether we have done our duty" (quoted from a newspaper clipping, in Schneider, *Reichsbischof Müller*, 131–32).

religious communities, namely, the community of those persons who, as distinct from the members of other religious communities, confess the Christian religion. There is no such thing as "church" as a general phenomenon in the history of religion, of which the Christian church would only be a particular case. In calling itself the body of Christ, the church is making a statement that has no analogy in the history of human religion and which cannot be understood at all by those outside the church. Everything the church says about its own nature must appear to the outside world as foolishness or presumptuousness. Thus all such statements will not only meet with lack of understanding but will be opposed by the world.

What church is, is unknown to any worldly body of knowledge, neither that of history nor that of sociology,

ates his people. Christ's people are the church. It is present everywhere where people are called by Christ, in the words of the gospel and in the sacraments, to conversion and faith. In this way the church becomes the communion of "saints." Its members are saints not because they are without sin; their holiness is not the fruit of human endeavor but depends solely on God's action, God's call. The church is therefore a community of sinners; it is a community of the godless, of people who are lost. Through God's forgiving action of justification, that is, only because God reaches out to them, people who are without God become God's children.

When the church looks upon its 392
people, it does not see any cause for self-glorification. It can say with certainty only that it is completely powerless and inadequate. This is why the church confesses that it does wrong, that it sins. On the other hand, when the church looks to Christ, whom it proclaims, it can only be full of praise, in the conviction that Christ is unconquerable. The church confesses that it is the communion of saints. Thus it is not subject to any judgment by the world. It stands under the Word of God, which puts to death and makes alive again—under God's judgment, which at the same time is always mercy.

What church is can only be understood from *within* the church, never from *outside* it. To human reason, the

and no statesman knows it on the basis of his craft. It can only be known through faith in Jesus Christ the Lord.

The prerequisite for church to exist is solely that Jesus of Nazareth, the Crucified and Risen One, is the Christ and the Lord. If he had not risen from the dead, if he were not the Lord to whom every knee shall bow, then there would be at the most a Christian religious community, but not a church. Church is that place, or more precisely, that place becomes church, where the One who, through the words of the gospel and through the sacraments, is truly and personally present as Lord, calls people to repentance and to faith, forgives
393 their sins, and gives them the gift of the Holy Spirit. There the church emerges as the *congregatio sanctorum*, the community of saints, that is, of justified sinners, the people of God, the body of Christ, the temple of the Holy Spirit. Thus the church is constituted not by human beings, not even by the faith or the moral qualities of persons, but only by Jesus Christ the Lord: *ubi Christus, ibi ecclesia.*[58] It does not owe its existence to the will of human beings. Its existence or nonexistence, therefore, does not depend on our good will or lack of good will but only on the sovereign will of God, whose almighty and loving Word calls

doctrine of the church is presumption or foolishness. No body of knowledge, and no statesman or government, can comprehend what the church is, except through faith in Jesus Christ the Lord, the faith that he gives.

[58.] "Where Christ is, there is the church."

people from the nations of the earth to be the people of God, wherever and whenever God pleases.

As people of God and body of Christ, hidden from the eyes of humankind, this church is nevertheless not a *civitas Platonica*[59] but rather a reality in the world. It is hidden within the visible institutions and social forms in which it enters into history. Only faith can recognize the true church in the outward expression of the forms that Christianity takes within history. And it is not the particular religious or moral qualities of these historical communities that make them recognizable as church but rather the presence of the pure teaching of the gospel and the administration of the sacraments according to their institution.[60] The Word and the sacraments of baptism and the Eucharist, the means of grace through which God is pleased, at any time or place, to give the gift of the Holy Spirit,[61] are the *sole notae ecclesiae*.[62] The holiness of the church consists solely in the words of the gospel, through which God justifies sinners and calls them into the holy company of the people of God.

Wherever on earth the pure gospel is preached aloud, there the one, holy, catholic church is a reality in

As people of God and body of Christ, the church is hidden from the eyes of humankind. It is nevertheless a reality in the world. Only faith can recognize the true church through the visible institutions and forms in which the church enters into history. The only marks by which it is recognized are the purity with which it teaches the gospel and its correct administration of the sacraments,[60] not the particular religious or moral status of its members.

394

Wherever on earth the pure gospel is preached aloud and the sacraments are administered according

[59.] Approx. "purely spiritual community."

[60.] See the Augsburg Confession VII, *Book of Concord*, 42.

[61.] See the Augsburg Confession V, *Book of Concord*, 41.

[62.] "Marks of the church" (according to the Augsburg Confession VII, "the gospel is purely preached and the holy sacraments are administered according to the gospel," *Book of Concord*, 42).

the world. Thus it is certain that the Word of God, the Word of the Creator and Perfecter, of the Judge and Reconciler, "shall not return to me empty."[63] Because the church bases itself solely on the presence of Jesus Christ in Word and sacrament, therefore the forms in which the ministry of preaching the word and administering the sacraments is carried out, and the forms in which the historical church organizes itself as an earthly *societas*,[64] are not of the essence of the church. No constitution was established for the church at its founding. However, this does not mean that the church has no need of outward forms and orders. When Jesus Christ chose the twelve apostles and sent them out into the world, he founded the church as an earthly entity that
395 appears in history. It is God's will that the church should take shape as a particular community among the institutions of human life (marriage, family, nation, state), within their context but distinct from them. For example, the preaching ministry was established from the foundation of the church, side-by-side with the offices, established by God, of the nation[65] and of worldly authority. However, the forms in which the church organizes itself in this world as a body incorporated under public law are taken from to their institution, there God gives faith through the Holy Spirit; there the one, holy, catholic church is a reality in the world. If either of these marks of the church is distorted or given short shrift, then it is no longer church but one among many religious communities and worldviews [Weltanschauungen].

[63.] See Isa. 55:11.

[64.] "Association."

[65.] "Nation [Volk]" crossed out and replaced with "father [Vater]" (in Bodelschwingh's handwriting?).

the world's example, and they remain part of the world. The church has not only the freedom but also the obligation to adapt itself in its outward forms to the various cultures and historical periods, so that the gospel may go forth into the world and be proclaimed by the church to each people in its own language.

With this statement we declare anew our allegiance to the church's teaching as set forth in Article 7 of the Augsburg Confession, and in Articles 5, 8, 14, and 28, which are indissolubly bound up with it, and as explained in the Apology of the Augsburg Confession, as a fundamental doctrine of the Protestant church. We reject these false doctrines:

1. That the church is a religious association formed by the gathering together of devout individuals (Enlightenment, pietism, liberalism);

2. That the true church is invisible, and that every empirical church is only an imperfect attempt to realize the ideal of the true church (idealism);

3. That there could be any marks of the true church other than the Word and the sacraments, particularly that moral or religious perfection on the part of its members is of the essence of the church (perfectionism); 396

4. That the unity of the church could depend on other things besides the unity of doctrine; that there could be a unity of the church and fellowship among churches where there is no unity of doctrine (unionism);

5. That the church has a constitution that is prescribed for it, and

that the existence of the true church depends on its presence (Roman Catholicism, Anglicanism, Presbyterianism, Congregationalism, Irvingianism,[66] etc.);

6. That the outward form of the church is of no importance, because the teaching of the gospel is not affected by any constitution (spiritualism);

7. That church government by the sovereign princes of the Reformation period could be anything other than a temporary and provisional order established by the *membra praecipua ecclesiae*[67] over against the anti-Christian papacy and the worldly bishops, who were no longer fulfilling their spiritual ministry but rather represented the estate of secular authority and were ruling the church as such (late Lutheran teaching of the Ordo Triplex[68] as the estates ruling the church);

8. That the state government as such could have the right to rule the church, especially the right to confer offices within it and to dismiss persons from office, and to make laws that affect the teachings of the church directly or indirectly (doctrine of

[66.] [Irvingianism was the chiliastic sect of the Scottish preacher Edward Irving, which protested the rationalism of Anglicanism and Presbyterianism in the mid-1800s. —LR]

[67.] "The leading church members."

[68.] "Three estates" (marriage, worldly authority, economic life; see also ed. note 31). The late Lutheran doctrine of the three estates is attributed to Johann Gerhard.

the absolute state, Erastianism,[69] caesaro-papism);[70]

9. That the church ought to be absorbed into the state and more or less renounce its independent existence as a body incorporated under public law (liberalism, socialism, doctrine of the totalitarian state);

10. That the church, not being tied *in its essence* to any particular nation, would not have to take into account, in its organization and in its preaching, the individuality of each particular ethno-national tradition [Volkstum] (internationalism); 397

11. That the church could be the religious organization for a nation, so that it would have to provide the religious foundation for that nation's ethno-national tradition [Volkstum], and that the territorial boundaries of that church should be the same as those of that nation (nationalism).

[The Bethel confession continued]

3(b). Ministry and Confession.

The Christian church acknowledges as its authority only the Word of God, as Christ testified to it in the gospel and as it is represented visibly in the sacraments. The proclamation of this Word and the administration of the sacraments as instituted by Christ are entrusted to the preaching ministry. It is a ministry of service to

[69.] [Erastianism was the view of Thomas Erastus that the sins of Christians should be punished by the state (rather than the church withholding the sacraments).—LR]

[70.] [Caesaro-papism is the doctrine that the power of secular government should be combined with the spiritual authority of the church or even be superior to it.—LR]

the Word and through the Word. It has no foundation before the Word or outside the Word, but stands upon the authority of the Word alone. As such, the preaching ministry does not belong to any individual or community but is a trust granted by the divine Word through the agency of a call from the Christian church-community. The Christian church-community has the duty and the right, at any time when it may be threatened with distortion of the divine Word, to confess and do honor to the Word by stating the doctrine that is recognized as correct over against that which is
398 in error. Such confessions are always to be examined with reference to the Word to ensure they are correct and are the norm for the ministry's service to the church-community.

We reject the false doctrine that makes the ministry an order that would take precedence over Word and sacrament and would be their source. We reject this doctrine in the form of the Roman church hierarchy and those who aspire to be like it,[71] and in the form of enthusiasm [Schwärmerei]. The power of the ministry depends neither on a historically established institution nor on the powers with which a human soul may be gifted. We therefore also protest against the attempt to apply the modern leadership [Führungs-] principle to the preaching ministry.

[71.] [A reference to the German Christians, whom Bonhoeffer viewed as a pseudo-Romanizing movement.—LR]

The preaching ministry is service to the Word of reconciliation and is therefore the opposite of any magical powers of leadership. (Cf. 1 Cor. 3:5; 2 Cor. 5:11ff.).[72]

As service to the Word of reconciliation, ministry lives by the word of the Holy Scriptures alone and can only be performed by taking this word as its source. The office of the ministry receives its mission neither from the nation, nor from the state, nor from any political and spiritual movement. The office of bishop is not by its nature set above that of the preaching ministry. Its superior position is that of the authority within the church-community. It is subject to the law of the Scriptures and of the confessions, and therefore it cannot ordain that the tie that binds the community to the confession be loosened or undone.

4. Church and Nation [Volk]

Because the foundation of the church is solely the presence of Jesus Christ, who has entered into history in Word and sacrament, the outward forms of the church's customs and its constitution are not part of its essence as church. They make it possible for the church to fulfill its duty to bring the gospel to all nations. The church enters with its preaching and its outward forms into the various peoples and into every age. Following

[72.] [See Bonhoeffer's discussion of the Führer principle in 2/8 and 2/9.—LR]

399

the example of the apostles, it can become "to the Jews as a Jew, to the Greeks, as a Greek," to the Germans, as a German, to the Chinese, as a Chinese, "so that I might by any means save some."[73]

This conformity to the Volk[74] encounters its boundaries in the content of the proclamation. This content alone, from the church's very essence, determines the ways and forms through which the church enters into history.

The message of the gospel is equally accessible, or equally inaccessible, to all peoples. For it is only God's Holy Spirit who can bring about faith in human beings and awaken consensus on the true confession. The communion of the confessing church extends across the borders between peoples. The boundaries of the Volk and church are never the same.

The church of Christ never floats over and above the peoples. It lives within them, and since the resurrection of Jesus Christ, it has never lived within only one people.

In every people to whom the church has brought its message, the church lives. The people is not the church; but the human beings who belong to both are in indissoluble

[73.] See 1 Cor. 9:20[–22].

[74.] [The German word used here, *Volksgemäßheit,* was an important term in Nazi (and German Christian) ideology that connoted conformity to the norms and values of an ethnically defined German "Volk." The text here is a rather complicated critique of the German Christians, who argued that biblical texts such as 1 Cor. 9:20 supported the idea of separate churches for separate ethnic groups and nationalities. In contrast, Bonhoeffer is arguing that the proclamation of the Scripture—as well as the church itself—transcends such divisions.—LR]

solidarity with both. They share in the guilt of their people. At the same time they are members of the people of God, citizens of the kingdom of heaven.

5. Church and State

The church teaches that worldly government is ordained by God and that everyone owes it obedience. Worldly government bears the sword, to defend against the disorder that is caused by the works of Christ's adversary. The state is established as a fatherly government over the people by the patience of God, to protect our lives and maintain public order and honor (A.C. XXIII, 55).[75] Both its dignity and its limitation are inherent in its office. Both the heathen[76] and Christians have such worldly authority over them, in the same measure. Thus all worldly govern- 400
ment, whether good or bad, stands not within the realm of salvation but rather within the realm of death. The church enters into this realm of death with its proclamation of Christ's resurrection and of salvation only through Christ. Only in Christ does the human being receive salvation and life before God. Thus the Word proclaimed by the church has a total claim on each person.

Worldly government and the church are both from God. They are separated by boundaries that cannot

[75.] See Apology of the Augsburg Confession, *Book of Concord*, 247.
[76.] [Regarding the translation of the German *Heiden*, see 2/12, ed. note 83.—LR]

be transgressed, but they are also wholly dependent on each other.

The church can never be absorbed by worldly government, that is, it can never be "built into" the structure of a state.[77] The content of its proclamation always places it over against all worldly authority.

Nevertheless, the church is bound together with worldly authority[78] in three ways:

1. Its word is addressed to the same human being whose life is preserved by the authority that bears the sword.

2. Its word tells this human being to obey the orders of the authorities as God's orders.

3. The church knows that, in its visible form, it too is subject to the orders of worldly government.

[77.] This statement is directed against the demand for the *Gleichschaltung* of church and state [the synchronization—essentially the nazification—of the church and other institutions into the Nazi Reich—LR], as upheld by the German Christians at their first Reich conference on April 3–5, 1933 (Gauger, *Chronik der Kirchenwirren*, 1:71). In May 1933, Professor Emanuel Hirsch expressed the German Christian viewpoint: "We therefore have no inherent right to resist the Protestant church's becoming 'church in the National Socialist state,' i.e., Reich church." He wanted the church to "develop an inherent kinship to the National Socialist state, above all to gain acceptance for the concept of leadership [*Führungsgedanken*], and to choose and educate properly those who are to lead the church" (Hirsch, "Die wirkliche Lage unserer Kirche," 183–84). In June 1933, Pastor Hans Schomerus argued similarly, developing the idea of the church's "Reich stature." He meant that the state should integrate the church "according to Reich law, by solemnly recognizing the doctrine set down in the confessional writings as the legitimate directive for a particular office, and by charging a bishop with exercising it as an office having the force of Reich stature" (Schomerus, "Kirche als Reichsstandschaft," 465; see also Ernst Wolf, *Barmen*, 124).

[78.] [The German word here (*Obrigkeit*) is sometimes best translated as "authority" and other times as "government," depending on context. The discussion here is sometimes broadly conceptual and general, thus "worldly authority." Other instances in this text and elsewhere in this volume or other *DBWE* volumes employ "government" (see 2/6, ed. note 6). The designation there is more specifically the state and its mandate as one of the authorities.—LR]

Worldly authority is bound together with the church only in that the latter is confined within its own orders by the right preaching of the gospel and thus does not become an instrument of the devil, who, in the end, seeks only to create disorder through which to destroy all life. This is the only service that worldly authorities should expect from the church. Here the church serves the state by keeping the human beings under state authority safe from the devil's deception, which would urge them to worship the state as the unlimited giver of life and of salvation. 401

The church and government come into conflict first of all when the church misunderstands its service as that of a state within the state, seeks to be a factor with political power, and wants the state to recognize membership in the church (through baptism) as a condition for state citizenship. In other words, church and state come into conflict when the church lacks the courage or the ability to serve the state solely through its preaching and confession according to the Scriptures.

Church and state come into conflict, second, when a worldly authority wants to use the church as its instrument; when the authority can no longer tolerate the church's witness to Christ as its only Lord; when the state can no longer bear to hear that its own dignity, in this world of sin, is forfeit to death.

We reject the false doctrine of the Christian state in any form. The

authorities, whether in a land of heathen or of Christians, only carry out their office rightly when they exercise the power of the sword rightly and remain within their boundaries. "The Word can have no emperor or judge, or protector, other than God alone" (W.A. 17.2, p. 108).[79] The state cannot presume to bring salvation to human beings. It cannot misuse the church as its moral and religious
402 foundation. It is false doctrine to think of the church as the soul or the conscience of the state.[80]

We reject any attempt to set up the visible rule of God on earth, through the church, as interference with the state's order of authority. This would mean making the gospel into law. The church can neither protect nor preserve earthly life. This remains the office of worldly authority.

6. The Church and the Jews[81]

The church teaches that God elected Israel, from among all the earth's peoples, to be the people of God. Israel was chosen solely by the power of God's word and in God's mercy, not because of any natural merit of

[79.] *Fastenpostille* (Lenten text), 1525.

[80.] Hossenfelder, for example, on April 22, 1933, referred to the church as the "nation's soul" (*Materialdienst*, 5:69).

[81.] The text of this section, "The Church and the Jews," while based on the original draft of Wilhelm Vischer, contains various alterations. See Vischer's theses for this section on the church and the Jews, published in Barth, *Briefe des Jahres 1933*, 598–99. [The more recent research by Andreas Pangritz has shed light on the differences between the versions of this essay as well as some of the internal debates within the group working on it. On August 21, 1933, Vischer had written to Barth: "The people around Bodelschwingh asked me to write some sentences on the church's position toward the Jews. I first referred them to the sixth point in your article in *Theol[ogische] Existenz* [see ed. note 87] against the German Christians. But they wanted it in more detail, such as some

its own (Exod. 19:5; Deut. 7:7–11). Jesus, the Christ promised by the Law and the Prophets, was rejected by the high council and the Jewish people according to the Scriptures. They wanted a national Messiah who would liberate them politically and make them masters of the world. But this, Christ Jesus was not, and did not do; he died at their hands, and for
their sake. Through the crucifixion 403
and raising from the dead of Christ Jesus, the dividing wall between Jews and Gentiles has been broken down (Eph. 2).[82] The place of the Old Testament people of the covenant has been taken not by another nation but rather by the Christian church, called out of, and within, all nations.[83]

God glorifies his overflowing faithfulness in remaining true to Israel according to the flesh, from which Christ was born in the flesh, despite

points about the unbaptized Jews. So then I put together what I hear the Bible saying on this. I am not surprised that the people who made this request (with the exception of Bonhoeffer) do not agree with what I have written" (Karl Barth-Archiv, Basel). It is obvious that Vischer here was referring to the original draft of the document, not the August version (which Barth only received from Bonhoeffer on September 9, 1933). Throughout Vischer's original draft, his positive statements about Jews and Jewish Christians were followed by refutations of the German Christian heresy. In the August version, these rebuttals were compiled into a single passage at the end of the chapter. This revision effectively obscured Vischer's train of thought in the essay, since the direct relationship between the individual rebuttals and the confessional statements that preceded each of them is no longer clear. See Pangritz, "Das Heil kommt von den Juden."—LR] In subsequent revisions in which Bonhoeffer was no long involved, this entire section was watered down considerably, especially with regard to its unambiguous characterization of and rejection of German Christian statements. It can be assumed that this in particular is the reason for Bonhoeffer's refusal to support the later revisions. See also the afterword, pp. 497–99.

[82.] Eph. 2:14.

[83.] [This theology, of course, is traditional supersessionism. While the covenant with Israel is acknowledged as still valid, the deicide charge is made here, and the history of the people of Israel is explained solely within the context of Christian salvation history.—LR]

all Israel's unfaithfulness and even after the crucifixion. God still wants to complete with the Jews the plan for redeeming the world that began with the calling of Israel (Rom. 9–11). This is why God has preserved, according to the flesh, a sacred remnant of Israel, which neither becomes absorbed into any other nation by emancipation and assimilation, nor becomes a nation among others through Zionistic or similar efforts, nor can be annihilated by measures such as those used by Pharaoh.[84] This sacred remnant has the *character indelebilis*[85] of the chosen people.[86] The church has received from its Lord the mission to call the Jews to conversion and to baptize those who believe in the name of Jesus Christ, for the forgiveness of sins (Matt. 10:5–6; Acts 2:38ff.; and 3:19–26). A mission to the Jews that refuses altogether to carry out baptisms of Jews because of cultural or political considerations is refusing to obey its Lord. Christ

[84.] Vischer was already speaking of the "sacred remnant" in this sense in late April 1933 ("Zur Judenfrage," 189); this formulation is also found in point 17 of Hans Ehrenberg's "72 Leitsätzen zur judenchristlichen Frage" [72 Guiding Principles on the Jewish Christian Question] of July–August 1933 (printed in K. D. Schmidt, *Bekenntnisse 1933,* 68). On Vischer's borrowing from Ehrenberg's ideas, see C.-R. Müller, *Bekenntnis und Bekennen,* 37–38, 40–41.

[85.] "Ineradicable character." [Vischer here is trying to underscore the permanence and indestructibility of God's covenant with Israel. The editor thanks Andreas Pangritz for this insight.—LR]

[86.] [Here Vischer's original draft continued: ", which is not to be confused with the 'yellow mark on the black background' with which the ethno-nationalists (*die Völkischen*) want to brand the Jews." This statement would have prevented any misunderstanding of *character indelebilis* as being of a racist or essentialist nature. In a similar fashion, Vischer in his essay "Zur Judenfrage" had differentiated the *character indelebilis* of the Jewish people from the racist branding of the Jews. Cf. Vischer, "Zur Judenfrage," 190. The editor thanks Andreas Pangritz for this information.—LR]

crucified is a stumbling block to the Jews and foolishness to the Gentiles (1 Cor. 1:22ff.). He represents the religious ideal of the Jewish soul no more than the religious ideal of any other people's soul. Neither can a Jew be given faith in Christ through flesh
and blood, but only through the Spirit 404
from the Father in heaven (Matt. 16:17).

The fellowship of those belonging to the church is determined not by blood nor, therefore, by race, but by the Holy Spirit and baptism.[87]

We reject any attempt to compare or confuse the mission of any other nation with that of Israel, which is part of salvation history.[88]

It can never in any case be the mission of any nation to take revenge on the Jews for the murder committed at Golgotha. "Vengeance is mine," says the Lord (Deut. 32:35; Heb. 10:30).[89] We reject any attempt to misinterpret God's special faithfulness to Israel in the flesh as proof for the religious significance of Jewish or any other culture.

[87.] Vischer borrowed this sentence verbatim from Karl Barth's *Theologische Existenz Heute* (June 1933, 52) as well as Barth's conclusion: "If the German Evangelical Church excludes Jewish Christians or treats them as second-class Christians, it ceases to be a Christian church" (ibid.); see also ed. note 81. For unknown reasons this concrete conclusion was omitted from the August draft of the Bethel confession. [Information provided by Carsten Nicolaisen, coeditor of *DBW* 12.—LR]

[88.] [This counters a claim made by the German Christians, who portrayed Germany as the new chosen people and Hitler as the Messiah.—LR]

[89.] It is striking that the section "On Christ" cites Heb. 10:29, thus recalling the guilt of *all* nations (see p. 398) but, in contrast to the verse quoted here, says nothing of a fundamental claim to revenge (see also C.-R. Müller, *Bekenntnis und Bekennen*, 42; and Mehlhausen, "Der Schriftgebrauch in Bekenntnissen," 225–26).

We object to the assertion that the faith of a Jewish Christian would, unlike that of a Gentile Christian, be a matter of race or blood, as a form of Judaistic enthusiasm [Schwärmerei].

We object to the attempt to make the German Protestant church into a Reich church for Christians of the Aryan race,[90] thus robbing it of its promise. This would set up a racial law at the entrance to the church,
405 making such a church itself legally into a Jewish Christian congregation.[91] We therefore oppose the establishment of congregations for Jewish Christians, because they would be based on the false premise that there is something particular about Jewish Christians at the same level as, for example, the special character that French refugee congregations in Germany have for historical reasons, or that Christians who have converted from Judaism should develop a particular Christianity appropriate to their race.[92] What is special about

[90.] See, for example, point 3 of the German Christian movement's Ten Principles of May 4, 1933: "The German Protestant Church of the Reich is the church of the German Christians, i.e., of Christians of the Aryan race" (Gauger, *Chronik der Kirchenwirren*, 1:77).

[91.] This and the preceding sentence were not in Vischer's draft and were evidently added by Bonhoeffer (see also Vischer, *Témoigne d'un Contemporain*, 118–19, and C.-R. Müller, *Bekenntnis und Bekennen*, 43–44 (the latter, however, does not take Vischer's draft into account). Bonhoeffer had similar arguments in his essay "The Church and the Jewish Question" (2/13), his memorandum "The Jewish-Christian Question as Status Confessionis" (2/14), and his theses on "The Aryan Paragraph in the Church" (2/16).

[92.] On this statement, see also Gerhard Kittel's text *Die Judenfrage*, published in the summer of 1933. Kittel had claimed that "the baptism of Jews has no effect on their Jewishness. . . . A Jew who converts becomes not a German but rather a Jewish Christian." There was therefore a need for "a Jewish Christian tradition . . . as the form which the religious life of Jewish Christians takes. . . . The goal, and the ideal, would be a Jewish Christian church" (70–71). In early summer 1933, the German Christians of Mecklenburg were already calling for "Protestant Christians of Jewish origin to be gathered into

Jewish Christians has nothing to do with their race or kind or their history, but rather with God's particular faithfulness to Israel according to the flesh. In fact, so long as Jewish Christians are not set apart legally in any way within the church, they serve as a living monument to God's faithfulness and a sign that the dividing wall between Jews and Gentiles has been broken down, and that faith in Christ must not be distorted in the direction of a national religion or a Christianity according to race. The Christians who are of Gentile descent must be
prepared to expose themselves to 406
persecution before they are ready to betray in even a single case, voluntarily or under compulsion, the church's fellowship with Jewish Christians that is instituted in Word and sacrament.[93]

Jewish Christian congregations" (K. D. Schmidt, *Bekenntnisse 1933*, 153), and Emanuel Hirsch, in early September 1933, advocated "that Jews newly converted to Christianity, and those of mixed race born from recent mixed marriages, should be gathered into special Jewish Christian congregations" ("Arier und Nichtarier," 20).

[93.] [Vischer's draft here reads: "The Christians of Germanic descent must be prepared to expose themselves to persecution before they are ready to betray in even a single case, voluntarily or under compulsion, the church's fellowship with Jewish Christians that is instituted in Word and sacrament." Vischer follows this with a concrete statement that was omitted from the August version: "Jewish Christians must, like others, have equal access to all offices of the church. If student regulations or any laws outside the church make theological study impossible for Jewish Christians, then the church must protest this and make a different path to the ministry possible for Jewish Christians." Vischer's original draft, therefore, called for concrete solidarity between those holding church offices and the Jewish Christians. Also, the final sentence of Vischer's draft concludes with a statement opposing an ethnically determined Christianity and an emphasis on a unity of humanity that is grounded both in a theology of creation and Christology: "God, who created the world, let all peoples descend from one blood and live on the entire earth, and determined in advance the ages and limits of their earthly home so that they would seek the Lord in order to sense and find him. Now, however, through the message of the gospel God places each people and every individual before the judgment of one man through whom he has decided to judge the entire earth (Acts 17). The duty of the Protestant church in Germany is to proclaim the gospel of Jesus Christ to the German people, for judgment and salvation through this one man; its duty is not, however,

7. On the End of All Things

The church teaches that Jesus Christ is the end of the world and its history. He who was born, crucified, and resurrected within history will come again to judge the living and the dead. Because the Christ of history, the Christ who is present, and the Christ who is to come are one and the same, in him the end time and the judgment are present now as well as in the future. ("The hour is *coming*, and is *now* here . . ." John 5:25.) Therefore, faith and hope are inseparable. Faith says, "now," "but now," while hope says "not yet." ("We are God's children *now*; what we will be has *not yet* been revealed," I John 3:2.) The unity of both is Christ, who is present to us in the commandment to love and thus brings the end time near.

As Christ went through death, so the whole world and each human, as a whole being, must go to their death. There is no way of going step-by-step, or progressing, from this world into the new world. Everything must pass through death. But as Christ was raised from the dead, so at the end time God will awaken the dead and call them before his judgment seat. Only those who believe can pass muster in this judgment. But who are those who believe, and who are those who do not believe? This question,

---

to create an ethnically determined (*artgemäßes*) German Christianity." This last statement, omitting Bonhoeffer's thesis about the "legalistic" character of the German Christians' "modern Jewish Christianity," is effectively the rejection (which Bonhoeffer calls for on p. 420) of the transformation of the Protestant church into "a Reich church of Christians of the Aryan race." The editor thanks Andreas Pangritz for this insight.—LR]

which we have to answer for ourselves, is the final thing that can be said about it here.

The new world of the resurrection will be a new heaven and a new earth. It is our earth that will be made new, the same earth on which the cross of Christ once stood. But it is a new earth; "the former things shall not be remembered" (Isa. 65:1[17]). God "will wipe away every tear from their 407
eyes. Death will be no more; mourning and crying and pain will be no more, for the first things have passed away" (Rev. 21:4).

Before the end, the Antichrist will come, disguised as the One sent from God, the Messiah, the Christ, aiming to lead the church into temptation. Dangerous in the world and even more dangerous in the church, he will bring a battle into Christ's community, and there will be a parting of the ways over him. History will end with Christ's community divided in two, struggling against the rule of the Antichrist. This end time of history, however, is "coming" and is already "now."

We reject the false doctrine that would seek to tear the world of hope apart from our world, so that the first has nothing to do with the second. We see this as an attempt to escape from the recognition that the present world is "now" already threatened and judged by the end time, and that Jesus Christ, the end of the world, already speaks his word to the world and demands our obedience. People put the emphasis on the "not yet," as the result both of unbending secularity and of pious escapism from the world. Both cases lie on the same level. Both are unable to think in terms of Christ as the end of the world; they think, as a matter of principle, only in worldly terms.

We reject the false doctrine that would see within the world a gradual development taking place that will culminate in the new world. Even that which is most noble in this world must go to its death. Christ had to go to the cross. Even the most devout must face the judgment. For our sake, Christ was cursed by God upon the cross. The outcome of this judgment yields no doctrine, neither the restoration of the entire world nor its eternal rejection. Only in prayer is it possible to speak about the outcome of this judgment.

We reject any version of the doctrine of the thousand-year reign [Reich] that clearly seeks to interpret certain historical events as the beginning of Christ's visible reign on earth.[94]

[94.] [The reference is simultaneously to Rev. 20:4 (the second coming of Christ) and the Nazi claim of inaugurating a thousand-year Reich for Germany.—LR]

16. Theses on "The Aryan Paragraph in the Church"[1] 408

The Aryan Paragraph in the Church

1. Radical version of the Aryan Paragraph:

Non-Aryans are not members of the German Reich Church[2] and are to be excluded through the establishment of their own Jewish Christian congregations.[3]

2. Second version of the Aryan Paragraph:

The law governing state officials is to be applied to church officials; thus employment of Jewish Christians as pastors should be discontinued, and none should be accepted for new employment.[4]

3. Third version of the Aryan Paragraph:

Although the Reich Church constitution has not adopted the Aryan paragraph, it has made clear by its silence that it recognizes the regulations affecting students, which are designed to exclude Jewish Christians from theological study, as binding on the church. Thus it accepts the future exclusion of Jewish Christians from the ministry of the church.[5]

Re: version 1. The exclusion of Jewish Christians from the church com- 409
munity destroys the substance of Christ's church, because

[1.] LKA EKvW, 5/1, Bestand 35, Fasc. 2; hectographed copy, with handwritten note in upper right-hand corner, "Sept. 1933," and beneath this, next to the title, "(Bonhoeffer)." See also *NL*, A 38,5; typewritten copy. Previously published in *GS* 2:62–69. These theses were written by the end of August 1933, shortly after the August version of the Bethel confession (2/15). They were discussed during preparations for the Old Prussian General Synod of September 5–6, 1933, by the "Gospel and Church" group (*Mündige Welt* 5:85–87; see also C.-R. Müller, *Dietrich Bonhoeffers Kampf*, 19–37).

[2.] See 2/14, ed. note 3.

[3.] See 2/15, ed. note 92.

[4.] The Law for the Reconstitution of the Civil Service of April 7, 1933, which contained the so-called Aryan paragraph, according to the third ordinance on its implementation of May 6, 1933, was "not applicable . . . to officials, employees and workers of religious societies recognized by public law" (*RGBl* 1:245; C. Nicolaisen, *Dokumente*, 1:35). However, on August 24, 1933, the Brandenburg provincial synod with its German Christian majority decided to introduce the Aryan paragraph into the church (including the provision that applied it to those with "non-Aryan" spouses as well; this provision applied to Reich officials as of June 30, 1933) and to submit a corresponding resolution to the Prussian General Synod of September 5–6, 1933 (Scholder, *Churches and the Third Reich*, 1:471–72). On the resolution's passage, see also 1/94.

[5.] It is not clear precisely which "regulations affecting students" Bonhoeffer refers to here. The first Ordinance on Implementation of the Law Prohibiting Overcrowding in German Schools and Universities of April 25, 1933, did not provide for a general exclusion of "non-Aryans" from higher education but rather limited the number of new "non-Aryan" admissions to 1.5 percent (*RGBl* 1:226; see also 2/14, ed. note 3). A few days earlier, however, on April 22, 1933, the Law on the Composition of Student Bodies in

first: it reverses the work of Paul, who assumed that through the cross of Christ the dividing wall between Jews and Gentiles had been broken down, that Christ has "made both groups into one" (Eph. 2),[6] that here (in Christ's church) there should be neither Jew nor Gentile . . . but rather all should be one.

second:[7] if the church excludes the Jewish Christians, it is setting up a law with which one must comply in order to be a member of the church community, namely, the racial law. It means that Jews can be asked at the door, before they can enter Christ's church in Germany, "Are you Aryan?" Only when they have complied with this law can I go to church with them, pray, listen, and celebrate the Lord's Supper together with them. But by putting up this racial law at the door to the church community, the church is doing exactly what the Jewish Christian church was doing until Paul came, and in defiance of him; it was requiring people to become Jews in order to join the church community. A church today that excludes Jewish Christians has itself become a Jewish Christian church and has fallen away from the gospel, back to the law.

410 The German Christians say:

The church is not allowed to undo or to disregard God's orders, and race is one of them, so the church must be racially constituted.[8]

We answer:

The given order of race is misjudged just as little as that of gender, status in society, etc. . . . In the church, a Jew is still a Jew, a Gentile a Gentile, a man a man, a capitalist a capitalist, etc., etc. But God calls and gathers them all together into one people, the people of God, the church, and they all belong to it in the same way, one with another. The church is not a community of people who are all the same but precisely one of people foreign to one another who are called by God's Word. The people of God is an order

---

Scholarly Institutions of Higher Learning limited new admissions to "students of German ancestry and mother tongue" (*RGBl* 1:215). Prussia's Ordinance on Regulation of Students of April 12, 1933, also required every student to present at registration a statement as to whether, according to the best of his or her knowledge and belief, "his or her parents and grandparents were of German ancestry" (*Zentralblatt*, 118), and individual regional governments (*Länder*) of the German Reich had already generally prohibited access to study for "non-Aryans" (see Adam, *Judenpolitik im Dritten Reich*, 68–70, esp. n. 234).

[6.] See Eph. 2:14.

[7.] The following statement is almost the same as in documents 2/13, pp. 368–69; 2/14, p. 372; and 2/15, pp. 420–21.

[8.] See 2/14, ed. note 3, and 2/15, ed. note 87.

over and above all other orders. "Who is my mother, and who are my brothers? . . . whoever does the will of my Father in heaven is my brother and sister and mother."[9] Race and blood are one order among those who enter into the church, but it must never become a criterion for belonging to the church; the only criterion is the Word of God and faith.

The German Christians say:

We don't want to take away from Jewish Christians the right to be Christians, but they should organize their own churches.[10] It is only a matter of the outward form of the church.

We answer:

(1) The issue of belonging to the Christian community is never an outward, organizational matter, but is of the very substance of the church. Church is the congregation that is called together by the Word. Membership in a congregation is a question not of organization but of the essence of the church.

(2) To make such a basic distinction between Christianity and the church, or between Christ and the church, is wrong. There is no such thing as the idea of the church, on one hand, and its outward appearance, on the other, but rather the empirically experienced church is the church of Christ itself. Thus to exclude people forcibly from the church community at the 411
empirical level means excluding them from Christ's church itself. That part of the church that excludes another is, of course, the one that is truly shut out—that is the particular danger of the German Christians' undertaking.

(3) When the church's organizers exclude anyone, they are interfering with the authority of the sacraments. Here in our church, Jewish Christians have been accepted, by the will of God, through the sacrament of baptism. Through baptism they are joined together with our church, and our church with them, by indissoluble ties. If the church that has baptized Jewish Christians now throws them out, it makes baptism into a ceremony, which implies no obligation on its part.

The German Christians say:

We are not so much concerned with these thousand Jewish Christians as with the millions of our fellow citizens who are estranged from God. For their sake, these others might in certain cases have to be sacrificed.

[9.] Matt. 12:48 and 50.

[10.] See 2/15, ed. note 92.

We answer:

We too are concerned for those outside the church, but the church does not sacrifice a single one of its members. It may even be that the church, for the sake of a thousand believing Jewish Christians that it is not allowed to sacrifice, might fail to win over those millions. But what good would it do to gain millions of people at the price of the truth and of love for even a single one? This could represent not gain but only loss, for the church would no longer be the church.

The German Christians say:

The German church people [Kirchenvolk] can no longer endure communion with Jews, who have done them so much harm politically.

We answer:

This is the very point where it must be made crystal clear: here is where we are tested as to whether we know what the church is. Here, where the Jewish Christian whom I don't like is sitting next to me among the faithful, this is precisely where the church is. If that is not understood, then
412 those who think they cannot bear it should themselves go and form their own church, but never, ever, can they be allowed to exclude someone else. The continuity of the church is in the church where the Jewish Christians remain.

In summary:

The church is the congregation of those who are called, where the gospel is rightly taught, and the sacraments are rightly administered,[11] and it does not establish any law for membership therein. The Aryan paragraph is therefore a false doctrine for the church and destroys its substance. Therefore, there is only one way to serve the truth in a church that implements the Aryan paragraph in this radical form, and that is to withdraw. This is the ultimate act of solidarity with my church. I can never serve my church in any other way than by adhering to the whole truth and all its consequences.

Re: version 2. Removal of Jewish Christians from the pastorate contradicts the nature of the ministry. Luther taught that through baptism all Christians are made priests, they all have the same rights, and each has the right

[11.] See the Augsburg Confession VII, *Book of Concord*, 42.

and the duty to obey and to teach the word of God.[12] The office of the ministry is conferred by the Christian community on a Christian who has already been consecrated a priest through baptism, and demands right teaching, Christian living, and spiritual gifts of the pastor. The pastor takes up this office as the call of Christ, and only an offense against one of these requirements can be grounds for the congregation to revoke this ministry.

If Jewish Christians are barred in principle from the pastorate, they become church members with *lesser rights.* To cite the biblical admonition, "Women should be silent in the churches,"[13] does not lead to any conclusion with regard to Jewish Christians as such. Either we consider this admonition as legally binding, in which case it still does not say anything about Jewish Christians' keeping silent in the churches, or we do not consider it legally binding, that is, women also are allowed to speak in the churches, in which case there is no possibility of forbidding Jewish Christians to speak
as a matter of principle. As soon as Jewish Christians are excluded, more- 413
over, the meaning of the ministry itself is destroyed, since it is subjected to the whim of the congregation. Ordination itself is then revoked and made invalid; the *ordinatio* is placed, in a disorderly way, at the mercy of the congregation.

The German Christians say:

For the sake of the patriotic sentiments of German church people, a leader in the church must be Aryan.[14]

We answer:

Church people must learn to pay attention not to the person of the pastor but rather to the pastor's proclamation. "What does it matter? Just this, that Christ is proclaimed in every way . . ."[15] If Paul, a Jew, had not proclaimed Christ to the heathen world, without worrying about any patriotic sentiment, there would never have been a German church.

[12.] Cf., for example, Luther, "That a Christian assembly or congregation has the right and power to judge all teaching . . . ," 1523 (*LW*, 39).

[13.] 1 Cor. 14:34.

[14.] See 2/14, ed. note 3, and Siegfried Nobiling's speech at the Reich Conference of the German Christians, April 3–5, 1933, during which he said, "Only a person without foreign blood can occupy a church appointment. . . . The ministry must be accessible only to those of pure Aryan blood" (Nobiling, "Kirchliches Führertum," 48ff.).

[15.] See Phil. 1:18 [see also Bonhoeffer's first annual report to his London parish of Sydenham, *DBWE* 13, 2/1, p. 301. The editor thanks Isabel Best for this reference.—LR]

This demand for the gospel to be preached by Aryans is a typical demand of those who are weak in the faith, so they want to set up legal restrictions in matters where, in truth, only faith and the Word of God has a say. This demand from the weaker members of the congregation might possibly be considered in exceptional individual cases, for pastoral reasons, to avoid giving serious offense. But in each such case the most earnest thought should be given to whether, for the sake of what church is about, the congregation should be asked to tolerate an offense to its sensibilities.[16] It is totally impossible, however, to allow the demands of the weak in the faith
414 to rule the church, because that means turning the freedom of the gospel into its opposite, a law.

The German Christians say:

The laws that apply to state officials must also apply to church officials; otherwise the church is placed in opposition to the will of the state.[17]

We answer:

This is precisely where the completely political character of all the German Christians' arguments about the Aryan paragraph is revealed. Seen in connection with current political events, they can appear only as the church emulating whatever the state does. However, the true service and loyalty that the church must render to the state consists never in blindly emulating its methods but only in the freedom of its own preaching and in displaying the form and character that properly belong to it as the church.

In summary:

The German Christians' demands destroy the substance of the ministry by making certain members of the Christian community into members with lesser rights, second-class Christians. The rest, those not affected by this demand, who remain privileged members, should prefer to stand by those with lesser rights rather than to benefit from a privileged status in the church. They must see their own true service, which they can still perform

[16.] This viewpoint was not shared by other church opposition speakers in Berlin. In addition to Künneth's earlier remark (1/58, ed. note 16), see Martin Niemöller's reaction to the introduction of the Aryan paragraph for pastors. Citing 1 Cor. 8, and in view of "the 'fragility' of the current situation," he called for a certain "restraint" on the part of church officeholders of Jewish descent, saying that it might be understandable for them not to be considered for "an office in the church government or an especially prominent position in home missions" (Niemöller, "Sätze zur Arierfrage," 270).

[17.] See ed. note 4.

for their church, in resigning from this *office of pastor as a privilege,* which is what it has now become.

Re: version 3. If regulation of the right to university study makes it impossible for Jewish Christians to become pastors, the church, for its part, must open new doors to the ministry for Jewish Christians and thereby protest, through its proclamation, against such measures that attack the substance of the ministry. If the church does not do so, it is guilty of responsibility for the entire Aryan paragraph.

The German Christians say: 415

The Aryan paragraph is an *adiaphoron,*[18] which doesn't affect the confession of the church.

We answer:

1. All that we have said above is evidence that the church and the ministry have been attacked in their substance, that is, the confession has been attacked.

2. Even if this were not the case, the following judgment on the part of the confessional writings would be true. "Thus, Paul submits and gives in to the weak in matters of food or days (Rom. 14:6). But he does not want to submit to false apostles, who wanted to impose such things upon consciences as necessary even in matters that were in themselves free and indifferent. Col. 2:16: 'Do not let anyone make matters of food or drink or the observation of festivals a matter of conscience for you.' And when in such a case Peter and Barnabas did give in to a certain degree, Paul criticized them publicly, as those 'who were not acting consistently with the truth of the gospel' (Gal. 2[:14]).

"For in such a case it is no longer a matter of external matters of indifference, which in their nature and essence are and remain in and of themselves free, which accordingly are not subject to either a command or a prohibition regarding their use or discontinuance. Instead, here it is above all a matter of the chief article of our Christian faith, as the Apostle testifies, 'so that the truth of the gospel might always remain' (Gal. 2:5). Such coercion and command *obscure and pervert the truth of the gospel, because either*

[18.] The Greek *adiaphoron* means a "matter of indifference." For the meaning of an *adiaphoron* in a confessional situation, see the quotation from the Formula of Concord that follows in the text. [See also 2/13, ed. note 14, regarding Bonhoeffer's contrast between the *status confessionis* and the *adiaphora.*—LR]

these opponents will publicly demand such indifferent things as a confirmation of false teaching, superstition, and idolatry for the purpose of suppressing pure teaching and Christian freedom or they will misuse them and as a result falsely reinstate them. . . .

"Thus, submission and compromise in external things *where Christian agreement in doctrine has not already been achieved strengthens idolaters in their idolatry.*"[19]

416 **17. Essay, "What Should a Student of Theology Do Today?"**[1]

What Should a Student of Theology Do Today?

One should, above all, only study theology out of the sincere opinion that one cannot choose any other course of study. Far less harm is done if many who might have become good pastors or teachers of religion instead become good lawyers or physicians than if a single person pursues theology who should not have done so. A large new generation of theological students is always a very ambiguous phenomenon.

One should not think that, as someone who truly had to study theology, one is superior to other students. For theological students will find in the course of their studies that the reasons that persuaded them that it must be theology or nothing will gradually fall away, and by the time they reach the end of a proper theological course they will have entirely different reasons for pursuing a career in theology—if indeed they are still convinced that they must do so—from those they had in the beginning.

One should not think it necessary to wait for particular experiences of "being called" to the ministry. A student who is simply gripped by the subject matter of theology and cannot turn away from it can consider that a calling. But certainly, it must be what theology is really about that enthralls the student—a real readiness to think about God, the Word, and the will of God, a "delight in the law of the Lord" and readiness to mediate on it "day

---

[19.] Cited from Article X of the Formula of Concord, paragraphs 13–14 and 16, in *Book of Concord*, 637–38. [The italicized passages were emphasized in the German document; they are not italicized in the English *Book of Concord*.—LR]

[1.] From *Literaturverzeichnis für die Vorlesungen an der Universität Berlin und an der Hochschule für Politik* (Index of References for Lectures at the University of Berlin and the School for Political Science); *Semester Review*, no. 12 (ending November 1, 1933), no page numbering. See also *NL*, A 31,5; typewritten copy; reprinted in *GS* 3:243–47. This essay has been included in this volume because of its relationship to Bonhoeffer's teaching in Berlin.

and night";[2] a real willingness to work seriously, to study, and to think. It is not the experience of a call but the determination to do sober, earnest, and responsible theological work that is the gateway to the study of theology.

One may bring to theological studies one's own passions, one's philosophical, ethical, pedagogical, patriotic, or social zeal. These belong to the 417
student as a whole person, and one must truly enter into theology with one's whole self. The person who is not driven to theological study at least in part by these very passions will certainly be a poor theologian. But theological students must then learn and know that the driving force in their lives and thinking, as theologians, can only come from the passion of Jesus Christ, our crucified Lord. The study of theology cannot be conquered by the overflowing vitality of one's own passion; rather, the real study of *theologia sacra*[3] begins when, in the midst of questioning and seeking, human beings encounter the cross; when they recognize the endpoint of all their own passions in the suffering of God at the hands of humankind, and realize that their entire vitality stands under judgment. This is the great turnaround, which for the course of study means the turn toward theological objectivity. Theological study no longer means revealing the passions of one's ego; it is no longer a monologue, no longer religious self-fulfillment. Rather, it is about responsible study and listening, becoming attentive to the Word of God, which has been revealed right here in this world; it is toning down one's self in the face of what is far and away the most important matter.

A young theological student should have the will to become a theologian in this sense, openly and honestly, or else waste no more time in pursuing the course. The real task of the theologian should not be a cause for shame, once the student discovers it; there should be no attempt to dress it up in all sorts of irrelevancies. Why should it be theological students and graduates who find it relevant and necessary, from their first semester until they reach the highest offices in the church, to talk disparagingly about theological studies? How can it be a good sign in them that they avoid the company of honest theologians from Paul to Augustine, from Thomas to Luther, and claim to have no need of what was immeasurably important to these teachers? How can such a facile setting aside of issues that were important to wiser and more serious people be evidence of anything but poorly concealed ignorance? How can such a student avoid being asked in astonishment: Do you really think you belong here, studying theology? 418

[2.] Ps. 1:2.

[3.] "Sacred theology."

Shouldn't you perhaps think of some more enticing, visible, imposing, in any case quite different place to be? Since when is a person especially qualified for a theological career who cares so little about theology as to talk as everyone else does about it? And ultimately, since when does it make someone a good Christian to presume to talk about things that he or she is far from understanding?

A young theological student should know that to pursue theology is to serve the true church of Christ, which is unwavering in confessing its Lord, and should live with this responsibility. It is detestable to see theological students fail to take this seriously and feel better about being seen as worldly than as dedicated to theology. With such an attitude, far from winning others over, one only invites their boundless and justified contempt and risks making the whole theological community a laughingstock once again, along with oneself. A theological student who likes to stand out, who likes to be made the center of attention at the expense of colleagues, in the end will achieve only the opposite. Moreover, those who like to display their worldliness will find that it actually plays dirty tricks on them. So it is really not clear at all how keeping all one's worldliness should be the decisive criterion for a good theological career.

One should prepare oneself, through the study of theology, to discern the spirits in Christ's church.[4] One should learn from the Holy Scriptures and the confessions of the Reformation what is the pure and true teaching of the gospel of Jesus Christ, and which are human teachings, human laws, false doctrines, and idolatry. One should learn, through these studies, not to turn black into white, but to call truth truth, and false doctrine false doctrine. One should think this through carefully, modestly, objectively, lovingly but also with boldness and complete determination, and in the same spirit bear witness to it. Whoever fails to do this must answer for it, to the Lord of the church that we serve! One should know where the wellspring of the church's life is found, and how it can become clogged
419 and poisoned. One must learn to recognize where and when the church of Christ reaches its hour of decision, when it is time for confession—the *status confessionis*.[5]

And if the church that one serves is in *status confessionis*, he is called upon to recognize that the gospel is being turned into a false doctrine; he must see with his trained vision that new and strange meanings are being concealed behind the old words—and he must say so out loud, openly, right

[4.] See 1 John 4:1.

[5.] [See the definition and discussion of *status confessionis* in 2/13, ed. note 14.—LR]

where he is. As a student of theology, no one can and should do otherwise than keep inquiring after the true gospel, ever more attentively and objectively, in ever more truth and love.

In such times one should in no way become emotional in one's thinking and action but remain completely sober. Especially at this point, one should not seek to play a role but rather read and study one's Bible as never before.

One should know, in such times, that under no circumstances are tactical considerations the way to serve one's church or the aims of theology; only the purest, most refined truth will do. Even with the best will in the world, tactical solutions only cloud and obscure the situation. The student of theology is the last one who should be thinking tactically and instead should carry on working with purely theological objectivity, in service to God.

One should, in such times, err on the side of being too quiet rather than too loud. For the false confidence of a loud voice has nothing to do with the assurance of repentance and the gospel.

Finally, one should know as a true theologian that, even where our knowledge of the gospel of Jesus Christ in its truth and purity keeps us away from false doctrines, we stand beside our brethren who have wandered and been misled, sharing their guilt, interceding and praying for them, knowing that our own life depends, not on our better knowledge or being on the right side, but on forgiveness.

One should, in such times of confusion, go back to the very beginning, to our wellsprings, to the true Bible, to the true Luther. One should keep on, ever more undaunted and joyfully, becoming a theologian ἀληθεύοντες ἐν ἀγάπῃ.[6]

[6.] "Speaking the truth in love" (Eph. 4:15).

PART 3
Sermons, Homilies, and Liturgies

1. Sermon on Revelation 2:4–5, 7 423
Berlin, Reformation Sunday, November 6, 1932[1]

Reformation Sunday, November 6, 1932

But I have this against you, that you have abandoned the love you had at first. Remember then from what you have fallen; repent, and do the works you did at first. If not, I will come to you and remove your lampstand from its place, unless you repent. . . . Let anyone who has an ear listen to what the Spirit is saying to the churches. To everyone who conquers, I will give permission to eat from the tree of life that is in the paradise of God.[2]

That we are in the eleventh hour of the life of our Protestant church, that we do not have much more time until it is decided whether our church is finished, or a new day is beginning for it—this should have become clear to us by now. We also ought to know that one does not comfort the dying, or revive them again, with trumpet calls. Trumpet fanfares belong at the funeral, when we think we have to drown out our cold silence with even colder noise, where decomposition is disguised with funeral wreaths and funereal music. It's like what children do when they are afraid to walk down a dark street—they whistle and stomp and make noise to get their courage up. It's an odd sort of deception—when your courage deserts you, you manufacture it, out of pure terror.

¶This sort of courage, which is really fear, this fearful courage and trumpet blowing, which only announce that death has already occurred—none 424
of us who are still involved in the life of the church can say we do not know about them. Reformation Sunday is the terrible day that has made them most familiar. Today, among the thousands of trumpet fanfares bearing

[1.] *NL*, A 33,10(b); typewritten. See also *NL*, A 33,10(a); handwritten; reprinted in *GS* 4:93–101 and *PAM* 1:328–36. The biblical text is marked in Bonhoeffer's Bible (Luther translation). According to *PAM* 1:328, the sermon was given at a university worship service at Dreifaltigkeitskirche (Trinity Church). Elections for the Reichstag (parliament) were being held that Sunday, (following a strike in Berlin that had caused a sensation; see ed. note 3). The Nazi party remained the strongest party, with 33.1 percent of votes cast, but won 2 million fewer votes than in the July 1932 Reichstag elections, while the Communists gained more than 600,000 votes. Dreifaltigkeitskirche in Berlin-Friedrichsstadt, where Friedrich Schleiermacher had served as a Reformed pastor, was blown up after World War II because its "vaulted cellar had served as the Nazi leaders' bunker" (Reich, "Schleiermacher als Gemeindepfarrer," 95n3).

[2.] Rev. 2:4–5, 7.

witness that Germany is at death's door,[3] others have joined in, shouting out to the world that the church is dying. Germany, in fear of its future, is drumming up its courage today with all manner of big, loud words, as long as they drive the terror of death out of its most secret heart. The church of the Reformation, which secretly knows that it is separated from the Reformation by an abyss and is already shuddering at the approach of death, sings with desperate courage, "A mighty fortress is our God . . . Lord of hosts is he, Jesus Christ, our Lord, God's only Son, adored"[4]—and fails to see that every time it says, "God," God actually turns against it. We sing, "A mighty fortress is our God." "If God is for us, who is against us?"[5] But God says, "But I have this against you . . ."

¶In celebrating the Reformation, the church can't leave old Luther in peace. He has to suffer for all the terrible things that are going on in the church today. Though he is dead, we prop him up in our church and make him hold out his hand, gesture toward the church, and keep saying over and
425 over those same self-confident words with all their pathos, "Here I stand—I can do no other."[6] We fail to see that this is no longer Luther's church, that Luther was distressed and agitated,[7] pushed all the way to the wall by the devil and in fear of God when he said, "Here I stand," and that these are hardly suitable words for us to speak. It is simply untruthful, or unforgivable heedlessness and arrogance, for us to take refuge behind these words. We can indeed do otherwise, or at least we should be able to, and it would cer-

[3.] The political crisis that ended the Weimar Republic was intensified greatly by the traffic strike in Berlin. On November 4, 1932, the *Kreuz-Zeitung* (no. 308-B) carried a headline on page 1, "To Be or Not to Be," and continued: "The traffic strike in Berlin, in which National Socialists and Communists stand shoulder to shoulder, is a storm signal of utmost seriousness. . . . The Papen government is responsible today for the fate of our nation and for the public order, and must immediately take all necessary measures, lest the disaster now threatening us run its course and throw our nation into chaos, possibly worse than the Thirty Years' War." On November 5, 1932 (no. 309-B), again on page 1, the headline was "The Strike—a Trial of Strength" and the subhead, "Terrorist Acts throughout the City—Bracht [Franz Bracht, the deputy Reich commissioner for Prussia] Mercilessly Takes Drastic Steps." A sentence below stated, "Imposition of a state of emergency will probably very soon become unavoidable, if the government does not intend to capitulate to the strikers." The strike did not end until Monday evening, November 7, 1932.

[4.] From Luther's Reformation hymn of 1528 (*Lutheran Book of Worship*, no. 228, verses 1 and 3).

[5.] Rom. 8:31.

[6.] This tradition is disputed; it appears that at the parliament of Worms in 1521, Luther answered the question as to whether he was willing to recant only with the words, "May God help me. Amen." See "Luther at the Diet of Worms," 1521 (*LW* 32:115).

[7.] Cf. Mark 14:33.

tainly bring us no honor before God or humankind if we could only do as we are now doing and not otherwise. Not one of us has taken that ultimate stand from which we can only pray to God, saying, "I can do no other; God help me." We can and should do otherwise. It must have resounded from pulpits thousands of times today: "I cannot do otherwise; here I stand." God, however, says, "But I have this against you . . ."

The Protestant church is observing its special day. Protest is among its traditional obligations. It may be protesting against quite a variety of things, but protest it must. This time it is strong protest against secularism in the form of godlessness, but of course also—perhaps especially this time—against Catholicism and its dangers (meaning, of course, only the political dangers).[8] Then there is protest against anything that binds us tightly, against dogma and authority, protest in favor of freedom of conscience and thinking, or individual freedom, protest against indecency and lack of faith, and protest against everyone who doesn't come to church and thus doesn't take much notice of this protest, of this Protestant day! Oh, how easily we protest, with what passion and self-confidence, since we have
a documented right to it. What a splendid day this is. "We protest!" is our 426
cry. But God says, "But I have this against you . . . ," meaning, "I protest." God protests—against whom? Against us and our protest! Can't we hear it? Protestantism is not about us and our protest against the world, but rather about God's protest against us: "But I have this against you . . ."

But we are still pretending, aren't we? When it comes down to it, we know very well that it is not about "A mighty fortress," nor about "Here I stand"; this is not the protest we are talking about. We know full well about God's protest against us, and we know that, most of all on Reformation Day, God is out in force against us. But we don't want to admit it, either to ourselves or to the world. We are afraid that we are not equal to facing God's offensive or protest; we are afraid we would look foolish in the eyes of God and the world if we admitted any such thing. That's why we make so much noise about this day, October 31,[9] hammering wrong ideas into the heads of thousands[10] of schoolchildren, only so that they don't notice our weakness, so that we can forget it ourselves.

[8.] Unlike Protestantism, Catholicism was represented clearly by a political party, the Center party, founded in 1870. It provided the Weimar Republic with several Reich chancellors. [Six of the Weimar chancellors were from the Center party.—LR]

[9.] Reformation Day is officially October 31. It was not a public holiday in Prussia; in many Protestant areas, worship was held only in schools on that day, and the churches celebrated the Reformation on the previous or following Sunday.

[10.] The handwritten version has "hundreds of thousands."

No, our time has run out for such solemn church feast days on which we put on an act for ourselves. Let us stop celebrating the Reformation that way! Let us lay the dead Luther to rest at long last, and instead listen to the gospel, reading his Bible, hearing God's own word in it. At the last judgment God is certainly going to ask us not, "Have you celebrated Reformation Day properly?" but rather, "Have you heard my word and kept it?"

¶So we had better let that word say to us, "But I have this against you, that you have abandoned the love you had at first." If only I had the power now to speak those words so that it would really hurt us to listen to them. It should hurt us—otherwise it wouldn't be God's word. But I see already that you are doing the same as with a bad novel, reading the happy ending of the story first, so you don't have to get too upset over what goes before it, so you can always say, "Well, it will all come out right in the end."

427 ¶"But I have this against you, that you have abandoned the love you had at first." The difference between what is here called "the love you had at first" and everything else we usually mean by these words can be succinctly stated: there is no other love besides this love. This love you had at first is the only love there is—for this is the love that comes from God and to God. Besides this love, this love you had at first, there is only hate, so that to abandon this love is to abandon God, to abandon one's brother or sister. It means that one can then only hate God and the world.

¶"But I have this against you, that you have abandoned the love you had at first" means that it was different at first; there was already a beginning in you too! There was a time, for you too, when something was happening. There was a time—wasn't there?—when you had something to do with God. You used to pray to God, to tell God your troubles and the evil you had done; there was a time when you loved God, when you thought you would try believing in God. There was also an effect on the world around you, in those days; something was really happening. You once loved the others, who so often annoy you and make things difficult for you, because you were thinking of God's love. There was a time when you thought God should be the Lord of your life, even the deepest hidden ground of it, and be Lord of all life that there is, and this indeed became true for you, as you went among the people around you with Jesus Christ in your thoughts and in your heart. "But I have this against you . . ."

Now let us turn to the church as a whole. Whatever became of that earliest time of grace, the time of the first Christians who called Jesus Christ the Lord of their lives and left their homes to serve him, when the fire was first lit and began to burn? When the coming of the kingdom of God was awaited with such great longing that it came down and entered into that waiting and took shape there in the most amazing way? Where has the time

gone that was described in the words: "Now the whole community was of one heart and soul, and no one claimed private ownership of any possessions, but everything they owned was held in common. With great power the apostles gave testimony to the resurrection of the Lord Jesus, and great
grace was upon them all" (Acts 4:32–33).[11] Where is it now, this church- 428
community that, because it knew of one divine miracle, the resurrection from death into life, thought all things must be possible for the one who believes,[12] believed in the power of grace, in the power of love for God, even to the point of loving others so much as to come down to them in their need and humbly help them? Where is the community of that first love, like a lamp set on a lampstand, a light from God in the midst of the world?

We may surely ask what good it does to recall the past. It is lost to us now. An individual might say: That was just my first love, my childish devotion. When I grew up and matured, I grew out of it. Of course it was nice then, but there was a lot of illusion in it. I've learned better; I've seen that the world is a bad place and not everything is possible, that we have to make compromises and settle for being less than we thought. This has certainly deadened me, but I'm wiser for it. This is just the way the church talks.

What can be the answer here? Do you think the first Christians, or the Reformation leaders and their first congregations, didn't know that the world is a bad place? What about those who saw their beloved Master being crucified by the world—didn't they know it? Indeed, they did, a thousand times better than we do. Just listen to the Bible, just read what Luther wrote. In fact, they knew something more, and it is crucial: they knew the reason why the world is evil, namely, hatred toward God and toward one's neighbor, the human love only for oneself. But now they had seen and heard how God conquered this hate, right in the midst of the world through Jesus Christ and his cross and his resurrection. They believed in this miracle of God's love here in the world, and so they loved God and their neighbors.

Back to you as an individual. Didn't you, too, once believe and know that hate has been overcome and that love is the right way? It may have been an illusion then; it may have been an illusion for you up to this very hour—who would vouch for what was going on in the past? But then hear the word spoken to you today: today it is not an illusion; it is true. You are being given God's own word for it: "I have this against you, that you have abandoned the love you had at first—that you have abandoned me."

[11.] Slight deviation from the NRSV translation to correspond to the German text.
[12.] See Mark 9:23.

429 "Remember then from what you have fallen; repent."[13] It was none other than this call that brought Luther to do what he did: "Remember then from what you have fallen; repent!" You should be burning and you are cold; you should wake up and you are sluggish; you should be hungry and you are full; you should believe and you are afraid; you should have hope and you are grasping for power; you should be loving and you won't come out of yourself; you should let Christ be your Lord and you interrupt when he speaks; you should be doing miracles with him and you are not even doing the most ordinary things.

¶"Remember then from what you have fallen; repent." The church of the Reformation is the church of those who expose themselves to this call, who let God be God here, who know that those who are standing are to watch out that they don't fall[14] and not boast that they are standing. Our church stands on God's Word alone, and it is that Word alone that makes us those who stand facing in the right direction. The church that stands in repentance, the church that lets God be God, is the church of the apostles and of Luther.

¶"Remember then from what you have fallen; repent, and do the works you did at first." This is essential. Without it, everything we have said here is meaningless.[15] It may not sound appropriate to be talking about works on Reformation Sunday, but it would be a dreadful misunderstanding of the gospel to say that faith and repentance are just something for our morning and evening devotions. Faith and repentance mean letting God be God, and that means also in what we do—especially in what we do, to be obedient to God.

¶Do the works you did at first—how much that needs to be said today. Nobody who knows the church today would complain that the church is doing nothing. No, the church is doing a tremendous amount, very seriously and even sacrificially. But we are all doing so many things that come second, third, and fourth; the church is not doing the works it did at first. And that is precisely why it is not doing what is crucial. We celebrate; we attend the events where we should be seen; we try to be influential; we set

[13.] The handwritten version continues here: "It was right, the way we began back then, but it was also wrong, because we fell away from it. The church has fallen away from the best it had, from that which only broke through again in the Reformation, from its Lord, from the love it had at first. Repent."

[14.] See 1 Cor. 10:12.

[15.] The handwritten version continues here: "To repent means to let God be God . . . that is why it also means do the works you did at first."

up a so-called Protestant movement;[16] we do Protestant youth work; we 430
provide social services and care for people; and we have anti-godless propaganda[17]—but are we doing the very first works, the ones that epitomize what we are all about? Do we love God and our neighbor with that first, passionate, burning love that is willing to risk everything except God? Are we really letting God be God? Are we putting ourselves and our church under God's guidance? If we were, things would have to look different—there would have to be some kind of breakthrough. But let us not fall into that most terrible of temptations and try to bring about that breakthrough ourselves. That is up to God alone. We must place ourselves at God's service; with the love we had at first, we must let God be wholly God. Perhaps then the words we read just now will come true: "Now the whole group of those who believed were of one heart and soul . . . everything they owned was held in common."

Now come the very serious words, "If not, I will come to you and remove your lampstand from its place, unless you repent." Here God is speaking with ultimate seriousness. The last hour has almost come for our church. God has been very patient and long-suffering. No one knows that day and hour.[18] It could break out at any moment and sweep everything away. We can already see things happening all around. God has been known to employ the strangest of instruments in working destruction. The story of Jerusalem's destruction by unbelievers[19] is beginning to take on a terrible relevance for us. However it may come—we had better not make up any fine words, today, about the heroic things we would do when such a breakdown comes—let God be the Lord.

This destroying God, before whom we bow, is the Lord of the Promise.
God alone knows his people; he is present, perhaps right here among us. 431
God alone knows to whom he is speaking when he says: "Let anyone who has an ear listen to what the Spirit is saying to the churches. To everyone who conquers, I will give permission to eat from the tree of life that is in

[16.] This probably alludes to the attempt to give Protestants political representation through the Christlich-Sozialen Volksdienst (Christian-Social Peoples' Service), just as the Catholics had long since done with their Center party (see the report on the "Leadership Conference of the Christian Social People's Service," with the headline "Gathering of the Protestant Movement," in the *Tägliche Rundschau*, no. 33, February 8, 1933). [The Christian-Social Peoples' Service won fourteen votes in the 1930 election.—LR]

[17.] Refers to the "Propaganda against the Godless," which was an important element in the systematic development of an apologetic for the church during the 1920s.

[18.] See Matt. 24:36.

[19.] Refers to the destruction of Jerusalem in the Roman-Jewish War, 70 CE.

the paradise of God." Will we be those people? Will we conquer? Will we be able to keep faith until the end? The future frightens us. But the Promise comforts us. Blessed are those who are called to it.

And now, when you leave the church, don't think about whether that was a fine or a poor Reformation service, but let us go soberly and do the works that came first. God be our help. Amen.

2. Homily on Daniel 10:1, 8, 16–19 Berlin, December 1, 1932[1]

Daniel 10 December 1, 1932

In the third year of Cyrus king of Persia a word was revealed to Daniel, who was named Belteshazzar. And the word was true, and it was a great conflict. And he understood the word and had understanding of the vision. . . . So I was left alone and saw this great vision, and no strength was left in me; my radiant appearance was fearfully changed, and I retained no strength. . . . And behold, one in the likeness of the sons of men touched my lips; then I opened my mouth and spoke. I said to him who stood before me, "O my lord, by reason of the vision pains have come upon me, and I retain no strength. How can my lord's servant talk with my lord? For now no strength remains in me, and no breath is left in me." Again one having the appearance of a man touched me and strengthened me. And he said, "O man greatly beloved, fear not, peace be with you; be strong and of good courage." And when he spoke to me, I was strengthened and said, "Let my lord speak, for you have strengthened me."[2]

432 I shall never forget the day when this text first made its impact on me. It was at a meeting of German and French young people, coming together on the common ground of the church, and our desire here was to talk very clearly and honestly about the things that lay between us. We wanted to submit ourselves with utmost seriousness to the commandment of God in

[1.] *NL*, A 33,19(a); handwritten, with note by Eberhard Bethge: "Thursday." See also *NL*, A 33,19(b); later written copy by Bethge. Previously published in *GS* 4:144–46 and *PAM* 1:337–39. According to *DB-ER*, 246, the service was [one of those Bonhoeffer conducted as chaplain] at the Technical College.

[2.] Verses selected at the discretion of the German editors. [Wording is from the RSV (1952); NRSV does not have "peace be with you."—LR]

our time, God's decree of peace on earth, goodwill among people.[3] And as we looked from Christ's call to the world to the real state of affairs in Europe and throughout the world, we were all filled with fear and dismay about our message. We felt something of what is said here of Daniel, that he felt wounded and weak in the presence of God's word; we would have been only too glad to free ourselves of the mission and the message of God. Then as we sat together, feeling rather frightened, a young Frenchman read out these words from the Bible. And when he came to the words "Fear not, peace be with you; be strong and of good courage," we all felt that afterward we could have said, "Let my lord speak, for you have strengthened us!"

None of us is totally without experience of such a moment—at least no one who has tried seriously to walk with God. When we are disturbed by chaos in our personal lives, and we can't cope with it anymore; when we feel as though every support keeps crumbling away, leaving us in free fall; when our lives go back and forth between good intentions and being ashamed of ourselves, and we can't avoid seeing clearly how little strength we have; when some incomprehensible stroke of fate, great suffering or a great passion, leaves us bewildered and feeling completely at the mercy of this fate; when we see how, through lack of faith and hope, we have given in and taken the wrong path in life; or, finally, when something breaks down in
our relations with friends, and all our good will isn't enough to get us back 433
together; in short, when we finally take seriously the whole of the human chaos in which we are involved, then it may suddenly come over us to say: God, I can't stand you anymore; keep out of my pitiful excuse for a life; I don't want to hear from you; I can't take it anymore. No, I don't even want to; I'm too far down in the muck. God, don't talk to me anymore; I don't want to talk to you either. God, we can't keep on like this.

¶This is just when what we have to do is listen again and hear again being said to us, as really to us: Peace . . . be of good courage, the courage that God gives . . . Then it's as if a mother takes away from her child the homework in which [he or she] has made so many mistakes and blots, and is now crying miserably about it, and puts a fresh sheet of paper in its place. Come on now, try again. Be of good courage. That's the way God talks to us when we are frightened at the very sight of ourselves.

And now this thing that happened to Daniel is taking place in a very particular case, which we today can understand as hardly anyone has before.

[3.] Luke 2:14. Bonhoeffer was probably referring to the German-French regional conference of the World Alliance at Westerburg Castle in Westerwald, July 12–14, 1932 (see *DBW* 11, 2/18, and *DB-ER*, 245–46).

God speaks: "Let me tell you . . . ," and Daniel can't stand to hear it. Can we stand it? Isn't it true of us too, that in this hopeless confusion and bewilderment, we say: God, you stay away too, [. . .][4] We already know how bad it is. But as soon as you turn up, then it's all over. That nameless fear . . . of hearing God's judgment on our people and what we have done . . . Be of good courage. What for? So that we, as men and women who have received strength, may hear God's voice speaking to God's people and make a new start at obeying and believing in God.

434 **3. Liturgy for a Seminar Worship Service**
Berlin, December 20, 1932[1]

Christmas Celebration 1932 in the Seminar

Choir: Be welcome here, O Jesus Christ . . .[2]

Pastor: Behold, I stand at the door and knock; if any one hears my voice and opens the door, I will come in to him and eat with him, and he with me.[3]

Congregation:
O Jesus Christ, all praise to thee,
Thou who art pleased a man to be;
To dwell with us thou dost not scorn,
And angels shout to see thee born,
Kyrieleis.

[4.] Illegible. The German editors suggest "but speak." [The context, however, can support "don't speak" as well.—LR]

[1.] *NL*, A 29,1 (4) b; carbon copy. See also *NL*, A 29,1 (4) a; handwritten. Reprinted in *GS* 6:207–9. The date of December 20, 1932, for the service has been deduced from letter 1/20. The place is not known. [Bonhoeffer took all the hymns from the *Evangelisches Gesangbuch*, the hymnal then in use in the German Lutheran church. Translator Isabel Best has taken the biblical citations from the Revised Standard Version (1971), since the language fits better with the translations found. For this liturgy we have also used translations from existing English hymnals as indicated. In some cases the text of the English translation is not a literal translation of the German hymn but conveys the meaning and certainly the liturgical rhythm of the German.—LR]

[2.] Probably the canon "Nun sei uns willkommen, Herre Christ, der du unser aller Herre bist, willkommen auf Erden" (Be welcome here, our Lord and Christ, you who are the Lord of all, we welcome you on earth) (*Neues Lied*, no. 36; *Evangelisches Gesangbuch*, no. 22).

[3.] Rev. 3:20.

The eternal Father's only Son
Now takes a manger for his throne;
With our poor flesh and our poor blood
Was clothed that everlasting good.
Kyrieleis.
The eternal Light to us descends,
Its brightness to the earth it lends,
And purely shines upon our night,
To make us children of the light.
Kyrieleis.
His love to show, surpassing thought,
God's Son this wondrous work hath wrought;
Then let us all unite to raise
Our song of glad, unceasing praise.
Kyrieleis.[4]

Pastor: There shall come forth a shoot from the stump of Jesse, 435
Congregation: and a branch shall grow out of his roots.
Pastor: And the Spirit of the LORD shall rest upon him,
Congregation: the spirit of wisdom and understanding,
the spirit of counsel and might,
the spirit of knowledge and the fear of the LORD.[5]
Pastor: Behold, God is my salvation; I will trust, and will not be afraid;
Congregation: for the LORD GOD is my strength and my song and my salvation.[6]
Pastor: The LORD is in his holy temple;
Congregation: let all the earth keep silence before him.[7]

Choir: Lo, how a rose e'er blooming . . .[8]

[4.] Translation here is from *The Lutheran Hymnary* (1935), no. 184, verses 1–2, 4, 7. Text by Luther (1524), trans. A. T. Russell (1851). [*Kyrieleis* = Lord, have mercy.—LR]

[5.] Isa. 11:1–2.

[6.] See Isa. 12:2.

[7.] Hab. 2:20.

[8.] The German hymn is "Es ist ein Ros entsprungen" (*Evangelisches Gesangbuch*, no. 30).

Pastor: Let us bring our prayers before God.

Congregation: Lord, such knowledge is too wonderful for me; it is too high, I cannot attain it.[9]

Pastor: Know the love of Christ, which surpasses all knowledge.[10]

Congregation: Lord, I am a person of unclean lips, and I dwell in the midst of a people of unclean lips.[11]

Pastor: If you return, I will restore you, and you shall stand before me.[12]

Congregation: Ah, Lord GOD! Behold, I do not know how to speak, for I am only a youth.

Pastor: Do not say, "I am only a youth"; for to all to whom I send you, you shall go, and whatever I command you, you shall speak.
Be not afraid of them, for I am with you to deliver you.[13]

Pastor and Congregation: I will lift up the cup of salvation
and call on the name of the LORD.[14]

436 Pastor: Rejoice in the Lord always; again I will say, Rejoice.[15]
For to us a child is born, to us a son is given;
and the government will be upon his shoulder.
and his name will be called "Wonderful Counselor, Mighty God, Everlasting Father, Prince of Peace."
Of the increase of his government and of peace there will be no end,
upon the throne of David, and over his kingdom,
to establish it, and to uphold it with justice and with righteousness
from this time forth and for evermore.[16]

[9.] See Ps. 139:6.
[10.] See Eph. 3:19.
[11.] See Isa. 6:5.
[12.] Jer. 15:19. [The Luther Bible has further "as my preacher."—LR]
[13.] See Jer. 1:6–8.
[14.] Ps. 116:13. [The Luther Bible has "and preach the name of the Lord."—LR]
[15.] Phil. 4:4.
[16.] Isa. 9:5–7.

Congregation: Come, and Christ the Lord be praising,
Heart and mind to Him be raising,
Celebrate his love amazing,[17]
Worthy folk of Christendom.

Choir: *In dulci jubilo*
Let us our homage show:
Our hearts' joy reclineth
In praesepio,
And like a bright star shineth
Matris in gremio.
Alpha es et O.

Congregation: Jacob's Star his advent maketh,
Soothes the longing heart that acheth;
And the serpent's head he breaketh,
Destroying all the powers of hell.

Choir: *O Jesu parvule,*
For thee I long always,
Comfort my heart's blindness
O puer optime
With all thy lovingkindness,
O princeps gloriae,
Trahe me post te.

Congregation: Gracious Child, we pray thee, hear us 437
From thy lowly manger cheer us,
Gently lead us and be near us
Till we join the angelic choir.

Choir: *Ubi sunt gaudia*
If they be not there?
There are angels singing
Nova cantica,

[17.] [This line of the English translation of this hymn differs from the German text, which could be translated: "Sing joyfully, let yourselves hear."—LR]

There the bells are ringing
In regis curia,
O, that we were there.[18]

Pastor: Blessed be the Lord God of Israel,
for he has visited and redeemed his people,
Congregation: and has raised up a horn of salvation for us
in the house of his servant David,
Pastor: as he spoke by the mouth of his holy prophets from of old,
Congregation: that we should be saved from our enemies,
and from the hand of all who hate us;
Pastor: to perform the mercy promised to our fathers,
and to remember his holy covenant,
Congregation: the oath which he swore to our father Abraham, to grant us
Pastor: that we, being delivered from the hand of our enemies,
might serve him without fear,
Congregation: in holiness and righteousness before him all the days of our life.
Pastor: And you, child, will be called the prophet of the Most High;
for you will go before the Lord to prepare his ways,
Congregation: to give knowledge of salvation to his people,
in the forgiveness of their sins,
Pastor: through the tender mercy of our God,
when the day shall dawn upon us from on high
438 Congregation: to give light to those who sit in darkness and in the shadow of death,
to guide our feet into the way of peace.[19]

[18.] [The text here is, in alternation, from Paul Gerhardt's German version of "Quem Pastores Laudavere," stanzas 1 and 5 (trans. J. Kelly) in *The Wartburg Hymnal,* stanza 7 from composite translation in *The Lutheran Hymnal* (1941), with Henry Suso's carol (trans. R. L. de Pearsall), stanzas 1, 2, and 6 (vs. 2 is from the *Oxford Book of Carols*).—LR]

[19.] Luke 1:68–79.

Pastor: Fear not: for, behold, I bring you good tidings of great joy,
which shall be to all people.
For unto you is born this day in the city of David a Savior,
which is Christ the Lord.
Glory to God in the highest,
and on earth peace, good will among people.[20]

Choir: I stand here at your manger . . .[21]

Pastor: Now the salvation and the power and the kingdom of our God
and the authority of his Christ have come.[22]
And he shall reign for ever and ever.[23]

Congregation: All my heart this night rejoices,
As I hear
Far and near
Sweetest angel voices;
"Christ is born," their choirs are singing,
Till the air
Everywhere
Now with joy is ringing.

For it dawns—the promised morrow
Of His birth
Who the earth
Rescues from her sorrow.
God to wear our form descendeth,
Of His grace
To our race
Here His Son he lendeth.

[20.] Luke 2:10–11, 14 [Citations are from the KJV and the NRSV.—LR]

[21.] "Ich steh an deiner Krippe hier," a popular German carol (*Evangelisches Gesangbuch*, no. 37).

[22.] Rev. 12:10.

[23.] Rev. 11:15.

439 Come then, let us hasten yonder,
Here let all
Great and small
Kneel in awe and wonder;
Love him who with love is yearning;
Hail the Star
That from far
Bright with hope is burning.[24]

Homily[25]
Prayer
Benediction

Congregation: All glory be to God on high,
Who hath our race befriended!
To us no harm shall now come nigh,
The strife at last is ended;
God showeth his good will toward men,
And peace shall dwell on earth again;
O thank him for his goodness![26]

4. Sermon on Matthew 8:23–27
Berlin, Second Sunday after Epiphany, January 15, 1933[1]

Matthew 8:23–27 January 15, 1933

And when he got into the boat, his disciples followed him. A windstorm arose on the sea, so great that the boat was being swamped by the waves; but he was asleep. And they went and woke him up, saying, "Lord, save us! We are perishing!" And he said to them, "Why are you afraid, you of little faith?" Then he got

[24.] [English translation from *Lyra Germanica*, no. 48, stanzas 1, 2, and 5, Paul Gerhardt, trans. Catherine Winkworth (1858).—LR]

[25.] Not extant.

[26.] [Translation used is from *The Lutheran Hymnary*, no. 2, stanza 1, trans. Catherine Winkworth (1863).—LR]

[1.] *NL*, A 33, 11(a); handwritten. See also *NL*, A 33,11(b); later written copy by Eberhard Bethge. Reprinted in *GS* 4:101–9 (indicating that the sermon was given at a vesper service in Trinity Church) and *PAM* 1:340–49. The German editors added the biblical text to the original manuscript.

up and rebuked the winds and the sea; and there was a dead calm. They were 440
amazed, saying, "What sort of man is this, that even the winds and the sea obey him?"

The overcoming of fear—that is what we are proclaiming here. The Bible, the gospel, Christ, the church, the faith—all are one great battle cry against fear in the lives of human beings. Fear is, somehow or other, the archenemy itself. It crouches in people's hearts. It hollows out their insides, until their resistance and strength are spent and they suddenly break down. Fear secretly gnaws and eats away at all the ties that bind a person to God and to others, and when in a time of need that person reaches for those ties and clings to them, they break and the individual sinks back into himself or herself, helpless and despairing, while hell rejoices.

¶Now fear leers that person in the face, saying: "Here we are all by ourselves, you and I; now I'm showing you my true face." And anyone who has seen naked fear revealed, who has been its victim in terrifying loneliness—fear of an important decision; fear of a heavy stroke of fate, losing one's job, an illness; fear of a vice that one can no longer resist, to which one is enslaved; fear of disgrace; fear of another person; fear of dying—that person knows that fear is only one of the faces of evil itself, one form by which the world, at enmity with God, grasps for someone. Nothing can make a human being so conscious of the reality of powers opposed to God in our lives as this loneliness, this helplessness, this fog spreading over everything, this sense that there is no way out, and this raving impulse to get oneself out of this hell of hopelessness.

¶Have you ever seen someone in the grip of fear? It's dreadful in a child, but even more dreadful in an adult: the staring eyes, the shivering like an animal, the pleading attempt to defend oneself. Fear takes away a person's humanity. This is not what the creature made by God looks like—this person belongs to the devil, this enslaved, broken-down, sick creature.

¶But the human being doesn't have to be afraid; we should not be afraid!
That is what makes the human being different from all other creatures. In 441
the midst of every situation where there is no way out, where nothing is clear, where it is our fault, we know that there is hope, and this hope is called: Thy will be done,[2] yes, thy will is being done. "This world must fall, God stands above all, his thoughts unswayed, his Word unstayed, his will

[2.] Matt. 6:10 [KJV].

forever our ground and hope."[3] Do you ask: How do you know? Then we name the name of the One who makes the evil inside us recoil, who makes fear and anxiety themselves tremble with fear and puts them to flight. We name the One who overcame fear and led it captive in the victory procession, who nailed it to the cross and committed it to oblivion; we name the One who is the shout of victory of humankind redeemed from the fear of death—Jesus Christ, the Crucified and Living One. He alone is Lord over fear; it knows him as its master; it gives way to him alone. So look to Christ when you are afraid, think of Christ, keep him before your eyes, call upon Christ and pray to him, believe that he is with you now, helping you . . . Then fear will grow pale and fade away, and you will be free, through your faith in our strong and living Savior, Jesus Christ.

Let's say there is a ship on the high sea, having a fierce struggle with the waves. The storm wind is blowing harder by the minute. The boat is small, tossed about like a toy; the sky is dark; the sailors' strength is failing. Then one of them is gripped by . . . whom? what? . . . he cannot tell himself. But someone is there in the boat who wasn't there before. Someone comes close to him and lays cold hands on his arms as he pulls wildly on his oar. He feels his muscles freeze, feels the strength go out of them. Then the unknown one reaches into his heart and mind and magically brings forth the strangest pictures. He sees his family, his children crying. What will become of them if he is no more? Then he seems to be back where he once was when he followed evil ways, in long years of bondage to evil, and he sees the faces of his companions in that bondage. He sees a neighbor
442 whom he wounded, only yesterday, with an angry word. Suddenly he can no longer see or hear anything, can no longer row, a wave overwhelms him, and in final desperation he shrieks: "Stranger in this boat, who are you?" And the other answers, "I am Fear." Now the cry goes up from the whole crew: "Fear is in the boat." All arms are frozen and drop their oars; all hope is lost. Fear is in the boat.

¶Then it is as if the heavens opened, as if the heavenly hosts themselves raised a shout of victory in the midst of hopelessness: "Christ is in the boat." Christ is in the boat, and no sooner has the call gone out and been heard than Fear shrinks back, and the waves subside. The sea becomes calm and the boat rests on its quiet surface. Christ was in the boat!

[3.] From Paul Gerhardt's hymn "Die güldne Sonne" (The Golden Sun), verse 8. Translation by Isabel Best.

We were along on that voyage, weren't we? and the call, "Christ is in the boat," was once our salvation too. And now, strangely enough, all of us are at sea again, on that voyage without faith, without hope, overwhelmed, in chains, in bondage, paralyzed by fear; we have lost heart, lost the joy of living, our limbs heavy as lead; each of us knows what it's like. Perhaps, or most likely, we don't even quite realize what has happened to us; we are already so used to this state of affairs that it seems natural to us, and we almost like it that way, all this misery around us and in our own lives. What would we do if we couldn't even complain anymore?

¶And that's the worst of it: we don't even want to find a way out. That is the final triumph of Fear over us, that we are afraid to run away from it and just let it enslave us. Fear has conquered us; it can be found among us in various forms. Some persons have become dull and insensitive and just live from one day to the next, brooding gloomily and doggedly along, but too apathetic to take their own lives. Others are noisy about their fear, pouring it out to everyone else in the form of crying and complaining. Still others, on the other hand, think they can drive out their fear with fine words and bold fantasies, and if they shout these words loudly enough it may seem to take care of things for a while. But those who know can recognize in such 443
empty words the horrifying power of fear all over again. Fear is in the boat, in Germany, in our own lives, and in the nave of this church—naked fear of an hour from now, of tomorrow and the day after. That is why we become apathetic, why we complain, why we intoxicate ourselves with this and that. What else is all the razzle-dazzle and drunkenness of New Year's Eve other than our great fear of a new era, of the future? Fear is breathing down our necks.

Those who would try to keep up their pride, as if all this had nothing to do with them, as if they didn't understand what it's all about, would hardly be human. No one human could fail to understand what the people of the world[4] have to be afraid of today.

But look here, right in the middle of this fearful world is a place that is meant for all time, which has a peculiar task that the world doesn't understand. It keeps calling over and over but always anew, in the same tone, the same thing: "Fear is overcome; don't be afraid. In the world you are frightened. But be comforted; I have conquered the world!"[5] Christ is in the

[4.] "The people of the world" (*Menschheit der Welt*) replaces "the German people" (*das deutsche Volk*).

[5.] John 16:33.

boat! And this place, where this kind of talk is heard and should be heard, is the pulpit of the church. From this pulpit the living Christ himself wants to speak, so that wherever he reaches somebody, that person will feel the fear sinking away, will feel Christ overcoming his or her fear.

¶"You of little faith, why are you so fearful?" In these words we must hear all the disappointment of Jesus Christ in his disciples and all his love for them. "Do you still not know that you are in God's hands, that where I am, God is? Why are you so fearful? Be of good courage, strong, firm, adult, sure, confident, not shaking with fear. Don't hang your heads; don't complain about what bad times these are . . . I am in the boat." And Christ is here, too, in the nave of this church. So why not hear him and believe him?

We have come here, very probably, because somehow or other we know that something in our lives needs to change, and because we think perhaps the church can somehow help us with this. We are aware of how meager,
444 how poor, how petty and shortsighted our lives have become. All of us see only our own worries and difficulties, and no longer those of others that may be a thousand times worse. Our affairs seem so enormous and infinitely important to us that we have become dulled toward anything else. This is the work of fear in us. And now we sense that we can't bear to be hemmed in like this anymore; it's suffocating. The call of the church cuts through this questioning and foreboding. There is one thing we are lacking: to believe that the almighty God is our Father and our Lord. To believe that for God, our greatest cares are like the worries of small children in their parents' eyes; that God can turn things around and dispose of them in no time at all; for God it's easy, not hard at all. We must believe that a thousand years in God's sight are like a day,[6] that God's thoughts are higher than our thoughts,[7] that God is with us in spite of everything. Let us receive the call of the church once again: You of little faith, why are you so fearful? In the midst of the storm, Christ is in the ship. Away with you, Fear! Let us see you, Lord Jesus, strong helper, Savior!

But now comes a host of objections and excuses. We say we would like to believe, but we simply can't anymore. The suffering is too great. Oh, but let's not take this kind of talk too seriously. You cannot believe? Well, neither can we. Do you want to believe?—in that case you already do, in a way, perhaps not very strongly, only a beginning, but perhaps a thousand times stronger than many others who think they are able to believe. Don't worry

[6.] See Ps. 90:4.
[7.] See Isa. 55:8–9.

about your faith, whether it is weak or strong. Just look to him in whom you believe, and speak to him: "Lord, increase our faith!"[8]

We say that it is not life's misery that frightens us, but rather our own sin that we fear; and that we need to fear it, so we won't be overcome by it! Again, that sounds so right, but it is really only a trick of fear itself. No, it is not true that we must be afraid of sin. Those who are afraid of it are already up to their necks in it. Fear is evil's net, spread to catch us. Once evil has made us afraid, confused us, we are in its clutches. Don't be afraid, be of
good courage . . . How can you meet the enemy with fear in your heart? You 445
of little faith, why are you so fearful? Isn't God greater than your sin? Let God grow strong in you; then sin is knocked down. Believe in God . . . Lord, strengthen our faith!

Now, finally, let the most depressed and despairing people speak, those who ask: Isn't our time up? Aren't the years of catastrophe, [of] utter decline and breakdown, the chaos of our lives, which no one can ignore, in both great and small things, the sign that God has let us go? God doesn't want us anymore. There's no more mercy coming our way from God. God is against us, and we have to accept it. It won't do to keep clinging if we aren't wanted. This is the cry out of the very depths of despair. There is only one thing that helps, and it is what the church does with any of us who thinks and feels this way. It takes the cross and places it before our eyes and asks: "Did God abandon him?" And since God did not abandon Jesus, we will not be abandoned by God, either.

¶Learn to recognize this sign in your own life. Learn to recognize and understand the hour of the storm, when you were perishing. This is the time when God is incredibly close to you, not far away. Right there, when everything else that keeps us safe is breaking and falling down, when one after another all the things our lives depend on are being taken away or destroyed, where we have to learn to give them up, all this is happening because God is coming near to us, because God wants to be our only support and certainty. God lets our lives be broken and fail in every direction, through fate and guilt, and through this very failure God brings us back; we are thrown back upon God alone. God wants to show us that when you let everything go, when you lose all your own security and have to give it up, that is when you are totally free to receive God and be kept totally safe in God. So may we understand rightly the hours of affliction and temptation,

[8.] Luke 17:5.

the hours in our lives when we are on the high seas! God is close to us then, not far away. Our God is on the cross.

The cross is the sign that stands in judgment on all the false security in our lives and restores faith in God alone. Be of good courage, be manly, be confident, be certain—that is what it says. Yes, but everything depends here
446 on making sure that one last, terrible misunderstanding does not arise. There is such a thing as false courage, false confidence . . . and this false confidence is itself only the most subtle form in which fear disguises itself. Let us return to our story.

When the disciples were climbing aboard the boat, they seemed quite confident; they seemed not at all afraid. Why were they confident? They looked at the lovely calm sea and saw no reason to worry. But as the wind and waves increased in force, the disciples lost their calm and fear grew in them. They gazed apprehensively at the wild sea. Its appearance had made them feel safe, but now fear was gaining the upper hand. The story says that Jesus was asleep. Only faith can sleep without a care—that is why sleep is a reminder of paradise—faith finds its safety in God alone. The disciples couldn't sleep; their security was gone; their confidence had been misplaced and now was lost. It was a false sense of security—it was only fear in disguise. This sense of security does not overcome fear but soon breaks down. Only the faith that leaves behind all false confidence, letting it fall and break down, can overcome fear. This is faith: it does not rely on itself or on favorable seas, favorable conditions; it does not rely on its own strength or on other people's strength, but believes only and alone in God, whether or not there is a storm. It is the only faith that is not superstition and does not let us slip back into fear but makes us free of fear. Lord, make this faith strong in us who have little faith!

But the other side of the coin is also true. When Christ is in the boat, a storm always comes up. The world tries with all its evil powers to get hold of him, to destroy him along with his disciples; it hates him and rises up against him. Christians surely know this. No one has to go through so much anxiety and fear as do Christians. But this does not surprise us, since Christ is the Crucified One, and there is no way to life for a Christian without being crucified. So we will suffer and make our way through together with Christ, looking always to him who [is] with us in the boat and can soon stand up and rebuke the sea, so that it becomes calm.

However, it does seem to be true, what you have surely all been quietly wanting to say for some time, that today Christ is no longer doing such
447 amazing things. He is so strangely hidden away that we often think he is no longer there at all! Dear brethren, what do we know about what Christ can do and wants to do for us, this very evening, if we will only call upon him as

we should, if we call out, "Lord, save us! We are perishing!" That was fear all right, but it was faith in the midst of fear, because it knew where help comes from, the only place. We say there are no miracles anymore . . . but what do we know really, you and I? We will certainly be ashamed of ourselves if one day we are allowed to see what God can do.

They were amazed, saying . . .[9] We can well understand their amazement. What sort of person is this on whom fear has no effect, who overcomes the fear in human life and takes away its power? By asking this question, we are already on our knees before him, praying to him, pointing to him, the wonder worker, and saying, This is God! Amen.

5. Sermon on Judges 6:15–16; 7:2; 8:23
Berlin, First Sunday in Lent, February 26, 1933[1]

Gideon
February 26, 1933 Judges 6:15–16; 7:2; 8:23

He responded [to the Lord], "But sir, how can I deliver Israel? My clan is the weakest in Manasseh, and I am the least in my family." The LORD said to him, "But I will be with you, and you shall strike down the Midianites, every one of them." . . . The LORD said to Gideon, "The troops with you are too many for me to give the Midianites into their hand. Israel would only take
the credit away from me, saying, 'I have delivered myself.'"[2] . . . Gideon 448
said to them, "I will not rule over you, and my son will not rule over you; the LORD will rule over you."

This is a passionate story about God's derision for all those who are fearful and have little faith, all those who are much too careful, the worriers, all those who want to be somebody in the eyes of God but are not. It is a story of God's mocking human might, a story of doubt and of faith in this God who makes fun of human beings, who wins them over with this mockery and

[9.] The ellipses in the manuscript undoubtedly indicate that Bonhoeffer planned, in giving the sermon, to cite the final sentence in the biblical text: "What sort of man is this, that even the winds and the sea obey him?"

[1.] *NL*, A 33,12(b); carbon copy. See also *NL*, A 33,12(a); handwritten. Previously published in *GS* 4:109–17 (indicating that the sermon was preached at a service for the conclusion of the semester in Trinity Church), and in *PAM* 1:349–58.

[2.] The Bible text says, "My own hand has delivered me." The text given here is also in Bonhoeffer's Luther Bible, along with various other handwritten markings of the text.

with love. So it is no rousing heroic legend—there is nothing of Siegfried in Gideon.[3] Instead it is a rough, tough, not very uplifting story, in which we are all being roundly ridiculed along with him. And who wants to be ridiculed, who can think of anything more humiliating than being made a laughingstock by the Lord of the world? The Bible often speaks of God in heaven making fun of our human hustle and bustle, of God's laughter at the vain creatures he has made. Here it is the powerful Sovereign One whose strength is unequaled, the living Lord, who carries on this way about his creatures. For him, who has all power in his hands, who speaks a word and it is done, who breathes forth his spirit and the world lives, or takes it away and the world perishes, who dashes entire nations to pieces, like potters' vessels[4]—for this God, human beings are not heroes, not heroic, but rather creatures who are meant to do his will and obey him, whom he forces with mockery and with love to be his servants.

So that's why we have Gideon and not Siegfried, because this doubter,[5] mocked by God, has learned his faith in the school of hard knocks.

In the church we have only *one* altar—the altar of the Most High, the
449 One and only, the Almighty, the Lord, to whom alone be honor and praise, the Creator before whom all creation bows down, before whom even the most powerful are but dust. We don't have any side altars at which to worship human beings.[6] The worship of God and not of humankind is what

[3.] Siegfried, the central figure in the saga of the Nibelungs, embodies the unconquerable warrior. [Figures such as Siegfried from the Teutonic legends were already being idealized in Nazi propaganda and in many German Christian sermons. See also ed. note 6.—LR]

[4.] See Pss. 33:9; 104:29–30; 2:9.

[5.] The phrase "because this doubter, mocked by God" replaces, already in the handwritten version, "that is why we have someone who doubts and believes, a fool whom God makes fun of, who has faith and victory dropped in his lap undeserved. And Gideon is important to us in the church not as the *one* valiant hero, the enthusiastic youth, but rather as one who . . ."

[6.] Bonhoeffer may be alluding to the adoration of Hitler with its religious overtones, which was found not only in German Christian circles but among National Socialists generally. On August 23, 1932, Hitler had sent a telegram expressing his solidarity to the storm troopers [SA members] sentenced to death for the murder of a Communist in Potempa, Upper Silesia. The newspaper *Völkischer Beobachter* reported that one of the condemned men hung the telegram on the wall of his cell, along with a note that said, "This telegram and his picture will be the small altar before which I shall pray daily" (quoted in Scholder, *Churches and the Third Reich*, 1:180). The sentence was commuted to life imprisonment by the end of 1932, and in March 1933 the men were freed in an amnesty for those who had been convicted of actions on behalf of National Socialism (see Kluke, "Der Fall Potempa"; regarding the Bonhoeffer family's opinion of this case, see *DB-ER*, 258).

takes place at the altar of our church. Anyone who wants to do otherwise should stay away and cannot come with us into God's house. Anyone who wants to build an altar to himself or to any other human is mocking God, and God will not allow such mockery.[7] To be in the church means to have the courage to be alone with God as Lord, to worship God and not any human person. And it does take courage. The thing that most hinders us from letting God be Lord, that is, from believing in God, is our cowardice. That is why we have Gideon, because he comes with us to the one altar of the Most High, the Almighty, and falls on his knees to this God alone.

In the church we also have only *one* pulpit, from which faith in God is preached and not any other faith, not even with the best intentions. This again is why we have Gideon—because he himself, his life story is a living sermon about this faith. We have Gideon because we don't want always to be speaking of our faith in abstract, otherworldly, unreal or general terms, to which people may be glad to listen but don't really take note of; because it is good once in a while actually to see faith in action, not just hear what it should be like, but see how it just happens in the midst of someone's life, in the story of a human being. Only here does faith become, for everyone, not just a children's game, but rather something highly dangerous, even ter-
rifying. Here a person is being treated without considerations or conditions 450
or allowances; he has to bow to what is being asked, or he will be broken. This is why the image of a person of faith is so often that of someone who is not beautiful in human terms, not a harmonious picture, but rather that of someone who has been torn to shreds. The picture of someone who has learned to have faith has the peculiar quality of always pointing away from the person's own self, toward the One in whose power, in whose captivity and bondage he or she is. So we have Gideon, because his story is a story of God glorified, of the human being humbled.

Here is Gideon, one person no different from a thousand others, but out of that thousand, he is the one whom God comes to meet, who is called into God's service, is called to act. Why is he the one, or why is it you, or I? Is it because God wants to make fun of me, in coming to talk with me? Is it God's grace, which makes a mockery of all our understanding? But what are we asking here? Isn't God entitled to call whomever God chooses, you or me, the highly placed or the lowly, strong or powerless, poor or rich, without our being entitled to start arguing about it straightaway? Is there anything we can do here other than hear and obey?

[7.] Gal. 6:7.

Gideon is supposed to liberate Israel from its bondage at the hands of the Midianites, an enemy nation with superior power. He, who is just like any of a thousand others, is called upon to do a phenomenal deed. He looks at himself and his own strength and then at the unconquerable might of the opposing side. He has nothing on his side—the enemy has it all. "He responded, 'But Lord, how can I deliver Israel?'" How am I supposed to accomplish this thing that you are calling me to do? Lord, it's too big a job; don't be cruel. Take it back, or let me see some help, give me armies, weapons, riches! God, you don't realize how wretched we are; look at this starving, weakened people; see how homelessness and lack of bread makes them doubt you; look how they bow down to other gods and not to you. How can I deliver Israel?" This Gideon is someone we know, isn't he? He has suddenly become very much alive for us. Gideon, we recognize your voice only too well; you sound just the same today as you did then.

The call comes to our Protestant church, just one like many others in the world: You are to redeem Israel; you are to set the people free from the
451 chains of fear and cowardice and evil that bind them. This call startles the church and troubles it profoundly, this church without influence, powerless, undistinguished in every way—why is it the one to be burdened with this call? It looks at the hopelessness of its proclamation; it looks at the apathy and the misery of those who are supposed to be listening and recognizes that it is not equal to the task. It looks upon its own inner emptiness and barrenness, and it says fearfully and reproachfully, *with what* am I supposed to redeem this people? How am I supposed to do this phenomenal thing? And then suddenly the call comes to us: Put an end to the bondage in which you are living; put an end to the mortal fear that gnaws at you, to the power of human desire that is burning you up, to your tormented and self-satisfied keeping to yourself. Put an end to your fear of other people and your vanity; set yourself free. Who would be willing to say that he or she has never heard this call and has never answered, as Gideon did: "Lord, *with what* am *I* supposed to do such great things?"

But then Gideon is silenced; today just as in those days, he's told to shut up. You're asking, "With what?" Haven't you realized what it means that this is God calling to you?[8] Isn't the call of God enough for you; if you listen properly, doesn't it drown out all your "with what" questions? "I will be with you"—that means you are not asked to do this with any other help. "It

[8.] In the German an older grammatical form is used here; cf., for example, the first scene in Goethe's *Faust,* part 1, in which the ghost conjured up by Faust appears and says, "Who is calling to me?"

is I who have called you; I will be with you; I shall be doing it too." Do you hear that, Gideon of yesterday and today? God has called you, and that is enough. Do you hear that, individual doubting Christian, asking and doubting Christian? God has plans for you, and that does mean you. Be ready and see to it. Never forget, even when your own powerlessness is grinding you down to the ground, that God has phenomenal, immeasurable, great plans for you. "I will be with you."

What does Gideon do? He goes out and has the trumpets blown, calls up an army from all the tribes, gathers around him whatever fighting forces he can find. Compared to the superior forces of the enemy, it is still only a small army, and Gideon hesitates to go into battle. Then, just as he is pitching his tents opposite those of the enemy, there comes God again, blocking his path. "Gideon, what have you done? Gideon, where is your faith? Look
at this army of yours; it's too big; Gideon, it was fear and doubt that made 452
you call up this army. The troops with you are too many for me. I'm not going to give you the victory this way. Then you would only take the credit for yourselves and say, 'We have delivered ourselves; we have gained the victory.' But I will have none of it." Fall down before your God and let God be your Lord; know that only God can save you. This is God's promise, and the word of God is more powerful than all the armies in the world.

Here the crucial question has been put: "Gideon, do you seriously believe in God your Lord, even here face-to-face with this terrifyingly dangerous enemy? Then, Gideon, send your massive army home; you don't need it. God is with you; the victory belongs to God and not to your army." What a phenomenal thing to ask, what a confusing encounter with the living God! There stands Gideon with his little army, hesitating to go out against the enemy's superior forces, and then God comes and laughs rudely in his face, makes fun of him: "Gideon, the troops with you are too many for me." Instead of bringing on huge amounts of weapons and armies, he calls for disarmament, meaning faith, faith; let your armies go home! How cruelly God makes fun of all human might; it's the bitterest of all tests of faith and makes God an incomprehensible lord and despot over the world. Isn't it crazy? Wouldn't Gideon have been torn apart inwardly, to have to give up the only forces that, from a human viewpoint, he could count on, here in the face of the enemy? What kind of wild God is this, zealous for his own honor, always standing in human beings' way and frustrating their plans, before they know it? Why does God frustrate us? Because God is opposed to the proud,[9] because human beings keep getting it wrong, however they

[9.] See 1 Pet. 5:5.

do it? Why do we always get it wrong? Because we are always trying for our own credit, and don't want to believe in God.

But Gideon believed and obeyed; he let his troops go home, and with every man who left him, his faith grew in this God who had made fun of him. And when they had all gone except for a tiny remnant, the victory was given into his hands. He believed, he obeyed, he gave God the glory, he renounced the honor for himself, and God kept the promise made.

Is this a tall tale like all the others? Anyone who says so has failed to understand that Gideon is still with us, that the old story of Gideon is being
453 played out in Christendom every day. "I will be with you in the face of the enemy . . ." What does Gideon do? What do we do? We rustle up all our own forces; we reach out for every means of help; we calculate, we weigh, we count; we arm ourselves with offensive and defensive weapons. Until then, suddenly and unexpectedly—nobody knows the hour—the living God is there and assails us again: "If you have faith, lay down your weapons; I am your weapon. Take off your armor; I am your armor. Put away your pride; I am your pride." Do you hear that, church of Gideon? Let God alone; let the word and the sacraments and the commandment of God be your weapons; don't look around for other help; don't be frightened. God is with you. "Let my grace be sufficient for you."[10] Don't try to be strong, mighty, famous, respected, but let God alone be your strength, your fame and honor. Or don't you believe in God?

¶It does seem crazy, doesn't it, that the church should not defend itself by every means possible in the face of the terrible threats coming at it from every side. What madness brought this Gideon into the world? But all this is only the foolishness of the Christian faith itself; that is what this story is [about]. It's not about the particular command that was given; it's not that which is valid for all the ages, but rather the foolishness, the stumbling block of living faith, which confesses, "With might of ours can naught be done, soon were our lost effected . . ."[11]

And you as an individual, you who have heard the call to free yourself from bondage, to loosen its chains and the grip of fear, you are already right back into acting from lack of faith. You think that by straining to exert all your energies, you can do it yourself, by putting all you have into it, because you want to control your own destiny. Then suddenly God himself is standing in your path, and there go all your fine plans again. "Lay down your

[10.] See 2 Cor. 12:9.

[11.] Luther's Reformation hymn "A Mighty Fortress" (1528) [translation from *The Lutheran Hymnal*, no. 262, verse 2.—LR]

weapons, for I am your weapon, and a thousand of your weapons are not equal to one of mine. Let me do what you cannot do. You want the honor of saying, 'I have delivered myself,' but this is not for you; give me the honor and the glory, believe in me. Let my grace be sufficient for you, for my power is made perfect in weakness."[12]

Gideon's warriors must have been flabbergasted; they must have shuddered when he gave them the order to go home. The church is always 454
astounded, and shudders, when it hears the voice of the One who commands it to renounce power and honor, to let go of all its calculations and let God alone do God's work. We shake our heads and are scandalized as we watch many a Gideon among us going his way. But how can that confound *us* who see in the midst of our church the cross, which is the sign of powerlessness, dishonor, defenselessness, hopelessness, meaninglessness, and yet is also where we find divine power, honor, defense, hope, meaning, glory, life, victory? Do we now see the direct line from Gideon to the cross? Do we see that the name of this line, in a word, is "faith"?

Gideon conquers, the church conquers, we conquer, because faith alone conquers. But the victory belongs not to Gideon, the church, or ourselves, but to God. And God's victory means our defeat, our humiliation; it means God's derision and wrath at all human pretensions of might, at humans puffing themselves up and thinking they are somebodies themselves. It means the world and its shouting is silenced, that all our ideas and plans are frustrated; it means the cross. The cross over the world—that means that human beings, even the most noble, go down to dust whether it suits them or not, and with them all the gods and idols and lords of this world. The cross of Jesus Christ—that means God's bitter mockery of all human grandeur and God's bitter suffering in all human misery, God's lordship over all the world.

¶The people approach the victorious Gideon with the final trial, the final temptation: "Be our lord, rule over us." But Gideon has not forgotten his own history, nor the history of his people . . . "The Lord will rule over you, and you shall have no other lord." At this word, all the altars of gods and idols fall down, all worship of human beings and human self-idolization. They are all judged, condemned, cancelled out, crucified, and toppled into the dust before the One who alone is Lord. Beside us kneels Gideon, who was brought through fear and doubt to faith, before the altar of the one and only God, and with us Gideon prays, Lord on the cross, be our only Lord. Amen.

[12.] See 2 Cor. 12:9.

455 **6. Sermon on 1 Peter 1:7b–9**
Berlin, Ascension Day, May 25, 1933[1]

Ascension Day
May 25, 1933 1 Peter 1:7b–9

. . . when Jesus Christ is revealed. Although you have not seen him, you love him; and even though you do not see him now, you believe in him and rejoice with an indescribable and glorious joy, for you are receiving the outcome of your faith, the salvation of your souls.

"Jesus, my joy"—that is what we have just sung,[2] and to be able to say that honestly, from the heart, is the meaning of a life lived with Christ. If there is someone to whom it sounds very foreign, or who hears nothing in it but mushy enthusiasm, then that person has never yet heard the gospel. Jesus Christ was made a human being for the sake of humankind in the stable at Bethlehem—rejoice, O Christendom.[3] Jesus Christ became the companion of sinners and sat among tax collectors and prostitutes—rejoice, O Christendom. Jesus Christ became a convicted criminal for the sake of convicts, on the cross at Golgotha—rejoice, O Christendom. Jesus Christ rose from death to life for the sake of all of us—rejoice, O Christendom. Jesus Christ, for the sake of his church, went from this earthly home to his heavenly kingdom—rejoice, O Christendom. Jesus Christ coming from God and returning to God—that is not a new world of problems, of questions and answers. That means it is not a new moral law, not a new burden added to the burdens people already have to carry. What it really means, above all, is the joy of God in the world, the joy of God catching fire in humanity, which is hungry for joy. In a thousand ways people today ask, where can we find joy? Church of Christ, you alone know the answer; say it out loud: Christ, my joy.

456 Christ's ascension has two meanings. It is Jesus's farewell to his disciples, to the world, which he loved. It was a long and hard road they had walked together. He had told them many things, but now the time had come when

---

[1.] *NL*, A 33,13(b); carbon copy. See also *NL*, A 33,13(a); handwritten. Previously published in *GS* 4:118–22 (indicating that this sermon was given in the Kaiser Wilhelm Gedächtnis Kirche [Kaiser Wilhelm Memorial Church], where Bonhoeffer was substituting for Gerhard Jacobi), and in *PAM* 1:358–63. Bible text as marked by hand in Bonhoeffer's Bible (Luther's version).

[2.] "Jesu, meine Freude," chorale by Johann Franck, *Lutheran Book of Worship*, no. 400 [where the title is "Jesus, priceless treasure," trans. Catherine Winkworth.—LR].

[3.] Refrain of the Christmas carol "O du fröhliche" ["O sanctissima"]. *Evangelisches Gesangbuch*, no. 44. Translation by Isabel Best.

he had to leave them alone. Now they had to be able to walk without always looking to him. Now the end of his time on earth had come. They had gone one last stretch of road together—then came the final moment; he laid his hands on them in blessing, and then he was taken from their sight. They were alone. The curtain had fallen. He had left this world of evil and gone home to his heavenly Father. Lord, have mercy on us. Rejoice, O Christendom; he has gone home to his Father; he is preparing a place for you, a home in his kingdom; he will take you home when his time comes.[4] Just wait—and rejoice. He will come again.

But how can people rejoice when they have been abandoned? How can those who are left orphans be comforted? How can those who are torn by homesickness be cheerful? You orphaned church, left alone in your homesickness for Jesus Christ and his ascension, your ascension, rejoice! For you are allowed to love him whom you cannot see; you are allowed to believe in him who is lost to your sight. And nobody can take your love and your faith from you. It is our church, the church living between Christ's ascension and his coming again, of which our text says: although you have not seen him, you love him; and even though you do not see him now, you believe in him. It is the church that stands alone in its waiting, alone in its faith, and that finds its joy in faith alone. Lord, teach this church, which does not see you, the true joy in Christ. Without rejoicing, there is no church. Let us talk today about joy in Christ.

Luther once said something like this: While he was on earth he was far away from us, but now that he is in heaven, he is close to us.[5] What does that mean? It means that now he is no longer king of the Jews but rather king of the whole world; it means that from heaven he reigns over his whole kingdom and is near, though not visible, and present to his whole church, 457
wherever it is scattered, among Jews and heathen, through all the world. He is close to us in his church, in his Word, in his sacrament, in love among the brethren. Here he comforts us who are abandoned; here he soothes our homesickness ever anew; here he takes us who are estranged from God, who are in barren, empty places, who don't know the way, who are alone, and makes us joyful in his Christly presence. Joy in the sermon, joy in the sacraments, joy in brothers and sisters—that is the joy of the believing church in its unseen, heavenly Lord.

Joy in the sermon—how hard that is for us people of today. That's because we are listening to the preacher and not to Christ. We turn our own joy

[4.] See John 14:2–3.

[5.] See Luther's sermon for Ascension Day, 1523 (*WA* 12:562, 24–26).

sour because we confuse earthly joy with heavenly joy. Our poor Protestant church doesn't offer us much earthly joy. Don't come looking for it here. But heavenly joy Christ can give us, even through his frail church, and we should look for it only from him, not from the preacher. In the sermon it is Christ who wants to visit us and wants to be himself our heavenly joy.

Joy in the sermon—joy in the sacraments—how much more we have lost of the latter than of the former. Joy in the sacraments—one might say that sounds Catholic. Maybe it does sound Catholic, but mainly it sounds archetypically Christian. Here the sacrament, the Lord's Supper with our heavenly Lord, is inexpressible joy in his presence; here the sacrament is the feast of joy for which a congregation of redeemed sinners gathers together, in the midst of this world of evil, and prays for the return of its heavenly king. Here the sacrament is the communion among brethren whose joy is in one another. Joy in the sacraments—that is the joy of the heart full of longing and desire for its God whom it has found; that is the anticipation in the hearts of strangers and homeless people, as they look forward to their eternal home and pray that it may come.

¶King of the church, Master of joy[6] beyond compare, give us great longing and desire, a mighty homesickness for you—and then come and com-
458 fort us with your ascension; make us certain of your promise, that one day the curtain that separates us from you will fall. We cannot see you, but we love you; we do not have you before our eyes, but we believe in you; we have plenty of sorrows and troubles, but your sermon and sacraments make us joyful. Lord, give more joy to your church; without joy in the sermon and joy in the sacraments, there is no church. Without the church, the whole world is joyless and miserable, and there is no end to hunger and thirst.

Joy of Ascension Day—we have to become very quiet inwardly before we can even hear the soft sound of this word. Joy comes to life in the quiet and the mystery. Indeed, this joy cannot be comprehended. But it is never what we can understand that brings us joy—it is that which we cannot understand but is true, real, and alive that sets us alight with joy. That is why real joy itself is always somewhat incomprehensible, both for others and for the person who feels it. Joy is simply there; the joy of Ascension Day is simply there, where the church speaks of Christ being exalted over all the world and of his return, where he himself meets his joyfully expectant church in the sacraments. That joy is there, not loud but soft and subdued, fearful of the world, fearful of sin—but it is there like the heavenly joy of servants who

[6.] See *Evangelisches Gesangbuch*, no. 198, stanza 6.

are up at night watching by candlelight until their beloved master comes home.[7] All our joy in Christ in this world is joy of anticipation—and who will admit out loud that he or she is looking forward to something? And yet what joy is stronger than the joy of anticipation?

Joy of anticipation—in expectation of what? In the expectation of the last things. For the Lord of heaven, who stills the hunger and thirst, the longing of his church-community, through the sacraments by faith—this Lord whom we cannot see, but whom we love nonetheless—he will come again. The curtain is opening. We shall see him face-to-face.[8] He will come back once again to this earth on which we are strangers, and he will lead the homeless, who in the church, through faith, have been hoping in God's new land, home to our heavenly Father. ". . . when Jesus Christ
is revealed. Although you have not seen him, you love him . . . and rejoice 459
with an indescribable and glorious joy, for you are receiving the outcome of your faith, the salvation of your souls." Then the church's time of waiting will be over, then the end of the time of faith will have come; then joy will no longer be veiled in fear and holding back; then will come the time of fulfillment, the time of everlasting seeing, when blessedness breaks in. Then he will appear, our brother the Lord, and his church will fall down before him in holy joy. "You . . . rejoice with an indescribable and glorious joy." Then the world and the church will fall away, and Jesus himself will be our joy. For here we have no lasting city, but we are looking for the city that is to come.[9]

¶Christ's ascension—the curtain falls, the church of faith waits, and its joy is the sacrament. Christ's coming again—heaven opens up. Home at last, our thirst is slaked—the community of the blessed sees the incomprehensible mystery. Its joy is Jesus Christ, none other than God. At present we are still strangers, wandering in the time between his ascension and his second coming, waiting long in hope and fear. But the ransomed of the Lord shall return with singing, and everlasting joy shall be upon their heads.[10] Rejoice, O Christendom. Amen.

[7.] See Luke 12:35–40; cf. also Bonhoeffer's 1926 Sunday school homily on this text (*DBWE* 9, 3/9).

[8.] See 1 Cor. 13:12.

[9.] Heb. 13:14.

[10.] See Isa. 35:10.

7. Sermon on Exodus 32:1–8, 15–16, 18–20, 30–35 Berlin, Sixth Sunday after Easter (Exaudi), May 28, 1933[1]

Exaudi Sunday, May 28, 1933 Exodus 32

When the people saw that Moses delayed to come down from the mountain, the
people gathered around Aaron, and said to him, "Come, make gods for us, who
shall go before us; as for this Moses, the man who brought us up out of the land
460 of Egypt, we do not know what has become of him." Aaron said to them, "Take
off the gold rings . . . of your wives, your sons, and your daughters, and bring
them to me." So all the people took off the gold rings . . . and brought them to
Aaron. He took the gold from them, formed it in a mold, and cast an image of a
calf; and they said, "These are your gods, O Israel, who brought you up out of
the land of Egypt!" When Aaron saw this, he built an altar before it; and Aaron
made proclamation and said, "Tomorrow shall be a festival to the LORD." They
rose early the next day, and offered burnt offerings and brought sacrifices of
well-being; and the people sat down to eat and drink, and rose up to revel.

¶The LORD said to Moses, "Go down at once! Your people, whom you brought up out of the land of Egypt, have acted perversely; they have been quick to turn aside from the way that I commanded them; they have cast for themselves an image of a calf, and have worshipped it and sacrificed to it, and said, 'These are your gods, O Israel, who brought you up out of the land of Egypt!'" . . .

¶Then Moses turned and went down from the mountain, carrying the two tablets of the covenant in his hands, tablets that were written on both sides, written on the front and on the back. The tablets were the work of God, and the writing was the writing of God, engraved upon the tablets. . . . Then [Moses] said . . . "It is the sound of revelers that I hear." As soon as he came near the camp and saw the calf and the dancing, Moses' anger burned hot, and he threw the tablets from his hands and broke them at the foot of the mountain. He took the calf that they had made, burned it with fire, ground it to powder. . . .

¶On the next day Moses said to the people, "You have sinned a great sin. But now I will go up to the LORD; perhaps I can make atonement for your sin." So Moses returned to the LORD and said, "Alas, this people has sinned a great sin; they have made for themselves gods of gold. But now, if you will only forgive their sin—but if not, blot me out of the book that you have written." But the LORD said to Moses, "Whoever has sinned against me, I will blot out of my

[1.] *NL*, A, 14(b); carbon copy. See also *NL*, A33, 14(a); handwritten. Previously published in *GS* 4: 123–29 (indicating that this sermon was given in the Kaiser Wilhelm Gedächtnis Kirche [Kaiser Wilhelm Memorial Church], where Bonhoeffer was substituting for Gerhard Jacobi), and in *PAM* 1:364–70. Bible text as marked and edited by hand in Bonhoeffer's Bible (Luther's version).

book. But now go, lead the people to the place about which I have spoken to you. . . . Nevertheless, when the day comes for punishment, I will punish them for their sin."

¶Then the LORD sent a plague on the people, because they made the calf—the one that Aaron made.

The priest against the prophet, the church of the world against the church of faith, the church of Aaron against the church of Moses—this eternal conflict in the church of Christ, and its resolution, is what we are going to hear about today.

Moses and Aaron, two brothers from the same tribe, with the same blood
and the same history, went part of the way side by side and then were torn 461
apart—Moses, the first prophet, and Aaron, the first priest; Moses, the one called out by God, the one chosen without regard for his person, the man who was slow of tongue, the servant of God who lived only by listening to the word of his Lord; Aaron, the man with the purple robe and the sacred crown, the priest who had been consecrated and sanctified, who was supposed to keep the people worshipping God. And now in our story, we have Moses alone, way up on the terrifying mountain with the living God, between life and death with the thunder and lightning, called to receive the law of God's covenant with God's people—and down in the valley the Israelites with their priest in his purple robe, making sacrifices but estranged from God.

Why did Moses and Aaron have to go against each other? Why couldn't they stand side by side and serve God together? Why are the church of Moses and the church of Aaron, the church of the Word and the church of the world, always breaking apart? The answer to this question is found in our text.

Moses is called by God to go up the mountain on behalf of his people. God wants to talk with him up there. The children of Israel know this; they know that Moses is standing up there on their behalf, struggling, praying, suffering. He wears no purple robe; he is not a priest; he is nothing, nothing at all but the servant who waits on the word of his Lord, who falls ill if he cannot listen to that word. He is nothing—but the prophet of his God. But the church of Aaron, the worldly church, cannot wait; it is impatient. Where is Moses anyway? Why doesn't he come back? We can't see him anymore. Where is he with his God? "We do not know what has become of him." Maybe he isn't there at all anymore—maybe he's dead.

¶These are the questions that the church of Aaron has in every age about the church of the Word. "We don't see it—what has it done, where are its accomplishments . . . surely it must be dead!" Don't we understand

that perhaps it is God who is keeping Moses up there on the mountain and hasn't let him go, because God still has something more to say to him—that maybe even today God doesn't let the church of Moses go, the church that wants to listen to God's word alone, but still has a word to say to that church in the stillness? Even God needs to have time with the prophets and the
462 church of God. Should we be impatient? Surely, the church of the Word is once again on Mount Sinai today, and in fear and trembling, amid the thunder and lightning, stands against the Word of God, waiting, believing, praying, struggling—and for whom? For the church of Aaron, for the church down there in the valley, for the church of the world. When the worldly church gets impatient and cannot wait any longer, that is the first step on its collision course with the church of the Word. It was always so and will always be so.

"We don't know what has become of this Moses. Come on, Aaron, you make us some gods to go before us." That is the second step that follows directly after the first. The church of the world, the church of the priests, wants something it can see. It doesn't want to wait any longer. It wants to go ahead and do something itself, take action itself, since God and the prophet aren't doing so. What is the priest there for anyway? What is the church doing there, if it is keeping them waiting? No, we need something in our church; we want to see something happen in our church. We don't want to wait. "You priests, you who are sanctified and consecrated, you owe us something. Come on, Priest Aaron, do your duty; see to the worship service. God has left us alone here, but we need gods! We need religion! If you can't prevail with the living God, then make us gods yourself!"

It's not really such a bad request that is being made here; actually, it's a pious request. They aren't saying, away with all gods, but rather, we need gods, we need religion, make us some. They aren't chasing the priest away either, but saying, do your job. Keep the people's religion alive, give them worship services. They really want to remain a church, with gods and priests and religion, but a church of Aaron—without God. And Aaron complies; he carries out his office for which he was consecrated; he pays attention to the people. He understands their impatience, their drive to do something, their pious raging only too well—and he complies. "Come here, all of you who have been abandoned by your God and your prophet; make yourselves a god who won't leave you anymore, an even finer, more splendid one than the God who left us. Bring precious jewelry and gold; bring it as an offering." And they all come, every one; they bring their precious sacrifice to
463 make their own idol. They tear off their ornaments and throw them into the molten mass, which Aaron then shapes into the glistening, monstrous form of the calf.

¶We hear it said that the masses aren't so ready to make sacrifices. But those who say so don't know the world very well! The human race is ready to make any sacrifice that allows it to celebrate itself, to worship its own accomplishments. The worldly church, the church of Aaron, is ready for any sacrifice if it can make its own god. Before the god that we have fashioned as it pleases us, the human race and the worldly church are happy to smile and kneel down. It is God who finds few prepared to sacrifice.

¶No, the church of Aaron spares no effort; it is not stingy; it spends lavishly on its god. Into the fiery heat of its idol it throws everything that it holds precious and worthwhile and holy. Everything must be spent on making the idol more glorious, so they all throw in whatever they can and want, each according to his or her own ideals, into the melting pot. Then the frenzy begins; the worldly church celebrates its triumph. The priest has demonstrated his power, so there he stands in the middle in his purple robe and his sacred crown, worshipping the work of his own hands . . . and all around him the people blissfully fall down and gaze at the idol that they have created by their own might and from their own sacrifices. Who would stand aside from this pious jubilation, this transport beyond compare, this great deed accomplished by human will and ability? Now the worldly church has its god . . . so come and sacrifice to it; be happy and play, eat, drink, dance, rejoice, get excited! You have a god again . . . These, Israel, are the gods who brought you up out of slavery. Come and see, and worship!

But there is rumbling on Sinai. God is showing Moses his faithless people. And Moses trembles for his people and hastily climbs down the mountain. He can already hear the jubilation and shouting of the dance, the frenzy of excitement. He can see his brother in his purple robe and the sacred crown, and in the middle the golden god of the worldly church, the worldly god, the idol, the priestly god. Then he is standing among them, the unexpected prophet, brandishing high in his hands the tablets of the law, so that everyone must see the writing engraved on them by the hand of God:
"I am the Lord your God, you shall have no other gods before me!"[2] The 464
worldly church is struck dumb with fear and horror at the sight; the frenzy is over—the living God has appeared in the midst of it and overwhelmed it. What will happen now? Then, in one incomparable and terrifying moment, the tablets of the law lie shattered next to the idolatrous image, and the idol itself is shattered and burnt up. That is the end of the worldly church, and it is God who has done it. God is still the Lord. Lord, have mercy . . .

[2.] The German text uses the version of the first commandment (Exod. 20:2–3) from the Nuremberg Catechism as printed in 1531 and 1558.

Priestly church and church of the Word, church of Aaron and church of Moses—this historic collision at the foot of Mount Sinai, the end of the worldly church and the appearance of the Word of God, is repeated in our church day after day, Sunday after Sunday. As the worldly church, which doesn't want to wait, which doesn't want to live by something unseen; as a church that makes its own gods, that wants to have a god that pleases it rather than asking whether it is itself pleasing to God; as a church that wants to do for itself whatever God does not do; as a church that is ready to make any sacrifice for the sake of idolatry, the glorification of human ideas and values—as a church that presumes divine authority for itself through its priesthood—it is as such a church that we come again and again to worship. And it is as a church whose idol lies shattered to pieces on the floor, as a church that has to hear anew, "I am the Lord your God" . . . as a church that is struck by this word and crumbles—it is as the church of Moses, the church of the Word, that we should depart from one another. The impatient church becomes the church of quiet waiting; the church that impetuously demands to be shown becomes the church of sober faith; the church of self-idolization becomes the church where the one and only God is worshipped. Will this church also be ready for such devotion and sacrifice?

But the matter did not end in brokenness. Once again Moses climbed the mountain. This time it was in order to pray for his people. He offered himself as sacrifice: "Blot me out along with my people; we are one and the same, Lord; I love my brothers and sisters." But God's answer was still dark
465 and frightening, threatening. Moses could not bring about reconciliation. Who will bring about reconciliation here? None other than he who is both priest and prophet, the man in the purple cloak and the crown of thorns, who stands before God and makes intercession for us, the crucified Son of the Father.

Here on his cross, all idolatry comes to an end. Here the whole human race, the whole church, is judged and pardoned. Here, God is wholly God, who does not tolerate any other gods but himself, but who is also wholly God in boundless forgiveness. We point to the cross as the church that is always both church of Moses and church of Aaron; we point to the cross and say: See, O Israel, this is your God who brought you up out of slavery, and who will lead you again. Come, believe and worship. Amen.

8. Sermon on Matthew 16:13–18,
Berlin, Sixth Sunday after Trinity, July 23, 1933[1]

July 23, 1933 Matthew 16:13–18

Now when Jesus came into the district of Caesarea Philippi, he asked his disciples, "Who do people say that the Son of Man is?" And they said, "Some say John the Baptist, but others Elijah, and still others Jeremiah or one of the prophets." He said to them, "But who do you say that I am?" Simon Peter answered, "You are the Messiah, the Son of the Living God." And Jesus answered him, "Blessed are you, Simon son of Jonah! For flesh and blood has not revealed this to you, but my Father in heaven. And I tell you, you are Peter, and on this rock I will build my church, and the gates of Hades will not prevail against it."

If we had our way, we would prefer to keep detouring around the decisions
confronting us. If we had our way, we would prefer not to be dragged into 466
this fight over the church.[2] If we had our way, we would rather not have to keep insisting on our cause and would gladly avoid the terrible danger of self-righteousness over against other people. If we had our way, we would remove ourselves tomorrow or better yet, today, join the quiet folk in the countryside, and leave the quarrel and self-righteousness to other people. But—God be thanked—it is not up to us. With God, we get just what we don't want. We are challenged to come out and make the decision; we cannot get out of it. Wherever we take our stand, we must also allow ourselves to be suspected of being self-opinionated, of speaking and acting against the others out of arrogance. We will not be spared any of this—making a decision means that we differ with others. Therefore, if we are honest, we will not hide from the significance of this day, today.

In the midst of the creaking and groaning of the church structures, which have been profoundly shaken and are collapsing and crumbling away here and there, we can still hear the promise of the eternal church, against which the gates of hell shall not prevail, the church on the rock, which

[1.] *NL*, A 33, 15; carbon copy. Previously published in *GS* 4:130–36 (with the indication that the sermon was preached on the Sunday of the church elections, in the Dreifaltigkeitskirche [Trinity Church]), and in *PAM* 1:371–77.

[2.] [Bonhoeffer preached this sermon on the very day of the national church elections, at a moment of great tension within the Protestant church. In a radio broadcast the evening before the church elections, Hitler himself had urged German Protestants to vote for the German Christians; Bonhoeffer and others like him had been working for the opposition "Gospel and Church" group. The German Christians would win two-thirds of the vote, setting the stage for the *Kirchenkampf*.—LR]

Christ has built and continues to build through all the ages. Where is this church? Where can we find it? Where can we hear its voice? Come, all of you who are asking this seriously, you who are left alone and lonely, who have lost your church. Let us go back to the Holy Scriptures, let us look together for the eternal church. Let anyone with ears to hear listen![3]

It is a lonely place where Christ has gone with his disciples, on the edge of a heathen region, where he can be alone with them. This is the place where, for the first time, he promises them, as his legacy, his eternal church. Not in the midst of the people, not at the visible climax of his ministry, but rather out here far away from the right-thinking scribes and the Pharisees, from the crowds who will sing "Hosanna" to him on Palm Sunday and then
467 on Good Friday shout, "Crucify him," he speaks to his disciples about the mystery and the future of his church. Evidently he meant that the building of this church could not begin with the scribes, the priests, or the crowds, but it was rather this little group of disciples, his followers, who were called to do it. Evidently he also did not consider Jerusalem, the city of the temple and the center of the people's life, as the right place for it, but instead he went to a quiet place where he could not hope for his announcement to make waves in any outward, visible way. And finally, he did not consider any great day of celebration as the proper time to speak about his church. Instead, he gave the promise of his church in the face of death, immediately before his first foretelling of his passion. So it is a church of a little flock, a church far out in a quiet place, a church in the face of death, about which we must be speaking here.

Jesus himself asks the decisive question, for which the disciples must have been waiting for some time, "Who do people say that the Son of Man is?" The answer is: "Some say you are John the Baptist, but others say you are Elijah, and still others say you are Jeremiah or one of the prophets." Opinions, nothing but people's opinions. The list of them could be extended as long as one wants . . . Some say you are a great man, others, that you are an idealist, others, that you are a religious genius, others, that you are a hero, the greatest of leaders. Opinions, more or less serious opinions—but Christ doesn't want to build his church on opinions.

¶So now he asks them directly, "But who do you say that I am?" In this unavoidable, face-to-face situation with Christ, there is no "perhaps," no "some say," no opinions anymore, but only silence, or else the one answer that Peter now gives: "You are the Messiah, the Son of the Living God."

[3.] Mark 4:9 et passim.

Here in the midst of the whirl of human opinions and perspectives, something truly new is visible. Here the name of God has been named; the name of the Eternal has been spoken; the mystery has been brought to light. This is no longer human thinking but rather the very opposite; this is divine revelation and confession of faith. "Blessed are you, Simon son of Jonah! For flesh and blood has not revealed this to you, but my Father in heaven. . . . 468
you are Peter, the rock, and on this rock I will build my church."

What is the difference between Peter and the others? Does he have such a heroic nature that he rises head and shoulders above them? He does not. Does he have unmatched strength of character? He does not. Does he have such unshakable loyalty? He does not. Peter is nobody really, nobody but a person who confesses, a person who has met Christ standing in his path and has recognized him, and who now confesses his faith in Christ. And this Peter, this confessing person, is now named as the rock on which Christ will build his church.

The church of Peter—that means the church on the rock, the church of confessing Christ. The church of Peter is not the church of opinions and views but rather the church of revelation; not the church that talks about "what people say" but the church in which Peter's confession is always being made and spoken anew, the church that does nothing else but always and only makes this confession, whether in singing, praying, preaching, or action. It is the church that only stands on the rock as long as it keeps doing this, but becomes the house built on sand that the wind blows down[4] if it dares to think of going another way, for whatever reason, or even to look away for a moment.

¶But being the church of Peter is not only something to be claimed with unalloyed pride. Peter, the confessing, believing disciple, denied his Lord on the same night that Judas betrayed him; Peter stood there by the fire that night and was ashamed, while Christ was standing before the high priest. Peter was the fearful one of little faith who sank into the sea. He was the disciple to whom Jesus said, "Get behind me, Satan!"[5] Even after that, he was the one who kept faltering, kept denying and falling down, a weak vacillator subject to the whim of the moment. The church of Peter is the church that shares his weakness, the church that also keeps denying Christ and falling down, being disloyal, of little faith, fearful, a church that again and again looks away from its mission and toward the world and its opinions. The church of Peter is the church of all those who are ashamed of their Lord, at 469

[4.] See Matt. 7:26–27.

[5.] See Matt. 26:69–75; 14:28–31; 16:23.

the very moment when they should be standing up for him . . .

But Peter is also the one of whom it is said that he went out and wept bitterly.[6] Of Judas, who also betrayed his Lord, it is said that he went out and took his own life.[7] That is the difference. Peter went out and wept bitterly. The church of Peter is the church that can not only confess, not only deny; it is the church that can also weep. By the rivers of Babylon—there we sat down and there we wept when we remembered Zion.[8] That is being church, for what does this weeping mean, if not that we have found the way back, that we are on our way home, that we are the prodigal son who falls weeping on his knees before his father?[9] The church of Peter is the church of divine sorrow, which leads to joy.

It's really shaky ground, isn't it? But it is still the rock, this ground; for this Peter, this reed bending in the wind, is called by God, taken prisoner by God, held fast by God. "You are Peter . . ." We are all Peter; not the pope, as the Catholics say, not this person or that person, but all of us who are just living by our confession of Christ, as fearful, disloyal persons of little faith, but who are held fast by God.

Yet it is not we who are to build, but God. No human being builds the church, but Christ alone. Anyone who proposes to build the church is certainly already on the way to destroying it, because it will turn out to be a temple of idolatry, though the builder does not intend that or know it. We are to confess, while God builds. We are to preach, while God builds. We are to pray to God, while God builds. We do not know God's plan. We cannot see whether God is building up or taking down. It could be that the times that human beings judge to be times for knocking down structures would be, for God, times to do a lot of building, or that the great moments of the church from a human viewpoint are, for God, times for pulling it down. It is a great comfort that Christ gives to the church: "You confess, preach, bear witness to me, but I alone will do the building, wherever I am pleased to do so. Don't interfere with my orders. Church, if you do your own part right, then that is enough. But make sure you do it right. Don't look for anyone's
470 opinion; don't ask them what they think. Don't keep calculating; don't look

[6.] Matt. 26:75 and Luke 22:62.

[7.] See Matt. 27:5.

[8.] Ps. 137:1.

[9.] See Luke 15:18–21.

around for support from others. Not only must church remain church,[10] but you, my church, confess, confess, confess" . . . Christ alone is your Lord; by his grace alone you live, just as you are. Christ is building.

And the gates of hell shall not prevail against you. Death is the great inheritor of everything that exists. This is as far as death goes. Right by the abyss of the valley of death is the foundation of the church, the church that confesses Christ as its life. The church has eternal life precisely there where death is reaching out for it, and death is reaching out for it precisely because it has eternal life. The church that confesses is the eternal church, for Christ is its protector. Its eternity is not visible to this world. It is not subject to challenge by the world, though the waves wash up over it and sometimes it looks completely covered over and lost. But victory belongs to the church, because Christ its Lord is with it and has overcome the world of death. Don't ask whether you can see victory but believe in the victory, for it is yours.

Our text is written in huge letters around the cupola of the great church of St. Peter, the church of the pope, in Rome.[11] Proudly this church points to its eternity, its visible victory over the world through all the centuries. Such glory, which our Lord did not desire for himself or put on, is not allowed us. But we may be certain that a glory immeasurably greater than this worldly glory is our destiny. Whether the people gathered are great or small, lowly or highly placed, weak or strong, if they confess Christ, the victory is theirs for eternity. "Fear not, little flock, for it is your Father's good pleasure to give you the kingdom."[12] "For where two or three are gathered in my name, there am I in the midst of them."[13] The city of God stands on a firm foundation.[14] Amen.

[10.] "Church must remain church" was the election campaign slogan of the "Gospel and Church" group, which opposed the German Christians in the church elections (see Scholder, *Churches and the Third Reich,* vol. 1, illustration no. 59).

[11.] It appears there in the Latin version of Matt. 16:18: "Tu es Petrus et super hanc petram aedificabo ecclesiam meam." Cf. also Bonhoeffer's diary from his 1924 trip to Italy (*DBWE* 9:83–84).

[12.] Luke 12:32 [in the more familiar RSV.—LR]

[13.] Matt. 18:20 [in the more familiar RSV.—LR]

[14.] Allusion to Ps. 87:1.

Ernst-Albert Scharffenorth

Editor's Afterword to the German Edition

This volume offers a perspective on one of the most important periods 471
in Bonhoeffer's life. Because much concerning Bonhoeffer's life in Berlin from 1932 to 1933 was never documented in written form, the biographical documents here cannot pretend to address all questions. This volume does, however, include documents from both spheres of Bonhoeffer's career as well as his important if not voluminous correspondence with two friends and with family members. Ultimately it is the political upheaval at the beginning of 1933 that gives this particular phase in Bonhoeffer's life its unique character. Hitler's appointment as chancellor of the Reich marks not only a profound caesura in Germany's own history; it also set into motion a dynamic in Bonhoeffer's own life that might allow us to characterize his life from this point onward as "sharing Germany's destiny."[1] Doing so, however, would precipitately equate the beginnings of Bonhoeffer's confrontation with the forces of National Socialism in 1933 with the kind of escalation he risked during the final phase of his life. Although one might quite legitimately draw a straight line from his position regarding the so-called Jewish question (2/13) to his participation in the coup against Hitler, one must acknowledge the qualitative distinction between the risky (double) life he led beginning in 1940, and the rather broad palette of commitments, contacts, and possibilities of self-expression still at his disposal in Berlin shortly before and after Hitler became chancellor. In the following

[1.] This was Eberhard Bethge's assessment of the third period in Bonhoeffer's life beginning in 1940 (see *DB-ER*, vii).

discussion I outline several characteristics of this particular phase of Bonhoeffer's life in Berlin in 1932–33, examining first his teaching activities at
472 the university, then his work with regard to the church and the ecumenical world, and concluding with a section on Bonhoeffer's confrontation with the political questions of that era.

I

As far as Bonhoeffer's teaching activity is concerned, one does indeed need to bear in mind that an especially important part of that activity is not represented in this volume. During the 1932–33 winter semester, Bonhoeffer lectured on "Creation and Sin" and then immediately published these lectures in 1933 as *Creation and Fall.*[2] Whereas all the other Berlin courses are represented only through student notes, *Creation and Fall* is a text in which Bonhoeffer himself is speaking, enabling us to discern more clearly than elsewhere what he was trying to communicate as an academic teacher in Berlin. In this respect, it is appropriate to examine the other courses from the perspective of that book and its fundamental concern.

In his exegesis of the first three chapters of Genesis, Bonhoeffer consciously places himself in the tradition of Karl Barth's commentary on Romans. Bonhoeffer, too, was concerned with presenting a postcritical interpretation of Scripture. The beginning of the Old Testament interested him not with respect to the various sources that historical-critical methodology might discern, but rather as an integral part of the Bible itself as the book of the church. His adoption of Karl Barth's initiative in understanding the Old Testament, however, represents only one side of Bonhoeffer's interpretation of Genesis, the side that is of interest with regard to the history of theology. The biographical background to Bonhoeffer's biblical understanding is also of considerable interest. *Creation and Fall* reflects Bonhoeffer's experience that the only people who grasp the real meaning of the Bible are those who discern within that book the message of the God who acts in the present.

One of the seminars documented in this volume—the one bearing a title that seems rather surprising to us today, namely, "Theologische Psychologie" (2/2),[3] exhibits a similar inclination. Bonhoeffer apparently concluded these "Dogmatic Exercises" with concrete guides for conducting one's life. What Hilde Pfeiffer Rannenberg and Wolf-Dieter Zimmermann

---

[2.] See *DBWE* 3. The German editor's discussion here draws on various ideas from the afterword to that volume.

[3.] [The translation of the title in this volume is "Theological Anthropology"; for an explanation of the title, see 2/2, ed. note 1.—LR]

noted here regarding "Christian practice," "Piety," "Knowledge of Sin," and 473
"Service" clearly shows that during this period their teacher was already reflecting on the theme of discipleship (*DBWE* 4). Following on *Creation and Fall,* this course is also of interest insofar as it shows Bonhoeffer developing his own relationship to the theology of Barth and Brunner. Although Bonhoeffer refers to Brunner's lecture on "biblical psychology" at the beginning of the course and provides a brief description of the three main directions Brunner distinguished within psychology, in the subsequent discussion he apparently referred only to Barth. That is to say, he did not engage in any further discussion of Brunner's program of eristics—which characterized the aforementioned lecture. Elsewhere, too, Bonhoeffer makes do by simply referring to this particular concern of Brunner's without further commentary.[4] That is, what Bonhoeffer actually did was adopt a key expression from Brunner and then pursue his own theological query concerning the believing soul under the presupposition of revelation. Bonhoeffer's impression was that contemporary theology—including that of Barth—had not yet answered the question. He attempted to answer it himself by taking ideas from *Act and Being*—in distinguishing between "faith" and "credulity"[5] and in examining self-knowledge, thinking, and action as three stages of reflection. Anyone reading the corresponding explications in this volume will understand why the students attending this course found it extremely challenging.[6]

Apart from the dispute with Heim, Bonhoeffer's lecture "Review and Discussion of New Publications in Systematic Theology" (2/1) was more accessible. Apparently Bonhoeffer had no intention of providing a genuinely comprehensive survey of recent publications in the field, and according to Wolf-Dieter Zimmermann, he even asked the students for their own recommendations at the beginning of the semester. When someone suggested Elert's recently published *Morphologie des Luthertums,*[7] Bonhoeffer declared
quite to the astonishment of his students, "I don't really understand it 474
enough."[8] What remained was in effect Bonhoeffer's own selection, reflecting his interest in ethics and dialectical theology, including mostly authors who had published in the periodical *Zwischen den Zeiten.* Similarly, his "Intro-

[4.] See. 2/1, p. 209. [Bonhoeffer had noted Brunner's program of eristics (apologetics) as a contrast of Brunner with Barth.—LR]

[5.] [See, for example, *DBWE* 2:128. *Gläubigkeit* in this volume has been translated as "devotion."—LR]

[6.] This was the recollection of Wolf-Dieter Zimmermann (*Wir nannten ihn Bruder Bonhoeffer,* 25–26).

[7.] ["Morphology of Lutheranism."—LR]

[8.] Zimmermann, *Wir nannten ihn Bruder Bonhoeffer,* 51.

duction to the current state of theology" was concerned primarily with the second edition (1922) of Barth's exegesis of the letter to the Romans. Bonhoeffer had already repeatedly adduced Barth's position in previous semesters,[9] the only new element being that he now apparently dispensed with any critical commentary. Was Bonhoeffer perhaps holding back because he himself was interested in seeing Barth appointed to Schleiermacher's chair at the university?[10] In any event, it is certainly striking that Bonhoeffer demonstrably dealt at some length with the ethics of Gogarten and Brunner while completely ignoring Barth as an ethicist—at least according to the lecture notes—despite Bonhoeffer's own reservations.[11]

Bonhoeffer decisively distanced himself theologically from Gogarten, whose conservatism Bonhoeffer found sufficiently traditional in the Lutheran sense but not entirely commensurate with the New Testament. What Bonhoeffer missed in Gogarten was a sense for the ambiguity of the state and an understanding for the task of concrete Christian ethics in the sense of "greater justice."[12] Bonhoeffer's critique of Brunner derived from a different source. As early as 1932, Bonhoeffer was already greatly anticipating Brunner's *Entwurf einer protestantisch-theologischen Ethik*[13] but became increasingly disappointed as he read it. Driven by the "question of whether it is possible for the concrete commandment to be proclaimed through the church," he found a "real gap" in this work; Bonhoeffer felt that what Brunner actually wrote was "extraordinarily paltry and even a real threat to the substance of the church."[14]

475 It was this very point that provided the point of departure for the public dispute toward the end of the 1932–33 winter semester.[15] At the beginning of 1933, Bonhoeffer was thus not really criticizing Brunner's overall theological initiative. Bonhoeffer apparently saw no problem there. The argument concerned the issue where Barth, too, had failed to satisfy him: namely, the question of the church's authority to issue concrete directives. The students' notes suggest that Bonhoeffer felt Brunner overly abbreviated

[9.] Concerning Barth's significance for Bonhoeffer, see the summary in the afterword to *DBWE* 11, sections IV and V.

[10.] See 1/30, esp. ed. note 8; and Ludwig, "Der Pazifist und Staatsfeind," 253.

[11.] Cf. 1/22.

[12.] See 2/1, p. 204. This expression also plays a role in the letter to Rößler (1/22).

[13.] [*Das Gebot und die Ordnungen: Entwurf einer protestantisch-theologischen Ethik*, which appeared in English as *The Divine Imperative: A Study of Christian Ethics*.—LR]

[14.] To Erwin Sutz at the beginning of August 1932 (*DBW* 11:100); see also the ambivalent judgment in Bonhoeffer's letter of May 17, 1932 (*DBW* 11:89).

[15.] Bonhoeffer had in the meantime had the opportunity to speak with Brunner in Switzerland (*DBW* 11:118).

this issue in an individualist fashion.[16] To avoid this himself, Bonhoeffer referred to the institution of a council,[17] thereby providing a theological recommendation designed to close a gap in Brunner's explication of the theology of God's Word. Bonhoeffer's theological grounding of this objection to Brunner's alleged individualism was doubtless inadequate, for why should it be viewed as fundamentally wrong for the church to take up the prophetic tradition in the first place? Although Brunner's view was undeniably correct at least in certain respects, his inclination to confine the broader ecclesiastical authority over concrete directives to the individual was unsatisfactory. Bonhoeffer referred to the decisions of the apostolic council (Acts 15:1–29), and his conclusion that authoritative directives could ultimately be issued only by a council rigorously shaped his own position amid the church disputes of his own age, first in the discussions concerning the "Jewish question,"[18] then in 1934 in connection with the peace question.[19]

This volume also does not fully document Bonhoeffer's teaching activity during his final semester in Berlin. His Hegel seminar has been published as a separate volume on the basis of Ferenc Lehel's notes.[20] Lehel's notes 476
as well as the lecture on Christology (2/12) show that even the considerable pressure of church politics during this semester did not distract Bonhoeffer from his intense theological work. In his Hegel seminar, he was concerned not with an ultimately political examination but with drawing the students' attention to his own theologically relevant discoveries in Hegel's philosophy of religion.[21] In contrast to the lectures on Christology, here Bonhoeffer was not really interested in any theological delimitation; the

[16.] See 2/1, p. 211.

[17.] [Bonhoeffer had in view an ecclesiastical council of the classic kind by which the ecumenical church makes binding doctrinal claims. He suggested this already in June 1933, in the debate between German Christians and the Young Reformation movement (see 1/58, the protocol on "The Struggle for the Church"), and he gave it prominence in his peace sermon at the ecumenical gathering of the World Alliance for Promoting International Friendship through the Churches in Fanø, 1934 (*DBWE* 13, 2/3). Both instances underscored what Bonhoeffer found wanting in Brunner's ethic, namely, the church's authority to issue concrete, binding directives (see *DBWE* 13, 2/3). See also note 18 here.—LR]

[18.] See esp. 2/13, which connects the possibility of the church engaging in "direct" political action to a conciliar decision (on the interpretation of this statement, see H. E. Tödt, *Theologische Perspektiven nach Dietrich Bonhoeffer*, 73).

[19.] See *DBWE* 13:307 and 309.

[20.] Cf. I. Tödt, *Dietrich Bonhoeffers Hegelseminar.*

[21.] Ibid., 138 and 10.

driving impetus was rather the possibility of learning—even in his own capacity as a critical theologian—from Hegel.

The lectures on Christology in the summer semester of 1933 represent the culmination of his academic activity in Berlin. Bonhoeffer had intensively prepared this theologically central theme[22] and during the brief semester taken every opportunity to articulate his own position with the utmost clarity, drawing on earlier works[23] and taking issue with his own theological teachers and models.[24] In his "critical or negative Christology," he exhaustively examined both the sense and the nonsense of various topoi concerning the doctrine of the person of Jesus within the history of theology and dogma; by contrast, his treatment of "positive Christology"—perhaps because of a lack of time—was rather brief. From the wealth of his ideas, I will note two details of particular importance for Bonhoeffer's theological position in this context.

First, it is worth noting that with respect to the Reformation's dispute concerning the Lord's Supper, Bonhoeffer advocated the Lutheran position without qualification. On this particular point, Bonhoeffer's contact with Barth and Brunner and his other, largely ecumenical experiences did not alienate him from his own theological heritage. Like his friend Franz Hildebrandt, Bonhoeffer insisted on the "EST" of the biblical tradition of the Lord's Supper,[25] defending the Lutheran doctrine of ubiquity against
477 Reformed objections. He was interested in the full integrity of Christ's presence and was unwilling to associate it explicitly with Christ's return still to come. It was only toward the end of the lectures that he referred to Christ's return, interpreting it there as the resolution of the stumbling block of humiliation and abasement.[26] Hence, although the eschatological element is thus not entirely lacking, Bonhoeffer did not perceive it as reason enough to investigate further the possible justification of the Reformed position.[27]

A second characteristic of Bonhoeffer's Christology emerges from a comparison with that of Brunner. Although Bonhoeffer was familiar with Brunner's "reflection on faith in Christ," he mentioned it in his lectures only as

[22.] Cf. Zimmermann, *Wir nannten ihn Bruder Bonhoeffer*, 49–50.

[23.] See in this regard Feil, *Theology of Dietrich Bonhoeffer*, 67–75, and Abromeit, *Geheimnis*.

[24.] See in this regard Abromeit, *Geheimnis*, 82–85.

[25.] See 2/12, pp. 345–46.

[26.] See 2/12, pp. 359–60.

[27.] Otto Weber later presented such a study (*Grundlagen der Dogmatik*, 2:707–9). Concerning the status of eschatology in these lectures, cf. also Krötke, "Der begegnende Gott," 29.

an aside, and even then only critically.[28] In defending the early church's faith in Christ as the true faith of the church, Brunner entered into extensive debate with liberal theology from Ritschl to Harnack.[29] Bonhoeffer, too, was interested in rehabilitating early church Christology, or more precisely the Chalcedonian formula. To that end, he could draw on Brunner's earlier distinction between the "who" and "how" questions,[30] albeit while expanding its meaning by using it not only to explicate the meaning of early church Christology itself but also to illuminate critically the attendant Protestant doctrinal development, particularly the doctrine of kenosis. Bonhoeffer also differed from Brunner insofar as he engaged in absolutely no criticism of Harnack, something prompted not merely out of reverential consideration for his Berlin teacher, but just as much by very substantive concerns. Quite in contrast to Brunner, Bonhoeffer was obviously intent on taking seriously Harnack's accomplishments in the field of dogmatic history. Bonhoeffer agreed with his teacher that the Chalcedonian formula used object-related categories, and to that extent Bonhoeffer's own Chris- 478
tology stayed close to that of his teacher Harnack[31]—even to the point of criticizing the doctrine of enhypostasia, whereas Brunner, as Bonhoeffer points out in his lectures, assessed that doctrine positively.[32]

His orientation toward dialectical theology notwithstanding, Bonhoeffer's own lectures on Christology did not simply negate the historical work of the liberal theology. Although he did indeed take note of its discoveries, he pressed the question regarding the meaning of object-oriented categories within the larger framework of contradictory statements about the person of Jesus Christ. His own judgment was that it was in precisely this way that object-oriented thinking was shattered, which only served to attest the mystery of the God-human and to cut short any further "how" questions. Here Bonhoeffer was able to combine loyalty to the kind of historical theology represented by Harnack with loyalty to the concerns of Brunner and Barth of positively incorporating early church theology. To that extent, Bonhoeffer's move here might even be described as an incorporation of

[28.] Bonhoeffer had expressed his disappointment in this work to Seeberg as early as 1928 (*DBWE* 10:122).

[29.] See Brunner, *Mediator*, 249–64.

[30.] Ibid., 232–33.

[31.] Concerning Harnack's influence on Bonhoeffer, see Kaltenborn, *Adolf von Harnack;* Staats, "Adolf von Harnack im Leben Bonhoeffers"; Staats, "Das patristische Erbe."

[32.] See 2/12, ed. note 95. Barth, too, had already come to a positive assessment of this doctrine as early as 1927 (*Christliche Dogmatik*, 264) and in a more general fashion defended the doctrine of the early church against the charge of intellectualism (255–57).

liberal theology into dialectical theology. While he acknowleded the problematic of early church terminology and concepts, the actual paradoxes of the Chalcedonian formula, rather than being criticized, were instead understood as being binding for any theological doctrine of the person of Jesus Christ.

II

Bonhoeffer's engagement on behalf of the World Alliance for Promoting International Friendship through the Churches is evident in three different texts in part 2 of this volume. The "Memorandum: 'The Social Gospel'" (2/4), which was conceived for work at the grassroots level, shows that Bonhoeffer was capable of carefully weighing the pros and cons before formulat-
479 ing his own position. Rather than focusing on coming to terms theologically with this American tradition, Bonhoeffer was concerned, on the one hand, with defending this movement's social engagement theologically and, on the other hand, with thwarting any Christian-ideological enhancement of democracy and countering any expectation of radical change within *this* world with an element of eschatological reserve, a position commensurate not only with his own Lutheran heritage but also with his orientation toward the Word-of-God theology of Barth and Brunner.

His theses on "Christ and Peace" (2/6) addressed the same ethical theme that shaped his own ecumenical engagement, namely, international peace. By contrast, Bonhoeffer's contributions to the ecumenical workshop in Dassel (2/10) attest more interest in dogmatic issues. Just as in the previous spring,[33] in 1933 Bonhoeffer was still intent on ensuring that efforts on behalf of ecumenical understanding did not neglect the critical question of truth. Peculiarly, he found little support for such concerns among other conference participants. The protocol reveals that with respect to both votes, Stählin opposed Bonhoeffer and did so in a rather surprising tone. Rather than commenting on Bonhoeffer's actual position, Stählin instead used the opportunity to criticize the young theologian as an advocate of Karl Barth's theology.[34] Bonhoeffer defended himself against this charge as little as against the charge that he did not understand the Pauline reference to the body of Christ in a sufficiently "real" fashion. Was Bonhoeffer silent because he felt that even this group no longer understood him? In any event, it is certainly striking that in Dassel he did not participate in the discussion of the very topic that demonstrably and intensely interested him:

[33.] See esp. the presentation in Ciernohorské Kúpele (*DBWE* 11, 2/14).

[34.] In turn, Bonhoeffer had vehemently opposed him at the first theological conference of the Provisional Bureau for ecumenical youth work (*DBW* 11:323–27).

the ecumenical movement's relationship "to the national and international movements of the present time."[35]

Bonhoeffer's correspondence with Henriod and Félice shows that domes- 480
tic German problems increasingly influenced and limited his own work in the World Alliance. World Alliance conferences in foreign countries now proceeded without Bonhoeffer, even when Henriod insisted that the international youth secretary be present. Conferences for which he was responsible were now canceled. As a result, Bonhoeffer had no further meetings with young French or Polish participants.[36] Unfortunately, he now no longer had time for the traditional goal of the World Alliance, namely, to promote international understanding through the participation of young Christians at such conferences, a goal that resonated in Bonhoeffer's homily of December 1, 1932 (3/2). Yet ecumenical conferences remained or became interesting because they offered an opportunity to find allies for the internal German debates. Bonhoeffer apparently chose his conferences from this perspective as well. Even though he had initially planned to travel to Basel, the meeting with French members of the World Alliance took place without him in early June 1933.[37] Bonhoeffer did not try to establish any bilateral understanding of what the church's task in Germany was to be, preferring instead to seek support on a broader front; as the World Alliance conference in Sofia shows, he was adept at exploiting such possibilities.[38]

A comparison of the conferences in Basel and Sofia shows how important it was in this organization, too, for the Germans not to distance themselves from their fellow Christians in other countries[39] and instead to acknowledge their concerns about violations of human rights in Germany. In Basel no genuine consensus was possible in assessing the situation. The French members of the World Alliance found no sympathetic ears for their own critical queries; even Siegmund-Schultze did not respond to the apology for the "German revolution" that was presented by the Nuremberg pastor Friedrich Bauer.[40] The participants in Sofia, however, did prepare an 481

[35.] See 2/10, ed. note 1, concerning the agenda of the Dassel conference.

[36.] [This is only the case for the period covered in this volume (12). Bonhoeffer resumed his ecumenical work in 1934, from London. See *DBWE* 13, documents 1/141; 1/145; 2/2; 2/3; and 2/3a.—LR]

[37.] See 1/38, ed. note 11.

[38.] [See 1/101.—LR]

[39.] This was certainly the case at the Life and Work conference in Novi Sad (the executive committee meeting on September 9–12, 1933); see *DB-ER*, 316; also C.-R. Müller, *Dietrich Bonhoeffers Kampf*, 55–57, and Boyens, *Kirchenkampf und Ökumene*, 1:59–66.

[40.] See the French protocol for this conference and the paper "Unsere Zusammenkunft" (Our Coming Together), which was delivered in an abbreviated form in Basel (WCC Archives, box 212-009).

official position statement on the German situation—even though the preliminary decision was not to issue such statements.[41] It was the position of the two German delegates, Bonhoeffer and Richter, that opened the way for this decision to be bypassed. Still affected by the recent introduction of the Aryan paragraph in Prussian churches, Bonhoeffer had already sent a telegraph asking Henriod to protest (1/94). By unofficially—and without enlisting Richter—informing Henriod and other foreign Christian colleagues about the political and ecclesiastical situation in Germany thoroughly and unequivocally,[42] Bonhoeffer directly contributed to the politically cautious but ecclesiastically unmistakable resolution that emerged. In the plenary session itself, both Bonhoeffer and Richter supported the World Alliance's decision. As Bell recounted, the two Germans were "courageous enough" to vote for the resolution.[43] They did, however, immediately visit the German legation. Nothing is known of the details of this meeting, in which they had to explain not only the criticism of the Reich Church and the church Aryan paragraph but also the statement deploring the state's anti-Jewish measures. The motivation for this visit is obvious: Bonhoeffer in particular, since he was about to travel to England, wanted to thwart any negative consequences of his participation in this resolution.[44] The report of the German legation to the Foreign Ministry in Berlin (1/103) suggests that he succeeded in this regard; the diplomatic representatives of the German Reich in Bulgaria downplayed the significance of the World Alliance conference and exonerated the German participants from any responsibil-
482 ity for criticism of the German Reich or of the Evangelical Church in Germany. Did Richter and Bonhoeffer perhaps veil from the legation their own roles with regard to the World Alliance's resolution? Or did they encounter a dialogue partner who shared their critical views and was willing to cover for the two ecumenists? The documents that exist offer no answers to these questions.

Bonhoeffer's church-related work at the Technical College in Berlin-Charlottenburg does not really exhibit any discernible high points. We do not know how his speech on the concept of Führer was received (2/9). Bonhoeffer did not even refer to it in his report to the consistory (1/54). According to this report, his entire work had already run aground in the

[41.] See Siegmund-Schultze in *Die Eiche* 21 (1933): 379. [For a description of the Sofia meeting and the text of its resolution, see *DB-ER*, 311–18.—LR]

[42.] See *DBWE* 13:22 and 31; and *DB-ER*, 314.

[43.] See 1/101, ed. note 1.

[44.] See in this regard *DBWE* 13:22–24; *DB-ER*, 317–20; as well as documents 1/107–8 and 2/16 in this volume.

1932–33 winter semester; neither his office hours nor devotional services elicited any interest—despite the detour through the student organizations. He also had to report to the consistory that he received only a few invitations to speak to the various organizations, although such visits did indeed often lead to "lively enough discussions." The only evidence of interest among the students at the Technical College that he could mention to his church superiors was the interest in his worship services at Trinity Church.[45]

Bonhoeffer presumably ceased working at the Technical College altogether in the summer semester 1933, concentrating instead on his university activities. Apart from his teaching duties, he also participated in the debate with the German Christians. He informed the Reich Chancellery that Ludwig Müller, the German Christian candidate for Reich bishop, could not count on the majority of students to support him (1/55 and 1/56). At the discussion meeting between the Young Reformation movement and the German Christians (1/58), Bonhoeffer was one of the main speakers and apparently made the strongest impression. Even the fact that Bonhoeffer was permitted to speak on behalf of the Young Reformation movement in June is noteworthy. At the beginning of May, when the opposi- 483
tion to the German Christians was forming, he was not yet welcome because of his solidarity with Dehn. He was also accused of being a socialist.[46] Hence Bonhoeffer's position in the Berlin church opposition had changed within a few weeks, even though he had not substantively modified his position. As before, none of the nationalist undertones that Barth criticized in this opposition[47] are discernible in Bonhoeffer's own position. Unlike his colleague Bronisch-Holtze, on June 22 Bonhoeffer said absolutely nothing about domestic political issues, instead confining his own remarks to the theological and ecclesiastical questions that had arisen because of the German Christians. Bonhoeffer understood the Aryan paragraph in the church—whose divisive significance Fabricius had doubted not without some justification[48]—as a touchstone for the validity of the confession, and he indicated the necessity of a binding conciliar decision regarding this issue. As surprising as this suggestion had to seem in view of the history of German Protestantism, this position elicited opposition only among

[45.] According to Wolf-Dieter Zimmermann's recollection, those students were actually a small group of theologians (*Wir nannten ihn Bruder Bonhoeffer*, 46–47).

[46.] See 1/44, ed. note 1, the information from Gertrud Staewen intended for Barth.

[47.] See Barth, *Theologische Existenz heute*, 30–34.

[48.] See his reference to the fact that not even the Young Reformation movement radically rejected this ordinance (1/58, ed. note 16).

the older speakers in the discussion.[49] The suggestion apparently made a stronger impression on the student participants at the meeting; Gertrud Staewen, who was vacationing on the Baltic coast at the time, was quickly informed and on June 26 already wrote and told Bonhoeffer that, considering the "Babylonian confusion of Christian discourse," the convocation of a council was now "really necessary" (1/62).

III

This volume contains only a selection of Bonhoeffer's sermons from this
484 period. His goal in those sermons was to confront his listeners directly with what God has to say here and now. None of these sermons deals with historical questions regarding the biblical texts. Just as he preferred to choose his own sermon texts instead of following the order of pericopes, he also felt free to omit individual verses. Through both criticism and encouragement, he was always primarily concerned with strengthening his listeners' faith in overcoming fear.

Bonhoeffer's sermons after Hitler came to power reveal a different tone, insofar as after the sermon on Gideon (3/5) Bonhoeffer no longer evoked the distinction between what is said to the individual and what is said to the church; as soon as the struggle for the church began, this traditional distinction had become obsolete. If one reads Bonhoeffer's sermons as a response to the political upheaval,[50] I think the most striking feature is that even here, Bonhoeffer makes no direct political statements. Potentially political allusions do occasionally appear: in February 1933 the assertion that Gideon is not to be confused with Siegfried (3/5); in July 1933 the assertion that Peter is not really to be understood as a heroic figure and that the church contained no secondary altars for venerating human beings (3/8). In none of his sermons after Hitler's rise to power, however, did Bonhoeffer try to influence the political actions of his listeners. In contrast to the ecclesiastical-political boundary drawn against the German Christians—to which the previous statements in any event also apply, and which led Bonhoeffer at the end of May to distinguish between the church of the Word and the world church of religion (3/7)—his sermons did not really focus on political questions. The guiding notion was rather Bonhoeffer's intention to articulate the message of God's gesture in Christ as something that can and indeed is meant to affect a person's entire life. Although from the pulpit Bonhoeffer did not articulate the political implications of

[49.] Prof. Schumann from Halle (cf. 1/58, p. 128).
[50.] According to Otto Dudzus (*PAM* 1:35).

that statement, he did articulate them unequivocally elsewhere, as is shown by his position regarding the so-called Jewish question.

Some scholars have criticized the freedom with which Bonhoeffer often 485
selected his own sermon texts.[51] It is indeed striking how radically Bonhoeffer differed from Barth on precisely this point. In publishing his own sermon of December 12, 1933, on Romans 15:5–13, Barth thought it appropriate to point out that he was addressing the "Jewish question" not on his own initiative, but rather because the text itself "required that one touch on" this issue.[52] By pointing out how one is bound to the lectionary, Barth wanted to show how preachers, rather than exercising freedom over against God's Word, were instead bound to serve it. Bonhoeffer took a different position toward the pericope order, though it was not really this position that prompted him to address the "Jewish question" in his sermon. Nor did Bonhoeffer otherwise fall prey to what Barth called the human presumption of "thematic sermons." Bonhoeffer did not, for example, engage "his" sermon text on May 28, 1933 (3/7),[53] as an occasion to identify the Confessing Christians with the church of Moses and the German Christians with the church of Aaron. Ultimately in this sermon he maintained that under the cross the church is "always both church of Moses and church of Aaron," which is also why he was able to conclude in the sense of the Reformation's *simul iustus ac peccator* with the summons, "come, believe and worship." Although in his sermon on the Sunday of the church elections (3/8) Bonhoeffer was clearly interested in drawing a line against the German Christians, he avoided any hint of ecclesial triumphalism. Those who listened closely could not mistake his criticism of the official election slogan, "The Church Must Remain the Church." Bonhoeffer considered it more appropriate to speak about confession on this particular Sunday; he understood the church of Peter as the church that must confess from within its own weakness, not as a church that might even consider trying to ensure its own continued existence: "No human being builds the church, but Christ alone."

IV 486

Bonhoeffer's particular contribution within the Berlin church opposition was his early and unqualified identification of the Aryan paragraph as a

[51.] On this point and Bonhoeffer's textual exegesis in general, see Wendel, *Studien zur Homiletik Dietrich Bonhoeffers*, 21–33 and 64–65.

[52.] See *Theologische Existenz heute* 5, 3 (emphasis in original not reproduced here).

[53.] Cf. in this regard the letter to Sutz, 1/67.

challenge on which the church would stand or fall. His brief text in English from mid-July (2/14), which tried to draw the ecumenical world's attention to the racist implications of the new church constitution, was not the first time he identified the Aryan paragraph as the *status confessionis* in this sense; his essay on "The Church and the Jewish Question" (2/13), completed on April 15, 1933, already made the same observation. Here he also insisted—unlike many of his colleagues in the church opposition against the German Christians—that the "Jewish question" also obligated the church with regard to state law.[54] Bonhoeffer also believed the confessional issue had been raised by the fact that Hitler's regime had begun to suspend the constitutionally guaranteed rights of German citizens; this could not be justified by a questionable "racial criterion." That is, Bonhoeffer was raising the crucial, critical question of principle at the very beginning of the anti-Jewish policies of Hitler's regime. He did not yet wish to rule out a certain unspecified latitude in the shaping of laws. But Bonhoeffer advocated the realization that this new "special law" represented a unique and grave deci-
487 sion to relinquish the principle of equality that is the foundation of modern constitutional law. Bonhoeffer believed that the new Jewish policies were fundamentally unacceptable and that the church was obligated to react, if necessary also in the form of a conciliar stand.

Those who were actually the subject of these statements apparently appreciated their significance more than did the church circles that Bonhoeffer was actually trying to influence. On July 28, 1933—that is, just after the German Christians rode to victory in the church elections—the *Jüdische Rundschau* reported two statements from Protestant quarters that raised "religious reservations of conscience against the German Jewish policies."[55] The *Jüdische Rundschau* related the first statement—one by

[54.] Walter Künneth saw no grounds here for uncompromising objection. On this and other statements from the churches, see Scholder, *Churches and the Third Reich,* 1:254–80, and Smid, *Deutscher Protestantismus.* Mecklenburg regional bishop Rendtorff also failed to recognize the heart of the challenge presented by the anti-Jewish policies of Hitler's regime, maintaining on the German Evangelical Church Committee that "for seventeen hundred years the Jews were subject to exceptional legal status with the complete concurrence of the church, their liberation being linked to the advancement of enlightened thinking. Such progressive thinking was not to be identified with Protestant norms." See the April 26, 1933, minutes of the Church Committee (DEKA), "Behandlung der Judenfrage" (Treatment of the Jewish Question), in Boyens, *Kirchenkampf und Ökumene,* 1:289–99, esp. 298. As document 2/13 in this volume shows, by this time Bonhoeffer had already taken a completely different position regarding the emancipation of the Jews (see in this regard p. 505 below).

[55.] *Jüdische Rundschau,* p. II, the report "Christentum und Judenfrage."

Johannes Müller, "the well-known preacher of Schloß Elmau"[56]—with an element of uneasiness. It then introduced Dietrich Bonhoeffer—"a son of the well-known Berlin psychiatrist"—as the author of "another Christian statement concerning the Jewish question." After summarizing his statements on the church's own position toward its members of Jewish descent in two sentences, it then related in greater detail how this theologian assessed the German Reich's new, anti-Jewish policies, reporting not only Bonhoeffer's belief that the church could not be permitted simply to accept these policies without some reaction but also his three-part enumeration of the various ways the church might react to state-sponsored injustice.

The problems that preoccupy scholars today, such as Bonhoeffer's reference to the curse on the Jewish people or his reference to admissible new possibilities for state laws,[57] received no mention in the *Jüdische Rundschau,* which focused instead on what was most important to those affected, namely, the question of just where members and representatives of the Evangelical Church stood in a situation in which cabinet-level decisions were suspending the equal rights of Jews without any kind of public or even parliamentary discussion.

Bonhoeffer addressed the "Jewish question" several times later as well, first in June, when he excluded the possibility that the Young Reformation 488
movement would discriminate against the Jews in any form in the church (1/58), then also in the previously mentioned statement to the ecumenical world (2/14), and finally in August in the position statement concerning the various forms of the Aryan paragraph in the church (2/16). In the same context, one might mention the Bethel confession (2/15) as well, on which Bonhoeffer worked intensively as long as he could,[58] although ultimately he did not agree with the final version. His letter explaining his disagreement with the final document that emerged from the various stages of evaluation and editing has been lost. All we have is his brief concluding assessment of the "Confession of the Fathers" edited by Martin Niemöller: "Too many cooks spoil the soup."[59]

Although the only thing directly documented is that Bonhoeffer no longer agreed with this confession, one can nonetheless surmise what might

[56.] ["Elmau castle," in Bavaria; Müller's movement was centered there. Müller had been active in the mission to proselytize Jews and was initially a supporter of National Socialism; hence the tone of the report.—LR]

[57.] See Smid, *Deutscher Protestantismus und Judentum,* 436–39.

[58.] See Bonhoeffer's August 20, 1933, letter to his grandmother (1/86) and the October 24, 1933, letter to Barth (*DBWE* 13, 1/2) and "Concerning the History of the Bethel Confession" in this volume.

[59.] Inscribed in the dedication on Rieger's copy (*NL-Bibl.* 11,4).

have prompted this disagreement. Because we do know with certainty that he believed the church would stand or fall by its decision on the "Jewish question" in 1933, the confession as edited by Niemöller would have to be measured as to whether it did indeed adhere to this line. Textual comparisons reveal three changes that Bonhoeffer could only have understood as the surrender of that position. In the version that he still supported, those responsible for the confession began with the assumption of "the human race as one united race in its origin and its final destination" and on the basis of both Scripture and creed rejected the "modern concept of race." In contrast, the final version cited Scripture and confession in speaking about the "truth concept of the modern concept of race," rejecting only those attempts to "place on the same level" "the natural phenomenon of race" with the "institutional orders" of marriage, authority, or people.[60]
489 Obviously the front that Bonhoeffer wanted to defend had retreated considerably. The confession was also seriously weakened in the section on the church and the Jews. The final version deleted the warning against any people presuming to "take revenge on the Jews for the murder committed at Golgotha."[61] Did they no longer view this as necessary in a confession that drew the line against the German Christians? Or did considerations of evangelization make the authors less inclined to criticize the regnant anti-Semitism too directly? It should be noted that this section initially concluded with the summons to maintain solidarity with persecuted Jewish Christians, a summons that also called upon the church itself to take an unequivocal position—quite in Bonhoeffer's sense—on behalf of those who were the objects of such discrimination. The final version exhibits none of the drama associated with this decision, a decision that did in any case point toward a church without privileges. Here, too, the focus was self-evidently on Christians of Jewish descent, whom the church naturally enough did not want to leave in the lurch. The summons to the church to act in solidarity, however, was now replaced by the assurance that the church should also grant privileges to Jews. In the style of what Bonhoeffer perceived as a rather suspicious insistence that "the church must remain the church," the final version now maintained that the church should grant to those Jews who "return home to acknowledge in Jesus . . . the Messiah

[60.] Compare the "August version," p. 388, with *Das Bekenntnis der Väter,* ed. Martin Niemöller, 24. [The phrases "the human race as one united race in its origin and its final destination" and the rejection of the "modern concept of race" are from the August version in this volume. The subsequent quoted phrases ("truth concept of the modern concept of race" etc.) are from the final version published in the Niemöller edition.—LR]

[61.] Compare the August version, p. 419, with *Das Bekenntnis der Väter,* ed. Niemöller, 35–36.

and Son of God" the same rights as those accorded "Gentile Christians."[62] Here, however, the authors were merely deceiving themselves and others concerning the real cost of discipleship, and Bonhoeffer could no longer affirm the document.

Given these differences, it is hardly surprising that Bonhoeffer did not want to be associated publicly with the final version, which had become a "soup" of opposition and accommodation. What is surprising is how facilely the Bethel participants dismissed Bonhoeffer's objections. Georg Merz explained it to Bodelschwingh as simply a result of Bonhoeffer being "too young" and having "slipped into academia too early and too one-sidedly."[63] At about the same time, the Berlin systematic theologian Arthur Titius 490
reached the opposite conclusion concerning his young colleague: "It is a great pity that our best hope in the faculty is being wasted on the church struggle."[64]

V

On February 6, 1933, Dietrich Bonhoeffer wrote to Reinhold Niebuhr, his former teacher in New York: "It would be precipitous to say even one word about the state of affairs here in Germany. It can scarcely be expected that nothing will substantially change here, whether economically, politically, or socially. But an even greater threat is a terrible barbarization of our culture, so that here, too, we will need to create a Civil Liberties Union in the coming period"(1/31).

Although these dense sentences are not easy to understand, the final words do provide a clue. Bonhoeffer's reference to the American Civil Liberties Union (ACLU) recalls the epoch in American history beginning in 1919 when all "aliens" were to be excluded. Bonhoeffer did not have to remind Niebuhr about the havoc that xenophobia and fear of Communism could cause in a state and society. He knew that Niebuhr had had similar experiences with American reactions to the alleged Bolshevik threat, racist prejudices, and false judgments, and that he was similarly familiar with the work of the ACLU, which embodied liberal opposition to the trend of denying basic rights to minorities and marginal groups.

Hence, without going into detail concerning the situation in Germany, Bonhoeffer had related to his American friend that the new regime, with

[62.] Compare the "August version," pp. 420–21, with *Das Bekenntnis der Väter*, ed. Niemöller, 36.

[63.] See the letter of November 24, 1933, to Bodelschwingh mentioned in "Concerning the History of the Bethel Confession," p. 512.

[64.] *DB-ER*, 221.

Hitler as Reich chancellor, offered grounds for genuinely grave concern and corresponding action. As far as is known, however, Bonhoeffer did not become engaged in any way during the following months to establish an
491 organization comparable to the ACLU. Instead, he chose more realistically to address an already existing, respected organization's responsibility with regard to the feared "cultural barbarization"; that is, he chose to confront the church with the "Jewish question" as a question of constitutional law, albeit—as mentioned above—without success.

Bonhoeffer's remarks to Niebuhr show that he expected the new regime to mount an immediate and serious attack on constitutionally guaranteed rights. In this context, he as well as other members of his family[65] understood Hitler and his party as decisive forces within the government coalition; that is, he shared neither the conviction of the centrist politician Franz von Papen that Hitler had merely been "engaged" and would soon become malleable enough[66] nor the surprisingly similar assessment of the leftist journalist Carl von Ossietzky, who believed the National Socialists would function merely as a ready troop of German nationalist "cavaliers."[67] Because we have no documentation of Bonhoeffer having made any remarks concerning the current political developments in Germany during this period,[68] we cannot really attribute to him any particular interest in current politics; that said, he did nonetheless develop a good sense for what
492 was actually at stake with regard to Hitler's chancellorship.[69] Although

[65.] See in this regard *DB-ER*, 257–59.

[66.] Cited after Hildebrand, *Das Dritte Reich*, 3.

[67.] As Ossietzky wrote on February 7, 1933, in his article "Kavaliere und Rundköpfe" (Cavaliers and Roundheads) in the *Weltbühne.* Ossietzky also noted that he did not expect this "regime of the united right wingers" to return to a parliamentary democracy, but that only changes moving toward a dictatorial regime could be expected. [Ossietzky was one of the first targets of the regime; he was arrested immediately after the Reichstag fire on February 28 and remained imprisoned until his death in 1938.—LR]

[68.] Concerning the earlier period, cf. Staats's remark that at the beginning of the 1930s in the United States, Bonhoeffer was yet untouched by contemporary politics (*DBWE* 10:610). Later (see *DBWE* 11) there are no statements on issues such as the presidential cabinet (i.e., on the nonparliamentary governance that had already begun under Brüning) or on the election gains made by the Nazi and Communist parties and the so-called Papen coup against Prussia's social democratic regime. Two letters from Bonhoeffer to Lehmann include fleeting reactions to the Reichstag elections during the summer of 1932; they are included in *DBWE* 11, 1/59a and 1/68a. Both letters reflect the picture that has emerged here.

[69.] Within the family, Bonhoeffer's father and especially the jurist Gerhard Leibholz, who was married to Bonhoeffer's twin sister, doubtless contributed to his developing opinions. See in this regard Strohm, *Theologische Ethik*, 54–147. In this work, Strohm

in his sermon on the Sunday of Reichstag elections (November 6, 1932, 3/1) he commented on the unmistakable signals of Germany's "death," he did not follow up this dark prognosis with any commentary on the election results. We have no evidence, for example, that Bonhoeffer viewed the considerable losses suffered by the Nazi party as a positive sign, that he was worried about the gains made by the Communist party, or that he pondered what real chance the Schleicher administration might have under the circumstances. It was only Hitler's own ascent to government that prompted him to react critically to developments in German politics.

Only a few days prior to these events, Bonhoeffer had already addressed an explosive topic in a radio broadcast. On February 1, 1933, he gave the address "The Younger Generation's Altered View of the Concept of Führer" (2/8). The concluding sentences of this address spoke about the leader [Führer] who becomes "the idol the led are looking for."[70] Because he had exceeded his time limit, however, these concluding, critical words were cut short in the broadcast.[71]

What was the focus of this address? Without mentioning Hitler's name, it nonetheless appears in hindsight as a remarkably early and clear criticism of the claims made by the National Socialist Reich chancellor.[72] In illustrating this point, I would take as my point of departure the fact that Bonhoeffer spoke in the context of a series of programs that, beginning January 11, 1933, was to present the "young generation" in six installments.[73] The series was thus concerned not with any direct and exclusively political question but with the new and major theme that arose around the turn of the 493
century and led after World War I to what amounted to a "mythologizing of youth."[74] This was connected to a selective perception of social reality, which was reflected in the lecture series as well; those who had planned the broadcasts apparently were not really interested in the situation of the youth among the working class.

Bonhoeffer's first position statement (2/8), published on January 28, 1933, followed the basic orientation of the broadcast series in addressing

tries to interpret Bonhoeffer's position primarily as the result of his intensive exchange with Leibholz. [But see the more recent critical study of Leibholz by Manfred Wiegandt, *Norm und Wirklichkeit*.—LR]

[70.] [2/9, p. 280.—LR]

[71.] See 1/29. [See esp. ed. note 3.—LR]

[72.] According to Christoph Strohm, *Theologische Ethik*, 124–25. Although Strohm analyzes the expansion into an address concerning the "Führer problem," he does not examine the genesis of the radio address.

[73.] See 2/9, ed. note 1.

[74.] Cf. Koebner, *Mit uns zieht die neue Zeit*, 10.

the issue of "leading the youth." His goal in this context was to go "beyond the vague and fantastic in order to have a clear vision."

Bonhoeffer began by opposing any glorification of youth. His ensuing explications also betrayed his distance from contemporary voices such as that of Ernst Gründel, who saw Germany's political future arising from the "sending forth of the young generation." The theme of "The Younger Generation's Altered View of the Concept of Führer" interested Bonhoeffer in a critical sense insofar as it involved the emergence of a new political and religious Führer concept, though one might keep in mind that he was not entirely opposed to the Führer expectations among the younger generation. What he was telling the readers of the radio magazine was that on February 1, 1933, he would delineate the justifications and limits of "leading and being led."

His typescript of the radio address largely adhered to the prescribed framework—even to the point of assuming that the younger generation was composed exclusively of males! Bonhoeffer described the profound transition from the youth movement's nonpolitical Führer concept to the "political-messianic idea of leader," which he thought characterized the youngest group, those men born in 1910. That is, the older members of the younger generation largely opposed rather than shared that political understanding. For Bonhoeffer, this dispute among young men concerning
494 the question of the authority of the Führer or the authority of office was one of "the most burning question[s] of the day." One might mention that Bonhoeffer's own position within this controversy involved connecting the function of the Führer to the nexus of social and political institutions, to the "orders of life." What is extremely important, however, is how he defined and developed the theme itself, beginning with the problem of how youth is to be guided and moving from that question to the role of young people in politics and thence to the problem of how political authority is to be understood in the first place.

In that sense, Bonhoeffer by no means conceived his radio address exclusively as a forum in which to take issue with Hitler and his party; such was, of course, certainly also an issue, since long before the "seizure of power" the leader of the NSDAP had imposed himself with such force upon the political landscape that even political opponents could not simply ignore him.[75] Moreover, Hitler's candidacy for Reich president in 1932 demonstrated unequivocally that he had his eye set on high office. Finally, one

[75.] As early as 1930 one could already read in *Das Junge Zentrum* (7, 1930): "We centrist young people do not want a democracy of the chaotic masses. We affirm the Führer. But it is not the Hitlers and Goebbels who are defining the figure of the Führer.

must also consider Hitler's actions in the Potempa case,[76] which the Bonhoeffer family followed both attentively and with disgust.[77] To the extent that Bonhoeffer's criticism of the Führer was from the outset certainly also directed at Hitler himself, it was directed primarily at Hitler as party leader.[78] Nor do Bonhoeffer's words suggest that in preparing and formulating the radio address he already anticipated that Hitler's second run 495
at "seizing power" was imminent. His implicit criticism of the man whose name would soon recede behind his function as Führer ultimately focused on only one side of a politically questionable constellation. The other side was the new mentality within the younger generation. At the beginning of 1933, Bonhoeffer had his eye on both, and with good reason, since it was not only Hitler's own claim to be the Führer that presented a problem but also—as Gründel's remarks demonstrate—the messianically tinged expectations of the Führer held among the younger generation itself.[79] Although this hope in a future savior for Germany was not tied specifically to the party leader Hitler at this time, demagogically adroit politicians such as Hitler and Goebbels were certainly capable of diverting it in that very direction.[80]

Hence the political situation in Germany that Bonhoeffer outlined in his radio address before the "seizure of power" describes a constellation that could potentially become extremely dangerous for Germany's political future. However, Bonhoeffer did not yet speak of any really serious threat to the constitution and political culture, something he first mentioned only in

---

The Führer as a son of the people [*Volk*]—the people as the entire strength of the nation itself, that is the Führer ideal of a 'young center'!" Cited in Götz von Olenhusen, *Jugendreich, Gottesreich, Deutsches Reich,* 40. But see also Carl von Ossietzky's assessment of Hitler at the beginning of 1933. On January 3, 1933, he wrote—believing that the Nazi party had already passed its political zenith—that "the great *völkisch Führer* with the external appearance and allurements of a gypsy chief may well have his day and then fade with it, but the evil, ugly instincts he evokes will not fade away so easily or quickly and will likely infect the entire public life in Germany for many years to come" ("Wintermärchen," 3).

[76.] See 3/5, ed. note 6.

[77.] See *DB-ER,* 257–58.

[78.] In this context one might remark critically that Bonhoeffer's categories do not do justice to the position of a party leader in the context of mass democracy. As already mentioned, he began with the alternative between the authority of the Führer or that of office and then spoke about how the Führer himself should function in the service of the "orders of life." In this sense, Bonhoeffer was working with a normative distinction instead of defining in a more objective fashion the function of political parties as such in the state.

[79.] Cf. 2/9, ed. note 14.

[80.] On this aspect of the history of the Third Reich, see Kershaw, *Hitler-Myth,* esp. 106–8.

the letter to Niebuhr (1/31) that alluded to Hitler's appointment as Reich chancellor. This discrepancy suggests that Bonhoeffer, too, was surprised by Hitler's appointment but then quickly recognized what was really at stake.

After the "seizure of power," Bonhoeffer publicly addressed the issue of the Führer principle twice more. The academic lecture "The Führer and the Individual in the Younger Generation" (2/9) shows how Bonhoeffer
496 reacted to the new situation. His first concern was to warn similarly against an overestimation of the authority of office. He then sharpened the responsibility of the individual before the ultimate authority, namely, God, and formulated an appeal to the responsibility of the Führer, maintaining that as the representative of those who were yet dependent, the Führer should bring about obedience and service to the "order of the state, the community," and provide guidance toward commensurate behavior.

After the Führer had moved into the Reich chancellery, of course, Bonhoeffer did indeed have to expand his criticism of the Führer with a warning against an overestimation of the authority of office. Bonhoeffer had assessed the situation with similar accuracy in summoning individuals to be responsible before God and in so doing warn them against self-accommodation and "synchronization" [Gleichschaltung]. Today we may find it rather surprising that he sought to obligate the Führer Hitler to fulfill his responsibility toward the "orders of life." Was this not a clear sign of political naïveté? Not necessarily, considering Bonhoeffer's critical assessment of the Hitler regime in the aforementioned letter to Niebuhr. A different interpretation seems more appropriate for this utterance, one made in a lecture at two Berlin colleges. As is well known, Luther concluded his own basic writing on "worldly authority" with a *Fürstenspiegel*, a piece offering guidance for the conduct of princes. From this perspective, it was precisely Bonhoeffer—who had serious reservations about Gogarten's Lutheran ethics—who was able to draw in a more direct fashion from Luther. What Bonhoeffer says about the task of the Führer does in any event stand objectively in the tradition of such a *Fürstenspiegel*, though instead of appealing primarily to the understanding of those in power, his addresses appealed to the judgment of his fellow citizens. In so doing he provided a critical standard for their own evaluation of the chancellor, who at the time was still using Christian formulations to establish credibility and support among the German people.[81] In this way, Bonhoeffer could avoid raising the suspi-

[81.] See the conclusion to the declaration on February 1, 1933: "May Almighty God take our work into his grace, properly shape our will, bless our understanding, and bestow upon us the trust of our people. For it is not for ourselves that we wish to fight, but for Germany" (cited according to the text in Nicolaisen, *Dokumente*, 1:2).

cion that he was overreaching his own competence as a theologian and yet still summon his listeners in the Berlin colleges—before the Reichstag election on March 5, 1933—to be mindful of their political responsibility. 497

From today's perspective, two additional details of his criticism of the Führer seem problematic. First, Bonhoeffer understood the *völkisch* myth of the Führer (and the Reich) to be a late offspring of the French Revolution, both instances allegedly involving the attempt to establish God's reign on earth. This criticism, of course, was not really original. Luther's battle against the enthusiasts [Schwärmer] helped turn eschatological reservation into a popular and effective argument against any radical political movement. What is noteworthy here is that Bonhoeffer was not shy about speaking out publicly after Hitler came to power. He dared to criticize the NSDAP and the entire political right—which, as was well known, clearly opposed the ideas of the French Revolution—in a fashion that could hardly have been sharper. His position also suggested that the commitment of the NSDAP and its Führer to the idea of "positive Christianity"[82] could not simply be blindly trusted. He did, however, adhere to a rather widespread view in not really fully articulating the meaning of the French Revolution, neglecting, for example, the contribution that the French declaration of human rights made to the development of modern constitutional law—making it all the more surprising that a few weeks later, in his discussion of the "Jewish question" (2/13), he expressed his confidence in an unrescindable concept of justice and law that can only be understood historically as a consequence of the French declaration of human rights. Within the span of just a few weeks, Bonhoeffer had thus revised his one-sided understanding of the French Revolution. Whereas in April 1933 he had come to realize that his own church ought to defend the emancipation of the Jews, Regional Bishop Rendtorff was still capable of defending the view—essentially the dominant opinion—that the church would be better advised *not* to become publicly engaged on behalf of this Enlightenment accomplishment.[83]

Even though in this instance one might say that Bonhoeffer engaged in a bit of early self-correction, elsewhere he did not really do so. His criticism 498
of authority "from below" obviously neglected the distinction between the populist legitimation of an authoritarian will of the Führer, on the one hand, and democratic legitimation through general, free elections and through public and parliamentary debate, on the other. At least as far as this problem was concerned, his brother-in-law Leibholz was already articulating more-precise categories by distinguishing between authoritarian

[82.] [The key phrase in paragraph 24 of the 1920 Nazi party platform.—LR]

[83.] Cf. his remarks as cited in ed. note 54.

and totalitarian states.[84] The inadequacies of Bonhoeffer's argumentation emerge even more clearly when confronted by the analysis of Sigmund Neumann, a lecturer at the Berlin College of Political Science who in 1932[85] had already ascertained in the NSDAP a "measure of democracy that is indispensable for any thoroughgoing politicization of broad classes of the population." Neumann characterized this form of democracy by maintaining that "it does, however, bear unequivocally 'Caesar-like' features; acclamation becomes virtually the only form by which one's own decisions are confirmed." This political scientist accordingly described the NSDAP as an "absolutistic party of integration," to be distinguished from the "democratic party of integration" of the Social Democrats. Bonhoeffer did not make such distinctions. Although his distinction between authority "from above" and "from below" seemed theologically unequivocal enough, it was ill-suited for articulating any sociologically precise distinction between different kinds of authority. Just as in his attempt to articulate the significance of the party leader within the weave of different political institutions,[86] Bonhoeffer was inclined to use dichotomous distinctions that were inadequate for identifying political phenomena within a mass democracy.

Is Bonhoeffer thus to be classified as an antidemocrat?[87] His opposition to Gogarten (2/1) already militates against this oversimplified conclusion. Bonhoeffer saw no reason to criticize the "system" of Weimar for any
499 lack of authority and thus to welcome the political turn of events in 1933. Second, one might certainly also note Bonhoeffer's repeated public warnings against any religiously determined understanding of the Führer and against granting unrestricted authority to such a political leader. Third, when Hitler did indeed begin to eviscerate the liberal parliamentary state, Bonhoeffer was immediately prepared to defend that "system" on a decisive point, namely, the "Jewish question," as a question of constitutional law, and to summon his own church to oppose such developments and to provide help to those affected by them. And even more: Bonhoeffer made an assertion unprecedented in the history of German Protestantism in maintaining that if mere objection alone could not prevent the state from turning justice into injustice and order into disorder, the church was obliged to abandon such "indirect" political action and move on to "direct" political

[84.] See in this regard Strohm, *Theologische Ethik*, 51–86.

[85.] See Neumann, *Die deutschen Parteien*; the following citations are from this volume, 109–10.

[86.] See ed. note 78.

[87.] This is the judgment of Nicolai Hammersen, *Politisches Denken im deutschen Widerstand*, whose thesis is based largely on Bonhoeffer's later statements (see 137, 150, 153, and 253–54). Concerning the essay on the Führer problem, see Hammersen, 248–49.

action. Those who read the materials in this volume carefully will inevitably see that during these months, months that were of such enormous significance for the history of both Germany and German Protestantism, one of Bonhoeffer's primary concerns was to defend the constitution of the Weimar Republic. From our own perspective, however, it seems regrettable that neither then nor later did Bonhoeffer really give democracy as a form of life the theological attention that, in the eyes of subsequent generations, it deserves.

Carsten Nicolaisen

Concerning the History of the Bethel Confession[1]

Because some of the pertinent source materials contradict each other, the 503
origin and editorial history of the Bethel confession cannot be determined definitively.[2] Nonetheless, we do know the following about Bonhoeffer's participation and his ultimate rejection of the changes subsequently made to the August version.

The initiative to formulate a confession came from the Young Reformation movement, which after the victory of the German Christians in the July 23, 1933, church elections resolved to "confront the new church leadership and the movement of the German Christians—the latter of which is determinative for the former—with the confessional question" and to clear up the situation with a "confession suitable for the times."[3] We can no longer determine for certain how and through whom Bonhoeffer was invited to work on what became known as the "Bethel confession." On the one hand, he already knew before July 26, 1933, that he would be traveling to Bethel;[4] on the other, the recommendations of Berlin theologians to Friedrich von Bodelschwingh that he enlist Bonhoeffer and the Erlangen

[1.] [This document appears as appendix 1 in *DBW* 12.—LR]

[2.] See in this regard *GS* 2:80–89; *DB-ER*, 300–303; G. C. Carter, *Confession at Bethel*, 61–148; C.-R. Müller, *Bekenntnis und Bekennen*, 13–21; Strohm, *Theologische Ethik*, 205–27; for a critical summary, see Lichtenfeld, *Theologie*.

[3.] See Martin Niemöller's theses "Die Jungreformatorische Bewegung und die Kirchenpolitik," 101.

[4.] See 1/75.

church historian Hermann Sasse to compose the text of a Lutheran confession date only from July 31 and August 1, 1933.[5]

Bodelschwingh, Bonhoeffer, and Georg Merz, one of the lecturers at the seminary in Bethel, met in Bethel for a preliminary meeting on August 5, the results of which Bodelschwingh then summarized that same day in a letter to Georg Schulz, the Barmen pastor and head of the Sydow Brethren:
504 "The wish has repeatedly arisen to work out a position statement concerning current questions from the perspective of the Lutheran confession in order to establish a firm basis within these disputes that might also provide support for lonely warriors. . . . We agreed that first a smaller circle of theologians [namely, Bonhoeffer, Merz, Sasse, and Schulz] meet here to begin this work"; the envisioned time period was August 15–20, 1933.[6]

The first two versions of the subsequent Bethel confession were then worked out between August 15 and 25 in Bethel under the patronage of Bodelschwingh himself.[7] Contrary to earlier scholarship, which considered the draft of the Bethel confession to have been authored only by Bonhoeffer and Sasse, the source materials as well as the text itself clearly show that Merz (but not Schulz) intensively participated.[8] Merz had already participated in the preliminary discussion on August 5; on August 16, 1933, immediately after the work began, he wrote to publisher Albert Lempp, "Mr. Sasse and Mr. Bonhoeffer, who have been here since yesterday to contribute to this theological endeavor, will be working with me this afternoon",[9] and at the annual conference of the German pastors ministering to foreign congregations in Great Britain, which met in Bradford, Yorkshire, on November 28, 1933, Bonhoeffer himself related that "at the beginning of September [he must mean August], Merz, Sasse, and [he] drafted a confession."[10] Those participating in the editorial work leading to the August version also included the Bochum pastor Hans Fischer, Bodelschwingh's colleague Gerhard Stratenwerth, and Wilhelm Vischer, an Old Testament scholar at the Bethel seminary.

[5.] Cf. 1/77 and 1/79.

[6.] C.-R. Müller, *Bekenntnis und Bekennen*, 196–97.

[7.] See also 1/86.

[8.] Concerning the specific participation of Merz in the composition of the draft and the additional editorial history of the Bethel confession, see Lichtenfeld, *Theologie*; Lichtenfeld also discloses various formulations and lines of thought from Merz in the text of the confession.

[9.] C.-R. Müller, *Bekenntnis und Bekennen*, 19.

[10.] *DBWE* 13:47 [actually Julius Rieger's notes of Bonhoeffer's remarks at that conference.—LR]; in *GS* 2:87, the final word in the citation incorrectly reads "finished" (*fertiggestellt*).

On August 31, 1933, Bodelschwingh sent the text to "an extended circle 505
of about twenty brothers with the ardent request to examine it and offer suggestions" and with the urgent summons to "get the corrected or expanded texts back to me by September 15, after which work on the final version will begin so that we can present that version in October."[11] It is possible that Bonhoeffer pushed for an earlier conclusion to the work so that the final version might be presented to the national synod on September 27, 1933.[12] On September 15, 1933, however, Bodelschwingh had to tell Karl Barth, who had just been solicited for an opinion as well,[13] that those working on the August version had "in the meantime become convinced that it was just not possible to conclude the work as quickly as originally hoped," and that he thought the second editorial conference might be held at the beginning of October.[14] This date also fell through, and the second editorial conference did not begin until the last ten days or so in October, when Bonhoeffer was already in London.[15] Before leaving for England, however, Bonhoeffer apparently returned once more to Bethel,[16] where he worked together at least with Fischer on the August version in light of the solicited opinions that had arrived in the meantime. This conclusion can be drawn from Fischer's own copy[17] and is consistent with his later recollection. When Eberhard Bethge was preparing the publication of the *Gesammelte Schriften* and queried Fischer about his recollections of the work on the Bethel confession, Fischer remarked on December
18, 1956, that "Dietrich Bonhoeffer and I spent several days cloistered in 506
Bethel"; Fischer also recalled the "sovereignty with which he examined and worked through the criticisms offered by those whose opinions had been solicited."[18] Nonetheless, even before he had seen the changes made to the August version by the second official editorial conference, Bonhoeffer complained from London in a letter to Barth on October 24, 1933, that "the Bethel confession, into which I truly had poured heart and soul,

[11.] Bodelschwingh's cover letter already dates from August 26, 1933 (*GS* 2:90–91; C.-R. Müller, *Bekenntnis und Bekennen*, 199. Müller does not, however, make it clear that she is reproducing the draft of the letter that Bodelschwingh himself altered). Müller also includes a list of those solicited for an opinion (194).

[12.] See in this regard *DB-ER*, 302–3, and C.-R. Müller, *Bekenntnis und Bekennen*, 45–46.

[13.] See 1/96 and 1/97.

[14.] C.-R. Müller, *Bekenntnis und Bekennen*, 200.

[15.] See in this regard C.-R. Müller, *Bekenntnis und Bekennen*, 70.

[16.] See in this regard also 1/100, ed. notes 3 and 5.

[17.] HA Bethel, 2/39–209,17.

[18.] *GS* 2:83.

met with almost no understanding."[19] On November 6, 1933, Merz then related to Bodelschwingh that the editorial work had been completed, but that he nonetheless felt it "urgently necessary that before publication the final version be sent to Bonhoeffer in London and to Professor Sasse in Erlangen. . . . Because both have participated since the very beginning, we really can't send this out into the world without considering their opinions once more."[20] Finally, on November 24, 1933, Merz sent Bodelschwingh Bonhoeffer's response to the "November version"—a response that has unfortunately been lost—adding: "'No mere trifle, but rather a catastrophe.' Or what else can we say about the cover letter of our friend Bonhoeffer? I can at most say that, in a way, I saw it coming and that throughout the meetings I could never rid myself of my apprehensions. I will say, though, that it's Bonhoeffer's own fault for having gone at this thing too precipitately and for having let go of it too hastily. Nothing good can come from such treatment. But we won't be able to make this clear to him because he is simply too young and slipped into academia too early and too one-sidedly."[21] For his own part, Bonhoeffer reported on November 28, 1933, at the pastoral conference in Bradford that the confession's "intent was spoiled by attempts to thwart it and by the strange course of action taken by Bodelschwingh. It is now being published, after having the (original)
507 intent spoiled by a few pastors."[22] These remarks may refer especially to the fact that Stratenwerth, in concurrence with Bodelschwingh, had on September 14, 1933, added Adolf Schlatter to the circle of those whose opinions were being solicited,[23] and that Schlatter's doubts were indeed then reflected by subsequent editorial changes.[24] In a missive to Stratenwerth on November 30, 1933,[25] Bodelschwingh also mentioned that Bonhoeffer rather harshly rejected the editorial changes that had been made in the meantime, and on December 5, 1933, Merz related to Martin Niemöller that "Bonhoeffer has resolutely rejected the reworked version and opposes it being published in the present form. Although I'm very

[19.] *DBWE* 13:23; see also *GS* 2:86 and 132.

[20.] C.-R. Müller, *Bekenntnis und Bekennen*, 204.

[21.] Ibid., 205; although *GS* 2:86 cites instead: "Bonhoeffer rejects the changes made to the first draft," this passage does not occur in the source itself.

[22.] *DBWE* 13:47 [actually Julius Rieger's notes of Bonhoeffer's remarks at that conference—LR].

[23.] HA Bethel, 2/39–96,24a–c; see also C.-R. Müller, *Bekenntnis und Bekennen*, 47.

[24.] C.-R. Müller, *Bekenntnis und Bekennen*, 47–49.

[25.] Ibid., 206.

sorry about all this, he is not entirely without blame himself, since after his initial stay in Bethel he was no longer able to work on it, a situation which may well have been justified."[26]

On the copy dedicated to Julius Rieger of the version that was published at the turn of 1933–34 with the title *The Confession of the Fathers and the Confessing Church: Presented for Your Consideration by a Circle of Protestant Theologians and Published in Their Name by Martin Niemöller,* Bonhoeffer ultimately wrote: "Too many cooks spoil the broth. An anonymous coauthor. D.B."[27]

[26.] *GS* 2:86.

[27.] *NL-Bibl.* 11,4.

Theses on Youth Work in the Church[1]

1. Since the days of the youth movement,[2] church youth work has often lacked that element of Christian sobriety that alone might enable it to recognize that the spirit of youth is not the Holy Spirit and that the future of the church is not youth itself but rather the Lord Jesus Christ alone. It is the task of youth not to reshape the church, but rather to listen to the word of God; it is the task of the church not to capture the youth, but to teach and proclaim the word of God. 508

[1.] [This document appears as appendix 2 in *DBW* 12.—LR] *NL*, A 32,5a); handwritten; cf. also *NL*, A 32,5b): (later?) typewritten copy with the title "Eight Theses on the Youth Work of the Church." Previously published in *GS* 3:292–93 (with Bethge's remarks that these represent "theses for a discussion, probably at the end of August 1933 in Berlin" on the basis of which Bonhoeffer purportedly delivered an address to the YMCA in London on April 24, 1934, on "Church and Youth"; cf. *DB-ER*, 323. [There is no document for Bonhoeffer's London address; Bethge's hypothesis is based on information from Julius Rieger; see *DB-ER*, 973n177.—LR]. The handwritten text bears neither title nor date. Arguments against this hypothetical dating include the fact that the text nowhere alludes to mid-1933 political or church-political problems; the choice is thus probably between an earlier (end of 1932/beginning of 1933) or later (London period) date. Dating the document earlier is supported by the paper, which bears the same watermark as three pieces with indisputable dates; see Bethge's handwritten remark in *NL*, A 32,5a), enumerating "Sermon January 15, 1933; Jewish question March 1933; radio February 1, 1933" (cf. in this volume documents 3/4; 2/14, ed. note 1; and 2/8), similarly Wolf-Dieter Zimmermann's recollection that Bonhoeffer composed the text at the beginning of 1933 (telephone communication to Hans Pfeifer on August 3, 1997). The occasion and site of this address must remain an open question. The text, however, suggests that Bonhoeffer was reflecting on a situation involving the position of Protestant youth work within the constituted church. Cf. in this regard Hans Lilje's piece "Die evangelische Jugendführung," which was already completed by the end of May 1932 and which reflects the state of the discussion at that point.

[2.] Concerning Bonhoeffer's assessment of the youth movement, see also the radio address on the concept of Führer in the young generation, composed around the turn of 1932–33: "The Younger Generation's Altered View of the Concept of Führer," 2/8.

2. Our question is not: What is youth and what rights does it have, but rather: What is the church-community and what is the place of youth within it?

3. The church-community includes those on earth whom God's dominion has torn away from the dominion of death and evil, those who hear
509 the word concerning the establishment of God's dominion among human beings in Jesus Christ and who obediently assemble around this word in faith. The church-community is Christ's presence as the true *Lord* and *Brother.* Being in the church-community means being in Christ; being in Christ means being in the church-community. Sacrifice, intercession, and confession are the acts of fellowship in the church-community.[3] It is only *within* the church-community that one can pass judgment *on* the church-community. By nature the church-community cannot be judged from the outside.

4. The church-community suspends the generational problem. Youth enjoys no special privilege in the church-community. It is to serve the church-community by hearing, learning, and practicing the word. God's spirit in the church has nothing to do with youthful criticism of the church, the radical nature of God's claim on human beings nothing to do with youthful radicalism, and the commandment for sanctification nothing to do with youthful impulse to better the world. "Christian" [and] "youth" is a rather harsh and not very credible word combination. The issue is not "modern" or "old fashioned," but rather solely our thinking concerning and from the perspective of the church.

5. The Bible judges youth quite soberly: Gen. 8:21; Isa. 3:5; Jer. 1:6; Eccl. 11:10; 1 Pet. 5:5; 2 Tim. 2:2 et passim.

6. Church youth work is possible only on the basis of addressing young people concerning their baptism and with the exclusive goal of having them hear God's word. It remains the act of the church-community toward its members. Every transgression of this boundary constitutes a betrayal of Christ's church-community.

7. It may well be that the youth do have the right to protest against their elders. If that be the case, however, the authenticity of such protest will be demonstrated by youth's willingness to maintain solidarity with the guilt of the church-community and to bear that burden in love, abiding in penitence before God's word.

[3.] This sentence was entered by hand in the text.

8. There is no real "church association"; there is only the church. The church youth association is not the youth of the church-community; that youth includes rather *all* baptized young people. Every church association as such already discredits the cause of the church. Such associations can only be perceived as makeshift entities, which as such have only relative significance.

Appendices

Appendix 1. Chronology of 1932–1933

1932 510

November	Winter semester begins. Bonhoeffer delivers lectures "Creation and Fall" (titled "Creation and Sin" the following semester) and "Review and Discussion of New Publications in Systematic Theology" and conducts a seminar on dogmatic exercises, "Theological Anthropology."
November 6	Sermon on Rev. 2:4–5, 7. Reichstag elections: the Nazi party loses 2 million votes compared to the elections of July 31, 1932. General Schleicher succeeds Franz von Papen as Reich chancellor.
December 1	Homily on Dan. 10:1, 8, 16–19.
December 3	Bonhoeffer's memorandum "The Social Gospel."
December 9–10	Bonhoeffer participates in the theological conference of the provisional bureau for ecumenical youth work in Berlin.
December 20	Seminar worship service.

1933

January 11	Altona confession.
January 15	Sermon on Matt. 8:23–27.
January 30	Reich president Hindenburg appoints Hitler as Reich chancellor.

	End of January/ beginning of February	Meeting of the Executive Committee of the World Alliance and the Administrative Committee of Life and Work in Berlin.
	February 1	Bonhoeffer's radio address "The Younger Generation's Altered View of the Concept of Führer."
	February 23	Bonhoeffer repeats his address on the Führer concept in expanded form at the Technical College in Berlin.
	February 26	Sermon on Judg. 6:15–16; 7:2; 8:23.
	February 27	Reichstag fire in Berlin.
	February 28	Hindenburg's emergency measures "for the protection of people and state" suspend essential basic democratic rights; this is followed by excesses against Communists and Social Democrats.
		Bonhoeffer loses the vote on his application for a pastorate at St. Bartholomew's in east Berlin.
511	Beginning of March	Bonhoeffer repeats his expanded address on the Führer concept at the College of Political Science in Berlin.
	March 5	Reichstag elections: the Nazi party and German National Peoples' Party [DNVP] win a combined 44.7 percent of the vote.
	March 6–10	Bonhoeffer participates in the ecumenical conference in Dassel.
	March 21	Opening ceremony of the Reichstag ("Day of Potsdam").
		Malicious Practices Act [Heimtückegesetz] passed.
	March 23	The Enabling Act grants dictatorial powers to Hitler.
	End of March/ beginning of April	Bonhoeffer develops theses concerning the question of the church membership of Jewish Christians.
	April 1	Boycott of Jewish businesses throughout the Reich.
	April 3–5	Reich conference of the German Christians in Berlin with the demand for a "synchronization of church and state."
	April 7	Law for the Reconstitution of the Civil Service with the so-called Aryan paragraph. Onset of the dismissal of Jewish and other "undesirable" civil servants from public service.

Mid-April — Bonhoeffer meets with Ehrenström, Henriod, and Schönfeld in Berlin.

April 16 — Bonhoeffer completes the essay "The Church and the Jewish Question."

April 23 — Church president Kapler issues a summons to reform the constitution of German Protestantism.

April 25 — Meeting of the German Evangelical Church Committee [Kirchenausschuss] in Berlin.
Hitler appoints Ludwig Müller "confidential adviser and plenipotentiary in questions concerning the Protestant church."

May — Summer semester begins. Bonhoeffer lectures on Christology and conducts a seminar on Hegel's philosophy of religion.

May 4 — Constitutional committee of the Church Federation [Verfassungsausschuss des Kirchenbunds] begins discussions about a new church constitution with the participation of Ludwig Müller.

May 6 — The German Christians deliver to President Kapler 512
"Ten Principles" demanding among other things that the new Reich church be a "church of the German Christians, that is, of Christians of Aryan race."

May 9 — Establishment of the Young Reformation Movement.

May 16 — New guidelines issued by the German Christians.

May 17 — The German Christians nominate Ludwig Müller as their candidate for Reich bishop.

May 19 — The Young Reformation Movement counters by nominating Friedrich von Bodelschwingh.

May 23 — Bonhoeffer loses the vote on his application for a pastorate at the Lazarus church in east Berlin.

May 25 — Sermon on 1 Pet. 1:7–9.

May 27 — Leaders of the regional churches elect Bodelschwingh Reich bishop; despite the German Christians' wild campaigns against him, Bodelschwingh takes office.

May 28 — Sermon on Exod. 32:1–8, 15–16, 18–20, 30–35.

June — Bonhoeffer's essay "The Church and the Jewish Question" is published.

June 7–8 — Franco-German World Alliance meeting in Basel; Bonhoeffer does not participate.

	June 19	Assembly of the German Student League [Deutsche Studentenschaft] on behalf of the German Christians. Most participants leave the auditorium when a resolution supporting Ludwig Müller is read. Bonhoeffer and Ernst Bronisch-Holtze report to the Reich chancellery concerning the assembly.
	June 21	Friedrich Siegmund-Schultze expelled from Germany.
	June 22	The "Working Committee of Protestant Students" [Arbeitsausschuss evangelischer Studenten] holds a counterassembly against the assembly of June 19 with about two thousand participants. As one of the main speakers, Bonhoeffer demands that a Protestant council issue binding doctrinal statements.
513	June 24	State commissioner August Jäger, appointed by the Prussian minister of culture, assumes leadership of all the regional churches in Prussia. Bodelschwingh resigns because of lack of support among church leaders.
	July 6	106 pastors from greater Berlin protest the installation of the state commissioner (sent to the Reich chancellor on July 12).
	July 11	Work on the new church constitution completed amid considerable political pressure.
	Before July 14	Bonhoeffer's memorandum "The Jewish-Christian Question as Status Confessionis."
	July 14	Publication of the new church constitution together with a Reich law confirming it and stipulating general church elections on July 23.
	Mid-July	Theodor Heckel inquires whether Bonhoeffer would accept a position in London as pastor to an overseas German congregation.
	July 18	Bonhoeffer and Jacobi protest to the Gestapo chief Diels in Berlin because of the confiscation of election materials of the Young Reformation movement; Diels threatens to send them to a concentration camp.
	July 20	Signing of the concordat between the Reich government and the Holy See initialed on July 8.
	July 22	In a radio address regarding the church elections, Hitler unequivocally supports the German Christians.

July 23	Sermon on Matt. 16:13–18. In the church elections, the German Christians win ca. two-thirds of all seats in the regional church administrations.	
July 24–25	The Young Reformation Movement withdraws from church politics and demands that a binding confession be formulated.	
July 28	Bonhoeffer travels to London and introduces himself to the German congregations of Sydenham and St. Paul on July 30–31.	
		514
August 4	The Old Prussian church senate elects Ludwig Müller as regional bishop of the Evangelical Church of the Old Prussian Union.	
August 5	Bonhoeffer in Bethel for preliminary talks concerning the Bethel confession.	
August 15–25	Work on the Bethel confession results in the August version.	
August 24	Meeting of the (majority German Christian) Old Prussian provincial synods to elect representatives for the general synod. The Berlin-Brandenburg provincial synod adopts the state "Aryan legislation" for church officials.	
August 29–September 4	International Youth Conference in Gland on Lake Geneva; because of church-political developments in Germany, Bonhoeffer does not participate.	
End of August	Bonhoeffer's theses titled "The Aryan Paragraph in the Church."	
September 5–6	The General Synod divides the Old Prussian church into dioceses, stipulates that sixteen of the nineteen representatives at the National Synod must be German Christians, and adopts the state Aryan paragraph.	
September 9	Bonhoeffer writes to Karl Barth asking for his position on the August version of the Bethel confession.	
September 11	Barth responds by letter.	
September 12	Establishment of the Pastor's Emergency League.	
September 15–20	Meeting of the World Alliance in Sofia, Bulgaria. Bonhoeffer and Julius Richter visit the German embassy in Sofia afterward.	

	September 24	Draft drawn up of the petition to the National Synod demanding that the introduction of the Aryan paragraph in regional churches be rescinded.
	September 27	National Synod convenes in Wittenberg. Ludwig Müller elected Reich bishop, but the issue of the Aryan paragraph is not addressed.
515	Beginning of October	In Bethel, Bonhoeffer and Hans Fischer work through the August version of the Bethel confession in light of the expert opinions that have arrived in the meantime. The official editorial conference, in which Bonhoeffer does not participate, does not take place until the final days of October.
	October 4	In a conversation with the Reich bishop, Bonhoeffer refuses to represent the cause of the German Christians in his London ministry.
	October 6	Bonhoeffer's discussion with Theodor Heckel.
	October 17	Bonhoeffer begins his ministry in London.

Appendix 2. Unpublished Material from Bonhoeffer's Literary Estate and Other Sources, 1932–1933

The following list of unpublished material includes document numbers 516
as cited in the Bonhoeffer *Nachlaß* volume (these are the numbers as they appear on the Bonhoeffer microfiche collection), as well as several documents from the Evangelisches Zentralarchiv in Berlin (EZA) and documents published in volume 5 of the early *Mündige Welt* compilation. The current archival location of the documents from *Mündige Welt* and from Glenthøj's *Zu Dietrich Bonhoeffers Eintritt in die ökumenische Arbeit* has not been established.

Addressee or Content	**Date**	***NL*/Archival Number /Publication**
To Renate Lepsius	November 18, 1932?	EZA, 51/P I d 9,1
To the Church Federation Office	November 24, 1932	Glenthøj, *Zu Dietrich Bonhoeffers Eintritt*
To Herbert Jehle	December 1, 1932	A 29,1 (6)
To Hans Schönfeld	December 5, 1932	A 28,3 (15)
To Renate Lepsius	December 6, 1932	EZA, 51/P I d 9,1
To Renate Lepsius	December 14, 1932	EZA 51/P III 1c
To Friedrich Siegmund-Schultze	January 18, 1933	*Mündige Welt*, 5:77
To the Association of German Students	February 1, 1933	A 29,1 (2)
To Friedrich Siegmund-Schultze	February 15, 1933	*Mündige Welt*, 5:77
Draft for a circular letter	before February 23, 1933	A 29,1 (8)
To Friedrich Siegmund-Schultze	March 11, 1933	EZA, 51/P I e 24,1
To Max Diestel	March 30, 1933	*NL* Anh. A7
To Friedrich Singer	July 23, 1933	A 39,1 (2)
Certificate for Franz Lehel	July 25, 1933	A 29,1 (7)
To Friedrich Singer	October 7, 1933	A 39,2 (6)
To Friedrich Singer	October 9, 1933	A 39,2 (7)
To Friedrich Singer	October 12, 1933	A 39,2 (8)

Appendix 3. Texts Published in *DBWE* 12 and in *Gesammelte Schriften* and *Mündige Welt*, vol. 5

	GS	***DBWE*** **12**	*GS*	***DBWE*** **12**
530				
	1:37	1/38	2:125	1/107
	1:38–39	1/67	2:126–27	1/96
	1:62–65	1/22	2:127–30	1/97
	1:104–12	2/4		
	1:179–81	2/10	3:23–24	1/27
			3:134–37	2/3
	2:19–21	2/8	3:138–59	2/5
	2:22–38	2/9	3:166–242	2/12
	2:39–40	1/21	3:243–47	2/17
	2:40–41	1/30	3:270–85	2/11
	2:41–42	1/37	3:286–91	2/7
	2:44–53	2/13	3:292–93	App. 2
	2:55	1/62		
	2:56–57	1/64	4:101–7	3/4
	2:58–59	1/69	4:109–17	3/5
	2:62–65	2/16	4:118–22	3/6
	2:70	1/94	4:123–29	3/7
	2:70–71	1/95	4:130–36	3/8
	2:71–73	1/98	4:144–46	3/2
	2:74–76	1/105		
	2:77–79	1/86	5:302–40	2/1
	2:91–119	2/15	5:341–58	2/2
	2:93–101	3/1	5:359–62	2/6
	2:120	1/70		
	2:121	1/71	6:207–9	3/3
	2:121–22	1/72	6:210	1/19
	2:122–23	1/75	6:218	1/10
	2:123	1/88	6:219	1/32
	2:124	1/87	6:226–27	1/9
	2:124	1/93	6:227	1/10

GS	*DBWE* 12
6:228	1/16
6:248	1/12
6:249	1/18
6:250–51	1/23
6:251–52	1/24
6:252	1/33
6:256–57	1/48
6:258–59	1/29
6:259–61	1/31
6:262–63	1/56
6:263–64	1/55
6:266	1/81
6:266–67	1/104
6:270–72	1/65
6:272–74	2/14
6:275–76	1/100
6:276–77	1/102
6:279–80	1/7
6:280–81	1/34
6:281	1/36
6:282	1/43
6:282	1/50
6:282–84	1/51
6:284–85	1/59
6:285	1/66
6:285–86	1/74
6:286	1/80
6:287	1/85

Mündige Welt	*DBWE* 12
5:57–59	1/1
5:63	1/28
5:64–65	1/59
5:65	1/74
5:65	1/80
5:69–71	2/6
5:74	1/16
5:75	1/23
5:75–76	1/24
5:78	1/33
5:92–93	1/45
5:93–94	1/56
5:94	1/55
5:100–101	1/65
5:103–4	2/14
5:110	1/102
5:122	1/78
5:123	1/82
5:124	1/91
5:126	1/107
5:127	1/108

Bibliography

1. Archival Sources and Private Collections

Dietrich Bonhoeffer's papers and personal library, as well as correspondence from others and relevant material in other archives, have been cataloged in the *Nachlaß Dietrich Bonhoeffer* volume compiled by Dietrich Meyer and Eberhard Bethge. All such citations in *DBWE* are indicated by *NL*, followed by the corresponding reference code within that published index. Not all this material is part of the actual Bonhoeffer Nachlaß in the Staatsbibliothek in Berlin; footnote citations of *NL* material from other archives also give the numbering from the respective archive. All the material listed in the Meyer and Bethge catalog, however, has been included on microfiches now located at the Staatsbibliothek in Berlin (previously at the Bundesarchiv in Koblenz) and in the Bonhoeffer Collection at Burke Library, Union Theological Seminary, New York. The designation *NL-Bibl.* in some bibliographic records indicates that a copy of the book was found in Bonhoeffer's surviving personal library.

Archiv der Evangelischen Lazarus-Kirchengemeinde, Berlin
Archiv der Evangelischen Michaelsbruderschaft, Kirchberg
Archives of the World Council of Churches, Geneva (WCC Archives)
    Bonhoeffer Box
    World Alliance for International Friendship through the Churches
        Box 212-003
        Box 212-009
Archives of Jørgen Glenthøj, Åbyhøj, Denmark
Bundesarchiv, Koblenz (BA Koblenz)
    Nachlaß Dietrich Bonhoeffer (fiches)
    Nachlaß Erich Seeberg
    R 43 II: Neue Reichskanzlei
        R 43 II/161

Bundesarchiv, Abt. Potsdam (BA Potsdam)
REM 1262
Center of Theological Inquiry, Princeton, New Jersey
Paul Lehmann Papers
Evangelisches Zentralarchiv, Berlin (EZA)
Bestand 1: Vorgängereinrichtungen der EKD
Bestand 5: Kirchliches Außenamt
Bestand 14: Konsistorium Berlin-Brandenburg
Bestand 50: Kirchenkampfarchiv
Bestand 51: Ökumenisches Archiv
Bestand 626: Nachlaß Friedrich Siegmund-Schultze
Geheimes Staatsarchiv, Berlin-Dahlem
Rep. 76, Bd. IV
Hauptarchiv der von Bodelschwinghschen Anstalten, Bethel (HA Bethel)
Bestand 2/39: Kirchenkampf und Euthanasie
Humboldt-Universität Berlin, Universitätsarchiv
Bestand Theologische Fakultät, 178
Karl Barth-Archiv, Basel
Landeskirchliches Archiv der Evangelischen Kirche von Westfalen, Bielefeld (LKA EKvW Bielefeld)
Bestand 5,1: Sammlung Wilhelm Niemöller
Bd. 35
Bd. 53
Landeskirchliches Archiv der Evangelisch-Lutherischen Kirche in Bayern, Nuremberg (LKA Nuremberg)
Personen XVIII: NL Stählin
Nr. 49
Nr. 63
Library of Congress, Annex, Washington, D.C.
Reinhold Niebuhr Papers
Luther Archives, Tübingen
The Royal Library, Copenhagen
Literary Estate of Bishop Ove Ammundsen
Zentralarchiv der Evangelischen Kirche in Hessen und Nassau, Darmstadt (ZEKHN)
Bestand 62: Privatdienstlicher Nachlaß D. Martin Niemöller
62/1000
62/1020
Zentral- und Landesbibliothek, Berlin (ZLB)
Nachlaß Adolf Deissmann

Private Collections (locations at time of *DBWE* publication)
Barbara Bayer-von Dohnanyi, Berlin

Eberhard Bethge, Berlin
Jørgen Glenthøj, Åbyhøj, Denmark
Herbert Jehle (in possession of his widow, Dieta Raisig), Ruckersville, Virginia
Ferenc Lehel, Szombathely, Hungary
Hilde Rannenberg-Pfeiffer, Lüneburg
Anneliese Schnurmann, London, England
Erwin Sutz, Herrliberg, Switzerland

2. Literature Used by Bonhoeffer

Althaus, Paul. *Grundriß der Dogmatik* (Outline for dogmatics). Erlangen: Merkel, 1929–32.

———. "Nomos und Erlösung" (Law and redemption). *Deutsches Volkstum* 15 (1933): 49–53.

Asmussen, Hans. "Wort und Bekenntnis Altonaer Pastoren" (Word and confession of the Altona pastors). *Der Vormarsch* 3 (1933): 34–36.

Augustine. "Confessionum libri tredecim." In *Corpus Scriptorum Ecclesiasticorum Latinorum,* vol. 33. Prague: Hoelder-Pichler-Tempsky, 1896. Translated by Maria Boulding as *The Confessions,* pt. 1, vol. 1, of *The Works of St. Augustine,* edited by John E. Rotelle, introduction and notes by Maria Boulding, OSB. Hyde Park, N.Y.: New City Press, 1997.

Barth, Karl. *Fides quaerens intellectum: Anselms Beweis der Existenz Gottes im Zusammenhang seines theologischen Programms.* Forschungen zur Geschichte und Lehre des Protestantismus, series 4, vol. 3. Munich: Chr. Kaiser, 1931. Translated by Ian W. Robertson as *Anselm: Fides Quaerens Intellectum; Anselm's Proof of the Existence of God in the Context of His Theological Scheme.* London: SCM Press; Richmond: John Knox Press, 1960; Pittsburgh: Pickwick Press, 1985.

———. *Der Römerbrief.* 2nd rev. ed. Munich: Chr. Kaiser, 1922. Translated from the 6th German edition by Edwin C. Hoskins as *The Epistle to the Romans.* London: Oxford University Press, 1960.

———. *Theologische Existenz heute!* Beiheft Nr. 2 of *Zwischen den Zeiten.* Munich: Chr. Kaiser, 1933. Translated by R. Birch Hoyle as *Theological Existence Today: A Plea for Theological Freedom.* London: Hodder & Stoughton, 1933; Lexington, Ky.: American Theological Library Association, 1962.

Bell, George Kennedy Allen. *A Brief Sketch of the Church of England.* London: SCM, 1929.

Bernanos, Georges. *Sous le soleil de Satan.* Paris: Plon-Nourrit et cie, 1926. Translated by J. C. Whitehouse as *Under Satan's Sun.* Lincoln: University of Nebraska Press, 2001.

Die Bibel oder die ganze Heilige Schrift des Alten und Neuen Testaments nach der deutschen Übersetzung D. Martin Luthers (The Bible or the entire Holy Scriptures of the Old and New Testaments according to the German translation of Dr. Martin Luther). Durchgesehen im Auftrag der Deutschen Evangelischen Kirchenkonferenz. Stuttgart: Mitteloktav-Ausgabe, 1911. *NL-Bibl.* 1 A 6.

Biedermann, Alois Emanuel. *Christliche Dogmatik* (Christian dogmatics). 2nd. rev. ed. Berlin: G. Reimer, 1885.

Brunner, Emil. "Die andere Aufgabe der Theologie" (The other task of theology). *Zwischen den Zeiten* 7 (1929): 255–76.

———. "Biblische Psychologie" (Biblical psychology). In *Gott und Mensch: Vier Untersuchungen über das personhafte Sein*, 70–100. Tübingen: J. C. B. Mohr (Paul Siebeck), 1930. Translated by David Cairns as *God and Man: Four Essays on the Nature of Personality.* London: SCM Press, 1936.

———. *Das Gebot und die Ordnungen: Entwurf einer protestantisch-theologischen Ethik.* Tübingen: J. C. B. Mohr (Paul Siebeck), 1932. *NL-Bibl.* 4, 6. Translated by Olive Wyon as *The Divine Imperative.* Philadelphia: Westminster Press, 1947.

———. *Der Mittler: Zur Besinnung über den Christusglauben.* Zürich: Zwingli Verlag, 1927. *NL-Bibl.* 3 B 15. Translated by Olive Wyon as *The Mediator: A Study of the Central Doctrine of the Christian Faith.* Philadelphia: Westminster Press, 1947.

Bultmann, Rudolf. "Welchen Sinn hat es, von Gott zu reden?" *Theologische Blätter* 4 (1925): 129–35. Translated by Louis Pettibone Smith as "What Does It Mean to Speak of God?" in *Faith and Understanding,* edited by Robert W. Funk, 53–65. Philadelphia: Fortress Press, 1987.

Diem, Hermann. "Glauben und Denken bei Karl Heim" (Faith and thought in Karl Heim). *Die Christliche Welt* (The Christian world) 46 (1932): 482–87 and 540–47.

Dostoyevsky, Fyodor Mikhaylovich. *Der Idiot.* Munich: R. Piper Verlag, 1922. Translated by Constance Garnett as *The Idiot.* New York: Modern Library, 1962.

Eddy, George Sherwood. *Facing the Crisis. A Study in Present Day Social and Religious Problems.* New York: G. H. Doran, 1922.

Ellwood, Charles Abram. *Christianity and Social Science: A Challenge to the Church.* New York: Macmillan, 1923.

———. *The Reconstruction of Religion: A Sociological View.* New York: Macmillan, 1922.

Eschweiler, Karl. "Zehn Gebote und Naturgesetz: Brief an Dr. Wilhelm Stapel" (The Ten Commandments and the law of nature: A letter to Dr. Wilhelm Stapel). *Deutsches Volkstum* 15 (1933): 53–59.

Evangelisches Gesangbuch für Brandenburg und Pommern (Protestant hymnal for Brandenburg and Pomerania). Berlin: Trowitzsch, 1931.

Fosdick, Harry Emerson. *Christianity and Progress.* New York: Fleming H. Revell, 1922.

Frick, Heinrich. *Das Reich Gottes in amerikanischer und deutscher Theologie der Gegenwart* (The kingdom of God in contemporary American and German theology). Gießen: Alfred Töpelmann, 1926.

Geß, Wolfgang Friedrich. *Das Dogma von Christi Person und Werk, entwickelt aus Christi Selbstzeugnis und den Zeugnissen der Apostel* (The dogma of the person and work of Christ, developed from Christ's own testimony and the testimonies of the apostles). Basel: C. Detloff, 1887.

Gogarten, Friedrich. *Ich glaube an den dreieinigen Gott: Eine Untersuchung über Glauben und Geschichte* (I believe in the triune God: An examination of faith and history). Jena: E. Diederichs, 1926. *NL-Bibl.* 3 B 29.

———. *Illusionen: Eine Auseinandersetzung mit dem Kulturidealismus* (Illusions: A debate with cultural idealism). Jena: E. Diederichs, 1926.

———. *Politische Ethik: Versuch einer Grundlegung* (Political ethics: Attempt at a foundation). Jena: E. Diederichs, 1932. *NL-Bibl.* 4, 14.

———. *Wider die Ächtung der Autorität* (Against the condemnation of authority). Jena: E. Diederichs, 1930.

Grisebach, Eberhard. *Gegenwart: Eine kritische Ethik* (The present: A critical ethic). Halle-Saale: M. Niemeyer, 1928.

Grosz, George. *Ecce homo* (Behold the man). 84 Blätter. Berlin: Der Malikverlag, 1923. Published in English as *Ecce Homo,* introduced by Henry Miller, 100 plates. 1923. Reprint, New York: Grove Press, 1966.

Gutmann, Bruno. *Freies Menschentum aus ewigen Bindungen* (Free human ways out of eternal bonds). Kassel: Bärenreiter-Verlag, 1928.

Hannoversches Sonntagsblatt (Hannover Sunday paper). Serial publication, Hannover, 1868–1941. Vol. 6, 1933.

Harnack, Adolf von. *Dogmengeschichte.* 5th rev. ed. Tübingen: J. C. B. Mohr, 1914. Translated from the 1st German ed. by Edwin Knox Mitchell as *Outlines of the History of Dogma.* London: Hodder & Stoughton; New York: Funk & Wagnalls, 1893. Reprint: Eugene, Ore.: Wipf & Stock, 2001.

———. *Lehrbuch der Dogmengeschichte.* Vols. 1–3. 4th newly revised and expanded ed. Tübingen: J. C. B. Mohr, 1909–10. *NL-Bibl.* 2 C 4, 17. Translated from the 3rd German ed. by Neil Buchanan as *History of Dogma,* 4 vols. Gloucester, Mass.: Peter Smith, 1976.

———. "Die Reden Pauls von Samosata an Sabinus (Zenobia?) und seine Christologie" (The speeches of Paul of Samosata concerning Sabinus and his Christology). In *Sitzungsberichte der Preußischen Akademie der Wissenschaften, Philosophisch-historische Klasse* (Session reports of the Prussian

Academy of Sciences, philosophical-historical class), 130–51. Berlin: Verlag der Akademie der Wissenschaft, 1924.

Harnack, Theodosius. *Luthers Theologie mit besonderer Beziehung auf seine Versöhnungs- und Erlösungslehre* (Luther's theology with special reference to his teaching on reconciliation and redemption). Erlangen: Theodor Blaesing, 1862, 1886.

Hartmann, Hans. *Die junge Generation in Europa* (The young generation in Europe). Berlin: Der Neue Geist Verlag, 1930. (Cf. *NL-Bibl.* 7 A 23, which erroneously attributes this book to Nicolai Hartmann.)

Hauptmann, Gerhart. *Der Narr in Christo, Emanuel Quint: Roman.* Berlin: S. Fischer, 1910. Translated by Thomas Seltzer as *The Fool in Christ, Emanuel Quint: A Novel.* New York: H. Fertig, 1976.

Hegel, Georg Wilhelm Friedrich. *Vorlesungen über die Philosophie der Geschichte.* Vol. 11 of *Sämtliche Werke.* Edited by V. H. Glockner. Jubiläumsausgabe in 20 Bänden (Collected works, 20-volume commemorative edition). Stuttgart: Frommann, 1928. Translated by John Sibree as *The Philosophy of History.* Mineola, N.Y.: Dover, 1956.

———. *Vorlesungen über die Philosophie der Religion.* Vol. 16 of *Sämtliche Werke.* Stuttgart: Frommann, 1928. Cf. *NL-Bibl.* 7 A 26. Translated by R. F. Brown, P. C. Hodgson, and J. M. Stewart as *Lectures on the Philosophy of Religion*, edited by Peter C. Hodgson, 3 vols. Berkeley: University of California Press, 1984–87. (Vol. 3 of the *Philosophie der Religion* was previously published as *The Christian Religion*, edited and translated by Peter C. Hodgson, based on the edition by Georg Lasson. Missoula, Mont.: Scholars Press, 1979.)

Heidegger, Martin. *Sein und Zeit.* In *Jahrbuch für Philosophie und Phänomenologische Forschung* (Annual for philosophical and phenomenological research), vol. 8. Halle: Niemeyer, 1927. Translated by Joan Stambaugh as *Being and Time: A Translation of* Sein und Zeit. Albany: State University of New York Press, 1996.

Heim, Karl. *Der evangelische Glaube und das Denken der Gegenwart: Grundzüge einer christlichen Lebensauffassung.* Vol. 1: *Glaube und Denken: Philosophische Grundlegung einer christlichen Lebensanschauung* (The Protestant faith and contemporary thought: Foundations for a Christian conception of life. Vol. 1: Faith and thought: Philosophical foundation of a Christian worldview). Berlin: Furche-Verlag, 1931. *NL-Bibl.* 3 B 34.

———. "Gott oder Verzweiflung." Tübinger Brief ("God or despair." Tübingen letter). *Die Furche* 18 (1932): 143–55.

———. "Zur Frage der philosophischen Grundlegung der Theologie: Antwort auf den Aufsatz von D. Th. Steinmann" (On the question of the philosophical foundation of theology: Reply to the essay by Dr. Th. Steinman). *Zeitschrift für Theologie und Kirche* 13 (1932): 175–90.

Herrmann, Wilhelm. *Der Verkehr des Christen mit Gott im Anschluß an Luther dargestellt.* 5th and 6th rev. eds. Stuttgart: J. Cotta, 1908. Translated and edited by Robert T. Voelkel as *The Communion of the Christian with God: Described on the Basis of Luther's Statements.* Philadelphia: Fortress Press, 1971.

Hertzler, Joyce Oramel. *The History of Utopian Thought.* London: Allen & Unwin, 1923.

Hildebrandt, Franz. *EST: Das lutherische Prinzip* (EST: The Lutheran principle). Studien zur systematischen Theologie 7 (Studies in systematic theology 7). Göttingen: Vandenhoeck & Ruprecht, 1931.

Hirsch, Emanuel. *Schöpfung und Sünde in der natürlich-geschichtlichen Wirklichkeit des einzelnen Menschen: Versuch einer Grundlegung christlicher Lebensweisung* (Creation and sin in the natural-historical reality of the individual person: Attempt at a foundation for Christian life instruction). Beiträge zur systematischen Theologie 1 (Contributions to systematic theology 1). Tübingen: J. C. B. Mohr (Paul Siebeck), 1931. *NL-Bibl.* 3 B 40.

Holl, Karl. "Luthers Urteile über sich selbst." In *Gesammelte Aufsätze zur Kirchengeschichte,* vol. 1: *Luther,* 326–58. Tübingen: J. C. B. Mohr (Paul Siebeck), 1927. Translated by H. C. Erik Midelfort as "Martin Luther on Luther" in *Interpreters of Luther: Essays in Honor of Wilhelm Pauck,* edited by Jaroslav Pelikan. Philadelphia: Fortress Press, 1968.

Jacob, Günter. *Der Gewissensbegriff in der Theologie Luthers* (The concept of conscience in the theology of Luther). Tübingen: J. C. B. Mohr, 1928.

James, William. *Die religiöse Erfahrung in ihrer Mannigfaltigkeit: Materialien und Studien zu einer Psychologie und Pathologie des religiösen Lebens.* Translated into the German by Georg Wobbermin. 2nd expanded ed. Leipzig: J. C. Hinrichs, 1914. English original: *The Varieties of Religious Experience: A Study in Human Nature.* New York: Longmans, Green, 1914.

Jelke, Robert. *Vernunft und Offenbarung* (Reason and revelation). Beiträge zur Förderung christlicher Theologie 36. (Contributions to the promotion of Christian theology 36). Gütersloh: C. Bertelsmann, 1932. *NL-Bibl.* 3 B 46.

Jones, Eli Stanley. *The Christ of the Indian Road.* New York: Abingdon Press, 1925.

Joyce, James. *Ulysses.* Paris: Shakespeare, 1922.

Kähler, Martin. *Der sogenannte historische Jesus und der geschichtliche, biblische Christus: Vortrag auf der Wuppertaler Pastoralkonferenz.* Leipzig: A. Deichart, 1892. Translated by Carl E. Braaten as *The So-Called Historical Jesus and the Historic Biblical Christ.* Philadelphia: Fortress Press, 1964.

Kierkegaard, Søren. *Die Krankheit zum Tode.* Vol. 8 of *Gesammelte Werke.* Jena: Diederichs, 1911. *NL-Bibl.* 7 A 43. Translated by Walter Lowrie as *Sickness unto Death.* Princeton, N.J.: Princeton University Press, 1941.

Knittermeyer, Hinrich. *Grenzen des Staates* (Boundaries of the state). Gegenwart: Deutsche Zeit- und Streitschriften 3 (The present: German periodicals and polemical pamphlets 3). Berlin: Edwin Runge, 1932.

Landshut, Siegfried. *Kritik der Soziologie: Freiheit und Gleichheit als Ursprungsproblem der Soziologie* (Sociological criticism: Freedom and equality as the original problem of sociology). Munich Leipzig: Duncker & Humboldt, 1929.

Löwith, Karl. *Das Individuum in der Rolle des Mitmenschen* (The individual in the role of fellow man). Munich: Drei Masken Verlag, 1928.

Luther, Martin. *Briefwechsel.* Vol. 14. 1912 ed. Edited by E. L. Enders. Frankfurt am Main: Schriften-Niederlage des Evangelischen Vereins, 1884–1978. Selected letters translated in *Luther's Works,* vols. 48–50. Philadelphia: Fortress Press, 1963–75.

———. *Tischreden.* Vols. 1-5 of *Werke: Kritische Gesamtausgabe.* Weimar: H. Böhlaus Nachfolger, 1912–. Partial translation by Theodore Tappert as *Table Talk,* vol. 54 of *Luther's Works.* Philadelphia: Fortress Press, 1967.

———. *Werke: Kritische Gesamtausgabe.* 58 vols. Weimarer Ausgabe. Weimar: H. Böhlau, 1883–. Translated as *Luther's Works,* vols. 1–30 edited by Jaroslav Pelikan, vols. 31–55 edited by Helmut Lehmann, complete works on CD-ROM. Minneapolis: Fortress Press; St. Louis: Concordia, 2002.

Mathews, Shailer. *The Church and the Changing Order.* New York: Macmillan, 1907.

McCown, Chester Carlton. *The Genesis of the Social Gospel: The Meaning of the Ideals of Jesus in the Light of Their Antecedents.* New York: Knopf, 1929.

Melanchthon, Philipp. "Loci communes rerum theologicarum seu hypotyposes theologicae." In *Corpus Reformatorum,* vol. 21, 81–227. Braunschweig: C. A. Schwetschke, 1854. Translated by Charles Leander Hill as *The Loci communes of Philip Melanchthon,* with a critical introduction by the translator, Charles Leander Hill, and a special introduction by Dean E. E. Flack. Boston: Meador, 1944.

Menken, Gottfried. *Schriften* (Writings). Vollständige Ausgabe (Complete edition), vol. 7. Bremen: J. G. Heyse, 1858.

Merz, Georg. "Christoph Blumhardt unter der Kritik der dialektischen Theologie" (Christoph Blumhardt critically viewed in light of dialectical theology). *Zwischen den Zeiten* 10 (1932): 541–50.

Müller, Hans Michael. "Credo, ut intelligam: Kritische Bemerkungen zu Karl Barths Dogmatik" (I believe, in order to understand: Critical comments on Karl Barth dogmatics). *Theologische Blätter* 7 (1928): 167–76.

———. "Priester und Laie: Zu Karl Heims neuem Werk" (Priests and laity: On Karl Heim's new work). *Zwischen den Zeiten* 9 (1931): 366–85.

Müller, Karl. *Der biblische Reich-Gottes-Gedanke im Lichte des Weltkrieges* (The biblical concept of the kingdom of God in light of the world war). Neukirchen: Buchhandlung des Erziehungsvereins, 1919.

Ein neues Lied: Ein Liederbuch für die deutsche evangelische Jugend (A new song: A songbook for German Protestant youth). Berlin-Dahlem, 1932.

Niebuhr, Reinhold. *Does Civilization Need Religion? A Study in the Social Resources and Limitations of Religion in Modern Life*. New York: Macmillan, 1927.

———. *Leaves from the Notebook of a Tamed Cynic*. Chicago: Willett, Clark & Colby, 1929.

Nietzsche, Friedrich. *Also sprach Zarathustra*. Nietzsche Werke, pt. 1, vol. 4. Stuttgart: Alfred Kröner Verlag, 1921. (Cf. *NL-Bibl.* 7 A 58.) Translated by Thomas Common as *Thus Spoke Zarathustra*. New York: Prometheus Press, 1993.

Otto, Rudolf. *Sünde und Urschuld: Und andere Aufätze zur Theologie*. Ergänzungsband II zu *Das Heilige*. Munich: Beck, 1932. Translated by Brian Lunn as *Religious Essays: A Supplement to "The Idea of the Holy."* London: Oxford University Press, 1931.

Page, Kirby. *Jesus or Christianity: A Study in Contrasts*. Garden City, N.Y.: Doubleday, 1929.

Quervain, Alfred de. *Das Gesetz des Staates: Wesen und Grenze der Staatlichkeit* (The law of the state: Essence and limit of statehood). Berlin: Furche Verlag, 1932. *NL-Bibl.* 4, 38.

Rauschenbusch, Walter. *Christianity and the Social Crisis*. New York: Macmillan, 1907.

———. *Christianizing the Social Order*. Boston: Pilgrim Press, 1912.

———. *For God and the People: Prayers of the Social Awakening*. Boston: Pilgrim Press, 1910. Translated by Minna Griebel and Heinrich Frick as *Für Gott und das Volk: Gebete der sozialen Erweckung*, with an appendix by C. H. Moehlmann and a picture of Rauschenbusch. Göttingen: Vandenhoeck & Ruprecht, 1928.

———. *A Theology for the Social Gospel*. New York: Macmillan, 1917. Translated by Clara Ragaz as *Die religiösen Grundlagen der sozialen Botschaft*. Zürich: Rotapfel-Verlag, 1922.

Rerum Novarum. In *Acta Sanctae Sedis* 23, 641–70. 1890–91. English translation edited by John Coleman and Gregory Baum in *Rerum Novarum: A Hundred Years of Catholic Social Teaching*. London: SCM Press; Philadelphia: Trinity Press International, 1991.

Ritschl, Albrecht. *Die christliche Lehre von der Rechtfertigung und Versöhnung*. Vol. 3. Bonn: A. Marcus, 1895. Cf. *NL-Bibl.* 3 B 58. Translated as *The*

Christian Doctrine of Justification and Reconciliation: The Positive Development of the Doctrine, edited by H. R. Mackintosh and A. B. Macauley, 2nd ed. Edinburgh: T & T Clark, 1902.

———. *Unterricht in der christlichen Religion*. 6th ed. Bonn: A. Marcus, 1903. *NL-Bibl.* 3 B 59. Translated as "Instruction in the Christian Religion," in *Three Essays*, by Albrecht Ritschl, translated by Philip Hefner. Philadelphia: Fortress Press, 1972.

Schaeder, Erich. *Das Geistproblem der Theologie: Eine systematische Untersuchung* (The problem of spirit in theology: A systematic examination). Erlangen: A. Deichert, 1924.

Schelling, Friedrich Wilhelm Joseph. *Philosophische Untersuchungen über das Wesen der menschlichen Freiheit und die damit zusammenhängenden Gegenstände*. Vol. 7 of *Sämtliche Werke*, part 1, 331–416. Stuttgart: Cotta, 1880. Cf. *NL-Bibl.* 7 A 71. Translated by Jeff Love and Johannes Schmidt as *Philosophical Investigations into the Essence of Human Freedom*. Albany: State University of New York Press, 2006.

Schleiermacher, Friedrich. *Der christliche Glaube nach den Grundsätzen der evangelischen Kirche im Zusammenhange dargestellt*. Dritter Teil. Neue unveränderte Ausgabe in vier Teilen. Bibliothek theologischer Klassiker 15: Schleiermachers Glaubenslehre 3. Gotha: Friedrich Andreas Perthes, 1889. Cf. *NL-Bibl.* 3 B 64. Translated, based on the 2nd German ed., as *The Christian Faith*, edited by H. R. Mackintosh and J. S. Stewart. Edinburgh: T & T Clark, 1928.

Schürer, Emil. *Geschichte des jüdischen Volkes im Zeitalter Jesu Christi*. Vol. 3: *Das Judentum in der Zerstreuung und die jüdische Literatur*. 2nd newly revised ed. Leipzig: J. C. Hinrichs, 1898. Translated by T. A. Burkill et al. as *The History of the Jewish People in the Age of Jesus Christ (175 BC–AD 135)*, revised and edited by Geza Vermes and Fergus Millar. Edinburgh: T & T Clark, 1973.

Schütz, Paul. *Säkulare Religion: Eine Studie über ihre Erscheinung in der Gegenwart und ihre Idee bei Schleiermacher und Blumhardt d. J.* (Secular religion: A study of its appearance in the present and the idea of it in Schleiermacher and Blumhardt the younger). Beiträge zur Systematischen Theologie 2. Tübingen: J. C. B. Mohr (Paul Siebeck), 1932.

Schweitzer, Albert. *Die Geschichte der Leben-Jesu-Forschung*. 2nd newly revised and expanded ed. Tübingen: Mohr, 1913. Translated by William Montgomery as *The Quest of the Historical Jesus: A Critical Study of Its Progress from Reimarus to Wrede*. New York: Macmillan, 1968.

Seeberg, Reinhold. *Lehrbuch der Dogmengeschichte*. Vol. 4/2: *Die Fortbildung der reformatorischen Lehre und die gegenreformatorische Lehre*. 3rd new rev. ed. Leipzig: A. Deichert (G. Böhme), 1920. *NL-Bibl.* 2 C 4, 44. Translated (abridged) by Charles E. Hay as *Textbook of the History of Doctrines,* 2 vols. in 1. Grand Rapids: Baker Book House, 1956. (The English translation was made in 1905 from a modified version of the German 1st ed.; it does not correspond in organization and pagination to the German 3rd ed. of vols. 2 and 3 used by Bonhoeffer.)

———. *System der Ethik* (A system of ethics). 2nd rev. ed. Leipzig: A. Deichert, 1920. *NL-Bibl.* 4, 46.

Silesius, Angelus (Johannes Scheffler). *Cherubinischer Wandersmann.* Halle an der Saale: M. Niemeyer, 1895. Translated by Maria Shrady as *The Cherubinic Wanderer.* Mahwah, N.J.: Paulist Press, 1986.

The Social Creed of the Churches. Adopted at the quadrennial meeting of the Federal Council of Churches of Christ in America, 1908 and December 1912 (revised). In *The Social Creed of the Churches,* edited by Harry F. Ward. New York: Abingdon Press, 1916.

Stählin, Wilhelm. "Die Einheit der christlichen Kirche und die Völker" (The unity of the Christian church and the peoples). *Die Eiche* 20 (1932): 332–33.

Stange, Erich. "Das Ergebnis der Aussprache über das Reich Gottes in Stockholm" (The outcome of the discussion in Stockholm concerning the kingdom of God). *Pastoralblätter für Predigt, Seelsorge und kirchliche Unterweisung* 86 (1926): 397–411.

Stapel, Wilhelm. *Der christliche Staatsmann: Eine Theologie des Nationalismus* (The Christian statesman: A theology of nationalism). Hamburg: Hanseatische Verlagsanstalt, 1932. *NL-Bibl.* 4, 49a.

———. "Juden, Heiden und Christen: Eine Antwort an Herrn Prof. D. Paul Althaus und an Herrn Prof. Dr. Karl Eschweiler" (Jews, Gentiles and Christians: A reply to Professor Dr. Paul Althaus and Professor Dr. Karl Eschweiler). *Deutsches Volkstum* 15 (1933): 59–62.

Steinmann, Theophil. "Noch einmal: Zur philosophischen Grundlegung der Theologie; Antwort an D. Heim" (Once more: On the philosophical basis of theology; reply to Dr. Heim). *Zeitschrift für Theologie und Kirche* 13 (1932): 289–306.

———. "Zur Auseinandersetzung mit Karl Heims philosophischer Grundlegung" (Toward a critical analysis of Karl Heim's philosophical basis). *Zeitschrift für Theologie und Kirche* 13 (1932): 27–50.

Tawney, Richard Henry. *The Acquisitive Society.* New York: Harcourt, Brace, & Howe, 1920.

Thomasius, Gottfried. *Christi Person und Werk: Darstellung der evangelisch-lutherischen Dogmatik vom Mittelpunkte der Christologie aus* (Christ's person and work: Presentation of evangelical Lutheran dogmatics from the center of Christology). Vol. 1: *Die Voraussetzungen der Christologie und die Per-*

son des Mittlers (The presuppositions of Christology and the person of the mediator). Erlangen: T. Bläsing, 1886.

Thurneysen, Eduard. "Schrift und Offenbarung" (Biblical text and revelation). *Zwischen den Zeiten* 2, no. 6 (1924): 3–30.

Titius, Arthur. "Der angelsächsische Aktivismus und Luther" (Anglo-Saxon activism and Luther). *Die Christliche Welt* 40 (1926): 665–75.

Troeltsch, Ernst. *Die Soziallehren der christlichen Kirchen und Gruppen*. Vol. 1 of *Gesammelte Schriften*. Tübingen: J. C. B. Mohr (Paul Siebeck), 1912. Translated by Olive Wyon as *The Social Teaching of the Christian Churches*, 2 vols., foreword by James Luther Adams. Louisville: Westminster John Knox, 1992.

Visser 't Hooft, Wilhelm Adolf. *The Background of the Social Gospel in America*. Haarlem, Netherlands: Tjeenk Willink, 1929. New ed. St. Louis: Bethany Press, 1962.

Vogel, Heinrich. *Allein und auch: Von der Sünde und vom Glauben* (Alone and more: Concerning sin and faith). Berlin: Furche-Verlag, 1930.

Ward, Harry Frederick. *The New Social Order: Principles and Programs*. New York: Macmillan, 1923.

———. *Our Economic Morality and the Ethic of Jesus*. New York: Macmillan, 1929.

———. *Which Way Religion?* New York: Macmillan, 1931. *NL-Bibl.* 7 B 27.

Weber, Max. *Die protestantische Ethik und der Geist des Kapitalismus*. Vol. 1 of *Gesammelte Aufsätze zur Religionssoziologie*, 17–206. Tübingen: Mohr, 1920. Translated by Talcott Parsons as *The Protestant Ethic and the Spirit of Capitalism*. Mineola, N.Y.: Dover, 2003.

Winkler, Robert. "Heim, Karl: Der evangelische Glaube und das Denken der Gegenwart" (Heim, Karl: The Protestant faith and modern thought). *Christentum und Wissenschaft* 7 (1931): 273–74.

The World Tomorrow. New York, 1918–. (Journal of the social gospel movement edited by Kirby Page and Reinhold Niebuhr.)

"Das Wort der Kirche zur Not und Verwirrung des öffentlichen Lebens" (The word of the church to need and confusion in public life). *Der Vormarsch* 3 (1933): 36–43.

"Das Wort und Bekenntnis Altonaer Pastoren in der Not und Verwirrung des öffentlichen Lebens" (The word and confession of Altona pastors in the crisis and confusion of public life). *Niederdeutsche Kirchenzeitung* 3 (1933): 21–26.

Wrede, William. *Das Messiasgeheimnis in den Evangelien: Zugleich ein Beitrag zum Verständnis des Markusevangeliums*. Göttingen: Vandenhoeck & Ruprecht, 1901. Translated by J. C. G. Greig as *The Messianic Secret*. Cambridge: J. Clarke, 1971.

Zoellner, Wilhelm. "Die una sancta ecclesia und die Einzelkirchen" (The one holy church and the individual churches). *Die Eiche* 20 (1932): 328–32.

3. Literature Mentioned by Bonhoeffer's Correspondents

Elert, Werner. *Ecclesia militans* (The militant church). 3 Kapitel von der Kirche und ihrer Verfassung (Chapter 3 on the church and its constitution). Leipzig: Dörffling & Franke, 1933.

Lietzmann, Hans. *Geschichte der alten Kirche.* Vol. 1: *Die Anfänge.* Berlin: W. de Gruyter, 1932. Translated by Bertram Lee Wolf from the 3rd German rev. ed. as *A History of the Early Church,* 4 vols. in 2. Cleveland: World, 1961.

Merz, Georg. "Mitteilungen und Hinweise" (Reports and recommendations). *Zwischen den Zeiten* 11 (1933): 374–76.

Sasse, Hermann. "Die deutsche Union von 1933: Ein Wort zur 'Verfassung der Deutschen Evangelischen Kirche'" (The German union of 1933: A statement on 'the constitution of the German Protestant Church'). *Theologische Blätter* 12 (1933): 274–80.

Schubring, Wilhelm, and Rudolf Köhler. "Karl Barth über Theologie und Mission" (Karl Barth on theology and mission). *Protestantenblatt* 65 (1932): 256–61.

4. Literature Consulted by the Editors

Abromeit, Hans-Jürgen. *Das Geheimnis Christi: Dietrich Bonhoeffers erfahrungsbezogene Christologie* (The mystery of Christ: Dietrich Bonhoeffer's experience-related Christology). Neukirchener Beiträge zur Systematischen Theologie 8 (Neukirchener contributions to systematic theology 8). Neukirchen-Vluyn: Neukirchener Verlag, 1990.

Adam, Uwe Dietrich. *Judenpolitik im Dritten Reich* (Policies on Jews in the Third Reich). Königstein: Droste Verlag, 1979.

Alston, Wallace, and Michael Welker, eds. "Dietrich Bonhoeffer: Bisher unveröffentlichte Briefe an Paul Lehmann." *Evangelische Theologie* 56 (1996): 465–75. German material translated by Matthias Gockel in "Dietrich Bonhoeffer: Previously Unpublished Letters to Paul Lehmann," *Theology Today* 53, no. 3 (1996): 289–98.

Altaner, Berthold, and Alfred Stuiber. *Patrologie: Leben, Schriften und Lehre der Kirchenväter.* Freiburg: Herder, 1978. Translated by Hilda C. Graef as *Patrology,* 2nd ed. New York: Herder & Herder, 1961.

Ayer, Joseph C. *A Source Book for Ancient Church History from the Apostolic Age to the Close of the Conciliar Period.* New York: Charles Scribner's Sons, 1952; AMS Press, 1970.

Barnett, Victoria. *For the Soul of the People: Protestant Protest against Hitler.* New York: Oxford University Press, 1992.

Barth, Karl. *Briefe des Jahres 1933* (Letters from the year 1933). Zürich: Theologischer Verlag Zürich, 2004.

———. *Die christliche Dogmatik im Entwurf* (Christian dogmatics in outline). Vol. 1: *Die Lehre vom Worte Gottes* (The doctrine of the Word of God). Munich: Chr. Kaiser, 1927.

———. "Das erste Gebot als theologisches Axiom" (The first commandment as theological axiom). *Zwischen den Zeiten* 10 (1932): 297–314.

———. *Die Kirche Jesu Christi* (The church of Jesus Christ). *Theologische Existenz heute* 5. Munich: Chr. Kaiser, 1933.

———. *Die kirchliche Dogmatik.* Vol. 1: *Die Lehre vom Wort Gottes: Prolegomena zur kirchlichen Dogmatik.* Erster Halbband. Zollikon-Zürich: Verlag der Evangelischen Buchhandlung, 1932. Translated by G. T. Thomson as *The Doctrine of the Word of God: Prolegomena to Church Dogmatics,* vol. 1/1. Edinburgh: T & T Clark, 1936. 2nd rev. ed., 1986.

———. "Die Theologie und die Mission in der Gegenwart" (Theology and mission in the present). *Zwischen den Zeiten* 10 (1932): 189–215.

———. *Vorträge und kleinere Arbeiten, 1909–1914* (Lectures and smaller works, 1909–1914). Karl Barth Gesamtausgabe, edited by Herbert Helms, Friedrich-Wilhelm Marquardt, Hans-Anton Drewes, and Hinrich Stoevesandt. Zürich: Theologischer Verlag, 1993.

Bauke, Hermann. "Christologie II." In *Die Religion in Geschichte und Gegenwart,* 2nd ed., vol. 1, cols. 1608–34. Tübingen: Mohr, 1927–31.

Baynes, Norman H., ed. *The Speeches of Adolf Hitler, 1922–1939.* 2 vols. London: Oxford University Press, 1942.

Die Bekenntnisschriften der evangelisch-lutherischen Kirche (The confessional texts of the Evangelical-Lutheran church). Published in the anniversary year of the Augsburg Confession 1930. 2 vols. Göttingen: Vandenhoeck & Ruprecht, 1930. See also Kolb and Wengert, *Book of Concord.*

Das Bekenntnis der Väter und die bekennende Gemeinde (The confession of the fathers and the confessing congregation). Zur Besinnung dargeboten von einem Kreise evangelischer Theologen und in ihrem Namen (Offered for reflection and in their name by a circle of Protestant theologians). Edited by Martin Niemöller. Munich: Chr. Kaiser, 1934.

Bergen, Doris L. *Twisted Cross: The German Christian Movement in the Third Reich.* Chapel Hill: University of North Carolina Press, 1996.

Bethge, Eberhard. *Dietrich Bonhoeffer: Theologe, Christ, Zeitgenosse.* Munich: Chr. Kaiser, 1986. Translated by Eric Mosbacher, Peter Ross, Betty Ross, Frank Clarke, and William Glen-Doepel as *Dietrich Bonhoeffer: A Biography,* under the editorship of Edwin Robertson, revised and edited by

Victoria Barnett, based on the 7th German ed. 1st Fortress Press ed., Minneapolis: Fortress Press, 2000.

Bismarck, Ruth-Alice von, and Ulrich Kabitz, eds. *Brautbriefe Zelle 92: Dietrich Bonhoeffer–Maria von Wedemeyer, 1943–1945.* Munich: Ch. H. Beck'sche Verlagsbuchhandlung, 1992. Translated by John Brownjohn as *Love Letters from Cell 92: The Correspondence between Dietrich Bonhoeffer and Maria von Wedemeyer, 1943–45,* with a postscript by Eberhard Bethge. London: HarperCollins, 1994; Nashville: Abingdon Press, 1995.

Bizer, Ernst. "Der 'Fall Dehn'" (The Dehn case). In *Festschrift für Günther Dehn,* edited by W. Schneemelcher, 239–61. Neukirchen: Verlag der Buchhandlung des Erziehungsvereins Neukirchen, 1957.

Bonhoeffer, Dietrich. *Dietrich Bonhoeffer Werke.* 17 vols. Edited by Eberhard Bethge et al. Munich: Chr. Kaiser; Gütersloh: Gütersloher Verlagshaus, 1986–99. Translated as *Dietrich Bonhoeffer Works,* Victoria J. Barnett, Wayne Whitson Floyd Jr., and Barbara Wojhoski, general editors, 17 vols. Minneapolis: Fortress Press, 1996–.

Vol. 1: *Sanctorum Communio: Eine dogmatische Untersuchung zur Soziologie der Kirche.* Edited by Joachim von Soosten. Munich: Chr. Kaiser Verlag, 1986. Translated by Reinhard Krauss and Nancy Lukens as *Sanctorum Communio: A Theological Study of the Sociology of the Church,* edited by Clifford J. Green. Minneapolis: Fortress Press, 1998.

Vol. 2: *Akt und Sein: Transzendentalphilosophie und Ontologie in der systematischen Theologie.* Edited by Hans-Richard Reuter. Munich: Chr. Kaiser Verlag, 1988. Translated by Martin Rumscheidt as *Act and Being: Transcendental Philosophy and Ontology in Systematic Theology,* edited by Wayne Whitson Floyd Jr. Minneapolis: Fortress Press, 1996.

Vol. 3: *Schöpfung und Fall: Theologische Auslegung von Genesis 1–3.* Edited by Martin Rüter and Ilse Tödt. Munich: Chr. Kaiser Verlag, 1989. Translated by Douglas Stephen Bax as *Creation and Fall: A Theological Exposition of Genesis 1–3,* edited by John W. de Gruchy. Minneapolis: Fortress Press, 1996.

Vol. 4: *Nachfolge.* Edited by Martin Kuske and Ilse Tödt. Munich: Chr. Kaiser Verlag, 1989. 2nd ed., Gütersloh: Chr. Kaiser/Gütersloher Verlagshaus, 1994. Translated by Barbara Green and Reinhard Krauss as *Discipleship,* edited by Geffrey B. Kelly and John D. Godsey. Minneapolis: Fortress Press, 2001.

Vol. 5: *Gemeinsames Leben: Das Gebetbuch der Bibel.* Edited by Gerhard Ludwig Müller and Albrecht Schönherr. Munich: Chr. Kaiser Verlag, 1987. Translated by Daniel W. Bloesch and James H. Burtness as *Life Together* and *Prayerbook of the Bible,* edited by Geffrey B. Kelly. Minneapolis: Fortress Press, 1996.

Vol. 6: *Ethik.* Edited by Ilse Tödt, Heinz Eduard Tödt, Ernst Feil, and Clifford Green. Munich: Chr. Kaiser Verlag, 1992. 2nd ed., Gütersloh: Chr. Kaiser/Gütersloher Verlagshaus, 1998. Translated by Reinhard Krauss and Charles West, with Douglas W. Stott, as *Ethics,* edited by Clifford J. Green. Minneapolis: Fortress Press, 2005.

Vol. 7: *Fragmente aus Tegel.* Edited by Renate Bethge and Ilse Tödt. Munich: Chr. Kaiser, 1994. Translated by Nancy Lukens as *Fiction from Tegel Prison,* edited by Clifford J. Green. Minneapolis: Fortress Press, 2000.

Vol. 8: *Widerstand und Ergebung* (Resistance and submission). Edited by Christian Gremmels, Eberhard Bethge, and Renate Bethge, with Ilse Tödt. Gütersloh: Chr. Kaiser/Gütersloher Verlagshaus, 1998.

Vol. 9: *Jugend und Studium: 1918–1927.* Edited by Hans Pfeifer, with Clifford Green and Carl-Jürgen Kaltenborn. Munich: Chr. Kaiser Verlag, 1986. Translated by Mary Nebelsick, with the assistance of Douglas W. Stott, as *The Young Bonhoeffer: 1918–1927,* edited by Paul Matheny, Clifford J. Green, and Marshall Johnson. Minneapolis: Fortress Press, 2001.

Vol. 10: *Barcelona, Berlin, Amerika: 1928–1931.* Edited by Reinhard Staats and Hans Christoph von Hase, with Holger Roggelin and Matthias Wünsche. Munich: Chr. Kaiser Verlag, 1991. 2nd ed., Gütersloh: Chr. Kaiser/Gütersloher Verlagshaus, 2005. Translated by Douglas W. Stott as *Barcelona, Berlin, New York: 1928–1931,* edited by Clifford J. Green. Minneapolis: Fortress Press, 2008.

Vol. 11: *Ökumene, Universität, Pfarramt: 1931–1932* (Ecumenical, academic, and pastoral work: 1931–1932). Edited by Eberhard Amelung and Christoph Strohm. Gütersloh: Chr. Kaiser Verlagshaus, 1994.

Vol. 12: *Berlin: 1932–1933.* Edited by Carsten Nicolaisen and Ernst-Albert Scharffenorth. Gütersloh: Chr. Kaiser/Gütersloher Verlagshaus, 1997. Translated by Isabel Best and David Higgins, with supplementary material translated by Douglas W. Stott, as *Berlin: 1932–1933,* edited by Larry L. Rasmussen. Minneapolis: Fortress Press, 2009.

Vol. 13: *London: 1933–1935.* Edited by Hans Goedeking, Martin Heimbucher, and Hans-Walter Schleicher. Gütersloh: Chr. Kaiser/Gütersloher Verlagshaus, 1994. Translated by Isabel Best as *London: 1933–1935,* with supplementary material translated by Douglas W. Stott, edited by Keith Clements. Minneapolis: Fortress Press, 2007.

Vol. 14: *Illegale Theologenausbildung: Finkenwalde, 1935–1937* (Theological education at Finkenwalde: 1935–1937). Edited by Otto Dudzus and Jürgen Henkys, with Sabine Bobert-Stützel, Dirk Schulz, and Ilse Tödt. Gütersloh: Chr. Kaiser/Gütersloher Verlagshaus, 1996.

Vol. 15: *Illegale Theologenausbildung: Sammelvikariate, 1937–1940* (Theological education underground: 1937–1940). Edited by Dirk Schulz. Gütersloh: Chr. Kaiser/Gütersloher Verlagshaus, 1998.

Vol. 16: *Konspiration und Haft: 1940–1945.* Edited by Jørgen Glenthøj, Ulrich Kabitz, and Wolf Krötke. Gütersloh: Chr. Kaiser/Gütersloher Verlagshaus, 1996. Translated by Lisa E. Dahill as *Conspiracy and Imprisonment: 1940–1945,* with supplementary material translated by Douglas W. Stott, edited by Mark S. Brocker. Minneapolis: Fortress Press, 2006.

Vol. 17: *Register und Ergänzungen* (Index and supplements). Edited by Herbert Anzinger and Hans Pfeifer, assisted by Waltraud Anzinger and Ilse Tödt. Gütersloh: Chr. Kaiser/Gütersloher Verlagshaus, 1999.

———. "Dein Reich komme! Das Gebet der Gemeinde um Gottes Reich auf Erden." In *Das kommende Reich,* Stimmen aus der deutschen christlichen Studentenbewegung 78. Berlin: Furche-Verlag, 1933. Translated in *DBWE* 12 as "Thy Kingdom Come! The Prayer of the Church-Community for God's Kingdom on Earth," 2/11, pp. 285–97. Also translated as "Thy Kingdom Come: The Prayer of the Church for God's Kingdom on Earth" in *Preface to Bonhoeffer: The Man and Two of His Shorter Writings,* by John Godsey, 28–47. Philadelphia: Fortress Press, 1965.

———. "Der Führer und der einzelne in der jungen Generation." *Der Rundfunk Hörer* 10, no. 5 (1933): 4. Translated in *DBWE* 12 as "The Führer and the Individual in the Younger Generation," 2/9, pp. 268–82. Also translated by Edwin Robertson and John Bowden as "The Leader and the Individual in the Younger Generation," in *No Rusty Swords,* 190–204. New York: Harper & Row, 1965.

———. *Gesammelte Schriften* (Collected writings). Edited by Eberhard Bethge. 6 vols. Munich: Chr. Kaiser Verlag, 1958–74. English selections edited by Edwin H. Robertson, translations by Edwin H. Robertson and John Bowden in *No Rusty Swords* (New York: Harper & Row, 1965), *The Way to Freedom* (New York: Harper & Row, 1966), and *True Patriotism* (New York: Harper & Row, 1973).

———. "Die Kirche vor der Judenfrage." *Der Vormarsch* 3 (1933): 171–76. Translated in *DBWE* 12 as "The Church and the Jewish Question," 2/13, pp. 361–70. Also translated in *No Rusty Swords,* 221–29. New York: Harper & Row, 1965.

———. *Predigten—Auslegungen—Meditationen 1925–1945* (Sermons, exegeses, meditations). 2 vols. Edited by Otto Dudzus. Munich: Chr. Kaiser Verlag, 1984, 1985.

———. "Rezension zu Robert Jelke, *Vernunft und Offenbarung.*" *Theologische Literaturzeitung* 57 (1932): 563–65. Translated in *DBWE* 12 as "Review of Robert Jelke, *Vernunft und Offenbarung,*" 2/3, pp. 233–35.

———. "Was ist Kirche?" *Der Vormarsch* 3 (1933): 8–10. Translated in *DBWE* 12 as "What Is Church?" 2/7, pp. 262–66. Also translated in *No Rusty Swords,* 153–57. New York: Harper & Row, 1965.

———. *Widerstand und Ergebung: Briefe und Aufzeichnungen aus der Haft.*

Edited by Eberhard Bethge. Munich: Chr. Kaiser, 1951. Expanded ed., 1970, 1985. Translated by Reginald H. Fuller as *Letters and Papers from Prison*, edited by Eberhard Bethge; translation revised by Frank Clarke et al., additional material translated by John Bowden for the enlarged edition published in London. London: SCM, 1971; New York: Macmillan, 1972; New York: Simon & Schuster, 1995.

———. "Zu Karl Heims *Glaube und Denken*." *Christentum und Wissenschaft* 8 (1932): 441–54. Translated in *DBWE* 12 as "On Karl Heim's *Glaube und Denken*," 2/5 , pp. 243–58. Also translated, abridged, as "An Assessment of Karl Heim," in *No Rusty Swords*, 347–59. New York: Harper & Row, 1965.

Boyens, Armin. *Kirchenkampf und Ökumene: Darstellung und Dokumentation* (The Church Struggle and the ecumenical movement: Description and documentation). Vol. 1: *1933–1939*. Munich: Chr. Kaiser, 1969, 1973.

Brackmann, Karl-Heinz, and Renate Birkenhauer, eds. *NS-Deutsch: "Selbstverständliche" Begriffe und Schlagwörter aus der Zeit des Nationalsozialismus* (Nazi-German: "Self-evident" concepts and slogans from the time of National Socialism). Glossar/Europäisches Übersetzer-Kollegium 4 (Glossary/ European Translators Collegium 4). Straelen: Straelener, 1988.

Braun, Hannelore, and Carsten Nicolaisen, eds. *Verantwortung für die Kirche: Stenographische Aufzeichnungen und Mitschriften von Landesbischof Hans Meiser 1933–1955* (Responsibility for the church: Stenographic notes and records of Provincial Bishop Hans Meiser 1933–55). Vol. 1: *Sommer 1933 bis Sommer 1935* (Summer 1933 to summer 1935). Arbeiten zur Kirchlichen Zeitgeschichte A 1. Göttingen: Vandenhoeck & Ruprecht, 1985.

Buber, Martin. "Offener Brief an Gerhard Kittel" (An open letter to Gerhard Kittel). *Theologische Blätter* 12 (1933): 248–50.

Büchmann, Georg. *Geflügelte Worte: Der Zitatenschatz des deutschen Volkes* (Familiar quotations: The treasury of sayings of the German people). 33rd printing, newly revised by W. Hofmann. Frankfurt am Main: Haude & Spener, 1981.

Busch, Eberhard. *Karl Barths Lebenslauf: Nach seinen Briefen und autobiographischen Texten*. Munich: Chr. Kaiser, 1975. Translated by John Bowden as *Karl Barth: His Life from Letters and Autobiographical Texts*. Grand Rapids: Wm. B. Eerdmans, 1994.

Carter, Guy Christopher. "Confession at Bethel, August 1933: Enduring Witness; The Formation, Revision and Significance of the First Full Theological Confession of the Evangelical Church Struggle in Nazi Germany." PhD. diss., Marquette University, Milwaukee, Wisconsin, 1987.

Conway, John. "Between Pacifism and Patriotism—a Protestant Dilemma: The Case of Friedrich Siegmund-Schultze." In *Germans against Nazism: Nonconformity, Opposition, and Resistance in the Third Reich; Essays in Honour of Peter Hoffmann*, edited by Francis R. Nicosia and Lawrence D. Stokes, 87–115. New York: Berg; distributed exclusively in the United States and Canada by St. Martin's Press, 1990.

Curti, Theodor. *Schweizer Geflügelte Worte* (Familiar Swiss quotations). Zürich: Art. Institut Orell Füzli, 1896.

Dehn, Günther, ed. *Die alte Zeit, die vorigen Jahre: Lebenserinnerungen* (The old time, the past years: A memoir). Munich: Chr. Kaiser, 1962.

———. *Kirche und Völkerversöhnung: Dokumente zum Halleschen Universitätskonflikt* (Church and the reconciliation of peoples: Documents on the university conflict in Halle). Berlin: Furche-Verlag, 1931.

Deutsches Pfarrerblatt (German pastors' gazette). Serial publication of the Reichsbund der Deutschen Evangelischen Pfarrervereine und Bund der Preussischen Pfarrervereine, Essen, 1900–1943. Vol. 37, 1933.

Dietrich Bonhoeffer: Einführung in seine Botschaft (Dietrich Bonhoeffer: Introduction to his message). Wuppertal-Barmen: Presseverband der Evangelischen Kirche im Rheinland, 1956.

Elert, Werner. *Morphologie des Luthertums*. 2 vols. Munich: Beck, 1931, 1932. Translated by Walter A. Hansen as *The Structure of Lutheranism*, 2 vols. St. Louis: Concordia Press, 1962.

Ericksen, Robert P. *Theologians under Hitler*. New Haven, Conn.: Yale University Press, 1985.

Das Evangelische Westfalen: Blätter für den Dienst an der Gemeinde (Protestant Westphalia: Materials for parish ministry). Serial publication, Witten. Vol. 9, 1932.

Evangelisches Gesangbuch (Protestant hymnal). Ausgabe für die Evangelische Landeskirche in Baden (Edition for the Protestant Church of Baden). Karlsruhe: Evangelischer Presseverband für Baden, 1996.

Das Evangelium im Dritten Reich: Das Sonntagsblatt der deutsche Christen (The gospel in the Third Reich: Sunday paper for German Christians). Serial publication, Berlin. Vol. 2, 1932–37.

Feil, Ernst. *Die Theologie Dietrich Bonhoeffers: Hermeneutik, Christologie und Weltverständnis*. Gesellschaft und Theologie, Systematische Beiträge 6. Munich: Chr. Kaiser; Mainz: Matthias-Grünewald-Verlag, 1971. Edition abridged by author and translated by Martin Rumscheidt as *The Theology of Dietrich Bonhoeffer*. Minneapolis: Fortress Press, 1985.

Field, David. "Dietrich Bonhoeffer." In *Empire: The Christian Tradition*, edited by Kwok Pui-lan, Don H. Compier, and Joerg Rieger. Minneapolis: Fortress Press, 2007.

Fischer, Franz. "Eindrücke von der Konferenz in Sofia" (Impressions of the conference in Sofia). *Die Kirchen am Werk: Mitteilungen*, no. 3 (October 1933): 6–7.

Frank, Franz Hermann Reinhold. *System der christlichen Sittlichkeit* (System of Christian morality). Zweite Hälfte (Part 2). Erlangen: A. Deichert, 1887.

Frank, Walter. *Hofprediger Adolf Stoecker und die christlichsoziale Bewegung* (Court preacher Adolf Stoecker and the Christian social movement). Mit 4 Bildbeilagen in Kupfertiefdruck. Berlin: R. Hobbing, 1928.

Fries, Willy. *Bilder im Sturm: Erinnerungen* (Pictures in the storm: A memoir). Amriswil: Amriswiler Bücherei, 1986.

———. *Gottlose: Eine Geschichte in Bildern* (Godless: A story in pictures). Erlenbach-Zürich: Eugen Rentsch, 1932.

Die Furche (The Furrow). Serial publication, Berlin. Vol. 19, 1933.

Gauger, Joachim. *Chronik der Kirchenwirren* (Chronicle of the church turmoil). 3 vols. Vol. 1: *Vom Aufkommen der "Deutschen Christen" 1932 bis zur Bekenntnis-Reichs-Synode im Mai 1934* (From the rise of the "German Christians" 1932 to the Confessing synod in May 1934). Elberfeld: J. Gauger, 1934–35.

Gerlach, Wolfgang. *And the Witnesses Were Silent: The Confessing Church and the Jews.* Translated and edited by Victoria J. Barnett from the German original, *Und die Zeugen Schwiegen.* Lincoln: University of Nebraska Press, 2000.

Glasenapp, Helmuth von. *Die nichtchristlichen Religionen: Das Fischer Lexikon A–Z.* Frankfurt am Main: Fischer Verlag, 1957. Translated by Eric Protter as *Non-Christian Religions A to Z: Based on the Work of Helmuth von Glasenapp,* edited under the supervision of Horace L. Friess. New York: Grosset & Dunlap, 1963.

Glenthøj, Jørgen, ed. *Dokumente zur Bonhoeffer-Forschung 1928–1945.* See *Mündige Welt.*

———. *Zu Dietrich Bonhoeffers Eintritt in die ökumenische Arbeit: Dokumente 1931–32* (Dietrich Bonhoeffer's entry into ecumenical work: Documents 1931–32). Fredericia, Denmark: Lohse, 1974.

Glombitza, Michael. *Die evangelisch-theologischen Fakultäten in Deutschland von 1933 bis 1945* (The Protestant theological faculties in Germany from 1933 to 1945) (typescript of state theological examination, Theologische Fakultät der Humboldt-Universität, Berlin). Berlin, n.d.

Goethe, Johann Wolfgang von. *Faust.* Vol. 3 of *Werke.* Hamburger Ausgabe. Edited by Erich Trunz. Munich: C. H. Beck, 1993. Translated by Stuart Atkins as *Faust 1 & 2,* vol. 2 of *Goethe's Collected Works.* Cambridge, Mass.: Suhrkamp, 1984.

Götz von Olenhusen, Irmtraud. *Jugendreich, Gottesreich, Deutsches Reich: Junge Generation, Religion und Politik 1928–1933* (Kingdom of youth, kingdom of God, German Reich: The younger generation, religion and politics 1928–1933). Cologne: Verlag Wissenschaft und Politik, 1987.

Green, Clifford J. *Bonhoeffer: A Theology of Sociality.* Grand Rapids: Wm. B. Eerdmans, 1999.

Grotefeld, Stefan. *Friedrich Siegmund-Schultze: Ein deutscher Ökumeniker und christlicher Pazifist* (Friedrich Siegmund-Schultze: A German ecumenist and Christian pacifist). Heidelberger Untersuchungen zu Widerstand, Judenverfolgung und Kirchenkampf im Dritten Reich 7. Gütersloh: Chr. Kaiser/Gütersloher Verlagshas, 1995.

Gründel, Ernst Günther. *Die Sendung der jungen Generation: Versuch einer umfassende revolutionären Sinndeutung der Krise* (The mission of the younger generation: Attempt at a comprehensive revolutionary sense of the crisis). Munich: Beck, 1932.

Hammersen, Nicolai. *Politisches Denken im deutschen Widerstand: Ein Beitrag zur Wirkungsgeschichte neokonservativer Ideen* (Political thought in the German resistance: A contribution to the history of neoconservative ideas). Beiträge zur Politischen Wissenschaft 67. Berlin: Duncker & Humblot, 1993.

Harling, Otto von. "Judenmission" (Mission to the Jews). In *Die Religion in Geschichte und Gegenwart*, 2nd ed., vol. 3, cols. 466–69. Tübingen: Mohr, 1927–31.

Heim, Karl. *God Transcendent: Foundation for a Christian Metaphysic.* Translated by Edgar Primrose Dickie from the 3rd ed. of *Glaube und Denken*, with an introduction and the revising aid of Edwyn Bevan. London: Nisbet, 1935; New York: Charles Scribner's Sons, 1936.

———. *Ich gedenke der vorigen Zeiten: Erinnerungen aus 8 Jahrzehnten* (I remember the earlier times: Recollections of 8 decades). 8 illustrations. Hamburg: Furche-Verlag, 1957.

Heimbucher, Martin. *Christusfriede—Weltfrieden: Dietrich Bonhoeffers kirchlicher und politischer Kampf gegen den Krieg Hitlers und seine theologische Begründung* (The peace of Christ—world peace: Dietrich Bonhoeffer's ecclesiastical and political struggle against Hitler's war and its theological grounding). Gütersloh : Chr. Kaiser, 1997.

Heine, Heinrich. *Almansor.* Vol. 5 of *Historisch-kritische Gesamtausgabe der Werke.* Edited by Manfred Windfuhr. Hamburg: Hoffmann & Campe, 1973–97.

Helmreich, Ernst Christian. *The German Churches under Hitler: Background, Struggle, and Epilogue.* Detroit: Wayne State University Press, 1979.

Henriod, Henry Louis. "Nationale und übernationale kirchliche Arbeit: Die Kirche und die allgemeine Not" (National and transnational church work: The church and the general crisis). *Die Eiche* 21 (1933): 260–69.

Herrmann, Wilhelm. *Dogmatik.* Gotha: L. Klotz, 1925. Translated by Nathaniel Micklem and Kenneth A. Saunders as *Systematic Theology.* New York: Macmillan, 1927.

———. *Offenbarung und Wunder* (Revelation and wonder). Gießen: Alfred Töpelmann, 1908.

Hielscher, Friedrich. *Das Reich* (The empire). Berlin: Das Reich, 1931.

Hildebrand, Klaus. *Das Dritte Reich.* Oldenbourg-Grundriß der Geschichte 17. Munich: Oldenbourg, 1979. Translated by P. S. Falla as *The Third Reich.* London: Allen & Unwin, 1984.

Hildebrandt, Horst, ed. *Die deutschen Verfassungen des 19. und 20. Jahrhunderts* (The German constitutions of the 19th and 20th centuries). 13th ed. Paderborn: Schöningh, 1985.

Hirsch, Emanuel. "Arier und Nichtarier in der deutschen evangelischen Kirche" (Aryans and non-Aryans in the German Protestant church). *Kirche und Volkstum in Niedersachsen* 1 (1933): 17–20.

———. *Die gegenwärtige geistige Lage im Spiegel philosophischer und theologischer Besinnung* (The present intellectual situation as reflected in philosophical and theological consciousness). Akademische Vorlesungen zum Verständnis des deutschen Jahres 1933. Göttingen: Vandenhoeck & Ruprecht, 1934.

———. "Die wirkliche Lage unserer Kirche" (The real situation of our church). *Pastoraltheologie* 29 (1933): 182–85.

Hitler, Adolf. *Mein Kampf: Eine Abrechnung.* Vol. 1. Munich: Franz Eher Nachf., 1926. Translated by Ralph Mannheim. New York: Houghton Mifflin, 1999.

Hodgson, Leonard. *The Second World Conference on Faith and Order, Held at Edinburgh, August 3–18.* New York: Macmillan, 1938.

Hofmann, Johann Christian Konrad von. *Encyklopädie der Theologie* (Theological encyclopedia). Nördlingen: C. H. Beck, 1879.

Huber, Ernst Rudolf, and Wolfgang Huber. *Staat und Kirche im 19. und 20. Jahrhundert* (State and church in the 19th and 20th centuries). Vol. 4: *Staat und Kirche in der Zeit der Weimarer Republik* (State and church in the time of the Weimar Republic). Berlin: Duncker & Humblot, 1988.

Huber, Wolfgang, and Tödt, Ilse, eds. *Ethik im Ernstfall: Dietrich Bonhoeffers Stellung zu den Juden und ihre Aktualität* (Ethics in the crisis: Dietrich Bonhoeffer's position regarding the Jews and its relevance). Internationales Bonhoeffer Forum: Forschung und Praxis 4. Munich: Chr. Kaiser, 1982.

Isaacson, Walter. *Einstein: His Life and Universe.* New York: Simon & Schuster, 2007.

Johnson, Donald Oscar. *The Challenge to American Freedoms: World War I and the Rise of the American Civil Liberties Union.* Lexington: University of Kentucky Press, 1963.

Jüdische Rundschau (Jewish Outlook). Serial publication, Berlin. Vol. 38, 1933.

Junge Kirche (Young Church). Serial publication, Göttingen. Vol. 1, 1933.

Kaltenborn, Carl-Jürgen. *Adolf von Harnack als Lehrer Dietrich Bonhoeffers* (Adolf von Harnack as Dietrich Bonhoeffer's teacher). Theologische Arbeiten 31. Berlin: Evangelische Verlagsanstalt, 1973.

Kattenbusch, Ferdinand. "Taufe II: Kirchenlehre" (Baptism II: Church doctrine). In *Realencyklopädie für protestantische Theologie und Kirche*, 3rd ed., 19:403–24. Graz: Akademische Druck- u. Verlagsanstalt, 1969–71.

Kershaw, Ian. *Der Hitler-Mythos: Volksmeinung und Propaganda im Dritten Reich*. Schriftenreihe der Vierteljahrshefte für Zeitgeschichte 41. Stuttgart: Deutsche Verlags-Anstalt, 1980. Translated as *The "Hitler Myth": Image and Reality in the Third Reich*. London: Clarendon Press; New York: Oxford University Press, 1987. Rev. ed., 2001.

Kierkegaard, Søren. *The Concept of Anxiety: A Simple Psychologically Orienting Deliberation on the Dogmatic Issue of Hereditary Sin*. Translation of *Begrebet angest* by Reidar Thomte. Princeton. N.J.: Princeton University Press, 1980.

———. Index volume to Kierkegaard, *Gesammelte Werke* (Collected works). Prepared by I. Jacobsen und H. Waechter with H. Gerdes. Düsseldorf: E. Diederich, 1969.

Die Kirchen am Werk: Mitteilungen. Bulletin of the Universal Christian Council for Life and Work and the World Alliance for International Friendship through the Churches. Geneva, 1933–38. Published in English as *The Churches in Action: Newsletter of the Universal Christian Council for Life and Work and the World Alliance for International Friendship through the Churches*. Quarterly. No. 1 (March 1933)–no. 18 (October 1938).

Kirchliches Gesetz- und Verordnungsblatt (Journal of ecclesiastical law and regulation). Berlin: 1928, 1933.

Kittel, Gerhard. *Die Judenfrage* (The Jewish question). Stuttgart: W. Kohlhammer, 1933.

Kluke, Paul. "Der Fall Potempa" (The Potempa case). *Vierteljahreshefte für Zeitgeschichte* 5 (1957): 279–97.

Knittermeyer, Hinrich. *Der Mensch der Erkenntnis: Entwurf einer kritischen Transzendentalphilosophie* (The person of knowledge: Outline of a critical philosophy of transcendence). Edited from the unpublished manuscript by Gusta Knittermeyer. Hamburg: F. Meiner, 1962.

Koebner, Thomas, et al., eds. *Mit uns zieht die neue Zeit: Der Mythos Jugend* (With us comes the new era: The myth of youth). Frankfurt am Main: Suhrkamp, 1985.

Kolb, Robert, and Timothy J. Wengert, eds. *The Book of Concord: The Confessions of the Evangelical Lutheran Church*. Translation of *Die Bekenntnisschriften der evangelisch-lutherischen Kirche* by Charles Arand, Eric Gritsch, Robert Kolb, William Russell, James Schaaf, Jane Strohl, and Timothy J. Wengert. Minneapolis: Fortress Press, 2000.

Das kommende Reich. Zwei Vorträge "Die biblische Botschaft vom Reiche Gottes" und "Dein Reich komme! Das Gebet der Gemeinde um Gottes Reich auf Erden" von Lic. Dr. Johannes Schneider und Lic. Dietrich Bonhoeffer. Privatdozenten an der Universität Berlin (Two lectures by Dr. Johannes Schneider and Dietrich Bonhoeffer, lecturers at Berlin University). Stimmen aus der deutschen christlichen Studentenbewegung, Nr. 78. Berlin: Furche-Verlag, 1933. Bonhoeffer lecture translated by John D. Godsey as "Thy Kingdom Come: The Prayer of the Church for God's Kingdom on Earth," in *Preface to Bonhoeffer: The Man and Two of His Shorter Writings,* by John Godsey, 28–47. Philadelphia: Fortress Press, 1965.

Koonz, Claudia. *The Nazi Conscience.* Cambridge, Mass.: Belknap Press of Harvard University Press, 2003.

Kretschmar, Georg. "Barmen 1934: Bekenntnis als Widerstand" (Barmen 1934: Confession as resistance). In *Die lutherischen Kirchen und die Bekenntnissynode von Barmen,* edited by Wolf-Dieter Hauschild, Georg Kretschmar, und Carsten Nicolaisen, 135–68. Göttingen: Vandenhoeck & Ruprecht, 1984.

Kreuz-Zeitung. Serial publication, Berlin. Vols. 85 and 86, 1932–33.

Krötke, Wolf. "Der begegnende Gott und der Glaube: Zum theologischen Schwerpunkt der Christologievorlesung D. Bonhoeffers" (The God who meets us and faith: On the theological core of Bonhoeffer's Christology lecture). In *Bonhoeffer-Studien: Beiträge zur Theologie und Wirkungsgeschichte Dietrich Bonhoeffers,* 25–35. East Berlin: Evangelische Verlagsanstalt, 1985.

Künneth, Walter. "Das Judenproblem und die Kirche" (The Jewish problem and the church). In *Die Nation vor Gott: Zur Botschaft der Kirche im Dritten Reich* (The nation before God: On the message of the church in the Third Reich), edited by Walter Künneth und Helmuth Schreiner, 90–105. Berlin: Wichern Verlag, 1933.

Das Leben Jesu in Bildern: Handzeichnungen und Radierungen von Rembrandt (The life of Jesus in pictures: Drawings and etchings by Rembrandt). Witten: Eckart-Verlag, 1963.

Lesser, Jonas. *Von deutscher Jugend* (On German youth). Berlin: Neff, 1932.

Lessing, Eckhard. "'Selbstständigkeit' und 'Freiheit' der Kirche: Eine Notiz zum Kirchenverständnis Dibelius' und Barths" ("Independence" and "freedom" of the church: A comment on Dibelius's and Barth's understanding of the church). *Kirchliche Zeitgeschichte* 2 (1989): 426–36.

Lichtenfeld, Manacnuc. *Lutherische Theologie im Bekennen: Georg Merz und das "Betheler Bekenntnis" 1933* (Lutheran theology in confession: George Merz and the "Bethel confession" 1933). Gütersloh: Gütersloher Verlagshaus, 1995.

Liefmann, Else. "Die Legende vom Antichrist und die Sage von Ahasver: Ihre Bedeutung für den Antisemitismus" (The legend of the Antichrist and the legend of Ahasuerus: Its meaning for anti-Semitism). *Judaica* 3 (1947): 122–56.

Lilje, Hans. "Die evangelische Jugendführung" (Protestant youth leadership). *Kirchliches Jahrbuch* 59 (1932): 283–321.

———. "Theologische Existenz und kirchliches Handeln (Gedanken zu Karl Barths Schrift *Theologische Existenz heute*)" (Theological existence and church action [Thoughts on Karl Barth's journal "Theological Existence Today"). *Junge Kirche* 1 (1933): 131–47.

Loofs, Friedrich. "Arianismus" (Arianism). In *Realencyklopädie für protestantische Theologie und Kirche*, 3rd ed., 2:6–45. Graz: Akademische Druck- u. Verlagsanstalt, 1969–71.

Ludwig, Hartmut. "Der Pazifist und Staatsfeind soll nicht länger deutsche Theologen erziehen: Dietrich Bonhoeffer und die Berliner Theologische Fakultät" (The pacifist and enemy of the state should no longer train German theologians: Dietrich Bonhoeffer and the Berlin theological faculty). *Berliner Theologische Zeitschrift* 13 (1996): 250–66.

Luther, Martin. *Deutsche Bibel* (German Bible). 7. Band. Kritische Gesamtausgabe (Critical edition). Weimar: 1931. Selected translation by Charles E. Jacobs and E. Theodore Bachmann (Prefaces to the Old Testament, Prefaces to the New Testament) in *Luther's Works*, vol. 35, 235–411. Philadelphia: Fortress Press, 1960.

———. *Werke.* Kritische Gesamtausgabe. Weimar 1883–. Translated as *Luther's Works*, vols. 1–30 edited by Jaroslav Pelikan, vols. 31–55 edited by Helmut Lehmann, complete works on CD-ROM. Minneapolis: Fortress Press; St. Louis: Concordia, 2002.

The Lutheran Hymnal. St. Louis: Concordia, 1941.

The Lutheran Hymnary. Minneapolis: Augsburg, 1935.

Lyra Germanica: Hymns for the Sundays and Chief Festivals of the Christian Year. Translated from the original German by Catherine Winkworth. London: George Newnes; New York: Charles Scribner's Sons, 1855.

Macfarland, Charles Stedman. *The New Church and the New Germany: A Study of Church and State.* New York: Macmillan, 1934.

Materialdienst (Documentation). Serial publication, published by Evangelischen Presseverband für Württemberg, Stuttgart. Vol. 5, 1933.

Maurenbrecher, Max Heinrich. *Der Heiland der Deutschen: Der Weg der Volkstum schaffenden Kirche* (The Savior of the Germans: The path of the church creating national heritage). Göttingen: Vandenhoeck & Ruprecht, 1930.

Mehlhausen, Joachim. "Der Schriftgebrauch in Bekenntnissen und grundsätzlichen Äusserungen zur Kirchenfrage aus der Anfangszeit des Kirchenkampfes" (The use of Scripture in confessions and basic statements to the question of the church from the time of the beginning of the Church Struggle). In *Sola Scriptura: Das reformatorische Schriftprinzip in der säkularen Welt* (Sola scriptura: The Reformation scriptural principle in the secular world), edited by Hans Heinrich Schmid and Joachim Mehlhausen, 213–28. Gütersloh: Gerd Mohn Verlag, 1991.

Merz, Georg. *Freiheit und Zucht: Die reformatorische Lehre von der Freiheit und ihrer Bedeutung für die Erziehung* (Freedom and discipline: Reformation teaching on freedom and its meaning for education). Munich: Chr. Kaiser, 1932.

———. "Mitteilungen und Hinweise" (Reports and advice). *Zwischen den Zeiten* 11 (1933): 374–76.

Meyer, Dietrich, and Eberhard Bethge, eds. *Nachlaß Dietrich Bonhoeffer: Ein Verzeichnis; Archiv-Sammlung-Bibliothek.* (Dietrich Bonhoeffer's literary estate: A bibliographical catalog; Archive, collection, library). Munich: Chr. Kaiser, 1987.

Mitteilungen der Deutschen Vereinigung des Weltbundes für internationale Freundschaftsarbeit der Kirchen (Reports of the German organization of the World Alliance for Promoting International Friendship through the Churches). Nos. 11 (March 1932), 12 (June 1932), 13 (May 1933). See also *Die Kirchen am Werk.*

Moeller van den Bruck, Arthur. *Das Dritte Reich.* Berlin: Der Ring, 1923. Abridged English edition translated by E. O. Lorimer as *Germany's Third Empire.* 1934; reprint, New York: H. Fertig, 1971.

Mohler, Arnim. *Die konservative Revolution in Deutschland 1918–1932* (The conservative revolution in Germany 1918–1932). Darmstadt: Wissenschaftliche Buchgesellschaft, 1989.

Mühlenberg, Ekkehard. "Apollinaris." In *Theologische Realenzyklopädie* 3:362–71. Berlin: Walter de Gruyter, 1978.

Mühling, Andreas. "Es hat diese Aussprache nun doch ihren Sinn: Anmerkungen zu Karl Ludwig Schmidt und der Neutestamentler-Erklärung des Jahres 1933" (This statement now does make sense: Comments on Karl Ludwig Schmidt and the 1933 statement of New Testament scholars). *Theologische Zeitschrift* 49 (1993): 353–64.

Müller, Christine-Ruth. *Bekenntnis und Bekennen: Dietrich Bonhoeffer in Bethel (1933); Ein lutherischer Versuch* (Confession and confessing: Dietrich Bonhoeffer in Bethel (1933); A Lutheran attempt). Munich: Chr. Kaiser, 1989.

———. *Dietrich Bonhoeffers Kampf gegen die nationalsozialistische Verfolgung und Vernichtung der Juden: Bonhoeffers Haltung zur Judenfrage im Vergleich mit Stellungnahmen aus der evangelischen Kirche und Kreisen des deutschen Widerstands* (Dietrich Bonhoeffer's struggle against the National Socialist persecution and genocide of the Jews: Bonhoeffer's position on the Jewish question compared with positions of the Protestant church and German resistance circles). Heidelberger Untersuchungen zu Widerstand, Judenverfolgung und Kirchenkampf im Dritten Reich 5. Munich: Chr. Kaiser, 1990.

Die Mündige Welt (The world come of age). Vol. 5: *Dokumentation zur Bonhoeffer-Forschung 1928–1945* (Documents on Bonhoeffer research, 1928–1945). Edited by Jørgen Glenthøj. Munich: Chr. Kaiser Verlag, 1969.

Nachlaß Dietrich Bonhoeffer. See Meyer and Bethge, *Nachlaß.*

Neiman, Susan. *Evil in Modern Thought: An Alternative History of Philosophy.* Princeton, N.J.: Princeton University Press, 2002.

Neumann, Sigmund. *Die deutschen Parteien: Wesen und Wandel nach dem Kriege* (The German parties: Nature and change after the war). Berlin: Junker & Dünnhaupt, 1932.

Nicolaisen, Carsten, ed. *Dokumente zur Kirchenpolitik des Dritten Reiches* (Documents on the church politics of the Third Reich). Vol. 1: *Das Jahr 1933* (The year 1933). Munich: Chr. Kaiser, 1971.

Nicosia, Francis R., and Lawrence D. Stokes, eds. *Germans against Nazism: Nonconformity, Opposition, and Resistance in the Third Reich.* New York: Berg, 1990.

Niemöller, Martin. "Die jungreformatorische Bewegung und die Kirchenpolitik" (The Young Reformation movement and church politics). *Junge Kirche* 1 (1933): 99–101.

———. "Sätze zur Arierfrage in der Kirche" (Comments on the Aryan paragraph in the church). *Junge Kirche* 1 (1933): 269–71.

Nobiling, Siegfried. "Kirchliches Führertum" (The church ideology of *Führer*). In *Volk und Kirche: Die amtlichen Berichte der ersten Reichstagung 1933 der Glaubenbewegung "Deutsche Christen"* (Nation and church: The official report of the first national conference 1933 of the faith movement "German Christians"), Schriftenreihe der "Deutschen Christen" 4, 43–49. Berlin, n.d.

Norden, Günther van. *Der deutsche Protestantismus im Jahr der nationalsozialistischen Machtergreifung* (German Protestantism in the year of the National Socialist seizure of power). Gütersloh: Gütersloher Verlagshaus Mohn, 1979.

———. *Kirche in der Krise: Die Stellung der evangelischen Kirche zum nationalsozialistischen Staat im Jahre 1933* (Church in crisis: The position of the Protestant church toward the National Socialist state in 1933). Düsseldorf: Pressverband der Evangelischen Kirche im Rhineland, 1963.

Nowak, Kurt. "Das Stigma der Rasse: Nationalsozialistische Judenpolitik und christliche Nichtarier" (The stigma of race: National Socialist politics toward the Jews and Christian non-Aryans). In *Der Holocaust und die Protestanten: Analysen einer Verstrickung* (The Holocaust and Protestants: Analysis of an entanglement), edited by Jochen-Christof Kaiser and Martin Greschat, Konfession und Gesellschaft 1, 73–99. Frankfurt am Main: Athenäum, 1988.

Ökumenisches Jahrbuch 1934/1935. (Ecumenical yearbook 1934–35). Edited by Friedrich Siegmund-Schultze. Zürich: M. Niehans, 1936.

Ossietzky, Carl von. "Kavaliere und Rundköpfe" (Cavaliers and Roundheads). *Die Weltbühne* 29 (1933): 193–95. Reprinted in *Die Weltbühne: Wochenschrift für Politik, Kunst, Wirtschaft.* Königstein: Athenäum Verlag, 1978.

———. "Wintermärchen" (Winter fairy tales). *Die Weltbühne* 29 (1933): 1–6. Reprinted in *Die Weltbühne: Wochenschrift für Politik, Kunst, Wirtschaft.* Königstein: Athenäum Verlag, 1978.

Oxford Book of Carols. London: Oxford University Press, 1964.

Pangritz, Andreas. "Das Heil kommt von den Juden: Die sogenannte 'Judenfrage' in der Diskussion zwischen Wilhelm Vischer, Karl Barth und Dietrich Bonhoeffer seit dem Jahr 1933" (Salvation comes from the Jews: The so-called "Jewish question" in discussion between Wilhelm Vischer, Karl Barth and Dietrich Bonhoeffer after 1933). Paper presented at the 10th International Bonhoeffer Congress, Prague, July 22–27, 2008.

Pascal, Blaise. *Pensées et Opuscules: Publiés avec une introduction, des notices et des notes par Léon Brunschvicg.* Paris: 1968. Translated by Honor Levi as *Pensées and Other Writings,* with introduction and notes by Anthony Levi. New York: Oxford University Press, 1995.

Petrick, Herbert. "Deutsche Mittelstelle für ökumenische Jugendarbeit" (German provisional office for ecumenical youth work). *Die Eiche* 19 (1931): 376–77.

Prolingheuer, Hans. *Der Fall Karl Barth: 1934–1935; Chronographie einer Vertreibung* (The case of Karl Barth: 1934–1935; Chronology of an expulsion). Neukirchen-Vluyn: Neukirchener Verlag, 1977.

Pugh, Jeffrey Carter. *Religionless Christianity.* London: Continuum, 2009.

Pui-lan, Kwok, Don H. Compier, and Joerg Rieger, eds. *Empire: The Christian Tradition.* Minneapolis: Fortress Press, 2007.

Rasmussen, Larry. *Dietrich Bonhoeffer: Reality and Resistance.* Louisville: Westminster John Knox Press, 2005.

Reich, Andreas. "Schleiermacher als Gemeindepfarrer: Die Dreifaltigkeitskirche als Ort pastoraler Existenz" (Schleiermacher as parish pastor: Trinity Church as a place of pastoral existence). *Berliner Theologische Zeitschrift* 12 (1995): 95–108.

Der Reichsbote (The Reich messenger). Serial publication, Berlin, 1873–1933. Vol. 61, 1933.

Reichsgesetzblatt (Reich legal gazette). Pt. 1. Berlin, 1933. Berlin: Reichsverlagsamt, 1871–1945.

Rexin, Manfred. "Machtergreifung und Widerstand im Spiegel von Rundfunkberichten" (Seizure of power and resistance as reflected in radio reports). In *Widerstand: Ein Problem zwischen Theorie und Geschichte* (Resistance: A problem between theory and history), edited by Peter Steinbach, 59–79. Cologne: Wissenschaft und Politik, 1987.

Rilke, Rainer Maria. *Letters to a Young Poet.* Translated with an introduction and commentary by Reginald Snell. Mineola, N.Y.: Dover, 2002.

Ritter, Adolf Martin. "Arianismus" (Arianism). In *Theologische Realenzyklopädie,* 3:692–719. Berlin: Walter de Gruyter, 1978.

Der Rundfunk Hörer (The radio listener). Serial publication, Berlin. Vol. 20, 1933.

Schjørring, Jens Holger. *Ökumenische Perspektiven des deutschen Kirchenkampfes* (Ecumenical perspectives on the German church struggle). Acta Theologica Danica 18. Leiden: E. J. Brill, 1985.

Schmidt, Jürgen. "Studien zur Vorgeschichte des Pfarrernotbundes" (Studies of the background history of the Pastors' Emergency League). *Zeitschrift für Kirchengeschichte* 79 (1968): 43–67.

Schmidt, Kurt Dietrich, ed. *Die Bekenntnisse und grundsätzlichen Äußerungen zur Kirchenfrage des Jahres 1933* (The confessions and fundamental statements on the church question in 1933). Göttingen: Vandenhoeck & Ruprecht, 1934.

Schmitt, Carl. *Der Begriff des Politischen.* Hamburg: Hanseatische Verlagsanstalt, 1933. Translated by George Schwab as *The Concept of the Political.* New Brunswick, N.J.: Rutgers University Press, 1976.

Schmitt, Franciscus Salesius. *Anselm von Canterbury: Proslogion; Untersuchungen.* Lateinisch-deutsche Ausgabe. Stuttgart: Frommann, 1962. Translated by Thomas Williams as *Proslogion: With the Replies of Gaunilo and Anselm.* Indianapolis: Hackett, 2001.

Schneider, Thomas Martin. *Reichsbischof Müller: Eine Untersuchung zu Leben, Werk und Persönlichkeit* (Reich Bishop Müller: An examination of his life, work and personality). Arbeiten zur Kirchlichen Zeitgeschichte B 19. Göttingen: Vandenhoeck & Ruprecht, 1993.

Scholder, Klaus. *Die Kirchen und das Dritte Reich.* Vol. 1: *Vorgeschichte und Zeit der Illusionen 1918–1934.* 2nd ed. 1977; Frankfurt: Propyläen/Ullstein, 1980. Translated by John Bowden as *The Churches and the Third Reich,* vol. 1: *Preliminary History and the Time of Illusions, 1918–1934.* London: SCM Press, 1987; Philadelphia: Fortress Press, 1988.

Schomerus, Hans. "Kirche als Reichsstandschaft" (Church as incorporated into the Reich). *Deutsches Volkstum* 15 (1933): 458–65.

Der Schwäbische Merkur (The Swabian mercury). Stuttgart. Vol. 148, 1933.

Seeberg, Reinhold. *Lehrbuch der Dogmengeschichte* (serial publication). Vol. 2: *Die Dogmenbildung der alten Kirche.* Leipzig: A. Deichert (G. Böhme), 1910. Translated, abridged, by Charles E. Hay as *Textbook of the History of Doctrines.* Grand Rapids: Baker Book House, 1956.

———. "Wunder" (Miracle). In *Realenzyklopädie für protestantische Theologie und Kirche,* 3rd ed., 21:558–67. Graz: Akademische Druck- u. Verlagsanstalt, 1969–71.

Shaw, Marvin C. "Naturalistic Theism and the Chicago School: Ames, Mathews, and Wieman." *Encounter* 49 (1988): 297–319.

Siegmund-Schultze, Friedrich, ed. *Ekklesia: Eine Sammlung von Selbstdarstellungen der christlichen Kirchen* (Ecclesia: A collection of self-portraits of Christian churches). Vol. 1: *Die britischen Länder: Die Kirche von England* (Britain: The Church of England). Gotha: L. Klotz, 1934.

———. *Rundschau: Vorträge in den Vereinigten Staaten* (A look around: Presentations in the United States). *Die Eiche* 21 (1933): 8–17.

Smid, Marikje. *Deutscher Protestantismus und Judentum 1932/1933* (German Protestantism and Judaism 1932/1933). Heidelberger Untersuchungen zu Widerstand, Judenverfolgung und Kirchenkampf im Dritten Reich 2. Munich: Chr. Kaiser, 1990.

Staats, Reinhart. "Adolf von Harnack im Leben Dietrich Bonhoeffers" (Adolf von Harnack in the life of Dietrich Bonhoeffer). *Theologische Zeitschrift* 37 (1981): 94–122.

———. "Das patristische Erbe in der Theologie Dietrich Bonhoeffers" (The patristic legacy in the theology of Dietrich Bonhoeffer). *Berliner Theologische Zeitschrift* 5 (1988): 178–201.

Stählin, Wilhelm. *Via Vitae: Lebenserinnerungen* (Via vitae: Life's memories). Kassel: Johannes-Stauda-Verlag, 1968.

Stern, Fritz. *Five Germanys I Have Known.* New York: Farrar, Straus & Giroux, 2006.

Strohm, Christoph. *Theologische Ethik im Kampf gegen den Nationalsozialismus: Der Weg Dietrich Bonhoeffers mit den Juristen Hans von Dohnanyi und Gerhard Leibholz in den Widerstand* (Theological ethics in the struggle against National Socialism: Dietrich Bonhoeffer's journey with the lawyers Hans von Dohnanyi and Gerhard Leibholz in the resistance). Heidelberger Untersuchungen zu Widerstand, Judenverfolgung und Kirchenkampf im Dritten Reich 1. Munich: Chr. Kaiser, 1989.

Tägliche Rundschau. Berlin. Vol. 52, 1933.

Tödt, Heinz Eduard. *Theologische Perspektiven nach Dietrich Bonhoeffer.* Edited by Ernst-Albert Scharffenorth. Gütersloh: Gütersloher Verlagshaus, 1993. Translated by David Stassen and Ilse Tödt as *Authentic Faith: Bonhoeffer's Theological Ethics in Context,* edited by Glen Harold Stassen. Grand Rapids: Wm. B. Eerdmans, 2007.

Tödt, Ilse, ed. *Dietrich Bonhoeffers Hegelseminar: Nach Aufzeichnungen von Ferenc Lehel* (Dietrich Bonhoeffer's Hegel seminar: From the notes of Ferenc Lehel). Internationales Bonhoeffer Forum: Forschung und Praxis 8. Munich: Chr. Kaiser, 1988.

Troeltsch, Ernst. *Die Absolutheit des Christentums und die Religionsgeschichte.* Lecture held at the meeting of the friends of *Die Christliche Welt* in Mühlacker on October 3, 1901. Expanded, with a preface. Tübingen: Mohr, 1929. Translated from the 3rd German ed. (1929) by David Reid as *The Absoluteness of Christianity and the History of Religions,* introduced by James Luther Adams. Richmond: John Knox Press, 1971.

Vischer, Wilhelm. "Témoigne d'un Contemporain" (Witness of a contemporary). *Revue d'Histoire et de Philosophie Religieuse* 64 (1984): 116–22.

———. "Zur Judenfrage: Eine kurze biblische Erörterung der Judenfrage im Anschluß an die Leitsätze eines Vortrags über die Bedeutung des Alten Testaments" (On the Jewish question: A brief biblical discussion in connection with the leading themes of a lecture on the meaning of the Old Testament). *Monatsschrift für Pastoraltheologie* 29 (1933): 185–90.

Völkischer Beobachter. Munich. Vol. 46, 1933.

Volk, Ludwig. *Das Reichskonkordat vom 20. Juli 1933: Von den Ansätzen in der Weimarer Republik bis zur Ratifizierung am 10. September 1933* (The Reich Concordat of 20 July 1933: From the beginnings in the Weimar Republic to the ratification on 10 September 1933). Veröffentlichungen der Kommission für Zeitgeschichte bei der Katholischen Akademie in Bayern B 5. Mainz: Matthias-Grünewald-Verlag, 1972.

Walker, Williston. *A History of the Christian Church.* 3rd ed. New York: Charles Scribner's Sons, 1970.

The Wartburg Hymnal. Chicago: Wartburg, 1918.

Weber, Otto. *Grundlagen der Dogmatik.* Vol. 2. Neukirchen: Verlag der Buchhandlung des Erziehungsvereins, 1962. Translated and annotated by Darrell L. Guder as *Foundations of Dogmatics,* vol. 2. Grand Rapids: Wm. B. Eerdmans, 1983.

Weiling, Christoph. *Die "Christlich-deutsche Bewegung": Eine Studie zum konservativen Protestantismus in der Weimarer Republik* (The "Christian-German movement": A study of conservative Protestantism in the Weimar Republic). Göttingen: Vandenhoeck & Ruprecht, 1998.

Weinel, Heinrich. "Völkische Bewegung II A und II B" (Nationalistic movement II A and II B). In *Die Religion in Geschichte und Gegenwart,* 2nd ed., vol. 5, cols. 1618–26. Tübingen: Mohr, 1927–31.

Weiße, Wolfram. *Praktisches Christentum und Reich Gottes: Die ökumenische Bewegung Life and Work 1919–1937* (Practical Christianity and the Kingdom of God: The ecumenical movement Life and Work 1919–1937). Kirche und Konfession 31. Göttingen: Vandenhoeck & Ruprecht, 1991.

Wendel, Ernst Georg. *Studien zur Homiletik Dietrich Bonhoeffers: Predigt-Hermeneutik-Sprache* (Studies in the homiletics of Dietrich Bonhoeffer: Sermon-hermeneutic-language). Tübingen: J. C. B. Mohr, 1985.

Wickham, Lionel R. "Chalkedon" (Chalcedon). In *Theologische Realenzyklopädie,* 7:668–75. Berlin: Walter de Gruyter, 1978.

Wiegandt, Manfred. *Norm und Wirklichkeit: Gerhard Leibholz (1901–1982); Leben, Werk und Richteramt.* Baden-Baden: Nomos, 1995.

Wieneke, Friedrich. *Deutsche Theologie im Umriß* (German theology in outline). Soldin: H. Madrasch, 1933.

Wiles, Maurice. *Archetypal Heresy: Arianism through the Centuries.* Oxford: Oxford University Press, 1996.

Wind, Renate. *Dietrich Bonhoeffer: A Spoke in the Wheel.* Translated by John Bowden. Grand Rapids: Wm. B. Eerdmans, 1992.

Wolf, Ernst. *Barmen: Kirche zwischen Versuchung und Gnade* (Barmen: Church between temptation and grace). Beiträge zur evangelischen Theologie 27. Munich: Chr. Kaiser, 1957.

The World Alliance for International Friendship though the Churches. *Annual Report.* Geneva: International Office, 1932–33 and 1933–34.

———. *Handbook of the World Alliance for International Friendship through the Churches: Covering the Period from Cambridge, September 1931, to Chamby, August 1935,* Geneva: International Office, 1936.

Wrede, William. *The Messianic Secret.* Translated by J. C. G. Grieg. Cambridge: J. Clarke, 1971.

Wünsch, Georg. "Christentum und Revolution" (Christianity and revolution). In *Die Religion in Geschichte und Gegenwart,* 2nd ed., vol. 4, cols. 2005–8. Tübingen: Mohr, 1927–31.

Zahn-Harnack, Agnes von. *Adolf von Harnack.* Berlin: W. de Gruyter, 1951.

Zentralblatt für die gesamte Unterrichts-Verwaltung in Preußen (Official publication for the whole administration of school instruction in Prussia). Berlin. Vol. 75, 1933.

Zimmermann, Wolf-Dieter, ed. *Begegnungen mit Dietrich Bonhoeffer.* Munich: Chr. Kaiser, 1969. Translated from the 1st German ed. by Käthe Gregor Smith as *I Knew Dietrich Bonhoeffer,* edited by Wolf-Dieter Zimmermann and Ronald Gregor Smith. London: Collins; New York: Harper & Row, 1966.

———. *Wir nannten ihn Bruder Bonhoeffer: Einblicke in ein hoffungsvolles Leben* (We called him Brother Bonhoeffer: Insights into a life full of hope). Berlin: Wichern-Verlag, 1995.

Index of Scriptural References

Index of Names

This index lists people mentioned in this volume, including authors and editors of literature cited in the notes. It provides brief profiles of the people listed and differs from the German edition by also including information about those whose work began after 1945, as well as additional information of interest to readers of the English edition. It does not include personal names that appear in book titles or only in the bibliography. When possible, dates of birth and death have been provided.

Index of Subjects

Greek Terms

Editors and Translators

Victoria J. Barnett (MDiv, Union Theological Seminary, New York) is general editor of the *Dietrich Bonhoeffer Works*, English edition, and director of church relations at the United States Holocaust Memorial Museum. She is the author of *Bystanders: Conscience and Complicity during the Holocaust* (Greenwood Press, 1999) and *For the Soul of the People: Protestant Protest against Hitler* (Oxford University Press, 1992) and the editor and translator of the new revised English edition of *Dietrich Bonhoeffer: A Biography*, by Eberhard Bethge (Fortress Press, 2000), as well as *And the Witnesses Were Silent: The Confessing Church and the Jews*, by Wolfgang Gerlach (University of Nebraska Press, 2000). In addition to numerous book chapters and articles, she is the author of the essay on Bonhoeffer on the U.S. Holocaust Memorial Museum Web site.

Isabel Best is a 1961 graduate of Oberlin College, where she studied English literature, French, and German. She has lived, studied, and worked in France, Germany, and Switzerland for over twenty-five years. She earned the Diploma in Translation from the Institute of Linguists, London, in 1996, while serving on the office staff of the Conference of European Churches in Geneva, Switzerland. Since then she has worked as a freelance translator for international organizations in Geneva, including the World Council of Churches, where her husband recently retired as an executive staff member. She has worked on several *DBWE* volumes and has also translated a forthcoming biography of Dietrich Bonhoeffer by Bonhoeffer scholar Ferdinand Schlingensiepen. She now lives in Belmont, Massachusetts.

David Warren Simons Higgins was born in Rochester, New York. A graduate of the University of Colorado, he earned a masters in history at the University of Warwick, England; he received his doctorate in history from the

University of Bremen in Germany. From 1989 to 1999, he lived and worked in Germany as an English teacher and translator. Since 1999, he has lived in Paris, France, where he teaches English in the French Foreign Ministry and continues his translation work. He is married and has one, bilingual son.

Larry L. Rasmussen is a U.S. Christian ethicist and the author of several works on Dietrich Bonhoeffer. He earned a doctorate from Union Theological Seminary, New York, with a dissertation on Bonhoeffer's ethics and resistance. From 1969 to 1972, he was a professor of religious studies at St. Olaf College, in Northfield, Minnesota. He served as professor of Christian ethics at Wesley Theological Seminary in Washington, D.C. from 1972 to 1986. In 1986, he became Reinhold Niebuhr Professor of Social Ethics at Union Theological Seminary, New York, a position he held until his retirement in 2004.

Douglas W. Stott is a freelance editor and translator. A graduate of Davidson College, Northwestern University, and Emory's Candler School of Theology, he also studied in Germany at the Philipps University in Marburg and at the University of Stuttgart. His translation credits include several volumes of the *Theological Dictionary of the Old Testament* and the *Exegetical Dictionary of the New Testament*; commentaries for the Old Testament Library; *DBWE* 10, *Barcelona, Berlin, New York: 1928–1931*, and *DBWE* 14, *Theological Education at Finkenwalde: 1935–1937*; and F. W. J. Schelling's *Philosophy of Art.* He was also on the translation team of volume 1 of *Religion Past and Present.* He is currently preparing an annotated English edition of the correspondence of Caroline Schlegel-Schelling.

Barbara Wojhoski studied art history at New York University, ancient history at the Philipps University in Marburg, Germany, and anthropology at Georgia State University, and has participated in archaeological excavations of Late Woodland Period sites in Arkansas. She has been a full-time freelance editor since 1995 for academic and denominational presses and has worked on projects ranging from a dictionary of the Miami-Illinois language to contemporary fiction translated from German to theological commentaries and philosophical works.